A
Planning Guide
To The
Preschool Curriculum

Revised Edition

THE CHILD
THE PROCESS
THE DAY

D1604895

Authors: Anne R. Sanford
Julia McLean Williams
Jeanne Cunningham James
Ann K. Overton

Editor: Jeanne Cunningham James

Art Direction:
Darious Oliver

Cover Illustration:
Beth Marcil   Gay Haff

Text Illustration:
Beth Marcil   Gay Haff
Bill Lunsford

Chapter Head Illustrations:
Sue Rusciano

Typesetting & Mechanicals:
Mary Rogers   Teresa Wright

A Planning Guide to the Preschool Curriculum - Revised: The Child, The Process, The Day

Published by
Kaplan Press
Winston-Salem, NC 27103
1983

ISBN # 0-88076-001-X

ACKNOWLEDGEMENTS:

Jane Findley, Patricia Miller, Annie Pegram, Linda Richey, Anne Sanford, and Barbara Semrau for writing the orginial manuscript.

Pat Doughty for her professional editing expertise.

Deborah Booth for the many units which she critiqued.

Brenda Bowen for the many units which she critiqued.

Ingrid Casterlow for critiqueing units.

The entire Outreach Staff for all their support and suggestions.

Donna Denney of Butler County, Kentucky for her inspiration to add a St. Patrick's Day unit and the many fine activities which she contributed to it and elsewhere in the book.

Cindy Ashburn of DeKalb County, Georgia for her thorough set of suggestions.

Margie Jones of Spencer County, Kentucky; Robert Franklin of Princeton, Kentucky; Betty Gore of Murray, Kentucky; Dee Dorsey of Learning Together, Raleigh, North Carolina; Susan Hunt of Fayetteville, North Carolina; Maureen Hohnhorst and Nancy Moore of Jacksonville, North Carolina.

Thomas F. Cunningham for his helpful additions.

CONTENTS

SECTION IV - APPENDICES

APPENDIX I - METHODS AND PRINCIPLES

APPENDIX II - SPECIFIC SKILLS

APPENDIX III - CHARTING THE UNIT GROUP LESSON

Section I - Curriculum

INTRODUCTION TO CURRICULUM

As teachers create more developmental programs for children, their needs for an organized guide to their planning increases. A guide to curriculum material, and activities which provide for individual developmental differences in children, helps teachers meet the needs of all students. Some say that normal children learn in spite of the teacher. Unfortunately, traditional early childhood teacher training leads a beginner to think that all children are self - motivated and learn from "discovery" experiences. However, many children (especially those with learning problems now being mainstreamed in Head Start, day care and public schools) require a well-planned program. A curriculum guide assists teachers in establishing and maintaining an in-depth, quality program.

Such an in-depth early childhood program provides the child with individual:
1) Learning Objectives
2) Direct Teaching Experience
3) Styles of Learning Adaptations
4) Environmental Structure (surroundings)
5) Reinforcement
6) Use of Learning Materials
7) Meaningful Curriculum

An in-depth program provides for prescriptive teaching starting from the existing skills which a teacher has observed and continuing with a program of small steps insuring success for each child.

WHO DETERMINES THE CURRICULUM?

The child, not the teacher, determines the curriculum. Identification of a child's strengths and weaknesses, based on normative data, offers educational direction to the teacher. Normative data refers to the ages at which the average child achieves essential skills. Instruments such as the Revised Learning Accomplishment Profile (Anne R. Sanford) enable the teacher to identify the child's skills (what he can and cannot do in all areas of development) and to program instruction based on his existing skills in these areas. Normative data on child development, sequenced in a hierarchy which moves from simplest to most difficult skills, provides the structure for teaching. The Unit Group Lesson of each lesson in this book provides an excellent example of a "hierarchy of responses" possible within a language lesson. Proper assessment and prescription identifies the individual child's level in the hierarchy. Instructional objectives are developed for the skills to be taught. Instructional objectives state a new skill or behavior which will be demonstrated by the child after he has been taught. These skills are observed and recorded by the teacher.

WHAT IS THE CURRICULUM?

The curriculum consists of the programmed arrangement of time, materials and tasks. The school environment is structured to meet the individual needs and developmental levels of each child. In addition to the unique characteristics of each child, there are common characteristics among children related to their environment or their world outside of school. Curriculum design for young children can take several forms:

(1) Individual lessons with all instructional objectives, teaching materials and daily work for the child being stored in a separate box for each child.

(2) The unit approach which focuses on the common characteristics and needs of children in teaching units of work such as Pets or Halloween.

(3) And, prehaps best, is a combination of both the unit approach for a portion of the day and time allotted for individual lessons during another portion of the day.

The curriculum may be developed entirely around unique characteristics and individual needs; or, through a unit topic approach, it may incorporate both individual and common characteristics of children.

The approach to curriculum activities suggested in this guide requires the teacher to design tasks and materials which focus on individual needs within the unit structure. While teaching the unit concept Winter, for instance, the teacher presents tasks for the children which differ from one child to the next, and expects each child to respond at his own level of development. Whatever approach is chosen, a good curriculum is one which individualizes activities and is designed to get active responses from all the children.

WHAT IS THE PROCESS FOR DEVELOPING A SYSTEMATIC CURRICULUM?

The teacher begins by finding out what the child can do through the use of normative data on child development. Two or three weeks may be set aside for this purpose at the start of the year. This assessment will determine the outcome of the teaching which goes on in that classroom. Individual long-range instructional objectives will be written by the teacher based on what the child can and cannot do in each area of development. These long-range objectives will be task analyzed into sub-skills which must be achieved before reaching the long-range objectives. The sub-objectives will then be sequenced in order of difficulty. This process is known as task analysis. Beginning where the child is now, the teacher moves toward the long-range objective by teaching one step at a time. Progressing step by step, one skill built upon the other, ensures success for the child.

WHAT ABOUT CURRICULUM EVALUATION?

The systematic curriculum has a continuous, built-in evaluation of both the teacher and the child. Teaching daily toward specific objectives enables the teacher to measure the child's progress and to determine the appropriateness of tasks and materials. Daily evaluation defines more clearly what should be taught the next day.

The teacher interested in a systematic approach to the curriculum should answer these questions:

1. Have you assessed each child in the different areas of development?

2. Have you written long-range and short-range objectives based on this assessment?

3. Have you planned for the child's success in each activity or lesson by expecting responses based on individual objectives?

4. Is the child reaching daily objectives set for him?

5. If the child is not reaching daily objectives set for him, have you evaluated your tasks, materials and teaching techniques, and revised the activity according to this evaluation?

WHAT ABOUT SUCCESS?

In a systematized learning situation the child succeeds more than he fails. How does the teacher ensure success?

1. Know the child, his level of functioning, before giving him a task. Begin on his individual level and stop just before he becomes frustrated.

2. Set appropriate learning objectives and task analyze them (break them down into a teachable order).

3. Teach small steps each day.

4. Reward each success with food, a hug, a smile, a star, etc. appropriate to the level and interests of the child.

5. Evaluate the child's progress each day.

6. Work with parents in planning successful home activities.

The purpose of this curriculum is to challenge the preschool teacher to develop a curriculum in which both LEARNING and TEACHING will take place. This type of curriculum ensures success and growth for both the teacher and the child. Here is a diagram which outlines the step-by-step process of developing a systematic curriculum.

PROCESS FOR CURRICULUM DEVELOPMENT

—— 1 ——
Assess Entry Behaviors
What are his skills in each area of development when he comes to you?

—— 2 ——
Determine Long-Range Objectives
What will he be able to do after you teach him in each area of development?

—— 3 ——
Task Analysis for Immediate Instructional Objectives
What skills must he learn before reaching the long-range objectives?

—— 4 ——
Sequence Instructional Objectives
Are you ensuring success by moving from his entry behavior to the next step in order of difficulty? Have you planned to teach the easiest first?

—— 5 ——
Program Materials, Tasks, and Responses
Have you gathered essential materials? Have you individualized the tasks? Do tasks require active responses from child? How will you know when he has met your objective?

—— 6 ——
Teach
1. Present material after getting attention by giving signal for attending.
2. For all new material have tasks which require active responses. Present material and test it out.
3. Help child make correct response by prompting, cueing, and/or modeling when necessary.
4. Reward appropriate responses immediately.
5. Correct inappropriate responses immediately; re-test.

—— 7 ——
Evaluate
1. Did child meet the objectives set for him today?
2. Were the objectives appropriate?
3. How many trials did he require?
4. Did your materials influence the learning?
5. Was attending behavior maintained? How?
6. Did you respond in a way to encourage child's appropriate action on other days?

—— 8 ——
Revise or Proceed
1. Do you need to change the teaching routine and materials but stick to present objectives?
2. If child is now doing or saying something new, he is learning. Build on these new skills by setting new objectives for the child.

8

Section II - The Unit Approach

INTRODUCTION TO THE UNIT APPROACH

A curriculum guide is a tool designed for the teacher to use in planning meaningful activities for learning. It is just that - a guide; not a recipe book containing all the steps in the cooking (teaching) process. To use the curriculum guide as it is intended, it is necessary that individualization and adaptation of activities, breakdown of learning tasks and correlation of activities be provided by the teacher, based upon the skills of the children. Specific techniques such as modeling, prompting and cueing are essential in planning and carrying out the teaching activities suggested (See Appendix I). However, your creativity and knowledge of the children with whom you work will complete the framework contained in this guide.

In addition to individual lessons, a unit approach is advocated, because all children need to learn certain information about themselves and their world. The objective of the unit approach is to help the teacher teach these basic facts, skills and abilities.

This curriculum guide is divided into six areas of skill development: (1) fine motor; (2) gross motor; (3) social; (4) self-help; (5) language; and (6) cognitive. Every teacher will want her curriculum to include each area. However, inclusion of each area is not enough. (Through random and haphazard teaching, these six areas can be included in any educational program.) What a good teacher wants is a systematic and thorough procedure for teaching specific skills in each area according to her assessment of each child and his level of functioning.

How is this done? Through the use of the Learning Accomplishment Profile Revised, informal observation, parental reports, and preschool tests, such as the Cooperative Preschool Inventory, each child's existing skills can be determined. From there, individual goals for learning should be formulated and written in each of the six areas of development for each child. These goals or instructional objectives might look something like Susan's:

OBJECTIVES FOR SUSAN - MARCH - MAY, 19--

Receptive Language
1. To be able to demonstrate an understanding of the words stop, up, down, fast, slow.
2. To understand the idea of taking a trip by telling what is involved: packing clothes, traveling to a place and returning home.

Expressive Language
1. Give full name upon request; first and last.
2. To tell **action** in pictures.
3. To be able to whisper.
4. To say a nursery rhyme.

Gross Motor
1. Stability of trunk muscles.
2. Stability of arm and shoulder muscles.
3. Stability of gross movements and balance.
4. Pedal trike.
5. Walk, instead of running, to carry out requests.

Fine Motor
1. Finger plays and touching of fingertips to thumb.
2. Hold magic marker and crayon with an approximate pincer grasp.
3. Put small pegs in peg board.
4. Tear paper and bits of clay off a hunk using a pincer grasp.
5. See folder for other activities which will be worked on.

Self-Help
1. To put on and remove cap and hang it up.
2. To hang up coat by collar.
3. To push button through hole to unbutton.
4. To verbalize toilet needs.

Cognitive
1. To be able to name colors - red, purple, yellow, blue, brown.
2. To associate the numeral 1 and one object or picture of one object.
3. To count two objects and two pictures of objects.
4. To match pictures of animals that are alike - (lotto).
5. To demonstrate difference between past and present, using yesterday, lask week and today as measures.

Pre-writing
1. Horizontal path tracing - with paint brush, chalk on board, tempera.
2. Vertical path tracing - with paint with water, chalk on board, tempera, magic marker and pencil.
3. To make a V stroke - with sand, fingerpaint, paint with water.

Social
1. To talk to strangers - say "hi" upon request and "bye" upon request.
2. To keep fingers out of mouth.
3. To say "thank you" when given something, without prompting.
4. To not put things found on floor into mouth.

The functional levels of the children and the specific instructional objectives set will determine the choice of activities within this guide. The teacher is provided with several options within each activity time. Therefore, the teacher's selectivity lies in the understanding of individual differences so that she may plan for adaptation of equipment, materials and teaching procedures, based upon the knowledge and assessment of her children's skills.

As you will discover, The Unit Group Lessons are based on the topic for the week. For example, when studying a unit on Garden Tools, the first Unit Group Lesson might be "hoe." Also note the way in which all activities during the day center around "hoe." Research data shows that repetition and a variety of experiences with a concept or object influence learning. The correlation of all activities around the concept in the group lesson is a major emphasis within the curriculum guide.

Within the Unit Group Lesson children respond on their individual levels. One child may be on the "touch" level while another may be on the "picture discrimination" level. The objective for each child is to move sequentially from his entering response level to the next higher skill level. He will continue to proceed to the next higher level task or skill in each developmental area.

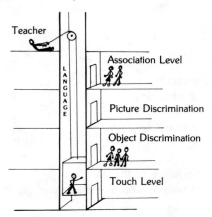

The following Hierarchy of Basic Skills to be Learned in the Group Lesson is suggested in planning meaningful, individualized lessons. The children will not all enter at the same level, nor will they proceed at the same rate to higher levels. They will not all reach the same level of achievement in the end.

A HIERARCHY OF BASIC SKILLS TO BE LEARNED IN THE UNIT GROUP LESSON

Unit on Musical Instruments
Monday - Unit Group Lesson "Drum"

(1)   Oral Language Response: "This is a drum," says the teacher. Child responds
        a. Sounds approximating word.
        b. One word - "drum".
        c. Two words - "a drum"; "see drum".
        d. Three words - "See a drum."
        e. Whole sentence - "I see a drum."

   Emphasize language responses within each step below. Ask every chance you get, "What did you touch?"
"Tell me what you found."

(2)   Touch Response: "Touch the drum."

(3)   Matching Responses: Using concrete objects and pictures: "Put the drum on the drum." (Use
        concrete objects first and later progress to flannel board cut-outs, pictures and abstract representations.)

(4)   Concrete Object Discrimination: Shown five real objects (including a drum) child is asked, "Show me
        the drum." "Where is the drum?"

(5)   Picture Discrimination: Shown five pictures, including a drum, child is asked to "Find the drum."
        "Find the picture of the drum."

(6)   Tactile Discrimination: Using a "feely box" or bag, child reaches in with hand, touches each object
        and finds the drum. He is not allowed to use his eyes in discriminating the "drum" from other objects.
        "Try and find the drum using your hands."

(7)   Sound Discrimination: Play the drum; then have child listen to musical sounds and be able to
        discriminate drum sound from other sounds. "When you hear the drum, raise your hand." "When
        you hear the drum, clap your hands."

(8)   Figure-Ground: To be able to identify the drum when it is part of a picture with other things in it.

(9)   Visual Closure (to be able to see a whole, when shown only a part): Shown a partially covered picture
        of a drum, children tell you what it is. "Look carefully; guess what this is."

(10)   Object Function: "Show me what we do with the drum." "Tell me what we do with the drum."

(11)   Association Skills: Things that go with the drum. Given a spoon, two wooden sticks, a napkin, etc.,
        say "Show me what goes with the drum."

(12)   Classification Skills: To what category or class of things does drum belong? "Is the drum a tool,
        musical instrument, or something we clean with?" Shown flannel board cutouts of toys, clothes or
        musical instruments, put the drum (cut out) with the right family.

(13)   Abstract Reasoning: Cause and effect relationships. "What would happen if?" "What do you think
        might happen next?" Example: "If I hit the top of the drum as hard as I could with my hand, what
        would happen?"

(14)   Concept Enrichment: Higher level language activities for use in mainstream settings where there are
        normal and bright students as well as students with delays. These are suggestions for expanding the
        concept.

Language skills should be emphasized at each and every step. Remember to:

(1) Encourage verbal responses always. Accept approximations to the word or words and later build whole words and sentences.

(2) Ask a question which requires a response on the child's individual level and which requires more than a "yes" or "no" answer.

(3) Model the desired response when necessary.

(4) Build sentences by further describing the concept. For example: Concept: ball. After the one word "ball" is clearly established in the child's repertoire of words, add
"a ball"
"is a ball"
"This is a ball."
"I see a ball."
"I see a _____ (big, red or green, etc.) ball."

(5) Gradually, add a little more to your expectations for each child's responses.

One child may need to move sequentially from imitating a one-word response to being able to answer "What is this?" Another child may enter the process at a higher level: being able to say phrases, and proceed from there to responding with complex sentences.

There are many more similarities than differences between educating the normal and the handicapped child. We have not dwelt much on the differences, because we believe that the educational goals should be the same. Although the educational needs of the normal and handicapped child may differ in terms of equipment, teaching techniques and teaching strategies, the overall goal of developing and increasing each child's potential is common to both.

OTHER ACTIVITIES IN THE CURRICULUM

Music Activities
Music activities are designed to be used with the whole group of children or subgroups. Each unit provides a choice of music activities and one or more can be used as time permits. The emphasis in music is on language and motor involvement in the singing.

Art Activities
Art activities are designed to reinforce and expand the concept which was introduced in the unit group lesson. The classroom teacher may choose one or more of the activities for all the children or provide different art experiences for individual children. Whenever possible, the art activities are presented from the simplest to the most difficult. The high correlation between art activities and fine motor skills may prompt the teacher to change an art experience to address the fine motor curriculum. The art curriculum places a greater emphasis on creativity than do the fine motor activities.

Snack Activities
Snack suggestions are included to provide for further development of the daily concept. In some cases the snack is significant in how it is served or obtained rather than in what is being served. If your center has limited choices of snack offerings, you will find the "how to serve" ideas most useful and adaptable to many different concepts.

Games Activities
Games are presented to enhance further development of the lesson concept in a multisensory, multidevelopmental approach. Many of the suggested games include auditory and visual components which are essential prerequisites for later learning.

Fine Motor Activities

Fine motor activities are designed to foster fine motor development while incorporating language skills. This feature of the curriculum also includes some tasks with strong visual development components such as eye-hand coordination, visual tracking and fixation skills. The fine motor tasks differ from the art activities in that they are structured specifically to develop the fine motor area of development.

Storytelling Activities

Storytelling and fingerplays are intended to promote additional language usage related to the daily concept. These activities include physical imitation skills which enhance body-in-space orientation and creative body movement. They also address skills of auditory memory and sequencing.

Gross Motor Activities

These are activities designed to foster the use and development of large muscles.

Cognitive Activities

The cognitive activities address intellectual functions such as reasoning, problem solving and knowledge. These curriculum are correlated with the cognitive index of the revised LAP and the LAP-D.

Enrichment Activities

The enrichment activities provide supplementary experiences for those centers which serve kindergarten children. Higher level cognitive activities, such as the alphabet, writing, language and arithmetic are incorporated in the enrichment curriculum.

Field Trip Activities

Suggested field trips are usually presented at the end of each unit. Field trips which are suggested during the week usually have a more narrow focus, such as a hike around the playground.

Visitor Activities

Descriptions of special visitors (ex. the carpenter) who may be invited to the class are designed to reinforce concept development.

The use of commerical materials will simplify implementation of the curriculum for the teacher. Some suggestions are:

Teaching Pictures from Kaplan Press which provide pictures of all of the concepts in the Curriculum Guide and are particularly useful for Figure-Ground activities.

Sewing Cards from Kaplan Press which provide lacing experiences correlated with many of the concepts included in the Curriculum Guide.

Story Sequence Cards from Kaplan Press which provide sequence stories for many of the concepts in the Curriculum Guide.

The Home Stretch published by Kaplan Press which provides suggestions for home activities which are correlated with the units of the Curriculum Guide.

POINTS TO REMEMBER

1. Small groups of six to eight children work best always.

2. When more than one activity is suggested for any area such as music or games, choose one or more that are most appropriate for your children. The activities within areas are sequenced from simplest to more difficult.

3. You will already know the tunes to the songs suggested.

4. You need no musical ability.

5. Materials suggested are readily available.

6. Activities are simple and do not require a lot of preparation.

7. This manual facilitates use of the Learning Accomplishment Profile.

REFERENCES

CURRICULUM DEVELOPMENT
1. Bangs, Tina, **LANGUAGE AND LEARNING DISORDERS OF THE PRE-ACADEMIC CHILD: WITH A CURRICULUM GUIDE,** Appleton Century Crafts, NY, 1968.

2. Becker, Englemann, Thomas, **TEACHING: A COURSE IN APPLIED PSYCHOLOGY,** Science Research Associates, Inc., 1971.

3. Hammill, Donald D., "Evaluating Children For Instructional Purposes", **EDUCATIONAL PERSPECTIVES IN LEARNING DISABILITIES,** John Wiley and Sons, Inc., NY, London, 1971.

4. Haring, Norris G., "The New Curriculum Design in Special Education", **EDUCATIONAL TECHNOLOGY,** May, 1970.

5. Smith, Robert M., **CLINICAL TEACHING: METHOD OF INSTRUCTION FOR THE RETARDED,** McGraw-Hill Book Company, NY, 1968.

INTRODUCTION TO THE UNIT APPROACH
1. Bangs, Tina, **LANGUAGE AND LEARNING DISORDERS OF THE PRE-ACADEMIC CHILD: WITH A CURRICULUM GUIDE,** Appleton Century Crafts, NY, 1968.

2. Bateman, Barbara, **THE ESSENTIALS OF TEACHING,** Dimensions Publishing Company, San Rafael, California, 1971.

3. Englemann, Siegfried, **CONCEPTUAL LEARNING,** Dimensions Publishing Company, San Rafael, California, 1969.

4. Haring, Norris G., "The New Curriculum Design in Special Education", **EDUCATIONAL TECHNOLOGY,** May, 1970.

Unit 1: Body Parts

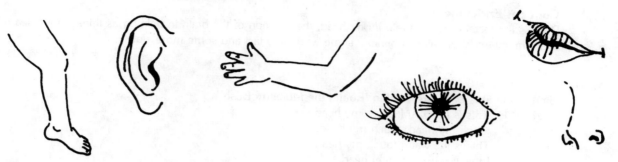

A developmental assessment should determine the functional levels of each child. Individual expectations are based on the assessment results.

Lesson 1: Head

Unit Group Lesson

1. **Match Concrete Objects**
   Present two heads. Say, "This is a head." Ask each child in turn to put the head with the head. Gradually increase number of irrelevant objects from which (s)he must select head to match.

2. **Discriminate Objects**
   Present several objects. Have each child touch the head in response to verbal direction, "Touch the head."

3. **Locate Own**
   Have each child touch his/her own head upon request: "Touch your head, (child's name)."

4. **Match Pictures**
   Present several pictures of common objects. Have each child match the pictures of the heads.

5. **Discriminate Pictures**
   Present a group of several unrelated pictures of objects. Have each child touch the picture of the head in response to verbal direction, "Touch the head."

6. **Figure-Ground**
   Present a "busy" picture with many visual distractions. Ask each child to find the picture of the head.

7. **Visual Closure**
   Partially cover each of several pictures with paper. Ask each child to find the picture of the head.

8. **Function**
   Ask, "What do we do with our heads?"

9. **Association**
   Ask, "What goes with the head?" Use related pictures or objects including hat, wigs, hair, etc., with several unrelated objects or pictures.

10. **Imitate Verbalization**
    Present a head and ask, "What is this? Say, 'Head'." The child will imitate "Head."

11. **Verbalize Label**

Present a head and ask, "What is this?" The child will respond, "Head."

12. **Concept Enrichment**

Discuss the location of the brain in the head; the function of the brain in helping us think, move, learn, and remember; differences in brains - some work very fast and some more slowly.

Music

1. Sing to the tune of "Here We Go 'Round the Mulberry Bush":

   Verse 1: This is the way I touch my head,
   touch my head, touch my head.
   This is the way I touch my head,
   I touch (child's name) head.

   Verse 2: This is the way I pat my head . . .
   Verse 3: This is the way I shake my head . . .
   Verse 4: This is the way I wash my head . . .

   Pantomime, "Touch my head." On the last line, touch a child's head and have the group sing the child's name.

2. Sing to the tune of "If You're Happy and You Know It":

   Verse 1: If you're happy and you know it, touch your head.
   If you're happy and you know it, touch your head.
   If you're happy and you know it,
   Then your face will surely show it;
   If you're happy and you know it, touch your head.

   Verse 2: If you're happy and you know it, pat your head.
   Verse 3: If you're happy and you know it, shake your head.

Art

1. Distribute pictures of bodies without heads from catalogs or magazines. Have the children paste the bodies, with matching heads, onto construction paper.
2. Using the above technique, have children paste animal heads on animal bodies.
3. Make a collage, either as a group or individual project. Have children cut out pictures of heads of various sizes and paste on construction paper or poster board.
4. Use light from slide projector to make a shadow silhouette of each child. Outline child's shadow profile with a pencil on black construction paper. Cut out black silhouette for each child. Mount pictures on white paper. Let children decorate silhouettes with pieces of lace doilies.

Snack

Eat sugar cookies made in Fine Motor #4.

Fine Motor

1. Have each child make a head with hair, eyes, nose, and mouth from clay or play dough.
2. Draw a picture of a head with all facial features on a piece of cardboard and punch holes on head where the hair should be. Have the children "sew" yarn on the head for hair.
3. Help children make "Rocky." Collect smooth rocks and have children add yarn hair and felt marker features on rocks for paper weights.
4. Make sugar cookies which look like heads. (See fig. 1A.)

Fig. 1A

Games

1. Have children put together a "Mr. Potatohead."
2. Let children use Velcro, magnet board, or masking tape to "Put the Head on the Girl (boy, dog, cat, etc.)." Play it like "Pin the Tail on the Donkey." Use blindfold, if it is acceptable to the children.
3. Play "Touch the Head". Have a child close his eyes (or use a blindfold) and touch another child's head. Then, let him guess which child he is touching.

Storytelling

1. Fingerplay: "Who Feels Happy":
    "Who feels happy, who feels gay?
    All who do, pat their heads this way.
    Who feels happy, who feels gay?
    All who do, nod their heads this way.
    Who feels happy, who feels gay?
    All who do, scratch their heads this way."
2. Read book about "Chicken Little."
3. Fingerplay: "Knock at the Door":
    "Knock at the door.   (Knock with fist on forehead.)
    Peep in.   (Peer through circled thumbs and
                                                        forefingers.)
    Turn the latch.   (Twist nose.)
    Walk in."   (Pretend to put finger in mouth.)

Gross Motor

Make cardboard picture of clown with hole cut in the place of the head. Have children take turns throwing a bean bag through the hole where the head is missing. (Volunteers could make target and head-shaped bean bags.)

Cognitive

1. Count how many heads each child in the class has.
2. Make a picture of a child with the head missing and ask, "What's missing?"
3. Put a series of profiles on the same page - some facing left and some facing right. Have a cue at the top and let the children mark those profiles that face the same way as the one at the top.

Enrichment

Have children match the correct number of heads to numerals on cards. On one side of each card, put a numeral; on the back of the card, put the same numeral and an appropriate number of circles for each numeral as a cue to the correct number. Make heads for matching. Have children work with cued sides of cards until they can progress to uncued sides. (See fig. 1B.)

Fig. 1B

Lesson 2: Eyes

Unit Group Lesson

1. **Match Concrete Objects**
    Present two eyes. Say, "This is an eye." Ask each child in turn to put the eye with the eye. Gradually increase number of irrelevant objects from which (s)he must select eye to match.

2. **Discriminate Objects**
    Present several objects. Have each child touch the eye in response to verbal direction, "Touch the eye."

3. **Locate Own**
   Have each child touch his/her own eye upon request: "Touch your eye, (child's name)."

4. **Match Pictures**
   Present several pictures of common objects. Have each child match the pictures of the eyes.

5. **Discriminate Pictures**
   Present a group of several unrelated pictures of objects. Have each child touch the picture of the eye in response to verbal direction, "Touch the eye."

6. **Figure-Ground**
   Present a "busy" picture with many visual distractions. Ask each child to find the picture of the eye.

7. **Visual Closure**
   Partially cover each of several pictures with paper. Ask each child to find the picture of the eye.

8. **Function**
   Ask, "What do we do with our eyes?"

9. **Association**
   Ask, "What goes with the eye?" Use related pictures or objects including glasses, mascara, etc., with several unrelated objects or pictures.

10. **Imitate Verbalization**
    Present an eye and ask, "What is this? Say, 'Eye'." The child will imitate "Eye."

11. **Verbalize Label**
    Present an eye and ask, "What is this?" The child will respond, "Eye."

12. **Concept Enrichment**
    Eyes have lashes and lids. Discuss what their functions are.

Music
1. Sing to the tune of "Here We Go 'Round the Mulberry Bush":
   Verse 1: This is the way I touch my eyes,
   Touch my eyes, touch my eyes,
   This is the way I touch my eyes,
   I touch (child's name) eyes.
   Verse 2: This is the way I close my eyes . . .
   Verse 3: This is the way I blink my eyes . . .
   Verse 4: This is the way I roll my eyes . . .
   Pantomime "Touch my eyes." On the last line touch a child's eyes and sing the child's name.
2. Sing to the tune of "Row, Row, Row Your Boat":
   Look, look with your eyes,   *(Cup hand around eyes.)*
   See what you can see.
   I see the boys and girls are here.   *(Point to boys and girls.)*
   I see a friend for me.   *(Pick a friend.)*
3. Sing, "I Have Two Eyes and They're Both the Same Size." (from Sesame Street).

Art
1. Help children make "play glasses." Have them cut a pair of circles from a plastic holder from canned beverage six pack and attach pipe cleaners for ear pieces. (See fig. 1C.)
2. Help children make a strip of paper with different pairs of eyes and a paper plate with nose and other features on it. Cut slits for the eye paper and let children select eyes. (See fig. 1P.)
3. Have each child paste pictures of eyes on outline of head and body and decorate the picture.

4.   Have children draw eyes on a blank face in sand, on chalkboard, with paint, or crayons and paper.

Fig. 1C

Fig. 1P

Snack

Play, "What Do Your Eyes See for Snack?" Present snack food and have children tell what they see. Partially hide the snack food. Talk about clues that help children identify food.

Fine Motor

1.   Have each child make a head from play dough or clay which includes eyes.
2.   Have children make masks from paper plates. Let them cut large holes for eyes. Suggest that children look at their eyes behind the mask in a mirror.
3.   Make puzzles of faces. (Either draw a face or use a large picture pasted on cardboard.) Cut out eyes for children to insert. For some children with better skills, cut out hair, mouth, nose, ears, etc. for them to insert.

Games

1.   Help children make a "World Watcher". Let them assemble toilet tissue tubes, yarn, hole puncher. Have each child paint or decorate the outside of two toilet tissue tubes. Punch holes in each of the top sides. Have children string yarn through the holes and hang the tubes around their necks. Let them go on a walk, "watching the world."(See fig. 1D.)
2.   Put old, empty eyeglass frames in the housekeeping corner.
3.   Play, "Peek-a-boo, Where Are You?" (Eyes closed.) "Here I Am." (Eyes open.)

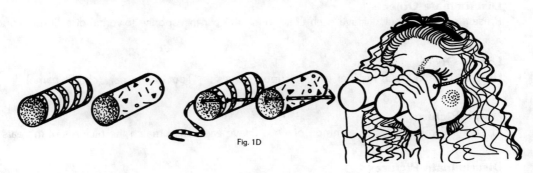

Fig. 1D

Storytelling

1.   Tell a flannelboard story using "My Face and My Body" flannelboard kit (Kaplan School Supply) or make body and face parts from felt and let children make up their own stories.
2.   Read "The Eye Book."
3.   Read "The Noisy Book," about Muffin the dog who got a cinder in his eye.
4.   Read a story about a child who has visual problems such as "Horses, Airplanes and Frogs," Mark Parker (Child's World), "Sally Can't See," Palle Peterson (John Day).

Gross Motor

1.   Take a walk and play, "I See Something."
2.   Play "Simon Says" (look up, look down, look all around).

Cognitive

1.   Let children taste things that look alike but are different such as salt and sugar, corn starch and powdered sugar and soda.
2.   Have children sort play cards by suit.
3.   Have children match pairs of eyes by color or size.
4.   Have children count eyes that each child has.

Enrichment

1. Help children make a mural of eyes. On one large sheet of paper, draw eye shapes. (Dot them for the children to complete.) Have children cut circles of brown, blue, green, and black and paste in the shapes. Have them add eyelashes and eyebrows. While working, discuss pairs of eyes, eye colors, eye shapes, etc. (See fig. 1E.)

2. Let children look through dark glasses, kaleidoscope, magnifying glass, and binoculars and describe what they see.

3. Have each child look at her eyes in a mirror and determine what color they are.

Fig. 1E

Lesson 3: Ears

Unit Group Lesson

1. **Match Concrete Objects**
    Present two ears. Say, "This is an ear." Ask each child in turn to put the ear with the ear. Gradually increase number of irrelevant objects from which (s)he must select ear to match.

2. **Discriminate Objects**
    Present several objects. Have each child touch the ear in response to verbal direction, "Touch the ear."

3. **Locate Own**
    Have each child touch his/her own ear upon request: "Touch your ear, (child's name)."

4. **Match Pictures**
    Present several pictures of common objects. Have each child match the pictures of the ears.

5. **Discriminate Pictures**
    Present a group of several unrelated pictures of objects. Have each child touch the picture of the ear in response to verbal direction, "Touch the ear."

6. **Figure-Ground**
    Present a "busy" picture with many visual distractions. Ask each child to find the picture of the ear.

7. **Visual Closure**
    Partially cover each of several pictures with paper. Ask each child to find the picture of the ear.

8. **Function**
    Ask, "What do we do with our ears?"

9. **Association**
    Ask, "What goes with the ear?" Use related pictures or objects including hearing aid, ear muffs, etc., with several unrelated objects or pictures.

10. **Imitate Verbalization**
    Present an ear and ask, "What is this? Say, 'Ear'." The child will imitate "Ear."

11. **Verbalize Label**

   Present an ear and ask, "What is this?" The child will respond, "Ear."

12. **Concept Enrichment**

   Discuss how people may hear differently. Some may be "hard of hearing" or "deaf." Use earphone (plug) from transistor radio to demonstrate hearing aid.

Music

1. Sing to the tune of "Here We Go 'Round the Mulberry Bush":
   Verse 1: This is the way I touch my ears,
   Touch my ears, touch my ears,
   This is the way I touch my ears,
   I touch (child's name) ears.
   Verse 2: This is the way I pat my ears . . .
   Verse 3: This is the way I pull my ears . . .
   Verse 4: This is the way I wash my ears . . .
   Pantomime "Touch my ears." On the last line, touch a child's ears and sing the child's name.
2. Sing to the tune of "If You're Happy and You Know It":
   If you're happy and you know it, touch your ears,   *(Touch ears.)*
   If you're happy and you know it, touch your ears.   *(Touch ears.)*
   If you're happy and you know it, then your face will
   surely show it.   *(Cup face and smile.)*
   If you're happy and you know it, touch your ears.   *(Touch ears.)*

Art

1. Have children tear or cut out pictures of ears and paste them on outlined picture of face and then decorate around the face.
2. Have children match animal ears.
3. Have children make a collage of pictures of ears cut from magazines, etc.

Snack

1. Make popcorn and use ears to hear it pop.
2. Eat crackly cereal, carrots, or celery to hear sounds of chewing.

Fine Motor

1. Have children press "Clickers" and "Squeekers" and listen to the sounds.
2. Have children play castinets and listen to sound.
3. Make cardboard puzzles with ears missing. Have children put "Ear" pieces in puzzle.

Games

1. Have children identify taped sounds of telephone, car horn, teacher's voice, dog barking, T.V. set, child's mother, etc. by touching correct pictures of source of sound or by verbalizing source of sounds.
2. Place three rhythm instruments in front of children. Let children close their eyes while teacher plays one hidden from sight. Ask one child to touch the instrument played.
3. Have children listen to a transistor radio with an ear plug, try on earrings, and talk on a telephone. Ask, "What do you hear?" or "What is on your ears?"
4. Seat group in a circle with hands behind backs. "It" is in center with eyes closed. One child shakes a bell and "it" tries to guess who made the jingle sound. The child discovered becomes "it."
5. Play "echo." Have children make the same sounds that come from behind a screen. Let them really enjoy these silly and happy sounds, whining, etc. Let 3 or 4 children go behind the screen. One speaks and the children on the other side identify him by his voice. One laughs and is identified, etc.

Storytelling

1. Make up a story about a boy with an earache who visits the doctor. Use pictures to illustrate. Ask children if they have had an earache.

2. Make up a story about a girl and her seashell. Bring a large shell for children to hold up to their ears to listen. Use pictures to illustrate.

Gross Motor
1. Play "Musical Chairs." Sit when the music stops. Children listen to music with ears.
2. Play "Statue-Statue." Have children make exercise movements until music stops and then "freeze" to become "statue."

Cognitive
1. Have children count ears on themselves and the others in class.
2. Place in envelope pairs of "cut-out" ears of people or animals. Let children match the ones which are alike.
3. Have children find things in the room which make noise.
4. Place objects in pairs of film cans. Have children match "sounds" of rice, screws, buttons, salt, or wooden beads.

Enrichment
1. Have children match ears to related animals, rabbit's ears to rabbit, etc. Use picture with ears on it for some children and pictures with part or all of ear missing for children with higher-level skills.
2. Clap blocks together in count of 2, 5, 3, 4, 6. Have children listen intently to how many claps and say how many claps.
3. Let children count animal ears and thereby determine how many animals there are. Two ears for each animal.

Lesson 4: Nose

Unit Group Lesson

1. **Match Concrete Objects**
   Present two noses. Say, "This is a nose." Ask each child in turn to put the nose with the nose. Gradually increase number of irrelevant objects from which (s)he must select nose to match.

2. **Discriminate Objects**
   Present several objects. Have each child touch the nose in response to verbal direction, "Touch the nose."

3. **Locate Own**
   Have each child touch his/her own nose upon request: "Touch your nose, (child's name)."

4. **Match Pictures**
   Present several pictures of common objects. Have each child match the pictures of the noses.

5. **Discriminate Pictures**
   Present a group of several unrelated pictures of objects. Have each child touch the picture of the nose in response to verbal direction, "Touch the nose."

6. **Figure-Ground**
   Present a "busy" picture with many visual distractions. Ask each child to find the picture of the nose.

7. **Visual Closure**
   Partially cover each of several pictures with paper. Ask each child to find the picture of the nose.

8. **Function**
   Ask, "What are noses used for?"

9. **Association**
   Ask, "What goes with the nose?" Use related pictures or objects including tissues, mouth, perfume, etc., with several unrelated objects or pictures.

10. **Imitate Verbalization**
    Present a nose and ask, "What is this? Say, 'Nose'." The child will imitate "Nose."

11. **Verbalize Label**
    Present a nose and ask, "What is this?" The child will respond, "Nose."

12. **Concept Enrichment**
    Discuss different types of smells.

Music
1. Sing to the tune of "Here We Go 'Round the Mulberry Bush":
   Verse 1: This is the way I touch my nose, etc.
   Verse 2: This is the way I scratch my nose, etc.
   Verse 3: This is the way I wipe my nose, etc.
2. Sing to the tune of "If You're Happy and You Know It":
   Verse 1: Touch your nose.
   Verse 2: Scratch your nose.
   Verse 3: Wiggle your nose.
3. Sing "My Little Nose Goes Wiggle, Wiggle, Wiggle" to the tune of "This is the Way We Wash Our Clothes":
   Verse 1: My little nose goes wiggle, wiggle,
            Wiggle, wiggle,
            Wiggle, wiggle,
            My little nose goes, wiggle, wiggle
            Wiggle, wiggle, wiggle.
   Verse 2: My little eyes go blink, blink, blink (review).
   Verse 3: My little head goes up and down (review).

Art
1. Have children paste a nose on a blank face or a face with two eyes and a mouth and decorate the border.
2. Have children make a nose collage from people and animal nose pictures. Obtain pictures from catalogs and magazines.
3. Give each child a giant nose and have her paint it.

Snack
1. Smell cinnamon and sugar and put it on bread. (BE SURE CHILDREN DO NOT SNIFF TOO CLOSELY.)
2. Eat food with strong aromas such as peanut butter, bacon, etc.

Fine Motor
1. Teach each child to wipe her nose.
2. Have children draw the nose on a picture of a face without a nose.
3. Have children sprinkle herbs and spices on wet glue. Let dry and smell.
4. Let the children use hand lotion and smell.
5. Let children use a flower magnet and a path on a cookie sheet or magnet board to path trace the flower to a nose.

Games

1.   Let children rub noses.
2.   Have children wipe cleansing cream off nose with leaves. Use mirror.

Storytelling

1.   Tell a flannelboard story of a little girl walking home from school. She smells flowers, hears birds, and sees a friend. It makes her very happy. She comes home and tells her mother what she smelled, heard, and saw. Use felt cut-outs of school, girl, mother, flowers, bird, and a boy to illustrate story.
2.   Talk about elephant's nose:
       An elephant goes like this and that.
       He's terribly big and terribly fat.
       He has no fingers.
       He has no toes.
       But goodness gracious, what a NOSE!
3.   Help children learn this fingerplay:
       10 little fingers
       10 little toes
       2 little eyes
       And a great big nose!

Gross Motor

      Have a potato race. Let the children use their noses to push balls or potatoes across floor to finish line.

Cognitive

1.   Have children match noses of different types of animals, people, pigs, dogs, cat, elephant, etc.
2.   Show children a picture of a face without a nose and ask, "What's missing?"
3.   Let children smell different odors. Prepare pairs of medicine bottles with alcohol, coffee, tobacco, dried onions, clovers, etc. Have child match those which are the "same." (Olfactory discrimination.)

Enrichment

      Have children draw the missing part on the picture from "Body Concept Ditto Masters." (D.L.M., 3505 N. Ashland Ave., Chicago, IL 60657.) Or, make a ditto master of a face and let children draw in missing part.

Lesson 5: Mouth

Unit Group Lesson

1.   **Match Concrete Objects**
      Present two mouths. Say, "This is a mouth." Ask each child in turn to put the mouth with the mouth. Gradually increase number of irrelevant objects from which (s)he must select mouth to match.

2.   **Discriminate Objects**
      Present several objects. Have each child touch the mouth in response to verbal direction, "Touch the mouth."

3.   **Locate Own**
      Have each child touch his/her own mouth upon request: "Touch your mouth, (child's name)."

4.   **Match Pictures**
      Present several pictures of common objects. Have each child match the pictures of the mouths.

5. **Discriminate Pictures**
   Present a group of several unrelated pictures of objects. Have each child touch the picture of the mouth in response to verbal direction, "Touch the mouth."

6. **Figure-Ground**
   Present a "busy" picture with many visual distractions. Ask each child to find the picture of the mouth.

7. **Visual Closure**
   Partially cover each of several pictures with paper. Ask each child to find the picture of the mouth.

8. **Function**
   Ask, "What do we do with a mouth?"

9. **Association**
   Ask, "What goes with the mouth?" Use related pictures or objects including teeth, lipstick, food, toothpaste, etc., with several unrelated objects or pictures.

10. **Imitate Verbalization**
    Present a mouth and ask, "What is this? Say, 'Mouth'." The child will imitate "Mouth."

11. **Verbalize Label**
    Present a mouth and ask, "What is this?" The child will respond, "Mouth."

12. **Concept Enrichment**
    Discuss fact that some children have difficulty talking, so it makes it hard to understand them. Discuss taste and the differences between tastes. Discuss different languages; how different-sounding words mean the same thing in different languages.

Music
1. Sing "If You're Happy and You Know It":
   Verse 1: If you're happy and you know it open your mouth.
   Verse 2: If you're happy and you know it close your mouth.
2. Sing to the tune of "Thumbkin":
   Open your mouth, open your mouth,
   Just like me, just like me.
   Now you can close it,
   Now you can close it,
   Close it tight, close it tight.

Art
1. Have children make a mouth collage from mouths cut from magazines and catalogs.
2. Put lipstick on each child and have her make a mouth print picture.
3. Have children do a soda straw painting. Place a teaspoon each of three different colors of thin tempera paint on a piece of paper (shiny finger paint paper would be good). Have children blow the paint around the paper and blend the colors where they overlap.
4. Provide the children with a table and mirror, vaseline, lipstick and tissues. Have the children imitate pictures from sequence story (Storytelling #3 of this lesson), or imitate teacher/child model, smiling, frowning, vaselining lips, painting lips red, opening mouth, and wiping mouth. (See fig. 1F & 1G.)

Fig. 1F

1. Smile   2. Frown   3. Put your finger in Vaseline.   4. Put Vaseline on your lips.   5. Paint your lips red.

Snack
1. During snack talk about eating and talking with our mouths. Have children chew fast and slowly. Mention that we kiss with our mouths (or lips). Have children try to eat without opening their mouths.
2. Talk about tastes of snack. Have lemonade before and after adding sugar.
3. Serve cinnamon toast and taste cinnamon and sugar.
4. Make milkshakes and add chocolate, strawberry, vanilla, and banana flavors. Sample each.

Fine Motor
1. Have children blow bubbles with straws in soapy water.
2. Have children blow out candles.
3. Have children blow up balloons. "This is the way I blow my balloon. (Puff, Puff, Puff) This is the way I pop my balloon - Pop! (Clap)."
4. Have children race ping pong balls across table by blowing.
5. Have children blow ping pong balls through a simple block maze on the table top. (Visual motor activity.)

Games
Prepare a gameboard with pictures of various body parts and cards with the same pictures. Ask child to identify picture on card. Then, have child put the card on the gameboard. Variation: using the same gameboard prepare cards with pictures that relate to that body part, (eg. eyes and eye glasses, head and hat, mouth and popsicle, eye and eye patch). Vinyl photographic album pages, with from two to nine pockets, make excellent lotto games and make it easy to vary the levels of the lotto games for children with different skill levels. (See fig. 1Q.)

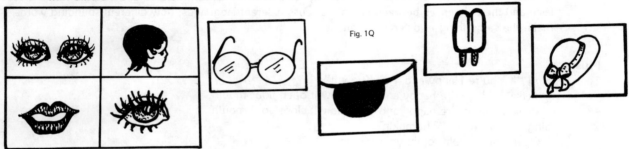

Fig. 1Q

Storytelling
1. Make up a story about a little boy whose mouth would not smile. Use pictures from magazines or flannel board cut-outs to illustrate.
2. Make up a story about the whale with a big mouth.
3. Use sequence cards as illustrated to make up a story about a smile, frown, etc.

Gross Motor
1. Let children have a potato race and use their mouths to push potatoes across floor.
2. Let children race carrying a boiled egg or other object on a spoon in the mouth.

Cognitive
1. How many mouths do we have? Do we have more eyes than mouths? Count each on the child and in pictures.
2. Discuss concepts of opened and closed by looking at mouths which are opened and closed as well as doors, windows, books, etc., which are opened and closed.
3. Discuss different tastes: sweet, sour, salty and bitter. Blindfold child and have him discriminate whether taste is salty, etc., or just identify food. Use peanut butter, jelly, lemon, sugar, salt, bitter chocolate, etc. Count each on the child and in pictures.

Enrichment

1. Match the correct lips. Make fit-together puzzle pieces for numerals one to five, (out of poster board or oaktag). Put a numeral on one lip and the correct number of dots on the other lip. Make puzzle self-correcting by having one notch for numeral 1, two for numeral 2, etc. Protect with clear plastic or laminate. Have children match upper and lower lips. (See fig. 1H.)
2. Have children trace around a mouth and the word mouth and color the mouth with "lipstick" crayon.

Fig. 1H

Lesson 6: Hair

Unit Group Lesson

1. **Match Concrete Objects**
   Present some hair. Say, "This is hair." Ask each child in turn to put the hair with the hair. Gradually increase number of irrelevant objects from which (s)he must select hair to match.

2. **Discriminate Objects**
   Present several objects. Have each child touch the hair in response to verbal direction, "Touch the hair."

3. **Locate Own**
   Have each child touch his/her own hair upon request: "Touch your hair, (child's name)."

4. **Match Pictures**
   Present several pictures of common objects. Have each child match the pictures of the hair.

5. **Discriminate Pictures**
   Present a group of several unrelated pictures of objects. Have each child touch the picture of the hair in response to verbal direction, "Touch the hair."

6. **Figure-Ground**
   Present a "busy" picture with many visual distractions. Ask each child to find the picture of the hair.

7. **Visual Closure**
   Partially cover each of several pictures with paper. Ask each child to find the picture of the hair.

8. **Function**
   Ask, "What does hair do?"

9. **Association**
   Ask, "What goes with the hair?" Use related pictures or objects including bobby pins, ribbons, hairbrush, comb, etc., with several unrelated objects or pictures.

10. **Imitate Verbalization**
    Present hair and ask, "What is this? Say, 'Hair'." The child will imitate "Hair."

11. **Verbalize Label**
    Present hair and ask, "What is this?" The child will respond, "Hair."

12. **Concept Enrichment**

Discuss differences in hair. Discuss names of hair colors. Discuss hair that is curly, straight, wavy, long, short, etc.

Music

1. Sing to the tune of "This is the Way We Wash Our Clothes":
   Verse 1: This is the way I touch my hair. . .   *(Pantomime movements.)*
   Verse 2: This is the way I brush my hair. . .
   Verse 3: This is the way I comb my hair. . .
2. Sing to the tune of "Where is Thumbkin":
   Verse 1: Comb your hair, comb your hair,   *(Pantomime.)*
   Just like me, just like me.   *(Pantomime.)*
   (Child's name) hair is pretty.   *(Touch child's hair.)*
   (Child's name) hair is pretty.
   So is (child's name).   *(Touch child's hair.)*
   So is (child's name).

Art

1. Have children paste cotton or yarn hair on pictures of heads.
2. Make pictures of boys and girls with no hair and have the children put the appropriate style of hair on appropriate body. Use either large pictures or teacher-made construction paper figures.
3. Have children paste spaghetti (straight hair), noodles, curled noodles (curly hair), etc., on a bald head with a face. Have children describe the hair on the head.
4. Let children use paper plates to make heads with all the features.
5. Have children make play dough or clay heads with eyes, ears, nose, mouth, and hair.

Snack

Have children get neat to eat by brushing and combing hair before snack.

Fine Motor

1. Have children brush and comb hair on dolls, teacher and each other.
2. Provide faces on large sheets of newsprint. Tape to table or at child level on bulletin board or wall. Have children add straight up and down strokes with crayons on the straight hair face and curly scribbles on the curly hair face.
3. Make sewing cards. Draw heads with all facial features on cardboard. Punch holes where the hair would be. Have the children "sew" the hair on the head. Vary the levels of difficulty.
4. Have children make hair with play dough and garlic press and glue onto pictures.
5. Help children braid yarn hair on a cardboard doll or real hair on a person.

Games

1. Encourage the children to play beauty parlor and barber shop.
2. Let children shampoo and comb doll's hair.
3. Let children try on different wigs and hair pieces.

Storytelling

1. Read *Straight Hair, Curly Hair* by August Goldin.
2. Make up a story about three boys who had red, black, and blond hair. Relate to children in class.
3. Make up a story about a girl's ponytails and pigtails. Illustrate with magazine pictures. Relate to children in class.

Gross Motor

Have children do full or partial headstands, with adult assistance.

Cognitive

1. Have children match hair samples. Collect trimmings from barber or beauty shop. Put each type in two jars. Have children match same kind.
2. Make pairs of faces with different hairstyles. Have children match those pairs which go together.
3. Discuss straight hair and curly hair.

Enrichment

1. Help children grow "hair" in a potato head. Have them scoop out part of a potato, put in soil and grass seed and put facial features on potato. When grass grows, give the potato a "hair cut." Start "hair" a week before needed.
2. Let children look at hair under a microscope.
3. Discuss differences among people in hair color, hair type, etc.

Field Trip

Visit a beauty parlor and/or barber shop.

Visitor

Have a hair stylist cut your hair at school.

Lesson 7: Body

Unit Group Lesson

1. **Match Concrete Objects**
   Present two bodies. Say, "This is a body." Ask each child in turn to put the body with the body. Gradually increase number of irrelevant objects from which (s)he must select bodies to match.

2. **Discriminate Objects**
   Present several objects. Have each child touch the body in response to verbal direction, "Touch the body."

3. **Locate Own**
   Have each child touch his/her own body upon request: "Touch your body, (child's name)."

4. **Match Pictures**
   Present several pictures of common objects. Have each child match the pictures of the bodies.

5. **Discriminate Pictures**
   Present a group of several unrelated pictures of objects. Have each child touch the picture of the body in response to verbal direction, "Touch the body."

6. **Figure-Ground**
   Present a "busy" picture with many visual distractions. Ask each child to find the picture of the body.

7. **Visual Closure**
   Partially cover each of several pictures with paper. Ask each child to find the picture of the body.

8. **Function**
   Ask, "What do our bodies do?"

9. **Association**

Ask, "What goes with the body?" Use related pictures or objects including arms, legs, clothes, etc., with several unrelated objects or pictures.

10. **Imitate Verbalization**

Present body and ask, "What is this? Say, 'Body'." The child will imitate "Body."

11. **Verbalize Label**

Present body and ask, "What is this?" The child will respond, "Body."

12. **Concept Enrichment**

Discuss different body types, heavy, thin, etc. This is a good time to discuss different skin colors, also.

Music
1. Sing to the tune of "Here We Go 'Round the Mulberry Bush":
   Verse 1: This is the way I touch my body,
   Touch my body, touch my body.
   This is the way I touch my body,
   I touch (child's name) body.
   Verse 2: This is the way I pat my body. . .
   Verse 3: This is the way I shake my body. . .
   Verse 4: This is the way I wash my body. . .
   Pantomime "touch my head." On the last line the teacher touches a child's head and the group sings the child's name.
2. Sing to the tune of "If You're Happy and You Know It":
   Verse 1: If you're happy and you know it, touch your body
   If you're happy and you know it, touch your body.
   If you're happy and you know it,
   Then your face will surely show it;
   If you're happy and you know it,
   Touch your body.
   Verse 2: If you're happy and you know it, pat your body.
   Verse 3: If you're happy and you know it, shake your body.

Art
1. Glue pre-cut heads from catalogs onto construction paper. Let the children glue the bodies onto the heads.
2. Repeat above activity with animal bodies and animal heads.
3. Supply cut out bodies of various sizes. Have the children glue them on construction paper or poster board.

Snack

Eat foods that help the body grow such as milk, protein, etc.

Fine Motor
1. Have the children make bodies and other parts of people from play dough.
2. Have children assemble cardboard body puzzles with brass fasteners.
   Let children punch their own holes in the parts. (See fig. 11.)

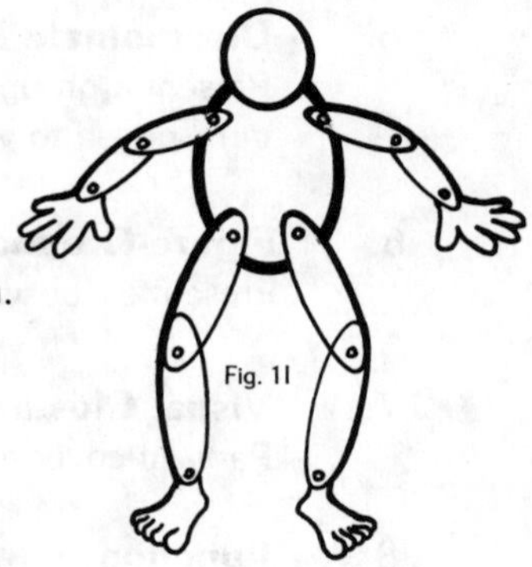

Fig. 11

Games

Let the children play "Tape the body on the girl" (boy, dog, cat, etc.). Use tape or magnets to attach the body to the arms, legs and head. Use blindfolds, if they are acceptable to the children.

Storytelling

1. Fingerplay "Who Feels Happy." Perform actions as rhyme indicates.
   Who feels happy, who feels gay?
   All who do clap their hands this way.
   Who feels happy, who feels gay?
   All who do wiggle their bodies this way.
   Who feels happy, who feels gay?
   All who do scratch their nose this way.

2. Fingerplay "Knock at the Door":

Knock at the door,	*(Knock on forehead.)*
Peep in.	*(Peer through circled thumbs and forefingers.)*
Turn the latch,	*(Twist nose.)*
Walk in.	*(Pretend to put finger in mouth.)*

Gross Motor

1. Have children crawl through boxes and inner tubes.
2. Have children twist hula hoops around body. Some children will only be able to step into hula hoops.

Cognitive

1. Ask, "How many bodies?" Have each child count how many bodies she has and how many bodies her teacher has.
2. Count how many bodies there are in the room.
3. Have children match cut-outs of sweaters to cut-outs of people and their bodies. (See fig. 1J.)

Fig. 1J

Enrichment

1. Have children decide which set of sweaters goes with which set of bodies.
2. Give children body cut-outs in three or more different sizes and have them arrange them from smallest to largest or largest to smallest.
3. Have each child lie on large paper and trace around the child. Have the child identify body parts on the outline and on herself.

Field Trip

Visit a health or body-building spa and watch how people exercise to keep their bodies in shape.

Lesson 8: Arm

Unit Group Lesson

1. **Match Concrete Objects**
   Present two arms. Say, "This is an arm." Ask each child in turn to put the arm with the arm. Gradually increase number of irrelevant objects from which (s)he must select arms to match.

2. **Discriminate Objects**
Present several objects. Have each child touch the arm in response to verbal direction, "Touch the arm."

3. **Locate Own**
Have each child touch his/her own arm upon request: "Touch your arm, (child's name)."

4. **Match Pictures**
Present several pictures of common objects. Have each child match the pictures of the arms.

5. **Discriminate Pictures**
Present a group of several unrelated pictures of objects. Have each child touch the picture of the arm in response to verbal direction, "Touch the arm."

6. **Figure-Ground**
Present a "busy" picture with many visual distractions. Ask each child to find the picture of the arm.

7. **Visual Closure**
Partially cover each of several pictures with paper. Ask each child to find the picture of the arm.

8. **Function**
Ask, "What do our arms do?"

9. **Association**
Ask, "What goes with the arm?" Use related pictures or objects including bracelets, watches, hands, etc., with several unrelated objects or pictures.

10. **Imitate Verbalization**
Present an arm and ask, "What is this? Say, 'Arm'." The child will imitate "Arm."

11. **Verbalize Label**
Present an arm and ask, "What is this?" The child will respond, "Arm."

12. **Concept Enrichment**
Discuss how the arm bends at the elbow and simulate some handicapping conditions. Make a "cast" by taping a file folder around arm or put one arm in a sling and have the child try to do things.

Music
1. Sing to the tune of "The Bear Went Over the Mountain":
   My arms are beginning to wiggle,   *(Wiggle arms.)*
   My arms are beginning to wiggle,
   My arms are beginning to wiggle,
   My arms are beginning to wiggle,
   Tra-la-la-la-la.
2. Sing "Hokey Pokey":
   I put my arm in.   *(Pantomime motions as indicated.)*
   I take my arm out.
   I put my arm in,
   And shake it all about.
   I do the hokey pokey,   *(Swing hips from side to side.)*
   And turn myself around,
   And that's what it's all about.

3. Sing to the tune of "Did You Ever See a Lassie?":
    Verse 1: Can you swing your arms, your arms, your arms?   *(Perform motions.)*
              Can you swing your arms, back and forth?
              Swing 'em this way.
              Swing 'em that way.
              Swing 'em this way.
              Swing 'em that way.
              Can you swing your arms back and forth?
    Verse 2: Can you wave your arms. . . .

Art
1. Help children make arm apple trees. Lay sheets of paper towel on cookie sheet. Cover lightly with brown tempera. Have each child place arm in paint up to elbow with hands stretched out. Print "tree" trunks from arm on newsprint or paper. Have children cut out apples and leaves for the arm apple tree and glue them on after the tree is dry.
2. Have children paint at the easel on large paper by moving their whole arms to make strokes.

Snack
Use arms for reaching for snack foods.

Fine Motor
1. Have children put together DLM Body Puzzle. Include only trunk, arms, hands and fingers, and head.
2. Have one child trace another child's arm. Use a large crayon or felt tip marker.
3. Help children make an arm out of cardboard or wood with two pieces and a brass fastener or bolt to flex the elbow joint.

Games
1. Play Simon Says. Include "wave arms, shake arms, pat arms, raise arms up, put arms down."
2. Have children arm wrestle.
3. Have children pretend to be airplanes with "propeller arms."

Storytelling
Fingerplay "Fold Your Arms Like Me":
    Verse 1: Roll your hands, roll your hands,
              As slowly, as slowly, as slow can be.
              Then fold your arms like me.
    Verse 2: Roll your hands, roll your hands,
              As fast, as fast, as fast can be.
              Then fold your arms like me.
    Verse 3: Clap your hands, clap your hands,
              As loudly, as loudly, as loud can be.
              Then fold your arms like me.
Do motions as words suggest.

Gross Motor
1. Let children have a relay race holding a paper plate with a large feather and one arm held behind back.
2. Have children use a balance beam, hold arms out and walk back and forth. (A piece of tape or rope stretched out on the floor can be used if a beam is not available.)
3. Let children crab walk on arms and legs.
4. Have children push a large ball along a tape line with a broom.
5. Have children hold a sheet with their arms. Have them go around in circles to right and left and make waves, or bounce nerf balls or balloons up and down.
6. Have children throw bean bags into box.
7. Have children throw rings cut from plastic lids onto an upright stick.
8. Let children swing golf clubs, tennis rackets, etc.

Cognitive

1. Have children count how many arms they have.
2. Have children identify arms and other body parts from shadows flashed behind a sheet with a strong light. You can use your body or cut-outs to make shapes.

Enrichment

1. Discuss wrist and elbow joints. The wrist has circular motions and the elbow can only move back and forth.
2. Have each child make a number bracelet suitable to her own counting skill.

Lesson 9: Hand

Unit Group Lesson

NOTE: Fingers can be studied at the same time as hand or as a separate topic by substituting fingers for hand in the Unit Group Lesson.

1. **Match Concrete Objects**
   Present two hands. Say, "This is a hand." Ask each child in turn to put the hand with the hand. Gradually increase number of irrelevant objects from which (s)he must select hand to match.

2. **Discriminate Objects**
   Present several objects. Have each child touch the hand in response to verbal direction, "Touch the hand."

3. **Locate Own**
   Have each child touch his/her own hand upon request: "Touch your hand, (child's name)."

4. **Match Pictures**
   Present several pictures of common objects. Have each child match the pictures of the hands.

5. **Discriminate Pictures**
   Present a group of several unrelated pictures of objects. Have each child touch the picture of the hand in response to verbal direction, "Touch the hand."

6. **Figure-Ground**
   Present a "busy" picture with many visual distractions. Ask each child to find the picture of the hand.

7. **Visual Closure**
   Partially cover each of several pictures with paper. Ask each child to find the picture of the hand.

8. **Function**
   Ask, "What does a hand do?"

9. **Association**
   Ask, "What goes with the hand?" Use related pictures or objects including rings, gloves, mittens, fingers, etc., with several unrelated objects or pictures.

10. **Imitate Verbalization**
    Present a hand and ask, "What is this? Say, 'Hand'." The child will imitate "Hand."

11. **Verbalize Label**
    Present a hand and ask, "What is this?" The child will respond, "Hand."

12. **Concept Enrichment**

Discuss joints in hands and fingers. Simulate not having the use of some fingers by taping thumb and pointer fingers together. Give the children some fine motor tasks to do.

Music

1. Sing to the tune of "Here We Go 'Round the Mulberry Bush":

    Verse 1: This is the way I clap my hands,
    Clap my hands, clap my hands.
    This is the way I clap my hands,
    Clap my two hands.

    Verse 2: This is the way I rub my hands.

    Verse 3: This is the way I shake my hands.

    Verse 4: This is the way I wash my hands.

2. Sing to the tune of "The Bear Went Over the Mountain":

    Verse 1: My fingers are starting to wiggle.
    My fingers are starting to wiggle.
    My fingers are starting to wiggle.
    Tra-la-la-la-la.

    Verse 2: My hands are starting to wiggle. . .

3. Make finger castinets. Use rubber bands to hold a big button on each child's middle finger and thumb and let him play.

Art

1. Have children make hand prints with tempera paint on paper.
2. Trace each child's hand. Have her color fingernails and rings on handprint.
3. Have children make rings from colored pipe cleaners.
4. Have children fingerpaint with fingerpaint, soapsuds, pudding, or shaving cream.
5. Have children make a handprint in plaster of paris.

Snack

Make sugar cookies in shape of hand. Trace around child's hand with blunt knife and bake the dough. During snack count the fingers and joke about cookies: "You're eating your fingers!"

Fine Motor

1. Have children put mittens or gloves on hand.
2. Have children assemble a puzzle of a hand. Make puzzles of different levels of complexity suitable to the children's skills.
3. Try on rings and bracelets.
4. Have children use fingers to screw lids onto various sizes of jars. Attach lids to board and have child screw on the jar.
5. Make a bolt board and have the children screw nuts onto bolts.
6. Have children pick up cotton balls with tongs.

Games

1. Let children paint their fingernails using tempera paint in fingernail polish bottles.
2. Let children use light from slide projector for hand shadows on a screen or white paper.

Storytelling

1. Fingerplay "Mittens":

    Slide your finger into the wide part,   *(Heel right hand forward.)*
    Make your thumb stand alone and tall.   *(Palm and finger together, thumb apart.)*
    When you put your mittens on,   *(Slide left hand over grouped fingers*
    You can't feel cold at all.   *and then over thumb.)*
    Give children real mittens.

2.   Fingerplay "Open, Shut Them":
    Open, shut them.
    Open, shut them.
    Give your hands a clap.
    Open, shut them.
    Open, shut them.
    Fold them in your lap.
    Creep them, creep them.
    Open wide your little mouth,
    But do not let them in.
    Make fingers follow the direction of the rhyme.

3.   Fingerplay "Right Hand, Left Hand":
    This is my right hand;
    I'll raise it up high.
    This is my left hand;
    I'll touch the sky.
    Right hand, left hand,
    Roll them around.
    Left hand, right hand,
    Pound, pound, pound.
    Raise hands and do as verse instructs.

4.   Fingerplay:
    I can knock with two hands   *(Knock, knock, knock.)*
    I can sock with two hands   *(Sock, sock, sock.)*
    I can tap with two hands   *(Tap, tap, tap.)*
    I can clap with two hands   *(Clap, clap, clap.)*

5.   Fingerplay:
    This little hand is a good little hand.   *(Hold up right hand.)*
    This little hand is his brother.   *(Hold up left hand.)*
    Together they wash and they wash and they
    wash.   *(Make washing motions.)*
    One hand washes the other.

Gross Motor
1.   Let children play frisbee.
2.   Have children clap hands behind back, run up to table and use mouths to pick up marshmallow or cookie from table.

Cognitive
1.   Count fingers on one hand. More advanced children may count to 10. Using water-color markers, put numeral on each finger from left to right. (See fig. 1K.)
2.   Have child reach under curtain to discriminate hand from foot on a friend on other side. "Find hand." "What do you find?" Child should respond, "Hand," "A hand," "I found a hand."
3.   Have children make tactile discrimination between rough and smooth textures by sorting things into two groups.
4.   Have each child select objects from "feely box" or "feely bag" in response to teacher's direction such as "Find the scissors," "Find the block," "Find the ball."

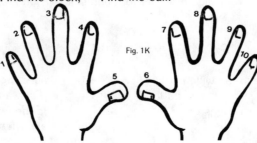

Fig. 1K

Enrichment

This activity takes two days. On day 1: cover a table or tape wrapping paper on the floor in a designated area. Have the children fingerpaint in one color on the entire sheet and let dry. On day 2: hang the paper on the bulletin board or tape on the wall at the child's level. Have all children and teachers add handprints in a contrasting color and make border of fingerpaints all the way around the edge. This makes a lovely bulletin board or wall hanging.

Lesson 10: Leg

Unit Group Lesson

1. **Match Concrete Objects**
    Present two legs. Say, "This is a leg." Ask each child in turn to put the leg with the leg. Gradually increase number of irrelevant objects from which (s)he must select leg to match.

2. **Discriminate Objects**
    Present several objects. Have each child touch the leg in response to verbal direction, "Touch the leg."

3. **Locate Own**
    Have each child touch his/her own leg upon request: "Touch your leg, (child's name)."

4. **Match Pictures**
    Present several pictures of common objects. Have each child match the pictures of the legs.

5. **Discriminate Pictures**
    Present a group of several unrelated pictures of objects. Have each child touch the picture of the leg in response to verbal direction, "Touch the leg."

6. **Figure-Ground**
    Present a "busy" picture with many visual distractions. Ask each child to find the picture of the leg.

7. **Visual Closure**
    Partially cover each of several pictures with paper. Ask each child to find the picture of the leg.

8. **Function**
    Ask, "What do legs do?"

9. **Association**
    Ask, "What goes with the legs?" Use related pictures or objects including pants, feet, knees, etc., with several unrelated objects or pictures.

10. **Imitate Verbalization**
    Present a leg and ask, "What is this? Say, 'Leg'." The child will imitate "Leg."

11. **Verbalize Label**
    Present a leg and ask, "What is this?" The child will respond, "Leg."

12. **Concept Enrichment**
    Discuss knee and ankle. Talk about not being able to use your legs. Simulate not being able to walk by using a wheelchair and trying to go through a maze.

Music
1.   Sing to the tune of "The Bear Went Over the Mountain":
          My legs are beginning to wiggle. . .
2.   Sing "Hokey Pokey":
          I put my leg in. . .
3.   Sing to the tune of "Oh, Dear, What Can the Matter Be?":
          Verse 1: See, see, see my legs walk.
                    See, see, see my legs walk.
                    See, see, see my legs walk.
                    They walk as slow (or fast) as can be.
          Verse 2: See, see, see my legs run. . .
          Verse 3: See, see, see my legs jump. . .
      Pantomime motions with song.

Art
1.   Have children paste animal legs on appropriate animal and paste human legs on pictures of boys and girls. Decorate pictures.
2.   Have children make a body-parts mobile. Trace each child's body and let them cut it out. Use a coat hanger for the shoulders and construction paper for the facial features and use string to assemble the parts.

Snack
1.   Hop to table to get snack.
2.   Sit Indian style (legs crossed) to eat snack.

Fine Motor
1.   Draw a boy (or girl) on child's hand so that legs are on the two middle fingers and hands are on the index and little fingers. Have the child walk the boy (or girl). (See fig. 1L.)
2.   Give child a ditto sheet with stick people drawn on it. Have child draw the missing legs. For more skilled children have a cue at the top of page and vary the stick people. (See fig, 1M.)
3.   Have children draw the missing parts of animal stick figures depending upon their skill levels. (See fig. 1N.)

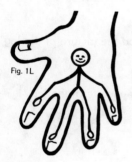
Fig. 1L

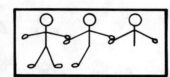
Fig. 1M

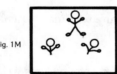

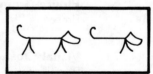
Fig. 1N

Games
1.   Play jumpfrog. If child cannot jump over another child, have her jump up from squatting position.
2.   Run relays using different series of commands such as
          "Run to the tree and come back,"
          "Run to the tree, then to the slide, and come back," and
          "Run to the tree, then to the slide, and then to the swing, and come back."
      (Auditory Memory)
3.   Have children hop on one leg, then the other; hop in a circle; hop turning around.
          Sing, "See, see, see my legs hop. . ." from Music #3.

Storytelling
      Make up a story about Tommy's legs that carry Tommy to the different activities in the center, eg., snack, playground, lunch room, etc. Use each child's legs in turn. Let the child select his own destination.

Gross Motor

1. Measure with a length of string how far a child can jump and let the child take the string home.
2. Let the children play "Jump the River." Put two pieces of rope parallel to each other and let children jump over. Start with ropes close together. Slowly move them further and further apart.

Cognitive

1. Have children identify the parts of the leg.
2. Use legs to emphasize fast and slow. Have children model moving their legs fast and slowly.
3. Have the children count the legs of the children in the class.

Enrichment

Have children cut out body parts and attach parts with brass fasteners to a body. (See fig. 10.)

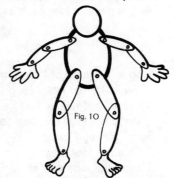

Fig. 10

Lesson 11: Foot

Unit Group Lesson

NOTE: Toes can be studied at the same time as foot or as a separate topic by substituting toes for foot in the Unit Group Lesson.

1. **Match Concrete Objects**
   Present two feet. Say, "This is a foot." Ask each child in turn to put the foot with the foot. Gradually increase number of irrelevant objects from which (s)he must select feet to match.

2. **Discriminate Objects**
   Present several objects. Have each child touch the foot in response to verbal direction, "Touch the foot."

3. **Locate Own**
   Have each child touch his/her own foot upon request: "Touch your foot, (child's name)."

4. **Discriminate Pictures**
   Present a group of several unrelated pictures of objects. Have each child touch the picture of the foot in response to verbal direction, "Touch the foot."

5. **Figure-Ground**
   Present a "busy" picture with many visual distractions. Ask each child to find the picture of the foot.

6. **Visual Closure**
   Partially cover each of several pictures with paper. Ask each child to find the picture of the foot.

7. **Function**
   Ask, "What do our feet do?"

8. **Association**
   Ask, "What goes with a foot?" Use related pictures or objects including sole, toes, shoes, socks, slippers, etc., with several unrelated objects or pictures.

9. **Imitate Verbalization**
   Present a foot and ask, "What is this? Say, 'Foot'." The child will imitate "Foot."

10. **Verbalize Label**

Present a foot and ask, "What is this?" The child will respond, "Foot."

11. **Concept Enrichment**

Discuss parts of foot such as ball, heel, arch, toes, etc.

Music

1. Sing to the tune of "My Little Hands Go Clap, Clap, Clap":
   Verse 1: My little feet go walk, walk, walk. . .
   Verse 2: My little feet go stamp, stamp, stamp. . .
   Verse 3: My little toes go wiggle, wiggle, wiggle. . .
2. Sing "Hokey Pokey":
   I put my foot in. . .
3. Sing to the tune of "Three Blind Mice":
   My foot has toes.
   My foot has toes.
   My foot has toes.
   My foot has toes.
   Whenever my feet are tickled
   My toes start to wiggle,
   My foot has toes.
   Have children take off shoes and socks to sing song. Tickle one child's foot when tickling is mentioned in song. Be sure every child has a turn.

Art

1. Have each child make a foot print by dipping foot in tempera paint and stepping on construction paper.
2. Let children paint with their toes.
3. Trace each child's foot. Let them cut it out and glue on paper. Have them decorate the foot.
4. Help each child trace around two feet together in shoes to make a butterfly and add feelers, eyes, etc. Color.

Snack

1. Put paper foot prints on floor in walking format. (Tarheels for Carolina fans.) Have children walk on foot prints to get snack and return to table.
2. Make foot-shaped sugar cookies and eat them. Count toes as the children bite them off.

Fine Motor

1. Have children remove and put on shoes and socks.
2. Have children paint toenails with polish.
3. Have children pick up pieces of clay with toes.
4. Let children walk in sandbox barefooted and pick up sand with toes.
5. Make a path tracing. Make a road on heavy paper on a metal surface, and have child move a magnet with feet glued on it from one end of the road to the other. (Eye-hand coordination)
6. Have children clip socks to a clothesline with spring clothespins.

Games

1. Have children locate body parts on stuffed animals or pictures of animals.
2. Take one shoe off each child's foot. Have children match missing shoes to owner's other shoe.

Storytelling

1.	Fingerplay "Runaway":

	I have two eyes to see with,
	I have two feet to run.
	I have two hands to wave with,
	And nose I have but one.
	I have two ears to hear with,
	And a tongue to say good-day.
	And two red cheeks for you to kiss,
	And now I'll run away.

	Point to parts of body mentioned. Run away on last line. It can be sung to tune of "Go In and Out the Window."

2.	On the flannelboard tell "Old Shoes, New Shoes."
3.	Recite and act out "This Little Piggy Went to Market."
4.	Read books: *The Foot Book* or *I Wish I Had Duck Feet.*

Gross Motor

1.	Have children stomp balloons with foot. Fasten balloons to floor with masking tape, if necessary.
2.	Have children respond to these instructions: "Can you walk on tip-toe as softly as a cat? Can you stomp across the room just like that? Can you march with your foot lifted high left, right, left, right? Can you hop on one foot, then the other?"
3.	Make oversized footprints (adult size) of foam rubber. Arrange on floor with tape. Let children follow them barefoot.
4.	Have children hop-a-long by clapping to the following rhyme: Hop, hop and do not stop until you touch the piano, the backdoor, the teacher's desk, the bookshelf, the blackboard, etc.
5.	Have children march to concepts. Play a marching record, talk about and act out:
	feet marching in place,
	feet marching in line, and
	feet marching in a parade (use American flags).

Cognitive

1.	Make feet in several sizes and have the children sequence them.
2.	Have children count how many feet each child has and compare it to number of heads, bodies, arms, hands, etc.
3.	Have children count how many toes each child has on each foot and both feet.
4.	Make life-sized cut-outs of three sizes of feet; baby, child and adult. Have children match their feet to determine which is child-sized.
5.	Let children wash socks of all colors and hang them to dry in correct pairs on a clothesline either outdoors or on a drying rack in the classroom.

Enrichment

1.	Outline a child's foot. Cut-out and let the children use it for measuring. "The table is as long as 6 of Sally's feet."
2.	Have the children fit the toes on the foot or feet. On heavy paper draw one or two feet and cut slots for inserting the toes. From separate heavy paper cut individual toes with long tabs for inserting in the slots and put the numerals 1-5 or 1-10 on the toes. Have the child insert the toes in the correct sequence from one to five or ten. A cue may be added by labeling each slot. (Numeral recognition, sequencing and fine motor activity.) Laminate all for durability.
3.	Have children find and cut out all kinds of feet and shoes from magazines and put them in a shoe box. Have each child reach in and pull out a "pair," tell color and to whom they could belong and where the shoes might be going. Talk about the word PAIR.
4.	In circle time or small group, children are rewarded for removing their shoes and socks by themselves by:
	a.	Painting their toe nails.
	b.	Tickling their toes with a feather.
	c.	Drawing a face on their big toe.
	d.	Making a footprint in a tray of damp sand.

Field Trip

1.   Visit a shoe store.
2.   Visit a clothing store and discuss clothing for each part of the body in a unit summary field trip.

Other Children's Records
"Bean Bag Rock" from **BEAN BAG ACTIVITIES & CO-ORD. SKILLS** (KIM)
"How Many Ways" from **BEAN BAG ACTIVITIES & CO-ORD. SKILLS** (KIM)
"My Hands Upon My Head" from **FINGERPLAY FUN** (EA)
"The Bean Bag" from **EASY DOES IT** (EA)
"Friends on the Floor" from **EASY DOES IT** (EA)
"Some Drifts to the Sky" from **EASY DOES IT** (EA)
"Hello" from **LEARNING BASIC SKILLS-VOC.** by Hap Palmer (EA)
"Spare Parts" from **IT'S A HAPPY FEELING**
"Turn Around" from **GETTING TO KNOW MYSELF** by Hap Palmer (Children's Music Center)
GET A GOOD START (KIM)
WALK LIKE THE ANIMALS (KIM)
"And One And Two" from **AND ONE AND TWO** (SCHOL)
"Head and Shoulder" from **LITTLE JOHNNY BROWN** (SCHOL)
"Otis O'Brian the Optician" from **BEGINNING SOUNDS & CAREERS**
"Clap Your Hands" from **AMERICAN FOLK SONGS** (FOLKWAY)
"Put Your Finger In the Air" from **ACTION SONGS & ROUNDS** (EA)
"Looby Lu" from **FOLK SONG CARNIVAL** (EA)
"Put Your Hands In the Air" from **LEARNING BASIC SKILLS VOL. 1** (EA)
"Open Them Shut Them" from **FINGERPLAY FUN** (EA)
"The Body Clap" from **TEMPO FOR TOTS** (MH)
"Hello World" from **TEMPO FOR TOTS** (MH)
"Squeeze a Shape" from **SHAPES IN ACTION** (KIM)
"Over and Under" from **SHAPES IN ACTION** (KIM)
"Playtime Parachute Fun" (KIM)
"Where is Thumbkin?" from **RAINDROPS** (MH)
"Follow the Leader" from **PLAY YOUR INSTRUMENTS** (SCHOL)
"Little Jack Horner" from **NURSERY RHYMES** (SCHOL)
"Mexican Hand-Clapping Song" from **THIS IS RHYTHM** (SCHOL)
SIMPLIFIED FOLK SONGS - SPECIAL ED. GRADES K-3 by Hap Palmer, (Children's Music Center)
GETTING TO KNOW MYSELF by Hap Palmer, songs about body awareness and body identification.
    (Children's Music Center)
MUSIC FOR THE 1'S AND 2'S by Tom Glazer, songs include "Where Are Your Eyes," "What Does Baby
    Hear?" and "Clap Hands." (Children's Music Center, EC2)

Other Children's Books
Brhrens, June. **WHAT I HEAR.** Chicago: Children's Press, 1980.
Brenner, Barbara. **BODIES.** New York: E.P. Dutton, 1973.
Brenner, Barbara. **FACES.** New York: E.P. Dutton, 1970.
Holzenthaler, Jean. **MY HANDS CAN.** New York: E.P. Dutton, 1978.
Howard, Katherine. **LITTLE BUNNY FOLLOWS HIS NOSE.** New York: Golden Press, 1971.
LeSeig, Theo. **THE EYE BOOK.** New York: Random House, 1978.

Related Parenting Materials
Cansler, Dot. **THE HOMESTRETCH.** Winston-Salem, NC 27113-5128: Kaplan Press, 1983.

Related Materials
TEACHING PICTURES. Winston-Salem, NC 27113-5128: Kaplan Press, 1983.
STORY SEQUENCE CARDS I, II. Winston-Salem, NC 27113-5128: Kaplan Press, 1983.
SEWING CARDS I, II, III. Winston-Salem, NC 27113-5128: Kaplan Press, 1983.

Unit 2: People & Family Members

A developmental assessment should determine the functional levels of each child. Individual expectations are based on the assessment results.

Lesson 1: Man

Unit Group Lesson

1. **Match Concrete Objects**
   Present two men. Say, "This is a man." Ask each child in turn to put the man with the man. Gradually increase number of irrelevant objects from which (s)he must select man to match.

2. **Discriminate Objects**
   When shown several objects have each child touch the man in response to verbal direction, "Touch the man."

3. **Match Pictures**
   Present several pictures of common objects. Have each child match the pictures of the men.

4. **Discriminate Pictures**
   Present a group of several unrelated pictures of objects. Have each child touch the picture of the man in response to verbal direction, "Touch the man."

5. **Figure-Ground**
   Present a "busy" picture with many visual distractions. Ask each child to find the man.

6. **Visual Closure**
   Partially cover each of several pictures with paper. Ask each child to find the picture of the man.

7. **Function**
   Ask, "What does a man do?"

8. **Association**
   Ask, "What goes with the man?" Use pictures or objects including grandpa, daddy, automobile, and several unrelated objects or pictures.

9. **Imitate Verbalization**
   Present a man and ask, "What is this? Say, 'Man'." The child will imitate "Man."

10. **Verbalize Label**
    Present a man and ask, "What is this?" The child will respond, "Man."

11.   **Concept Enrichment**
         Discuss facts that daddy is a man, grandpa is a man, and uncle is a man.

Music
1.   Sing to the tune of "The Farmer In The Dell":
         Verse 1:   A daddy is a man
                    A daddy is a man
                    Oh, ho, I know, I know
                    A daddy is a man.
         Verse 2:   A grandpa is a man
                    A grandpa is a man
                    Oh, no, I know, I know
                    A grandpa is a man.
2.   Sing to the tune of "The Muffin Man":
         Verse 1:   Oh, do you know the mailman
                    The mailman, the mailman
                    Oh, do you know the mailman,
                    That lives in Chapel Hill?
         Child may add verses about different men they know (eg. grocery man, policeman, fireman, etc.).
3.   Sing "Fat Man, Skinny Man" to tune of "Did You Ever See a Lassie?":
         Verse 1:   Did you ever see a fat man,
                    a fat man, a fat man?
                    Did you ever see a fat man
                    Walk down the street?
         Verse 2:   Did you ever see a skinny man?
         Verse 3:   Did you ever see a tall man?
         Verse 4:   Did you ever see a short man?
         Use pictures to illustrate each size man. Teacher can use large and short as a verse.
4.   Sing to the tune of "Mary Had a Little Lamb":
         My daddy helps me (ride my bike),
         (Ride my bike), (ride my bike).
         My dady helps me (ride my bike)
         And I love him very much.
         Have children name other things that their daddies help them do. Substitute other activities for "ride
         my bike."

Art
1.   Make a "Man Collage." From "people" pictures (various pictures of men, women, boys, girls, and
         babies cut out from catalog) have children find the pictures of men and paste on construction paper.
         Ask during activity, "Is a man a person?" Children will answer "Yes." Refer to the "people" in the
         pictures during the activity. A lower functioning child may need to choose "men" pictures from a
         group of "men" pictures. This will begin a "People" book.

3.   Give pictures of a man's body in parts (head, arms, trunk, legs). Have the children paste the parts on
         an outline of a man.

4.   Help children make a "Family Album" by using actual photographs of children's families for the
         children, daddy, and grandpa pages.
5.   Have children fingerpaint a daddy and his son. Children may need to be shown how to make stick
         people with one finger. Make comments, "The daddy is big. The son is little."
6.   Have children make tin can stilts. After children have made them and are standing on them; you may
         comment, "You are tall (big) like your daddy."
         Directions: Punch two holes on either side of two cans. Slip a piece of strong cord through each can.
         Adjust length of cords for each child. Child stands on can and holds cord. Use cans of various sizes.
         Stilts made from large fruit cans may be harder to manipulate than stilts from tortilla cans. Each child
         will need different sized stilts. (See fig. 2A.)

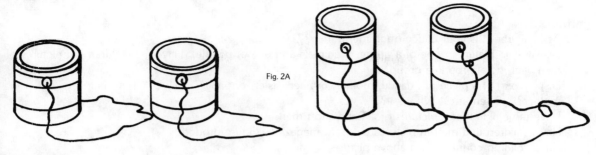
Fig. 2A

Snack

Dress like a man or daddy for snack.

Fine Motor

1. Have children do path tracing activities such as: Take a man to his car, take daddy to his children, and take grandpa to grandchild. Make a variety of levels of difficulty according to the skills of the children.
2. Have children make a man from clay by making a ball for the head, large "pancake" for the body, and long and short "snakes" for arms and legs and drawing facial features with their fingers.
3. Have children make gingerbread men and decorate with squeeze tubes of frosting.
4. Have children put together "Daddy" puzzles - either commerical or teacher-made.
5. On a ditto sheet, have children connect dots in the picture of a hat. The hat is on "Daddy's" head. Children can color picture.

Games

1. Have children dress men paper dolls. Discuss what men wear.
2. Let children play "dress-up":
   a. Each child gets a turn to dress up in men's clothing. Teacher may ask "David, will you wear this when you grow to be a man?"
   b. Let the children find an article of men's clothing from a box of mixed clothing and put it on.
3. Let children play house: Children pretend to be mother, daddy, children, and baby. Take pictures and display on bulletin board.

Storytelling

1. Make story cards or use flannel board, and tell the story of "The Gingerbread Man."
2. Use fingerplay and sing "Thumbkin."

   Where is Thumbkin? Where is Thumbkin?
   Here I am.   *(Left hand, wiggle thumb)*
   Here I am.   *(Right hand, wiggle thumb)*
   Here I am.   *(Left hand, wiggle thumb)*
   How are you today Sir?   *(Right hand, wiggle thumb)*
   Very well, I thank you.   *(Left hand, wiggle thumb)*
   Run away,   *(Left hand disappears behind back)*
   Run away.   *(Right hand disappears behind back)*
   Verse 2: Where is Pointer?   *(index finger)*
   Verse 3: Where is Tall man?   *(3rd finger)*
   Verse 4: Where is Ring man?   *(4th finger)*
   Verse 5: Where is Pinky?   *(5th finger)*
3. Tell the story of "The Three Bears." Read the story from a book or tell the story using sequence cards or pictures to illustrate. Have the children find the Papa or Daddy Bear.
4. "Pinnochio" - tell a simplified version of this story. Use pictures to illustrate. Explain how the little old man wanted to be a father and wanted to have a child to love.
5. Use the "Family Album" made in art. Have each child tell about "father" and show his picture.

Gross Motor

1. Have children run and try to catch the child who is the "Gingerbread Man." Everyone says: "Run, run, as fast as you can. You can't catch me; I'm the Gingerbread Man." Outside activity.
2. Let children be a daddy and push babies in a baby carriage around an obstacle course.

Cognitive

1. Ask children, "Is your daddy (mommy) a man?"
2. Display two pictures: one of a group of animals and one of people. Have the children put pictures of men with the appropriate group.
3. Display part of a piece of "daddy, mother, brother, sister, or baby." Ask children "Is this daddy or mother?" Then ask, "Who is it?"
4. Have the children sort pictures of tall and short men.
5. Have children find men in pictures cut from magazines (figure ground).
6. Have children count men in above pictures.

Enrichment

1. Make a family: Using magazines, let the children cut out pictures of people and paste them on a large sheet of paper. Ask the children to name the family members they have cut out. Have the children count the members in the "family" they have made and tell how many there are.
2. Place paper at five separate places on the walls at child level. Part of this activity should be completed as each new concept is studied. On each sheet put a cue picture (it may be a stick figure) of Man, Woman, Boy, Girl and Baby. Each day have some children find pictures of man, woman, boy, girl or baby as appropriate. Add the above pictures to unrelated pictures and have the children sort the pictures of men from non-men, men from women and so on as the number of pictures increases in the week. When all children have had some sorting activity, Begin pasting some of the day's people on the correct paper on the wall.

Lesson 2: Woman

Unit Group Lesson

1. **Match Concrete Objects**
    Present two women. Say, "This is a woman." Ask each child in turn to put the woman with the woman. Gradually increase number of irrelevant objects from which (s)he must select woman to match.

2. **Discriminate Objects**
    Present several objects. Have each child touch the woman in response to verbal direction, "Touch the woman."

3. **Match Pictures**
    Present several pictures of common objects each child match the pictures of the women.

4. **Discriminate Pictures**
    Present a group of several unrelated pictures of objects. Have each child touch the picture of the woman in response to verbal direction, "Touch the woman."

5. **Figure-Ground**
    Present a "busy" picture with many visual distractions. Ask each child to find the woman.

6. **Visual Closure**
    Partially cover each of several pictures with paper. Ask each child to find the picture of the woman.

7. **Function**
    Ask, "What does a woman do?"

8. **Association**
    Ask, "What goes with the woman?" Use pictures or objects including woman, mommy, automobile, grandma, with several unrelated objects or pictures.

9. **Imitate Verbalization**

   Present a woman and ask, "What is this? Say, 'Woman'." The child will imitate "Woman."

10. **Verbalize Label**

   Present a woman and ask, "What is this?" The child will respond, "Woman."

11. **Concept Enrichment**

   A mommy is a woman; a grandma is a woman, an aunt is a women.

Music

1. Sing to the tune of "The Farmer in the Dell":

   Verse 1: A mama is a woman.

   Verse 2: A grandma is a woman.

2. Sing to the tune of "Did You Ever See a Lassie?":

   Did you ever see a fat woman. . .?

   Did you ever see a skinny woman. . .?

   Did you ever see a tall woman. . .?

   Did you ever see a short woman. . .?

3. Sing "A Big Sweet Kiss" to tune of "This Is the Way We Wash Our Clothes":

   I give my mother a big sweet kiss,

   A big sweet kiss, a big sweet kiss,

   I give my mother a big sweet kiss,

   Before I come to school

   (Blow a kiss after song)

4. Sing "My Mother Helps Me" to tune of "Mary Had A Little Lamb":

   My mother helps me (get dressed),

   (Get dressed), (get dressed);

   My mother helps me (get dressed),

   And I love her very much.

   Have children suggest ideas for the song, (e.g. "tie my shoes," "button my coat," etc.).

Art

1. Have the children paste a dress and a hat on the picture of a woman.
2. Have the children continue "Family Album" by using actual photographs of children's relatives.
3. Have the children make a class "Family" photograph album. During the week (at snack time, during free play, etc.) bring out the photograph album and say, "Find John's mother," "Find Ellen's sister," etc.
4. Have the children paint a picture of their mothers. Make frames for the pictures with poster board. The frames can be decorated by the children with felt tip pens, crayons, painted macaroni, etc.
5. Have the children continue "People" book with a woman collage.

Snack

   Dress like a woman or mother for snack and serve snack family-style out of bowls.

Fine Motor

1. Have the children lace a "Woman" lacing card.
2. Have the children do path tracing such as, "Take a mother to child or baby."
3. Ask the children to put together a "Mother" puzzle - either commerical or teacher-made.
4. Have the children "cook" like Mother by rolling or patting out dough, kneading dough, sifting flour, stirring, pouring a liquid, etc.
5. Have children turn the pages of the books created in Art today and yesterday.

Games

1. Have each child's mother tape a passage on a tape recorder. Play the tape to the group of children. Ask, "Whose mother is this?" (Auditory Discrimination).

2.   Play "Ring-a-Round Mother" with children. A child pretends to be mother. Let the child decide how he will "be" mother. Have women's clothes and accessories, household items, etc., available. Children form a ring around "mother" and sing:

> Ring around mother;
> Ring around mother;
> Quickly, quickly,
> We all fall down.

Children take turns being mother.

3.   Play "Mother, May I?" with children. One child plays "Mother". Other children stand in a line approximately ten feet in front of "Mother". The "mother" gives each child individually some direction. Examples: "Mother, may I take two baby steps?" Mother says, "Yes, you may." Child may then carry out instruction. Teacher may want to play "Mother."

Storytelling

1.   Use the flannel board to tell "The Old Woman in the Shoe." Use pictures from a storybook or make felt cut-outs to illustrate the shoe, old woman, and children. Count the children and be sure children can identify the old woman.

2.   Make a five card sequence story of a woman planting, hoeing, watering, and harvesting her garden and eating the vegetables (Each card illustrates one activity). Initially tell the story using two cards, (e. g. planting and watering the garden). Build up to a sequence of five events. Let children tell the story and/or put the cards in order.

3.   "The Three Bears" - either read the story from a book or tell the story using sequence cards or pictures to illustrate. Have the children find the Mama Bear.

4.   Read or tell "Old Mother Hubbard". - Use a storybook, sequence cards, or pictures.

Gross Motor

Let children be a mommy and push babies in a baby carriage around an obstacle course.

Cognitive

1.   Use the "Family Book" made in art and have each child tell about his mother and show her/his pictures.

2.   Display a poster with pictures of three different groups of people: a teacher and her class, a family group, and a group of children playing. Ask, "Does Mother belong in the classroom, with the children, or with the family?" Children will put the pictures of the mother with the picture of the family (classifying family members).

3.   Ask the children, "Is your mommy (daddy) a woman?"

4.   Cut women's pictures from a catalog in half and let the children match the halves.

Enrichment

1.   Let the children use clothespins to make figures representing their families. (See fig. 2B.)

2.   Continue the Together Activity from Enrichment #2 Lesson 1.

Have the children work on the woman wall. Add women to the sorting table.

Some children may only be able to sort women from non- women.

Some children will be able to sort women, men and other.

Fig. 2B

Lesson 3: Boy

Unit Group Lesson

1. **Match Concrete Objects**

Present two boys. Say, "This is a boy." Ask each child in turn to put the boy with the boy. Gradually increase number of irrelevant objects from which (s)he must select boy to match.

2. **Discriminate Objects**
Present several objects. Have each child touch the boy in response to verbal direction, "Touch the boy."

3. **Match Pictures**
Present several pictures of common objects. Have each child match the pictures of the boys.

4. **Discriminate Pictures**
From a group of several unrelated pictures of objects, each child touch the picture of the boy in response to verbal direction, "Touch the boy."

5. **Figure-Ground**
Present a "busy" picture with many visual distractions. Ask each child to find the boy.

6. **Visual Closure**
Partially cover each of several pictures with paper. Ask each child to find the picture of the boy.

7. **Function**
Ask, "What does a boy do?"

8. **Association**
Ask, "What goes with the boy?" Use pictures or objects including boys in class, toys, etc., with several unrelated objects or pictures.

9. **Imitate Verbalization**
Present a boy and ask, "What is this? Say, 'Boy'." The child will imitate "Boy."

10. **Verbalize Label**
Present a boy and ask, "What is this?" The child will respond, "Boy."

11. **Concept Enrichment**
Discuss fact that boys are sons, brothers, and cousins, and nephews.

Music
1. Sing to the tune of "Farmer In The Dell":
   Verse 1: The farmer takes a boy (girl).
   Verse 2: The farmer takes a son (daughter).
2. Sing: "I Have A Friend" to tune of "Paw Paw Patch":
   I have a friend, his name is David,
   I have a friend, his name is David,
   I have a friend, his name is David,
   And my friend is a boy.

Art
1. Have children paste eyes, nose, mouth, and ears on a boy's face and decorate his clothing.
2. Have children make a boy stick puppet by using a small paper plate or stiff paper disc and tongue depresser. Let children use magic markers to make features, yarn for hair and wall paper scraps for clothing. (See fig. 2C.)
3. Have children continue "People" book with a boy collage.
4. Have children continue "Family Album" for those children who have boys in their family.

Fig. 2C

Snack

Serve the boys' snack first. Say, "Give the boys cookies" and "Give the boys juice."

Fine Motor

1. Have children do a path tracing, such as, "Take a boy to his bicycle."
2. Play String and Pass Relay. Put the boys on one team and the girls on the other. Have each team member string one button and pass the string to the next person.
3. Place large sheets of newsprint or butcher paper on the floor and let the children draw the members in their families with magic markers. When the children have completed their pictures, ask them to point to and name the members of their family. Label the members as the children identify them. Ask the children to tell their last name (family name) and write "The _____ Family" at the top of each child's picture. Display the pictures.

Games

1. Play "Find the Boys" by blindfolding a child. Tell him/her to feel a child's head (especially hair) and tell if the child is a boy or girl.
2. Play "Tape the Hat on the Boy." Play like "Pin the Tail on the Donkey," but do not use pins.
3. Let children make rock boys.

Storytelling

1. Teacher can tell and/or sing the story of "Little Boy Blue" using teacher-made sequence story cards.
   Little Boy Blue come blow your horn'
   The sheep in the meadow,
   The cows in the corn
   Where is the boy who tends the sheep?
   Under the haystack fast asleep.
2. Read "Jack and the Beanstalk."
3. Read "Three Pigs."
4. Read a story about the Bear Family by Jan and Stan Berentain.

Gross Motor

Place boys on one team and girls on the other and have them race around an obstacle course.

Cognitive

1. Make a cue sheet with a boy at the top. Have the children select boys from other objects. Let the children mark the boys.
2. Help children count the boys wearing red and then count boys wearing blue. Count the boys in class and those who are brothers.
3. Have boys demonstrate front, last and middle positions in a short line.

Enrichment

1. Let the boys in the class do all the special jobs (passing out cups, holding the door, etc.) for the day.
2. Continue the Together Activity from Enrichment #2 Lesson 1. Have the children work on the boy wall. Add boy to the sorting table. Some children may only be able to sort boys from non-boys. Some children will be able to sort women, men, boy and other.

Lesson 4: Girl

Unit Group Lesson

1. **Match Concrete Objects**
   Present two girls. Say, "This is a girl." Ask each child in turn to put the girl with the girl. Gradually increase number of irrelevant objects from which (s)he must select girl to match.

2. **Discriminate Objects**
   Present several objects. Have each child touch the girl in response to verbal direction, "Touch the girl."

3. **Match Pictures**
   Present several pictures of common objects. Have each child match the pictures of the girls.

4. **Discriminate Pictures**
   Present a group of several unrelated pictures of objects. Have each child touch the picture of the girl in response to verbal direction, "Touch the girl."

5. **Figure-Ground**
   Present a "busy" picture with many visual distractions. Ask each child to find the girl.

6. **Visual Closure**
   Partially cover each of several pictures with paper. Ask each child to find the picture of the girl.

7. **Function**
   Ask, "What does a girl do?"

8. **Association**
   Ask, "What goes with the girl?" Use pictures or objects including the girls in class, toys, etc., with several unrelated objects or pictures.

9. **Imitate Verbalization**
   Present a girl and ask, "What is this? Say, 'Girl'." The child will imitate "Girl."

10. **Verbalize Label**
    Present a girl and ask, "What is this?" The child will respond, "Girl."

11. **Concept Enrichment**
    Girls are daughters, sisters, cousins, and nieces.

Music
1. Sing to the tune of "The Farmer In the Dell":
   Verse 1: The farmer takes a girl (boy).
   Verse 2: The farmer takes a daughter (boy).
2. Sing "Going to Dance" to tune of "Mulberry Bush":
   Verse 1: Come along girls, (boys) we're going to dance;
   Going to dance; going to dance;
   Come along girls, we're going to dance;
   Early in the morning.
   Verse 2: Don't we look pretty when we're dancing,
   When we're dancing, when we're dancing,
   Don't we look pretty when we're dancing,
   Early in the morning.
   Begin the song and motion to girls (or boys) to join you. Have children hold hands and walk in a circle as they sing. Eventually, phase out any motions. Let the children decide if they are a boy or girl and if they should be in circle.
3. Sing "Mary Had A Little Lamb."

Art
1. Have children spatter paint a girl silhouette. Cut out paper doll of a girl. Give each child a paper doll. (Precut) Use it for spatter painting.

2. Have children make a girl stick puppet by using a small paper plate
    or circle of stiff paper, gluing onto a stick, putting features on with
    magic markers and using yarn bits for hair and wallpaper scraps for
    a dress or skirt. (See fig. 2D.)
3. Have children continue "People" book with a girl collage.
4. Have children continue "Family Album" for those children who
    have girls in their family.
5. Have children paint a paper table cloth for the family dinner at
    snack time. Groups of 8-10 can eat the family dinner.

Fig. 2D

Snack
1. Serve the girls first. Say, "Give the girls cookies," and "Give the boys juice."
2. Have children plan, cook and serve a family dinner. Help them set the table and serve family style out
    of bowls. Use names Mother, Daddy, Aunt, Uncle and Grandmother.

Fine Motor
1. Have children do a path tracing, such as, "Take the girl to her dog," or "Take the doll to the girl."
2. Have children paste girl's features on an outlined face. Make Family Member lacing cards by cutting
    out large pictures from magazines of various family members, gluing them on poster board, covering
    them with contact paper, cutting the figures out of the poster board and punching holes around the
    outside of the figures. Let the children lace them with shoe strings.

Games
1. Make two posters one for girls and the other for boys. Take or obtain photographs of every child. Let
    each child paste his photograph on the appropriate poster. As (s)he fastens it the child will identify
    his/her own category. "I am a girl (boy)."
2. Let girls do all the helping activities in the classroom today.
3. Make available clothes, shoes hats, purses, etc., worn by different members of a family. Let the
    children take turns dressing up like various family members. Have the other children guess which
    family member they are supposed to be. Tell the child to "dress up" like a certain family member.
    (The child has to choose the appropriate clothing for that member and dress himself with or without
    assistance from the teacher or another child).

Storytelling
1. Fingerplay or sing: "Ha, Ha, This-A-Way."
    Verse 1: When I was a little girl, little girl,
              Little girl, (child points to self)
              When I was a little girl, five years old (child holds up fingers)
              Chorus: Ha, ha, this-a-way,
              Ha, ha, this-a-way, (child pantomimes laughing or laughs)
              Ha, ha, this-a-way,
              Then, oh, then.
    Verse 2: Ma-ma bought me a little sled, little sled, little sled,
              Ma-ma bought me a little sled,
              Then, oh, then.
              Chorus
2. Recite poem: "Jack and Jill."
3. Read the story: "Goldilocks and the Three Bears;
                     "Little Red Riding Hood"
4. Read Berenstain Bear stories.
5. Say "Little Bo Peep."

Gross Motor

1. Play "Pass and Stack Relay." Divide into boy and girl teams. Pass a tray. Each child adds a block to the tray.
2. Play "Kick the Can" or "Ball Down a Track," alternating girls and boys.

Cognitive

1. Make a cue sheet with a girl at the top. Selecting from girls and distractions, have the children mark the girls.
2. Have the children count girls who are sisters, nieces, cousins and wearing red.
3. Have a girl occupy first, last or middle positions. Have children name the position occupied by the girl.

Enrichment

1. Using the same family member magazine pictures as in Fine Motor #2, ask the child to make families by choosing the pictures of family members named (Name various family member combinations). Then let a child name family members and have another child make the families. Have a child make families with different numbers of members. Say, "Can you make a family with 3 members?" Then let the child choose three family members from the pictures. Continue activity using different numbers of members.
2. Continue Together Activity from Enrichment #2 Lesson 1. Have the children work on the girl wall. Add girl to sorting table. Some children may only be able to sort girls from non-girls. Some children will be able to sort women, men, boy, girl and other.

Lesson 5: Baby

Unit Group Lesson

1. **Match Concrete Objects**
   Present two babies. Say, "This is a baby." Ask each child in turn to put the baby with the baby. Gradually increase number of irrelevant objects from which (s)he must select baby to match.

2. **Discriminate Objects**
   Present several objects. Have each child touch the baby in response to verbal direction, "Touch the baby."

3. **Match Pictures**
   Present several pictures of common objects. Have each child match the pictures of the babies.

4. **Discriminate Pictures**
   Present a group of several unrelated pictures of objects. Have each child touch the picture of the baby in response to verbal direction, "Touch the baby."

5. **Figure-Ground**
   Present a "busy" picture with many visual distractions. Ask each child to find the baby.

6. **Visual Closure**
   Partially cover each of several pictures with paper. Ask each child to find the picture of the baby.

7. **Function**
   Ask, "What does a baby do?"

8. **Association**
   Ask, "What goes with the baby?" Use pictures or objects including diapers, babies, etc, with several unrelated objects or pictures.

9. **Imitate Verbalization**

    Present a baby and ask, "What is this? Say, 'Baby'." The child will imitate "Baby."

10. **Verbalize Label**

    Present a baby and ask, "What is this?" The child will respond, "Baby."

11. **Concept Enrichment**

    Discuss care of babies. "If a baby cries, what does it mean?" "If the baby's bottle is too hot (cold) what could someone do to make it just right?"

Music
1. Sing "Rock A Bye Baby." The children may want to rock "baby" in cradle or in a rocking chair.
2. Sing "Jane Has A Little Baby" to the tune of "Mary Had A Little Lamb":
    Jane has a little baby, little baby, little baby,
    Jane has a little baby, and she is soft and sweet.
3. Sing "Baby's Sleeping" to tune of "Are You Sleeping":
    Baby's sleeping, baby's sleeping
    Sleep, sleep, sleep,
    Baby is a-sleeping, baby is a-sleeping,
    Sleep, sleep, sleep,
    Sleep, sleep, sleep,
    Children may want to rock baby in arms while singing.

Art
1. Let children make a "Baby Collage" by pasting pictures on contruction paper. Include pictures of objects a baby uses (e.g. crib, stroller, high chair, etc.).
2. Help children assemble all collages from previous days and make "People Book." Children can design a cover for book. See Fine Motor #2 for today.
3. Help children assemble the "Family Album." Include a page for those children who have babies in their families or include a baby picture of each child. Children can potato print cardboard covers. See Fine Motor #2 for today.

Snack
1. Eat teething biscuits.
2. Have a baby food tasting center. Children may bring baby food that little brother or sister eats.
3. Eat finely mashed foods.

Fine Motor
1. Let children do a path tracing, such as, "Take a baby to its mother."
2. Let children punch holes for assembling "People" book and "Family Album."
3. Dress a baby doll.
4. Make Family Member Puzzles by cutting out large magazine pictures of various family members, pasting them on construction paper, covering with contact paper, and cutting the pictures into pieces to make puzzles, (making some with just a few pieces and some with more pieces). Place each puzzle in a large envelope with names of members written on the outside. Have the child put the puzzle together and then tell which family member he has made.

Games
1. Have the children get a baby doll ready for bed by bathing, powdering, and dressing it. They may want to bottle, burp, and rock the baby. Teacher may ask, "What are you doing to the baby? Is the baby sleepy (hungry)?"

2.   Talk about and act out with a doll:
        talking to a baby
        touching a baby
        holding a baby
        faces to show a baby
        a song to sing to a baby
        how to walk when baby is sleeping

Storytelling
1.   Fingerplay: "Toys for Baby":

Here's a ball for baby,	*(Make a ball with thumbs and*
Big and soft and round.	*forefingers.)*
Here is baby's hammer,	*(Make hammer with fist.*
See how it can pound.	*Pound in other hand.)*
Here is baby's music,	*(Hold fingers up facing each other.)*
Clapping, clapping so.	*(Clap.)*
Here are baby's soldiers,	*(Hold fingers up straight.)*
Standing in a row.	
Here is baby's trumpet,	*(Pretend to blow with fists in*
Toot-to-toot-to-too.	*front of mouth.)*
Here's the way that baby,	*(Play peek-a-boo with fingers.)*
Plays at Peek-a-boo.	
Here's a big umbrella	*(Cup hand and put finger under*
To keep the baby dry.	*for handle.)*
Here is baby's cradle,	*(Make cradle of arms.)*
Rock-a-baby-bye.	

     This fingerplay may be used in parts. Pictures or objects can be used to illustrate.
2.   Use large story cards for the story, "The Three Bears." Emphasize that baby bear is little and has a little dish, little chair and little bed.
3.   Tell the following fill-in story, "Baby's Bath": One night it was time for baby to go to bed. Before she went to bed her mother decided to give her a bath. So, she filled the tub with (water). She got out (soap) and washcloth. Then she put the (baby) in the tub. The baby splashed and played, She liked her bath. When the baby got out of the tub, her mother dryed her with a (towel). Now the baby was clean! Use pictures of actual objects to fill in blanks for non-verbal children.

Gross Motor
1.   Create an obstacle course for the children to push doll carriages around. Let them take turns.
2.   Let the children wrap dolls in baby blankets and walk the babies in strollers.

Cognitive
1.   Emphasize big and little by dusting powder on a doll's/baby's hands and feet. Print on a dark piece of paper. Dust powder on a child's hands and feet. Print on a dark piece of paper and compare to baby's.
2.   Have children identify baby sounds from other voices when they are talking and crying.
3.   Classify family members by cutting pictures from magazines of different family members and having the children put all the mothers, fathers, sisters, brothers, grandpas, grandmas, and babies in different stacks.

4.   Let the children pack a diaper bag from a table full of objects, choosing baby objects from assorted objects on the table.

Enrichment

1.   Display large magazine pictures of various family groups. Ask the children to find and point to a mother, father, grandma, grandpa, sister, brother, and baby. Have those children who can point to and name the various family members. Help each child decide which family is most like his family.

2.   Using the same magazine pictures, let the children count the number of members in each family group. Write the corresponding numeral under each family picture and let the children trace, copy, or write numeral himself.

3.   Have a pocket shoe bag with numerals on the pockets. Let the children put correct number of babies in the pockets. Use tiny baby dolls or babies cut from heavy paper. (See fig. 2E.)

Fig. 2E

4.   Cut babies and carriages from posterboard. Put dots on the babies' sunsuits and corresponding numerals on the carriages. Mount the carriages on a manilla folder. Leave the top open, so a baby can be put in the carriage. Let the children match the dots on the babies sunsuits to the numbers on the baby carriages by placing the babies in the correct carriages. (See fig. 2F.)

Fig. 2F

5.   Finish Together Activity from Enrichment #2 Lesson 1 by having the children work on the baby wall. Add baby to the sorting table. Some children may only be able to sort babies from non-babies. Some children will be able to sort women, men, boys, firls, babies and others.

Other Children's Records
"Sweet Little Baby" from **ABIYOYO** (FLKW)
"Little Boy" from **FINGER GAMES** (EA)
"Little Baby" from **AND ONE AND TWO** (SCHOL)
"Jumping W/Variations" from **AND ONE AND TWO** (SCHOL)
"The Muffin Man" from **NURSERY RHYMES** (SCHOL)
"Georgie Porgie" from **NURSERY RHYMES** (SCHOL)
"Hush Little Baby" from **FOLK SONG CARNIVAL**
"He's Got The Whole World in His Hands" from **FOLK SONG CARNIVAL**
"Getting Along" from **OOOO WE'RE HAVING FUN** (RP)
"He's Got the Whole World in His Hands" from **LITTLE JOHNNY BROWN** (SCHOL)

Other Children's Books
Berenstain, Stan and Berenstain, Jan. **HE BEAR, SHE BEAR.** New York: Random House, 1974.
Fassler, Joan. **HOWIE HELPS HIMSELF.** Chicago: Albert Whitman & Co., 1975.
Krasilovsky, Peter. **THE VERY LITTLE BOY.** New York: Doubleday & Co., 1953.
Krasilovsky, Peter. **THE VERY LITTLE GIRL.** New York: Doubleday & Co., 1953.
Spier, Peter. **PEOPLE.** New York: Doubleday & Co., 1980.
Hallinan, P.K. **WE'RE VERY GOOD FRIENDS, MY BROTHER AND I.** Chicago: Children's Press, 1973.
Keats, Ezra Jack. **PETER'S CHAIR.** New York: Harper & Row, 1967.
Peterson, Jeanne. **I HAVE A SISTER, MY SISTER IS DEAF.** New York: Harper & Row, 1977.
Stecher, Miriam B. and Randell, Alice. **DADDY AND BEN TOGETHER.** New York: Lothrop, Lee & Shepard Co., 1981.
Scott, Ann Herbert. **SAM.** New York: McGraw Hill, 1967.

Unit 3: Autumn

A developmental assessment should determine the functional levels of each child. Individual expectations are based on the assessment results.

Lesson 1: Leaf

Unit Group Lesson

1. **Match Concrete Objects**
   Present two leaves. Say, "This is a leaf." Ask each child in turn to put the leaf with the leaves. Gradually increase number of irrelevant objects from which (s)he must select leaves to match.

2. **Discriminate Objects**
   Present several objects. Have each child touch the leaf in response to verbal direction, "Touch the leaf."

3. **Match Pictures**
   Present several pictures of common objects. Have each child match the pictures of the leaves.

4. **Discriminate Pictures**
   Present a group of several unrelated pictures of objects. Have each child touch the picture of the leaf in response to verbal direction, "Touch the leaf."

5. **Figure-Ground**
   Present a "busy" picture with many visual distractions. Ask each child to find the leaf.

6. **Tactile Discrimination**
   Put some leaves and some very different textured objects in a "feely box." Say, "Find the leaf."

7. **Visual Closure**
   Partially cover each of several pictures with paper. Ask each child to find the picture of the leaf.

8. **Function**
   Ask, "Why do trees have leaves?"

9. **Association**
   Ask, "How do the branches hold onto the leaves?" Use pictures or objects including trees, branches, etc., with several unrelated objects or pictures. Talk about things made from wood.

10. **Imitate Verbalization**
    Present a leaf and ask, "What is this?" Say, 'Leaf'." The child will imitate "Leaf."

11.   **Verbalize Label**

Present a leaf and ask, "What is this?" The child will respond, "Leaf."

12.   **Concept Enrichment**

Discuss and look at different types of leaves.

Music

1.   Slowly sing "Autumn Leaves" to the tune of "Mary Had a Little Lamb":

Falling, falling, autumn leaves,
Autumn leaves, autumn leaves,
Falling, falling, autumn leaves,
Falling on the ground.
Whirling, whirling, autumn leaves,
Autumn leaves, autumn leaves,
Whirling, whirling, autumn leaves,
Whirling all around.

Have children move like slowly falling leaves (falling slowly to the ground), then like leaves whirling in the air (spinning round and round).

2.   Sing "Leaves" to the tune of "Pop Goes the Weasel":   *(Pantomime motions.)*

Round and round and round and round,
Down, down, down - oh
Now the leaves are on the ground.
Jump in the leaves.

3.   Sing "Rake the Leaves" to the tune of "Row, Row, Row Your Boat":

Rake, rake, rake the leaves
Rake, John, rake.
Rake, rake, rake the leaves
Rake, John, rake.

Have children pantomime raking or sing while raking leaves outside.

Art

1.   Have children use leaves gathered from a nature hike to make a leaf collage or a leaf man.
2.   Have children make a leaf silhouette by spatter painting around a leaf. Place paper and leaf in a shallow box to prevent excess of spattering. Have children dip a toothbrush in paint and use a popsicle stick to spatter the paint.
3.   Have children paint with red and yellow at the easel.

Snack

1.   Have grape leaves stuffed with meat.
2.   Eat leaf-shaped cookies. (See Fine Motor #3.)

Fine Motor

1.   Make leaf sewing cards in different levels of difficulty. Use full colors. Have each child sew a "leaf" sewing card.
2.   Help children press leaves in wax paper using an iron. Let children arrange leaves on bottom layer of wax paper. Help with the pressing. Let the children frame the pictures with strips of construction paper.
3.   Help children make sugar cookies in the shapes of leaves. Let them frost them in yellow, red and orange frosting.
4.   Spread a sheet on the floor. Have the children gather leaves in a box and put the box on the sheet. Let them "crunch" the leaves with their hands and listen to the sound of crunching leaves.

5.   Have child path trace floating leaves as illustrated. (See fig. 3A.)

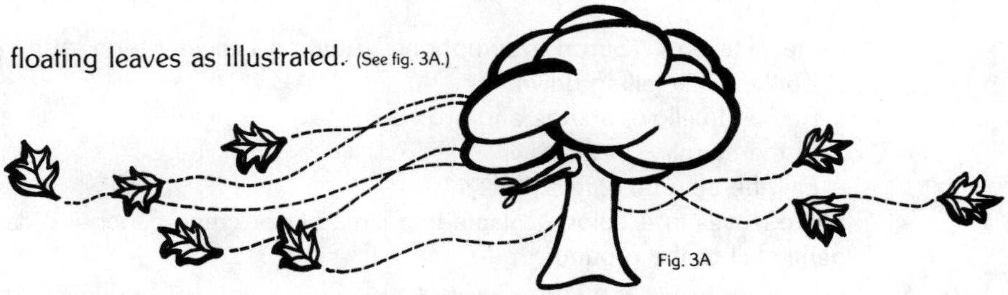

Fig. 3A

Games

1.   "Find the Leaf." Arrange various objects on a table (e.g., block, doll, paper cup, leaf, etc.). Blindfold child and lead him to the table. Child must find the leaf by touching the objects. (Tactile Discrimination)

2.   Domino Game: Make domino cards of different colored and shaped leaves. Child must pick up card and lay it down on table, matching it to another card. (See fig. 3B.)

Fig. 3B

3.   Play the "twister game" with leaves on a mat. Direct children to put hands and feet in different spots. Tape construction paper leaves of different shapes and colors on a mat. Make a large spinner with matching leaves. Let children put hands or feet on leaf spun. (See fig. 3C.)

Red Leaf	Yellow Leaf	Orange Leaf
Green Leaf	Brown Leaf	Multi-color Leaf

Fig. 3C

Storytelling

1.   Fingerplay "Pretty Leaves":
     Pretty leaves are falling down   *(Hands above head, fingers wiggling slowly coming down to sides.)*

     See them lying on the ground.   *(Stoop down, patting here and there.)*
     Trees are bending in the breeze.   *(Sway body back and forth.)*
     Don't you love the falling leaves?   *(Hands above head, slowly coming down.)*

2.   Make up a story about the last leaf to fall off the tree. Use cut-outs of a tree and fall-colored leaves made from pictures, felt, or construction paper.

Gross Motor

1.   Have children rake several piles of leaves. Have children race and jump into the leaves.

2.   Sing to the tune of "Are You Sleeping":
     Leaves are floating
     Leaves are floating   *(Children do floating motions with hands or hold cut-*
     Floating down   *out autumn leaves in their hands, bright leaves*
     Floating down   *attached to heavy yarn to twirl.)*
     Now they all are resting
     Now they all are resting
     On the ground
     On the ground
     (Substitute "twirling" for floating.)

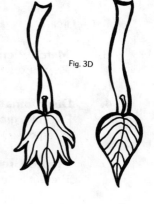
Fig. 3D

3.   Attach leaf cut-outs the children have made to strips of cloth or streamers of crepe paper (heavy lines in shape of leaf). Have children sing the song using these in each hand. (See fig. 3D.)

4. Tune: Haydn's "Surprise Symphony" Autumn Leaves. Sing to the children; listen for the colors:
    Softly, softly falling down
    Red and yellow, orange and brown
    In the country, in the town
    Fall the autumn leaves.
    Make leaves in 4 colors. Staple to a streamer or crepe paper and dance to the music. Let the leaves gently fall to the ground.

Cognitive

1. Make a cue sheet. Have child mark an "X", encircle or color every leaf on a page with pictures of various objects. Draw a "leaf" at the top of the page. The number of leaves and objects on a page depends upon level of the child. Initially only one leaf with one object (or no object) may be appropriate. Increase number as child's level increases.
2. Compare a dry leaf to a green leaf.
3. Drop different items: block, book, cotton, autumn leaf. Talk about quiet sound of the leaf.
4. Sponge print shape leaves. On a sheet with a shape cue, print leaves with the same shape. Add
5. Have children put leaves on a tree drawn on poster board. Using material that will stick to poster, have the children follow your directions. Depending on the child's level, you may request: "Put a yellow leaf on the tree, a green leaf on the top branch, a red leaf on the largest branch, two leaves on the tree, a leaf on the tree," etc.
6. Have children paste construction paper leaf on partially hidden outline of a leaf. Start with one picture to be matched and increase number and difficulty with increased skill of children.

Enrichment

Collect 10 different shapes of leaves from outdoors. Paste or attach to cardboard. Talk about differences. Relate to differences in people. Have matching leaf shapes to match ones on board. Let children match them.

Lesson 2: Tree

Unit Group Lesson

Unit Group Lesson

1. **Match Concrete Objects**
    Present two trees. Say, "This is a tree." Ask each child in turn to put the tree with the tree. Gradually increase number of irrelevant objects from which (s)he must select tree to match.

2. **Discriminate Objects**
    Present several objects. Have each child touch the tree in response to verbal direction, "Touch the tree."

3. **Match Pictures**
    Present several pictures of common objects. Have each child match the pictures of the trees.

4. **Discriminate Pictures**
    Present a group of several unrelated pictures of objects. Have each child touch the picture of the tree in response to verbal direction, "Touch the tree."

5. **Figure-Ground**
    Present a "busy" picture with many visual distractions. Ask each child to find the tree.

6. **Visual Closure**
   Partially cover each of several pictures with paper. Ask each child to find the picture of the tree.

7. **Function**
   Ask, "What do trees do?"

8. **Association**
   Ask, "What goes with the trees?" Use pictures or objects including leaves, branches, nuts, squirrels, etc., with several unrelated objects or pictures. Talk about things made from wood.

9. **Imitate Verbalization**
   Present a tree and ask, "What is this?" Say, 'Tree'." The child will imitate "Tree."

10. **Verbalize Label**
    Present a tree and ask, "What is this?" The child will respond, "Tree."

11. **Concept Enrichment**
    Discuss different types of trees. Discuss how the trees look in different seasons.

Music
1. Sing "Ring Around the Tree" to the tune of "Ring Around the Rosey":
   Ring around the tree,
   Ring around the tree,
   Lea-eves, lea-eves,
   We all fall down.
   Sing the song outside with the children holding hands and forming a ring around a tree.
2. Sing "Here We Go Walking" to the tune of "Frere Jacques":
   Here we go walking,
   Here we go walking,
   Around the tree,
   Around the tree.
   Sing the song outside. Have children form a line, hold hands, take turns being leader, and choose the trees to walk around.
3. Sing "Old MacDonald":
   Old MacDonald had a farm.
   E-I-E-I-O
   And on this farm he had a tree.
   E-I-E-I-O
   With a tree here, a tree there,
   Here a tree, there a tree,
   Everywhere there were trees.
   Old MacDonald has some trees.
   E-I-E-I-O.

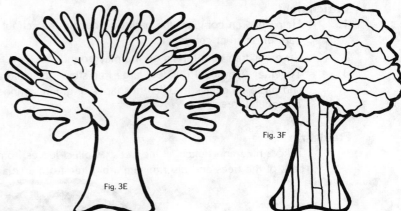

Fig. 3E

Fig. 3F

Art
1. Have children put hand prints onto a class tree. (See fig. 3E.)
2. Have children sponge-paint fall colors (leaves) on a drawn outline of tree.
3. Have children paste brown strips on a paper for tree trunks, tear small colored pieces for the leaves and cover the ground under the tree with leaves. (See fig. 3F.)

Snack
1. Think of pretzels as great tree trunks and branches.
2. Let each child eat the raisins from her "raisin tree" made in Fine Motor #4.

Fine Motor

1. Have children connect dots that are in the shape of a tree. (Make copies of these so child can have several copies.) Have them color the tree fall colors.
2. Make a road and two trees on a large piece of paper. Have children drive a small car from one tree to the other. Vary the difficulty of the road for children of different ability levels.
3. Have children tear leaves and glue on a picture of a tree trunk.
4. Give each child a small branch and some raisins. Let her make a raisin tree and eat it for snack.
5. Let children make a gum drop tree as above.
6. Let children blow watery brown paint on a light-colored paper using drinking straws and add paper or crayon leaves to make a Fall tree.

Games

Play "Ring Around a Tree" on the school grounds or around a potted plant or pretend tree.

Storytelling

Tell a sequence story of how "The Tree Changes Colors." Start with a green tree in summer and describe the changes from the summer to the spring.

Gross Motor

Blow a whistle and say, "Touch a tree," or "Find a tree," and have children run to a tree. Model activity if necessary. Ask, "What did you find?" (Visual Discrimination)

Cognitive

1. Bring a big branch into the classroom. Have each child attach colored leaves according to instructions such as "Put on two orange leaves", "Put on a leaf like this one", "Put on three leaves", etc. so the branch becomes a Fall tree. Use the leaves for color recognition, matching, and counting.
2. Make big and little trees and have children compare big trees and little trees.
3. Use paper leaves with a strip of magnet tape behind for sorting and matching colors on a metal tree (or paper tree on a metal background).
4. Have children paste construction paper tree on partially hidden outline of a tree. Start with one picture to be matched and increase number and difficulty with increased skill by children.

Enrichment

1. Help children compare the bark on trees on the school grounds and note rough bark, smooth bark, bark of different colors, etc.
2. Have children count trees on the playground.
3. Together Activity. Provide a large tree shape for children to work on together. Have children cut out and paste on circles in different shapes of green, orange, brown, and yellow to make a beautiful tree. (See fig. 3G.)

Field Trip

Take a hike and notice all the trees. Collect leaves from the trees. Have children feel and smell the bark of the trees and discriminate a big tree from a small tree.

Fig 3G

Unit Group Lesson

1. **Match Concrete Objects**
   Present two nuts. Say, "This is a nut." Ask each child in turn to put the nut with the nut. Gradually increase number of irrelevant objects from which (s)he must select nuts to match.

2. **Discriminate Objects**
   Present several objects. Have each child touch the nut in response to verbal direction, "Touch the nut."

3. **Match Pictures**
   Present several pictures of common objects. Have each child match the pictures of the nuts.

4. **Discriminate Pictures**
   Present a group of several unrelated pictures of objects. Have each child touch the picture of the nut in response to verbal direction, "Touch the nut."

5. **Figure-Ground**
   Present a "busy" picture with many visual distractions. Ask each child to find the nut.

6. **Visual Closure**
   Partially cover each of several pictures with paper. Ask each child to find the picture of the nut.

7. **Function**
   Ask, "What do we do with nuts?"

8. **Association**
   Ask, "What goes with the nuts?" Use pictures or objects including trees and squirrels with several unrelated objects or pictures.

9. **Imitate Verbalization**
   Present a nut and ask, "What is this?" Say, 'Nut'." The child will imitate "Nut."

10. **Verbalize Label**
    Present a nut and ask, "What is this?" The child will respond, "Nut."

11. **Concept Enrichment**
    Discuss different nuts and their uses.

Music

1. Sing "Gathering Nuts" to the tune of "Here We Go 'Round the Mulberry Bush":
   Here we come gathering nuts,
   Gathering nuts, gathering nuts,
   Here we come gathering nuts
   On a fall day.
   Sing outside during the nature hike or inside during a game of "Find the Acorns" as in Games.

2.   Sing "Acorns Falling" to the tune of "Are You Sleeping":
        Acorns falling, acorns falling,
        From the tree, from the tree.
        Pick up all the acorns, pick up all the acorns,
        Off the ground, off the ground.

Art
1.   Have children make a nut collage using real nuts.
2.   Have children paint with nut colors at the easel.
3.   Have each child trace the outline of an acorn with a cotton swab or paintbrush dipped in brown paint (depending upon skill of child).

Snack
Serve children assortments of nuts such as a "party mix" made from many kinds of nuts. Have a mixture for the children (peanuts, almonds, etc.) and a mixture to share with birds and squirrels.

Fine Motor
1.   Help children use various methods for cracking nuts such as hand cracker or hammer and board.
2.   Have children connect dots in the shape of an acorn and color the acorn after completed.

Games
1.   Play find the acorn. Inside the classroom, have children find felt or construction paper acorns that have been hidden. Let them pretend to be hungry squirrels.
2.   Outside give children paper bags and encourage them to find as many acorns as they can.

Storytelling
Tell a story about "The Acorn Hunt."
    Two squirrels look all over the forest for acorns. They cannot find the acorns although the acorns are under a tree. The squirrels look behind trees, under rocks, and in the river. They even ask a bear. Finally they ask a child, "Where are the acorns?" The child has seen them all along under the tree. Use pictures, a flannelboard, or puppets to illustrate. Make sure the children see the acorns under the tree.

Gross Motor
Have children gather nuts into a basket and then carry the basket of nuts through an obstacle course.

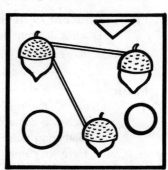

Fig. 3H

Cognitive
1.   Have children sort nuts by type, such as acorns with acorns, etc.
2.   Have children sort nuts into light and dark colors.
3.   Have children arrange nuts from smallest to largest in an egg carton using upper half of carton as a cue, by gluing appropriate nuts in it. Some children will not need cues. Use different types of nuts for different sizes.
4.   Have children draw lines from one nut to matching nuts. (See fig. 3H.)
5.   Have a treasure hunt. Hide nuts and make a picture of the classroom and mark hidden nuts. Let children gather as many as they can find.

Enrichment

1. Together Activity: Provide several varieties of nuts. Have children sort them according to variety and size. Let them arrange the nuts in rows, circles, or patterns. Then have them make a tree gluing nuts on according to variety with the largest variety at the bottom. (See fig. 31.)

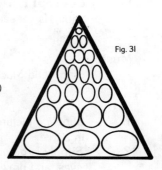

Fig. 31

2. Make numbered "nut" boxes and have children put the correct number of nuts in each box.

3. Help children sort, count and weigh nuts. Decide whether five acorns are heavier than five chestnuts, etc. Talk about gravity or what happens when one drops a nut.

4. Take a walk and find nuts from trees such as acorns from oak trees, hickory trees, etc.

Lesson 4: Squirrel

Unit Group Lesson

1. **Match Concrete Objects**
    Present two squirrels. Say, "This is a squirrel." Ask each child in turn to put the squirrel with the squirrel. Gradually increase number of irrelevant objects from which (s)he must select squirrel to match.

2. **Discriminate Objects**
    Present several objects. Have each child touch the squirrel in response to verbal direction, "Touch the squirrel."

3. **Match Pictures**
    Present several pictures of common objects. Have each child match the pictures of the squirrels.

4. **Discriminate Pictures**
    Present a group of several unrelated pictures of objects. Have each child touch the picture of the squirrel in response to verbal direction, "Touch the squirrel."

5. **Figure-Ground**
    Present a "busy" picture with many visual distractions. Ask each child to find the squirrel.

6. **Visual Closure**
    Partially cover each of several pictures with paper. Ask each child to find the picture of the squirrel.

7. **Function**
    Ask, "What do squirrels do?"

8. **Association**
    Ask, "What goes with the squirrels?" Use pictures or objects including nuts, trees, etc., with several unrelated objects or pictures.

9. **Imitate Verbalization**
    Present a squirrel and ask, "What is this?" Say, 'Squirrel'." The child will imitate "Squirrel."

10. **Verbalize Label**
    Present a squirrel and ask, "What is this?" The child will respond, "Squirrel."

11.   **Concept Enrichment**
      Squirrels eat seeds and nuts including peanuts. They live and play in trees. They have long, bushy tails.

Music

Sing "Old MacDonald Had a Squirrel" to the tune of "Old MacDonald Had a Farm."

Art

1.   Supply a picture of a tree and small pictures of squirrels (animal stamps). Have children paste squirrels in a tree.
2.   Supply large outline of squirrel for each child. Have children glue fake fur on a squirrel's tail, color in eyes, and draw whiskers (straight lines) on squirrel.
3.   Let children make squirrel collages with pictures of squirrels and fake fur scraps.

Snack

1.   Eat peanuts like squirrels do. Save the shells to let the children glue on a collage.
2.   Make homemade peanut butter. Eat and compare to manufactured peanut butter.

Fine Motor

1.   Have each child put glue on outline of squirrel, sprinkle sawdust on picture, and shake off loose sawdust. Display or take home.
2.   Make squirrel sewing cards by gluing pictures of squirrels onto cardboard and punching holes around them. Have each child sew a squirrel sewing card with brown or black yarn.
3.   Have children make a squirrel's "tail" by stuffing old panty hose into a single panty hose leg. Attach to child by tying around his/her waist.
4.   Have children do a path tracing activity. Using pictures drawn on a large poster board, make a squirrel run to his home in the tree. Child can use crayon or felt tip marker. Or use a stuffed toy animal and let child move the squirrel to the tree. "Where is the squirrel going?" "Where does the squirrel live?" Child may respond, "tree," "a tree," "in the tree," or "The squirrel lives in the tree."

Games

Have children use masking tape or magnets to attach tails to squirrel. Play it like "Pin the Tail on the Donkey."

Storytelling

1.   Fingerplay "Two Little Squirrels":

Two little squirrels	(Thumbs of both hands point up, fingers rolled into fists.)
Sat upon a limb.	
One named Jack,	(Point with right thumb.)
One named Jim.	(Point with left thumb.)
Run away Jack,	(Right thumb disappears behind back.)
Run away Jim.	(Left thumb disappears behind back.)
Come back Jack,	(Right thumb returns to original position.)
Come back Jim.	(Left thumb returns to original position.)

2.   Fingerplay "Five Little Sqirrels":

One, two, three, four, five,	(Count fingers.)
Five little squirrels sitting in a tree;	
Said this little squirrel, "What do I see?"	(Point to each finger in turn.)
Said this little squirrel, "I see a gun!"	
Said this little squirrel, "Oh, let's run!"	
Said this little squirrel, "I'm not afraid."	
Said this squirrel, "Let's sit in the shade."	
Bang! went the gun, and they all ran away.	(Clap hands sharply and hide behind back.)

If appropriate to the children's levels, discuss how guns hurt animals.

3. Flannel Board: Make up a simple story about a squirrel and his home in the tree using a flannelboard. Include a baby squirrel or a squirrel "family." Squirrels gather corn and nuts to eat and have fun chasing each other.

Gross Motor
Play a circle game with the "dog" running after the "squirrel."

Cognitive
1. Have each child pretend to be a squirrel (use props of paper ears and bushy tails). Instruct each child to put "one acorn in tree" "two acorns in tree," etc., appropriate to the child's counting abilities. Make a tree with a hole in it from poster board.
2. Make squirrels in several different sizes and have children sequence them from smallest to largest and largest to smallest.

Enrichment
1. Together Activity: Make a large squirrel on the wall at child level. Have children use small crumpled brown paper wads to fill in tail and use brown paper squares to fill in the body.
2. Talk about flying squirrels. Find out all about flying squirrels and make up a story about a flying squirrel.
3. Talk about "squirrel words" and act out: scamper, nibble, dart.

Field Trip
Take a nature hike around school or a park. Give children paper sacks to hold items they find.

Lesson 5: Football

Unit Group Lesson

1. **Match Concrete Objects**
    Present two footballs. Say, "This is a football." Ask each child in turn to put the football with the football. Gradually increase number of irrelevant objects from which (s)he must select football to match.

2. **Discriminate Objects**
    Present several objects. Have each child touch the football in response to verbal direction, "Touch the football."

3. **Match Pictures**
    Present several pictures of common objects. Have each child match the pictures of the footballs.

4. **Discriminate Pictures**
    Present a group of several unrelated pictures of objects. Have each child touch the picture of the football in response to verbal direction, "Touch the football."

5. **Figure-Ground**
    Present a "busy" picture with many visual distractions. Ask each child to find the football.

6. **Tactile Discrimination**
    Put some footballs and some very different textured objects in a "feely box." Say, "Find the football."

7. **Visual Closure**
    Partially cover each of several pictures with paper. Ask each child to find the picture of the football.

8. **Function**
   Ask, "What do we do with a football?"

9. **Association**
   Ask, "What goes with the football?" Use pictures or objects including helmets, pads, uniforms, etc., with several unrelated objects or pictures.

10. **Imitate Verbalization**
    Present a football and ask, "What is this?" Say, 'Football'." The child will imitate "Football."

11. **Verbalize Label**
    Present a football and ask, "What is this?" The child will respond, "Football."

12. **Concept Enrichment**
    Discuss terms in football such as touchdown, goal post, field, helmet, cheerleader, etc., for understanding. Discuss that it usually is played in the fall and winter seasons.

Music
1. Sing "A Big Football" to the tune of "This is the Way We Wash Our Clothes":
   I give my friend a big football,
   Big football, a big football,
   I give my friend a big football,
   A big football, bi-ig fo-otball.
   Have children form a circle and have a child with a football walk around group while group sings song. At end of song, the child chooses someone to take her place until each child has a turn.
2. Sing "John Has a Big Football" to the tune of "Mary Had a Little Lamb":
   John has a big (little) football,
   Big football, big football.
   John has a big football,
   That he will throw to me.
   Have children sing the song substituting children's names in appropriate places. Use a big and a little football and be sure that each child has a turn.

Art
1. Have children make a football collage. Let them get pictures of players and footballs from sports magazines and catalogs and glue them on brown construction paper.
2. Have children outline a football with glue, sprinkle grits (colored brown with tempera paint) over outline, and shake off loose grits. Let them add other decorations.
3. Let children paint with brown paint at the easels.

Snack
Have a stadium snack of popcorn and hot dogs.

Fine Motor
1. Make football sewing cards in a variety of levels of difficulty. Have each child sew a football sewing card appropriate to her own level.
2. Make a football puzzle for each child from paper and let each paste puzzle together on the outline of a football. Vary the number of pieces according to the skill levels of the children.
3. Cut "footballs" from cardboard. Let each child lace across one to make "X's." Vary the number of holes with the skill level of each child. (See fig. 3J.)

Fig. 3J

Games

Make "goal posts" with colored tape on each end of a table and put center line across the middle. Have the children take turns kneeling at the end of the table and blowing ping pong balls. The side that blows a ball over the goal line gets a "touchdown." Keep score by adding one point per touchdown or multiples of a number for more advanced children.

Storytelling

Find a good action picture from a sports magazine. Have the children help make up a story about the picture. Include the words football, touchdown, run, quarterback, etc. as appropriate for the language skills of the children.

Gross Motor

1. Play catch with the football. (The soft sponge type is best.) Use different sized footballs.
2. Let the children run for a touchdown. Have a child catch a ball (large and easy to catch) thrown by another child and run to the "goal." Yell, "Touchdown!" Be sure each child scores a touchdown.
3. Hang a football in a net bag (orange bag) on a tree or pole. Have children run up and kick it.

Cognitive

1. Have children sort footballs from non-footballs. Use real balls or pictures depending upon level of child.
2. Prepare cue sheets with football at the top, and baseballs, tennis balls, basketballs, etc., mixed in with footballs. Have children mark the footballs. Vary the level of complexity according to the skills of the children.
3. Have children sort football from non-football items.

Enrichment

Organize a football experience. Have some children be the team, some the cheering crowds, some the snack sellers, some the cheerleaders, etc.

Field Trip

Visit a football team's practice session.

Visitor

Have a football player, dressed in uniform visit the class. Let children try on helmet and hold his football.

Other Children's Records
"Posture Exercises" from **LEARNING, BASIC SKILLS-HEALTH & SAFETY** (EA)
"Growing" from **LEARNING BASIC SKILLS VOL. I** (EA)
"Autumn Song" from **LOOK AT THE HOLIDAY** (GA)
"Autumn Season" from **JAMBO** (SCHOL)
"Songs About Trees" from **RHYTHMS OF CHILDHOOD**

Other Children's Books
Kessler, Ethel and Kessler, Leonard. **ALL FOR FALL.** New York: Parent's Magazine Press, 1974.
Monecure, Jane. **FALL IS HERE.** Elgin, Ill.: Child's World, 1975.
Zolotow, Charlotte. **SAY IT!** New York: Greenwillow Books, 1980.

Related Parenting Materials
Cansler, Dot. **THE HOMESTRETCH.** Winston-Salem, NC 27113-5128: Kaplan Press, 1983.

Related Materials
TEACHING PICTURES. Winston-Salem, NC 27113-5128: Kaplan Press, 1983.
STORY SEQUENCE CARDS I, II. Winston-Salem, NC 27113-5128: Kaplan Press, 1983.
SEWING CARDS I, II, III. Winston-Salem, NC 27113-5128: Kaplan Press, 1983.

Unit 4: Clothing

A developmental assessment should determine the functional levels of each child. Individual expectations are based on the assessment results.

Lesson 1: Hat

Unit Group Lesson

1. **Match Concrete Objects**
    Present two hats. Say, "This is a hat." Ask each child in turn to put the hat with the hat. Gradually increase number of irrelevant objects from which (s)he must select hat to match.

2. **Discriminate Objects**
    Present several objects. Have each child touch the hat in response to the verbal direction, "Touch the hat."

3. **Match Pictures**
    Present several pictures of common objects. Have each child match the pictures of the hats.

4. **Discriminate Pictures**
    Present a group of several unrelated pictures of objects. Have each child touch the picture of the hat in response to the verbal direction, "Show me the hat."

5. **Figure-Ground**
    Present a "busy" picture with many visual distractions. Ask each child to find the hat.

6. **Visual Closure**
    Partially cover each of several pictures with paper. Ask each child to find the picture of the hat.

7. **Function**
    Ask, "What do we do with a hat?"

8. **Association**
    Ask, "What goes with the hat?" Use pictures or objects including coat, shoe, gloves, etc. with several unrelated objects or pictures.

9. **Imitate Verbalization**
    Present a hat and ask, "What is this? Say, 'Hat'." The child will imitate "Hat."

10. **Verbalize Label**
    Present a hat and ask, "What is this?" The child will respond, "Hat."

11. **Concept Enrichment**

Discuss fire hats, soldier hats, cowboy hats. Classify hats by type - warm weather versus cold weather; professional versus non-professional, etc.

Music

1. Sing to the tune of "Here We Go 'Round The Mulberry Bush":

Verse 1: We put on our hat when it is cold
When it is cold, when it is cold;
We put on our hat when it is cold,
Early in the norming.

(Use different types of hats and have children imitate the motions of putting on a hat.)

Verse 2: We put on our hat when it is rainy. . .
Verse 3: We put on our hat when it is snowy. . .

You and children may want to make up new verses or vary the ones given, (e.g. (child) puts his hat on his head).

2. Sing to the tune of "The More We Get Together":

When (child) puts a hat on,
A hat on, a hat on.
When (child) puts a hat on,
We will clap for him.

(The named child puts on a hat, and the others clap for him/her)

3. Sing to the tune of "Mary Had A Little Lamb": You and the class can make-up a song using the children and what they are wearing as the subject of the song. Follow this model:

(Janet) has a blue and white hat,
Blue and white hat, blue and white hat.
(Janet) has a blue and white hat,
It is on her head.

The children will be very proud of their clothes.

Art

1. Have the children sponge a design on paper for the paper hat in Fine Motor #1 today.
2. Have the children cut or tear pictures of hats from catalogs. Let the children paste the pictures on paper.
3. Make a soldier hat by folding paper. You should help the child fold and crease the paper. Staple it to keep it together. The children can decorate it. Make it out of construction paper, newspaper, paper sacks, etc. (See fig. 4A.)

Fig. 4A

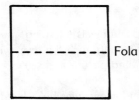 Fola
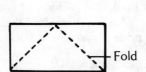 Fold
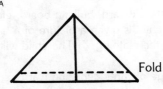 Fold
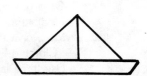

Snack

1. Eat snack while wearing paper hats made by children.
2. Have children wear chef's hats when preparing snack.

Fine Motor

1. Have the children make dress-up bonnets with flowers and streamers. Cut out 12" circles. Cut a radius. Fold and tape or staple at the cut. Attach decorations such as flowers, pieces of ribbon, lace, stickers, etc. Attach ribbon ties with staples. (See fig. 4B.)
2. Cut construction paper into large feathers. Have the children fringe them with scissors. Attach the feathers to the paper hats made in Art #3 today.
3. Have the children put their paper hats on when it is time to out.
4. During dress-up period give the children a variety of hats to try on. Have the children put the hats on themselves.

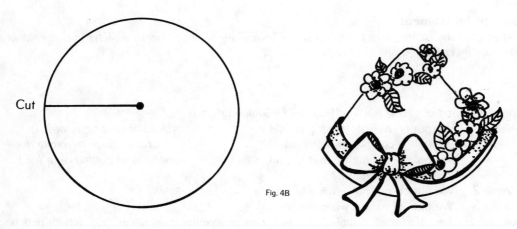

Cut

Fig. 4B

Games

1. Play: "Who's Wearing The Hat?" Put a hat in front of a child's face. Ask, "Who's wearing the hat?" Let everyone guess.
2. Some children may enjoy dressing the "New Friends" dolls during this unit.

Storytelling

1. Flannel Board: Have available the figures of a boy and a girl and different types of clothing. Have children, one at a time, put an article of clothing on figures. As they put on the clothing ask, "What are you putting on the boy's head?" The child responds appropriately. Ask, "What do you want to put on the boy, (child)?" The child responds and you ask, "Where does it go?"
2. Have the following hats on display for the children to see: ski hat, rain hat, football helmet, man's hat, woman's hat, baseball hat, etc. Have children try on the hats. Then, hold up a hat and ask children, "Who wears this hat?" Children respond to question.
3. Read *Caps For Sale* by Esphyr Slobodkina.

Gross Motor

1. Play musical "Pass The Hat." The child left with the hat, when the music stops, is out.
2. Make an obstacle course (indoors or outdoors). Let children get hat and run obstacle course. Hang the hat on a hook by climbing steps to hang hat.

Cognitive

1. On a poster (blackboard, bulletin board, etc.) put three pictures of groups of objects (clothing, toys, food). Each child is given a picture of a hat. Ask, "Where does the hat belong, with the toys, with the food, or with the clothing?" The child will place his picture with the clothing picture and say, "Clothing."
2. Use three large pictures depicting warm, sunny weather, rainy weather, and snowy weather. Hold up a rain hat, and ask, "When do you wear this hat?" The child may respond by pointing to the correct picture or saying, "Rain," "In the rain" or "When it rains." Hold up a winter hat and repeat the question. Pointing to picture of a warm day, say "Do you wear a hat when it is hot?" The child responds "no." Pointing to picture of rainy day, say "Do you wear a hat when it rains?" "Yes." "Do you wear a hat when it snows?" "Yes." Note that some children may wear sun bonnets in the hot weather, therefore a "yes" answer can be appropriate.
3. Let children try on different hats, (e.g. nurse's cap, fireman's hat, policeman's hat, father's hat, mother's hat, chef's hat) then tell what the person who wears the hat does.
4. Put all the children's hats in a pile on the table. Have child match a hat to its owner. Every child should get a turn at matching.
5. Have the children sort pictures. Give each child in turn twenty pictures of various objects, including clothes. The children sort the pictures - pulling out clothing items, especially hats, and putting them in a "clothes" box (shoe box, cigar box, etc.).

Enrichment

1. Make helmets out of plastic milk cartons. Talk about times you would wear a helmet:
   a. to play football,
   b. to ride a motorcycle,
   c. as protection for a child who has trouble standing and sitting,
   d. to build a building.
   (Coordinate with New Friends doll who wears a helmet.)

2. Together Activity: Make a clothing store. In a corner or work area, "build" a clothing store with large cardboard boxes. Make or provide: (See fig. 4C.)
   a. a basket of socks to match before you "buy",
   b. shelves for folded garments,
   c. a cardboard box with a pole through it for hanging garments,
   d. a belt rack and tie rack on which belt buckles and ties fit,
   e. a curtained off area for "changing", and
   f. a full length mirror for looking at garments.
   Display garments sorted by criteri like color, size (big, little), types of clothing etc. depending upon your emphasis for the day.

   Children can:
   a. select and try on outfits,
   b. sort garments according to various criteria as indicated above,
   c. fold garments and put them on shelves,
   d. staple price tags on garments,
   d. model outfits.

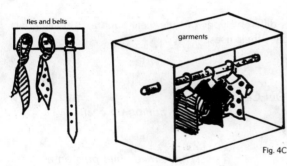
ties and belts
garments
Fig. 4C

a place for folded garments

Basket of socks to match before you buy

Visitor

Pretend to be a visiting relative coming in with a suitcase of clothing that will tell what you plan to do in your visit.

Lesson 2: Coat

Unit Group Lesson

1. **Match Concrete Objects**
   Present two coats. Say, "This is a coat." Ask each child in turn to put the coat with the coat. Gradually increase number of irrelevant objects from which (s)he must select coat to match.

2. **Discriminate Objects**
   Present several objects. Have each child touch the coat in response to the verbal direction, "Touch the coat."

3. **Match Pictures**
   Present several pictures of common objects. Have each child match the pictures of the coats.

4. **Discriminate Pictures**
    Present a group of several unrelated pictures of objects. Have each child touch the picture of the coat in response to the verbal direction, "Show me the coat."

5. **Figure-Ground**
    Present a "busy" picture with many visual distractions. Ask each child to find the coat.

6. **Visual Closure**
    Partially cover each of several pictures with paper. Ask each child to find the picture of the coat.

7. **Function**
    Ask, "What do we do with a coat?"

8. **Association**
    Ask, "What goes with the coat?" Use pictures or objects including coat, shoe, pants, dress, etc. with several unrelated objects or pictures.

9. **Imitate Verbalization**
    Present a coat and ask, "What is this? Say, 'Coat'." The child will imitate "Coat."

10. **Verbalize Label**
    Present a coat and ask, "What is this?" The child will respond, "Coat."

11. **Concept Enrichment**
    Compare human's coats to animal coats. Discuss different types of outerwear such as: heavy coats, light coats, rain coats, jackets, sweaters, etc. Discuss their uses.

Music
1. Sing to the tune of "This is The Way We Wash Out Clothes":
    Verse 1: We put on our coat when it is cold   *(Pantomine putting on coat)*
    Verse 2: We put on our coat when it is snowy
2. Sing to the tune of "The More We Get Together":
    When (child) puts a coat on,   *(The named child puts on a*
    A coat on, a coat on.   *coat, and the other clap for*
    When (child) puts a coat on,   *him/her.)*
    We will clap for him.
    You may need to assist with coat.

Art
1. Have children cut or tear pictures of coats for a coat collage.
2. Give the children pictures of a child wearing a coat. Have children either decorate the coat the way they want or follow your instructions (e.g. "Color the coat blue").
3. "Dressing" paper dolls. Have a parent or volunteer cut out large paper dolls (about 20" tall) from newspaper. Have the children add clothing - whatever is being discussed - shirt, shorts, sweater, etc. with water color markers. Keep this type of paper doll on hand, as they can be used for many activities through out the year. (See fig. 4D.)

Fig. 4D

Snack
    Wear coats and go outside for snack in the playground.

Fine Motor

1. Have the children draw buttons or paste real buttons on a picture of a coat.
2. Let the children learn to put on and take off their coats. Teach them to put coats on by the "over the head" method. Put the coat on the floor, inside up. The child stands at the neck (head) place, leans down and puts arms inside sleeves. Then the child swings the coat over his head so that it's on.
3. Let the children help each other with buttons and zippers on coats.
4. Take a dress maker's form to class. Place it at the height of the child. Practice buttoning skills with a coat placed on the form. (See fig. 4E.)
5. Tape a large smiling face on the back of a chair. Hang a garment around the chair for buttoning practice. (See fig. 4F.)

Fig. 4E

Fig. 4F

Games

1. Have the children turn coats inside out and right side out again.
2. Play "Tape The Coat On The Child." Play like "Pin The Tail On The Donkey," but use two-sided tape or magnets. Make a coat and child outline of heavy paper. Attach the outline of the child to a wall or metal surface. Let the children "attach" the coat to the child. (Some children may not want to be blindfolded.)

Storytelling

Show the children a large picture of a family dressed up to go out. The family members have on their coats and hats. Ask the children to describe how they are dressed and where they might be going. Have the class help to make up a story about the family.

Gross Motor

Make obstacle course for relay race. Have two child-sized chairs with coats hanging on the backs. Divide the children into teams. The children go through a simple obstacle course (over 3 books, under chairs, etc.) to get to the coats. (The complexity of the obstacle course will vary with the children's level of development.) Take the coat from the chair, turn it wrong-side-out and re-hang it on the chair and return to start. The next child repeats the process doing the opposite (right-side out), etc. (See fig. 4G.)

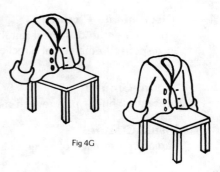

Fig 4G

Cognitive

1. Have each child dress a doll with a coat and hat, pretend he or she is going to the store, and it is very cold outside.
2. Put all of the children's coats in a pile on a table. A child matches a coat to its owner. Every child should get a turn at matching.
3. Have children sort button coats and zipper coats into different piles. Use pictures for more advanced children.
4. Paste coats of different colors on paper. Give the children this paper and a collection of different colored hats. Have the children paste the hats next to the matching coat.
5. Hang two clothes lines and cut many pairs of variously sized paper coats from construction paper. Depending on the developmental level of the children:
   1. Have the child sequence coats from large to small and vice-versa. Provide a model for the child who needs it.
   2. Create a sequence of coats. Have the child copy the sequence or reverse the sequence.

Enrichment

1. Use a shoe bag with numerals on the pockets. Have the children put coats with different numbers of buttons into the correct shoe bag pocket (one button to numeral 1, etc.).
2. Create a fabric match activity by cutting different coats from different fabrics. Have the children match them with each other. Vary textures and discuss different textures.

Field Trip

Bundle up in coats and take a walk.

Visitor

Invite a mother who has a fur coat. Let the children touch the soft fur.

Lesson 3: Shoe

Unit Group Lesson

1. **Match Concrete Objects**
   Present two shoes. Say, "This is a shoe." Ask each child in turn to put the shoe with the shoe. Gradually increase number of irrelevant objects from which (s)he must select shoe to match.

2. **Discriminate Objects**
   Present several objects. Have each child touch the shoe in response to the verbal direction, "Touch the shoe."

3. **Match Pictures**
   Present several pictures of common objects. Have each child match the pictures of the shoes.

4. **Discriminate Pictures**
   Present a group of several unrelated pictures of objects. Have each child touch the picture of the shoe in response to the verbal direction, "Show me the shoe."

5. **Figure-Ground**
   Present a "busy" picture with many visual distractions. Ask each child to find the shoe.

6. **Visual Closure**
   Partially cover each of several pictures with paper. Ask each child to find the picture of the shoe.

7. **Function**
   Ask, "What do we do with a shoe?"

8. **Association**
   Ask, "What goes with the shoe?" Use pictures or objects including a hat, coat, pants, dress, etc. with several unrelated objects or pictures.

9. **Imitate Verbalization**
   Present a shoe and ask, "What is this? Say, 'Shoe'." The child will imitate "Shoe."

10. **Verbalize Label**
    Present a shoe and ask, "What is this?" The child will respond, "Shoe."

11. **Concept Enrichment**
    Talk about different types of footwear, such as shoes, boots, sandals, slippers, etc. Discuss the uses of the different types of footwear. Discuss parts of shoes (heel, tongue, etc.).

Music

1. Sing to the tune of "This Is The Way We Wash Our Clothes":

    This is the way we put on our shoes,   *(Pantomine putting on shoes)*
    Put on our shoes, put on our shoes,
    This is the way we put on our shoes,
    Before we go skipping around (hopping, jumping, etc.).   *(Skip around)*

2. Sing to the tune of "Mary Had A Little Lamb":

    (Jane) is wearing tennis shoes, tennis shoes, tennis shoes.
    (Jane) is wearing tennis shoes,
    And they are on her feet.

3. Sing to the tune of "The More We Get Together":

    When (child) puts a shoe on,   *(The named child puts on a*
    A shoe on, a shoe on.   *shoe, and the others clap for*
    When (child) puts a shoe on,   *him/her).*
    We will clap for her.

Art

1. Give each child a page with a series of shoes pasted on it. Only one shoe from a pair is pasted on the paper. The remaining shoe is in an envelope. The children take the shoes from the envelope, paste them next to the matching shoe on the page. Let the children decorate the border of the paper.

2. Let the children match pictures of shoes to outlines of shoes that are drawn on construction paper. Use pictures of sneakers, boots, sandals, men's shoes, high heels, etc. Let the children paint the shoes.

Snack

1. Have everyone wear fancy shoes taken from the housekeeping area to snack.
2. Have each child pack his lunch or snack in a clean shoebox.

Fine Motor

1. Have the children "lace" a shoe sewing card, a large man's shoe, or a lacing board (8½ x 11)

2. Let the children learn and practice putting on and taking off their shoes and other types of footwear.
3. Let the children learn and practice tying (or buckling) their shoes.
4. After children learn to take off their own shoes and socks, reward them by painting their toenails red.

Games

1. "Find Your Shoe." Take one shoe from each child and hide them all at one time. Each child looks for his shoe. When he finds it, he puts it on and sits in his chair.
2. Have the children walk on dewy grass, then on paper or the sidewalk to see footprints.
3. Have many kinds of shoes (rain boots, dress-up shoes, cowboy boots, Indian moccasins, bedroom slippers, etc.) in the housekeeping corner.

Storytelling

Tell the Mother Goose story, "The Little Old Lady Who Lived In A Shoe." Use a flannel board or story cards to illustrate the story.

Gross Motor

Make paper shoe prints across the floor. Let the children walk on the shoe prints. Make sure some are close together, some far apart. Have some with one shoe print directly in front of and touching another. Have the children walk forward and backwards on the shoe prints.

Cognitive

Have the children associate shoes with other clothing. Have the children select items from a table of clothing items that the teacher asks, "What do you wear with shoes?" The child will pick up a pair of socks. The teacher may hold up various items and ask, "Do you wear gloves with shoes on your feet?"

2. Place one shoe from each child on a table. The child who is "it" takes a shoe from the pile and places it next to the owner's foot (matching shoes). Give each child a turn.

3. Use vinyl photo album pages to make a LOTTO game with pictures of clothes. The photo album pages are available in different sizes with from 4 to 9 pockets per page. Lotto games can be made with varying levels of difficulty. Use large pictures and less pockets for an easier game. Slip pictures into the pockets and have matching pictures on index cards. Have the children play as a lotto game or use for matching.

4. Have a collection of many pairs of shoes for the children to select "PAIRS" of shoes.

Enrichment

1. Supply graph paper with different sized squares. Trace around the foot of each child. Help each child count how many squares his/her foot touches. Vary the complexity of the "graph" paper according to counting level of child. (See fig. 4H.)

2. Have the children use shoes as measuring sticks. "The Table is the same length as (5) of (Sally's) shoes (feet)." (See fig. 4I.)

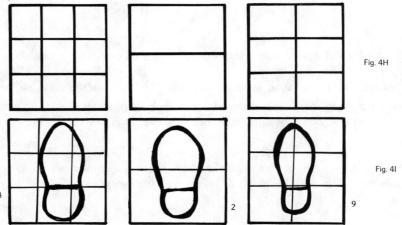

Fig. 4H

Fig. 4I

Visitor

Invite parent with all their shoes to tell where they wear each pair - (even their old gardening shoes).

Lesson 4: Glove

Unit Group Lesson

1. **Match Concrete Objects**
Present two gloves. Say, "This is a glove." Ask each child in turn to put the glove with the glove. Gradually increase number of irrelevant objects from which (s)he must select glove to match.

2. **Discriminate Objects**
Present several objects. Have each child touch the glove in response to the verbal direction, "Touch the glove."

3. **Match Pictures**
Present several pictures of common objects. Have each child match the pictures of the gloves.

4. **Discriminate Pictures**
Present a group of several unrelated pictures of objects. Have each child touch the picture of the glove in response to the verbal direction, "Show me the glove."

5. **Figure-Ground**
Present a "busy" picture with many visual distractions. Ask each child to find the glove.

6. **Visual Closure**
   Partially cover each of several pictures with paper. Ask each child to find the picture of the glove.

7. **Function**
   Ask, "What do we do with gloves?"

8. **Association**
   Ask, "What goes with the glove?" Use pictures or objects including a hat, coat, shoes, pants, dress, etc. with several unrelated objects or pictures.

9. **Imitate Verbalization**
   Present a glove and ask, "What is this? Say, 'Glove'." The child will imitate "Glove."

10. **Verbalize Label**
    Present a glove and ask, "What is this?" The child will respond, "Glove."

11. **Concept Enrichment**
    If the children are able to understand more than one concept, teach mitten as well as glove. Discuss handwear such as, mittens, rubber gloves, gardening gloves, work gloves, etc. Discuss the uses of these items.

Music
1. Sing to the tune of "This Is The Way We Wash Our Clothes":
   Verse 1 - We put our gloves on our hands
   (Pantomime putting on gloves.)

2. Sing to the tune of "Mary Had A Little Lamb":
   (John) has gloves with snowmen on them.
   Snowmen on them, snowmen on them
   (John) has gloves with snowmen
   And they keep his hands warm.

3. Sing to the tune of "The More We Get Together":
   When (child) puts his gloves on,
   His gloves on, his gloves on,
   When (child) puts his gloves on,
   We will clap for him.
   (The named child puts on gloves, and the others clap for him/her.)
   Help each child put his gloves on if necessary.

Art
1. Draw around each child's hands and fingers to make a picture of a pair of gloves. Have the children color the gloves.
2. Have the children paste a pair of "gloves" (construction paper) on a pair of hands drawn on paper. The children must put the right glove on the right hand and the left glove on the left hand. They should cover the hand completely "to keep it warm."

Snack
Let the children try to pick up snack with gloves on their hands. Use stick pretzels, peanuts, oyster crackers, or other small items for snack.

Fine Motor
1. Let the children put on their gloves when it is time to go out.
2. Let the children outline the picture of a glove with glue. Then place heavy yarn on the glue. Use a volunteer to plan and conduct activity with small groups.

Games

1. Have a big box of different types of gloves for children to use for pretending.
2. Make finger puppets from glove "fingers." Cut fingers off light colored gloves and draw faces on them. Let the children wear them on their fingers for puppets.

Storytelling

1. Tell the story of "The Three Little Kittens" who lost their mittens. Use pictures to illustrate. The teacher should dramatize.
2. Do the fingerplay "Mittens" by Marion F. Grayson

    Slide your fingers into the wide part,   *(Hold right hand forward, palm fingers together - thumb apart.)*

    Make your thumb stand alone and tall.
    When you put your mitten on,   *(Slide left hand over grouped fingers and then over thumb.)*

    You won't feel cold at all.
    Have the children use their mittens as they follow the directions. Discuss when you wear mittens and gloves.

Gross Motor

1. Have a jumping glove relay. The teams consist of two children. Each child jumps to the glove box, puts on a pair of gloves, jumps back and gives the gloves to another child. That child puts the gloves on, jumps to the box, and puts them back. For different levels of children, this can be done with walking, hopping, skipping, etc.
2. Have the children push a cage or medicine ball (a large heavy ball available in most elementary schools) around with gloved hands.

Cognitive

1. Use real mittens in three different sizes. Let the children try them on their hands. Discuss which fit, which are too little and which are too big.
2. Make construction paper mittens in three different sizes: small, medium and large. Have each child put them in correct order big to small or small to big.
3. Make a sequencing activity with clothesline, clip clothes pins and different pairs of gloves. Have each child match the sequence created by teacher. Some children will be able to reverse the sequence.
4. Provide a basket with all the children's mittens and gloves. Sort out in "PAIRS."
5. Provide mittens and glove shapes cut from wallpaper or fabric with different designs. Have the children match them by design. (See fig. 4J.)

 Fig. 4J

Enrichment

1. Make sets of matching gloves, hats, and coats cut from paper. Have the children match correct outfits by color or pattern.
2. Make a game: "Count the Fingers on the Gloves." Make a large set of gloves out of poster board. Put the numbers 1-10 on the fingers from left to right. (Laminate). Have the children count the fingers. Some children can trace over the given numerals. Some children can copy the numerals below the given ones.

Field Trip

Visit a department store. Visit the men's, women's, children's and baby's departments. Look at clothes in the store. Have the children try on clothes (hats, sweaters). The teacher and children should complement each child on how nice he/she looks. Have the children look in a mirror. Discuss the trip when back at school. Take pictures at the clothing store. Have pictures of the children trying on clothes, looking in the mirror, etc. Post these in the classroom.

Visitor

Invite someone to come to the class as "Mary Mixed-Up." Ask visitor to dress in clothing put on incorrectly with pairs mixed up, etc. Let the children identify what is wrong.

Lesson 5: Pants and Shirt

Unit Group Lesson

1. **Match Concrete Objects**
   Present two pants and shirts. Say, "This is a pants and shirt." Ask each child in turn to put the pants and shirt with the pants and shirt. Gradually increase number of irrelevant objects from which (s)he must select pants and shirt to match.

2. **Discriminate Objects**
   Present several objects. Have each child touch the pants and shirts in response to the verbal direction, "Touch the pants and shirt."

3. **Match Pictures**
   Present several pictures of common objects. Have each child match the pictures of the pants and shirt.

4. **Discriminate Pictures**
   Present a group of several unrelated pictures of objects. Have each child touch the picture of the pants and shirt in response to the verbal direction, "Show me the pants and shirt."

5. **Figure-Ground**
   Present a "busy" picture with many visual distractions. Ask each child to find the pants and shirt.

6. **Visual Closure**
   Partially cover each of several pictures with paper. Ask each child to find the picture of the pants and shirt.

7. **Function**
   Ask, "What do we do with pants and shirt?"

8. **Association**
   Ask, "What goes with the pants and shirt?" Use pictures or objects including a hat, coat, shoe, glove, dress, etc. with several unrelated objects or pictures.

9. **Imitate Verbalization**
   Present pants and a shirt and ask, "What is this? Say, 'Pants and shirt'." The child will imitate "Pants and shirt."

10. **Verbalize Label**
    Present pants and a shirt and ask, "What is this?" The child will respond, "Pants and shirt."

11. **Concept Enrichment**
    Discuss dress up pants and shirts and play pants and shirts. Look at different ones and decide if they are for play or dress up.

Music

1. Sing "This Is The Way I Put On My Pants" to tune of "This Is The Way We Wash Our Clothes":

    This is the way I put on my pants,   *(Teacher and children*
    Put on my pants, put on my pants.   *panomine putting on pants*
    This is the way I put on my pants,   *and zipping them.)*
    Zip, zip, zip!

2. Sing "Button Your Shirt" to the tune of "Are You Sleeping?":

    Button your shirt,   *(Have children pantomine*
    Button your shirt,   *buttoning their shirts.)*
    Up the front
    Up the front
    Button up your shirt
    Button up your shirt
    Up the front
    Up the front.

Art

1. Have each child make a pants collage. Children tear or cut out pictures of pants and paste them on paper.
2. Have children paste pants and shirts on a large posterboard as a group project. Display poster in room.
3. Give children large ditto outline of boy and girl. Have children paste various articles of clothing on outline. Vary the activity by having the children draw on and color the clothing. Children can also decorate the clothing with potato or sponge designs.

Snack

Have a fancy snack with pretty napkins and have children wear dress-up pants and shirts.

Fine Motor

1. Teach the children to put on and take off their own pants during toileting. Teacher may want to help until child can be entirely on his own.
2. Teach the children to zip the zippers in their pants.
3. Have the children outline with glue a pair of pants in a picture. Sprinkle colored grits on the glue and shake off excess. Display picture.
4. Make several puzzles of a child composed of the different articles of clothing and the body parts. One puzzle should include pants, shirt, shoes, and appropriate body parts. Another should include a dress, shoes, pretty hat, and appropriate body parts.
5. Make a doll clothing puzzle by making a child shape and clothing to fit on the shape. Cut the clothing into two or more pieces. Some children need simpler puzzles than others. Some suggested variations are: to make the puzzle pieces in three basic colors. Have the children sort and match the colors to get the clothing the same color. Make the puzzle outline on the doll and have the children match the pieces to the outline. (See fig. 4K.)

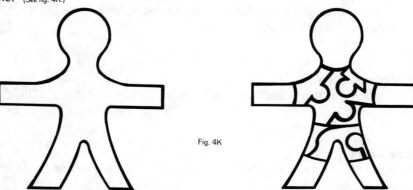

Fig. 4K

6. Have the children button their own shirts. If buttons are too small to manipulate, a small vest with large buttons and button holes can be made for buttoning practice.
7. Have the children hang real (small) pants and shirts on a clothesline.
8. Have the children hang pants and shirts cut from magazines on clothesline.

Games

1. Have dolls for children to dress with pants and shirts. Use bigger dolls for less skilled children.
2. Encourage the children to play "dress-up like Mommy and Daddy" by having a box of old clothes with Daddy's pants, Mommy's dresses, etc.
3. Pack a suitcase or laundry basket full of clothes. Have each child pull out a garment and tell the apropriate time to wear that garment.

Storytelling

1. Make a sequence story by showing pictures which show a boy or a girl getting dressed. Talk about what the child puts on first, second, etc. Each child has a turn putting the pictures in order. Start the story with three pictures. Make task more difficult by increasing the number of pictures.
2. Show and Tell: Let the children voluntarily stand in front of the class and show the clothes they are wearing. Encourage them to label and describe what they are wearing. You and the children can make comments like "Oh! That's pretty," and "I like your pants."

Gross Motor

1. Have a three-legged walking race by pinning the legs of pairs of childrens' pants together and having the children race.
2. Have a tug of war using an old pair of adult pants as the rope.

Cognitive

1. Take a piece of doll clothing (pants, shirt, etc.) from a box and names it. Have child find another article just like yours. The child names it and puts it on a doll.
2. Make "pants" cue sheets and "shirt" cue sheets. A cue sheet has the model pictured at the top of the page. The child marks all those items on the page that are the same as the cue. (See fig. 4L.)
3. Have the children match patterns of clothes hung on a line: pants, shirts, dress.
4. Let children match red pants to a red shirt, blue pants to a blue shirt, etc.

Cognitive

5. On a poster, blackboard, or bulletin board put three pictures of groups of objects (clothing, toys, foods). Each child is give a picture of a pair of pants. The teacher asks, "Where do the pants belong, with the toys, the food, or the clothing?" Child will place his picture with clothing picture and say "Clothing." Repeat the activity with shirt.

Fig. 4L

Enrichment

Make pants number puzzles which are SELF-CORRECTING. Make each pair of pants with a numeral on one leg and the corresponding numbers of patches on the other leg. Cut each pair so that it is unique and the correct answer only matches with the correct numeral. (See fig. 4M.)

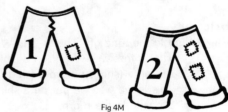

Fig 4M

Visitor

Invite someone to come to class as "Mary Mixed-Up;" dressed in clothing put on incorrectly with pairs mixed up, etc. Let the children identify what is wrong.

Lesson 6: Dress

Unit Group Lesson

1. **Match Concrete Objects**
   Present two dresses. Say, "This is a dress." Ask each child in turn to put the dress with the dress. Gradually increase number of irrelevant objects from which (s)he must select dress to match.

2. **Discriminate Objects**
    Present several objects. Have each child touch the dress in response to the verbal direction, "Touch the dress."

3. **Match Pictures**
    Present several pictures of common objects. Have each child match the pictures of the dress.

4. **Discriminate Pictures**
    Present a group of several unrelated pictures of objects. Have each child touch the picture of the dress in response to the verbal direction, "Show me the dress."

5. **Figure-Ground**
    Present a "busy" picture with many visual distractions. Ask each child to find the dress.

6. **Visual Closure**
    Partially cover each of several pictures with paper. Ask each child to find the picture of the dress.

7. **Function**
    Ask, "What do we do with a dress?"

8. **Association**
    Ask, "What goes with the dress?" Use pictures or objects including a hat, coat, gloves, pants, shoes, shirt, etc. with several unrelated objects or pictures.

9. **Imitate Verbalization**
    Present a dress ask, "What is this? Say, 'Dress'." The child will imitate "Dress ."

10. **Verbalize Label**
    Present a dress and ask, "What is this?" The child will respond, "Dress."

11. **Concept Enrichment**
    Discuss different types of dresses such as party dresses, school dresses, etc. Talk about the uses of the different types of dresses.

Music

1. Sing to the tune of "This Is The Way We Wash Our Clothes":
    This is the way we put on a (shirt)
    Put on a (shirt), put on a (shirt),
    This is the way we put on a shirt
    So early in the morning.
    Have the boys sing about putting on pants, shirts, shoes, hats, coats and gloves. Have the girls sing about putting on pants, shirts, blouses, dresses, shoes, coats, hats and gloves. Have the children pantomine actions of dressing as they sing.

2. Sing to the tune of "Mary Had A Little Lamb":
    (Susan) has a pretty (green) dress,
    Pretty (green) dress, pretty (green) dress,
    (Susan) has a pretty (green) dress
    And she is all dressed up!

3. Sing to the tune of "The More We Get Together":
    When (child) puts a dress on,   *(The named child puts on a*
    A dress on, a dress on,   *dress, and the others*
    When (child) puts a dress on,   *clap for her.)*
    We will clap for her.

Art

1. Give the children an envelope of clothing pictures cut from catalogs. Have the children pick out the dress pictures and paste on paper to make a collage.

2. Give the children an envelope of cut-outs of dresses. Each dress will be shaped and sized differently. The children match and paste dresses to dress outlines, pre-drawn by you. Use gross differences of size and shape for some children.

3. Make single doll shapes at least 24 inches high, and outline dresses for the doll shapes. Have the children decorate the dresses for the dolls with: stripes, sponge prints, stickers, lick 'n' stick polka dots, plaids (draw beads lines and have children trace in colors) etc. Some children can cut their own dresses. Let all children dress the doll shapes. (See fig. 4N.)

 Fig. 4N

Snack

Let the children come to snack in an outfit from the dress-up section of the classroom.

Fine Motor

1. Draw a dress on the blackboard or on chart paper. Let the children take turns drawing circles for buttons and straight lines for stripes on the drawing.

2. Have the children paste buttons on construction paper dresses. Then let them use crayons to decorate dresses. The teacher supplies "dresses," cut before hand.

3. Let the children hang real dresses on a clothes line.

Games

1. Have a variety of items in the dress-up section of the classroom including clothes (large child or small adult for easy wear), jewelry, ties, boots and shoes, hats, lace, etc.

2. During transition from one activity or location to another, use the following game: Say, "All the children wearing dresses, line up at the door." "All boys wearing tennis shoes go to the snack table," etc.

3. Play a "Go Touch" game. Ask the children to touch different articles of clothing such as "Go touch Mary's dress." Let the children take turns being teacher.

4. Let the children take turns washing the clothes of the "New Friends" dolls or doll clothes from the housekeeping corner.

Storytelling

1. Use puppets to tell a story about a little girl who goes to the store to buy a dress. At the end of the story have the puppet talk to the children. Include such things as "Mary, I like your red dress." and "Children with shoes on, stand up."

2. Tell a sequence story about "Visiting A Department Store" and talk about seeing different things, including clothes. Let the children retell the story in sequence.

Gross Motor

1. Have one child (or yourself) wear a dress and hold the skirt out like a bucket. Have the children toss beanbags into the "bucket."

2. Have the children pass a box of dresses around the circle to music. The child who has it when the music ends tries on a dress.

Cognitive

1. Make paper dresses out of wallpaper samples. Cut them in half and have the children match the halves.

2. Study the concepts of big and little: Let the children dress in big dresses or dresses which are too little. Have them tell whether the dress they are wearing is too large or too small for them.

3. Have the children match fabric samples of different textures and designs.

Enrichment

Have a parent or volunteer come in as a surprise visitor dressed in the following way:

a. ½ hair braided or in pony tail, ½ smoothly combed
b. Shirt inside out and backwards. Masking tape in a strip down the front.
c. A wristwatch on her ankle.
d. Eye glasses with no glass.
e. Socks on her hands.
f. Unmatched shoes on wrong feet.
g. Lipstick on ½ of mouth.
h. Freckles on ½ of face.

Have children sit down or stand in a circle around visitor and tell what is wrong.

Field Trip

Visit a department store and look at dresses in the girl's department and in the women's department. Notice the differences in the sizes.

Visitor

A mother comes to school with several of her dresses. Let her tell where she wears them. Talk about pleats, pockets, ruffles, etc.

Related Children's Records

"My Shoes Went Walking" from **COME AND SEE THE PEPPERMINT TREE** (EA)
"What Are You Wearing" from **LEARNING BASIC SKILLS VOL. 1** (EA)
"Umbrella, Raincoats, and Boots or Galoshes" from **RAINDROPS** (MH)
"One, Two, Buckle My Shoe" from **AND ONE AND TWO** (SCHOL)
"Diddle, Diddle, Dumpling" from **NURSERY RHYMES** (SCHOL)
"Where Are My Pajamas?" from **ABIYOYO** (FLKW)
"The Dress" from **COME AND SEE THE PEPPERMINT TREE** (EA)

Related Children's Books

Barrett, Judi. **ANIMALS SHOULD DEFINITELY NOT WEAR CLOTHING.** New York: Atheneum, 1970.
Keats, Ezra Jack. **JENNIE'S HAT.** New York: Harper & Row, 1966.
Kellogg, Stephen. **THE MYSTERY OF THE MISSING RED MITTEN.** New York: Dial Press, 1974.
Moncure, Jane Belk. **TRY ON A SHOE.** Elgin, Ill.: Child's World, 1973.
Watanable, Shiegeo. **HOW DO I PUT IT ON?** New York: Philomel Books, 1980.
Watson, Pauline. **THE WALKING COAT.** New York: Walker & Co., 1980.

Related Parenting Materials

Cansler, Dot. **THE HOMESTRETCH.** Winston-Salem, NC 27113-5128: Kaplan Press, 1983.

Related Materials

TEACHING PICTURES. Winston-Salem, NC 27113-5128: Kaplan Press, 1983.
STORY SEQUENCE CARDS I, II. Winston-Salem, NC 27113-5128: Kaplan Press, 1983.
SEWING CARDS I, II, III. Winston-Salem, NC 27113-5128: Kaplan Press, 1983.

Unit 5: Halloween

A developmental assessment should determine the functional levels of each child. Individual expectations are based on the assessment results.

Lesson 1: Pumpkin

Unit Group Lesson

1. **Match Concrete Objects**
   Present two pumpkins. Say, "This is a pumpkin." Ask each child in turn to put the pumpkin with the pumpkin. Gradually increase number of irrelevant objects from which (s)he must select pumpkin to match.

2. **Discriminate Objects**
   Present several objects. Have each child touch the pumpkin in response to the verbal direction, "Touch the pumpkin."

3. **Match Pictures**
   Present several pictures of common objects. Have each child match the pictures of the pumpkins.

4. **Discriminate Pictures**
   Present a group of several unrelated pictures of objects. Have each child touch the picture of the pumpkin in response to the verbal direction, "Touch the pumpkin."

5. **Figure-Ground**
   Present a "busy" picture with many visual distractions. Ask child to find the pumpkin.

6. **Visual Closure**
   Partially cover each of several pictures with paper. Ask child to find the picture of the pumpkin.

7. **Function**
   Ask, "What do we do with a pumpkin?"

8. **Association**
   Ask, "What goes with the pumpkin?" Use pictures or objects including black cat, mask, witch, ghost, etc. with several unrelated objects or pictures.

9. **Imitate Verbalization**
   Present a pumpkin and ask, "What is this? Say, 'Pumpkin'." The child will imitate "Pumpkin."

10. **Verbalize Label**
    Present a pumpkin and ask, "What is this?" The child will respond, "Pumpkin."

11. **Concept Enrichment**

Discuss how a pumpkin grows and that it is a vegetable. Talk about times and places where we usually eat pumpkin.

Music

1. Sing "Shining Pumpkin" to tune of "Baa, Baa Black Sheep":
   Pumpkin, pumpkin, shining bright,
   That's how I know it's Halloween night.
   BOO!

2. Sing "Jack-O-Lantern" to the tune of "London Bridge Is Falling Down":
   Jack-O-Lantern shining bright,
   Shining bright, shining bright,
   Jack-O-Lantern shining bright,
   Shining in the night.

3. Sing "Did You Ever See A Pumpkin?" to tune of "Did You Ever See A Lassie?":
   Did you ever see a pumpkin, a pumpkin, a pumpkin?
   Did you ever see a pumpkin, on Halloween night?
   Repeat.

Art

1. Have the children paint a pumpkin stencil with orange paint and use black paint to put on eyes, mouth, and nose.
2. Let the children draw facial features on a real pumpkin. Carve the pumpkin following their drawing.
3. Have the children paste a construction paper pumpkin on a partially hidden outline of a pumpkin in a pumpkin patch. Start with one pumpkin to be matched and increase number and difficulty according to the skills of the children.

Snack

1. Have pumpkin pie.
2. Have pumpkin bread.
3. Have pumpkin seeds. When you clean the Jack-O-Lantern, save the seeds. Rinse them and put them in a jelly roll pan. Spread out and sprinkle with salt. Bake in a 250-300⁰ oven until dry and crisp. Turn them frequently.

Fine Motor

1. Have the children paste pre-cut parts on a pumpkin face.
2. Have the children outline a pumpkin with glue. Sprinkle orange-colored grits on the picture. Shake off the excess. Display them and let the children take them home.
3. Have the children connect dots in a pumpkin shape. Color the pumpkin orange.
4. Have the children cut pumpkin for pie or bread.
5. Have the children do a sewing card of a pumpkin.

Games

1. Make a feely box out of a cardboard box. Cut a hole in the side. Put various Halloween articles in box. Child puts hand through hole and feels for the pumpkin (tactile discrimination).
2. Play a game of "Ring Around the Pumpkin." Sing to tune of "Ring Around the Rosey." Put jack-o-lantern in center of room. The children form a circle around it and sing.
3. Play a game of "Tape the Mouth on the Pumpkin." The children are blindfolded and are directed to tape the mouth on the pumpkin. Some children should not be blindfolded. Help children to the pumpkin after turning them around in circles. (Use a magnet and magnetic surface if one is available).

Storytelling

1. Do a fingerplay "Five Little Pumpkins"

  Five little pumpkins sitting on a gate, *(Hold hand up and move each finger as it talks).*
  The first one said, "Oh my, it's getting late."
  The second one said, "There are witches in the air."
  The third one said, "But we don't care."
  The fourth one said, "Let's run and run and run!"
  The fifth one said, "I'm ready for some fun."
  Whooo-oo-oo went the wind and out went the lights, *(Close hand.)*
  And the five little pumpkins rolled out of sight. *(Roll hand behind back).*
  NOTE: A bulletin board showing five pumpkins on a gate would illustrate the story.

2. Tell a story about the little pumpkin in the pumpkin patch. He grew so big that he became a jack-o-lantern on Halloween. Use pictures or felt cut-outs on flannel board to illustrate.

3. Recite "Pick-A-Pick-A-Pumpkin"

  Pick-a-pick-a-pumpkin
  From the pile
  We can make his eyes
  And a great big smile
  Pick-a-pick-a-pumpkin
  Round and clean
  Then we'll be ready for Halloween
  Halloween
  Halloween
  Then we'll be ready for Halloween.

Gross Motor

Have a pumpkin toss. Let the children toss bean bags into a large plastic pumpkin or waste can decorated like a pumpkin.

Cognitive

1. Have four large pictures depicting four holidays (Halloween, Christmas, Valentine's Day, Easter) displayed in the room. Give each child a picture of a pumpkin. Ask the child, "Where does the pumpkin belong?" "Put the pumpkin where it belongs." Help the child fasten the pumpkin on or under the correct poster.

2. Draw pumpkins on construction paper. Make pairs of pumpkins with the same facial expression. Cover with clear contact paper. Cut out and have children find the pumpkin pairs that are alike.

Enrichment

1. Make a Jack-O-Lantern. Discuss what we do to the pumpkin to make a Jack-O-Lantern? "We cut out the top; clean the middle; roast seeds for snack and cut out eyes, nose, mouth." Sit around the Jack-O-Lantern and tell stories and sing songs.

2. Together picture: "Pumpkin Patch." Help the children make a pumpkin patch with pumpkin vines, pumpkins and leaves. Make the vines by cutting large spirals from green construction paper. Hang them up and let them run along the edges of the room or on a designated table. Sponge paint

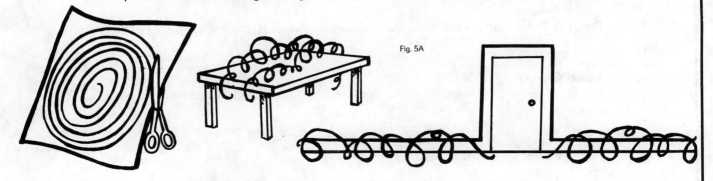

Fig. 5A

pumpkins and add to the vines. When sponge painting, the paint should be thick and placed in flat containers, a small amount at a time. Show children how to dip the sponge on the flat side - without pressing and paint on paper with an ''up-down'' motion rather than smearing motion. Let the children

Fig. 5B

experiment using newspaper for painting, before painting the pumpkins. Cut large green leaves and let the children glue them to the vine. (See fig. 5A. & fig. 5B.)

Field Trip
Take the children to a market, a farm or a pumpkin patch to buy a pumpkin.

Visitor
Pretend a pumpkin is a visitor. Give him a face, a hat, a pipe and give him a name. Include the ''visitor'' in conversation.

Lesson 2: Black Cat

Unit Group Lesson

1. **Match Concrete Objects**
    Present two black cats. Say, ''This is a black cat.'' Ask each child in turn to put the black cat with the black cat. Gradually increase number of irrelevant objects from which (s)he must select black cat to match.

2. **Discriminate Objects**
    Present several objects. Have each child touch the black cat in response to the verbal direction, ''Touch the black cat.''

3. **Match Pictures**
    Present several pictures of common objects. Have each child match the pictures of the black cats.

4. **Discriminate Pictures**
    Present a group of several unrelated pictures of objects. Have each child touch the picture of the black cat in response to the verbal direction, ''Touch the black cat.''

5. **Figure-Ground**
    Present a ''busy'' picture with many visual distractions. Ask child to find the black cat.

6. **Visual Closure**
    Partially cover each of several pictures with paper. Ask child to find the picture of the black cat.

7. **Function**
    Ask, ''What do we do with a black cat?''

8. **Association**
    Ask, "What goes with the black cat?" Use pictures or objects including pumpkin, witch, ghost, mask, etc. with several unrelated objects or pictures.

9. **Imitate Verbalization**
    Present a black cat and ask, "What is this? Say, 'Black cat'." The child will imitate "Black cat."

10. **Verbalize Label**
    Present a black cat and ask, "What is this?" The child will respond, "Black cat."

11. **Concept Enrichment**
    Discuss other colors that cats come in. Ask, "Why are black cats associated with Halloween?"

Music
1. Sing "Halloween's Here" to tune of "Twinkle, Twinkle, Little Star":
    Halloween has come at last,
    Witches, ghosts and big black cats,
    Funny faces around a-bout,
    People laugh and people shout.
    Pumpkins shine and cats meow,
    Meow, Meow, Meow, Meow,
    Halloween has come at last
    Witches, ghosts, and big black cats.
    BOO! BOO!
2. Sing "Did You Ever See A Black Cat?" to the tune of "Did You Ever See A Lassie?"
    Did you ever see a black, a black cat, a black cat?
    Did you ever see a black cat on Halloween night?   *(Short meow.)*
    Repeat.
3. Sing "Black Cat" to tune of "Mary Had A Little Lamb":
    Verse 1: We saw a black cat,
              Black cat, black cat.
              We saw a black cat
              On the night of Halloween.
    Verse 2: He was stretching out his paws.   *(Make a scratching motion.)*
              Out his paws, out his paws.
              He was stretching out his paws.
              On the night of Halloween.

Art
1. Have the children paste head, tail, and legs on the body of a cat. Have a finished cat available.
2. Make cat's faces. Have children make cat's whiskers. Depending on the level of the child, do the following: (See fig. 5C.)
    a. Have child paste pre-cut whiskers in designated place on cat's face.

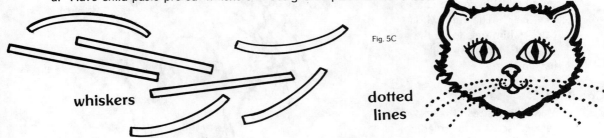

whiskers   Fig. 5C   dotted lines

    b. Have child paste pre-cut whiskers on cat's face.
    c. Have child tear out whiskers from black construction paper and paste on cat's face.
    d. Have child cut out whiskers from black construction paper and paste on cat's face.

3.   Help children make cat masks. Give each child a paper bag. Help children draw a big grin for the cat's mouth. Have children paste on paper ears and whiskers. Tie a bright bow around the child's neck to hold the sack in place.

Snack
1.   Eat Halloween candies which are in the shape of black cats.
2.   Eat Black Cat Cake (chocolate cake decorated with black cat frosting).
3.   Have milk because cats like milk.

Fine Motor
1.   Have the children do a path tracing which takes a black cat to a pumpkin.
2.   Help the children make cats from clay or playdough. Make the bodies and have the children mold heads, legs, and tails from the balls. Pinch and pull from a single ball so that the head, legs and tail do not fall off and disappoint child.

Games
1.   Make a Feely Box and have a black cat as one of the objects.
2.   Pretend you are a black cat and act like a cat.

Storytelling
1.   Fingerplay: "Cat and Kittens":

There was a cat, smooth and black	*(Hold up thumb.)*
With her kittens four,	*(Hold up four fingers.)*
She went to sleep on her back	*(Close hand.)*
By the kitchen door.	

2.   Fingerplay: "Black Cats":

Two big black cats,	*(Point thumbs of both hands up and roll fingers into fists)*
Sat upon a wall.	
One named Peter	*(Point with right thumb)*
One named Paul.	*(Point with left thumb.)*
Run away, Peter	*(Peter thumb disappears behind back.)*
Run away, Paul.	*(Paul thumb disappears behind back.)*
Come back, Peter	*(Return thumb to original position.)*
Come back, Paul.	*(Return thumb to original position.)*

NOTE: You can make finger puppets to illustrate.

Gross Motor
1.   Have the children creep, walk, and jump like a cat. See suggested records at the end of this unit.
2.   Play "Catch the Cat." Put cat whiskers and a black tail on a child. Everyone chases the "cat." The child who catches him gets to be the next cat. Let every child have a turn.

Cognitive
1.   Make three sizes of black cats. Discuss small, medium and large with the children.
2.   Sort black cats from non-black cats.

Enrichment

    Make black cats from construction paper (Some children may be able to help cut.) Number the cats with chalk. Dotted numerals provide outlines for those children who need them.

Field Trip

1.   Visit a local animal shelter to see cats.
2.   Take a walk in the neighborhood. Look for cats, especially black ones.

Visitor

    Invite a cat lover to come with kittens or cats to show with the class.

Lesson 3: Witch

Unit Group Lesson

1.   **Match Concrete Objects**
    Present two witches. Say, "This is a witch." Ask each child in turn to put the witch with the witch. Gradually increase number of irrelevant objects from which (s)he must select witch to match.

2.   **Discriminate Objects**
    Present several objects. Have each child touch the witch in response to the verbal direction, "Touch the witch."

3.   **Match Pictures**
    Present several pictures of common objects. Have each child match the pictures of the witches.

4.   **Discriminate Pictures**
    Present a group of several unrelated pictures of objects. Have each child touch the picture of the witch in response to the verbal direction, "Touch the witch."

5.   **Figure-Ground**
    Present a "busy" picture with many visual distractions. Ask child to find the witch.

6.   **Visual Closure**
    Partially cover each of several pictures with paper. Ask child to find the picture of the witch.

7.   **Function**
    Ask, "What does a witch do?"

8.   **Association**
    Ask, "What goes with the witch?" Use pictures or objects including pumpkin, black cat, ghost, mask, etc. with several unrelated objects or pictures.

9.   **Imitate Verbalization**
    Present a witch and ask, "What is this? Say, 'Witch '." The child will imitate "Witch."

10.   **Verbalize Label**
    Present a witch and ask, "What is this?" The child will respond, "Witch."

11.   **Concept Enrichment**
    Discuss witches. Let children talk about witches and express their concerns.

Music
1. To the tune of "Did You Ever See A Lassie?" sing "Did You Ever See a Witch?"
2. Sing "Little Witch" to tune of "I Had a Rooster":
    I had a little witch by the garden gate,
    And that little witch was my playmate.
    That little witch went whoo, whoo, whoo,
    Whoo, whoo, whoo, whoo, whoo, whoo, whoo.

Art
1. Have the children paste a black hat on a witch which the teacher has drawn on construction paper. Tell the children to "Put the hat ON the witch's head."
2. Have the children "paint" hair on the witch picture with glue. Place thick, black yarn on the glued section for the witch's hair.

Snack
Drink Witch's Brew (see Gross Motor #1) and eat "black" apples (apple wedges dipped in chocolate).

Fine Motor
1. Make a path trace activity of a witch on a broom going for a ride in the sky.
2. Have the children outline a witch's broom with glue. Shake brown-colored grits on the outline. Shake off the excess. Display the picture.

Games
1. Play a game of "Ring Around the Witch" sung to the tune of "Ring Around A Rosey." Have the children form a circle. They sing and walk around the "witch" in the center. The child in the center should be wearing a witch's hat and cape and riding a broom. Every child should have a turn.
2. Make a domino game. Prepare domino cards using Halloween stickers. Let the children match cards or play as a regular domino game. (See fig. 5E.)

Fig. 5E

Storytelling
1. Witch, Witch
    Witch, witch where do you fly?   *(Fly.)*
    Over the moon and under the sky.
    Witch, witch, who do you eat?   *(Eat.)*
    Little black apples from Hurricane Street.
    Witch, witch, what do you drink?   *(Drink.)*
    Vinegar, blacking, and good red ink.
    Witch, witch, where do you sleep?   *(Sleep.)*
    Up in the clouds where the pillows are cheap.
2. Tell a story about the friendly witch who could not find her broom on Halloween night. Use props of witch's hat, witch's cape, and broom when telling story. Children may enjoy suggesting story ending.

Gross Motor
1. Stir witches brew (lemonade, cider, etc.) in a big pot or caldron.
2. Ride broomsticks around the yard.

Cognitive
1. Have the children count witches hats. (See fig. 5F.)
2. Have the children sequence different sized witches hats. (See fig. 5G.)
3. Have the children match different sized witches to different sized hats. (See fig. 5H.)
4. Make witches hats with numerals on them. Have matching numerals on cards. Let the children match the numerals to the correct witches hats. (See fig. 5I.)
5. Cut witches from construction paper and have the children glue them on the broom drawn on paper.

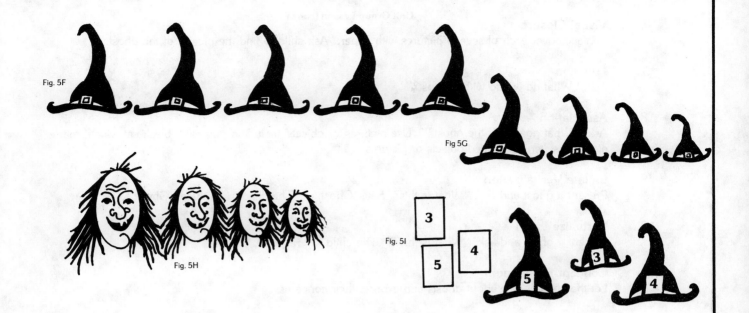

Fig. 5F

Fig 5G

Fig. 5H

Fig. 5I

Enrichment

Make witch's brooms with 1 to 10 straws. Make witches with the numerals 1-10 on them. Let the children match the witch to the broom with the correct number of straws. (See fig. 5J.)

Fig. 5J

Visitor

Invite a "witch" to the class.

Lesson 4: Ghost

Unit Group Lesson

1. **Match Concrete Objects**
    Present two ghosts. Say, "This is a ghost." Ask each child in turn to put the ghost with the ghost. Gradually increase number of irrelevant objects from which (s)he must select ghost to match.

2. **Discriminate Objects**
    Present several objects. Have each child touch the ghost in response to the verbal direction, "Touch the ghost."

3. **Match Pictures**
    Present several pictures of common objects. Have each child match the pictures of the ghosts.

4. **Discriminate Pictures**
    Present a group of several unrelated pictures of objects. Have each child touch the picture of the ghost in response to the verbal direction, "Touch the ghost."

5. **Figure-Ground**
    Present a "busy" picture with many visual distractions. Ask child to find the ghost.

6. **Visual Closure**
    Partially cover each of several pictures with paper. Ask child to find the picture of the ghost.

7. **Function**
    Ask, "What do we do with a ghost?"

8. **Association**
    Ask, "What goes with the ghost?" Use pictures or objects including pumpkin, black cat, witch, mask, etc. with several unrelated objects or pictures.

9. **Imitate Verbalization**
    Present a ghost and ask, "What is this? Say, 'Ghost '." The child will imitate "Ghost."

10. **Verbalize Label**
    Present a ghost and ask, "What is this?" The child will respond, "Ghost."

11. **Concept Enrichment**
    Let the children talk about ghosts and express their concerns.

Music
1. Sing to the tune of "Baa, Baa Black Sheep":
    Who is the ghost wrapped up in a sheet,
    Who comes to the door, saying,
    Trick or treat!
    Have a child covered in a sheet come to the door saying, "Trick or treat!" You and the other children sing to the child.
2. Sing to the tune of "Did You Ever See A Lassie?":
    Did you ever see a ghost....
    At the end of the song add BOO!

Art
1. Make a ghost stencil. Have the children make a ghost with white paint on purple or blue paper.
2. Help the children make a ghost. Stuff one facial tissue in the center of a white handkerchief (or cloth square). Tie the handkerchief with a string to form a head. Supply black construction paper eyes. The child pastes eyes on the "ghost" or draws them with a magic marker. (See fig. 5K.)
3. Have the children spatterpaint (white paint) a ghost on black construction paper.

Fig. 5K

Snack
Have sugar cookies in the shape of ghosts made in Fine Motor #4 today.

Fine Motor
1. Let the children draw eyes on a ghost drawn on blackboard.
2. Let the children trace a ghost outline on black construction paper. Use white chalk.
3. Draw dots in the shape of a ghost. Have the children connect the dots.
4. Help the children make ghost cookies. Cut the ghost shapes from sugar cookies and bake. Let the children ice them with white frosting and supply black gumdrops or jellybeans for eyes.

Games
1. Make a feely box with a ghost and other things inside. Let the children find the ghost.
2. Have the children dress in a sheet and say "Boo!" You can model activity.
3. Play "Ring Around the Ghost."

Storytelling

1. Fingerplay: "The Friendly Ghost":

I'm a friendly ghost - almost!	*(Point to yourself.)*
And I can chase you, too.	*(Point to child.)*
I'll just cover me with a sheet,	*(Pretend to cover youself, ending with hands over face.)*
And then call "Boo!" to you.	*(Uncover face quickly and then call out BOO!)*

    You may want to use a real sheet to introduce fingerplay.

2. Poem: "A Ghost":

A ghost lives in our house,	*(Use pictures or a ghost finger puppet to illustrate.)*
in our house, in our house,	
A ghost lives in our house at Halloween time.	
He bumps	*(Pantomine movements to this part.)*
and he jumps	
and he thumps.	
He knocks	*(Pantomine movements to this part.)*
and he rocks	
and he rattles at the locks.	
A ghost lives in our house, in our house,	
in our house	
A ghost lives in our house at Halloween time	

3. Tell a story of a friendly ghost who came to dinner on Halloween night. Use a finger puppet ghost. Make it by tying a handkerchief on an index finger.

Gross Motor

Have the children pretend to be ghosts. Walk on tiptoes, quietly. Stand with hands together and arms at side and be invisible. Move and dance to spooky music.

Cognitive

1. Make "Feeling" faces. Use two circles for each and attach them to drinking straws or ice cream sticks putting the circles back to back. Use three different ones to play "How Do I Feel". Make up a list of situations typical of children's experiences such as "Bobby's ice cream cone fell in the dirt." and "Susie got a birthday present." These can be used with individual children to help them express feelings also. (See fig. 5L.)

2. Make cue sheets with a ghost at the top and ghosts and distractors beneath. Let the children mark the ghosts like the one at the top.

  Fig. 5L

Enrichment

Make GHOST NUMBER PUZZLES. Draw ghosts on white poster board. Write numerals on the left half of the ghosts and draw dots on the right half to correspond to the numeral. Cover with clear contact paper. Cut ghosts out and then cut each ghost in half differently so that only the correct halves can match. Have the children do the puzzles.

Lesson 5: Mask

Unit Group Lesson

1. **Match Concrete Objects**
   Present two masks. Say, "This is a mask." Ask each child in turn to put the mask with the mask. Gradually increase number of irrelevant objects from which (s)he must select mask to match.

2. **Discriminate Objects**
   Present several objects. Have each child touch the mask in response to the verbal direction, "Touch the mask."

3. **Match Pictures**
   Present several pictures of common objects. Have each child match the pictures of the masks.

4. **Discriminate Pictures**
   Present a group of several unrelated pictures of objects. Have each child touch the picture of the mask in response to the verbal direction, "Touch the mask."

5. **Figure-Ground**
   Present a "busy" picture with many visual distractions. Ask child to find the mask.

6. **Visual Closure**
   Partially cover each of several pictures with paper. Ask child to find the picture of the mask.

7. **Function**
   Ask, "What do we do with a mask?"

8. **Association**
   Ask, "What goes with the mask?" Use pictures or objects including pumpkin, black cat, witch, ghost, etc. with several unrelated objects or pictures.

9. **Imitate Verbalization**
   Present a mask and ask, "What is this? Say, 'Mask'." The child will imitate "Mask."

10. **Verbalize Label**
    Present a mask and ask, "What is this?" The child will respond, "Mask."

11. **Concept Enrichment**
    Discuss masks. Let the children try on masks and get accustomed to them.

Music
1. Sing "Oh, Do You Have A Mask?" to tune of "Oh, Do You Know The Muffin Man?":
   Oh, do you have a mask, a mask, a mask?
   Oh, do you have a mask for Halloween night?

   Yes, I have a mask, a mask, a mask.
   Yes, I have a mask for Halloween night! Boo!
   After singing the song the children hold up masks to their faces and yell "Boo!"

2. Sing "Trick or Treating" to tune of "Are You Sleeping?":

> Trick or treating, trick or treating,
> Boo! Boo! Boo!
> Boo! Boo! Boo!
> Trick or treating, trick or treating,
> I scare you!
> I scare you!

Art

1. Make masks of poster board or cardboard. Cut them out and let the children add colors and ribbons to tie on. (See fig. 5M.)
2. Let the children make trick or treat bags by pasting Halloween decals (pumpkin, black cat, witch, ghost) or bags. Use for trick or treating. (See fig. 5N.)
3. Let the children make paper bag masks. Provide paper bags that will fit over the childrens' heads, cut out eyes, provide hair, ears, etc., and let the children create their own heads.

Fig 5M

Fig. 5N

Snack

Have everyone wear masks to snack and guess each person.

Fine Motor

1. Let each child make a noise maker from two individual foil pie tins. Punch holes around both edges of tins. Let the children sew tins together with open sides facing each other. Put dry beans or kernels of rice or corn inside. Help as much as necessary and tie a loop of yarn at the top for a handle. Cut orange circles to fit the bottoms of the pie tins, and let the children paste pumpkin faces on them. Use for trick or treating.
2. Let the children "sew" around a mask sewing card.
3. Cut Halloween masks out of black paper. Let the children decorate the masks with bits of paper, yarn or paper hair, etc. (See fig. 5O.)

Fig. 5O

Games

1. Make a tape recording of Halloween noise makers. Have the children match the sound to an object, which is one of many objects on a table. Ask, "What do you hear?" The child picks up a noise maker and says, "whistle," "a whistle," or "I hear a whistle."
2. Have the children pretend they are trick or treating. One child goes out of the room and closes the door. The child knocks on the door, says, "Trick or treat" or "Boo!" The teacher puts candy in the child's sack and looks under mask, "Oh, its (child)!" Let each child have a turn.

Storytelling

Tell a story about a child who was afraid of masks. He refused to wear one for Halloween. Let the children make up the ending.

Gross Motor

Make a simple obstacle course for the children. Let the children walk it wearing masks.

Cognitive
1. Make many masks in three different colors. Have the children match them by color.
2. Have children point to both eyes in a mask.
3. Make masks out of different textured materials. Have the children match them by texture.

Enrichment

Have a pretend box with different masks in it. Tell about what "pretend" means. Pretend you are:

a mouse

a giraffe

an alligator

a monkey

a jack-o-lantern

an invisible man

a ghost

a witch

a pirate

a black cat, etc.

Field Trip

Take children trick or treating. Notify people you will be coming so they will have treats for the children. The children dress in costume or wear their masks, carry their sacks, and make noise with their noise makers. Children will say "Boo!" or "Trick or treat."

Visitor

Have a teacher or parent dress up in costume and mask and come to classroom. Talk about pretend.

Other Children's Records

"Pumpkin Man" from **ACTION SONGS & ROUNDS** (EA)

"What Can We Be For Halloween?" from **HOLIDAY SONGS** (KIM)

"Have A Good Time on Halloween Night" from **HOLIDAY SONGS** (ES)

"The Black Pussy Cats" from **ACTION SONGS FOR SPECIAL DAYS** (KIM)

"Jack-O-Lantern" from **ACTION SONGS FOR SPECIAL DAYS** (KIM)

"Dress Up on Halloween" from **ACTION SONGS FOR SPECIAL DAYS** (KIM)

"The Round Fat Pumpkin" from **ACTION SONGS FOR SPECIAL DAYS** (KIM)

"The Merry Brownies" from **ACTION SONGS FOR SPECIAL DAYS** (KIM)

" Five Little Pumpkins" from **SONGS IN MOTION-HOLIDAY** (EA)

Related Children's Books

Bridwell, Norman. **CLIFFORD'S HALLOWEEN.** Englewood Cliffs, N.J.: Four Winds Press, 1966.

Freeman, Don. **TILLY WITCH.** New York: Viking Press, 1969.

Keats, Jack Ezra. **THE TRIP.** New York: Greenwillow Books, 1978.

Kraus, Robert. **HOW SPIDER SAVED HALLOWEEN.** New York: E.P. Dutton, 1973.

Mooser, Stephen. **THE GHOST WITH THE HALLOWEEN HICCUPS.** New York: Avon Books, 1878.

Vigna, Judith. **EVERYONE GOES AS A PUMPKIN.** Chicago: Albert Whitman & Co., 1977.

Related Parenting Materials

Cansler, Dot. **THE HOMESTRETCH.** Winston-Salem, NC 27113-5128: Kaplan Press, 1983.

Related Materials

TEACHING PICTURES. Winston-Salem, NC 27113-5128: Kaplan Press, 1983.

STORY SEQUENCE CARDS I, II. Winston-Salem, NC 27113-5128: Kaplan Press, 1983.

SEWING CARDS I, II, III. Winston-Salem, NC 27113-5128: Kaplan Press, 1983.

Unit 6: Pets

A developmental assessment should determine the functional levels of each child. Individual expectations are based on the assessment results.

Lesson 1: Cat

Unit Group Lesson

1. **Match Concrete Objects** (Use toys.)
   Present two cats. Say, "This is a cat." Ask each child in turn to put the cat with the cat. Gradually increase number of irrelevant objects from which (s)he must select cat to match.

2. **Discriminate Objects**
   Present several objects. Have each child touch the cat in response to the verbal direction, "Touch the cat."

3. **Match Pictures**
   Present several pictures of common objects. Have each child match the pictures of the cats.

4. **Discriminate Pictures**
   Present a group of several unrelated pictures of objects. Have each child touch the picture of the cat in response to the verbal direction, "Touch the cat."

5. **Figure-Ground**
   Present a "busy" picture with many visual distractions. Ask each child to find the cat.

6. **Visual Closure**
   Partially cover each of several pictures with paper. Ask each child to find the picture of the cat.

7. **Function**
   Ask, "What does a cat do?"

8. **Association**
   Ask, "What goes with the cat?" Use pictures or objects including dog, bird, fish, turtle, etc. with several unrelated objects or pictures.

9. **Imitate Verbalization**
   Present a cat and ask, "What is this? Say, 'Cat'." The child will imitate "Cat."

10. **Verbalize Label**
    Present a cat and ask, "What is this?" The child will respond, "Cat."

11. **Concept Enrichment**
     Discuss cat homes, sounds, food, fur, toys, etc. Encourage children to describe their cats.

Music

1. Sing "I Love My Kitty" to the tune of "Down In The Valley":
    I love my kitty (cat), my kitty loves me.
    I love my kitty, my kitty loves me.
    I love my kitty, meow, meow, meow, meow.
    I love my kitty, meow, meow, meow, meow.

2. Sing "Old MacDonald":
    Old MacDonald had a farm,
    E-I-E-I-O
    And on this farm he had a cat,
    E-I-E-I-O
    With a meow-meow here, meow-meow there,
    Here meow, there meow
    Everywhere a meow.
    Old MacDonald had a farm,
    E-I-E-I-O
    Have the children hold pictures of various pets. A child stands when his picture is named. Conclude the song with a last verse of "Old MacDonald had some pets."

3. Sing "Where Can the Kitty Be?" to the tune of "Oh, Dear What Can the Matter Be?"
    Oh, dear, where can the kitty be?   *(Show a picture of a cat*
    Oh, dear, where can the kitty be?   *asleep in a basket.)*
    Oh, dear, where can the kitty be?
    She's in her basket (bed) asleep.

4. Sing, "I Have a Little Kitten as sweet as sweet can be
    He curls up on my bed and purrs a song to me."

Art

1. Have the children make a cat collage. Give children an envelope of "pet" pictures. The children choose cat pictures and paste on paper.

2. Have the children paste fake fur scraps on an outline of a cat. Use a cat for each child or a large one for the whole class.

3. Help the children make a cat out of a paper bag and stuff with newspaper. Use pipe cleaners or toothpicks for whiskers and ears cut from construction paper.

4. Give each child a large and a medium-sized circle of black, brown or white. Have the children paste the circles on paper, add two small triangle ears, add yarn whiskers, and add a tail of yarn. (See fig. 6A.)

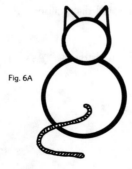

Fig. 6A

Snack

1. Have animal crackers and milk.
2. Eat Cat Face sandwiches. Have the children pinch the corners of bread for ears. Add peanut butter, raisin eyes, and pretzel whiskers. Have ingredients on the table with one cat face prepared on a plate. The children can prepare at one table and sit at another table to eat. (See fig. 6B.)

Fig. 6B

3. Drink warm milk at snack time and try to "lap" it up like a cat.

Fine Motor

1. Have the children draw whickers on a picture of a cat. (See fig. 6C.)
2. Let the children do path tracings of "Take the cat to his food." and "Take the cat to her kittens."
3. Make cue sheets by putting a picture of a cat at the top and a cat and other pets below. The children have to mark all cats on the sheet. The first one can have the same kind of cat pictured. The next one can have different breeds of cats pictured. (Animal stamps may be used to make this.)
4. Use the picture from Activity 1 of a cat's face. The children cover the cat face with fur (strips of fake fur or yarn). (See fig. 6C.)

Fig. 6C

Games

1. Present cat sounds. The teacher models. "The cat says, 'Meow'." Children imitate, "Meow." The teacher asks "What does the cat say?" The children respond, "Meow." Display two animals (one a cat). "Who says 'Meow'?" The child will select cat.
2. Use a furry bathroom mat to let children take turns being the kitty. Each one gets on all fours with the rug across his back. The other children take turns "petting" the kitty gently. (Discuss how to pet gently, and how to stroke the fur.) The kitty should meow and purr when the hand touches gently and snarl when it is rough. (See fig. 6D.)
3. Put toy cats in the housekeeping corner.

Fig. 6D

Storytelling

1. Find a picture which shows children playing with, or taking care of, the cat. Have the class help describe what the children are doing. Ask the children to "Find the cats (kittens)."
2. After reading a book about a cat to the children, show them all the pictures again from the beginning. Ask the children to "Find the cat food," "Find the cat's bed," etc.
3. On a flannel board place a cat with a part missing. Ask, "What is missing?" The children name the part missing and the place the correct part on the board from a box of spare parts.
4. Visit a pet shop. Take pictures of the trip. Make a sequence story. "What happened first?" (Polariod pictures would provide immediate reinforcement of trip).
5. Sing (or say) "The 3 Little Kittens" (who lost their mittens). Use as a counting activity or flannel board story.

Gross Motor

1. Have the children curl up like a cat. "Purr." Then stand up and stretch like a cat. Everyone imitates a cat getting up and down.
2. Play a rhythm game. Have the children stand in a circle and play appropriate music so the children can "jump like a cat, run like a cat, stretch like a cat, curl up like a cat, etc."

Cognitive

1. Present a cat bed or cat basket (as cat's home). Have the child put a picture of a cat in a picture of a cat's bed. "Put the cat in his basket (bed)."
2. Present three pictures of pet homes (basket, bed, doghouse, birdcage, goldfish bowl, or turtle dish). Give the child a picture of a cat. "Where does the cat live?" The child will put the cat in his basket (bed) and say, "basket (bed)."
3. Have the children use a pocket chart for matching animal pictures and asociating an animal with his home. Make a pocket chart from poster board, tag board, etc., staple two rows of pockets one beneath the other. On the top row put an animal card on each pocket. On the bottom row put associated homes of the animals. The children match animals by putting cat with cat, dog with dog, etc. Then they associate homes by putting cat with cat basket, dog with dog house. Some children may not be ready to match anything but cat. Leave the other pictures off and add them as the animals are added each day. Have sets of many cat cards, etc.

4. Present a cat sound on tape. Imitate the sound. Request that a child imitate the sound. Ask the child, "What does the cat sound like?" The child verbalizes the cat sound.

5. Have the children discriminate fur from non-fur textures by sorting the two types into shoe boxes. Put a cue on each shoe box.

Enrichment

Together Activity: Draw an outline of a giant cat with heavy magic marker. Have a parent bring bits of cotton print cloth scraps. Tape the cat to a wall at child level. Have the children glue on the bits of cloth in sections to make a Calico Cat. (See fig. 6E.)

Fig. 6E

Field Trip

Visit pet store or home where cats are pets.

Lesson 2: Dog

Unit Group Lesson

1. **Match Concrete Objects** (Use toys.)
Present two dogs. Say, "This is a dog." Ask each child in turn to put the dog with the dog. Gradually increase number of irrelevant objects from which (s)he must select dog to match.

2. **Discriminate Objects**
Present several objects. Have each child touch the dog in response to the verbal direction, "Touch the dog."

3. **Match Pictures**
Present several pictures of common objects. Have each child match the pictures of the dogs.

4. **Discriminate Pictures**
Present a group of several unrelated pictures of objects. Have each child touch the picture of the dog in response to the verbal direction, "Touch the dog."

5. **Figure-Ground**
Present a "busy" picture with many visual distractions. Ask each child to find the dog.

6. **Visual Closure**
Partially cover each of several pictures with paper. Ask each child to find the picture of the dog.

7. **Function**
Ask, "What does a dog do?"

8. **Association**

Ask, "What goes with the dog?" Use pictures or objects including cat, bird, fish, turtle, etc. with several unrelated objects or pictures.

9. **Imitate Verbalization**

Present a dog and ask, "What is this? Say, 'Dog'." The child will imitate "Dog."

10. **Verbalize Label**

Present a dog and ask, "What is this?" The child will respond, "Dog."

11. **Concept Enrichment**

Discuss dog homes, sounds, foods, toys. Discuss different types of dogs.

Music

1. Sing "Bingo":
   There was a boy who had a dog,
   And Bingo was his name,
   Oh! B-I-N-G-O, B-I-N-G-O,
   B-I-N-G-O,
   And Bingo was his name-O.
2. Sing "How Much Is that Doggy in the Window?"
   How much is that doggy in the window,
   The one with the waggly tail?
   How much is that doggy in the window,
   I wonder if he is for sale?
3. Sing "This Old Man."
4. Sing "I Love My Dog" to the tune of "Down In The Valley":
   I love my doggy, my doggy loves me.
   I love my doggy, my doggy loves me.
   I love my doggy, bow wow, bow wow, bow wow, bow wow.
5. Sing "Old MacDonald" with a dog verse. Conclude with "Old MacDonald had some pets."

Art

1. Make a candle resist of a dog. Have the children trace around an outline of a dog with a candle. Apply a light brown water color wash. The area where the candle was put should remain free of paint.
2. Let the children make dog masks from paper plates. Use fake fur ears and pipe cleaners for whiskers.
3. Cut out an animal picture. Glue it onto plain paper. Let the children draw or paint a background.

Snack

Paste a picture of a dog on the bottom of a glass. When the drink is "all gone," the child will see the dog.

Fine Motor

1. Help the children make a dog out of clay or play dough. Show the children how to pinch and pull from the dog body so that the head and tail do not fall off.
2. Prepare a path tracing of "Take the dog to his bone." and "Take the dog to his doghouse."
3. Make a cue sheet similar to the one for cat and substitute dog. (See Lesson #1 Fine Motor #3.)
4. Let the children tear bits of brown (two shades of brown) and black paper for the Enrichment activity.
5. Let the children glue pictures (or gummed labels) of dogs on tongue depressors to use for book marks.

Games

1. Show a picture of an animal. Have the children make the appropriate animal sound. The children then listen to a taped animal sound. From three pictures of animals, the children find the picture of the animal making the sound.
2. Set up a "pet shop." The children can come to the "store" and buy a pet (stuffed animals or pictures).

3. Have a "Dog Catcher" find dogs hidden in classroom.
4. Put toy dogs in the housekeeping area.

Storytelling

Show and Tell: Let the children bring their pets to school. They describe it, tell what it eats, and how it sounds. You read a book about a pet like one the children brought.

Gross Motor

Have the children rest "like dogs" (all curled up) then jump up and race around barking.

Cognitive

1. Have each child count the number of feet a dog has.
2. Have the children put the spots on the dog. Have a series of dogs with different numerals. The children put the correct number of spots on each dog.
3. Have the children match pictures of dogs by type, such as Scottie, Poodle, etc.
4. Continue the pocket chart from Lesson #1 Cognitive #3. Emphasize dog and doghouse today.

Enrichment

Together Activity: Draw an outline of a giant dog and a dog bowl with heavy black magic marker. Tape to the wall as though it were sitting on the floor. Let the children cover the dog with bits of brown and black construction paper (torn) glued on one piece at a time. (Use paper torn in Fine Motor #4) (See fig. 6F.)

   a. Tear bits of paper of brown and black.
   b. Sort paper bits into containers according to color.
   c. Glue paper onto dog shape.
   d. After the dog is completed, add white spots.
   e. Name the dog.
   f. Write a story about him.
   g. Fill the dog bowl with "dog food." (bits of brown paper, brown colored cotton balls, etc.)
   h. Print dog's name on bowl.

Fig. 6F

FIDO

Field Trip

1. Visit the veterinary hospital. Talk about how to care for dogs.
2. Visit an animal shelter.

Visitor

Invite a person whose dog knows tricks or is a show dog.

Lesson 3: Bird

Unit Group Lesson

1. **Match Concrete Objects** (Use toys.)
   Present two birds. Say, "This is a bird." Ask each child in turn to put the bird with the bird.
   Gradually increase number of irrelevant objects from which (s)he must select bird to match.

2. **Discriminate Objects**
   Present several objects. Have each child touch the bird in response to the verbal direction, "Touch the bird."

3. **Match Pictures**
   Present several pictures of common objects. Have each child match the pictures of the birds.

4. **Discriminate Pictures**
   Present a group of several unrelated pictures of objects. Have each child touch the picture of the bird in response to the verbal direction, "Touch the bird."

5. **Figure-Ground**
   Present a "busy" picture with many visual distractions. Ask each child to find the bird.

6. **Visual Closure**
   Partially cover each of several pictures with paper. Ask each child to find the picture of the bird.

7. **Function**
   Ask, "What does a bird do?"

8. **Association**
   Ask, "What goes with the bird?" Use pictures or objects including dog, cat, fish, turtle, etc. with several unrelated objects or pictures.

9. **Imitate Verbalization**
   Present a bird and ask, "What is this? Say, 'Bird'." The child will imitate "Bird."

10. **Verbalize Label**
    Present a bird and ask, "What is this?" The child will respond, "Bird."

11. **Concept Enrichment**
    Discuss bird homes, sounds, food, toys and types of birds used for pets.

Music

1. Sing "Mary Had A Little Bird" to the tune of "Mary Had A Little Lamb":
   > Mary had a little bird,
   > Its feathers were fun to show.
   > And everywhere that Mary went
   > Her bird was sure to go.

2. Sing "Feed the Bird" to the tune of "Row, Row, Row Your Boat":
   > Feed, feed, feed the bird   *(Pantomine feeding a bird.)*
   > Feed the bird some seed.
   > Feed, feed, feed the bird,
   > Feed the bird some seed.

Art

1. The teacher supplies a cut-out of a bird with its wings spread. The children glue real or paper feathers on the bird. Hang the bird from the ceiling for display.
2. Give each child a bird shape. Let him add feather marks and eyes. Hang on the "telephone wire." (Black yarn strung on the bulletin board). Birds should be different colors. (See fig. 6G.)

Fig. 6G

Snack

1. Eat peanut butter balls since birds like peanut butter.
2. Serve toasted seeds such as sunflower, sesame, pumpkin.

Fine Motor

1. Make a path tracing of "Take a bird to his birdcage." and "Take a bird to the birdseed."
2. Have the children connect dots that make an outline of a bird. The children can paste a bird into the outline.
3. Let the children outline a picture of a bird with bird seeds.
4. Have the children outline a bird cage over a bird outline. (They may color the bird first.) (See fig. 6H.)

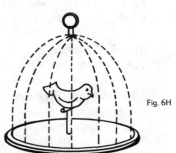

Fig. 6H

Games

Use the birds from Art #2. Staple a string to the bird's back. Let the children fly the birds to different places in the room. (See fig. 6I.)

Fig. 6I

Storytelling

Fingerplay: "Two Little Birds"
Two little birds sitting on a hill,
One named Jack and the other named Jill.
Fly away Jack; fly away Jill
Come back Jack; come back Jill.

(Close fists, extend thumbs.)
(Talk to each thumb.)
(Toss thumbs over shoulder separately.)
(Bring back fists separately with thumbs extended.)

Gross Motor

1. Make up action rhymes for children to do:
    "Little birds, little birds, flop to the tree. . . . .back to me!
    Little birds, little birds, hop to the door. . . . .sit on the floor!"
2. Have a Feather Race. Have the children blow feathers on the floor from start to stop line. Let children "race" one at a time.

Cognitive

1. Have the children match birds by types.
2. Have the children match birds by color: yellow, green, etc.
3. Continue the pocket chart from Lesson #1 Cognitive #3. Emphasize bird and birdhouse today.

Enrichment

1. Together Activity: Make a large bird. Hang it on the wall. Have children glue on real or paper feathers. Each child glues on a specific number, one, two, etc.
2. Cut bird shapes and wings from different colors. Have the children add eyes and a bill to the bird and glue string to the center of the wing. Have them fold the wings and staple on the bird. They can run to make the birds fly. (See fig. 6J.)

Fig. 6J

Field Trip
Take a bird walk. Watch for different kinds of birds and listen for bird sounds.

Visitor
1.   Invite a "bird watcher" to come with a bird book and binoculars.
2.   Invite a person with a pet bird.

Lesson 4: Goldfish

Unit Group Lesson

1.   **Match Concrete Objects** (Use toys.)
     Present two goldfishes. Say, "This is a goldfish." Ask each child in turn to put the goldfish with the goldfish. Gradually increase number of irrelevant objects from which (s)he must select goldfish to match.

2.   **Discriminate Objects**
     Present several objects. Have each child touch the goldfish in response to the verbal direction, "Touch the goldfish."

3.   **Match Pictures**
     Present several pictures of common objects. Have each child match the pictures of the goldfishes.

4.   **Discriminate Pictures**
     Present a group of several unrelated pictures of objects. Have each child touch the picture of the goldfish in response to the verbal direction, "Touch the goldfish."

5.   **Figure-Ground**
     Present a "busy" picture with many visual distractions. Ask each child to find the goldfish.

6.   **Visual Closure**
     Partially cover each of several pictures with paper. Ask each child to find the picture of the goldfish.

7.   **Function**
     Ask, "What does a goldfish do?"

8.   **Association**
     Ask, "What goes with the goldfish?" Use pictures or objects including dog, cat, bird, turtle, etc. with several unrelated objects or pictures.

9.   **Imitate Verbalization**
     Present a goldfish and ask, "What is this? Say, 'Goldfish'." The child will imitate "Goldfish."

10. **Verbalize Label**
     Present a goldfish and ask, "What is this?" The child will respond, "Goldfish."

11.   **Concept Enrichment**
      Discuss other types of pet fish. Talk about how fish breathe.

Music

1.   Sing "Have You Seen My Goldfish?" to tune of "Oh, Do You Know The Muffin Man?":
     Oh, have you seen my goldfish, my goldfish, my goldfish?   *(Hold up picture of a goldfish*
     Oh, have you seen my goldfish in his his goldfish bowl?   *in a bowl?)*

2.   Sing: "All the fish are swimming in the water,
              All the fish are swimming in the water,
              All the fish are swimming in the water,
              Bubble, bubble, bubble, bubble, SPLASH!"

Art

1.   Have the children make a stuffed fish. Supply two fish shapes cut from construction paper. Have the children paste on the eyes and decorate their fish. Staple around the sides with the children's help. Let the children stuff it with tissue. Then staple it closed.

2.   Let the children paint a fishbowl on paper (a circle). Give each child three cuts-outs of goldfish to paste "in" his/her fishbowl.

3.   Let the children draw fish pictures with crayons. "Wash" over with watery blue paint for an "underwater" effect.

4.   Let the children make an aquarium from two paper plates, drawn fish, and blue cellophane. Cut out the center of one paper plate and a plate-sized blue cellophane circle for each child. Let each child decorate the center of the other paper plate and glue on goldfish. Assemble the child's drawing, a cellophane circle and an open paper plate. Staple around the edges.

Snack

Eat "goldfish" crackers.

Fig. 6K

Fine Motor

1.   Make a path tracing of "A goldfish swimming to the aquarium." and "A goldfish swimming under a shell."

2.   Have children glue or paste "scales" on a fish shape. Scales may be made with all kinds of materials: bits of styrofoam, cut up cartons, cut up egg cartons, large sequins, round styrofoam packing material, etc.

3.   Have children do pattern tracing. Make a goldfish for each child. Let him draw over the marks with circles, curved lines, and straight lines (tail). Make the length and thickness of the lines harder or easier depending upon the needs of the individual child. (See fig. 6K.)

4.   Together Activity: Make a giant fish. On old newspapers or wrapping paper draw a large fish in dark magic marker. Divide it into sections with a child's name on each one. Put it on a table or on the wall at child level. Have the children glue on wadded tissue paper in their area in shades of yellow and orange. Let one child make the eye from black tissue paper. (See fig. 6L.)

5.   Together Activity: Let children fill a huge red goldfish bowl with goldfish they cut out. (See fig. 6M.)

Fig. 6L

Fig. 6M

Games

1.   Play a game: "Catch the Fish" during water play. Have the children catch the fish as instructed: "Catch one fish." "Catch the blue fish." "Catch the large fish." Make different colors and sizes of fish from sponges.

2.   "Go Fishing." Make a "fishing rod" by tying a string with a large magnet on the end of a yardstick. "Fish" are made from construction paper with a paper clip in the mouth. The fish are put in a large fishbowl or empty aquarium tank. The children go fishing by lowering the magnet into bowl. Ask, "What did you catch?" A blue cloth or designated floor area for lake may be used instead of tank or bowl. (See fig. 6N.)

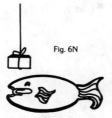

Fig. 6N

Storytelling
Fingerplay: "This Is The Way the Animals Talk"
This is the way the dog talks
Bow-wow Bow-wow   *(Children make appropriate animal sound.)*
This is the way the cat talks
Meow, meow.
This is the way the bird talks
Chirp-chirp, Chirp-chirp.
This is the way the fish talks
(no sound)   *(All mouths quiet, no sound.)*
This is the way the children talk,
Hurrah, Hurrah.

Gross Motor
1.   Have the children get on the floor and pretend to swim like fish. Then have them make motions like people swimming.
2.   If a pool is available, have children really swim.

Cognitive
1.   Make three sizes of goldfish; small, medium and large. Have children sort the goldfishes by size. They can also sequence them from small to large or large to small.
2.   Give the children fish bowl shapes and have them glue or draw different numbers of goldfish in the bowls.
3.   Continue the pocket chart from Lesson #1 Cognitive #3. Emphasize fish and fishbowl.

Enrichment
Together Activity: Stick a giant paper fish bowl on the wall. Have the children path trace water in blue crayon, paste lots of goldfish into bowl, and paste pebbles in bottom of bowl. (See fig. 6O.)

Fig. 6O

Field Trip
Visit an aquarium or fish supply store.

Visitor
Invite a person to school who has a small aquarium. Look at supplies to care for fish in an aquarium.

Lesson 5: Turtle

Unit Group Lesson

1. **Match Concrete Objects** (Use toys.)
   Present two turtles. Say, "This is a turtle." Ask each child in turn to put the turtle with the turtle. Gradually increase number of irrelevant objects from which (s)he must select turtle to match.

2. **Discriminate Objects**
   Present several objects. Have each child touch the turtle in response to the verbal direction, "Touch the turtle."

3. **Match Pictures**
   Present several pictures of common objects. Have each child match the pictures of the turtles.

4. **Discriminate Pictures**
   Present a group of several unrelated pictures of objects. Have each child touch the picture of the turtle in response to the verbal direction, "Touch the turtle."

5. **Figure-Ground**
   Present a "busy" picture with many visual distractions. Ask each child to find the turtle.

6. **Visual Closure**
   Partially cover each of several pictures with paper. Ask each child to find the picture of the turtle.

7. **Function**
   Ask, "What does a turtle do?"

8. **Association**
   Ask, "What goes with the turtle?" Use pictures or objects including dog, cat, fish, bird, etc. with several unrelated objects or pictures.

9. **Imitate Verbalization**
   Present a turtle and ask, "What is this? Say, 'Turtle'." The child will imitate "Turtle."

10. **Verbalize Label**
    Present a turtle and ask, "What is this?" The child will respond, "Turtle."

11. **Concept Enrichment**
    Discuss land turtles and sea turtles. Talk about pet safety. Snapping turtles exist in the wild and can be dangerous.

Music
1. Sing "My Turtle" to the tune of "Did You Ever See A Lassie?" :
   Have you seen my turtle, my turtle, my turtle?
   Have you seen my turtle with his hard shell.
2. Sing "Old MacDonald Had a Farm", include all the animals studied in this unit and end with "Old MacDonald Had Some Pets."

Art
1. Have children paste one picture of a pet on a page and paste the appropriate home on the same page. Staple them together and make a booklet. Add a cover which the children will decorate.

Fig. 6P

2. Let children make a collage using pet food (dry cat food, dry dog food, milkbone, bird seed, fish flakes, turtle flakes).
3. Let each child make a turtle paperweight by painting a small stone and adding a felt turtle head and feet. (See fig. 6P.)
4. Use the same shapes for the head and feet; glue on to paper dessert or a cereal bowl. Paint the bowl. Mark turtle shell design on top. (see fig. 6Q.)

Fig. 6Q

Snack

Eat chocolate and peanut turtles (made by pouring melted chocolate over pretzel sticks or Chinese fried noodles and peanuts).

Fine Motor

1. Have the children make a turtle out of clay with your help. The body of the turtle can be a ball. The shell can be a "pancake" placed over the body. Children scratch a design in the shell with a pencil. Use plastic forks for feet.
2. Sew a turtle sewing card.
3. Make holes in pairs of paper plates, insides together.
    Cut out turtle heads, legs and tails for each child.
    Help the child staple these to one of his paper plates,
    then join paper plates and sew them together with green yarn.
    Have children decorate the top of the shell with magic markers. (See fig. 6R.)

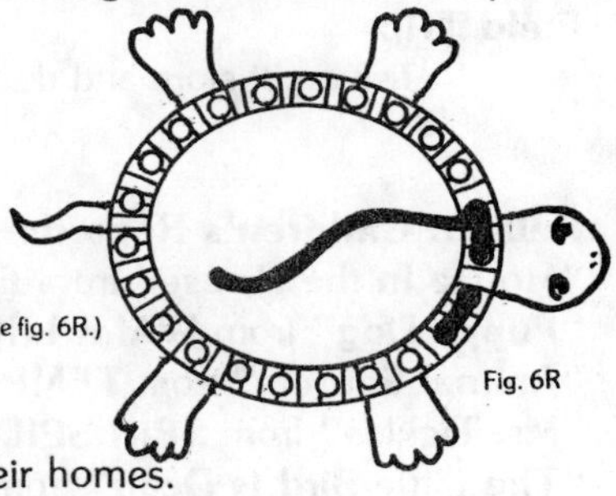

Fig. 6R

Games

1. Set up the housekeeping corner with real or pretend turtles and their homes.
2. Pretend to be turtles and catch insects.

Storytelling

1. Learn the fingerplay:
    "I had a little turtle.
    I thought he was dead   (Balled fist.)
    I tapped him on the back   (With other hand.)
    And out popped his head.   (Out points finger.)

2. Fingerplay: "There Was A Little Turtle," by Rachel Lindsay.
    There was a little turtle,   (Make a small circle with hands.)
    He lived in a box,   (Make a box with both hands.)
    He swam in a puddle,   (Wiggle hand.)
    He climbed on the rocks.   (Climb finger of one hand up over the other.)
    He snapped at a mosquito,   (Clap hands.)
    He snapped at a flea,   (Clap hands.)
    He snapped at a minnow,   (Clap hands.)
    He snapped at me.   (Point to self.)
    He caught the mosquito,   (Hold hands up, palms facing forward; quickly bend fingers shut.)

    He caught the flea,   (Same motion.)
    He caught the minnow   (Same motion.)
    But, he didn't catch me.   (Bend fingers only half way shut.)

Gross Motor

1. Have children walk like a turtle on all fours.
2. Make turtle bean bags. Toss into a waste can decorated as a turtle pond.
3. Play a rhythm game. Have the children stand in a circle and play appropriate music so the children can "jump like a cat, run like a dog, fly like a bird, swim like a fish and walk like a turtle." This can be played without music by having a child hold up a picture of one of the named animals as a cue of which to imitate.

Cognitive

1. Have a turtle hunt. Hide turtles and have the children find them. Hide some in the open, so they can be found easily. Hide a few under things with only a head or tail showing. Ask, "What did you find?" Let the children take turns hiding turtles. This is a good outdoor activity.
2. Make a map of the classroom and mark a spot with a hidden turtle. Help the children to find the turtle. Some children may also be able to find the turtle if the map is rotated 90° in relationship to the classroom.
3. Continue the pocket chart from Lesson #1 Cognitive #3. Emphasize turtle and turtle bowl today.

Enrichment

1.	Let the children match the turtle to the correct bowl. Have bowls with one to ten pebbles in them. Print a numeral on each turtle. Let each child put the turtles in the correct bowls. This can be done with toy turtles and plastic bowls or with pictures cut from tagboard and covered with plastic.

2.	Together Activity: Make a background scene for turtles on a big sheet of paper. Cut turtles out of sponge. Let the children decorate the background and then add the sponge turtles. (See fig. 6S.)

Field Trip

Visit a pet store and discuss all animals studied during the week.

Fig. 6S

Related Children's Records

"Mouse In the House" from **FIDDLE-EE-FEE** (RP)

"Puppy Dog" from **WALK LIKE THE ANIMALS** (KIM)

"Animal Sounds" from **TEMPO FOR TOTS** (MH)

"Mr. Tickles" from **SPIN SPIDER SPIN** (EA)

"The Little Bird Is Dead" from **SPIN SPIDER SPIN** (EA)

"Robin Red Breast" from **LOOK AT THE HOLIDAYS** (GA)

"It's Raining Cats and Dogs" from **MY STREET BEGINS AT MY HOUSE** (SCHOL)

"Two Little Black Birds" from **COUNTING GAME & RHYTHMS** (SCHOL)

"The Cuckoo" from **RHYTHMS OF CHILDHOOD** (SCHOL)

"Wake Up Little Sparrow" from **RHYTHMS OF CHILDHOOD** (SCHOL)

"Where Has My Little Dog Gone" from **THIS IS RHYTHM** (SCHOL)

"My Dog Has Fleas" from **THIS IS RHYTHM** (SCHOL)

"Val Vandiveer the Veterinarian" from **BEGINNING SOUNDS AND CAREERS** (UPB)

Related Children's Books

Barton, Byron. **JACK AND FRED.** New York: Macmillian Publishing Co., 1974.

Keats, Ezra Jack. **PET SHOW.** New York: Macmillian Publishing Co., 1972.

Moncure, Jane Belk. **PETS ARE SMART.** Chicago: Children's Press, 1976.

Skorpen, Liesel Moak. **ALL THE LASSIES.** New York: Dial Press, 1970.

Spier, Peter. **THE PET SHOP.** Garden City, N.Y.: Doubleday & Co., 1981.

Related Parenting Materials

Cansler, Dot. **THE HOMESTRETCH.** Winston-Salem, NC 27113-5128: Kaplan Press, 1983.

Related Materials

TEACHING PICTURES. Winston-Salem, NC 27113-5128: Kaplan Press, 1983.

STORY SEQUENCE CARDS I, II. Winston-Salem, NC 27113-5128: Kaplan Press, 1983.

SEWING CARDS I, II, III. Winston-Salem, NC 27113-5128: Kaplan Press, 1983.

Unit 7: Thanksgiving

A developmental assessment should determine the functional levels of each child. Individual expectations are based on the assessment results.

Lesson 1: Turkey

Unit Group Lesson

1. **Match Concrete Objects**
    Present two turkeys. Say, "This is a turkey." Ask each child in turn to put the turkey with the turkey. Gradually increase number of irrelevant objects from which (s)he must select turkey to match.

2. **Discriminate Objects**
    Present several objects. Have each child touch the turkey in response to the verbal direction, "Touch the turkey."

3. **Match Pictures**
    Present several pictures of common objects. Have each child match the pictures of the turkeys.

4. **Discriminate Pictures**
    Present a group of several unrelated pictures of objects. Have each child touch the picture of the turkey in response to the verbal direction, "Touch the turkey."

5. **Figure-Ground**
    Present a "busy" picture with many visual distractions. Ask each child to find the turkey.

6. **Visual Closure**
    Partially cover each of several pictures with paper. Ask each child to find the picture of the turkey.

7. **Function**
    Ask, "What do we do with a turkey?"

8. **Association**
    Ask, "What goes with the turkey?" Use pictures or objects including feathers, pumpkin pie, pilgrim, etc. with several unrelated objects or pictures.

9. **Imitate Verbalization**
    Present a turkey and ask, "What is this? Say, 'Turkey'." The child will imitate "Turkey."

10. **Verbalize Label**
    Present a turkey and ask, "What is this?" The child will respond, "Turkey."

11.   **Concept Enrichment**

Show a large picture of a Thanksgiving dinner, and let the children point to foods according to direction. For example, "Find the turkey." "Show me the pumpkin pie."

Music

1.   Sing "Turkey, Turkey Run Away, Run Fast on Thanksgiving Day" to the tune of "Baa, Baa Black Sheep":

Turkey, turkey, run away,
Run fast on Thanksgiving Day.
Run, run, run, run, run, run, run
Run, run, run, run, run, run, run
Turkey, turkey, run away,
Run fast on Thanksgiving Day.

2.   Sing "Gobble, Gobble, Gobble" to the tune of "London Bridge":

The turkey goes gobble, gobble, gobble;
  gobble, gobble, gobble, gobble, gobble, gobble;
The turkey goes gobble, gobble, gobble,
  on Thanksgiving Day.

3.   Sing to the tune of "10 Little Indians":

1 little, 2 little, 3 little turkeys, etc.
10 Thanksgiving turkeys   *(Hold up fingers as each number is sung.)*

4.   Dance to "Turkey In the Straw."

Art

1.   Have the children construct turkeys by using paper plates with pre-cut paper head, feathers, and feet. Use the plate as the body. Have the children paste the pants and color the feathers.

2.   Give each child a paper plate and an envelope of Thanksgiving food (magazine pictures). Ask the children to paste the turkey on the plate and put the dressing next to the turkey, etc.

3.   Let the children trace around their fingers and hand or another child's to draw a turkey. Have the children add legs, eyes, etc. and color the "feathers." (See fig. 7A.)

4.   Help the children make a turkey puppet using a lunch bag and a paper plate on which children have colored feathers. Glue the paper plate to the back of the bag. Glue on eyes and a beak to the folded bottom of the bag and glue a wattle under the folded bottom. (See fig. 7B.)

Fig. 7A

Fig. 7B

Snack

1.   Eat cooked turkey. Eat (white and dark meat, giblets). Talk about location of each part on the turkey.

2.   Eat the turkey apples made in Fine Motor #5 today.

Fine Motor

1.   Have the children paste feathers on an outline of a turkey.

2.   Have the child use small blocks to build a fence to enclose miniature toy turkeys. Number concepts are developed by asking the child to place one or two turkeys inside the fence.

3.   Have the children stick paper feathers and a turkey head onto opposite ends of a pine cone, which is lying on its side.

4.   Let children make turkey apples for snack. Each child makes feathers by pushing raisins and small marshmallows onto toothpicks. Let them stick the feather into the back of the apple and add a marshmallow on a toothpick for a head.

Games

1. Use toy plastic foods to improve visual memory. Select three foods and place them on a plate. Have the child watch. After a few seconds, remove the foods and ask the child to identify the foods. Let the children take turns being teacher.

2. Construct a large paper turkey with the tail missing. Set out pre-cut red, yellow, blue, and green paper tail feathers and give directions to the children as to the color and number of feathers to put on the turkey such as "Put on a red tail feather." "Find a tail feather this color," (holding up a specific color feather).

3. Place a toy turkey, duck, and bird on table. Demonstrate the sound each one makes and have the children imitate. The child turns his back to teacher and listens while the teacher produces one of the sounds. The child turns and points to the appropriate toy. This game enhances auditory discrimination.

Storytelling

1. Make up a story about "Thanksgiving Dinner". Tell about a little boy and little girl getting ready for Thanksgiving dinner. They count silverware, fold napkins, and set the table. Then, they serve the food. Dramatize the story by letting the children get ready for Thanksgiving dinner, using pretend food (toy food, pictures, or imaginary food) and asking the child what he wants, such as "What part of the turkey do you want?" "Do you need anything else?"

2. Tell this turkey story with turkeys taped on fingers. Five fat turkeys are we. We sat all night in a tree when the cook came around we couldn't be found. So that's why were here you see. (See fig. 7C.)

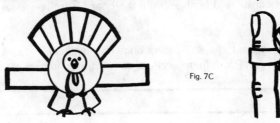

Fig. 7C

Gross Motor

1. Play "Gobble, Gobble." Let the children be "turkeys" and have a "base" (pen). One child is the "hunter." The "turkeys" go looking for food and when the leader calls "gobble, gobble," the "hunter" tries to catch some of the "turkeys" before they can return to "base." Those caught become "hunters" until all "turkeys" are caught.

2. A variation is that the "turkeys" run from one end of the play area to the other. The "hunter" tries to catch the "turkeys" before they get "home."

Cognitive

1. Make a cue sheet with a turkey at the top and many turkeys interposed with other items below the cue. Have the children mark the turkeys. Vary the number of turkeys and objects on a page according to the level of the child. Initially only one turkey with one object (or no object) may be appropriate. Increase number as the child's skill increases.

2. Collect some turkey eggs. How do they differ from chicken eggs? Scramble some of each. How do they taste?

3. Collect turkey feathers. Let the children wash them in soap and water to remove oil and then dye the white feathers different colors by dipping them in dye. (Homemade dye can be made by boiling onion skills for yellow, cranberries for red, and spinach leaves for green.)

4. Have the children put five feathers on five turkeys. Draw five turkeys without tails. Let the children draw five feathers on each. (See fig. 7V)

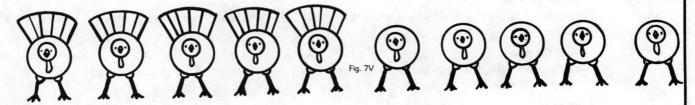

Fig. 7V

Enrichment

1. Let children use scissors to cut the top of a paper plate for feathers. Add head and feet. (See fig. 7W)
2. Let each child stuff a small brown lunch bag half full of crumpled newspapers. Secure the opening and splay out the end for feather area. Add colors, colored paper, or cut to fringe. Add head and legs.

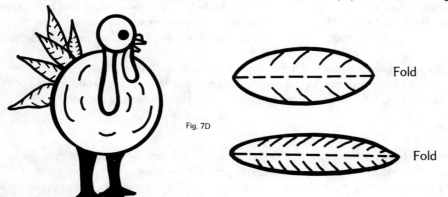

Fig. 7D

Fold

Fold

Fig. 7W

3. Together Activity: On the bulletin board put a large circular turkey body, head and feet. Let the children color the turkey and have each child cut oval paper feathers. Let the children fold the feathers and staple to the bulletin board. Add feathers until the board is full. (See fig. 7D.)

Field Trip

1. Visit a turkey farm. Observe the turkeys. Collect eggs and feathers.
2. Take a hike and gather leaves. Press them and use to form the tail of a cardboard turkey.

Lesson 2: Pilgrim

Unit Group Lesson

1. **Match Concrete Objects**
    Present two pilgrims. Say, "This is a pilgrim." Ask each child in turn to put the pilgrim with the pilgrim. Gradually increase number of irrelevant objects from which (s)he must select pilgrim to match.

2. **Discriminate Objects**
    Present several objects. Have each child touch the pilgrim in response to the verbal direction, "Touch the pilgrim."

3. **Match Pictures**
    Present several pictures of common objects. Have each child match the pictures of the pilgrims.

4. **Discriminate Pictures**
    Present a group of several unrelated pictures of objects. Have each child touch the picture of the pilgrim in response to the verbal direction, "Touch the pilgrim."

5. **Figure-Ground**
    Present a "busy" picture with many visual distractions. Ask each child to find the pilgrim.

6. **Visual Closure**
    Partially cover each of several pictures with paper. Ask each child to find the picture of the pilgrim.

7. **Function**
    Ask, "What did the pilgrims do?"

8. **Association**

   Ask, "What goes with the pilgrim?" Use pictures or objects including pilgrim hat, turkey, feather, Indian, etc. with several unrelated objects or pictures.

9. **Imitate Verbalization**

   Present a pilgrim and ask, "What is this? Say, 'Pilgrim'." The child will imitate "Pilgrim."

10. **Verbalize Label**

    Present a pilgrim and ask, "What is this?" The child will respond, "Pilgrim."

11. **Concept Enrichment**

    Talk about the pilgrims coming on the Mayflower to this country. Indians helped them survive the first winter. After the first harvest, they all celebrated with a big feast. We remember their feast with one of our own.

Music

1. Sing "Pilgrim" to the tune of "Did You Ever See A Lassie?":
   Verse 1: I am a pilgrim, a pilgrim, a pilgrim   *(Have the children wear pilgrim*
             I am a pilgrim and I wear a hat.   *hats which they made in Art #3.)*
   Verse 2: I'm friends with the Indians, the Indians, the Indians.
             I'm friends with the Indians,
             And grow all my food.
2. Sing "Pilgrim Had A Big Turkey" to the tune of "London Bridge":
   The Pilgrim had a big turkey, big turkey, a big turkey,   *(bi-ig or tur-key)*
   The Pilgrim had a big turkey and he kept him in a fence.
3. Sing up, then down the scale.
   Thanksgiving Day will soon be here.
   It comes around but once a year.
4. Sing traditional songs the Pilgrim children may have sung (see Gross Motor #2).

Art

1. Have the children make a collection of pictures of things for which we are thankful, (e.g., fathers, mothers, sisters, brothers, pets, homes) on construction paper.
2. Have the children paste up a collection of things for which the Pilgrims were thankful, (e.g., friends, foods, houses, clothes, Indians) on construction paper.
3. Help the children make a pilgrim hat from construction paper. Cut two pieces of black paper shaped like the illustration. Staple them together. Add a band and buckle. (See fig. 7E.)

Staple

Fig. 7E

Staple ⊢   ⊣ Staple

4. Have the children make Mayflowers using:
   a. A walnut shell, a toothpick anchored in Playdoh, and a triangle-shaped paper sail.
   b. A plastic lid and drinking straw and a triangle of paper.
   c. A bar of floating soap, a toothpick and a triangle of paper.
   Sail in a pan of water from "Europe" to "America."   (See fig. 7F.)

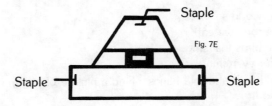

a.   Fig. 7F   b.   c.

Snack

1. Make cranberry relish and emphasize that it is one of the foods pilgrims ate on Thanksgiving. If possible, visit a grocery store and let the children shop for the ingredients.

  Recipe: 4 cups frozen fresh cranberries
       1 orange
       2 cups sugar

  Using a food grinder, let the children grind the cranberries and orange together. Stir in the sugar. Chill in a refrigerator. Eat on soda crackers.

2. Tape a picture of a pilgrim on the side near the bottom of the child's glass. As he finishes his drink, he will see the pilgrim.
3. Be thankful for snack.
4. Start snack with a table blessing:
  Thank you for the world so sweet.
  Thank you for the food we eat.
  Thank you for the birds that sing.
  Thank you God for everything.

Fine Motor

1. Have children do a path tracing of "Take the turkey to the pilgrim" and "Take the pilgrim to the feast."
2. Have each child connect dots that are in the shape of a pilgrim's hat and color the hat black.
3. Have the children sew a pilgrim hat sewing card.

Games

1. Have the children play "Tape the Hat on the Pilgrim." Have each child tape that hat on the pilgrim's head. Depending upon the child's level, blindfold child, turn him around, and lead the child to the pilgrim poster and say, "Put the hat on the pilgrim's head." (Some children may just want to close their eyes and turn around and not be blindfolded.)
2. Demonstrate giving by giving children treats and having them verbalize or gesture "Thank you." Tell the children "The pilgrims gave thanks for their food."

Storytelling

1. Display a poster of pilgrims eating Thanksgiving dinner. Tell the story of how they worked together, gathered their food, and celebrated the first harvest. Ask the children to "find the pilgrims" in the picture (Figure Ground).
2. Tell the Thanksgiving Story from Lesson #1 again. Let the children dramatize it again. Start the meal with a table blessing:
  Thank you for the world so sweet.
  Thank you for the food we eat.
  Thank you for the birds that sing.
  Thank you God for everything.

  Have the children bow heads and fold hands. Find a picture of pilgrims praying and display it in the room. Call attention to it.

3. Fingerplay: "Five Little Pilgrims"
  Five little pilgrims on Thanksgiving Day,   *(One hand up, fingers extended -*
  The 1st one said, "I'll have cake if I may,"   *move each finger as it talks.)*
  The 2nd one said, "I'll have turkey roasted,"
  The 3rd one said, "I'll have chestnuts toasted,"
  The 4th one said, "I'll have pumpkin pie,"
  The 5th one said, "Oh! Cranberries I spy."
  But before they ate any turkey or dressing,
  All the pilgrims said a Thanksgiving blessing. *(Touch hands in prayer.)*

4. Read "The Thanksgiving Story," Dalgliesh or "The Pilgrim's First Thanksgiving," McGovern.
5. Have the children dramatize the trip on the Mayflower.

Gross Motor
1. Have the children dress in Pilgrim costumes.
2. Let the children play traditional games the Pilgrim children may have played such as: Hokey Pokey; Mulberry Bush; Skip To My Lou; Oats, Peas, Beans; Looby Loo; Did You Ever See A Lassie?' Go Round and Round the Village; A'hunting We Will Go; London Bridge; Bluebird Through My Window.

Cognitive
Tell the children the Pilgrims had to make everything they used. Let them make things the Pilgrims made:
a. Rub oil on grocery bags and use for windows for (Lincoln Log) cabins or block cabins.
b. Make candles. Melt parafin wax. Remove from heat. Dip string in the wax, then into water. Repeat about 20 times. Use the candles.

Enrichment
1. Use authentic information to practice math skills with "Mayflower Math" or "Pilgrim Problems" such as:

   There were 5 men, 2 women and 3 children on the Mayflower. Were there more men or women? etc. Use plastic people to demonstrate.

2. Use a cut-out Pilgram hat for a tachistoscope for a vocabulary list. Cut poster board into a hat shape. Make cuts where buckle would go. Use a strip of paper with words on it spaced far enough apart that only one word at a time shows through the opening. Thread it through the cuts so only one word shows at a time. (See fig. 7G.)

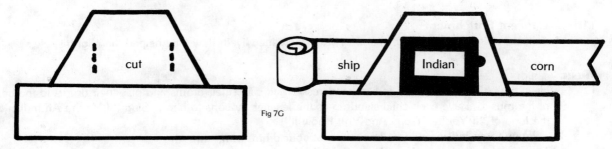

Fig 7G

Field Trip
1. Visit a historical site, an old village or settlement to see how the Pilgrims might have lived.
2. Tour the restored "Mayflower" or other old sailing ships.

Visitor
Invite someone to come wearing traditional Pilgrim clothes.

Lesson 3: Indian

Unit Group Lesson

1. **Match Concrete Objects**
   Present two Indians. Say, "This is a Indian." Ask each child in turn to put the Indian with the Indian. Gradually increase number of irrelevant objects from which (s)he must select Indian to match.

2. **Discriminate Objects**
   Present several objects. Have each child touch the Indian in response to the verbal direction, "Touch the Indian."

3. **Match Pictures**
   Present several pictures of common objects. Have each child match the pictures of the Indians.

4. **Discriminate Pictures**

Present a group of several unrelated pictures of objects. Have each child touch the picture of the Indian in response to the verbal direction, "Touch the Indian."

5. **Figure-Ground**

Present a "busy" picture with many visual distractions. Ask each child to find the Indian.

6. **Visual Closure**

Partially cover each of several pictures with paper. Ask each child to find the picture of the Indian.

7. **Function**

Ask, "What did the Indians do?"

8. **Association**

Ask, "What goes with the Indian?" Use pictures or objects including feathers, tepee, pilgrim, turkey, etc. with several unrelated objects or pictures.

9. **Imitate Verbalization**

Present an Indian and ask, "What is this? Say, 'Indian'." The child will imitate "Indian."

10. **Verbalize Label**

Present an Indian and ask, "What is this?" The child will respond, "Indian."

11. **Concept Enrichment**

Talk about Indians. Discuss what they wore, how they lived, how they helped the pilgrims, etc.

Music

1. Have the children wear their Indian headdresses and carry their drums and play their drums to the beat of the music. Have each child stand up as the teacher motions to him . Sing "If You're An Indian" to the tune of "If You're Happy And You Know It":

   If you're an Indian and you know it, beat your drum, rum, tum, tum.
   If you're an Indian and you know it, beat your drum, rum, tum, tum.
   If you're an Indian and you know it, then your drum will surely show it.
   If you're an Indian and you know it, beat your drum.

2. Dance heel - toe to Indian music.

3. Take brown work gloves; sew a pom pom on each finger tip: add a tiny feather; sing "One little, two little, three little Indians" moving the finger Indians with the music. (See fig. 7H.)

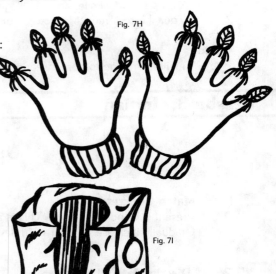

Fig. 7H

Fig. 7I

Art

1. Have each child make an Indian drum from an old shortening can with the plastic top taped down or an empty oatmeal box, etc. Have them decorate the construction paper and cover the outside of the can with it.

2. Have each child make an Indian feather headband by pasting feathers on strips of stiff construction paper. Fasten the paper around the child's head with staples or paper clips.

3. Help each child make Indian vests: Use brown grocery bags with fringed edges. Let each child decorate his vest. (If the paper bag is crumpled it will look more like leather.) (See fig. 7I.)

Snack

1. Have everyone make original American breads (corn bread, johnnycake, Anadama Bread) made from corn.

122

2. Have everyone make homemade butter from whipping cream. Beat (shake) until the cream becomes solid. Drain off the "buttermilk" or whey. Add a little salt and spread.
3. Eat seeds and nuts served from an Indian bowl or basket.
4. Pop popcorn and eat it for snack.

Fine Motor
1. Make path tracings of "Take the Indian to his tepee," and "Take the Indian to the cornfield."
2. Teach the children an Indian war whoop. Have them pat their mouth with their hand as they yell.
3. Cut sandpaper to fit inside a lid. Glue inside. Have children use markers to make Indian designs or symbols. Make triangles, squares, circles. Follow design with fingers.
4. Have children trace and complete Indian designs. These designs can be pattern traced on brown paper bags which have been crumpled to resemble "leather." Indian costumes or tepees can be decorated with the designs. Put designs on a semicircle and make tepees to add to Indian village in Enrichment #1. Trace Indian designs; complete Indian designs. (Make pattern simple or complex according to the level of the child.) (See Fig. 7X)
5. Have children pattern trace designs on Indian bowls. (You draw designs on large paper bags.) (See fig. 7J.)

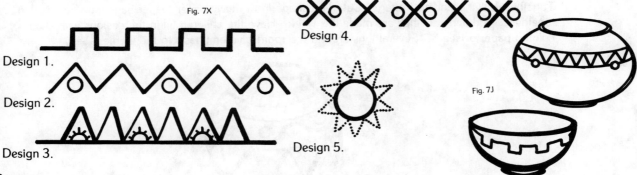

Fig. 7X

Design 1.

Design 2.

Design 3.

Design 4.

Design 5.

Fig. 7J

Games
1. Let the children dance like Indians while one child plays the drum.
   Model dancing and Indian war whoop (pat mouth while yelling). Let the children take turns playing the drum.
2. Let the children select Indian names (Running Bear, Eagle Feathers, Moon Flower, etc.). Make name tags and call each other by Indian names for a day.
3. Use kernels of corn for markers in a board game.
4. Play "The Indian Says" like "Simon Says."

Storytelling
1. Tell a simple story of Thanksgiving. Tell how the pilgrims and Indians were friends. Explain how they shared their food. Use pictures to illustrate.
2. Fingerplay: "Ten Little Indians." Hold fingers up when appropriate. Only sing about "Five Indians," if ten is not appropriate. Refer to Indian boys and Indian girls.
3. Read *Let's Be Indians,* Parish, or *Little Way,* McGovern.

Gross Motor
1. Bean Bag Toss: Have the children throw a bean bag in the Indian box. Decorate a box (or waste can) with Indian pictures to make the Indian box.
2. Obstacle Course: Have the children move one at a time through an obstacle course either inside or outside. At the end of the course place a tepee where the children can rest. Crawling through a tunnel, walking a balance beam, walking between taped lines on the floor, climbing up and over an indoor jungle gym, etc.
3. Make a corn trail. Pick up the kernels as you go.
4. Let Indian tribes (groups of children) follow a trail ("blazed" ahead of time by teacher who has put colored paper or shapes along the way to be discovered and followed by the Indians using their bright eyes).

Cognitive

1. Have the children make bracelets and necklaces by stringing shells, macaroni, beads and straw segments. Provide a pattern for the children to follow. Prepare yarn for stringing by dipping the ends in white glue and letting them dry flat.
2. Have the children make canoes from pieces of bark. Float them. Discuss which ones work better than others and why?
3. Try drying foods before eating them. Remind the children that long ago there was no refrigeration.
4. Play an Indian dice game. Fill cans with the same number of pebbles. Let the children roll dice, have them remove from the can as many pebbles as the number they roll. Play until all cans are empty. (See fig. 7K.)

Fig. 7K

Enrichment

1. Create an Indian village in the sand table or on a table using tepees, canoes, and totem poles with plastic Indians, animals, and other things.
2. Together Activity: Indian Pottery - Cut a jug shape from heavy paper (paper bags glued or stapled together). Add items as they are made this week. Have the children fill-in the designs with shapes, colored paper or seeds. Several jugs around the room give emphasis to the theme. (See fig. 7L.)

Fig. 7L

3. Divide the children in the classroom into tribes. Put an emblem on their foreheads such as sun tribe, moon tribe, and star tribe. Plan a pow wow. Have all tribes come wearing headdresses with the tribal colors and emblem.

Field Trip

If no Indian village or museum is available, visit a weaver, basket maker, or potter to see cloth, baskets, or bowls being made.

Visitor

Have an Indian visit. Ask if (s)he will dress in authentic Indian dress.

Lesson 4: Tepee

Unit Group Lesson

1. **Match Concrete Objects**
   Present two tepees. Say, "This is a tepee." Ask each child in turn to put the tepee with the tepee. Gradually increase number of irrelevant objects from which (s)he must select tepee to match.

2. **Discriminate Objects**
   Present several objects. Have each child touch the tepee in response to the verbal direction, "Touch the teepee."

3. **Match Pictures**
    Present several pictures of common objects. Have each child match the pictures of the tepees.

4. **Discriminate Pictures**
    Present a group of several unrelated pictures of objects. Have each child touch the picture of the tepee in response to the verbal direction, "Touch the tepee."

5. **Figure-Ground**
    Present a "busy" picture with many visual distractions. Ask each child to find the tepee.

6. **Visual Closure**
    Partially cover each of several pictures with paper. Ask each child to find the picture of the tepee.

7. **Function**
    Ask, "What do we do with a tepee?"

8. **Association**
    Ask, "What goes with the tepee?" Use pictures or objects including Indian, tomahawk, house, pilgrim, etc. with several unrelated objects or pictures.

9. **Imitate Verbalization**
    Present a tepee and ask, "What is this? Say, 'Tepee'." The child will imitate "Tepee."

10. **Verbalize Label**
    Present a tepee and ask, "What is this?" The child will respond, "Tepee."

11. **Concept Enrichment**
    Discuss other types of Indian homes such as log houses, hogans, etc.

Music
1. Sing "Where Does the Indian Live?" to the tune of "Mulberry Bush":
    Where, oh where, does the Indian live?
    Indian live? Indian live?
    Where, oh where, does the Indian live?
    He lives in a tepee. (te-ee-pee)
2. Sing "The Big Tepee" to the tune of "Mary Had A Little Lamb":
    The Indian has a big tepee, a big tepee, a big tepee,
    The Indian has a big tepee
    And that is where he lives.

Art
1. Cut each child a circle of paper to make a tepee. Have the children decorate around the circle with patterns. You or the child can cut a pie-shaped wedge from the circle and staple it into a cone. Then cut or tear out space for a door. Give each child a toy Indian for his tepee.
2. Figure-Ground Activity: Have the child glue a tepee or tepees on top of the one(s) he has found in his picture. Before hand you should create a picture like the illustration. Use simple and more complex pictures depending upon the child's developmental level. Let the child decorate the picture.

Snack
    Eat snacks taking turns inside a tepee, or sitting Indian style.

Fine Motor
1. Have the children connect dots in the shape of a tepee and let the children paste an Indian in the tepee when finished.
2. Have the children sew a tepee sewing card.

3. Have each child make a tepee. Draw background of "pine trees." Color tepee brown or draw a design. (See fig. 7M.)

 Fold to this line.

Fig 7M

Draw a background of "pine trees."

Fold corner to dot.

Color Tepee brown or draw a design.

4. Use brown grocery bags. Have each child wad up a bag tightly and spread it out. Do this several times to make the bag look like leather. Outline tepees on it, cut out and have the children decorate them.

Games

1. Make a tepee in the block area or outside. Use a blanket thrown over a climbing toy for the tepee. Have the children wear their Indian headbands, carry their drums, pretend they are Indians, live in tepees and do Indian dances outside the tepee using the war whoop.
2. Make lotto cards picturing different colors and different designs of tepees and matching single cards. Have the children match the tepees or play it as a regular lotto game. (See fig. 7N.)

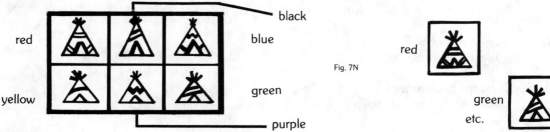

Fig. 7N

Storytelling

1. Use pictures to illustrate a story about an Indian girl and an Indian boy who are neighbors. Show the tepees in which the children live.
2. Fingerplay "Tepee":

Once there was an Indian girl.	(Hold up one index finger.)
And a little Indian boy.	(Hold up other index finger.)
They were very, very happy.	(Use index fingers to point to smile on your face.)
Living in their Indian tepees.	(Put tips of index fingers together to make a tepee shape.)

Gross Motor

1. Make a tepee by covering a card table with a sheet. Have the children run an obstacle course going through the tepee and around other objects.
2. Outline a masking tape tepee on the floor. Have the children "run around the tepee, jump over the tepee, lie down beside, and jump in the tepee."

Cognitive

1. Cut tepees our of wallpaper scraps and have children match those with the same design.
2. Tell the children to count the suns on the tepee and open the flap to see if they are correct.
3. Give each child a paper with a picture of a house and a tepee, and a picture of a child and an Indian. Ask, "Where does the Indian live?" and have the children paste the picture of the Indian next to the tepee. Ask, "Where does the boy (or girl) live?" Have children paste the picture of the child next to the house. (See fig. 7O.)

 Fig. 7O

Enrichment

1.   Together Activity: Help the children make an Indian village with a forest and tepees on a mural. Have them made evergreen trees from triangles of green paper and rectangles of brown paper. Glue these to the mural for the forest. Have the children make tepees from large triangles of tan paper (grocery sacks are excellent) on which they draw or trace Indian designs and cut and fold back a flap. Glue the tepees to the mural in the form of a village. (See fig. 7P.)

Fig. 7P

Green triangles

Brown rectangle

2.   Build a giant tepee. Start with poles tied with rope. Add "leather" made of bags or brown wrapping paper. Have children paint designs. Hold a "Pow Wow" inside. (See fig. 7Q.)

Fig. 7Q

Visitor

Invite a father and son from an Indian Tribe to visit wearing their costumes.

Lesson 5: Pumpkin

Unit Group Lesson

1. **Match Concrete Objects**
Present two pumpkins. Say, "This is a pumpkin." Ask each child in turn to put the pumpkin with the pumpkin. Gradually increase number of irrelevant objects from which (s)he must select pumpkin to match.

2. **Discriminate Objects**
Present several objects. Have each child touch the pumpkin in response to the verbal direction, "Touch the pumpkin."

3. **Match Pictures**
Present several pictures of common objects. Have each child match the pictures of the pumpkins.

4. **Discriminate Pictures**
Present a group of several unrelated pictures of objects. Have each child touch the picture of the pumpkin in response to the verbal direction, "Touch the pumpkin."

5.   **Figure-Ground**
     Present a "busy" picture with many visual distractions. Ask each child to find the pumpkin.

6.   **Visual Closure**
     Partially cover each of several pictures with paper. Ask each child to find the picture of the pumpkin.

7.   **Function**
     Ask, "What do we do with a pumpkin?"

8.   **Association**
     Ask, "What goes with the pumpkin?" Use pictures or objects including pie, turkey, squash, etc. with several unrelated objects or pictures.

9.   **Imitate Verbalization**
     Present a pumpkin and ask, "What is this? Say, 'Pumpkin'." The child will imitate "Pumpkin."

10. **Verbalize Label**
     Present a pumpkin and ask, "What is this?" The child will respond, "Pumpkin."

11. **Concept Enrichment**
     Discuss uses of pumpkin (eg. making pie, Jack-o-lanterns, and eating the seeds).

Music
1.   Sing "Pumpkin Pie" to the tune of the "Campbell's Soup Song":
        Pumpkin pie,
        Pumpkin pie,
        Yum, yum, yum,
        I like pumpkin pie.
2.   Sing "Taste a Pumpkin" to the tune of "Did You Ever See A Lassie?":
        Did you ever taste a pumpkin, a pumpkin, a pumpkin,
        Did you ever taste a pumpkin, a pumpkin pie?
        It's tasty, it's sweet;
        It's good to eat.
        Did you ever taste a pumpkin, a pumpkin pie?

Art
1.   Have the children paste a pumpkin pie puzzle onto a paper plate. (The puzzle pieces should be in pie wedge shapes.)
2.   Let the children paint a pumpkin orange and its stem green.
3.   Have the children cut out or tear orange construction paper to decorate a pumpkin which is outlined in black magic marker on white paper.
4.   Dry and have children use pumpkin seeds for a collage. Dry the seeds on a shallow pan in a 250° oven turning frequently.

Snack
1.   Prepare pumpkin cookies (either regular sugar cookies in a pumpkin shape or actual pumpkin cookies) or pumpkin pie. If a pumpkin pie is made, use the pumpkin carved from the fresh one used in Fine Motor #2 for today.
2.   Eat pumpkin seeds which have been sprinkled with salt and roasted in a 250° oven in a shallow pan. (Turn frequently.)

Fine Motor
1.   Let the children make a pumpkin (a ball) out of orange play dough and add green play dough at the top for the stem.
2.   Have the children help scoop out a real pumpkin using hands and a spoon. Keep the pumpkin for making a pumpkin pie or pumpkin cookies and use the seeds for roasting.

3. Have the children sew a pumpkin sewing card.

4. Ask children to path trace lines on a pumpkin shape. Make the activity simple to complex according to the levels of children. (See fig. 7R.)

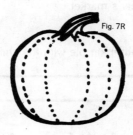

Fig. 7R

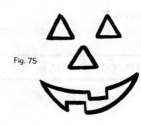

Fig. 7S

5. Use the same pumpkin drawn in #4. Have the children change it into a Jack-O-Lantern by gluing on 3 triangles and a mouth shape. (See fig. 7S.)

6. Ask children to cut pumpkin vines with a spiral line drawn in black marker. Make lines according to child's cutting ability. (Thicker/shorter lines for lesser ability and thinner/longer lines for greater ability.) (See fig. 7T.)

Fig. 7T

Games

Play a game of "Find the Pumpkin." Hide a small plastic pumpkin in the room. Have the children try to find it. Initially put the pumpkin in a very conspicuous place, then gradually make it harder to find. Say, "Find the pumpkin." When the pumpkin is found, ask, "Where did you find it?" Use a map showing the location for some children. Let the children take turns hiding the pumpkin.

Storytelling

Fingerplay: "Five Little Pumpkins"

Five little pumpkins sitting on a gate,　　　　　　　　*(Hold hand up and move*
The 1st one said, "Oh, my it's getting late."　　　　　*each finger as it talks.)*
The 2nd one said, "There's a storm in the air."
The 3rd one said, "But we don't care."
The 4th one said, "Let's run and run and run."
The 5th one said, "I'm ready for some fun."
Whooo went the wind, and out went the lights.　　　　*(Close hand.)*
And the five little pumpkins rolled out of sight.　　　　*(Roll hands behind back.)*

Gross Motor

Pumpkin Toss: Use a medium sized plastic pumpkin and have the children toss the pumpkin back and forth. Have the children face each other and throw it. Make sure they are not too far away from each other. Say, "Catch the pumpkin." and "What did you catch?" after it is caught.

Cognitive

1. Let the children cut pumpkins of different sizes from construction paper. Use them for sorting, counting and sequencing by size.

2. Have the children plant pumpkin seeds in small pots in the classroom.

Enrichment

Together Activity: Make a pumpkin patch on a long roll of paper. Let the children draw or path trace pumpkins in orange. Add pumpkin vines, cut in Fine Motor #6, and paste on leaves you have made. (See fig. 7U.)

Fig. 7U

Field Trip

Visit a pumpkin farm or farmer's market.

Visitor

Invite a parent to prepare a pumpkin pie with the children.

Lesson 6: Feast

Unit Group Lesson

1. **Match Pictures**

   Present pictures of two feasts. Ask each child in turn to put the feast with the feast. When shown several pictures of common objects, the child will match the pictures of the feasts.

2. **Discriminate Pictures**

   Present a group of several unrelated pictures of objects. Have each child touch the picture of the feast in response to verbal direction, "Touch the feast."

3. **Figure-Ground**

   Present a picture of a feast. Ask each child to find the turkey in the feast. Continue activity by locating the other foods.

4. **Visual Closure**

   Partially cover each of several pictures with paper, Ask child to find the picture of the turkey in the feast.

5. **Function**

   Ask, "What do we do at a feast?"

6. **Association**

   Ask, "What goes with the feast?" Use pictures or objects including turkey, pumpkin pie, cranberry sauce, etc. with several unrelated objects or pictures.

7. **Imitate Verbalization**

   Present a feast and ask, "What is this? Say, 'Feast'." The child will imitate "Feast."

8. **Verbalize Label**

   Present a feast and ask, "What is this?" The child will respond, "Feast."

9. **Concept Enrichment**

   Discuss a menu for a feast, i.e., turkey, pumpkin pie, mashed potatoes, cornbread, Indian pudding, cranberry relish, squash, cabbage salad or other items traditional in the area. Parents may contribute some items already prepared and the rest of the day's activities should be devoted to preparing, eating, and cleaning up the feast.

Music

1. Sing "Whistle While You Cook" to the tune of "Whistle While You Work":

   Whistle while you cook
   Whistle while you cook
   Come on get smart
   Tune up and start
   To whistle while you cook.

2. For recipes involving corn sing the song "Jimmy Crack Corn."

Art

1. Let the children make placemats by gluing cut-out food on a large piece of construction paper and fringing the edges with scissors.
2. Let the children make a table cloth by decorating a sheet with squeeze bottles full of thin tempera paint or food coloring and water.
3. Ask the children to do a "glad" wall in the room with pictures all the things that make us glad at Thanksgiving, including feast foods like turkey, pumpkin, etc.

Snack

1. Have a feast.
2. Serve popcorn if the feast is to be eaten for lunch.

Fine Motor

With close supervision have children:
  a. Cut all necessary vegetables, etc., for feast.
  b. Grind or mash corn for recipes (use some commerical cornmeal if needed).
  c. Grind or mash cranberries and make relish, sauce, muffins, or cake.
  d. Shave or grate carrots for carrot and raisin salad or cabbage salad.
  e. Wash dishes after feast is over.

Games

Let the children imitate popcorn by playing "Pop Goes the Weasel."

Storytelling

Tell the story of the first Thanksgiving feast. Build a Mayflower from a large box. Dramatize the Thanksgiving story in sequence:
  1. There were some people called Pilgrims who were unhapopy in their country.
  2. They got on a big ship called the Mayflower to go to another land.
  3. They were met by the Indians and they became friends.
  4. They had a feast together after the first harvest and called it Thanksgiving.

Gross Motor

1. Let the children move tables and chairs into a festive arrangement.
2. Have the children climb step stools to decorate the classroom with Thanksgiving decorations.

Cognitive

1. Help the children make popcorn and count kernels while doing it.
2. Tell a child to look at a table setting or feast. Remove one or more item(s) while the child's back is turned. Have the child tell "What's Missing?"
3. Let the children match, sort, group, and classify real food.
4. Recall the feast afterwards by gluing pictures of what was eaten on to paper plates. Use pictures of what was and was not eaten, so that the children really have to remember.

Enrichment

1. Help the children make a handwritten menu.
2. Help the children make name cards for each person's place.
3. Have children set table, serve foods, and have the feast.

Field Trip

Set up the feast in a particular place in school and have children "go" to the feast. Talk about appropriate manners at a feast.

Visitor

Invite a Mother. Let her tell how she prepares Thanksgiving dinner. Maybe she can help the children make a "feast" item.

Related Children's Records
"Turkey" from **ADVENTURES IN SOUND** (MH)
"Ten Little Indians" from **FINGERPLAY FUN** (EA)
"The Turkey Wobble" from **HOLIDAY SONGS** (DIM)
"Things I'm Thankful For" from **HOLIDAY SONGS** (EA)
"The Pilgrims" from **ACTION SONGS FOR SPECIAL OCCASION** (KIM)
"The Indians" from **ACTION SONGS FOR SPECIAL OCCASION** (KIM)
"The Strutting Turkey" from **ACTION SONGS FOR SPECIAL OCCASION** (KIM)
"Over the River and Through the Woods" from **SONG IN MOTION-HOLIDAY** (KIM)
"Parachute Pow Wow" from **PLAYTIME PARACHUTE FUN** (KIM)
"Floating Cloud" from **PLAYTIME PARACHUTE FUN** (KIM)
"Old Tom Turkey" from **LOOK AT THE HOLIDAYS** (GA)
"Maori Indian Battle Chant" from **YOU'LL SING A SONG** (SCHOL)

Related Children's Books
Child, Lydia. **OVER THE RIVER AND THROUGH THE WOODS.** New York: Coward, McCann & Geoghegan, 1974.
Devlin, Wende and Devlin, Harry. **CRANBERRY THANKSGIVING.** New York: Parent's Magazine Press, 1971.
Hilert, Margaret. **WHY WE HAVE THANKSGIVING.** Chicago: Follet Publishing Co., 1982.
Janice. **LITTLE BEAR'S THANKSGIVING.** New York: Lothrop Lee & Shepard Co., 1967.
Marilue. **BABY BEAR'S THANKSGIVING.** New York: Harper & Row, 1978.
Moncure, Jane Belk. **OUR THANKSGIVING BOOK.** Elgin, Ill.: Child's World, 1976.

Related Parenting Materials
Cansler, Dot. **THE HOMESTRETCH.** Winston-Salem, NC 27113-5128: Kaplan Press, 1983.

Related Materials
TEACHING PICTURES. Winston-Salem, NC 27113-5128: Kaplan Press, 1983.
STORY SEQUENCE CARDS I, II. Winston-Salem, NC 27113-5128: Kaplan Press, 1983.
SEWING CARDS I, II, III. Winston-Salem, NC 27113-5128: Kaplan Press, 1983.

Unit 8: Buildings

A developmental assessment should determine the functional levels of each child. Individual expectations are based on the assessment results.

Lesson 1: School

Unit Group Lesson

(CAUTION: If only pictures are available, use them for number 1 and omit numbers 2 and 3.)

1. **Match Concrete Objects**
    Present two schools. Say, "This is a school." Ask each child in turn to put the school with the school Gradually increase number of irrelevant objects from which (s)he must select school to match.

2. **Discriminate Objects**
    Present several objects. Have each child touch the school in response to the verbal direction, "Touch the school."

3. **Match Pictures**
    Present several pictures of common objects. Have each child match the pictures of the schools.

4. **Discriminate Pictures**
    Present a group of several unrelated pictures of objects. Have each child touch the picture of the school in response to the verbal direction, "Touch the school."

5. **Figure-Ground**
    Present a "busy" picture with many visual distractions. Ask each child to find the school.

6. **Visual Closure**
    Partially cover each of several pictures with paper. Ask each child to find the picture of the school.

7. **Function**
    Ask, "What do we do in a school?"

8. **Association**
    Ask, "What goes with the school?" Use pictures or objects including school bus, children, teachers, books, etc. with several unrelated objects or pictures.

9. **Imitate Verbalization**
    Present a school and ask, "What is this? Say, 'School'." The child will imitate "School."

10. **Verbalize Label**
    Present a school and ask, "What is this?" The child will respond, "School."

11.   **Concept Enrichment**

Discuss how children get to school. Discuss the different activities that happen at school.

Music

1.   Sing "Come to School" to the tune of Campbell's Soup song "Um Um Good":
Come to school
Come to school.
You and I-I
Will come to school.

2.   Sing "The People on the Bus Go Up and Down." Line chairs up to make a school bus.
Verse 1: The people on the bus go up and down,   *(Have the children get up and*
Up and down,   *down.)*
Up and down.
The people on the bus go up and down. Up
and down.
Verse 2: The wipers on the bus go swish, swish, swish.   *(Hands move left to right.)*
Verse 3: The horn on the bus goes beep, beep, beep.   *(Children act out honking*
horn.)

Add other appropriate verses.

Art

1.   Have the children make posters to decorate school halls.
2.   Make each child a sewing card by reinforcing a picture of a school with cardboard and punching holes through which the children sew colorful yarn. Let children take pictures home.
3.   Have each child outline a school shape with glue and red yarn, then decorate.
4.   Together Activity: Provide a large rectangular outline of a school building with bricks outlined in different sizes. Have the children cut bricks outlined on red construction paper and match to the sizes on the building. Let them add windows made from yellow squares with panes outlined in black. Add shrubs and flowers or autumn leaves, depending upon the season. (See fig. 8A.)

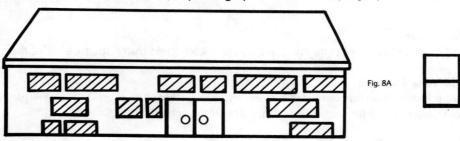

Fig. 8A

Snack

Have snack from school lunch pails.

Fine Motor

Fig. 8B

Tape Drawing to Block

(DRAWING)

(TAPE)

(BLOCK)

(Side View)

1.   Prepare path tracings of "Take the children to school." Make a map showing the path to school. Use simple paths for some children and more complex paths for others.
2.   Draw a large map with each child's house pictured and his name. Make roads (straight and curved) and have each child begin at the starting point (school) and drive a toy car to his own house.
3.   Make roads on a table top with colored tape. Make a house shape on a block (tape house to block). Have the children drive cars to their address. (See fig. 8B.)
4.   Give each child a drawing of a schoolroom. Let the children glue children cut from catalogs in the schoolroom.

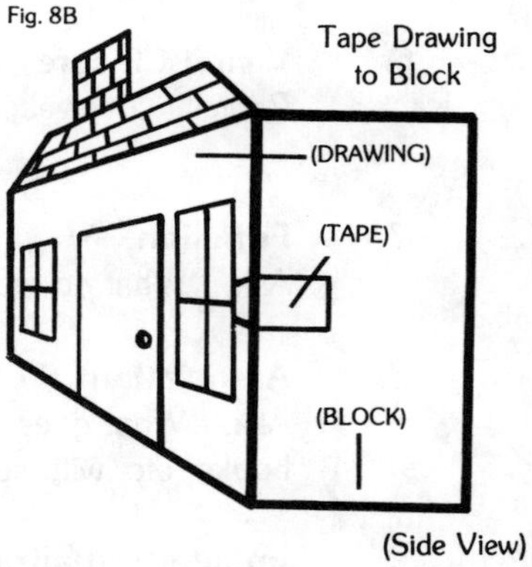

Games

1.   Play school and let the children take turns being the teacher and directing other children in activities.
2.   In block area, build a school and provide toy children and school buses to use in this activity.
3.   Arrange chairs in the form of a bus. Have the children take turns being bus driver and riding the bus to school.

Storytelling

1. On a flannel board with figures of children, teacher, and classroom objects. Make up a story, relating the teacher figure to the children figures. The children will enjoy becoming the teacher and telling a story.

2. Tell the story about Mr. Lincoln living with his teacher because:
   a. there wasn't a school,
   b. he wanted to learn,
   c. the teacher cared about him.

Gross Motor

1. Have the children go through an obstacle course which leads to a school. Have the children sing "Here We Go To School" to the tune of "Here We Go 'Round the Mulberry Bush."

2. Make "blueprints" of school buildings ranging from simple to complex according to children. Laminate the blueprints and collect for use year after year. Have the children use them to build buildings. (See fig. 8C.)

Cognitive

1. Talk about different building materials (wood, bricks, etc.). Use some of each for building towers or buildings.

2. Count the windows in the schoolroom.

3. Make a picture of a school and let the children count the windows in the picture. Each window opens to reveal its number. (See fig. 8D.)

Enrichment

1. Together Activity: Schoolbus - Make a schoolbus. Get a large box. Cut out windows. Have the children paint the box "school-bus" yellow, print SCHOOL BUS on the side by tracing it with black tempera, paint black circles for wheels and use it for dramatic play. (See fig. 8E.)

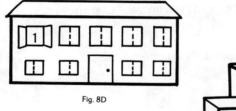

Fig. 8D

Fig. 8E

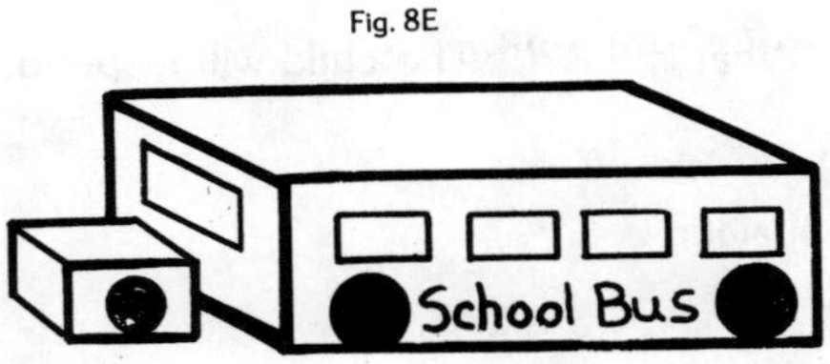

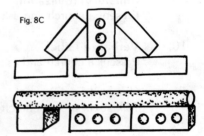

Fig. 8C

2. Add playground equipment to the school building from Art #4 today. Have children cut-out pictures of playground equipment and arrange around the school building.

Field Trip

Visit other schools and see how they are made.

Visitor

Invite a principal or a teacher to come visit and tell about what they do. Other visitors who work in the school such as a lunch room worker or custodian would also be appropriate.

Lesson 2: Church

Unit Group Lesson

(CAUTION: If only pictures are available, use them for number 1 and omit numbers 2 and 3.)

1. **Match Concrete Objects**
   Present two churches. Say, "This is a church." Ask each child in turn to put the church with the church Gradually increase number of irrelevant objects from which (s)he must select church to match.

2. **Discriminate Objects**

   Present several objects. Have each child touch the church in response to the verbal direction, "Touch the church."

3. **Match Pictures**

   Present several pictures of common objects. Have each child match the pictures of the churches.

4. **Discriminate Pictures**

   Present a group of several unrelated pictures of objects. Have each child touch the picture of the church in response to the verbal direction, "Touch the church."

5. **Figure-Ground**

   Present a "busy" picture with many visual distractions. Ask each child to find the church.

6. **Visual Closure**

   Partially cover each of several pictures with paper. Ask each child to find the picture of the church.

7. **Function**

   Ask, "What do we do in a church?"

8. **Association**

   Ask, "What goes with the church?" Use pictures or objects including a pulpit, pews, school, minister, etc. with several unrelated objects or pictures.

9. **Imitate Verbalization**

   Present a church and ask, "What is this? Say, 'Church'." The child will imitate "Church."

10. **Verbalize Label**

    Present a church and ask, "What is this?" The child will respond, "Church."

11. **Concept Enrichment**

    Talk about proper church behavior.

Music

1. Sing to tune of "Are You Sleeping, Brother John":

   Church bells ringing.   *(Children can play small bells.)*
   Church bells ringing.
   Ding, Ding, Dong.
   Ding, Ding, Dong.
   Church bells ringing.
   Church bells ringing.
   Ding, Ding, Dong.
   Ding, Ding, Dong.

2. Go to a church and listen to someone play the church organ.

Art

1. Prepare a figure-ground picture of a church partially hidden by lines. Have the children paste a cut-out of a church on a partially hidden outline of a church and decorate the church. Start with one picture to be matched and increase the number and difficulty as children increase in skill.

2. Have each child put glue on an outline of a church and sprinkle on glitter, sand or grits. Then have each draw flowers, shrubbing, and people around the church.

3. Let the children make a "church" book by pasting pictures of various churches in books and decorating a cover.

Snack

Use church behavior during snack. Depending upon local custom sit quietly and eat quietly or sing church songs during snack.

Fine Motor

1. Make sewing cards of cardboard cut-outs of a church. Punch holes around the edges. Let the children sew the holes with brightly colored yarn.
2. Make church puzzles by cutting churches mounted on cardboard into pieces. Outline the chuch on construction paper and let each child build the puzzle on the outline. Each separate piece can be outlined and/or color-coded if necessary. Make the puzzles in several levels of difficulty.
3. Have each child build a church out of small blocks or out of Lincoln Logs.

Games

1. Have the children walk on a straight or curved road, made with strips of masking tape placed one foot apart, to the "church" at the end of the "road." Tell the children, "Stay on the road, let's go to the church." Demonstrate.
2. Play a pretend game of "What Do You Do - In a Pew?": sing songs, listen to the minister, take up offering, sit quietly, etc. Role play "What you do NOT do in a pew": eat supper, say a rhyme, punch a friend, etc. Build a pretend "pew" by lining up chairs in 2 long rows.

Storytelling

1. Make up a story of a little child who knew how to behave properly in church. Have the children contribute ideas about his behavior.
2. Tell a "Church" story. Each time the word chuch is used the children will clap or raise their hands.
3. Have everyone turn back to back, and clap fingers togethers. Have the children place index fingers straight up and touching, then turn hands over, and wiggle fingers still clasped together while reciting the following: (See fig. 8F.)

> Here is the church
> Here is the steeple
> Open the door
> And see all the people.

Fig. 8F

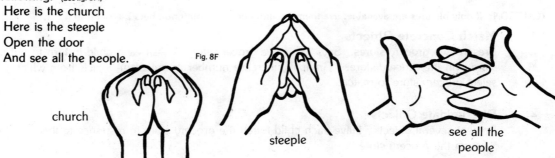

church

steeple

see all the people

Gross Motor

1. Set up a balance beam on the path to the "church." (A picture on the wall.) Have the children walk backwards and forwards, some may be able to hop across to "church." While doing it, encourage them to keep their eyes on the steeple.
2. Have children practice walking quietly "down the aisle" of an imaginary church on tiptoe.
3. Visit a church with many steps at the entrance and have the children walk up and down the steps.

Cognitive

1. Make pairs of churches with differences between pairs and let the children match the identical ones. Make less obvious differences for higher level children.
2. Make construction paper churches in different heights. Have the children sequence the churches from shortest to tallest.

Enrichment

1. Have the children make a church wall mural. Write the word, "churches" on the top of a large piece of newsprint or butcher paper. Place it on the floor and let the children cut pictures of different kinds of churches from magazines and paste them on the paper.

2. Make a tall church using a tall drinking cup box as a spire in a shorter rectangular box. Paint the boxes. Have the children make stained glass windows by gluing bits of shiny colored paper on outlined windows. (See fig. 8G.)

3. Together Picture: Have the children make a giant stained glass window. Provide a shape with black divisions. Use tissue or construction paper scraps to cover the "glass" pieces. (See fig. 8H.)

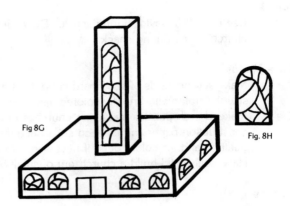

Fig 8G

Fig. 8H

Field Trip
1. Go to one or more churches. Emphasize "quiet" and sitting still in church. Act out these concepts in the real church.
2. Listen to someone play the church organ.

Visitor
Invite a rabbi, a minister, priest or organist to visit the classroom. Have them wear any special clothing that goes with their jobs.

Lesson 3: Grocery Store

Unit Group Lesson

(CAUTION: If only pictures are available, use them for number 1 and omit numbers 2 and 3.)

1. **Match Concrete Objects**
   Present two grocery stores. Say, "This is a grocery store." Ask each child in turn to put the grocery store with the grocery store. Gradually increase number of irrelevant objects from which (s)he must select grocery store to match.

2. **Discriminate Objects**
   Present several objects. Have each child touch the grocery store in response to the verbal direction, "Touch the grocery store."

3. **Match Pictures**
   Present several pictures of common objects. Have each child match the pictures of the grocery stores.

4. **Discriminate Pictures**
   Present a group of several unrelated pictures of objects. Have each child touch the picture of the grocery store in response to the verbal direction, "Touch the grocery store."

5. **Figure-Ground**
   Present a "busy" picture with many visual distractions. Ask each child to find the grocery store.

6. **Visual Closure**
   Partially cover each of several pictures with paper. Ask each child to find the picture of the grocery store.

7. **Function**
   Ask, "What do we do at a grocery store?"

8. **Association**
   Ask, "What goes with the grocery store?" Use pictures or objects including food, grocery cart, cash register, etc. with several unrelated objects or pictures.

9. **Imitate Verbalization**

   Present a grocery store and ask, "What is this? Say, 'Grocery store'." The child will imitate "Grocery store."

10. **Verbalize Label**

    Present a grocery store and ask, "What is this?" The child will respond, "Grocery store."

11. **Concept Enrichment**

    Have children identify food items found in a grocery store. They can discuss the section of a store where the various things would be found: produce, dairy, frozen foods, cleaning products, paper products, etc.

Music

Use the classroom grocery store as in Games for this activity. Give each child two or three common foods (milk, apple, banana, meat, corn). The children may have all the same items. Hold up one item at a time such as meat. Sing to the tune of the Campbell's Soup song "Um Um Good":

Grocery Store	*(Have the child or children*
Grocery Store	*holding the appropriate item*
Put the meat (apple, corn, banana, etc.)	*put it in the grocery store.)*
In the grocery store.	

Art

1. Get some old advertising posters or displays from a grocery store and have the children make additional decorations on them.
2. Let the children decorate grocery bags for use in Gross Motor #2. They can glue paper scraps, mark with magic marker or crayon, or "paint" with paper scraps or tempera. Some children may want to put the "name" of the grocery store on their paper bags.

Snack

Select and buy foods from the classroom or a real grocery store to have for snack.

Fine Motor

1. Make a path tracing of "Take a child to a grocery store" and "Take the cart to the check-out." Begin with a 1½ inch wide horizontal path and then go to narrower paths. Some children may be ready for curved half-inch paths. The paths should lead from left to right. Large crayons, magic markers, pieces of sponge nailed to a thread spool (for child with less finger/hand control), or small metal cars can be used.
2. Have children wrap "meat" in waxed paper or plastic wrap.
3. Prepare a figure-ground picture of a grocery store partially hidden by lines. Have the children paste a grocery store onto the grocery store outline.

Games

Set up a grocery store in the classroom. Find a real grocery cart or use a wagon, stroller or carriage. Give children play money. (It is not necessary for them to know the value of money, just that they use it as exchange for food.) Bring in real cans, boxes, pictures, or real food for the children to "buy." The children take turns playing the cashier, or grocery man/woman. Model (demonstrate) selecting food, putting it in the cart, and paying for it.

Storytelling

1. Read *The Supermarket* by Anne and Harlow Rockwell.
2. Put grocery items in a bag. Start a story called "This morning I went to the grocery store and I bought": (reach in bag and pull out item) "a loaf of bread to make sandwiches"; "a head of lettuce to make a salad"; or "laundry soap to wash the clothes."

Gross Motor

1.   Have the children roll a "grocery cart" through the "store" (chairs arranged in rows), to the check-out stand.

2.   Let the children play "grocery" boy and bag groceries and take them to the "car."

Cognitive

1.   Provide large brown bags full of "groceries" and have the children "sort" the groceries as they take them out of the bags and store on shelves. Parents can provide bags filled with empty boxes and cans with bottoms cut out.

2.   On a flannel board have a lay-out of a store with areas for meat, vegetables, fruit, etc. and cut-outs of various foods. After putting one of each kind of food in the appropriate place in the store, have the children come up and place their fruits, meat, vegetables, etc. in the appropriate place. (Classification activity).

3.   Have children distinguish food items from other concrete objects in the categories of clothing, tools, and animals. Do this only after a thorough explanation and demonstration of food items found in a grocery store and after identifying food items. The children can put the food objects in a box painted to look like a grocery store.

4.   Present a large picture of a grocery store, many magazine pictures, and newspaper ads of items such as furniture, flowers, tools, animals and food. Have the children find the food and paste it on the picture of the grocery store. Say, "Let's put the food on the grocery store." Ask the children to say "Grocery store." Demonstrate the task, assist and praise success.

Enrichment

1.   Have the children select groceries from the store:
        a. to cook for breakfast,
        b. to take on a picnic,
        c. to put in the freezer, and
        d. to chop up for soup.

2.   Put colored dots on cans, boxes, etc., used in the classroom "grocery store." Let children "pay" for items with the same numbers of chips as the dots on their purchase.

3.   Set up a grocery store with aisles in which groceries are sorted according to types, such as produce, dairy, etc. Some children may be able to make signs to identify each area of the store.

Field Trip

1.   Go to a grocery store to buy snacks for the next week. Let each child put an item in the cart and pay the cashier with money you give him. A child may receive change which he returns to you. The activity includes selecting food, pushing cart, paying, and receiving change. Every child should participate in some way. Give praise for participation.

2.   Give each child a picture of a grocery item before going to the store. Help each find the item at the store.

Visitor

Invite a "bag boy" to school. Have him demonstrate what he does.

Lesson 4: Gas Station

Unit Group Lesson

(CAUTION: If only pictures are available, use them for number 1 and omit numbers 2 and 3.)

1.   **Match Concrete Objects**
        Present two gas stations. Say, "This is a gas station." Ask each child in turn to put the gas station with the gas station.   Gradually increase number of irrelevant objects from which (s)he must select gas station to match.

2. **Discriminate Object**
    Present several objects. Have each child touch the gas station in response to the verbal direction, "Touch the gas station."

3. **Match Pictures**
    Present several pictures of common objects. Have each child match the pictures of the gas station.

4. **Discriminate Pictures**
    Present a group of several unrelated pictures of objects. Have each child touch the picture of the gas station in response to the verbal direction, "Touch the gas station."

5. **Figure-Ground**
    Present a "busy" picture with many visual distractions. Ask each child to find the gas station.

6. **Visual Closure**
    Partially cover each of several pictures with paper. Ask each child to find the picture of the gas station.

7. **Function**
    Ask, "What do we do at a gas station?"

8. **Association**
    Ask, "What goes with the gas station?" Use pictures or objects including gas hose, car, tow truck, gas pump, etc., with several unrelated objects or pictures.

9. **Imitate Verbalization**
    Present a gas station and ask, "What is this? Say, 'Gas station'." The child will imitate "Gas station."

10. **Verbalize Label**
    Present a gas station and ask, "What is this?" The child will respond, "Gas station."

11. **Concept Enrichment**
    Discuss the functions of a gas station such as providing gas to make cars go, putting oil in cars, repairing cars, etc.

Music

Sing to the tune of "Here We Go 'Round the Mulberry Bush":
  This is the way we pump the gas,   *(Model actions with a*
  Pump the gas,   *toy car and black hose.)*
  Pump the gas.
  This is the way we pump the gas
  Right into your car.

Art
1. Have the children paint a large box to use as a gas pump.
2. Have the children paste pictures of cars beside gas pumps on pictures of service stations. Then the children can decorate their gas stations.
3. Make a gas station by painting a large cardboard box. Put a roof on it, then paste on windows and doors. Make outlines of cars and trucks on each side. Give the children cut-outs to match outlines. (Some children can cut their own.) Have the children match and glue the cut-outs to the outlines on the box.

Snack

Have milk for snack so that the cartons can be used for garages for small cars.

Fine Motor

1. Make a sewing card with many cars around a gas pump. Make a yarn gas hose, attach one end to the pump and punch holes in each car. Have the children pump gas by putting gas hose in each car's tank. (See fig. 8I.)

2. Help children use well-rinsed milk cartons as blocks to build a gas station. Put yarn on the sides of smaller cartons for gas pumps. (See fig. 8J.)

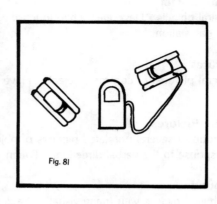

Fig. 8I

Fig. 8J

Games

In the block area set up a service station. Let the children pretend to drive cars to the station. They say, "I want gas," "Fill it up," "Regular, please." Each child plays station attendent, puts gas in car and receives money. Demonstrate by driving the first "car."

Storytelling

Make up a story about a car that ran out of gas. Let the children think up all kinds of things to do to get the gas in the car such as telephoning the garage, getting a wrecker to tow the car, pushing the car off the road, walking to get gas in a gas can, and having the garage man come in his "pick-up truck."

Gross Motor

1. Let the children wash the teacher's car.
2. Let the children wash the school riding toys.
3. Outside - draw a large straight or curved road in dirt and designate a place for a service station (with box, blocks, tire, etc.). Have the children drive tricycles on the road, stop for gas, a car wash, a tire check, or other automotive work. Use the gas pump made in Art #1.
4. Have on hand a tire for the children to roll, "repair", and jump on.

Cognitive

1. Put the teacher's car on a lift (at a real gas station) and have the children look under it. Look under the hood. Look at "Where the gas goes into the car," "Where the oil goes into the car" etc.
2. Show the children a picture of a gas station and let them choose, from various pictures of related and unrelated objects, the objects related to a gas station (gas pump, car, gas hose), and paste them on the picture of the station. Model the task with one picture.

Enrichment

1. Make garages out of milk cartons covered with construction paper. Put a numeral on each one. Put a numeral on each car. Have the children drive the correct car into the correct garage.
2. Together Activity: Place dots (in the form of a gas station) on a large sheet of paper. Have the children connect the dots with a yardstick and crayons. Have some hold the stick and some mark. When the lines are connected they have made a gas station. Have some children add large squares and others divide them into 8 sections to look like garage doors. Add doors, wadded green tissues for shrubbery and tall milk cartons for gas pumps.

Field Trip

This field trip may be most beneficial as the first activity of the day. Go to a service station to get gas in car, have oil checked, windows washed, etc. This trip will strengthen concept if it precedes the group lesson.

Visitor

Invite an auto mechanic to the classroom with his tools.

Unit Group Lesson

(CAUTION: If only pictures are available, use them for number 1 and omit numbers 2 and 3.)

1. **Match Concrete Objects**
   Present two houses. Say, "This is a house." Ask each child in turn to put the house with the house. Gradually increase number of irrelevant objects from which (s)he must select house to match.

2. **Discriminate Objects**
   Present several objects. Have each child touch the house in response to the verbal direction, "Touch the house."

3. **Match Pictures**
   Present several pictures of common objects. Have each child match the pictures of the house.

4. **Discriminate Pictures**
   Present a group of several unrelated pictures of objects. Have each child touch the picture of the house in response to the verbal direction, "Touch the house."

5. **Figure-Ground**
   Present a "busy" picture with many visual distractions. Ask each child to find the house.

6. **Visual Closure**
   Partially cover each of several pictures with paper. Ask each child to find the picture of the house.

7. **Function**
   Ask, "What do we do in a house?"

8. **Association**
   Ask, "What goes with the house?" Use pictures or objects including lawn, chimney, roof, etc., with several unrelated objects or pictures.

9. **Imitate Verbalization**
   Present a house and ask, "What is this? Say, 'House'." The child will imitate "House."

10. **Verbalize Label**
    Present a house and ask, "What is this?" The child will respond, "House."

11. **Concept Enrichment**
    Discuss different types of houses such as mobile homes, apartments, houseboats, one-story, two-story, etc. Discuss materials used to make houses.

Music

1. Sing to the tune of "Here We Go 'Round The Mulberry Bush":

I give my friend a little house	*While everyone sings, one child walks around*
Little house	*the group holding a small toy model of a*
Little house	*house. He picks a "friend" and gives him the*
I give my friend a little house	*house. That child then takes a turn.*
Little house.	

2. Have the children bring in snapshots of their homes. Make a bulletin board displaying them with the child's name underneath. At music time, have the children sit in a group near the bulletin board. Sing to the tune of "Oh, Tannenbaum" ("Oh, Christmas Tree") all sing and clap:

Go find your house	*(Clap)*
Go find your house	*(The child goes to bulletin board and touches*
Oh, Tommy,	*his own house.)*
Go find your house.	

Art
1. Make an outline of a house and cut additional houses into two or more pieces. Have the children paste the cut-out houses on the outline.
2. Have children build houses from scraps of wood and glue them together.
3. Write each child's name (and address) on a cut-out house. Have the child color the house the colors of his/her own house.
4. Flatten out light-weight cardboard boxes. Have the children make a room by making windows and picture shapes on the walls and rug shapes for the floor. Tape up the sides, add doll furnture and figures for creative play. (See fig. 8K.)

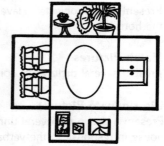

Fig. 8K

Snack
1. Have each child bring a snack from home.
2. Eat snack in the "house" area of the room.

Fine Motor
1. Model building a house with small blocks, then have the children build the same house. (See fig. 8L.)

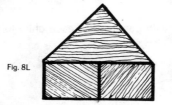

Fig. 8L

3 blocks or more

2. Have the children paste beans one at a time within outline of house. Use different colored beans for different parts of the house.
3. Have the children make a house booklet from folded paper which is cut to give a "roof" effect. Let them draw a front to look like a house and draw or glue pictures inside for different rooms. (See fig. 8M.)

Fig. 8M

4. Let the children make log homes with Lincoln Logs.
5. Let the children use strips of brown paper to build a log house on paper. Use short strips and long strips. Older children can draw in background of trees. (See fig. 8N.)

Fig. 8N

Games

1. Encourage the children to play house in the housekeeping area and role play family members.
2. Outside: form circle, join hands, and have each child take turns going in and out of circle through joined arms.

   Sing: Go in and out the window
   Go in and out the window
   Go in and out the window
   As we have done before.
3. Provide a doll house and furnishings for free play.

Storytelling

1. Fingerplay: Here is a nest for the robin.   *(Cup hands.)*
   Here is a hive for the bee.   *(Make fists.)*
   Here is a hole for the bunny.   *(Thumb and fingers make "hole.")*
   And here is a house for ME!   *(Fingers touching.)*
2. Read the story "The Three Little Pigs" to the children. Ask them what kinds of materials the pigs used to build their houses. Then have the children say the lines of the story that were repeated by the pigs and the wolf. Let the children take turns acting out the story of "The Three Little Pigs."
3. Tell a story about the kind of house Mr. Lincoln lived in as a boy. (A log cabin.)
4. Tell a story, with pictures, of the kinds of houses animals live in: nests, caves, underground tunnels, beaver dams, etc.

Gross Motor

1. Have the children rearrange the furniture in the housekeeping corner.
2. Have the children sweep the house.
3. Have the children vacuum the house.
4. Let the children build houses with large blocks.

Cognitive

1. Present houses with parts missing and have the children identify the missing parts.
2. Have the children match pairs of different types of houses with each other.
3. Draw different numbers of cabins on long sheets of paper and provide a place at the end of the row for a numeral. Count the cabins. Draw on long sheet, fill in correct number or find out of 3 numbers the correct one. (Increase numbers for children with greater skills.) (See fig. 80.)

Fig. 80

Enrichment

1. Make a "house" out of a box large enough for one or two children.
2. Help the children make shoe box houses. Have each child bring a shoe box and paint it a house color. Give the children rectangles of paper on which squares and rectangles have been dotted and have them path trace the lines and glue these onto their shoe boxes for windows. Help each child make a door. Make a roof design on construction paper and have the children add shingle marks and glue the roof onto the house. Provide a house sign with each child's name and address. The houses can be used as part of a miniature town and the children can drive cars to "John's house," etc.

3.   Together Activity: Make two large house shapes. Make brick shapes on one and wood siding stripes on the other. Make dotted roof patterns. Have some children cut brick shapes from red, pink, or brown construction paper and others cut siding strips from white construction paper. Have the children glue them on to the appropriate house. Other children can follow the dots for the roof shingles. Others can add shurbs, flowers or whatever is seasonal.

Field Trip
1.   Take trips to take a picture of each child in front of his home. Make an album at school of these pictures.
2.   Take a walk to look at nearby houses.
3.   Visit an apartment complex and play on the playground.

Related Children's Records
"Ken Kelly the Kindergarten Teacher" from **BEGINNING SOUNDS & CAREERS** (UBB)
"Mr. Gilly the Grocer" from **BEGINNING SOUNDS & CAREERS** (UBB)

Related Children's Books
Breinburg, Petronella. **SHAWN GOES TO SCHOOL.** New York: Thomas Y. Crowell, 1973.
Burton, Virginia Lee. **THE LITTLE HOUSE.** Boston: Houghton-Mifflin Co., 1942.
Keats, Ezra Jack. **APT. 3.** New York: Macmillan Publishing Co., 1971.
Rockwell, Anne and Rockwell, Harlow. **THE SUPERMARKET.** New York: Macmillan Publishing Co., 1979.
Spier, Peter. **VILLAGE BOOK LIBRARY.** Garden City, N.J..: Doubleday & Co., 1981.

Related Parenting Materials
Cansler, Dot. **THE HOMESTRETCH.** Winston-Salem, NC 27113-5128: Kaplan Press, 1983.

Related Materials
TEACHING PICTURES. Winston-Salem, NC 27113-5128: Kaplan Press, 1983.
STORY SEQUENCE CARDS I, II. Winston-Salem, NC 27113-5128: Kaplan Press, 1983.
SEWING CARDS I, II, III. Winston-Salem, NC 27113-5128: Kaplan Press, 1983.

Unit 9: Musical Instruments

A developmental assessment should determine the functional levels of each child. Individual expectations are based on the assessment results.

Lesson 1: Drum

Unit Group Lesson

1. **Match Concrete Objects**
   Present two drums. Say, "This is a drum." Ask each child in turn to put the drum with the drum. Gradually increase number of irrelevant objects from which (s)he must select drum to match.

2. **Discriminate Objects**
   Present several objects. Have each child touch the drum in response to verbal direction, "Touch the drum."

3. **Match Pictures**
   Present several pictures of common objects. Have each child match the pictures of the drums.

4. **Discriminate Pictures**
   Present a group of several unrelated pictures of objects. Have each child touch the picture of the drum in response to verbal direction, "Touch the drum."

5. **Figure-Ground**
   Present a "busy" picture with many visual distractions. Ask each child to find the drum.

6. **Visual Closure**
   Partially cover each of several pictures with paper. Ask each child to find the picture of the drum.

7. **Function**
   Ask, "What do we do with a drum?"

8. **Association**
   Ask, "What goes with the drum?" Use pictures or objects including drumsticks, tambourine, horn, etc., with several unrelated objects or pictures.

9. **Imitate Verbalization**
   Present a drum and ask, "What is this? Say, 'Drum'." The child will imitate "Drum."

10. **Verbalize Label**
    Present a drum and ask, "What is this?" The child will respond, "Drum."

11. **Concept Enrichment**

Say "A drum is a pounding instrument." Ask the children to name some other pounding instruments such as cymbals, castinets.

NOTE: Spools on the end of pencils make nice drumsticks.

Music

1. Auditory Discrimination of sound of drum: Behind a screen, play various instruments one at a time. Have each child tell which is the drum in response to the question, "Is this a drum?" Begin with only two or three instruments, the non-drum sounds should be very different from the drum sound.

2. Have a rhythm activity. Have the children play drums to a marching record. Model rhythm and have children imitate. After practice allow children to march and play.

3. Play the beat of each child's name. "Ma-ry," "Jon-a-than." Give a beat for each syllable in child's name.

Art

1. Have the children make drums from oatmeal boxes and coffee cans with masking tape and paint. Make drumsticks from dowels with tape or a wooden knob on the end. Let the children paint the drums and drumsticks or glue on decorations.

2. Make a picture of a drum. Have each child decorate his drum with sequins and glitter.

Snack

Tap out rhythms for chewing while children eat snack.

Fine Motor

1. Have the children make drums out of clay.

2. Make drum lacing cards. Punch holes around the outline of a drum. Vary size and number of holes depending upon ability level of children. Use shoe strings or dip ends of string in Elmer's glue and let dry.

3. Have the children do a path tracing of "Take the drumsticks to the drum." and "Take the drum to the child." Some children should use magic markers, large crayons, or large paint brushes before using pencils for path tracing activities.

Games

1. Hide a drum in the room or in the playground and have the children find it.

2. Play "Who's Playing the Drum": Have three children sit with their backs to group. Two of them pretend to play the drum, one actually plays. Let the other children guess who is really playing.

3. Use identical glasses (bottles) with different amounts of water (colored if desired) in each one of the glasses. Let the children tap the glasses on the rim softly and listen to the sounds. Play a tune by tapping the rims. (See fig. 9A.)

Fig. 9A

Storytelling

1. Make up a story of a boy who loses his drum and looks in many places. He finally finds it in an unexpected place.

2. Read *The Boy With a Drum.*

3. Have a rhythm story of "I've Got A Rhythm."

Listen to my rhythm.
I've got a rhythm.
Can you do it, too?
This is my rhythm.
Listen.
Can you do it, too!"

(Have each child tell the story and make up his own rhythm. Have the children imitate his rhythm.)

(Child plays rhythm)
(Others imitate.)

Gross Motor

1. Play Musical Chairs by having the teacher or a child beat the drum as children march around the chairs. When drum beat stops all must find a chair. This can be played with as many chairs as children.
2. Play Follow The Leader by letting the leader play drum while marching, walking, jumping, or doing any body movement and have the other children imitate.

Cognitive

1. Have the children select drums from a group of instruments.
2. Have the children sort pounding and non-pounding instruments.
3. Make pairs of construction paper drums with shapes on them. Have the children match the shapes.

Enrichment

1. Have the children complete a picture of the drum and the word "Drum." (See fig. 9B.)
2. Count out beats on drum. 1, 2, 3, 4, 5, 6, 7, 8, 9, 10. Feel the rhythm (beat) of one's own pulse (in neck, wrist, etc.). Imitate on a drum.

Field Trip

Examine drums in a music store with the class.

Fig. 9B

Lesson 2: Horn

Unit Group Lesson

1. **Match Concrete Objects**
   Present several pictures of common objects. Have each child match the pictures of the horns. Gradually increase number of irrelevant objects from which (s)he must select horn to match.

2. **Discriminate Objects**
   Present several objects. Have each child touch the horn in response to verbal direction, "Touch the horn."

3. **Match Pictures**
   When shown several pictures of common objects, have each child match the pictures of the horns.

4. **Discriminate Pictures**
   Present a group of several unrelated pictures of objects. Have each child touch the picture of the horn in response to verbal direction, "Touch the horn."

5. **Figure-Ground**
   Present a "busy" picture with many visual distractions. Ask each child to find the horn.

6. **Visual Closure**
   Partially cover each of several pictures with paper. Ask each child to find the picture of the horn.

7. **Function**
   Ask, "What do we do with a horn?"

8. **Association**
   Ask, "What goes with the horn?" Use pictures or objects including drum, tambourine, clarinet, flute, etc., with several unrelated objects or pictures.

9. **Imitate Verbalization**

Present a horn and ask, "What is this? Say, 'Horn'." The child will imitate "Horn."

10. **Verbalize Label**

Present a horn and ask, "What is this?" The child will respond, "Horn."

11. **Concept Enrichment**

Tell the children that a horn is a blowing instrument. Ask the children to name some other blowing instruments such as kazoo, recorder, etc.

Music

1. Auditory Discrimination of sound of horn: Behind a screen play various instruments one at a time. Have each child tell which is the horn. Use drum and horn for less advanced children and more instruments for more advanced children.
2. Review name and function of drum, model use of horn and have the children play the drum and the horn while marching.
3. Play a cassette tape on which you have recorded sounds of the drum and the horn and one or two non-musical sounds. Place the drum and horn in the middle of the table. When the sound of the drum or horn is heard, ask the children to touch the drum or horn.

Art

1. Help the children make a toilet tube kazoo with waxed paper. Have the children decorate the tube with small pieces of paper and hum in the open end. (See fig. 9C.)
2. Have the children drip watery paint on paper and blow on it with straws to make interesting designs.
3. Have children paint with gold or silver paint at the easel today.

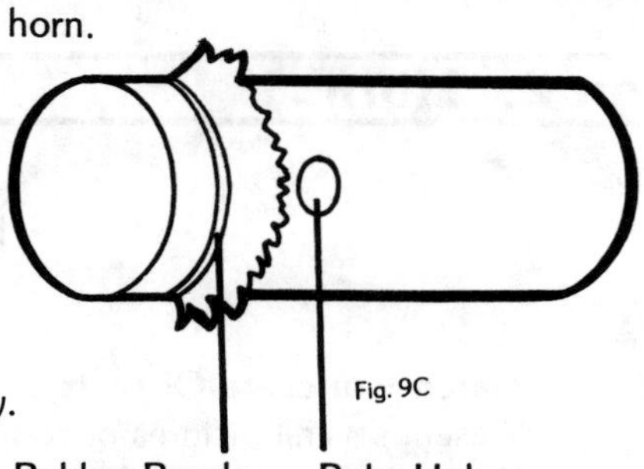

Fig. 9C

Rubber Band   Poke Hole

Snack

Call everyone to snack by blowing a horn.

Fine Motor

1. Make puzzles by pasting simple pictures of a horns on cardboard and cutting them into pieces. Sequence the difficulty by cutting puzzles into two, three, four, and five pieces. One child may work a puzzle of two pieces while another may have one of five pieces.
2. Practice manipulating the valves of a real trumpet.
3. Paste pieces of paper horn together over an outline of a horn. Pieces can be of various colors and choosen by children. Model the task by actually pasting a horn together as the children observe.
4. Create a Figure Ground activity and let the children find the hidden shapes of horns and paste on cut-outs of horns. Vary the confusion of the picture and the number of horns with the ability of the child. (See fig. 9D.)

Fig. 9D

Games

Play find the horns. Paste many pictures of horns around the room, some in obvious places, some not so obvious. Have all children look for horns and collect the pictures they find or call out when they find a picture.

Storytelling

1. Use puppets to tell a story of a child (animal, etc.) who could not play a horn. His friends taught him how.
2. Tell and act out this story with children.

   If I had a horn (drum, etc.) horn, horn
   If I had a horn, Oh how I would play.
   Toot dee and toot day
   1-2-3-4 hours a day
   If I had a horn (to play).

Gross Motor

Play "Follow the Leader." Give each child a horn. Let the children take turns outside being "leader" for a parade. All play horns and march imitating the leader. Give each child an opportunity to be a leader.

Cognitive

1. Present two, three or four different musical instruments. Have the children close their eyes. Hide one instrument and have the children tell which one is missing.
2. Use long and short paper-tube kazoos to let the children identify which is long and which is short.
3. Make horns of different colors of construction paper. Have the children match the horns by color.

Enrichment

1. Play horns and drums together.
2. Discuss the fact that horns that are made of brass and that there are a number of brass instruments such as the trumpet, coronet, french horn, tuba, and trombone.

Lesson 3: Tambourine

Unit Group Lesson

1. **Match Concrete Objects**
Present two tambourines. Say, "This is a tambourine." Ask each child in turn to put the tambourine with the tambourine. Gradually increase number of irrelevant objects from which (s)he must select tambourine to match.

2. **Discriminate Objects**
Present several objects. Have each child touch the tambourine in response to verbal direction, "Touch the tambourine."

3. **Match Pictures**
Present several pictures of common objects. Have each child match the pictures of the tambourines. tambourines.

4. **Discriminate Pictures**
Present a group of several unrelated pictures of objects. Have each child touch the picture of the tambourine in response to verbal direction, "Touch the tambourine."

5. **Figure-Ground**
Present a "busy" picture with many visual distractions. Ask each child to find the tambourine.

6. **Visual Closure**
Partially cover each of several pictures with paper. Ask each child to find the picture of the tambourine.

7. **Function**
Ask, "What do we do with a tambourine?"

8. **Association**
Ask, "What goes with the tambourine?" Use pictures or objects including bells, cymbal, etc., with several unrelated objects or pictures.

9. **Imitate Verbalization**

Present a tambourine and ask, "What is this? Say, 'Tambourine'." The child will imitate "Tambourine."

10. **Verbalize Label**

Present a tambourine and ask, "What is this?" The child will respond, "Tambourine."

11. **Concept Enrichment**

Tell the children that a tambourine is a shaking instrument. Talk about other instruments that are shaken such as maracas, bells, etc.

Music

1. Review names and use of drum and horn and add the tambourine to the group of instruments. Have a few children model use of each. Have a parade with each child choosing his instrument. March and play with or without an accompanying record.
2. Tap out a rhythm and asks the children to imitate. Let children take turns tapping out a rhythm.
3. Auditory Discrimination of sound of tambourine: Behind a screen play various instruments one at a time. Have each child tell which is the tambourine in response to the question, "Is this a tambourine?"

Art

Make tambourines by using aluminum pie plates, bottle tops and string. Punch holes around the rims of the pie plates and through the bottle tops. Let the children loop a short piece of string through the hole in pie plate and through bottle tops and tie. The more bottle tops at each hole the better the tambourine. Decorate the plates with streamers.

NOTE: If aluminum pie plates are unavilable, strong paper plates may be used. (See fig. 9E.)

Fig. 9E

Pie Plate — String — Bottle Cap

Snack

Serve snack on "tambourine" trays (the tambourines made in Art).

Fine Motor

1. Ask children to paste cut-outs of tambourines on pieces of construction paper on which there have been drawn outlines of tambourines. Use two or three sizes as a size discrimination task.
2. Prepare a Shape Discrimination Activity. Have children paste cut-outs of drum, horn, and tambourine on construction paper on which the three outlines have been drawn. Strengthen the follow-up on drum and horn by having children re-name and pantomime the playing of each instrument.

Games

1. Give out cards with pictures of drums, horns, and tambourines. Give five to each child. Shuffle and deal so that each child has a varying number of instruments. Call out a name of an instrument ("drum") and ask children with pictures of drums to throw one in a pile in the center of the table. Keep calling names of all three instruments until one child throws in all his cards and becomes the "winner." Continue until all children become winners. (This game works better with a small group of three to five children.)
2. Make a Feely Box. Place one of the three instrument studied (horn, drum, tambourine) in a box with a hole in one side large enough for the child's hand. Have each child reach in, feel the instrument, and name it. If he can not, show and name the instrument, put it back in the box, let him feel it again and give him another opportunity to name it.

Storytelling

Make up a story about a monkey who played a tambourine in many different places such as in a tree, in school, at the grocery store, in church. Let the children name places and decide the reaction of others to the monkey's playing.

Gross Motor
Have a relay race passing the tambourine. Child runs, plays the tambourine and carries it to a designated area. Child must say "tambourine" before he passes it on to next child. Divide the children into teams. Have a child from each team run carrying a tambourine to a designated spot, shout TAMBOURINE and run back playing it. Each child passes the tambourine to another child on his team. Let the "race" continue until all children have had at least one turn.

Cognitive
1. Place the drum, tambourine, and horn on a table with other objects (shoes, fruit, clothing, cars, etc.). Ask the children to find the "things that are musical instruments."
2. Make pairs of shakers out of film cans with different things inside rice, sand, salt or small beans, etc. Have the children find the matching sounds. (Good for Aditory Discrimination, especially for visually impaired children.)
3. Play a tape on which you have recorded the sounds of the drum, the horn, and the tambourine. Place all three instruments on the table, and have the children identify by touching or naming (or both) the instrument they hear.

Enrichment
Glue 2 paper plates together with (pinto) beans inside. Decorate.
Put crepe paper streamers around.
Shake to rhythm music. Keep beat of music. (See fig. 9F.)

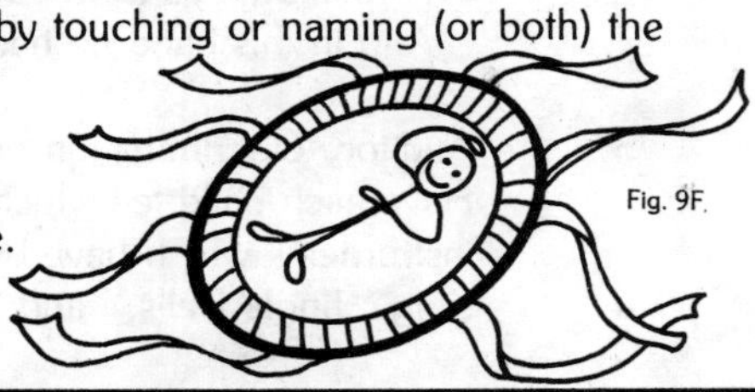

Fig. 9F.

Lesson 4: Bells

Unit Group Lesson

1. **Match Concrete Objects**
   Present two bells. Say, "This is a bell." Ask each child in turn to put the bell with the bell. Gradually increase number of irrelevant objects from which (s)he must select bell to match.

2. **Discriminate Objects**
   Present several objects. Have each child touch the bell in response to verbal direction, "Touch the bell."

3. **Match Pictures**
   Present several pictures of common objects. Have each child match the pictures of the bells.

4. **Discriminate Pictures**
   Present a group of several unrelated pictures of objects. Have each child touch the picture of the bell in response to verbal direction, "Touch the bell."

5. **Figure-Ground**
   Present a "busy" picture with many visual distractions. Ask each child to find the bell.

6. **Visual Closure**
   Partially cover each of several pictures with paper. Ask each child to find the picture of the bell.

7. **Function**
   Ask, "What do we do with a bell?"

8. **Association**
   Ask, "What goes with the bell?" Use pictures or objects including clapper, tambourine, drum, etc., with several unrelated objects or pictures.

9. **Imitate Verbalization**

    Present a bell and ask, "What is this? Say, 'Bell'." The child will imitate "Bell."

10. **Verbalize Label**

    Present a bell and ask, "What is this?" The child will respond, "Bell."

11. **Concept Enrichment**

    Tell the children that bells are shaking instruments like the tambourine and maracas.

Music

1. Review the names and how to play the other three instruments (drum, horn, tambourine). Add bells and form a rhythm band.
2. With instruments from above sing "Old MacDonald Had a Band":
    And in this band he had some bells   *(A drum, a horn, etc.)*
                                               (Point to child who has that instrument to play it.)
3. Auditory Discrimination of sound of bells. Behind a screen, play various instruments one at a time. Have each child tell which is the bell in response to the question, "Is this a bell?" Include all instruments which have been taught in the unit.
4. Sing "Jingle Bells," and let the children shake bells during the song.

Art

1. Let the children paste cut-outs of drum, horn, tambourine, and bells onto pre-outlined shapes on a sheet of paper. Have each child name the shapes. Let the children decorate the paper.
2. Help the children make Nail Bells - use many nails, (big, medium, small, fat, thin). Tie the heads of the nails with two inch string and tie the other end around a stick suspended from strings. Strike the various sized nails with a very large nail or screw to hear "bell" tones. Use at least five or six nails per child's stick. This may be dangerous for some children. SUPERVISE CAREFULLY. Let children paint the sticks with water color paints. (See fig. 9G.)

Fig 9G

Snack

Ring bells to indicate that it is time for snack.

Fine Motor

1. Have children follow outlined picture of a bell with glue and sprinkle glitter, sand, salt or grits onto the glue. Prepare cut-out clappers, and let the children glue them in correct spots. The more skilled children can cut their own clappers. (See fig. 9H.)
2. Let the children ring bells of different sizes. Jingle bells will not ring unless held by the tiny handle which makes this a good exercise for practicing the pincer grasp.   (See fig. 9I.)

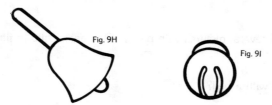

Fig. 9H   Fig. 9I

Games

Name a child "it" for first turn. Tell him to close his eyes and ask another child to play bells in some area of the room. Have "him" point to the area in which he hears the bells. Let those two children choose two others to take their places.

Storytelling

Have the children tell an Experience Story about making nail bells in Art #2 today. Have the children tell what they did first, next, and so on in making the nail bells. Write it down in story form as the children tell it and read it back to the children. Follow reading with questions: "Now what did we do first?" "Then what did we do?"

NOTE: For non-verbal children who are able to express ideas through gestures, this will also be appropriate.

Gross Motor

1. Hang a bell from a tree limb or doorway just above the children's heads. Have the children jump up to ring the bell.
2. Have a bell relay: Use tap bells and place one on each of two chairs. Have the children run, ring the bell and run back to the end of the line. Vary the activity by having more than two chairs with numbers placed on the backs. Then the children must ring the bells in sequence. (See fig. 9J.)

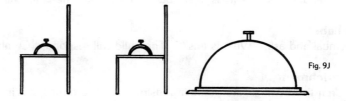

Fig. 9J

Cognitive

1. Have different sized bells. Let children sequence from biggest to smallest and listen to differences in the sounds of the bells.
2. Put numerals on some bells and have the children ring each bell the correct number of rings.

Enrichment

Visit places or tell stories about the use of different kinds of bells such as: door bell, alarm bell, fire bell, bicycle bell, school bell, cow bell and jingle bell.

Field Trip

Make arrangements with a local church to ring the church bell.

Lesson 5: Cymbal

Unit Group Lesson

1. **Match Concrete Objects**
   Present two cymbals. Say, "This is a cymbal." Ask each child in turn to put the cymbal with the cymbal. Gradually increase number of irrelevant objects from which (s)he must select cymbal to match.

2. **Discriminate Objects**
   Present several objects. Have each child touch the cymbal in response to verbal direction, "Touch the cymbal."

3. **Match Pictures**
   Present several pictures of common objects. Have each child match the pictures of the cymbals.

4. **Discriminate Pictures**
   Present a group of several unrelated pictures of objects. Have each child touch the picture of the cymbal in response to verbal direction, "Touch the cymbal."

5. **Figure-Ground**
Present a "busy" picture with many visual distractions. Ask each child to find the cymbal.

6. **Visual Closure**
Partially cover each of several pictures with paper. Ask each child to find the picture of the cymbal.

7. **Function**
Ask, "What do we do with a cymbal?"

8. **Association**
Ask, "What goes with the cymbal?" Use pictures or objects including drum, tambourine, horn, bells, etc., with several unrelated objects or pictures.

9. **Imitate Verbalization**
Present a cymbal and ask, "What is this? Say, 'Cymbal'." The child will imitate "Cymbal."

10. **Verbalize Label**
Present a cymbal and ask, "What is this?" The child will respond, "Cymbal."

11. **Concept Enrichment**
Tell the children that cymbals are pounding instruments like drums, castinets, etc.

Music
1. Auditory Discrimination of sounds of the cymbal: Repeat this activity (see Lesson #4, Music #3) with each of the instruments studied in this unit.
2. Review, name and use each instrument studied in this unit, add cymbals and have a rhythm band. If there are not enough cymbals to go around, use pot lids or something similar.
3. Give a concert: Have the children arrange the chairs in a semi-circle which you have marked on the floor. Use tape crosses or short strips of tape to indicate chair arrangement. Have a music stand, platform and baton for the conductor (you or a child). Have children choose and play instruments under the direction of the conductor.

Art
1. Make cymbals from aluminum pie plates. Attach a piece of elastic to the center for fingers to hold. Decorate the pie plate with pictures.
2. Make finger cymbals with bottle caps and elastic for fingers. Glue elastic to the bottle caps. (See fig. 9M.)
3. Discrimination Activity. Have the children paste cut-outs of all five instruments on pre-outlined shapes on sheet of paper. Let them decorate the sheet with magic markers.

Snack
1. "Glue" a gumdrop handle on a wafer cookie with frosting. Eat the "cymbal." (See fig. 9K.)
2. Call the children to snack with a cymbal.

Fine Motor
1. Make cardboard or pieplate cymbals: Use small corks as handles. Attach to cardboard with glue (dry overnight) or attach to aluminum pie plates with thumbtacks. Ask the children to "play" the cymbals in time to music. March in place with cymbals. Play "Follow the Leader" to the side, over head, behind legs, around a friend, etc. with cymbals. (See fig. 9L.)
2. Let children play finger cymbals made in Art #2.

Fig 9M

Fig. 9K

Fig. 9L

Games

Play a rhythm game: Have one child clang the cymbals at different paces (slow, faster, very fast) and have the other children move to the beat by walking, sliding, running, jumping, etc. Give each child a turn at being leader. You should model responses to the beat.

Storytelling

Tell this flannel board story about the "Cymbal Family."

The cymbal family was traveling along whey they met a drum (children name drum when you show cut-out). "What do you do?", they asked the drum. Children say, "I say, 'boom, boom." "Maybe we could play together," said the cymbals. "Clang, Clang." (You and children pantomime playing cymbals and say "clang, clang").

Repeat the story and add the horn, tambourine, and bells. At end, all play together and are happy. Hold up each cut-out, pantomime playing and saying the different sounds one after the other.

Gross Motor

1. Have the children play cymbals and march in time to music.
2. Have the class march in time to music. At a given signal, stop and count the beat of the music with the cymbals 1-2-3-4, then continue to march.

Cognitive

1. Prepare a Size Discrimination: Have children match and paste different sizes of round cut-outs (cymbals) on pre-outlined sheets of paper. Match to appropriate size.
2. Make paper cymbals in different sizes and colors. Have the children sort first by color then by size.

Enrichment

Listen to classical music which has cymbals playing frequently. Have the children hold up their hands, play the cymbal, or stand up when the cymbal sounds.

Field Trip

Visit a school band practice and let the children point out the instruments they have studied. Arrange to let them touch or hold some of the instruments in the band.

Related Children's Records

"Join In the Game" from **FOLK SONG CARNIVAL** (EA)
"Let's Hide the Tambourine" from **LEARNING BASIC SKILLS II** (EA)
"Beat the Drum for George Washington" from **HOLIDAY** (EA)
"Rhythm No. 2 With Drum" from **ADVENTURES IN RHYTHM** (SCHOL)
"Rhythm No. 3 With Drum" from **ADVENTURES IN RHYTHM** (SCHOL)
"Kaluba, Beat the Drum" from **I KNOW THE COLORS IN THE RAINBOW** by Ella Jenkins (EA)

Related Children's Books

Isadora, Rachel. **BEN'S TRUMPET.** New York: Greenwillow Books, 1979.
Keats, Ezra Jack. **APT. 3.** New York: Macmillan Publishing Co., 1971.
Kredenser, Gail. **ONE DANCING DRUM.** New York: S.G. Philips, 1971.
Lionni, Leo. **GERALDINE, THE MUSIC MOUSE.** New York: Pantheon Books, 1979.
McClosky, Robert. **LENTIL.** New York: Viking Puffin Books, 1978.
Stecher, Miriam and Kandell, Alice. **MAX, THE MUSIC MAKER.** New York: Lathrop, Lee & Shepard Co., 1980.

Related Parenting Materials

Cansler, Dot. **THE HOMESTRETCH.** Winston-Salem, NC 27113-5128: Kaplan Press, 1983.

Related Materials

TEACHING PICTURES. Winston-Salem, NC 27113-5128: Kaplan Press, 1983.
STORY SEQUENCE CARDS I, II. Winston-Salem, NC 27113-5128: Kaplan Press, 1983.
SEWING CARDS I, II, III. Winston-Salem, NC 27113-5128: Kaplan Press, 1983.

Unit 10: Toys

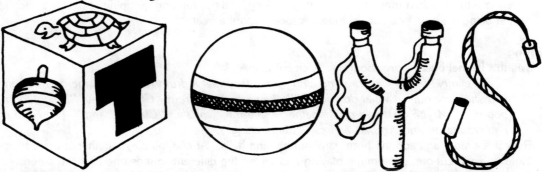

A developmental assessment should determine the functional levels of each child. Individual expectations are based on the assessment results.

Lesson 1: Ball

Unit Group Lesson

1. **Match Concrete Objects**
   Present two balls. Say, "This is a ball." Ask each child in turn to put the ball with the ball. Gradually increase number of irrelevant objects from which (s)he must select ball to match.

2. **Discriminate Objects**
   Present several objects. Have each child touch the ball in response to the verbal direction, "Touch the ball."

3. **Match Pictures**
   Present several pictures of common objects. Have each child match the pictures of the balls.

4. **Discriminate Pictures**
   Present a group of several unrelated pictures of objects. Have each child touch the picture of the ball in response to the verbal direction, "Touch the ball."

5. **Figure-Ground**
   Present a "busy" picture with many visual distractions. Ask each child to find the ball.

6. **Tactile Discrimination**
   Put a ball and some very different objects in a "feely box." Say, "Find the ball."

7. **Visual Closure**
   Partially cover each of several pictures with paper. Ask each child to find the picture of the ball.

8. **Function**
   Ask, "What do we do with a ball?"

9. **Association**
   Ask, "What goes with the ball?" Use pictures or objects including a doll, dishes, rope, blocks, etc. with several unrelated objects or pictures.

10. **Imitate Verbalization**
    Present a ball and ask, "What is this? Say, 'Ball'." The child will imitate "Ball."

11. **Verbalize Label**
    Present a ball and ask, "What is this?" The child will respond, "Ball."

12.   **Concept Enrichment**
        Discuss games that are played with a ball.

Music

1.   Sing "I Give My Friend A Big, Red Ball" to the tune of "Here We Go 'Round the Mulberry Bush": Other words may be substituted for big (little) and red (other color). Have the children sit in a circle, one child begins with the ball and at the end of the song gives the ball to his "friend." All name the friend, and he then carries the ball to give to another friend while all sing the song.
2.   Sing "The Very Little Ball" from *Action Songs for all Occasion* (EA).
3.   Bounce balls to the rhythm of music, "What are we doing?" "Bouncing the ball." "Good."

Art

1.   With large brush and choice of colors, let the children paint big balls on large paper.
2.   Build structures with various sized styrofoam balls. Use white glue and decorate with paint, sequins, junk.

Snack

        Have small "balls" of fruit or candy or homemade peanut butter balls. The children name "ball." Talk about big and little balls.

Fine Motor

1.   Make sewing cards. Make colorful cardboard cut-outs of balls. Punch holes the size and number to meet the child's needs. Let the children sew with shoe strings or string with ends hardened from dipping in white glue.
2.   Let children decorate large cut out cardboard balls (circle) by gluing on small objects such as beans, cotton balls, bits of junk jewelry, colored pop corn, etc. (A good art activity also).
3.   Let children form sheets of newspaper into a ball shape and throw into a box on the table.

Games

1.   Play "Hot Potato" with a ball for the potato.
2.   Play basketball with a bottomless box for the hoop.
3.   Have children stand in two lines facing each other. Ask them to toss the ball across and work down the line.

Storytelling

1.   Experience Story - "What did we do today with a ball?" As children tell what the activities were, write what they say (in their words) on large paper.
2.   Hold a large ball of string with one end dangling. Say, "Once there was a big ball of string. Some children and a teacher wanted to use it. The teacher wanted to use it to tie a balloon (pull some string). And the ball got smaller, and smaller." (Give the end of the string to a child and have him tell why he wants to use it, pulling the string more and more). All say together, "And the ball got smaller and smaller." (Each child has a turn to tell how he will use the string, to pull off more). Repeat together each time, "And the ball got smaller and smaller." Make an ending to the story: The ball though now tiny, was happy to be used by the children.

Gross Motor

1.   Have the children stand in a circle with one child (or teacher at first) in the center. The person in the middle turns slowly, calls a child's name and tosses the ball to that child, who catches it. He then takes a turn in the center and the first child rejoins the circle.
2.   Have a relay race with balls. Use running relay or "over-under" relay.
3.   Have children toss a large ball into a box or large wastebasket. This is a good hand-eye and gross motor activity.
4.   Have the children pass balls to each other (2 children as partners), roll or bounce balls to each other.
5.   Have a relay involving a ball. The first child on each team runs up and throws a ball in a basket, runs back and tags the next child in line.

Cognitive

1.   Explain the roundness of balls; have the children name other round things.
2.   Explain that a picture of a ball is a circle. Find other things in pictures and around room that are circles.
3.   Size Discrimination - have the children paste cut out balls of different sizes on matching outlines of different sizes.

Enrichment

Organize teams to play a ball game. Make "uniforms" out of fabric rectangles cut at the neck. Use two colors of fabric (one for each team). Paint numbers and names on the "uniforms" and pin sides together on children.

Field Trip

Visit a ball park or playground where ball games can be watched.

Visitor

Invite a uniformed ball player (baseball, soccer, basketball, etc.) to come visit the class. A high school coach may be willing to bring a whole team.

Lesson 2: Doll

Unit Group Lesson

1.   **Match Concrete Objects**
Present two dolls. Say, "This is a doll." Ask each child in turn to put the doll with the doll. Gradually increase number of irrelevant objects from which (s)he must select doll to match.

2.   **Discriminate Objects**
Present several objects. Have each child touch the doll in response to the verbal direction, "Touch the doll."

3.   **Match Pictures**
Present several pictures of common objects. Have each child match the pictures of the dolls.

4.   **Discriminate Pictures**
Present a group of several unrelated pictures of objects. Have each child touch the picture of the doll in response to the verbal direction, "Touch the doll."

5.   **Figure-Ground**
Present a "busy" picture with many visual distractions. Ask each child to find the doll.

6.   **Visual Closure**
Partially cover each of several pictures with paper. Ask each child to find the picture of the doll.

7.   **Function**
Ask, "What do we do with a doll?"

8.   **Association**
Ask, "What goes with the doll?" Use pictures or objects including blocks, dishes, ball, jump rope, doll clothes, doll carriage, etc. with several unrelated objects or pictures.

9.   **Imitate Verbalization**
Present a doll and ask, "What is this? Say, 'Doll'." The child will imitate "Doll."

10. **Verbalize Label**

Present a doll and ask, "What is this?" The child will respond, "Doll."

11. **Concept Enrichment**

Display and discuss different types of doll such as baby dolls, teenage dolls, storybook characters, dolls from other countries, etc.

Music

1. Have three or four dolls for the children to use. Let the children manipulate the dolls. For example, have them "dance" to a record. Ask "Who is dancing?" "What are the dolls doing?"
2. Hold a large doll, moving its legs, arms, body to music. Have the children do what the doll does. Use slower music at first, then faster.
3. Sing "The Mechanical Toys" from *Action Songs for All Occasion* (EA).

Art

1. Have children paste cut-outs of a doll's body part together to make a doll on a pre-drawn outline, or if the parts are large, paste them together and put a rubber band through the head. This enables the child to make the doll walk, dance or bounce. Model the pasting, naming the body parts as they are being pasted together.
2. Use a pre-drawn outline of a large doll. Give the children bits of fabric, colored paper, beans, sequins, yarn, etc. to dress the doll and make its hair.

Fig. 10A

Snack

1. Make gingerbread people or other cookies shaped like dolls.
2. Cut a slice of bread with a "person" cookie cutter. Decorate it with food and eat the "doll."

Fine Motor

1. Let the children dress and undress dolls.
2. Use large "paper" (cardboard) dolls. Let the children dress and undress the dolls according to the weather. (Hot-weather clothes, cold-weather clothes.)
3. Make a dot-to-dot picture of a doll. The children can connect the dots, then color the doll. (See fig. 10A.)

Games

1. All eyes closed. One child hides a doll in the room or on the playground. The children open their eyes and the teacher asks, "Who can find the doll?" The child marks the doll's hiding place on a classroom map.
2. Have dolls in the housekeeping area for family play. Select dolls that can be dressed, undressed, and bathed with water.
3. Present three dolls to a group. Explain that dolls are very different in size, color, sex, clothing, etc. Talk about the outstanding features of each and have the children talk about each. Have the children close their eyes while the teacher hides one doll. "Which one is missing?"

Storytelling

1. Use classroom dolls to "act out" a story. This provides a good model for pretend play with dolls on other days.
2. Show a Raggedy Ann doll. Read a story about Raggedy Ann. Be familiar enough with the story to adapt the words to the language level of the children.

Gross Motor

1. Put doll(s) in a doll carriage. Have the children push it over a pretend route (uphill, downhill, under a swing set, over or on a chalk line, etc.).
2. Pull dolls in a wagon. Let some children be the dolls. They can be limp (flop) like Raggedy Ann and Andy or sit stiffly like other dolls.

Cognitive

1. Have paper dolls with two identical sets of clothes. Say to the child, "Match this dress to the doll who is wearing a dress exactly like this one?"

2. Have dolls in three sizes. Ask, "Which doll is largest?" "Which is smallest?" Have the children put the dolls in order - large to small.

Enrichment
1. Let children make simple doll clothes.
2. Let children make simple rag clothes.
3. Let children hang doll clothes on a clothes line using spring-type clothespins.

Field Trip
Visit a toy store and see the dolls.

Visitor
1. Have a doll collector bring some dolls.
2. Have a parent or volunteer demonstrate ways to make dolls and clothes.

Lesson 3: Block

Unit Group Lesson

1. **Match Concrete Objects**
Present two blocks. Say, "This is a block." Ask each child in turn to put the block with the block. Gradually increase number of irrelevant objects from which (s)he must select block to match.

2. **Discriminate Objects**
Present several objects. Have each child touch the block in response to the verbal direction, "Touch the block."

3. **Match Pictures**
Present several pictures of common objects. Have each child match the pictures of the blocks.

4. **Discriminate Pictures**
Present a group of several unrelated pictures of objects. Have each child touch the picture of the block in response to the verbal direction, "Touch the block."

5. **Figure-Ground**
Present a "busy" picture with many visual distractions. Ask each child to find the block.

6. **Visual Closure**
Partially cover each of several pictures with paper. Ask each child to find the picture of the block.

7. **Function**
Ask, "What do we do with a block?"

8. **Association**
Ask, "What goes with the block?" Use pictures or objects including a doll, dishes, jump rope, etc. with several unrelated objects or pictures.

9. **Imitate Verbalization**
Present a block and ask, "What is this? Say, 'Block'." The child will imitate "Block."

10. **Verbalize Label**
Present a block and ask, "What is this?" The child will respond, "Block."

11. **Concept Enrichment**
Explain to the children that blocks are squares, rectangles, triangles, and sometimes semicircles. Have the children find other objects in the room that are these shapes or look like blocks.

Music

1. Play a rhythm record. Have the children clap various sized blocks together in time with music.
2. Make sand blocks by gluing sandpaper to some blocks. Model how to use them by scraping them together. Let the children play them to music. Place large blocks a few feet apart in two rows. Have the children march to music around or between the blocks according to your instructions given Repeat the instructions often.

Art

1. Have a small group of children sit at a table. Give each child ten or fifteen small one-inch wooden cubes. Models different ways to build with small blocks, then let the children build whatever they like.
2. Get small wood scraps from a lumber company. Have the children build their own imaginative structures, using glue or nails, and paint them.
3. Use scrap lumber "blocks" as a base for a stabile (a mobile type structure on a stand) or for gluing onto cardboard for a collage.

Snack

1. Cut cheese (different kinds) into blocks. Have the children stack them, use them for building and then eat!
2. Make Jello blocks (Knox Blox). Let children eat them with their fingers.

Fine Motor

1. Have the children make patterns with blocks to match the teacher's patterns or patterns on cards (excellent perceptual motor activity). Use bigger blocks for less advanced children.
2. Let the children hammer nails into lumber "blocks."
3. Do block-stacking on the floor. Lie down on floor with 4 children - each person with 5 small alphabet blocks. Arrange them in a pattern, and then let the children copy the pattern with their blocks. (See fig. 10B.)
4. Have the children use their pincer grasp (thumb and index finger) to imitate a robot picking up small 1" cubes and loading them in a dump truck.

Fig. 10B

Games

Using large cardboard building blocks, have a contest to see who can build the highest tower before it topples over. Give each child a turn. This can be played outside as well as inside.

Storytelling

Show children a real brick. Pass it around the group pointing out that it is heavy, rough, very strong, and hard to break. Emphasize that "a brick is a block also and houses can be made of bricks." Read the story of the "Three Little Pigs" or use flannel board characters. At the end of the story, pass the brick around again. Repeat characteristics (heavy, strong) and let the children tell why the wolf could not blow down the house of bricks.

Gross Motor

1. Have many large blocks of different shapes and sizes in a conspicuous place (in middle of the floor) for the children to build houses, trains, cars, etc.
2. Build a "road," "bridge," or "river" with two lines of blocks. Have the children walk inside the "road" or "bridge" or jump over the "river," etc.

Cognitive

1. Have the children sort blocks by shape, size, or color into containers.
2. Put blocks in a long line (high tower). Count to see how many are used.
3. Have colored blocks. Give directions such as "What can you show me with two green blocks."

Enrichment

1. Make directions more difficult. "What can you make with two green, one red, and tree blue blocks?" "Today is the 6th. What can you make using only six blocks?"
2. Ask, "How many little blocks are used to make an area the size of this larger box?" Then show the children how to find this out by filling the box with blocks. Have the children help count the blocks.

3.   Build model buildings (homes, school, airport), that children have seen or are familiar with, with blocks.

4.   Help children use blocks, people, animals, cars, and other props to make a city.

Field Trip

1.   Visit a lumber yard. Watch wood being cut (sawed) into lengths. Let each child bring back a "block" of wood.

2.   Visit another classroom to see (show) different ways blocks can be used. An instant camera could be taken along and pictures taken for a reminder when the children return to their classroom.

Visitor

Have a teacher (parent) come in and demonstrate ways to use blocks (ramps, bridges, etc.).

Lesson 4: Dishes

Unit Group Lesson

1.   **Match Concrete Objects**
Present two dishes. Say, "This is a dish." Ask each child in turn to put the dish with the dish. Gradually increase number of irrelevant objects from which (s)he must select dish to match.

2.   **Discriminate Objects**
Present several objects. Have each child touch the dish in response to the verbal direction, "Touch the dish."

3.   **Match Pictures**
Present several pictures of common objects. Have each child match the pictures of the dishes.

4.   **Discriminate Pictures**
Present a group of several unrelated pictures of objects. Have each child touch the picture of the dish in response to the verbal direction, "Touch the dish."

5.   **Figure-Ground**
Present a "busy" picture with many visual distractions. Ask each child to find the dish.

6.   **Visual Closure**
Partially cover each of several pictures with paper. Ask each child to find the picture of the dish.

7.   **Function**
Ask, "What do we do with a dish?"

8.   **Association**
Ask, "What goes with the dish?" Use pictures or objects including food, doll, jump rope, etc. with several unrelated objects or pictures.

9.   **Imitate Verbalization**
Present a dish and ask, "What is this? Say, 'Dish'." The child will imitate "Dish."

10.   **Verbalize Label**
Present a dish and ask, "What is this?" The child will respond, "Dish."

11.   **Concept Enrichment**
Discuss the names for all the different dishes: plate, cup, saucer, soup bowl, bread plate, dessert dish, platter, teapot, etc.

Music

1. Let the children use a real tea set or they can imitate the teacher who uses a real tea set. Sing to the tune of "Here We Go 'Round the Mulberry Bush":

    a. This is the way we drink our _____.

    b. This is the way we eat our _____.

    c. This is the way we cut our _____.

    d. This is the way we pour our _____.

2. Show the children a real tea pot or toy tea pot. Label the handle and spout and have the children name handle and spout. Have the children show function by pouring from the tea pot. Sing this song:

    I'm a little tea pot

    Short and stout   *(Or fat.)*

    Here is my handle.   *(Arm makes handle.)*

    Here is my spout.   *(Arm out to side.)*

    When I get all steamed up,

    Then I shout.   *(Blow or whistle.)*

    Just tip me over,   *(Bend body to side.)*

    Pour me out.

3. Sing "Here's A Cup" from *Finger Games* (EA).

Art

1. Have three or four parts of a dish set (cup, plate, glass, fork, knife, pot) outlined on a placemat. Have the children match cut-outs to the appropriate outline, paste them on and decorate the placemat.

2. Have the children mold plates, cups, bowls and other parts of a dish set from natural clay or play dough, which will harden. In a few days, they may want to print the pieces.

Snack

Use a set of dishes for serving snack. Let the children pour their own juice from a pitcher, eat their snack using knives, forks, spoons, plates. Discuss the use of each part of the set of dishes.

Fine Motor

1. Have a picture of a cup and other dishes cut into a puzzle. Let the children put the cup and other dishes together. Make several puzzles of each dish in different degrees of difficulty.

2. Have a picture of a cup and other dishes cut into a puzzle. Let the children put the cup and other dishes together. Make several puzzles of each dish in different degrees of difficulty.

Games

1. Give one or two pieces of a tea set to each child in a small group. Ask, "Who has a cup?" (or plate, or fork, or pitcher, etc.). "Hold it up high." "What is it?" The child names it. Say, "Show us what you do with a cup." Each child has at least one turn.

2. Have a tea set on a table when the children come in that morning and encourage them in the dramatic play of eating together, serving each other, and talking about what they are eating.

Storytelling

1. For language and following directions: give a piece of a tea set to each child (small group of children). Have a small table in front of the children. Have a comical puppet say, "Oh dear, oh dear, where is my tea set? I'm so hungry. Hi, boys and girls. Do you have my tea set?" The children answer, "Yes." Ask, "Who has my cup?" The child holding the cup says, "I have your cup" (non-verbal children hold up cup and say "c" or "cu" or "cup"). The puppet says, "Please put it on the table for me." Repeat actions and verbalizations for each piece. Say, "Oh, now I have my tea set. I can eat. Thank you boys and girls. Good-bye." He begins to eat.

2. Read a story which uses dishes such as "Miss Suzy," "The Three Bears" (porridge bowls), "The Man Who Didn't Wash His Dishes," etc.

Gross Motor

1. Imitate cup, plate, pot, in sequence to music to "I'm a Little Teapot."

   "I'm a litte tea cup look at me
   I'm a little plate flat as can be
   Now I'm a pot with my handle sticking out
   Stand me up and I'll shout. YEAH!"

   Repeat rhythmically and sequentially several times. (See fig. 10C.)

2. Place a set of dishes on the floor. Have the children "walk around,"
   "tiptoe beside," "jump over," etc. the dishes.

cup

plate

Fig. 10C

pot

Cognitive

1. Have some cups and saucers. Let the children match the cups to the saucers. Ask, "How many more cups do we need? Do we have enough for all the boys and girls here today?"
2. Count knives, forks, and spoons. Have the children match them to see if each knife can be placed with a fork and spoon.
3. Let the children be a life-sized set of dishes. Have them place themselves on the carpet "placemat." Let each one describe use.

Enrichment

1. Have the children match related objects, cup and saucer, spoon and fork, etc.
2. Have the children draw or paste pictures of appropriate food or drink next to or in parts of a set of dishes.
3. Let children use cut-outs from magazines to make a "place setting" - a (construction paper) place mat, plate, knife, fork, spoon, cup, etc. The more advanced children can cut their own.

Field Trip

1. Visit a pottery store to see sets of dishes.
2. Visit a potter and watch dishes being made.

Visitor

Invite a potter to come in and show some dishes (s)he has made.

Lesson 5: Rope

Unit Group Lesson

1. **Match Concrete Objects**
   Present two ropes. Say, "This is a rope." Ask each child in turn to put the rope with the rope. Gradually increase number of irrelevant objects from which (s)he must select rope to match.

2. **Discriminate Objects**
   Present several objects. Have each child touch the rope in response to the verbal direction, "Touch the rope."

3. **Match Pictures**
   Present several pictures of common objects. Have each child match the pictures of the ropes.

4. **Discriminate Pictures**
   Present a group of several unrelated pictures of objects. Have each child touch the picture of the rope in response to the verbal direction, "Touch the rope."

5. **Figure-Ground**
   Present a "busy" picture with many visual distractions. Ask each child to find the rope.

6. **Visual Closure**

Partially cover each of several pictures with paper. Ask each child to find the picture of the rope.

7. **Function**

Ask, "What do we do with a rope?"

8. **Association**

Ask, "What goes with the rope?" Use pictures or objects including blocks, ball, dishes, etc. with several unrelated objects or pictures.

9. **Imitate Verbalization**

Present a rope and ask, "What is this? Say, 'Rope'." The child will imitate "Rope."

10. **Verbalize Label**

Present a rope and ask, "What is this?" The child will respond, "Rope."

11. **Concept Enrichment**

Look at ropes of different thicknesses. Take some ropes apart to see how they are made. Demonstrate simple rope making.

Music
1. Pantomime jumping rope to a rhythm record. Model the action by actually jumping rope.
2. Give the children short pieces of rope. Let them move the ropes to music.
3. Sing jump rope rhythms such as "Teddy Bear" (turn around, touch the ground, etc.).

Art
1. Help the children make a simple macrame wall hanging.
2. Let the children make a collage picture using pieces of rope, spaghetti, drinking straws and other long cylindrical shapes.
3. "Frame" a picture that a child has made with a thick piece of rope glued around the outside. (See fig. 10D.)

Fig. 10D

Snack
1. Make "ropes" out of peanut butter play dough, cookie dough, (or biscuit) etc. Cook, if needed, and eat.
2. Eat spaghetti which has been cooked and seasoned.
3. Eat licorice or other "rope" candies.

Fine Motor
1. Find different ropes and bring them into the classroom. Take some ropes apart and examine them.
2. Have the children use ropes to tie knots.
3. Let the children make some rope by braiding string of different sizes and colors.
4. Make each child a jump rope. Cut the rope to fit the child's height. Let each child wrap tape round and round the ends of his rope to make hand grips.

Games
1. Put two ropes side by side. Have the children "jump the river." Slowly move the rope further and further apart so the children must jump farther.
2. Put a rope on the ground. Let the children walk "on the snake." Try it with partners. Then let the rope curve. Let the children "walk the rope" that way, too.

Storytelling
Make up a story of a rope, that was used for many things such as roping cattle, hanging clothes (clothesline), tying up a box, etc. and, finally as a jump rope for some children. Use pictures or flannel board pieces to illustrate the story.

Gross Motor

1.	Have two children, each hold one end of a rope. Starting with the rope lying on the ground, have each child in line jump over. When all the children have had a turn, the rope is raised one or two inches. Call out directions "jump over," and have the children say these words as they complete the action.

2.	Have two children, each hold one end of rope, slowly bring rope up and over the head of a child. Have everyone call out "jump." This represents a beginning step in learning to jump rope.

3.	Take a long rope and turn it around slowly. Let the children jump over the rope. Wiggle the rope, and let the children jump over the "snake."

Cognitive

1.	Use a rope to make a big circle on the floor or ground. Have the children walk "around" the rope, "jump in" the rope circle, "walk on" the rope circle, "sit in" the rope circle, etc. Stress the vocabulary.

2.	Use rope to make circles, squares, triangles, and other shapes.

3.	Have each child measure a rope with his feet. "This rope is 3 and a little more of Johnny's feet."

Enrichment

1.	Use rope to mark sets of things. "Circle with the rope all the balls, red triangles, dolls, etc." or "Place all the blocks inside the rope circle."

2.	Hold a rope about 4 feet off the ground. Let the children go under it without touching it. Lower it a few inches. Let the children try again. See who can get under it when the rope is the lowest.

Field Trip

1.	Go to a toy store. Help the children find and touch the toys you have learned about. Try to have enough money to purchase one toy from the toy store.

2.	Visit a craft store. Look at the ways ropes are used in macrame.

Visitor

1.	Have a parent come in to demonstrate the art of macrame.

2.	Invite a Boy Scout to visit and demonstrate knot-tying with ropes.

3.	Have someone come and make real rope for the children.

Related Children's Records
"Here's A Cup" from **FINGER GAMES** (EA)
"The Mechanical Toys" from **ACTION SONGS FOR ALL OCCASIONS** (EA)
"The Very Little Ball" from **ACTION SONGS FOR ALL OCCASIONS** (EA)

Related Children's Books
Freeman, Don. **CORDUROY.** New York: Viking Press, 1968.
Kellogg, Stephen. **MYSTERY OF THE MAGIC GREEN BALL.** New York: Dial Press, 1978.
Lionni, Leo. **ALEXANDER AND THE WINDUP MOUSE.** New York: Pantheon Books, 1969.
Walsh, Ellen Stoll. **BRUNUS AND THE NEW BEAR.** Garden City, N.Y.: Doubleday & Co.
Zolotow, Charlotte. **WILLIAM'S DOLL.** New York: Harper & Row, 1972.

Related Parenting Materials
Cansler, Dot. **THE HOMESTRETCH.** Winston-Salem, NC 27113-5128: Kaplan Press, 1983.

Related Materials
TEACHING PICTURES. Winston-Salem, NC 27113-5128: Kaplan Press, 1983.
STORY SEQUENCE CARDS I, II. Winston-Salem, NC 27113-5128: Kaplan Press, 1983.
SEWING CARDS I, II, III. Winston-Salem, NC 27113-5128: Kaplan Press, 1983.

Unit 11: Winter Holidays

A developmental assessment should determine the functional levels of each child. Individual expectations are based on the assessment results.

Lesson 1: Hanukkah Candle

Unit Group Lesson

1. **Match Concrete Objects**
    Present two Hanukkah candles. Say, "This is a Hanukkah candle." Ask each child in turn to put the Hanukkah candle with the Hanukkah candle. Gradually increase number of irrelevant objects from which (s)he must select Hanukkah candles to match.

2. **Discriminate Objects**
    Present several objects. Have each child touch the Hanukkah candle in response to verbal direction, "Touch the Hanukkah candle."

3. **Match Pictures**
    Present several pictures of common objects. Have each child match the pictures of the Hanukkah candles.

4. **Discriminate Pictures**
    Present a group of several unrelated pictures of objects. Have each child touch the picture of the Hanukkah candle in response to verbal direction, "Touch the Hanukkah candle."

5. **Figure-Ground**
    Present a "busy" picture with many visual distractions. Ask each child to find the Hanukkah candle.

6. **Visual Closure**
    Partially cover each of several pictures with paper. Ask each child to find the picture of the Hanukkah candle.

7. **Function**
    Ask, "What do we do with Hanukkah candles?"

8. **Association**
    Ask, "What goes with the Hanukkah candle?" Use pictures or objects including draydel, decorations, Christmas, etc. with several unrelated objects or pictures.

9. **Imitate Verbalization**
    Present a Hanukkah candle and ask, "What is this? Say, 'Hanukkah candle'." The child will imitate "Hanukkah candle."

10. **Verbalize Label**
Present a Hanukkah candle and ask, "What is this?" The child will respond, "Hanukkah candle."

11. **Concept Enrichment**
Discuss meaning of Hanukkah. The candles are kept in a special stand called a Menorrah.

Music
1. Sing this traditional Hanukkah song.
"Oh Hanukkah, oh Hanukkah
A festival of joy
A merry time, a happy time
For every girl and boy."
2. Sing "I Have a Litte Draydel":

I have a little draydel
I made it out of clay
And when it's good and ready
Oh draydel I shall play.
Draydel, draydel, draydel
I made it out of clay
Draydel, draydel, draydel
Now it's time to play.
3. Sing "We Wish You a Happy Hanukkah" to the tune of "We Wish You a Merry Christmas."

Art
1. Glue 6 popsicle sticks together to make a star and cover with glitter or paint. (See fig. 11A.)
2. Make a Menorrah from an upside down egg carton using six and three "bumps" taped (glued) together. Paint the egg carton. Put popsicle sticks (which have "fire" glued or painted on one end) into each "bump." (See fig. 11B.)

Fig. 11A

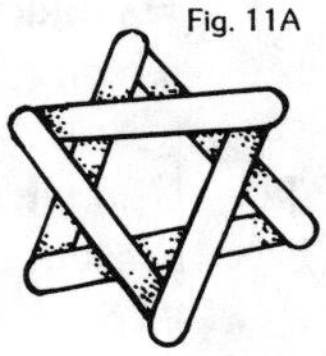

Fig. 11B

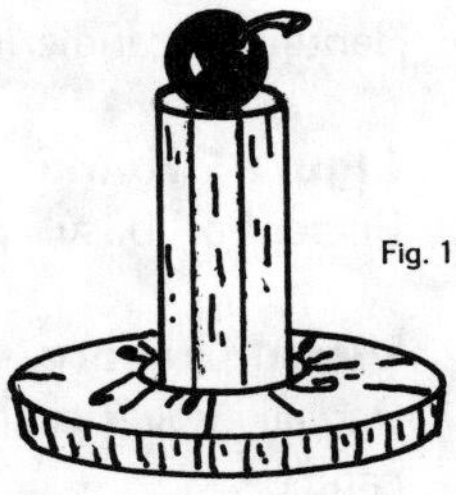

Snack
1. Make and eat a "candle" using a pineapple ring base, half a banana as the candle and a cherry as the flame. (See fig. 11C.)
2. Serve latkes (potato pancakes).

Fig. 11C

Fine Motor
Make a menorrah from clay. Use cut drinking straws for candles.

Games
Have draydels for each child to spin. (Draydels are small tops with Hebrew letters on the four faces.) (See fig. 11D.)

Fig. 11D

Storytelling
1. Tell the Hanukkah Story. The Eternal light in the temple was to be kept burning all the time. There was enough oil for only a couple of days. The Jewish people went to get oil, but it took eight days. It was a mircle that the Eternal light kept burning for the whole eight days.

Gross Motor

Let the children "spin" like draydels. The teacher can "spin" each one by turning the child's hands which are held over his/her head. (See fig. 11E.)

Fig. 11E

Cognitive

1. Have a Jewish parent bring in a Menorrah and light the candles. Count the candles as they are lighted. One candle is kept as the candle to light the others.
2. Give each child a picture of a menorrah. Have them glue the correct number of candles on the menorrah. Write the number nine.

Enrichment

Make a giant menorrah. Put on the wall at the childrens' level. Glue bits of brown or gold paper for the base, white tissue paper for the candles and shiny golden paper for the candle flames.

Lesson 2: Christmas Tree

Unit Group Lesson

1. **Match Concrete Objects**
   Present two Christmas trees. (Use small models if you do not have life-size trees available.) Say, "This is a Christmas tree." Ask each child in turn to put the Christmas tree with the Christmas tree. Gradually increase number of irrelevant objects from which (s)he must select Christmas tree to match.

2. **Discriminate Objects**
   Present several objects. Have each child touch the Christmas tree in response to verbal direction, "Touch the Christmas tree."

3. **Match Pictures**
   Present several pictures of common objects. Have each child match the pictures of the Christmas tree.

4. **Discriminate Pictures**
   Present a group of several unrelated pictures of objects. Have each child touch the picture of the Christmas tree in response to verbal direction, "Touch the Christmas tree."

5. **Figure-Ground**
   Present a "busy" picture with many visual distractions. Ask each child to find the Christmas tree.

6. **Visual Closure**
   Partially cover each of several pictures with paper. Ask each child to find the picture of the Christmas tree.

7. **Function**
   Ask, "What do we do with a Christmas tree?"

8. **Association**
   Ask, "What goes with the Christmas tree?" Use pictures or objects including presents, decorations, etc. with several unrelated objects or pictures.

9. **Imitate Verbalization**

    Present a Christmas tree and ask, "What is this? Say, 'Christmas tree'." Child will imitate "Christmas tree."

10. **Verbalize Label**

    Present a Christmas tree and ask, "What is this?" The child will respond, "Christmas tree."

11. **Concept Enrichment**

    Discuss the fact that Christmas trees are evergreens, therefore they do not lose their leaves. They have a triangular shape and are green.

Music

1. Sing "Oh, Christmas Tree." Simplify the words for children who cannot process original version to:
    Oh, Christmas tree   *(Children walk around a real*
    Oh, Christmas tree   *tree singing.)*
    Oh, pretty, green Christmas tree.
2. Do Christmas caroling: Act out going to a "door," holding caroling "books," and singing Christmas songs. (Also turning pages, holding books individually or together.) Tiptoe to add an element of Christmas surprise.
3. Sing to the tune of "Mulberry Bush":
    a. Here is a lovely Christmas tree - so early in the morning.
    b. Here is a horn (doll, drum, cookie, etc.) for the Christmas tree.
    c. Here are the lights for the Christmas tree (flutter fingers).
    d. Here stands the pretty Christmas tree.

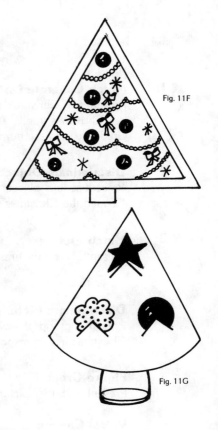

Fig. 11F

Art

1. Help the children make Christmas trees from cone-shaped cups (snow-cone cups, cone-shaped spindles from a textile mill, or styrofoam cones) paint, cotton, beads, sequins, glitter, and glue.
2. Have the children arrange 3 triangles on a sheet of paper to form an evergreen tree, add a small rectangular brown "trunk," and decorate the tree.
3. Let the children outline a green tree shape with strips of gold foil, red paper, etc. Decorate inside the outline with bits of decoration such as foil from red cards, paper cut apart into tiny snowflakes, etc. (See fig. 11F.)

Snack

1. Serve cookies shaped like Christmas trees, made in Fine Motor today. Use toy Christmas trees as a centerpiece. Talk about shape of cookies, color of toy tree and allow children to express Christmas tree ideas.
2. Make a large cone tree from green tagboard and a bottle trunk. Cut slots in paper for cookies. After each child removes a cookie to eat, he can replace it with a decoration he has made. (See fig. 11G.)

Fig. 11G

Fine Motor

1. Have everyone use Christmas tree cookie cutter and make cookies. Decorate with tiny candy "sprinkles." Have children put cookies on the pan and go to the oven with you.
2. Let each child with a cookie cutter cut a hole in center of shape of cookie dough and drop in one colored Life-Saver which melts to give a stained glass window effect.
3. Have the children cut small triangles in three shades of light green for the Enrichment #1 Together Activity.
4. Help the children cut balls of bright colored foil to add to the Christmas tree in different sizes for Enrichment #1.
5. Let the children cut simple shapes from old Christmas cards to add to the Christmas tree in Enrichment #1 today.

6.   Cut trees from green paper. Let the children use a hole puncher to punch each tree full of holes. Put each over another bright colored paper for "lights."

7.   Have the children decorate a pine cone or v-shaped paper cup with whipped Ivory Flakes that have been tinted green with food color or paint. Decorate with Macaroni, etc.

8.   Let the children punch holes in different colors of paper and glue the tiny circles on a green tree.

Games

1.   Place a Christmas tree or small tree in center of floor or outside. Run, walk, crawl, jump, gallop around the tree. Emphasize action words as well as preposition "around."

2.   Hide tiny Christmas trees around the room or outside. Have a Christmas tree hunt.

Storytelling

Use a flannel board and a cut-out of a large, 12" Christmas tree, small flannel cut-outs of decorations and things which are not decorations (stove, clothes, food, furniture) all placed on flannel board.

Teacher: "Hello, boys and girls. I am a Christmas tree."	*(Holds up tree and moves it around group)*
(TREE) "I need some decorations. Can you help me?"	
Children: "Yes, we can help you."	*(Put tree on flannel board.)*
Child: "I can give you a star. (Ball, cane Santa, etc.)"	*(Each child selects and places a decoration on the tree.)*
Teacher: "Oh, thank you, (child's name)."	

After the tree is very full of decorations, he is very happy.

Gross Motor

Play "Ring Around the Christmas Tree" like "Ring Around the Rosey" with a tree in the middle.

Cognitive

1.   Make a cue sheet. At top of the paper put an outline of a Christmas tree. Have other identical tree outlines on the paper, mixed with different objects. Ask the children to "Find all the Christmas trees and mark them with your crayon." Model how to mark on chalkboard or paper. Vary the number of objects different from tree according to the skill level of each child.

2.   Help children associate the Christmas tree with Christmas. Place small object including a toy Christmas tree on a table. Ask, "What do we see at Christmas time?" Help each child identify the Christmas tree.

Enrichment

1.   Together Activity: Put a giant triangular tree shape in dark green with black lines on the wall or bulletin board. Let the children glue the triangles cut in Fine Motor #3 onto the black lines. The triangles are lighter shades of green. Add bright balls and simple shapes from Fine Motor #4 & 5 in different sizes over the triangles. (Several of these on the walls of the classroom provide a beautiful Christmas atmosphere in January. Balls may be taken off by the children and snow cotton balls added.) (See fig. 11H.)

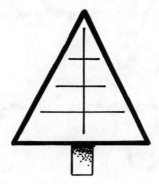 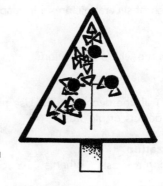

Fig. 11H

2. Trace each child's hand on green construction paper. Write his/her name on the hand. Cut out hands and arrange in form of a tree with a brown rectangle as a base. Put a star on top cut from yellow or gold paper. (See fig. 111.)

3. Help children make Christmas tree decorations for the class tree:
   a. Paper chains: Cut red and yellow construction paper into strips 6" x 1". Have the children glue the ends of each piece to make rings. After the first ring, put each succeding strip through the previous one and glue it.
   b. Styrofoam balls: Stick with toothpicks, spray paint, and add glitter, and a string to hang.
   c. Gum balls (from sweet gum tree): Paint , add glitter, and a string to hang.
   d. Egg cup bells: Paint egg carton sections, glue on colored salt, glitter, put yarn through top for hanging and attach a small bell to end of yarn inside egg cup.
   e. Glue popsicle sticks together in various shapes, add paint, glitter, yarn for hanging.
   f. "Stained Glass" cookies may be hung on tree.

Fig. 111

Lesson 3: Decoration

Unit Group Lesson

1. **Match Concrete Objects**
   Present two decorations. Say, "This is a decoration." Ask each child in turn to put the decoration with the decoration. Gradually increase number of irrelevant objects from which (s)he must select decoration to match.

2. **Discriminate Objects**
   Present several objects. Have each child touch the decoration in response to verbal direction, "Touch the decoration."

3. **Match Pictures**
   Present several pictures of common objects. Have each child match the pictures of the decoration.

4. **Discriminate Pictures**
   Present a group of several unrelated pictures of objects. Have each child touch the picture of the decoration in response to verbal direction, "Touch the decoration."

5. **Figure-Ground**
   Present a "busy" picture with many visual distractions. Ask each child to find the decoration.

6. **Visual Closure**
   Partially cover each of several pictures with paper. Ask each child to find the picture of the decoration.

7. **Function**
   Ask, "What do we do with a decoration?"

8. **Association**
   Ask, "What goes with the decoration?" Use pictures or objects including Christmas tree, etc. with several unrelated objects or pictures.

9. **Imitate Verbalization**
   Present a decoration and ask, "What is this? Say, 'Decoration'." Child will imitate "Decoration."

10.   **Verbalize Label**
      Present a decoration and ask, "What is this?" The child will respond, "Decoration."

11.   **Concept Enrichment**
      Discuss some things which are used as decorations or formal decorations such as shiny paper, glitter, bright colors, evergreens, candles, holly & berries, wrapping paper, stockings, greeting cards, etc.

Music
1.   Sing "Jingle Bells." (Measuring spoons on a ring make lovely "Jingle Bells.")
2.   Sing "Deck the Halls."

Art
1.   Dye pasta green and dry. Cut the middle from a paper plate. Let children glue green pasta onto plate and add red bow for a wreath.
2.   Have the children decorate newsprint with potato print stars or red and green circles for Christmas wrapping paper.

Fig. 11J

Fig. 11K

3.   Prepare a GREETING TAPE all around the room with greetings cut from cards. Cut a long narrow strip of paper (use adding machine tape.) Let the children cut words from old Christmas cards and glue them onto the paper. Then hang it around the room. (See fig. 11J.)
4.   Together Activity: Help the children make a giant Christmas card. Have the group decide on the words that they want to include. Make dotted outlines of the words. Let some children trace over the outlines to complete the words. Other children should draw, cut or tear decorations for the card. (See fig. 11K.)

Snack
1.   Make and drink egg nog. (One egg to 1½ cups of milk, vanilla and sugar to taste).
2.   Make and drink "wassail." (Hot apple cider with a stick of cinnamon for flavor and stirring.)

Fine Motor
1.   Let children do a path tracing of "Christmas decoration to Christmas tree." and "Christmas gift to a Christmas tree." Vary the difficulty of the path for the different levels of children.
2.   Have children cut red berries and holly leaves and use them to make small Christmas greeting cards. (See fig. 11L.)
3.   Provide red (or paint red) and white pipe cleaners. Have children twist one of each color together and bend into a "cane."
4.   Help children wrap "surprises" chosen from toy shelf, etc., in Christmas wrapping.
5.   Have children cut paper shapes using cookie cutters as stencils, and decorate them with glitter and other things. Hang around the classroom.

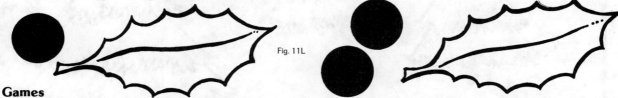

Fig. 11L

Games
1.   Play "Pin the Decoration on the Tree": Put a large tree on wall; blindfold each child; point him in the direction of the tree; and have him pin or tape a colorful decoration on tree.

Storytelling

Recite "Twas the Night Before Christmas." Emphasize the stockings being hung.

Gross Motor

Have children hang decorations around the classroom. Let them use steps and small ladders and bend and reach to decorate.

Cognitive

1. Have children do a classification task. Place many objects on the table. Make sure that some are Christmas decorations, some not decorations. Say, "Find all the decorations and put them in the box."
2. Put different shapes on a cut-out Christmas tree. Have extra shapes for the children to match. (See fig. 11M.)

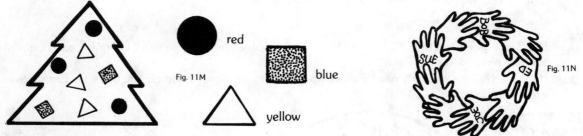

Fig. 11M — red — blue — yellow — Fig. 11N

Enrichment

1. Trace each child's hand on green construction paper. Write the child's name on his/her hand. Cut out "hands" and paste them in a circle to form a "Hand Wreath." (See fig. 11N.)
2. Together Activity: Make a Christmas Forest.
   Hang a long sheet of paper at child level. Have children:

   a. Glue or staple on brown tree trunks. (Small strips of brown construction paper.)
   b. Paint triangles in three sizes and fringe the bottoms. Attach them above the trunks.
   c. Add red, silver, and gold decorations.
   d. Make up a story about "What Could Happen in a Christmas Forest?" (See fig. 11O.)

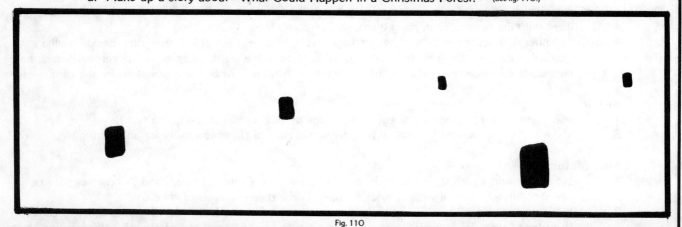

Fig. 11O

Lesson 4: Santa Claus

Unit Group Lesson

1. **Match Concrete Objects**
   Present two Santa Clauses. Say, "This is a Santa Claus." Ask each child in turn to put the Santa Claus with the Santa Claus. Gradually increase number of irrelevant objects from which (s)he must select Santa Claus to match.

2. **Discriminate Objects**
   Present several objects. Have each child touch the Santa Claus in response to verbal direction, "Touch the Santa Claus."

3. **Match Pictures**
   Present several pictures of common objects. Have each child match the pictures of the Santa Claus.

4. **Discriminate Pictures**
   Present a group of several unrelated pictures of objects. Have each child touch the picture of the Santa Claus in response to verbal direction, "Touch the Santa Claus."

5. **Figure-Ground**
   Present a "busy" picture with many visual distractions. Ask each child to find the Santa Claus.

6. **Visual Closure**
   Partially cover each of several pictures with paper. Ask each child to find the picture of the Santa Claus.

7. **Function**
   Ask, "What do we do with a Santa Claus?"

8. **Association**
   Ask, "What goes with the Santa Claus?" Use pictures or objects including sleigh, reindeer, etc. with several unrelated objects or pictures.

9. **Imitate Verbalization**
   Present a Santa Claus and ask, "What is this? Say, 'Santa Claus'." Child will imitate "Santa Claus."

10. **Verbalize Label**
    Present a Santa Claus and ask, "What is this?" The child will respond, "Santa Claus."

11. **Concept Enrichment**
    Discuss story of Santa Claus.

Music

1. For children with little language sing to the tune of "Where is Thumbkin?"
   Santa Claus
   Santa Claus
   Ho, Ho, Ho
   Ho, Ho, Ho
   Santa Claus
   Santa Claus
   Ho, Ho, Ho
   Ho, Ho, Ho
   (Modify all songs to fit the children's language ability.)

2. Sing "Santa Claus Is Coming To Town." Emphasize actions in song by acting out words like "better watch out," "better not pout," "cry." Use toy Santa and sleigh to act out Santa's coming to town. Sing only the first verse with most pre-school children.

3. Sing "Here Comes Santa Claus."

Art

1. On pre-drawn outlines of Santa have children glue cotton balls or cotton for beard, mustache, and hat trim.

2. Have children paste parts of Santa's face or whole body together. Allow children to paste as they choose after you model task.

3. Make a giant poster of Santa (a pre-drawn outline). Have children paint Santa with large paint brushes in appropriate colors. Let them glue on cotton or cotton balls for bear, mustache, hat and suit trim.

Snack

Have Santa sandwiches: Spread a circle of bread with peanut butter. Make raisin eyes and nose, red candy mouth, cream cheese for frosting mustache and beard and a construction paper hat. (See fig. 11P.)

Fig. 11P

Fine Motor

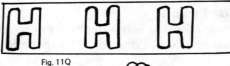
Fig. 11Q

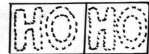
Fig. 11W

1. Have children put glue on a circular outline of Santa's face and sprinkle with glitter and salt.

2. Make a word tape. Have the children make H's over an outline from black strips of paper and put an O next to each H. Use these tapes or HO HO cards all around the room. (See fig. 11Q.)

3. Put dotted HO HO on cards. Have children trace over them and decorate border of the cards. (See fig. 11W.)

4. Have children use a 5-pointed star to make Santa. (See fig. 11R.)

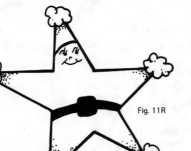
Fig. 11R

Games

1. On large heavy paper draw a large "map." Draw a house for each child with his name on it. Have children draw 1½" wide roads (some straight and some very curvy depending on skill). Each child starts at beginning point and drives toy plastic Santa and sleigh to his house.

2. Prepare a language activity for small groups. Fill a large bag with little presents, one for each child. Pretend to be Santa, call each child up, ask him to feel the present, shake it, and guess what is in it. Have the child tell the whole group, and put present back in bag. When each child has had a turn, hand out the gifts and let the children open them.

Storytelling

1. Recite "Twas The Night Before Christmas." (Change words which are unfamiliar to the children.) Put a lot of expression - body, facial, and vocal - into the reading.

2. Make a flannel board story with cut-outs of Santa without a hat, Santa's hat, a boot, a box, a ball, a baby, a banana, and a boy. Tell how Santa has lost his hat and is very worried. He asks the children if they have seen it. He begins to look.

Children respond to each queston as Santa asks children; "No-o-o."
Santa, "Is it in the boot?"
Santa, "Is it in the box?"
Santa, "Is it on the baby?"
Santa, "Is it under the banana?"
Santa, "Is it under the ball?"
Santa, "Oh dear, where is my hat?" Place the boy on flannel board. He says, "Santa, is this your hat?" He puts it on Santa." Santa, "Ho, ho, ho, thank you little boy. Now I have my hat."

Gross Motor

1. Paint or draw a large picture of Santa with his toy bag on cardboard. Cut out a large hole at the top of his bag. Children throw bean bags or ball "into Santa's bag."
2. Have each child carry a bag of toys around an obstacle course.

Cognitive

1. Have children make Santa Claus from paper plates. Ask, "How many paper plates do we need for each child in the group?"; "Do we need more, less, or the same number of red paper hats?"; "Do we need more, less, or the same number of cotton balls?"; and "Do we need more, less, or the same number of buttons for eyes?" (See fig. 11S.)

Fig. 11S

2. Prepare an activity sheet to make a large picture of a toy bag for each child. Cut pictures of toys and other things from a catalog. Have each child sort toys from non-toys and glue some toys on Santa's bag. This activity may also be done with a real bag and real objects.

Enrichment

1. Have a large Santa (December) calendar with numbers 1-25 on Santa's beard. Each day cover a number with a cotton ball. By vacation time Santa's beard will be covered!
2. Together Activity: Santa. Provide a large Santa outline. Have children cover fur areas: beard, eyebrows, etc., by pulling aparts wips of cotton balls; use blue scraps of paper for eyes, red scraps for hat and cheeks, nose, mouth, berries, green scraps for leaves and glue the pieces onto the picture.

Field Trip

Visit Santa at local shopping center.

Lesson 5: Reindeer

Unit Group Lesson

1. **Match Concrete Objects**
   Present two reindeer. Say, "This is a reindeer." Ask each child in turn to put the reindeer with the reindeer. Gradually increase number of irrelevant objects from which (s)he must select reindeer match.

2. **Discriminate Objects**
   Present several objects. Have each child touch the reindeer in response to verbal direction, "Touch the reindeer."

3. **Match Pictures**
   Present several pictures of common objects. Have each child match the pictures of the reindeer.

4. **Discriminate Pictures**
   Present a group of several unrelated pictures of objects. Have each child touch the picture of the reindeer in response to verbal direction, "Touch the reindeer."

5. **Figure-Ground**
   Present a "busy" picture with many visual distractions. Ask each child to find the reindeer.

6. **Visual Closure**
   Partially cover each of several pictures with paper. Ask each child to find the picture of the reindeer.

7. **Function**
   Ask, "What do we do with a reindeer?"

8. **Association**
   Ask, "What goes with the reindeer?" Use pictures or objects including sleigh, Santa Claus, etc. with several unrelated objects or pictures.

9. **Imitate Verbalization**
   Present a reindeer and ask, "What is this? Say, 'Reindeer'." The child will imitate "Reindeer."

10. **Verbalize Label**
    Present a reindeer and ask, "What is this?" The child will respond, "Reindeer."

11. **Concept Enrichment**
    Santa Claus has eight reindeer pulling his sleigh. Rudolph, the red-nosed reindeer, also helps pull Santa's sleigh sometimes.

Music

Show pictures of reindeer, one with a red nose. Ask children: "Which one is different?" "How is it different?" "Red nose, right." "Let's sing a song about a reindeer who has a red nose." "Rudolph, the Red-nosed Reindeer." If children know the song, have them play bells to rhythm of the song. For children with little language, simplify the words by repeating:

"Rudolph the red-nosed reindeer
Had a very shiny nose
Rudolph the red nosed reindeer
Had a very shiny nose."   *(Point to nose.)*

Art

1. Draw outlines of reindeer's heads for each child. Let the children spread white glue on the outlines and sprinkle sand on the glue. For fuzzy reindeer skin let the children glue on fuzzy fabric. Have children verbally label antlers and other features of the head.
2. On pre-drawn head of a reindeer let children glue twigs for antlers. Verbally label antlers.
3. Make a brown headband and a pair of antlers for each child. Let children glue the antlers to the headband and decorate the headband.

Snack

1. Eat cookies made in Fine Motor #2 today.
2. Bring snack foods to the table in a sleigh pulled by reindeer.

Fine Motor

1. Have children path trace "A reindeer to a sleigh." and "Rudolph to the other reindeer."
2. Help children cut, bake and decorate reindeer and sleigh cookies.
3. Make a reindeer rein from strips of brown construction paper. Glue together and decorated with glue and glitter. Have children punch holes and tie on small jingle bells. (See fig. 11T.)

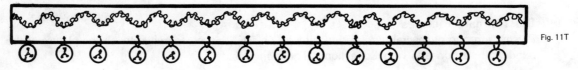

Fig. 11T

4. Let children fingerpaint in white "snow." Make a playground for the deer. Use shaving cream or white fingerpaint as the snow.

Games

1.   Arrange 5 chairs with one in front. A "reindeer" sits in the lead chair and holds a cloth strap to which small bells have been pinned. As they sing, the driver shakes the reins and the bells ring. (Sing "Jingle Bells.") (See fig. 11U.)

2.   Put a reindeer in the middle and play "Ring Around the Reindeer" like "Ring Around the Rosey." Let children take turns being reindeer.

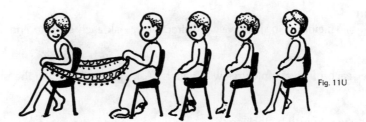

Fig. 11U

Storytelling

Tell the story of Rudolph on the flannel board or with some pictures from a book. Reduce length of story and adapt language to the individual needs of your groups. Paper clipping sections of a book that you do not want to show eases the "reading" of the story.

Gross Motor

1.   Gallop and run like reindeer. Pull sleighs (wagons) loaded with toys for Christmas.

2.   Put a rope through the front of a large cardboard box (sleigh). Have two or three children wear their reindeer headbands and pull another child in the box.

Cognitive

1.   Make a cue sheet with a reindeer (cue) at the top and reindeer and other animals or objects on the rest of the page. Have the children mark all other pictures on the page that are the same as the cue.

2.   Prepare a classification task. Place objects on a table, some reindeer and some non-reindeer. Have reindeer (toys) differ in size, color, and position of body. Have each child find "all the reindeer" and puts them in a container.

3.   Have children look at reindeer with "pairs" of antlers. Stress that reindeer have "pairs" of antlers, ears, and eyes.

Enrichment

1.   Make construction paper reindeer and construction paper sleighs. Put different numerals on the sleighs. Let the children count out the correct number of reindeer for each sleigh.

2.   Tell the complete story of "Rudolph the Red-nosed Reindeer" and let the children talk about the feelings that Rudolph had. Discuss why the others rejected him. Stress that someone who is different can still be a friend and playmate.

Lesson 6: Stocking

Unit Group Lesson

1.   **Match Concrete Objects**
Present two Christmas stockings. Say, "This is a stocking." Ask each child in turn to put the stocking with the stocking. Gradually increase number of irrelevant objects from which (s)he must select stocking match.

2.   **Discriminate Objects**
Present several objects. Have each child touch the stocking in response to verbal direction, "Touch the stocking."

3. **Match Pictures**
    Present several pictures of common objects. Have each child match the pictures of the stocking.

4. **Discriminate Pictures**
    Present a group of several unrelated pictures of objects. Have each child touch the picture of the stocking in response to verbal direction, "Touch the stocking."

5. **Figure-Ground**
    Present a "busy" picture with many visual distractions. Ask each child to find the stocking.

6. **Visual Closure**
    Partially cover each of several pictures with paper. Ask each child to find the picture of the stocking.

7. **Function**
    Ask, "What do we do with a stocking?"

8. **Association**
    Ask, "What goes with the stocking?" Use pictures or objects including Santa Claus, Christmas tree, etc. with several unrelated objects or pictures.

9. **Imitate Verbalization**
    Present a stocking and ask, "What is this? Say, 'Stocking'." The child will imitate "Stocking."

10. **Verbalize Label**
    Present a stocking and ask, "What is this?" The child will respond, "Stocking."

11. **Concept Enrichment**
    Study different types of Christmas stockings. In Holland children place their wooden shoes on the doorstep instead of hanging stockings.

Music

1. Sing to the tune of "Here We Go Round the Mulberry Bush":
    I give my friend a stocking (sto-cking)   *(Have a child carry a stocking around the*
    Stocking, stocking   *circle and give it to another at the end of*
    I give my friend a stocking   *the song.)*
    Christmas stocking.

2. Give each child a small stocking which he hides behind his back. Sing to the tune of "Where is Thumbkin?":
    Where is stocking?
    Where is stocking?
    Here it is.
    Here it is.   *(Each child holds stocking up.)*
    I have a stocking.
    I have a stocking.   Fig. 11X
    Here it is.
    Here it is.
    This is a good language builder which focuses on the pronouns it and I.

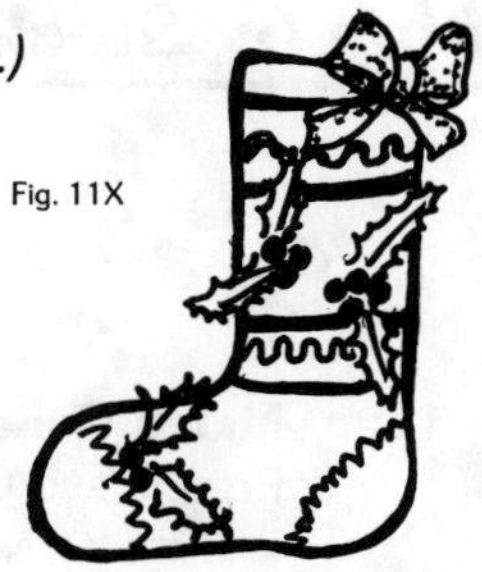

Fig. 11X

Art

1. Make Christmas stockings. Materials: two 12" long felt pieces cut in simple stocking shape for each child, hole puncher, colorful yarn, white glue, felt cut-outs for decoration, glitter, and sequins. Punch holes through both pieces of felt ½" apart. The day before you use it, dip one end of measured yarn in white glue to harden for sewing. Children sew pieces together in any style and decorate.

2. Teacher cuts giant Christmas stocking out of poster paper (brown wrapping paper). Lay it on floor. Have children decorate by painting, pasting scraps of fabric, cotton, junk jewelry, coloring, glittering, any way at all. Have a variety of materials available. Hang in room after decorating. (See fig. 11X.)

Snack
1. Serve snack out of Christmas stockings.
2. Let children roll dates in confectioner's sugar, eat some and give some away.

Fine Motor
1. Make sewing cards in shape of a Christmas stocking. Have children sew around them with shoe laces or yarn or string which has had ends stiffened with white glue.

2. Have children "stuff" stockings with surprises chosen from around the room.
3. Outline in dark marker on red and brown construction paper, bricks in sizes to fit the spaces on the fireplace in Enrichment #1. Have the children cut out the bricks.

Games
Have a stocking treasure hunt. Hide stocking in room or outside. Have children find the stockings.

Storytelling
Recite "Twas the Night Before Christmas." Emphasize the stockings being hung and have the children act out hanging stockings.

Gross Motor
1. Let children climb the jungle gym or climb up stairs to hang and retrieve stockings.
2. Have a relay race in which the children must walk, run, jump, hop, or skip carrying a gift to a Christmas stocking. Put the gift in and run back.

Cognitive
1. Cut Christmas stockings from paper with different patterns. Have children match the pairs of stockings.
2. Have children pick out items or pictures of items from a basket that would be small enough to fit into a stocking at Christmas.

Enrichment

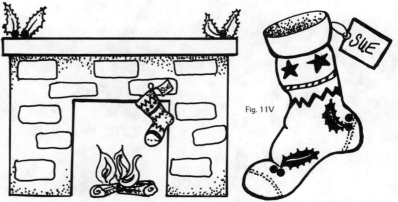

Fig. 11V

Together Activity: Make a fireplace from cardboard box or large boxes and outline bricks. Have children glue bricks cut in Fine Motor #3 today onto the outlines. (Bricks may be placed at random.) Let everyone decorate top of mantle with evergreens and candles. Have children hang stockings made in art after adding name tags for each child. (See fig. 11V.)

Field Trip
Go to a department store to visit Santa. Have children identify the concepts learned this week: Christmas tree, decorations, Santa Claus, reindeer, stocking, and Hanukkah Candles.

Related Children's Records
"My Christmas Wish" from HOLIDAY SONGS
"What A World We'd Have If Christmas Lasted All Year Long" from HOLIDAY SONGS (EA)
"Santa Claus Is Coming" from ACTION SONGS FOR ALL OCCASIONS (EA)
"Santa's Helpers" from ACTION SONGS FOR ALL OCCASIONS (EA)
"Pack Up The Sleigh" from WITCHES BREW (EA)
"Jingle Bells" from SONGS IN MOTION-HOLIDAY (EA)
"O Christmas Tree" from SONGS IN MOTION-HOLIDAY (EA)
"The Christmas Bell Story" from LOOK AT THE HOLIDAY (GA)

Related Children's Books

Budhill, David. **CHRISTMAS TREE FARM.** New York: Macmillan Publishing Co., 1974.

Brown, Margaret Wise. **ON CHRISTMAS EVE.** Reading, Mass.' Addison-Wesley Publishing Co., 1961.

Ets, Marie Hall. **NINE DAYS TO CHRISTMAS.** New York: Viking Press, 1959.

Goffstein, M.B. **LAUGHING LATKES.** New York: Farrar Straus-Girox, 1980.

Moncure, Jane Belk. **OUR CHRISTMAS BOOK.** Elgin, Ill.: Child's World, 1977.

Simon, Norma. **HANUKKAH IN MY HOUSE.** New York: United Synagogue Book Service, 1960.

Related Parenting Materials

Cansler, Dot. **THE HOMESTRETCH.** Winston-Salem, NC 27113-5128: Kaplan Press, 1983.

Related Materials

TEACHING PICTURES. Winston-Salem, NC 27113-5128: Kaplan Press, 1983.

STORY SEQUENCE CARDS I, II. Winston-Salem, NC 27113-5128: Kaplan Press, 1983.

SEWING CARDS I, II, III. Winston-Salem, NC 27113-5128: Kaplan Press, 1983.

Unit 12: Winter

A developmental assessment should determine the functional levels of each child. Individual expectations are based on the assessment results.

Lesson 1: Snow

Unit Group Lesson

Note: If real snow is not available, use pictures for numbers 1 and omit numbers 2 and 3.

1. **Match Concrete Objects**
    Present snow. Say, "This is snow." Ask each child in turn to put the snow with the snow. Gradually increase number of irrelevant objects from which (s)he must select snow to match.

2. **Discriminate Objects**
    Present several objects. Have each child touch the snow in response to verbal direction, "Touch the snow."

3. **Match Pictures**
    Present several pictures of common objects. Have each child match the pictures of the snow.

4. **Discriminate Pictures**
    Present a group of several unrelated pictures of objects. Have each child touch the picture of the snow, in response to the verbal direction, "Touch the snow."

5. **Figure-Ground**
    Present a "busy" picture with many visual distractions. Ask each child to find the snow.

6. **Visual Closure**
    Partially cover each of several pictures with paper. Ask each child to find the picture of the snow.

7. **Function**
    Ask, "What do we do with snow?"

8. **Association**
    Ask, "What goes with the snow?" Use pictures or objects including snowman, ice, winter coat, etc. with several unrelated objects or pictures.

9. **Imitate Verbalization**
    Present snow and ask, "What is this? Say, 'Snow'." The child will imitate "Snow."

10. **Verbalize Label**
    Present snow and ask, "What is this?" The child will respond, "Snow."

11.   **Concept Enrichment**
Discuss the fact that snow is cold. Have children name other cold things.

Music

1.   Sing to the tune of "Here We Go 'Round the Mulberry Bush":
The white snow falls (fa-alls) down, down, down
Down, down, down   *(Arms and hands move down, fingers, wiggle.)*
Down, down, down
The white snow falls (fa-alls) down, down, down
All all-all on the ground   *(Move whole body to floor.)*

2.   Sing to the tune of "Are You Sleeping, Brother John":
Verse 1: We are cold.   *(Have children jump in places.)*
We are cold.
Let's get warm.
Let's get warm.
Repeat.

Verse 2: Make a snowball.
Make a snowball.
Throw it now.   *(Throwing motion.)*
Throw it now.
Make a snowball.
Make a snowball.
Throw it now, throw it now.
Repeat action with wiggle, run in place, rub hands together, put on a coat, wrap a scraf around neck,
and get under a blanket substituted for jump in place.

3.   Do Creative Rhythm/Body Movement. To soft instrumental music, have children act out snow falling,
drifting, blowing, and coming to the ground. Model movements.

Art

1.   Whip Ivory Flakes with a little water to make "snow." Let the children feel, squeeze, mold it into
shapes, use it like fingerpaint or put it on cardboard soup bowls for an igloo effect when it dries.

3.   Begin a mural for the whole week, to be added to each day. On a large paper put leafless trees drawn
on by you. Have the children glue cotton or white packing material on the ground and branches to
make snow.

Snack

1.   If there is plenty of snow on the ground make snow cream. Add milk, sugar, and vanilla to snow. Let
the children do the stirring and serving.
2.   Make and eat snow cones. (Crushed ice with juice concentrate poured on top.)
3.   Lick and stick marshmallows together. Then eat.

Fine Motor

1.   Make snowball sewing cards from paper plates. Punch holes around the edges. Let the children use
white string or yarn.
2.   Let children make pictures in rice or salt.
3.   Make outline of a town scene and let the children follow the dark lines with "snow" (white cotton balls
on small marshmallows, licks & sticks). (See fig. 12A.)

Fig. 12A

Games

1. Have a contest to see, "How long can you hold a snowball?", "Who can hold it the longest?" and "It makes your hands feel cold!"
2. Divide the class into teams and give each team a cup of snow. Determine which cup stays frozen the longest. Have children pass cup around to each member of the team when their hands get too cold from holding it.

Storytelling

Use a flannel board to tell the story of snow coming down (small paper flakes) and covering the ground (cotton), and children playing with snowballs and snowmen.

Gross Motor

1. If snow is on the ground, have everyone go outside, make snowballs, and play in the snow.
2. Have a snowball relay. A child carries a "snowball" (styrofoam ball) to a designated point, returns and hands it to next child.
3. Let children have a snowball fight with large cotton balls, wadded-up tissue paper, or white yarn balls.

Cognitive

1. Have children look at the roundness of snowballs. Help children identify other round things in the classroom.
2. Have children watch snow melt and discuss why this happens.

Enrichment

1. Let the children make letters in rice or shaving cream.
2. Have the children punch holes from waxed paper and put waxed paper holes into a jar full of water. Make sure the lid is tightly secured. Let the children shake a snowstorm.

Lesson 2: Snowman

Unit Group Lesson

1. **Match Concrete Objects**
   Present snowman. Say, "This is snowman." Ask each child in turn to put the snowman with the snowman. Gradually increase number of irrelevant objects from which (s)he must select snowman to match.

2. **Discriminate Objects**
   Present several objects. Have each child touch the snowman in response to verbal direction, "Touch the snowman."

3. **Match Pictures**
   Present several pictures of common objects. Have each child match the pictures of the snowmen.

4. **Discriminate Pictures**
   Present a group of several unrelated pictures of objects. Have each child touch the picture of the snowman, in response to the verbal direction, "Touch the snowman."

5. **Figure-Ground**
   Present a "busy" picture with many visual distractions. Ask each child to find the snowman.

6. **Visual Closure**
   Partially cover each of several pictures with paper. Ask each child to find the picture of the snowman.

7. **Function**

Ask, "What do we do with a snowman?"

8. **Association**

Ask, "What goes with the snowman?" Use pictures or objects including snow, brown top hat, etc. with several unrelated objects or pictures.

9. **Imitate Verbalization**

Present snowman and ask, "What is this? Say, 'Snowman'." The child will imitate "Snowman."

10. **Verbalize Label**

Present snowman and ask, "What is this?" The child will respond, "Snowman."

11. **Concept Enrichment**

Discuss the fact that snow is cold. Have children name other cold things. Ask, "What happens if a snowman gets warm?"

Music

1. Use snowman masks made in Art #1. Have the children hold masks behind them and sing to tune of "Where is Thumbkin?", "Where Is Snowman":

  Verse 1: Where is snowman?
      Where is snowman?
      Here I am!   *(Hold masks in front of face.)*
      Here I am!
      I am a snowman
      I am a snowman
      Here I am!
      Here I am!
  Verse 2: Make a snowman.   *(Pantomime making a snowman.)*
      Make a snowman.
      Make it now.
      Make it now.
      Repeat.

2. Sing "Frosty the Snowman."

Art

1. Have the children make snowman faces from paper plates, black construction paper for facial features and hats, and a stick taped to the bottom for holding. Model the pasting task. Cut holes for the eyes. The face can be held up as a snowman mask.
2. Add to the mural begun in Lesson #1 Art #3. Cut out snowmen. (The more skilled children can cut their own.) Have the children cover them with glue and cotton balls. Add these to the snow scene.
3. Have the children use chalk on black construction paper to make a snowman. Provide an outline for those children who need the cue.
4. Have the children paint a stencil of snowman. Tape the stencil to the tablets to hold it securely.

Snack

1. Model making marshmallow snowmen. Add raisins for eyes, nose, mouth, buttons, then eat. Let the children make and eat theirs.
2. Make or buy snowman cookies.

Fine Motor

1. Do a path tracing of "Take the hat to the snowman." and "Take the snowball to the snowman." Vary the difficulty of the paths to suit each child's ability.
2. Have the children blow styrofoam balls across the table. Make a track with masking tape.
3. Have children follow the dotted outline of a snowman on paper with a marker.

4.   Together Picture: SNOWMAN HILL
       Tape a large sheet of paper on the floor or on a table. Draw a hill with circles for the children to trace.
       Draw at least one complete snowman. Have the children trace circles, complete snowman, add
       features, add small snowballs (circles), and make snow fall on picture (cotton pieces). (See fig. 12B.)

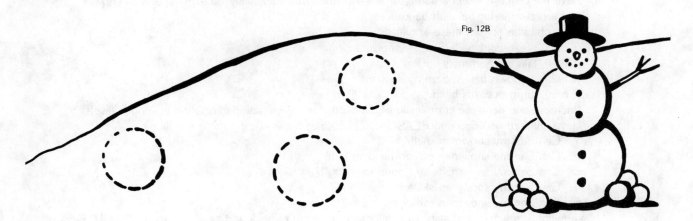

Fig. 12B

Games

1.   Make a snowman outside.
2.   Play "ring around the snowman."
3.   Hide cut-out snowmen. Let the children find them.
4.   Make large cut-out snowman. Have the children tape the eyes (nose, hat, etc.) on the snowman. Use
       tape or magnet to attach the missing part.

Storytelling

1.   Repeat flannel board story from Lesson #1 Storytelling. Have the children tell more of story this time.
2.   Tell a squence story:
          a. Snow falls
          b. Covers ground
          c. Children build snowman
          d. Sun shines on snowman
          e. Snowman melts, all snow is gone
       Tell the story, then the children help by telling "what comes next."
3.   Read *Katy and the Big Snow* by Burton or *Snow* by Eastman.

Gross Motor

1.   Have children toss "snow balls" at snowman mounted on the front of a trash can.
2.   Place two pictures of snowmen on floor a foot apart. Keep moving these further apart. Have each
       child jump from one snowman to the next.
3.   Have the children pretend to melt like snowmen, slowly sinking to the floor.

Cognitive

1.   Have several pairs of cut-out snowmen dressed exactly alike. Have the children find the two snowmen
       that match.
2.   Use 3 sizes of white circles. Help the children make a snowman using the largest circle at the bottom,
       the smallest circle for the snowman's head. "Where else could we use circles?" (eyes, nose, etc.)
       "Would those circles be big or little?"
3.   Have the children cut white circles and put them together for a snowman. Then have them follow
       these verbal directions:
          a. Draw the snowman a hat, a scarf, and some mittens in the same color.
          b. Match all the snowmen who are wearing the same colors.
          c. Count the number of snowmen wearing red, blue, green, etc.

Enrichment

1. Cut 18", 15" and 12" circles one of each. Have the children form a circle and cover them with tufts of cotton pulled from cotton balls. Then have:

    a. One child make a snowman from in the center of the circle.

    b. Have the children select a name for the snowman that starts with the same sound as snow.

    c. Add a rectangle for hat with band.

    d. Have children act out these activities:

    (Child), please sit beside Sammy snowman.

    (Child), take off Sammy's hat.

    (Child), lie down beside Sammy snowman.

    (Child), jump over his head.

    (Increase and decrease complexity of directions for appropriate participation at various levels)

    e. Have children participate in REASONING activities by answering these questions:

    1. Can Sammy snowman melt?

    2. Can Sammy snowman put on his own hat?

    3. Can Sammy snowman say "good morning"?

    4. Can Sammy snowman skate on the pond?

    5. Can Sammy snowman roll down the hill?

2. Make twenty snowmen and staple a small piece of velcro at neck and head of each. Make 10 pairs of caps and scarves in different colors or designs and staple velcro to the back of each. Have children match the caps and scarves by color. Decrease and increase numbers of pairs with which each child works according to his ability. This activity may also be done with different designs or patterns on the caps and scarves for high level children. (See fig. 12C.)

Fig. 12C

Lesson 3: Sled

Unit Group Lesson

1. **Match Concrete Objects**

    Present two sleds. Say, "This is a sled." Ask each child in turn to put the sled with the sled. Gradually increase number of irrelevant objects from which (s)he must select sled to match.

2. **Discriminate Objects**

    Present several objects. Have each child touch the sled inresponse to verbal direction, "Touch the sled."

3. **Match Pictures**

    Present several pictures of common objects. Have each child match the pictures of the sleds.

4. **Discriminate Pictures**

Present a group of several unrelated pictures of objects. Have each child touch the picture of the sled, in response to the verbal direction, "Touch the sled."

5. **Figure-Ground**

Present a "busy" picture with many visual distractions. Ask each child to find the sled.

6. **Visual Closure**

Partially cover each of several pictures with paper. Ask each child to find the picture of the sled.

7. **Function**

Ask, "What do we do with a sled?"

8. **Association**

Ask, "What goes with the sled?" Use pictures or objects including snow, snowman, cold weather clothing, etc. with several unrelated objects or pictures.

9. **Imitate Verbalization**

Present sled and ask, "What is this? Say, 'Sled'." The child will imitate "Sled."

10. **Verbalize Label**

Present sled and ask, "What is this?" The child will respond, "Sled."

11. **Concept Enrichment**

Discuss the fact that wheels are good on the ground, but sleds have runners because flat surfaces are better on snow. Name other snow transportation that uses runners or flat surfaces for movement. (Skis, ice skates, toboggan, snowshoes, etc.).

Music

1. Sing to the tune of "A-Hunting We Will Go":

   A-sledding we will go
   A-sledding we will go
   We'll hold on tight
   And sit just right
   And down the hill we go.
   We-e-e-e!

   Provide a real sled for the children to sit on. Use a toy sled to show children how sled moves down a hill (draw hill on chalkboard). Sing song and demonstrate sled in motion.

2. Sing to the Campbell's Soup commerical "Um Um Good":

   Sammy, Sammy,   (Name each child in the class.)
   Verse 1 - Can you go and find the sled.   (Help child perform each activity.)
   Verse 2 - Put the box on the sled.
   Verse 3 - Take John to the sled.
   Verse 4 - Put the book under the sled.
   This is an excellent language activity.

3. Sing to the tune of "Here We Go Round the Mulberry Bush":

   a. Johnny walk around the sled (real or picture) so early in the morning   (Have the named child
   b. Johnny jump over the sled (real or picture) so early in the morning   perform the activities.)
   c. Johnny step on the sled (real or picture   so early in the morning
   Give each child a turn.

Art

1. Prepare a Figure-Ground activity by creating a busy picture with a sled in it. Have each child decorate the sled.

2. Have the children paste cut-outs of sleds (different sizes and positions) on pre-drawn outlines which match. (Vary the difficulty according to the child's level of functioning.) Let the children decorate the picture.
3. Have the children use play dough to make sleds with children riding them.
4. Add to the mural begun in Lesson #1 Art #3. Let them decorate some of the sled cut-outs from #2 above and add to the scene.

Snack
1. Use a real sled as a table for eating snack. Eat white foods such as popcorn, milk, etc. while seated on or around the sled.
2. Make "sleds" from bread or cookie dough. Let the "sleds" go "down the hill" into the stomach.

Fine Motor
1. Prepare a path tracing of "A child riding a sled to his house," and "A child taking his sled to the top of the hill." Vary the degree of difficulty according to the abilities of the children. Have each child do one which is appropriate for his level.
2. Make cardboard sleds and have the children decorate them. Glue catalog cut-outs of people onto sleds. The more adept children can cut out their own sleds.
3. Have the children make a cut-out sled to guide along a path made on the table with parallel pieces of tape. (See fig. 12D.)

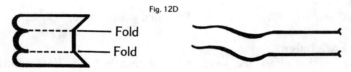

Fig. 12D

— Fold
— Fold

Games
1. Let the children use cardboard sleds to race down an inclined plane.
2. Have the children play board games with small cut-out sleds as the markers.

Storytelling
1. Have a film showing sledding. Find one in the library under "Winter Fun," winter games, or winter sports.
2. Make up a flannel board story about the "Sled That No One Wanted." Bobby did not want it because he was too big for it. Susie did not want it because it never snowed. Let the children help you choose other reasons why people did not want the sled. At the end the sled finds someone who wants it.
3. Make up a story about a sled which was broken. Tell how sad he felt when he saw all other sleds racing down the hill. He had difficulty accepting the fact that he could no longer slide down the hill. One day a lady found him. Her plants were dying because the floor of her house was too cold and she had no place to put the plants. She took the sled home and fixed him so he could hold up her plants. He liked having such beautiful plants sit on him and she was happy becuase her plants were healthy.

Gross Motor
1. Ride on real sleds if possible.
2. Let the children slide down grassy hills in boxes if there is no snow.
3. Flatten out a large box, put ropes through it, and let the children pull each other on the "sled."

Cognitive
1. Bring in a real sled and study it. Have children look at the runners under the seat. Talk about positions for riding on the sled. Let the children try different positions (sitting, tummy down, etc.). Have children look at the steering mechanism, etc.
2. How many children can sit on a sled at one time? Do this and have the children count how many.
3. Help the children associate the sled with the season: Show a winter picture and a summer picture. Have each child touch and label the winter picture in response to teacher's question, "Do we use a sled in the summer or in the winter?" Include appropriate toys for each season. Trikes for summer, a sled for winter. Point to each picture and have the children act out cold feeling for winter, hot feeling for summer.

Enrichment

1. Bring in a real sled and measure it. Use different measurement tools. For example: "How many toy sleds make up a big sled?"
2. Have the children find answers to: "What in our classroom is longer than the sled?" "Shorter?" Stand the sled up. Measure to children's heights.
3. Ask, "What are sleds made from?" and "How are they made?"

Lesson 4: Ice

Unit Group Lesson

1. **Match Concrete Objects**
   Present two pieces of ice. Say, "This is ice." Ask each child in turn to put the ice with the ice. Gradually increase number of irrelevant objects from which (s)he must select ice to match.

2. **Discriminate Objects**
   Present several objects. Have each child touch the ice in response to verbal direction, "Touch the ice."

3. **Match Pictures**
   Present several pictures of common objects. Have each child match the pictures of the ice.

4. **Discriminate Pictures**
   Present a group of several unrelated pictures of objects. Have each child touch the picture of the ice in response to the verbal direction, "Touch the ice."

5. **Figure-Ground**
   Present a "busy" picture with many visual distractions. Ask each child to find the ice.

6. **Visual Closure**
   Partially cover each of several pictures with paper. Ask each child to find the picture of the ice.

7. **Function**
   Ask, "What do we do with ice?"

8. **Association**
   Ask, "What goes with the ice?" Use pictures or objects including snow, cold weather clothing, sled, etc. with several unrelated objects or pictures.

9. **Imitate Verbalization**
   Present ice and ask, "What is this? Say, 'Ice'." The child will imitate "Ice."

10. **Verbalize Label**
    Present ice and ask, "What is this?" The child will respond, "Ice."

11. **Concept Enrichment**
    Discuss differences between snow and ice. Discuss how trees look in icy weather. Use the words icicles, sleet, hail, etc.

Music

Have the children hold large picture of winter trees. Sing to the tune of the Campbell's soup commerical: "Um Um Good":

> It is winter
> We have no leaves
> Here we stand
> Icy winter trees.   *(Blow like the wind.)*

Art

1. Have the children make a crayon picture on medium dark paper, and paint all over it with equal parts of epsom salts and water. "Ice crystals" will appear when the liquid dries.
2. Help the children make winter trees. Gather twigs outside, glue several together, and stick them in a small cup of dirt.
3. Add to the mural begun in Lesson #1 Art #3. On other white paper have the children paint an icy lake, river and other icy patches by using a paint made from a drop or two of blue food cloring and half as much warm water as epsom salts. Let the paint cool and thicken so it will not run. After the paint is dry, cut out the pieces and glue them onto the mural.

Snack

1. Color water with food coloring and freeze. Use in drinks.
2. Have or make ice cream.

Fine Motor

1. Have each child follow dot-to-dot outline of a winter tree with icicles on it.
2. Put a twiggy branch in a container of dirt. Attach paper leaves lightly. Provide paper icicles. Let the children blow off the leaves and replace them with icicles.
3. Draw several "stick-figure" ice skaters on blackboard (at child level) or on large sheet of paper taped at child level or flat on a table. Have the children scribble swirls with strokes across the "ice." (See fig. 12E.)

Fig. 12E

Games

Have the children "skate" around the room. Then when Jack Frost (teacher) touches them, they "freeze." When the sun (child with sun mask) touches them they "melt" and skate again.

Storytelling

1. Make large picture cards showing the sequence of tree growth:
    a. full summer tree
    b. colorful fall tree
    c. bare winter tree with ice around it
    d. spring tree with green buds
    After telling the story of how a tree changes from season to season, mix up the four pictures and let children put them in sequence. Then have a child tell the story and show the cards.
2. Make a sequence story to use in Cognitive 3. Show how water becomes ice. Show in pictures: Water; Water in a tray: Tray in freezer; Ice coming out of tray. Tell the children the story and let them retell it.

Gross Motor

1. Let the children knock down icicles with bean bags.
2. Pretend to ice skate to music. Encourage children to be "graceful."

Cognitive

1. Freeze ice cubes in different shapes. See Storytelling #2.
2. Ask "Is water always wet?" Show that the answer is "No." by touching paper to ice and noticing that it is dry.

3.	Watch ice melt. What does it become?

Enrichment
1.	Put things on an ice cube (penny, salt, paper clips, etc.). What happens?
2.	Try different ways to melt an ice cube (in water, wrapped in a paper towel, etc.). Time each method and decide which way helps the ice last longest.
3.	Show that water gets bigger when it freezes by filling a plastic container to the top with water and freezing it. The ice comes over the top of the container and may even break the container.

Lesson 5: Cold-Weather Clothing

Unit Group Lesson

1.	**Match Concrete Objects**
Present two pieces of cold-weather clothing. Say, "This is cold-weather clothing." Ask each child in turn to put the cold-weather clothing with the cold-weather clothing. Gradually increase number of irrelevant objects from which (s)he must select cold-weather clothing to match.

2.	**Discriminate Objects**
Present several objects. Have each child touch the cold -weather clothing in response to verbal direction, "Touch the cold-weather clothing."

3.	**Match Pictures**
Present several pictures of common objects. Have each child match the pictures of the cold-weather clothing.

4.	**Discriminate Pictures**
Present a group of several unrelated pictures of objects. Have each child touch the picture of the cold-weather clothing, in response to the verbal direction, "Touch the cold-weather clothing."

5.	**Figure-Ground**
Present a "busy" picture with many visual distractions. Ask each child to find the cold-weather clothing.

6.	**Visual Closure**
Partially cover each of several pictures with paper. Ask each child to find the picture of the cold-weather clothing.

7.	**Function**
Ask, "What do we do with cold-weather clothing?"

8.	**Association**
Ask, "What goes with the cold-weather clothing?" Use pictures or objects including snow, snowman, sled, etc. with several unrelated objects or pictures.

9.	**Imitate Verbalization**
Present cold-weather clothing and ask, "What is this? Say, 'Cold-weather clothing'." The child will imitate "Cold-weather clothing."

10.	**Verbalize Label**
Present cold-weather clothing and ask, "What is this?" The child will respond, "Cold-weather clothing."

11.	**Concept Enrichment**
Discuss clothing for other temperatures. Compare the thickness of clothing for different seasons.

Music

1. Sing to the tune of "Row, Row, Row Your Boat":

    Blow, blow, blow the wind   *(Blow.)*
    Put on your hat and coat   *(Pantomime action.)*
    Brrr, brrr, brrr, brrr   *(Arms across chest.)*
    Winter time is here.

2. Sing to the tune of "Are You Sleeping?":

    We-e are co-old.   *(Have everyone jump in place.)*
    We-e are co-old.
    Let's get warm.
    Let's get warm.
    Repeat

    Substitute wiggle in place, run in place, rub hands together, put on a coat, wrap a scarf around neck, and get under a blanket for jumpin place.

Art

1. Add to mural started in Lesson #1 Art #3. Draw simple figures of boys and girls standing in the snow. Say, "Look at these boys and girls, they are cold. What do they need?" Let the children tell what they need and come to the mural to show where that particular article of clothing goes. Then let the children paint, color or paste in winter clothing such as hats, mittens, coats, boots, etc.

2. On a pre-drawn outline of a boy or girl, have the children paste paper or fabric winter clothes. You may need to have these pre-cut.

3. Have the children find pictures of "winter clothes" in a magazine and cut them out and paste them on paper.

Snack

Eat snack while wearing mittens.

Fine Motor

1. Cut paper mittens for each child. Let the children punch holes in the tops of the mittens and hook them together with a piece of yarn. The more skilled children can cut their own mittens.

2. Have the children trim winter clothing with "fur" made of tufts of cotton. Provide caps, mittens and scarves in bright color paper with lines to follow for adding "fur." Let the children fringe the ends of the scarves. Put the winter clothing on paper dolls made of newspaper. (See fig. 12F.)

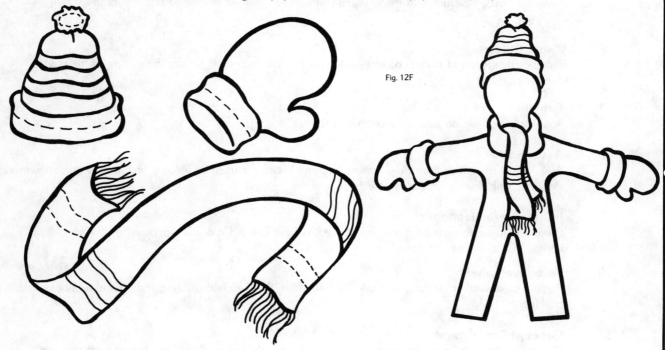

Fig. 12F

3. Have the children path trace a string to tie the mittens together so the child cannot lose them. Use simple paths for lower functioning children and more complex paths for higher functioning children. (See fig. 12G.)

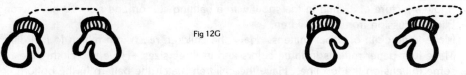

Fig 12G

4. Punch holes in a brown, black, or red tagboard boot. Let the children "lace" with a long shoe lace. (See fig. 12H.)

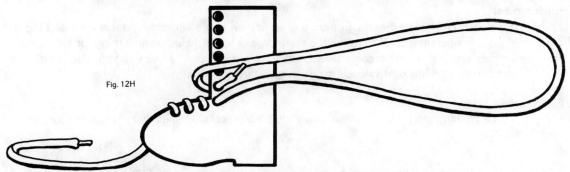

Fig. 12H

5. Give each child mitten shapes cut or outlined in heavy black for cutting. Let them decorate with stripes or border, outline the top with cotton tufts of "fur," and staple on heavy yarn so that mittens can hang around their necks. (See fig. 12I.)

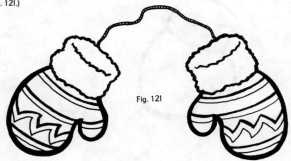

Fig. 12I

Games
1. Set up a store with a mixture of summer and winter clothes. Send the children to the store with play money (toy play money, or money made from construction paper) to buy winter clothes. Talk with them about what they buy and why it is or is not winter clothing.
2. Make a feely box. Place a piece of ice and another object in the box. Let each child find the thing that is cold.
3. Have cold-weather child and doll clothes in the housekeeping corner.

Storytelling
1. Make up a story of a girl going out to play on a cold winter day. She goes out, comes back in for a sweater, goes out, back in for a coat, out, etc. (hat, gloves, scarf, boots, etc.).
2. Read *Pelle's New Coat.*

Gross Motor
1. Have the children divide in to two teams. The first child on each team runs to a box of winter clothing (coat, mittens), puts on something, runs back. The next child goes to the box and gets a different piece of clothing.
2. Have everyone learn to put his/her own winter clothing on. They can put coats "over the head" and mittens on hands. Have extras for practice.

Cognitive
1. Make cut-out hats, coats, and mittens of different colors. Let the children match which are the same color.

2. Prepare a classification task. Place pictures of winter clothing and summer clothing. Have the children find all the winter clothing and put it in a box.
3. Show a picture of a child in the snow with a bathing suit on and ask, "What's wrong with this picture?" Elicit discussion from the children.
4. Make large cloth or paper mittens. Have the children reach into mitten to feel different objects.
5. Make four paper mittens in three colors and in three sizes. Have two clotheslines. Use clips to hang some mittens on the top line. Have the children match the pattern in the bottom line.

Enrichment
1. Have each child copy the design from a given mitten to a plain mitten to make a matching mitten. (See fig. 12J.)
2. Make a temperature chart to go with a thermometer which helps plan clothing for different temperatures. It can be made with cut-outs from old catalogs. Have children glue cut-outs of appropriate clothing next to each major temperature. (See fig. 12K.)

Field Trip
Visit a clothing store. Look at the winter clothing especially things that are suitable for very cold weather.

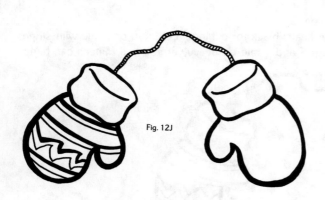

Fig. 12J

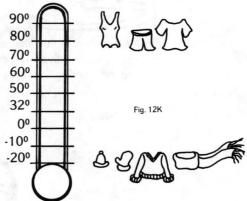

Fig. 12K

Related Children's Records
"Angels In the Snow" from **GET A GOOD START**
"I Love the Winter" from **LOOK AT THE HOLIDAYS** (GA)
"Winter Season" from **JAMBO** (SCHOL)
"Pease Porridge Hot" from **NURSERY RHYME** (SCHOL)
"Winter" from **THIS IS RHYTHM** (SCHOL)
"Posture Exercises" from **LEARNING BASIC SKILLS-HEALTH & SAFETY** (EA)

Related Children's Books
Hader, Berta and Hader, Elmer. **THE BIG SNOW.** New York: Macmillan Publishing Co., 1948.
Keats, Ezra Jack. **THE SNOWY DAY.** New York: Viking Press, 1962.
Miles, Betty. **A DAY OF WINTER.** New York: Albert A. Knopf, 1961.
Moncure, Jane Belk. **WINTER IS HERE!** Elgin, Ill.: Child's World, 1975.

Related Parenting Materials
Cansler, Dot. **THE HOMESTRETCH.** Winston-Salem, NC 27113-5128: Kaplan Press, 1983.

Related Materials
TEACHING PICTURES. Winston-Salem, NC 27113-5128: Kaplan Press, 1983.
STORY SEQUENCE CARDS I, II. Winston-Salem, NC 27113-5128: Kaplan Press, 1983.
SEWING CARDS I, II, III. Winston-Salem, NC 27113-5128: Kaplan Press, 1983.

Unit 13: Living Room

A developmental assessment should determine the functional levels of each child. Individual expectations are based on the assessment results.

Lesson 1: Sofa

Unit Group Lesson

1. **Match Concrete Objects** (Use toys.)
   Present two sofas. Say, "This is a sofa." Ask each child in turn to put the sofa with the sofa. Gradually increase number of irrelevant objects from which (s)he must select sofa to match.

2. **Discriminate Objects**
   Present several objects. Have each child touch the sofa in response to verbal direction, "Touch the sofa."

3. **Match Pictures**
   Present several pictures of common objects. Have each child match the pictures of the sofas.

4. **Discriminate Pictures**
   Present a group of several unrelated pictures of objects. Have each child touch the picture of the sofa in response to verbal direction, "Touch the sofa."

5. **Figure-Ground**
   Present a "busy" picture with many visual distractions. Ask each child to find the sofa.

6. **Visual Closure**
   Partially cover each of several pictures with paper. Ask each child to find the picture of the sofa.

7. **Function**
   Ask, "What do we do with a sofa?"

8. **Association**
   Ask, "What goes with the sofa?" Use pictures or objects including cushions, chair, living room table, T.V., etc., with several unrelated objects or pictures.

9. **Imitate Verbalization**
   Present a sofa and ask, "What is this? Say, 'Sofa'." The child will imitate "Sofa."

10. **Verbalize Label**
    Present a sofa and ask, "What is this?" The child will respond, "Sofa."

11.   **Concept Enrichment**
Discuss different types of sofas. Sofas are used in living rooms and family rooms. Sofas have different names such as couch, divan, love seat, etc.

Music
1.   Sing to the tune of "Three Blind Mice":
Three little sofas,   *(Show 3 toy or picture sofas.)*
Three little sofas,
Take one away and we have
Two little sofas.   *(Hide one, show two.)*
Repeat for two then one sofa.
2.   Sing to the tune of "The Farmer in the Dell":
I walk to find the sofa   *(Have each child identify the sofa in a group*
I walk to find the sofa   *of objects.)*
Hi-ho the deery-o
I walk to find the sofa.
(Substitute run, gallop, hop and skip for walk.)

Art
1.   Let children find pictures of sofas in home decorating magazines, cut out (with help from teacher if necessary), and paste on construction paper.
2.   Draw on large paper, a line drawing of a furnished living room for each child. Have each child paste sofa on the appropriate outlined space. Each day the child will paste another piece of living room furniture in the proper place.
3.   Make a large mural of a living room with a sofa outline. Have the children paste bits of fabric on the sofa.

Snack
Eat snack sitting on (or pretending to sit on) a sofa. Talk about being careful of spills.

Fine Motor
1.   Have the children glue beans or rice on outline of sofa.
2.   Do path tracing of "A girl going to sit on a sofa." and "A boy going to sit on a sofa."
3.   Use stickers or crayons to decorate a sofa outline.

Games
1.   Play "Go Fish" for a sofa. Tie a magnet on the end of a string which is attached to a yard stick. Place a paper clip on pictures of various objects, including some sofas. Spread out the pictures and let the child "fish" for the sofa pictures.
2.   Play drop the sofa like "Drop the Handkerchief." One child drops a toy sofa behind another child in circle; that child picks it up and chases the first child.
3.   Have a sofa available for the doll house. Discuss which room is appropriate for it.

Storytelling
Tell a flannel board story. Cut out pictures of various rooms in the house and a flannel cut-out of a sofa. Make up a story about a little sofa looking for a place to live. The sofa interacts with the children and asks them: "Is this my room?" "Why not?" "Why?"

Gross Motor
1.   Arrange chairs to be a "sofa." Walk, run, skip, etc. to sit on the sofa.
2.   Play a relay game carrying the doll house sofa.
3.   Make a "sofa" out of large blocks.

Cognitive

1. Make sofas out of wallpaper scraps. Cut them in half and have the children match the correct pieces together.
2. If a real sofa is available "How many children can sit on the (chair) sofa?" Seat the children and count them.
3. Think up how many different ways a child can use a sofa.

Enrichment

1. Construct a sofa out of boxes, scraps of lumber, and cloth.
2. Put a real sofa in a quiet corner for reading and looking at books.

Lesson 2: Table

Unit Group Lesson

1. **Match Concrete Objects**
    Present two tables. Say, "This is a table." Ask each child in turn to put the table with the table. Gradually increase number of irrelevant objects from which (s)he must select table to match.

2. **Discriminate Objects**
    Present several objects. Have each child touch the table in response to verbal direction, "Touch the table."

3. **Match Pictures**
    Present several pictures of common objects. Have each child match the pictures of the tables.

4. **Discriminate Pictures**
    Present a group of several unrelated pictures of objects. Have each child touch the picture of the table in response to verbal direction, "Touch the table."

5. **Figure-Ground**
    Present a "busy" picture with many visual distractions. Ask each child to find the table.

6. **Visual Closure**
    Partially cover each of several pictures with paper. Ask each child to find the picture of the table.

7. **Function**
    Ask, "What do we do with a table?"

8. **Association**
    Ask, "What goes with the table?" Use pictures or objects including sofa, lamp, T.V., chair, etc., with several unrelated objects or pictures.

9. **Imitate Verbalization**
    Present a table and ask, "What is this? Say, 'Table'." The child will imitate "Table."

10. **Verbalize Label**
    Present a table and ask, "What is this?" The child will respond, "Table."

11. **Concept Enrichment**
    Discuss differences between living room tables and kitchen tables, such as: height, size, material made from, etc.

Music

1. Sing to the tune of "Farmer in the Dell":
    Around the table we go,
    Around the table we go,
    Hi-ho the deery-o,
    Around the table we go.
    (For "around," substitute other prepositions as "under" or "over," or "behind.")
2. Sing to the tune of "Pop, Goes the Weasel":
    All around the classroom
    We look for the baby
    Where is the baby?
    Under the table.
    (Sing again substituting "on," "beside," and "behind" for "under.")

Art

1. Continue the mural from Lesson 1, Art #3. On the mural make outlines of various living room tables. Have children decorate them with brown construction paper, scraps of woodtone contact paper, wall paper, or thin wood scraps.
2. Have the children build a small table out of cardboard and wooden blocks or scrap lumber.
3. Let the children paint a large box cut in the shape of a living room table.
4. Have each child continue individual living room picture from Lesson 1 Art #2 and glue on pictures of tables.

Snack

Eat snack on living room tables if possible.

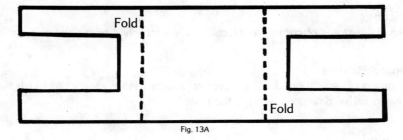

Fig. 13A

Fine Motor

1. Help each child cut a table out of construction paper. Fold legs down. (See fig. 13A.)
2. On a low table, have children roll a table tennis ball back and forth over the center or between a masking tape path.

Games

1. Put a sheet of large cloth over a folding table. Let the children get under the table.
2. Play table games.
3. Make sure there are living room tables in the housekeeping corner and dollhouse.

Storytelling

Make up a story about a tree which became a table and was used in many ways such as for eating, for art work, for changing a baby's diaper, etc.

Gross Motor

1. Divide the class into three teams. Have a child from each team run to a box of toys which includes some toy tables. Find a table, run back, pass the table to the next child who runs to the box and puts the table back in it. Continue until all children have had several turns.
2. Have the children go over, under, and around a coffee table.
3. Have each child try to roll a ball under a table without bumping the table's legs.

Cognitive

1. Display pictures of a living room, bathroom, kitchen, and bedroom. Give each child a picture of a living room table and sofa. Ask, "Which room has the table and sofa?" The child brings the picture to the appropriate room.

2. Make a list of materials from which tables are made.

3. Give the child tables in three or more different sizes. Have them sequence them from small to large.

Enrichment

Tables in Our House: Give each child a paper with the outline of a house. Have them cut out the house and name the rooms in it. Then have the child match tables cut from catalogs with each room.

Lesson 3: Chair

Unit Group Lesson

1. **Match Concrete Objects** (Use toys.)
    Present two chairs. Say, "This is a chair." Ask each child in turn to put the chair with the chair. Gradually increase number of irrelevant objects from which (s)he must select chair to match.

2. **Discriminate Objects**
    Present several objects. Have each child touch the chair in response to verbal direction, "Touch the chair."

3. **Match Pictures**
    Present several pictures of common objects. Have each child match the pictures of the chairs.

4. **Discriminate Pictures**
    Present a group of several unrelated pictures of objects. Have each child touch the picture of the chair in response to verbal direction, "Touch the chair."

5. **Figure-Ground**
    Present a "busy" picture with many visual distractions. Ask each child to find the chair.

6. **Visual Closure**
    Partially cover each of several pictures with paper. Ask each child to find the picture of the chair.

7. **Function**
    Ask, "What do we do with a chair?"

8. **Association**
    Ask, "What goes with the chair?" Use pictures or objects including sofa, living room, table, lamp, T.V., etc., with several unrelated objects or pictures.

9. **Imitate Verbalization**
    Present a chair and ask, "What is this? Say, 'Chair'." The child will imitate "Chair."

10. **Verbalize Label**
    Present a chair and ask, "What is this?" The child will respond, "Chair."

11. **Concept Enrichment**

Discuss differences between living room chair and other chair. Discuss sitting in a chair.

Music

1. Teach the children to play "Musical Chairs." Have enough chairs for each child. Before playing the game instruct the children to listen for the stop cue:

   a. Have children walk around chairs. Teacher says, "stop" without music.

   b. Have children walk around chairs. Teacher pairs her verbal signal "stop" with the stopping of music.

   c. When the children have learned to stop on the verbal command paired with the stopping of music, fade the verbal cue, teach them to listen for the stopping of the music only.

2. Sing to the tune of "Farmer in the Dell":

   The chair is behind the teacher,
   The chair is behind the teacher,
   Hi-ho the deery-o,
   The chair is behind the teacher.

   Substitute "under the table," "in the hall," "beside Sally." Procedure: You or a child places the chair in a new location for each verse. This reinforces learning of prepositions.

Art

1. Continue the mural from Lesson #1 Art #3. Makes outlines of several chairs in living room and have children glue on fabric scraps to cover each chair.

2. Make chairs out of bottle caps and match sticks. Glue sticks on for legs and backs of chairs.

3. Continue individual living room picture begun in Lesson #1 Art #2 by pasting in pictures of chairs.

Snack

Sit on a living room chair for snack.

Fine Motor

1. Outline a simple living room chair. Children can cut it out and decorate with bits of wallpaper.

2. Cut a living room chair from construction paper for each child. Outline each child's name on a chair and have him follow the outline with glue and sprinkle on glitter or sand. Let dry and each child has a tactile name to use for practicing writing his name.

Games

1. Have a child sit in a chair with his back to the group. Point to a child who walks up behind the child in the chair, disguises his voice, and says, "I see you in the chair." He then returns to his seat, and the child must guess who spoke to him. If he guesses correctly he earns another turn; if not, the child who spoke gets the turn.

2. Play musical chairs again to reinforce the rules of the game.

Storytelling

Tell the story of "Goldilocks and the Three Bears." Emphasize the chairs.

Gross Motor

1. Have children get in the chair, then out of the chair.

2. Throw a medicine ball or other large ball in the chair.

Cognitive

1. With a flannel board use cut-outs of various objects including some chairs. The chairs should be different in size, shape, and color. Place a group of cut-outs on the flannel board. Say, "Some of these are chairs and some are not chairs. Find all the chairs." Help each child to identify all the chairs.

2. Mix up all of the chairs with children's names made in Fine Motor #2 today. Help each child find his own name. See how many other names the children can identify.

Enrichment

Left-right, in-out, behind: Have the children form a line behind a chair facing its back. The child who is it must go to the left, right, in, out or behind the chair as directed. When he does all the instructions another child has a turn.

Lesson 4: Lamp

Unit Group Lesson

1. **Match Concrete Objects**
   Present two lamps. Say, "This is a lamp." Ask each child in turn to put the lamp with the lamp. Gradually increase number of irrelevant objects from which (s)he must select lamp to match.

2. **Discriminate Objects**
   Present several objects. Have each child touch the lamp in response to verbal direction, "Touch the lamp."

3. **Match Pictures**
   Present several pictures of common objects. Have each child match the pictures of the lamps.

4. **Discriminate Pictures**
   Present a group of several unrelated pictures of objects. Have each child touch the picture of the lamp in response to verbal direction, "Touch the lamp."

5. **Figure-Ground**
   Present a "busy" picture with many visual distractions. Ask each child to find the lamp.

6. **Visual Closure**
   Partially cover each of several pictures with paper. Ask each child to find the picture of the lamp.

7. **Function**
   Ask, "What do we do with a lamp?"

8. **Association**
   Ask, "What goes with the lamp?" Use pictures or objects including shade, switch, living room table, etc., with several unrelated objects or pictures.

9. **Imitate Verbalization**
   Present a lamp and ask, "What is this? Say, 'Lamp'." The child will imitate "Lamp."

10. **Verbalize Label**
    Present a lamp and ask, "What is this?" The child will respond, "Lamp."

11.   **Concept Enrichment**
       Discuss safety with electric lamps. Children should not plug and unplug lamps.

Music

Use a real lamp as a prop and have it connected to electric outlet. Sing to the tune of "Hickory Dickory Dock":

    The la-amp makes a light,
    The lamp makes a light,
    On-off, on-off
    The lamp makes a light.

Art

1.   Continue the mural begun in Lesson #1 Art #3. Outline several lamps in picture. Let children paint the lamps or decorate colored shiny paper.

2.   Continue individual picture begun in Lesson #1 Art #2. Add lamps to the living room picture.

Snack

Have a lamp on the table during snack.

Fine Motor

1.   Have the children turn a lamp on and off. It is a good fine motor activity.

2.   Mount a variety of switches on a wooden board, and let children turn them on and off.

3.   Glue cut-out pieces of a lamp together. Demonstrate by assembling a real lamp, then model the gluing tasks. Show the bulb under the shade. (See fig. 13B.)

Fig. 13B

Games

Play "What's Missing?" Use a real lamp as a prop. Have children close their eyes. Hide part of the lamp such as: shade, bulb, or base, or leave it unplugged. Let children open eyes and guess what is missing.

Storytelling

Make up a story about a lamp who stayed lit to help a child find his room and keep him from being afraid. Give children the opportunity to express their fears of the dark.

Gross Motor

With a real lamp as a prop have the children walk, run, jump, hop or skip to the lamp.

Cognitive

1.   Use real lamps and have the children put one shade with each lamp. Stress that a shade goes with each lamp.

2.   Have construction paper lamps and shades. Have children match correct shade to lamp by color.

Enrichment

Have five or more real lamps with different switches all plugged in. Teach children to turn them on and off. Have other children count how many different types each child can make work.

Lesson 5: T.V.

Unit Group Lesson

1. **Match Concrete Objects**
   Present two T.V.'s. (use toy T.V.'s if real ones are not available.) Say, "This is a T.V.." Ask each child in turn to put the T.V. with the T.V.. Gradually increase number of irrelevant objects from which (s)he must select T.V. to match.

2. **Discriminate Objects**
   Present several objects. Have each child touch the T.V. in response to verbal direction, "Touch the T.V.."

3. **Match Pictures**
   Present several pictures of common objects. Have each child match the pictures of the T.V.'s.

4. **Discriminate Pictures**
   Present a group of several unrelated pictures of objects. Have each child touch the picture of the T.V. in response to verbal direction, "Touch the T.V.."

5. **Figure-Ground**
   Present a "busy" picture with many visual distractions. Ask each child to find the T.V..

6. **Visual Closure**
   Partially cover each of several pictures with paper. Ask each child to find the picture of the T.V..

7. **Function**
   Ask, "What do we do with a T.V.?"

8. **Association**
   Ask, "What goes with the T.V.?" Use pictures or objects including sofa, chair, lamp, etc., with several unrelated objects or pictures.

9. **Imitate Verbalization**
   Present a T.V. and ask, "What is this? Say, 'T.V.'." The child will imitate "T.V.."

10. **Verbalize Label**
    Present a T.V. and ask, "What is this?" The child will respond, "T.V.."

11. **Concept Enrichment**
    Discuss safety around the T.V.. Don't sit too close. Always have a lamp on in the room when watching T.V.. Never touch the back or bottom of the T.V..

Music

Sing one or two popular, current commercial jingles from T.V.

Art

1. Have each child bring in a shoe box. Help child cut out one side for a T.V. screen. Have child wrap pre-cut paper around index finger and tape together to form a cylinder, draw face on cylinder, and add string or yarn to tip for hair. Each child has a finger puppet to perform in the shoe box T.V. (See fig. 13C.)

2.   Continue the classroom mural begun in Lesson #1 Art #3 by adding a T.V. Cut a hole and use plastic wrap for screen. Then have children make pictures to put on T.V.

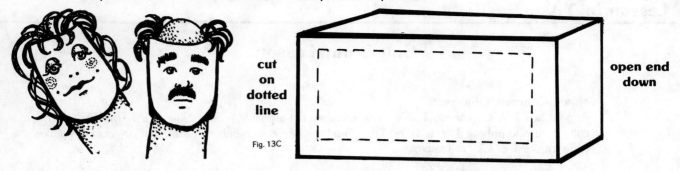

cut on dotted line

Fig. 13C

open end down

3.   Have each child continue his individual living room picture from Lesson #1 Art #2 and glue on a T.V.

Snack

Have snack on T.V. tables served in T.V. dinner trays.

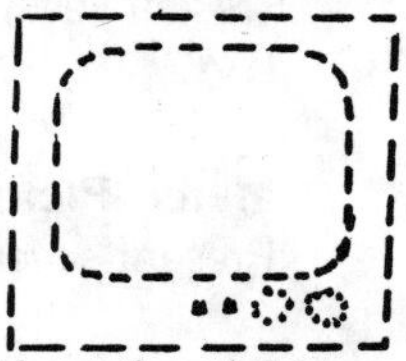

Fine Motor

1.   Have each child follow dotted lines to draw a T.V. set and screen. (See fig. 13D.)
2.   Make a sewing card. Outline a T.V. and punch holes around the T.V. screen. Have the children outline the screen with yarn.
3.   Make room puzzles from large magazine pictures of different living rooms and paste them on poster board. Cover with contact paper and cut into puzzle pieces. Make different numbers of pieces for different levels of children. Have the children put the pieces together and identify the room.

Fig. 13D

Games

1.   Get a large appliance box such as one in which a stove or refrigerator is packed. Cut out a rectangular area for a T.V. screen. Paint knobs on the outside. Let children stand inside and perform on T.V. Later this same box may be used as a store front, a puppet stage, a house, or any other large structures.
2.   Have pieces of living room funiture in the housekeeping corner. Encourage children to role play living room behavior.

Storytelling

Have the children use the shoe box T.V.'s and finger puppets made in art. Let a few children come in front of the group to tell and act out a short story.

Gross Motor

Use the T.V. made for Games #1. Have the children toss bean bags, sponge balls or basketballs into the top of the box. When they succeed, they can see their balls on T.V.

Cognitive

1.   Count the things in the class living room. Use the large living room mural made in "Art" for this unit or a plastic covered picture of a living room. Have the children count the items in the room.
2.   Make T.V.'s from construction paper and put related pictures on pairs of screens, such as a cup on one and a saucer on another. Have the children match the T.V.'s that have related items. (Make the related pairs out of the same color paper to provide a cue to the correct answer.)

Enrichment

Make T.V.'s out of poster board and cut different sized screens. Put 1 sticker on the smallest screen, 2 on the next etc. Put the corresponding numeral on the matching T.V. Cover with contact paper for durability. Have children match the correct screen to the correct T.V.

Field Trip

1. Go to a furniture store. Have the children find all the living room furniture studied in this unit. Verbalize labels for the different furniture seen.

2. Visit a house with a living room which contains all the components studied in this unit.

Related Children's Records

"Show Me" from **LEARNING BASIC SKILLS-VOC.** (EA)

"Rhythms Around the Chair" from **AND ONE AND TWO** (SCHOL)

Related Children's Books

Hurd, Thatcher. **THE OLD CHAIR.** New York: Greenwillow Books, 1978.

Johnson, John. **THIS IS MY HOUSE.** New York: Golden Press, 1981.

Mayer, Mercer. **LITTLE MONSTER AT HOME.** New York: Golden Press, 1978.

Tornborg, Pat. **SPRING CLEANING.** New York: Golden Press, 1980.

Related Parenting Materials

Cansler, Dot. **THE HOMESTRETCH.** Winston-Salem, NC 27113-5128: Kaplan Press, 1983.

Related Materials

TEACHING PICTURES. Winston-Salem, NC 27113-5128: Kaplan Press, 1983.

STORY SEQUENCE CARDS I, II. Winston-Salem, NC 27113-5128: Kaplan Press, 1983.

SEWING CARDS I, II, III. Winston-Salem, NC 27113-5128: Kaplan Press, 1983.

Unit 14: Kitchen

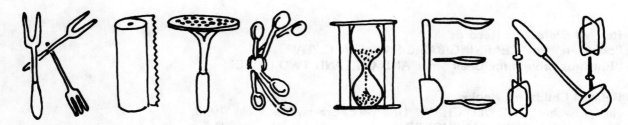

A developmental assessment should determine the functional levels of each child. Individual expectations are based on the assessment results.

Lesson 1: Stove

Unit Group Lesson

1. **Match Concrete Objects** (Use toys.)
    Present two stoves. Say, "This is a stove." Ask each child in turn to put the stove with the stove. Gradually increase number of irrelevant objects from which (s)he must select stove to match.

2. **Discriminate Objects**
    Present several objects. Have each child touch the stove in response to the verbal direction, "Touch the stove."

3. **Match Pictures**
    Present several pictures of common objects. Have each child match the pictures of the stoves.

4. **Discriminate Pictures**
    Present a group of several unrelated pictures of objects. Have each child touch the picture of the stove in response to the verbal direction, "Touch the stove."

5. **Figure-Ground**
    Present a "busy" picture with many visual distractions. Ask each child to find the stove.

6. **Visual Closure**
    Partially cover each of several pictures with paper. Ask each child to find the picture of the stove.

7. **Function**
    Ask, "What do we do with a stove?"

8. **Association**
    Ask, "What goes with the stove?" Use pictures or objects including oven, toaster, pot, pan, etc. with several unrelated objects or pictures.

9. **Imitate Verbalization**
    Present a stove and ask, "What is this? Say, 'Stove'." The child will imitate "Stove."

10. **Verbalize Label**
    Present a stove and ask, "What is this?" The child will respond, "Stove."

11. **Concept Enrichment**

A stove is used for cooking. Name other things used for cooking. Name other appliances that are used for cooking such as the oven and the toaster. Discuss stove safety: it's hot, etc.

Music

1. Sing to the tune of "Mary Had A Little Lamb":

At the stove we stir and stir,   *(Pantomime holding pot and stirring.)*
Stir and stir, stir and stir.
At the stove we stir and stir
As we cook our food.

At the oven we mix and bake,   *(Pantomime mixing and putting in the oven.)*
Mix and bake, mix and bake.
At the oven we mix and bake
As we cook our food.

2. Sing to the tune of "Hickory Dickory Dock":

We cook our food in the pot.
Watch out! The stove is hot.
Don't get too close.
You'll burn your nose,
As we cook in the pot.

Art

1. Begin a kitchen mural on one wall of the classroom. Have the children cut out and glue bits of shiny paper on outlines of cooking appliances which the you have made.
2. Help the children make an oven out of a box; have everybody paint and decorate it.
3. Let the children decorate gingerbread men cookies or pictures with frosting. (See Fine Motor #4 and Snack #2 today.)

Snack

1. Toast bread in a toaster and spread with jelly, peanut butter, or butter.
2. Eat the gingerbread men baked in Fine Motor #4 and decorated in Art #3 today.
3. Eat canned soup cooked on a stove (or hot plate).

Fine Motor

1. Make a floor plan of a kitchen on a large piece of paper for each child. Include outlines of: the stove, refrigerator, sink, a cabinet with pots, pans and trays, a cabinet with groceries, and a cabinet with dishes. Cut out stove shapes to fit the outline and let each child glue his onto his own picture.
2. Have the children find pictures of stoves in magazines, cut them out, with help if necessary, and paste them on paper for a stove collage.
3. Have the children assemble a stove from cut out shapes (basic shapes of a stove and four "eyes") and paste on paper.
4. Let the children help make gingerbread men. They can mix the ingredients, roll the dough, cut the shapes, put them on pans and go to the oven. They can take cooled cookies off the pans.

Games

1. Set out several toy stoves, ovens, and toasters, pots and pans, clay or play dough, and spoons - for free play or dramatic play.
2. Let one child pretend to cook with a toy stove, oven, toaster, pots, pans and spoons in front of small group. Have child describe what is being cooked and let the children guess what it is.

Storytelling

Read (or use flannel board cut-outs) the story of the Gingerbread Man.

Gross Motor

1. Pretend you are the bread! Down into the toaster. (Children squat down.) Now you are done and up you pop. (Children jump up.)
2. Have a relay race. The first child gets the "cookie" from the oven and runs to the table with it; the next child carries the "cookie" from the table to the oven. Continue until all have had several turns. If you make the "cookie" fairly heavy the arm muscles will work harder.

Cognitive

1. Ask, "Where does the stove go?" and hold up pictures of rooms of the house with the stove blocked out or not shown in the kitchen. Have each child point to and name the room which answers the question.
2. Have the children "find all the stoves" when shown a group of objects including some stoves of different colors, shapes and styles.
3. Have the children sort pictures of stoves, ovens and toasters into groups. Have more divisions for brighter children.
4. Put 1 slice of toast in each opening of a toaster. Use a real toaster and stress that it is one piece of toast per opening.
5. Use actual or pictures of a two- and four-slice toaster; have the children match the number of construction paper slices of toast to the appropriate toaster. Example: two slices of toast to the two slice toaster. Stress that one slice of toast goes into one opening.

Enrichment

1. Make a toaster and two slices of toast from construction paper. For each numeral 1-5, put a numeral on the toaster, the word on one piece of toast and the correct number dots on the other piece of toast. Cut slots in the toaster. Have the child put the toast into the slots of the correct toaster. Laminate all materials for durability. (See fig. 14A.)
2. Make many gingerbread men from brown construction paper and ovens from different colors. Put a color word on each gingerbread man and let the children match him to the oven which is the correct color. (Provide a color cue on some by using a label which matches the oven.) (See fig. 14B.)

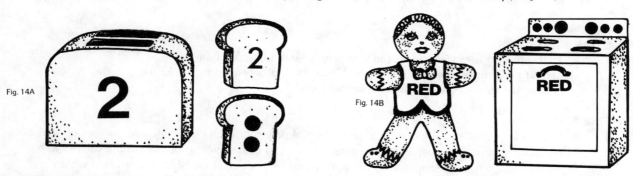

Fig. 14A Fig. 14B

Lesson 2: Pot

Unit Group Lesson

1. **Match Concrete Objects**
   Present two pots. Say, "This is a pot." Ask each child in turn to put the pot with the pot. Gradually increase number of irrelevant objects from which (s)he must select pot to match.

2. **Discriminate Objects**
   Present several objects. Have each child touch the pot in response to the verbal direction, "Touch the pot."

3. **Match Pictures**

Present several pictures of common objects. Have each child match the pictures of the pots.

4. **Discriminate Pictures**

Present a group of several unrelated pictures of objects. Have each child touch the picture of the pot in response to the verbal direction, "Touch the pot."

5. **Figure-Ground**

Present a "busy" picture with many visual distractions. Ask each child to find the pot.

6. **Visual Closure**

Partially cover each of several pictures with paper. Ask each child to find the picture of the pot.

7. **Function**

Ask, "What do we do with a pot?"

8. **Association**

Ask, "What goes with the pot?" Use pictures or objects including stove, food, refrigerator, etc., with several unrelated objects or pictures.

9. **Imitate Verbalization**

Present a pot and ask, "What is this? Say, 'Pot'." The child will imitate "Pot."

10. **Verbalize Label**

Present a pot and ask, "What is this?" The child will respond, "Pot."

11. **Concept Enrichment**

Discuss the fact that we cook in pots, pans, and on cookie sheets. Stress that things for cooking are hot.

Music

Sing "I'm a Little Teapot":

I'm a little teapot	
Short and stout.	*(Pantomime.)*
Here is my handle.	*(Put hand on hip.)*
Here is my spout.	*(Other hand out as spout.)*
When I get all steamed up,	
Then I shout,	
"Tip me over,	*(Pantomime tipping and*
And pour me out."	*pouring.)*

Art

1. Let the children use clay to make play pots for cooking. If you have access to a kiln, fire the clay. If not, harden it in the oven.

2. Make sandpaper cut-outs of pots, pans and cookie sheets. Have the children make a rubbing. Tape thin paper over sandpaper items and have the children discover what is underneath by rubbing over the paper with the side of a crayon.

3. Continue classroom mural from Art #1, Lesson #1 of this unit. Have the children glue bits of foil paper on pots, fill pots with macaroni and beans, put appropriate items on cookie pans, etc.

Snack

1. Eat something which has been cooked or heated in a pot, such as soup, warm applesauce, pudding, etc.

2.   Make hot chocolate with water in a teapot.
3.   Eat soup made from vegetables the children have cleaned, cut and put in the pot. See Fine Motor #3 and Cognitive #1 today.

Fine Motor
1.   Have each child add pots, pans and trays to the kitchen picture started in Lesson #1 Fine Motor #1.
2.   Use a horseshoe magnet to move a small pot along a path laid out with masking tape on a large piece of poster board. The child pulls the pot along with the magnet and tries to stay between the lines. (Aluminum is non-magnetic.)
3.   Let the children clean and cut vegetables for soup. See Cognitive #1 today.

Games
Put pots, pans and trays in the kitchen corner and encourage the children to "cook" with them.

Storytelling
1.   Find a story of Johnny Appleseed planting seeds with his pot on his head.
2.   Read *Stone Soup* by Marcia Brown.

Gross Motor
1.   Have the children toss bean bags into different sized pots with or without keeping score.
2.   Potato Race: get the potato to the pot by rolling it across the floor. Let the children use nose, stick, small broom, etc. depending on their skill level.
3.   Have each child balance a pan on his head and walk along a carpet strip on the floor. Turn the pan rim down and use a fairly well fitting one for each child.

Cognitive
1.   Help children make soup for snack using pictorial recipe sequence cards.
2.   Provide pots in several different sizes which fit inside each other. (See fig. 14C.) Let the children stack them and nest them together. Decide which way is best for storage.

Fig. 14C

Enrichment
1.   Have the children count the ingredients for the soup based on the recipe cards as each is being added.
2.   Provide one-, two-, three- and four-quart pots. Let the children experiment to determine how many of the one-quart pots it takes to fill each of the others.

Visitor
Have someone visit with a chef's hat and help cook soup with the children.

Lesson 3: Refrigerator

Unit Group Lesson

1.   **Match Concrete Objects** (Use toys.)
Present two refrigerators. Say, "This is a refrigerator." Ask each child in turn to put the refrigerator with the refrigerator. Gradually increase number of irrelevant objects from which (s)he must select refrigerator to match.

2. **Discriminate Objects**

   Present several objects. Have each child touch the refrigerator in response to the verbal direction, "Touch the refrigerator."

3. **Match Pictures**

   Present several pictures of common objects. Have each child match the pictures of the refrigerators.

4. **Discriminate Pictures**

   Present a group of several unrelated pictures of objects. Have each child touch the picture of the refrigerator in response to the verbal direction, "Touch the refrigerator."

5. **Figure-Ground**

   Present a "busy" picture with many visual distractions. Ask each child to find the refrigerator.

6. **Visual Closure**

   Partially cover each of several pictures with paper. Ask each child to find the picture of the refrigerator.

7. **Function**

   Ask, "What do we do with a refrigerator?"

8. **Association**

   Ask, "What goes with the refrigerator?" Use pictures or objects including ice, stove, milk, etc., with several unrelated objects or pictures.

9. **Imitate Verbalization**

   Present a refrigerator and ask, "What is this? Say, 'Refrigerator'." The child will imitate "Refrigerator."

10. **Verbalize Label**

    Present a refrigerator and ask, "What is this?" The child will respond, "Refrigerator."

11. **Concept Enrichment**

    Use other names for refrigerator. Discuss fact that refrigerators are used for storing food. Discuss other places to store food. What would happen to foods if the refrigerator stopped working? What is the difference between the refrigerator and the freezer sections?

Music

1. Sing to the tune of "Did You Ever See a Lassie":

   Did you ever see a refrigerator open and close,
   Open and close, open and close?
   Did you ever see a refrigerator open and close?

2. Sing to the tune of "Here Wo Go Round the Mulberry Bush":

   This is the way we put milk in the refrigerator,   *(Pantomime movements.)*
   Milk in the refrigerator, milk in the refrigerator.
   This is the way we put milk in the refrigerator
   So early in the morning.
   Repeat with other refrigerated items such as eggs, butter, cheese, etc.

3. Sing to the tune of "Ten Little Indian Boys":

   One little, two little, three little shelves;   *(Count out on fingers.)*
   Four little, five little, six little shelves;
   Seven little, eight little, nine little shelves;
   Ten little shelves for food.

Art

1. Continue kitchen mural begun in Lesson #1 Art #1 by letting the children paint the refrigerator and use stickers to put up their drawings.
2. Have the children fingerpaint with finger paints stored in a pantry, finger paints from the refrigerator, and look at one container that was stored in the freezer. Compare textures.
3. Make a pantry, refrigerator, and freezer from small cardboard cartons. Let the children paint them to suit their taste.

Snack

1. Help the children get ice from the freezer, put it in glasses and pour juice over it. Ask, "How does it taste, hot or cold?"; "What makes it cold?"; "Where did we get the ice?" Taste juice without ice.
2. Eat refrigerator cookies. Ask "Are they still cold?"
3. Use ice cube trays and toothpicks to make popsicles with juice from pantry. Compare them to juice from refrigerator. Let the children eat them.

Fine Motor

1. Contine the kitchen picture from Lesson #1, Fine Motor #1 by letting each child decorate his own refrigerator.
2. Prepare path tracings of "Take ice cream to the freezer," "Milk to the refrigerator," "Meat to the refrigerator," etc. Vary the difficulty according to the levels of the children.
3. Put magnetic stripping around an outline of a refrigerator on a metal sheet and have the children pull it off. If you cannot get magnetic stripping, have children put refrigerator magnets on and off "refrigerator."
4. Slice refrigerator cookies. Have children pick up a piece and put on cookie sheet. Ask, "How do they feel before they are cut?"
5. Have children open juice cans with a can opener.

Games

Make a fishing game. Put paper clips on pictures of refrigerators (different colors, shapes, etc.) and other things. Attach a magnet to the end of a string which is tied to a stick. Spread the pictures on the floor and let the children fish for the refrigerator pictures.

Storytelling

Make up a story about a refrigerator which could not stay cold. Talk about how the milk got sour, the meat went bad, the lettuce wilted, the ice cream melted etc. Have some real things to show if possible.

Gross Motor

Open and close doors of the big kitchen refrigerator. Get large containers of juice or milk off the shelf and put them back on shelf.

Cognitive

1. Make a large refrigerator and have children sort items to put in the refrigerator from things which do have to be kept cold.
2. Take the children to the kitchen and have them put their hands in the refrigerator. "How does it feel?" "Is it hot or cold in the refrigerator?" Touch the ice in the freezer. Touch the things in the pantry. Ask, "Are they cold?"
3. Present pictures of things that go in the refrigerator, freezer, or pantry boxes made in Art #3 today.

Enrichment

1. Demonstrate how ice turns to water and water disappears when heated.
2. Let the children put eggs in an egg carton and count them. Use hard-cooked eggs or something to represent eggs like beans, ping pong balls, etc. The idea is to have one "egg" for each cup in the egg carton. Talk about "12 makes a dozen."
3. Place cups of juice in both the refrigerator and freezer parts of a refrigerator. Talk about how the refrigerator is cold and the freezer is colder. Let the children try to feel the differences.

Lesson 4: Cabinet

Unit Group Lesson

1. **Match Concrete Objects** (Use toys.)
   Present two cabinets. Say, "This is a cabinet." Ask each child in turn to put the cabinet with the cabinet. Gradually increase number of irrelevant objects from which (s)he must select cabinet to match.

2. **Discriminate Objects**
   Present several objects. Have each child touch the cabinet in response to the verbal direction, "Touch the cabinet."

3. **Match Pictures**
   Present several pictures of common objects. Have each child match the pictures of the cabinets.

4. **Discriminate Pictures**
   Present a group of several unrelated pictures of objects. Have each child touch the picture of the cabinet in response to the verbal direction, "Touch the cabinet."

5. **Figure-Ground**
   Present a "busy" picture with many visual distractions. Ask each child to find the cabinet.

6. **Visual Closure**
   Partially cover each of several pictures with paper. Ask each child to find the picture of the cabinet.

7. **Function**
   Ask, "What do we do with a cabinet?"

8. **Association**
   Ask, "What goes with the cabinet?" Use pictures or objects including sink, refrigerator, stove, pots, food, etc., with several unrelated objects or pictures.

9. **Imitate Verbalization**
   Present a cabinet and ask, "What is this? Say, 'Cabinet'." The child will imitate "Cabinet."

10. **Verbalize Label**
    Present a cabinet and ask, "What is this?" The child will respond, "Cabinet."

11. **Concept Enrichment**
    Discuss things that are stored in kitchen cabinets. List and show them.

Music

Sing to the tune of "Did You Ever See A Lassie?":
(Child's name), can you find the cabinet!
The cabinet, the cabinet.
(Child's name), can you find the cabinet,
And show it to us?

Substitute " stove" and "refrigerator" for verses 2 and 3 if they have been studied this week.

Art

1. Continue the kitchen mural begun in Lesson #1 Art #1 by having the children decorate an outline of a cabinet. Use wood tone wallpaper scraps or real wood scraps.
2. Have the children paste drawn or cut-out pictures of dishes, glasses, pots and other objects on pre-drawn outlines of cabinet shelves.
3. Let the children decorate pictures of kitchen cabinets with collage scraps.

Snack

1. Eat on dishes from a dish cabinet.
2. Eat food from the food storage cabinet.

Fine Motor

1. Contine the kitchen begun in Lesson #1 Fine Motor #1 by having the children decorate their cabinets and paste them on appropriate outline today.
2. Help the children make cabinets by gluing shoe boxes together.
3. Make a lock board or lock box of the various types of cabinet locks and let the children practice opening them.

Games

Make a pictorial map of the classroom. Make a path from one item to another for the child to follow. Have the children end up at a cabinet.

Storytelling

Make up a story of a sad empty cabinet waiting for a family to fill it with dishes and food.

Gross Motor

Have each child race to a cabinet, open door, get a dish, then race back to next person and pass dish. The next person races to put it into cabinet and returns to touch the next person's hand, etc. until all have participated.

Cognitive

1. Open a cabinet in the room. Have child find the cabinet which is "open" and find the cabinet which is "closed." Then ask the children to open and/or close a cabinet door.
2. Discuss the things we keep in cabinets in the kitchen, at home and at school.
3. Have the children sort different things or pictures from catalogs to put into different cabinets. Use shoe boxes for sorting.

Enrichment

1. Have the children count the cabinets in the classroom.
2. Have children help make labels for each cabinet which indicates its contents (paper, games, etc.).

Lesson 5: Sink

Unit Group Lesson

1. **Match Concrete Objects** (Use toys.)
   Present two sinks. Say, "This is a sink." Ask each child in turn to put the sink with the sink. Gradually increase number of irrelevant objects from which (s)he must select sink to match.

2. **Discriminate Objects**

Present several objects. Have each child touch the sink in response to the verbal direction, "Touch the sink."

3. **Match Pictures**

Present several pictures of common objects. Have each child match the pictures of the sinks.

4. **Discriminate Pictures**

Present a group of several unrelated pictures of objects. Have each child touch the picture of the sink in response to the verbal direction, "Touch the sink."

5. **Figure-Ground**

Present a "busy" picture with many visual distractions. Ask each child to find the sink.

6. **Visual Closure**

Partially cover each of several pictures with paper. Ask each child to find the picture of the sink.

7. **Function**

Ask, "What do we do with a sink?"

8. **Association**

Ask, "What goes with the sink?" Use pictures or objects including pots, pans, stove, refrigerator, dishes, etc., with several unrelated objects or pictures.

9. **Imitate Verbalization**

Present a sink and ask, "What is this? Say, 'Sink'." The child will imitate "Sink."

10. **Verbalize Label**

Present a sink and ask, "What is this?" The child will respond, "Sink."

11. **Concept Enrichment**

Discuss different types and sizes of sinks. Discuss other ways to wash dishes, (dishwasher, dishpan, etc.) and other types of cleaning done in a kitchen.

Music

1. Place a box in front of a small group. Give each child a toy dish and an empty dishwashing liquid bottle. Act out and sing to the tune of "Here We Go Looby Loo":

   We put the dishes in.   (Children put dishes in box.)
   We put the soap in.   (Squeeze the "soap" into box.)
   Turn water on and S-h-h, S-h-h, S-h-h   (Hand gesture.)
   The dishes come out clean.   (Take dishes out.)

2. Sing to the tune of "This Is The Way We Wash Our Clothes":
   Verse 1: This is the way we wash the dishes
   Verse 2: This is the way we dry the dishes

Art

1. Add a sink to the classroom mural begun in Lesson #1 Art #1 of this unit.
2. Let the children squirt different colored thin tempera paint around the classroom sink, let it dry and then clean it with scouring powder.

Snack

Have the children wash their own dishes after snack, clean up the table and sweep the floor near the table.

Fine Motor

1. Have each child add a sink to his kitchen picture begun in Lesson #1 Fine Motor #1 and take home the completed picture.
2. Have the children use an egg beater to whip up soap suds in the sink.
3. Use the soap suds on a table for finger painting.

Games

1. Hide pictures of sinks around the room, some in full sight and obvious other partially hidden, and others completely hidden. Ask, "Who can find the sink?" and let children hunt together.
2. In a small group, have children take turns at the sink (toy sink, or plastic tub) and wash toy dishes in real soapy water. Model washing the dishes then give each child a turn.

Storytelling

Make up a story about a sink which was all plugged up. The water could not drain out of it. The sink says "gurgle, gurgle, gurgle." When it is fixed and the water finally drains out.

Gross Motor

Have the children fill the "sink" with buckets of water and then bail it out with buckets.

Cognitive

1. Cut "sinks" out of different colors of construction paper. Sort sinks by color. Use two colors for some children and more colors for other children.
2. Make a set of cards with pictures in upper left hand corner of stove, pot, refrigerator, cabinet, and sink. On small cards place pictures of pans, refrigeratored dishes, ice cream, milk, dishes, etc. Match small pictures to appropriate large pictures.

Enrichment

Put a stopper in the sink, fill with water, and look at different things that will and will not float.

Field Trip

Visit a restaurant or other institutional-sized kitchen to see large appliances, utensils and storage areas.

Related Children's Records
"All Around the Kitchen" from **AMERICAN FOLK SONGS** (FOLKWAYS)
ADVENTURES IN SOUND (MH)
"Kitchen Stuff" from **COME & SEE THE PEPPERMINT TREE** (EA)

Related Children's Books
Mercer, Mayer. **LITTLE MONSTER AT HOME.** New York: Golden Press, 1978.
Rockwell, Harlow. **MY KITCHEN.** New York: Greenwillow Books, 1980.
Sendak, Maurice. **IN THE NIGHT KITCHEN.** New York: Harper & Row, 1970.
Weissman, Cynthia. **BREAKFAST FOR SAMMY.** Englewood Cliffs, N.J.: Four Winds Press, 1978.

Related Parenting Materials
Cansler, Dot. **THE HOMESTRETCH.** Winston-Salem, NC 27113-5128: Kaplan Press, 1983.

Related Materials
TEACHING PICTURES. Winston-Salem, NC 27113-5128: Kaplan Press, 1983.
STORY SEQUENCE CARDS I, II. Winston-Salem, NC 27113-5128: Kaplan Press, 1983.
SEWING CARDS I, II, III. Winston-Salem, NC 27113-5128: Kaplan Press, 1983.

Unit 15: Bedroom

A developmental assessment should determine the functional levels of each child. Individual expectations are based on the assessment results.

Lesson 1: Bed

Unit Group Lesson

1. **Match Concrete Objects** (Use doll furniture.)
    Present two beds. Say, "This is a bed." Ask each child in turn to put the bed with the bed. Gradually increase number of irrelevant objects from which (s)he must select bed to match.

2. **Discriminate Objects**
    Present several objects. Have each child touch the bed in response to verbal direction, "Touch the bed."

3. **Match Pictures**
    Present several pictures of common objects. Have each child match the pictures of the beds.

4. **Discriminate Pictures**
    Present a group of several unrelated pictures of objects. Have each child touch the picture of the bed in response to verbal direction, "Touch the bed."

5. **Figure-Ground**
    Present a "busy" picture with many visual distractions. Ask each child to find the bed.

6. **Visual Closure**
    Partially cover each of several pictures with paper. Ask each child to find the picture of the bed.

7. **Function**
    Ask, "What do we do with beds?"

8. **Association**
    Ask, "What goes with the bed?" Use pictures or objects including sheets, pillows, blankets, etc. with several unrelated objects or pictures.

9. **Imitate Verbalization**
    Present a bed and ask, "What is this? Say, 'Bed'." Child will imitate "Bed."

10. **Verbalize Label**
    Present a bed and ask, "What is this?" The child will respond, "Bed."

11.   **Concept Enrichment**
       Discuss different sizes and types of beds, such as twin, double, king-sized, bunk, trundle, water, etc.

Music

1.   Sing to the tune of "This Is The Way We Wash Our Clothes":
      Verse 1: This is the way we make our bed,
                Make our bed, make our bed,
                This is the way we make our bed,
                Early in the morning.
      Verse 2: First we put the sheet on . . .
      Verse 3: Next we put the blanket on . . .
      Verse 4: Then we put the pillow on . . .
      You and children make up a doll's bed.

2.   Sing to the tune of "Are You Sleeping, Brother John?":
      Are you sleeping, are you sleeping,
      In your bed, in your bed?
      Are you sleeping,
      Are you sleeping,
      In your bed,
      In your bed?

3.   Sing "The Bed is in the Bedroom" to the tune of "The Farmer in the Dell":
      The bed is in the bedroom.
      The bed is in the bedroom.
      Hi - ho, I know
      The bed is in the bedroom.

Art

1.   Have the children cut or tear out pictures of beds from catalogs and paste on paper.
2.   Have each child make a small doll bed. Supply small boxes (gelatin box, tea box, etc.), squares of sheeting (cut up old sheets), fabric squares (fabric samples), and squares of colored sponge. Have the children glue or paste the sheet on box. Fabric square is used for a blanket and the sponge square for a pillow. Sing song "This is the Way We Make Our Bed" as in Music #1 while assembling the beds.
3.   Begin a bedroom mural. Hang a large piece of paper on the wall at child level. Outline the bed. Let the children "make" a bedspread by covering the bed with fabric scraps.

Snack

Pretend to be eating in bed so eat a snack like fruit that does not leave crumbs in the "bed."

Fine Motor

1.   Have each child draw a bed by connecting dots in a rectangular shape. After the dots are connected, have each child paste a girl or boy dressed in pajamas in bed.
2.   Have each child paste a construction paper "blanket" on the outline of a "bed."
3.   Have the children "quilt" a cover for the bed by gluing felt designs on a fabric square. Let the more skilled children cut the felt.

Games

1.   Display some dollhouse furniture on a table. Ask the children, "What do you sleep on?" Have a child find a bed. Continue with other pieces of furniture. "What do you sit on?" "What do you take a bath in?" (Indicate Use.)
2.   Set up a dollhouse bedroom. Let the children pretend to be putting a doll to sleep, waking it up, and dressing it. Say, "Put the baby to bed," "Wake up, baby," and "Touch the baby in bed."
3.   Make up a doll bed. Put a pillowcase, sheets, blanket and pillow in a box with other items (clothes, toys, hairbrush and comb, towels, washcloths, potholders, etc.). Ask each child to bring an item from the box to be used in making the bed. Say, "Yes, the sheet goes on the bed." Leave the doll bed and accessories in the housekeeping corner.

Storytelling

1. Read and tell the story of "The Three Bears" using a picture book or story cards. Ask children to find the bed, find the baby bear's bed, and touch daddy bear's bed. (Figure Ground)

2. Tell a simple story about a child going to bed. Use sequence pictures to illustrate. Have five sequence pictures including the following: 1. child taking bath; 2. child putting on pajamas; 3. child brushing teeth; 4. child kissing parents goodnight; 5. child in bed. Begin with a simple story using cards #1 and #5. Let children take turns tell the story and arranging the cards in the correct order. Make story more difficult by adding card #2. Repeat procedure of telling story and letting children tell the story. Then add cards #3 and #4.

3. Fingerplay: "Five Little Piggies"

   It's time for my piggies to go to bed,
   The nice, big, mother piggy said.   *(Wiggle right thumb.)*
   Now I shall count them to see   *(Hold up left hand.)*
   If all my piggies have come back to me,
   One little piggy, two little piggies,   *(Count fingers.)*
   Three little piggies dear,
   Four little piggies, five little piggies,
   Yes, they are all here.

Gross Motor

1. Have a race to bed. Set up a box with a coverlet as the bed. Have the children race through an obstacle course to get to the bed. Set the timer so they can beat the clock.

2. Make a bed on top of high place on the playground. Have children climb to get into bed and climb down (or slide down if there is a slide).

3. Make an obstacle course with places for child to act out sequence story in Storytelling #2 of this lesson.

Cognitive

1. Help each child make a shoe box bedroom. Give each child a shoe box whose sides have been flattened. Have her decorate it with rugs, windows and doors. From an envelope containing pictures of things to sleep on such as various sized beds, a crib, a bassinet, a hammock, a sleeping bag, a water bed, etc. The child selects a "bed" for her shoe box room glue it into his bedroom.

2. Have the children sort picture cards (pictures pasted on file cards) of big beds and little beds; baby beds and big beds; different types of beds such as bunks, cots, regular beds, twin, etc.; animal beds (basket, padded box) from "people" beds; and furniture by room (kitchen, bedroom, bathroom, living room.)

3. On a flannel board, group pictures of four rooms of equipment and /or furniture (bedroom, living room, bathroom, and kitchen). Give the child a picture of a bed. Ask the child, "Where does the bed belong?" Child will place the picture with the bedroom grouping.

Enrichment

Make beds with dotted covers (from 1 to 10 dots) and children in pajamas with corresponding numerals on them. Have the children match the children to the correct beds. The bed with single dot goes with pajamas numbered "1", etc. Color coding the pajamas and beds simplifies the activity and makes it self-correcting.

Lesson 2: Chest

Unit Group Lesson

1. **Match Concrete Objects** (Use doll furniture.)
   Present two chests. Say, "This is a chest." Ask each child in turn to put the chest with the chest. Gradually increase number of irrelevant objects from which (s)he must select chest to match.

2. **Discriminate Objects**
Present several objects. Have each child touch the chest in response to verbal direction, "Touch the chest."

3. **Match Pictures**
Present several pictures of common objects. Have each child match the pictures of the chests.

4. **Discriminate Pictures**
Present a group of several unrelated pictures of objects. Have each child touch the picture of the chest in response to verbal direction, "Touch the chest."

5. **Figure-Ground**
Present a "busy" picture with many visual distractions. Ask each child to find the chest.

6. **Visual Closure**
Partially cover each of several pictures with paper. Ask each child to find the picture of the chest.

7. **Function**
Ask, "What do we do with chests?"

8. **Association**
Ask, "What goes with the chest?" Use pictures or objects including drawer, clothes, bed, dresser, etc. with several unrelated objects or pictures.

9. **Imitate Verbalization**
Present a chest and ask, "What is this? Say, 'Chest'." Child will imitate "Chest."

10. **Verbalize Label**
Present a chest and ask, "What is this?" The child will respond, "Chest."

11. **Concept Enrichment**
Discuss the difference between a bed, dresser, and a chest of drawers.

Music
1. Sing "My Clothes" to the tune of "The Bear Went Over the Mountain":
    Verse 1: I need to get dressed,
        I need to get dressed,
        I need to get dressed
        So I can go to school.
    Verse 2: My clothes are in the chest,
        My clothes are in the chest,
        My clothes are in the chest
        Folded nice and neat.
    Verse 3: First I'll get my underwear;
        Second I'll get my shirt;
        Then I'll get my pants;
        And my socks too!
    Verse 4: Now I'm all dressed,
        Now I'm all dressed,
        Now I'm all dressed
        I'm ready for school.
Pantomime the song or use pictures to illustrate.

2. Sing "Chest of Drawers" to the tune of "Here We Go Round the Mulberry Bush":
> My clothes are in the chest of drawers,
>> Chest of drawers, chest of drawers;
> My clothes are in the chest of drawers,
>> And the chest is in the bedroom.

Use a picture to illustrate.

Art
1. Have the children tear or cut out pictures of chests and paste on paper for a collage.
2. Help the children make a small doll chest. Have them stack three Q-Tip boxes or match stick boxes on top of each other, glue together and paint or color with magic markers.
3. Continue the bedroom mural begun in Lesson #1 Art #3 by having the children paint a chest of drawers on paper and gluing it to the mural.

Snack
Eat a layer cake or gelatin dessert made in layers.

Fine Motor
1. Supply an incomplete ditto picture of a chest. Have the children draw lines to make the chest of drawers. Instruct children to "start on green; stop on red" and "draw a straight line." (See fig. 15A.)

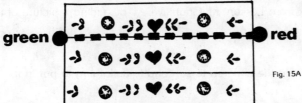

Fig. 15A

2. Make a path tracing of "Take a child to his chest of drawers to get some clean clothes," and "Put the clean clothes in the chest of drawers."
3. Have each child cut out a chest of drawers from a sheet of construction paper. (See fig. 15B.)

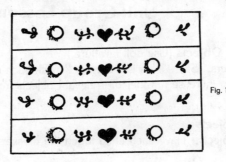

Fig. 15B

Games
1. Partially hide a doll house chest. Have the children hunt for it. The child who finds it gets to hide it again.
2. Make a feely box. Place plastic dollhouse furniture in the box and show a piece of furniture. The child finds the matching piece by feeling in the box (Tactile Discrimination). Vary the activity by showing the child a picture of the furniture, instead of the actual object.

Storytelling
1. Present a large picture of a child's room. Explain that this is where a little girl or boy sleeps, keeps his/her clothes, and keeps his/her toys. Ask children if they have their own bedrooms. Ask the children if they have a bed, dresser, chest, desk, closet, etc. Let children describe their bedrooms. Have children find the chest in the picture. "Point to the chest." "Touch the chest." (Figure Ground).
2. Tell a story about how a mother puts clean clothes in the child's chest of drawers for him to wear. Include how the mother washed, dried, folded and put the clothes away.

Gross Motor

Have the children race from a box to a chest with a piece of clothing and put it in a drawer. Provide an obstacle course to run. Stress fact that the child takes the clothing OUT of the box and puts it IN the chest.

Cognitive

1. Match drawers to chest. Have a picture of a chest with one drawer in it. Have each child match the remaining drawers according to color or design on the chest. (See fig. 15C.)

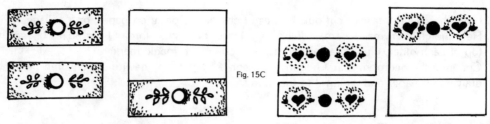

Fig. 15C

2. Display four pictures: 1. Daddy shaving in the bathroom. 2. A child asleep. 3. A family watching T.V. in the living room. 4. Mother cooking in kitchen. Give the child a picture of a chest. Ask the child, "Does the chest belong in the bathroom, in the bedroom, in the living room, or in the kitchen?" Have the child place the picture with the bedroom picture and respond, "Bedroom." "In the bedroom." or "The chest belongs in the bedroom."
3. Continue the bedroom shoe box from Lesson #1 Cognitive #1 by adding a picture of a chest from an envelope full of bedroom items.

Enrichment

Get a real chest of drawers and help the children to sort and fold clothing to put in it.

Lesson 3: Dresser

Unit Group Lesson

1. **Match Concrete Objects** (Use doll furniture.)
    Present two dressers. Say, "This is a dresser." Ask each child in turn to put the dresser with the dresser. Gradually increase number of irrelevant objects from which (s)he must select dresser to match.

2. **Discriminate Objects**
    Present several objects. Have each child touch the dresser in response to verbal direction, "Touch the dresser."

3. **Match Pictures**
    Present several pictures of common objects. Have each child match the pictures of the dressers.

4. **Discriminate Pictures**
    Present a group of several unrelated pictures of objects. Have each child touch the picture of the dresser in response to verbal direction, "Touch the dresser."

5. **Figure-Ground**
    Present a "busy" picture with many visual distractions. Ask each child to find the dresser.

6. **Visual Closure**
    Partially cover each of several pictures with paper. Ask each child to find the picture of the dresser.

7. **Function**

Ask, "What do we do with a dresser?"

8. **Association**

Ask, "What goes with the dresser?" Use pictures or objects including drawer, clothes, bed, chest, etc., with several unrelated objects or pictures.

9. **Imitate Verbalization**

Present a dresser and ask, "What is this? Say, 'Dresser'." Child will imitate "Dresser."

10. **Verbalize Label**

Present a dresser and ask, "What is this?" The child will respond, "Dresser."

11. **Concept Enrichment**

Discuss difference between a chest and a dresser (a dresser has a mirror).

Music

1. Sing "The Dresser is in the Bedroom" to the tune of "The Farmer in the Dell":
   The dresser is in the bedroom,
   The dresser is in the bedroom.
   Hi - ho, I know
   The dresser is in the bedroom.

2. Sing "My Clothes" to the tune of "The Bear Went Over the Mountain":
   Verse 1: I need to get dressed,
   I need to get dressed,
   I need to get dressed
   So I can go to school.
   Verse 2: My clothes are in the dresser,
   My clothes are in the dresser,
   My clothes are in the dresser
   Folded nice and neat.
   Verse 3: First I'll get my underwear;
   Second I'll get my shirt;
   Third I'll get my pants;
   And my socks too!
   Verse 4: Now I'm all dressed,
   Now I'm all dressed,
   Now I'm all dressed
   I'm ready for school
   Pantomime the song or use pictures to illustrate.

Art

1. Have the children tear or cut out pictures of dressers and paste on paper as a dresser collage.
2. Help the children make a small doll dresser. Supply the following materials: several halves of a Q-Tip box; small piece of cardboard for the mirror backing; a small piece of aluminum foil to fit cardboard; and a knotted (large knot) piece of yarn. Let the children paint the dresser, glue the aluminum foil on the cardboard backing, string the yarn through the holes in the "dresser drawers" and glue drawers together. Knot the yarn after it is strung and fasten "mirror" to back of Q-Tip boxes. (See fig. 15D.)
3. Continue the bedroom mural from Lesson #1 Art #3 by having the children paint a dresser, make a mirror with aluminum foil and cardboard, and glue it on the mural.

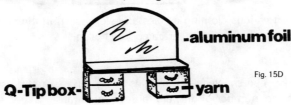

-aluminum foil

Q-Tip box-   -yarn

Fig. 15D

Snack

Get snack from the dresser made in Art #2 today. Example: raisins in one drawer, peanuts in another drawer, etc.

Fine Motor

1. Supply an incomplete dresser picture. Have the children draw lines from green to red to complete the dresser drawers. (See fig. 15E.)

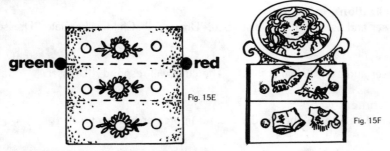

Fig. 15E

Fig. 15F

2. Have children paste appropriate clothing pictures on picture of a dresser and paste a child's face on mirror. (See fig. 15F.)
3. Have each child cut out the dresser from #2 above if he has adequate cutting skills.

Games

1. Decorate a large cardboard shipping box as a bedroom. Paint some of the furniture on the walls. Lay a blanket on the floor for the "bed." Let the children pretend to be sleeping, waking up, etc.
2. Play "Guess Which Drawer?" Use a teacher-made Q-Tip box dresser, doll-dresser, or real dresser, guess where the various articles of clothing are kept. Clothes can be pictures cut from catalogs, doll or baby clothes or real child clothes.

Storytelling

Show a large picture of a child's room. Have children find the dresser in the picture. "Point to the dresser." "Touch the dresser."

Gross Motor

Have the children throw a bean bag in the dresser drawer. Provide a real dresser drawer or a pretend one painted on a cardboard box for the target. Different sized drawers can be given different scores or used for children at different levels.

Cognitive

1. Continue the bedroom shoe box from Lesson #1 Cognitive #1. From an envelope of bedroom items, have children select dresser. "Find something in a bedroom you keep your clothes in." "What do you keep your clothes in?" Then glue it in their room.
2. Have the children match the model on the drawer and put pictures from catalogs, of pants, shirts, socks, underpants, and pajamas onto drawer that has similar picture. This activity can be done with a real dresser and real clothing. (See fig. 15G.)

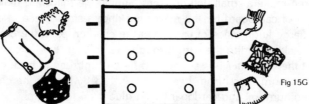

Fig 15G

3. Have the children sort various clothing articles and store them in the correct drawers. Sorting can be done on clothing type, color or any other category chosen.

Enrichment

Let the children make cue sheets with numerals at the top. Count dresser drawers and match the dressers with the correct number of drawers to each numeral.

Unit Group Lesson

1. **Match Concrete Objects** (Use doll furniture.)
   Present two desks. Say, "This is a desk." Ask each child in turn to put the desk with the desk.
   Gradually increase number of irrelevant objects from which (s)he must select desk to match.

2. **Discriminate Objects**
   Present several objects. Have each child touch the desk in response to verbal direction, "Touch the desk."

3. **Match Pictures**
   Present several pictures of common objects. Have each child match the pictures of the desks.

4. **Discriminate Pictures**
   Present a group of several unrelated pictures of objects. Have each child touch the picture of the desk in response to verbal direction, "Touch the desk."

5. **Figure-Ground**
   Present a "busy" picture with many visual distractions. Ask each child to find the desk.

6. **Visual Closure**
   Partially cover each of several pictures with paper. Ask each child to find the picture of the desk.

7. **Function**
   Ask, "What do we do with a desk?"

8. **Association**
   Ask, "What goes with the desk?" Use pictures or objects including chest, pens, paper, bed, etc., with several unrelated objects or pictures.

9. **Imitate Verbalization**
   Present a desk and ask, "What is this? Say, 'Desk'." Child will imitate "Desk."

10. **Verbalize Label**
    Present a desk and ask, "What is this?" The child will respond, "Desk."

11. **Concept Enrichment**
    Discuss the similarities between a desk, a bed, a chest, and a dresser. Discuss the differences between a desk, a bed, a chest and a dresser.

Music
1. Sing "A Desk" to the tune of "Did You Ever See A Lassie?":
   Verse 1: I have a desk,
   A desk, a desk;
   I have a desk,
   And it's in my bedroom.
   Verse 2: I keep my books there,
   My books there, my books there;
   I keep my books there;
   On my desk.

2.   Sing "The Desk in the Bedroom" to the tune of "Bingo":
          Verse 1: There was a kid who had a desk,
                    In his bedroom.
                    He had a desk, he had a desk, he had a desk,
                    In his bedroom.
          Verse 2: And on this desk there were some pencils,
                    On the desk in his bedroom.
                    He had some pencils, he had some pencils, he had some pencils
                    On the desk in his bedroom.
          Verse 3: And on this desk there was some paper . . .
                    See Verse 2.
          Repeat Verse 1.

Art
1.   Give each child a paper with bedroom furniture outlined on it and an envelope of pictures of bedroom furniture. Have the children match the picture to its outline and paste it on the paper. Then decorate the wallpaper in the bedroom.
2.   Have the children tear or cut out pictures of desks and paste on paper.
3.   Continue the bedroom mural from Lesson #1 Art #3. Give the children scraps of wood colored paper and real wood to cover the desk outline on the mural. Let them add drawer pulls and desk accessories to complete the desk.

Snack
Store snack in a desk.

Fine Motor
1.   Make a path tracing of "Take a child to his desk." and "Take some pencils to the desk."
2.   Have children "draw" a crayon and a piece of paper on a "desktop" by connecting dots. (See fig. 15H.)

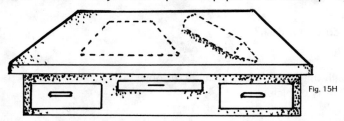

Fig. 15H

3.   Let children glue pictures on construction paper cut-outs of a pencil box of crayons, paper, scissors, and ruler on a desk top. Children match the picture to the outline drawn on the desk. Children are instructed to be careful and not glue over the lines. They should apply the glue only within the outline on the desk.

Games
1.   Put a desk in the middle of a large area and have the class play "Ring Around the Desk."
2.   Provide a desk, if possible, and office materials in the housekeeping area so the children can play with them.

Storytelling
1.   Show a large picture of a child's room. Have children find the desk (and chair) in the picture. "Point to the desk." "Touch the desk." (Figure Ground)
2.   Make up a story about a little boy or girl who wanted a desk and chair in his/her room. (S)He had to draw and write on the floor and his/her pictures were always dirty. On day on his/her birthday his/her mother and daddy surprised him/her with a desk and chair.

Gross Motor
Have the children fill a desk with paper. Let them use unopened packages of paper and fill desk drawers with paper.

Cognitive

1. How is a desk the same as a bed, a chest, and a desser. How is a desk different from a bed, a chest, and a dresser?
2. Have each child continue the shoe box bedroom by adding a desk from an envelope full of bedroom items.
3. Make ten pairs of desks which are indentical within the pairs, but slightly different between the pairs. Mix them and have the children match the pairs. Provide pairs with grosser or finer differences depending upon the skill development of the children.

Enrichment

1. Fill a desk with office materials, blank checks, pens, etc. Let the children play office.
2. Discuss the different types of drawers in desks and their uses. The file drawer is used for file folders, the middle drawer for pencils, rulers, etc.

Lesson 5: Closet

Unit Group Lesson

1. **Match Concrete Objects**
   Present two closets. (If only pictures are available, present pictures for number 1 and omit numbers 2 and 3.) Say, "This is a closet." Ask each child in turn to put the closet with the closet. Gradually increase number of irrelevant objects from which (s)he must select closet to match.

2. **Discriminate Objects**
   Present several objects. Have each child touch the closet in response to verbal direction, "Touch the closet."

3. **Match Pictures**
   Present several pictures of common objects. Have each child match the pictures of the closets.

4. **Discriminate Pictures**
   Present a group of several unrelated pictures of objects. Have each child touch the picture of the closet in response to verbal direction, "Touch the closet."

5. **Figure-Ground**
   Present a "busy" picture with many visual distractions. Ask each child to find the closet.

6. **Visual Closure**
   Partially cover each of several pictures with paper. Ask each child to find the picture of the closet.

7. **Function**
   Ask, "What do we do with a closet?"

8. **Association**
   Ask, "What goes with the closet?" Use pictures or objects including coats, shirts, etc., with several unrelated objects or pictures.

9. **Imitate Verbalization**
   Present a closet and ask, "What is this? Say, 'Closet'." Child will imitate "Closet."

10. **Verbalize Label**
    Present a closet and ask, "What is this?" The child will respond, "Closet."

11.   **Concept Enrichment**
       Discuss things that can be stored in a clothes closet. Discuss other types of closets such as cleaning, coat, linen, broom, food (pantry), etc.

Music

1.   Sing "Clothes in my Closet" to the tune of "The Bear Went Over the Mountain":
             I have clothes in my closet,
             I have clothes in my closet,
             I have clothes in my closet,
             And shoes too!

2.   Sing "Oh, My Closet" to the tune of "Clementine":
             Oh my closet, oh, my closet,
             Oh my closet is a mess!
             I have got to clean my closet,
             So it will look its best!
       You and children clean out a closet in the classroom. Make up new verses while cleaning the closet.

Art

1.   Give each child a teacher-made "closet." Make the "closets" by pasting one sheet of construction paper on another. The top sheet has a door cut and folded. Have the children paste pictures of clothes in the closets. Some children may be able to make their own closets. (See fig. 15l.)

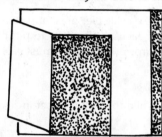

Fig. 15l

2.   Let the children paint closet doors with clear water.
3.   Finish the bedroom mural begun in Lesson #1 Art #3 of this unit. Let the children paint a closet door and glitter a string handle on a closet outline on the mural.

Snack

       Go to a closet and get the snack for the day.

Fine Motor

1.   Help children open and close the closet door in the classroom.
2.   Have children draw a doorknob (a circle) on a closet door (a large rectangle) drawn on the blackboard.
3.   Make a "closet" from cardboard and attach it to a flannel board. Each child picks up a felt cut-out dress and puts it "in" the closet. The child picks up the felt piece using thumb and index finger, "opens" closet door, and places piece on flannel board.
4.   Make a closet out of a small box or milk carton. Have the children cut a closet door in it.

Games

1.   Display three pictures: 1. an open closet; 2. a kitchen cabinet; and 3. a medicine cabinet. Ask, "Where do you hang your clothes?" Have children pick correct picture. (Indicate use.)
2.   Play "Hide and Seek" in the room. Have some children hide in the closet. "I see Nick hiding in the closet!"

Storytelling

1.   Use a picture of a child's room. Have children find the closet in the picture. "Point to the closet." "Touch the closet." (Figure Ground)

2. Tell a story about the closet who was sad because he had no clothes hanging in him. Use the flannel board closet. Make the closet frown and smile by placing a construction paper mouth on the door. Conclude the story by having a little girl go to a clothing store and buy some new clothes. Have children put felt cut-outs in closet. Change the closet's frown to a smile. (See fig. 15J.)

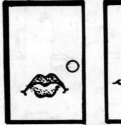

Fig. 15J

Gross Motor
Hang clothes on hanger and put into closet or on a rod that represents the closet.

Cognitive
1. Make pairs of different types of clothing, cut out of construction paper. Have the children follow a pattern arranged by teacher or another child. Some children may be able to reverse the pattern.

Fig. 15K

2. Have children sort clothes that can be hung in a closet from those which must be stored in a dresser or chest. (See fig. 15K.)
3. Have each child finish his/her shoe box bedroom by adding the closet and taping up the walls.

Enrichment
Make a variety of closets out of shoe boxes. Have the children place pictures of appropriate things into the correct closet.

Field Trip
1. Visit a furniture store. Tour the bedroom displays. "What a pretty dresser!" "Such a comfortable bed!"
2. Go to someone's house to see a real bedroom, preferably one that has all the items from the unit.

Related Children's Records
"Show Me" from **LEARNING BASIC SKILLS-VOC.** (EA)

Related Children's Books
Barrett, Judi. **I HATE TO GO TO BED.** Englewood Cliffs, N.J.: Four Winds Press, 1977.
Brown, Margaret Wise. **GOODNIGHT MOON.** New York: Harper & Row, 1947.
Hoban, Russell. **BEDTIME FOR FRANCIS.** New York: Harper & Row, 1960.
Rockwell, Anne. **THE AWFUL MESS.** Englewood Cliffs, N.J.: Four Winds Press, 1973.
Sendak, Maurice. **WHERE THE WILD THINGS ARE.** New York: Harper & Row, 1973.

Related Parenting Materials
Cansler, Dot. **THE HOMESTRETCH.** Winston-Salem, NC 27113-5128: Kaplan Press, 1983.

Unit 16: Bathroom

A developmental assessment should determine the functional levels of each child. Individual expectations are based on the assessment results.

Lesson 1: Toilet

Unit Group Lesson

1. **Match Concrete Objects** (Use toys.)
   Present two toilets. Say, "This is a toilet." Ask each child in turn to put the toilet with the toilet. Gradually increase number of irrelevant objects from which (s)he must select toilet to match.

2. **Discriminate Objects**
   Present several objects. Have each child touch the toilet in response to verbal direction, "Touch the toilet."

3. **Match Pictures**
   Present several pictures of common objects. Have each child match the pictures of the toilets.

4. **Discriminate Pictures**
   Present a group of several unrelated pictures of objects. Have each child touch the picture of the toilet in response to verbal direction, "Touch the toilet."

5. **Figure-Ground**
   Present a "busy" picture with many visual distractions. Ask each child to find the toilet.

6. **Visual Closure**
   Partially cover each of several pictures with paper. Ask each child to find the picture of the toilet.

7. **Function**
   Ask, "What do we do with a toilet?"

8. **Association**
   Ask, "What goes with the toilet?" Use pictures or objects including shower, toilet paper, tub, mirror, etc. with several unrelated objects or pictures.

9. **Imitate Verbalization**
   Present a toilet and ask, "What is this? Say, 'Toilet'." The child will imitate "Toilet."

10. **Verbalize Label**
    Present a toilet and ask, "What is this?" The child will respond, "Toilet."

11. **Concept Enrichment**
    Discuss good toilet hygiene.

Music

1. Sing "The Toilet" ("The Potty") to the tune of "The Farmer In the Dell":
   The toilet's in the bathroom;
   The toilet's in the bathroom;
   Hi ho, I know;
   The toilet is in the bathroom.

2. Sing "Flush the Toilet" ("Potty") to the tune of "The Bear Went Over the Mountain":
   Remember to flush the toilet;
   Remember to flush the toilet;
   Remember to flush the toilet;
   In the bathroom.

Art

1. Have the children tear or cut out pictures of bathroom fixtures and paste on paper.
2. Have the children match pictures of bathroom fixtures to the correct outlines of those fixtures on construction paper.
3. Have the children decorate a picture of a toilet seat with magic markers.
4. Have a large piece of paper on the wall at child level. Have the children begin a bathroom mural by painting the walls around the outlines of a toilet, tub, shower, sink, and mirror. Put a decorated toilet on mural.

Snack

Wash hands after toileting and before snack.

Fine Motor

1. Have children get their own toilet paper during toileting.
2. Have children flush the toilet when they are finished.
3. Put a target on the backside of the toilet bowl. Instruct the boys to "hit the target."
4. Provide a picture of a toilet and let the children trace around it and color in the lines.

Games

Children listen to bathroom sounds and are asked to identify them. Some examples of sounds are: person taking a shower (have person sing!); water running into tub; water draining out of tub; toilet flushing; water running into sink; water draining from sink; the squeaking of the medicine cabinet door; the splashes of someone taking a bath; etc. Vary the activity by having the child match the sound to a picture. (Auditory Discrimination)

Storytelling

Make up a story about a child who did not use the toilet. Describe how he eventually learned to use a potty chair and then the toilet and stopped wearing diapers. Let the children contribute ideas to the story.

Gross Motor

1. Make an obstacle course with a doll house an the end of it. Have each child carry a doll house bathroom fixture to the doll house around, over, under and through an obstacle course.
2. Have the children push a cageball to the bathroom.

Cognitive

1. Arranges five groups of bathroom fixtures (toilets, tubs, showers, sinks, mirrors), each with a variety of colors and shapes of fixtures. For example, a grouping of toilets would include old and new toilets, different colored toilets, different shaped toilets, and toilets with coverings on them. Give each child a picture of a toilet. Ask each child individually, "Put it where it belongs" and point to the five groups. Have the child place his picture with the grouping of toilet pictures.
2. Provide cardboard toilets in two or more sizes. Have children sequence them from big to little.
3. Provide pictures of different types of toilets such as regular toilets, camping toilets and baby toilets. Have the children sort them.

4. Make a distinction between big and little toilets. Babies use potty chairs and "big people" use big toilets. Provide pictures or a real potty chair for comparison to a big toilet.

Enrichment
1. Help the children make and put on a toilet seat cover.
2. Help the children study the workings of the flushing mechanism of a toilet.

Lesson 2: Shower

Unit Group Lesson

1. **Match Concrete Objects** (Use toys.)
   Present two showers. Say, "This is a shower." Ask each child in turn to put the shower with the shower. Gradually increase number of irrelevant objects from which (s)he must select shower to match.

2. **Discriminate Objects**
   Present several objects. Have each child touch the shower in response to verbal direction, "Touch the shower."

3. **Match Pictures**
   Present several pictures of common objects. Have each child match the pictures of the showers.

4. **Discriminate Pictures**
   Present a group of several unrelated pictures of objects. Have each child touch the picture of the shower in response to verbal direction, "Touch the shower."

5. **Figure-Ground**
   Present a "busy" picture with many visual distractions. Ask each child to find the shower.

6. **Visual Closure**
   Partially cover each of several pictures with paper. Ask each child to find the picture of the shower.

7. **Function**
   Ask, "What do we do with a shower?"

8. **Association**
   Ask, "What goes with the shower?" Use pictures or objects including soap, towel, tub, shower curtain, etc., with several unrelated objects or pictures.

9. **Imitate Verbalization**
   Present a shower and ask, "What is this? Say, 'Shower'." The child will imitate "Shower."

10. **Verbalize Label**
    Present a shower and ask, "What is this?" The child will respond, "Shower."

11. **Concept Enrichment**
    Discuss differences between a shower and a bath. Discuss names of fixtures in a shower.

Music

1.   Sing "Take A Shower" to the tune of "The Bear Went Over the Mountain":
   Verse 1:   John took a shower;
                  John took a shower;
                  John took a shower;
                  And he got all wet!
                  He got all wet;
                  He got all wet.
                  John took a shower;
                  And he got all wet!
   Verse 2:   He used some soap;
                  He used some soap;
                  He used some soap;
                  And washed himself clean!
                  Washed himself clean;
                  Washed himself clean.
                  He used some soap;
                  And washed himself clean!
   Make up new verses. Pantomime taking a shower.
2.   Sing "Wash the Dirt Away" to the tune of "Anchors Aweigh":
   Wash the dirt away,
   Wash the dirt away,
   We'll get into the shower
   And turn the water on to warm
   Wash the dirt, wash the dirt away
   We'll get into the shower
   Wash the dirt away, away, away!

Art

1.   Have the children paste paper dolls on a picture of a shower and color the water streaming down.
2.   Help the children make shower curtains out of cloth for the above pictures and decorate them with potato prints. Gather the shower and staple it on the shower picture above.
3.   Continue the mural begun in Lesson #1 Art #4. Have the children decorate curtain first. (An old shower curtain can be decorated with crayon or permanent magic markers.) Then add it to the shower on the mural.

Snack

1.   Have snack served in waterproof plastic bags.
2.   Wear shower caps to snack.

Fine Motor

1.   Provide each child with a picture of a shower head at the top of the page and a child's head at the bottom of the page. Children make the water hit the child's head. Children use either a blue crayon or blue felt tip pen.
2.   Practice turning faucets on and off.
3.   Have the children practice folding a wash cloth.

Games

1.   Let the children give a doll a shower and wash the doll's hair. Hook up a portable hose and shower head. Let the children hold doll in tub and give the doll a shower.
2.   Make a feely box and place plastic dollhouse furniture fixtures in the box. Show a bathroom fixture and have each child find the matching piece by feeling in the box. (Tactile Discrimination) Vary the activity by showing the child a picture of a fixture, instead of the actual object.

Storytelling

Make up a story about the "dirtiest kid there ever was." Start the story with the following: "Once there was a kid - a dirty kid - a real dirty kid. He must have been the dirtiest kid there ever was. Do you know what he did to get dirty? (Children suggest things. You listen.) Well, I'll tell you. . ." Make up story of why this kid was always so dirty and end the story with the following: "So the kid came home to take a shower. He (or she) got in the shower and washed and washed and washed. He washed all day and he washed all night. He even ate supper in the shower. Finally he was shining clean. And do you know what? He's the cleanest kid there ever was!" Change ending to suit the story, if needed. Do let the "kid" end up in the shower.

Gross Motor

1. Practice washing body while pretending to be in the shower. First wash head, then shoulders, etc. "Be sure to scrub between your toes."
2. Make an obstacle course leading to the shower on the mural. Have the children go through it to get to the shower.

Cognitive

1. Provide a variety of shower pictures cut from catalogs. Let children sort shower from non-shower bathroom fixtures.
2. Discuss hot, cold and warm. Stress the importance of checking the temperature of the water before getting into a shower. Practice testing the water to find the warm one.

Enrichment

Provide small squares of colored cardboard (poster board). Have the children use them to make tile floors (and/or walls) for a bathroom in a box. Put in doll fixtures. Use the "tiles" to make a shower inside a shoe box to make a shower.

Lesson 3: Tub

Unit Group Lesson

1. **Match Concrete Objects** (Use toys.)
   Present two tubs. Say, "This is a tub." Ask each child in turn to put the tub with the tub. Gradually increase number of irrelevant objects from which (s)he must select tub to match.

2. **Discriminate Objects**
   Present several objects. Have each child touch the tub in response to verbal direction, "Touch the tub."

3. **Match Pictures**
   Present several pictures of common objects. Have each child match the pictures of the tubs.

4. **Discriminate Pictures**
   Present a group of several unrelated pictures of objects. Have each child touch the picture of the tub in response to verbal direction, "Touch the tub."

5. **Figure-Ground**
   Present a "busy" picture with many visual distractions. Ask each child to find the tub.

6. **Visual Closure**
   Partially cover each of several pictures with paper. Ask each child to find the picture of the tub.

7. **Function**
   Ask, "What do we do with a tub?"

8. **Association**
   Ask, "What goes with the tub?" Use pictures or objects including soap, towel, washcloth, shower, etc., with several unrelated objects or pictures.

9. **Imitate Verbalization**
   Present a tub and ask, "What is this? Say, 'Tub'." The child will imitate "Tub."

10. **Verbalize Label**
    Present a tub and ask, "What is this?" The child will respond, "Tub."

11. **Concept Enrichment**
    Discuss wash tubs, old-fashioned laundry tubs, and baby tubs. Discuss differences between a shower and a tub.

Music

Sing "Splish, Splash" to the tune of "Twinkle, Twinkle Little Star":
   Splish, splash in the tub;
   Get some soap and rub-a-dub-dub.
   Wash your face carefully,
   Remember your elbows and your knees.
   Splish, splash in the tub;
   Get some soap and rub-a-dub-dub.

Art
1. Have children paste "three kids in a tub." See Storytelling #2, today. Supply pictures of tubs of different colors and small pictures (or illustrations) of children. Direct, "Paste one girl in the red tub," etc.
2. Have the children paste a girl or boy in a tub with a rubber duck and paste blue cellophane paper over them in the tub part to make it look like water.
3. Continue the mural begun in Lesson #1 Art #4 today. Add a tub to the mural. Paint it a special color.

Snack

Serve snack in a doll tub.

Fine Motor
1. Make a path tracing of "Take a dirty child to the tub." and "Take a washcloth to a child." Vary the level of paths according to the level of each child.
2. Have each child color a tub of water blue. Tell children not to "spill the water" (color out of lines). (See fig. 16A.)

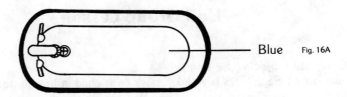

Blue   Fig. 16A

Games
1. Provide a baby tub to give a doll a bath. Let the children soap, rinse, and dry off the doll. Then have them dress the doll.
2. Put tub toys, towels and washclothes in the housekeeping area.

Storytelling

1. Have the children help tell a fill-in story. "It was time for Janie to go to bed. So she went to the bathroom to take a bath. She ran the water in the (tub). She took off her clothes and got into the water in the tub. She scrubbed all over with a (washcloth) and (soap). Then she got out of the tub and dried off with a (towel). Then she put her (pajamas) on. Janie was ready for bed." Have pictures of tub, washcloth, soap, towel, and pajamas and hold the appropriate picture up when you name it. Tell the story again. Let children fill in the blanks either by naming the item or finding the correct picture.

2. Fingerplay: "Rub-a-dub-dub"
   Verse 1: Rub-a-dub-dub;
   Three kids in a tub;   *(Hold up three fingers.)*
   Washing their hands and feet.   *(Pantomime washing hands and feet.)*
   Rub-a-dub-dub;
   Three kids in a tub;   *(Hold up three fingers.)*
   Won't they be clean and sweet?
   Verse 2: Washing their hands and knees
   Hope they don't get cold and sneeze!   *(Sneeze.)*

   Dramatize poem. Have children sit in cardboard box (tub) and "wash" themselves with paper towels or dry washclothes. Change number of kids in tub for a variation. Make up new verses.

Gross Motor

Use any type of tub to let the children practice climbing in and out of it. Be sure tub is steady and child gets help if he needs it.

Cognitive

1. Provide tubs and people in different sizes. Have children match person with properly sized tub. Use toys if available. Children with higher-level skills can use pictures.

2. Hold items such as towel, washcloth, soap, sheets, pillowcases, etc. up one at a time. Ask the children, "Does this go in a bathroom?" Vary the activity by placing the articles on a table. "Find something that belongs in the bathroom."

3. Count tubs. Provide a shoebag with numerals on the pockets. Have the children put the correct number of tubs (pictures) in each pocket.

Enrichment

Cover a large rectangular-shaped box with a sheet tucked in all around. This is the bathtub. From a basket full of cleaning supplies let the children choose the things you can use in taking a bath such as soap, washcloth, toy duck, bubble bath, sponge, shampoo, etc. Other items to have in basket include dishwashing liquid, a truck, a dishtowel, a whisk broom. Pretend to bathe in the tub. Wash your face, your knees, your ears, etc.

Lesson 4: Sink

Unit Group Lesson

1. **Match Concrete Objects** (Use toys.)
   Present two sinks. Say, "This is a sink." Ask each child in turn to put the sink with the sink. Gradually increase number of irrelevant objects from which (s)he must select sink to match.

2. **Discriminate Objects**
   Present several objects. Have each child touch the sink in response to verbal direction, "Touch the sink."

3. **Match Pictures**
Present several pictures of common objects. Have each child match the pictures of the sinks.

4. **Discriminate Pictures**
Present a group of several unrelated pictures of objects. Have each child touch the picture of the sink in response to verbal direction, "Touch the sink."

5. **Figure-Ground**
Present a "busy" picture with many visual distractions. Ask each child to find the sink.

6. **Visual Closure**
Partially cover each of several pictures with paper. Ask each child to find the picture of the sink.

7. **Function**
Ask, "What do we do with a sink?"

8. **Association**
Ask, "What goes with the sink?" Use pictures or objects including soap, water, towel, washcloth, toothbrush, etc., with several unrelated objects or pictures.

9. **Imitate Verbalization**
Present a sink and ask, "What is this? Say, 'Sink'." The child will imitate "Sink."

10. **Verbalize Label**
Present a sink and ask, "What is this?" The child will respond, "Sink."

11. **Concept Enrichment**
Discuss different types of sinks and laundry tubs.

Music
1. Sing "In the Bathroom Sink" to the tune of "This Old Man":
   Wash your hands;   *(Pantomime washing hands.)*
   Brush your teeth;   *(Pantomime brushing teeth.)*
   Do it all in the bathroom sink.
   With a brush, brush,   *(Pantomime brushing teeth.)*
     scrub, scrub.   *(Pantomime washing hands.)*
   Quicker then a wink,   *(Wink.)*
   You'll be finished with the bathroom sink!
2. Sing "This Is the Way. . ." to the tune of "This Is the Way We Wash Our Clothes":
   Verse 1: This is the way we brush our teeth,
             Brush our teeth, brush our teeth;
             This is the way we brush our teeth;
             Using the bathroom sink.
   Verse 2: This is the way we wash our hands,
   Children and teacher make-up new verses. Pantomime each verse.

Art
1. Have each child cut out pictures of bathroom fixtures and assemble a picture of a bathroom.
2. Have children tear or cut out pictures of bathroom sinks and paste on paper for a sink collage.
3. Continue the mural begun in Lesson #1 Art #4. Add a bathroom sink to the mural. Have children decorate a wood cabinet around it with wood tone scraps of wall paper or thin wood scraps.

Snack
Wash hands in a sink before snack.

Fine Motor

1. Have children wash and dry their own hands during toileting. Let the children use soap, pull their own paper towels from the dispenser, and turn the water on and off.
2. Fill a sink with soapy water. Have children blow bubbles using straws.
3. Have children brush their teeth after lunch everyday. Let them put toothpaste on their brush with help from the teacher.

Games

Let children pretend to be Daddy at the sink (girls too!). Let each stand on a foot stool so the child can see himself in mirror. Put shaving cream in his hand and let him smear it on his face. Give child a bladeless razor. "Shave like your daddy."

Storytelling

Have the children help tell a fill-in story. Use the same story as used in Lesson #3 Storytelling #1. Add to that story the following: "After Janie put her pajamas on she decided to brush her teeth. So she stood up at the sink and turned the water on. She put toothpaste on her toothbrush and brushed her teeth. Then Janie went to bed."

Gross Motor

Put large square of paper (sink) on the floor - give directions to walk, run, jump to: top, bottom, right side, left side, on, beneath, above, and beside the "sink."

Cognitive

1. Cut out sinks from catalogs or construction paper and have the children sort them by color.
2. Count the sinks in response to number words. Provide a number of sinks which the children can count. Say, "Give me two sinks," etc. Have each child give the correct response.
3. Learn hot and cold faucets. Practice testing the water with a fingertip before putting the whole hand under it. Stress the importance of not putting hands under or into hot water. Test containers of water to find the warm one which is best for washing.

Enrichment

1. Clean the bathroom sink.
2. Make a collage of pictures of things to use in cleaning a sink and relate to a sink in other ways.

Lesson 5: Mirror

Unit Group Lesson

1. **Match Concrete Objects**
   Present two mirrors. Say, "This is a mirror." Ask each child in turn to put the mirror with the mirror. Gradually increase number of irrelevant objects from which (s)he must select mirror to match.

2. **Discriminate Objects**
   Present several objects. Have each child touch the mirror in response to verbal direction, "Touch the mirror."

3. **Match Pictures**
   Present several pictures of common objects. Have each child match the pictures of the mirrors.

4. **Discriminate Pictures**
   Present a group of several unrelated pictures of objects. Have each child touch the picture of the mirror in response to verbal direction, "Touch the mirror."

5. **Figure-Ground**

   Present a "busy" picture with many visual distractions. Ask each child to find the mirror.

6. **Visual Closure**

   Partially cover each of several pictures with paper. Ask each child to find the picture of the mirror.

7. **Function**

   Ask, "What do we do with a mirror?"

8. **Association**

   Ask, "What goes with the mirror?" Use pictures or objects including sink, brush, comb, shower, etc., with several unrelated objects or pictures.

9. **Imitate Verbalization**

   Present a mirror and ask, "What is this? Say, 'Mirror'." The child will imitate "Mirror."

10. **Verbalize Label**

    Present a mirror and ask, "What is this?" The child will respond, "Mirror."

11. **Concept Enrichment**

    Observe that things look backwards in a mirror.

Music

1. Sing "Oh Mirror" to the tune of "O Christmas Tree":
   Verse 1: Oh, mirror   *(Children look in large mirror.)*
           Oh, mirror,
           Look at me smile in the mirror!
   Verse 2: Oh, mirror,
           Oh, mirror,
           I see me in the mirror.
   Make up new verses based upon what children do in front of mirror.

2. Sing "In Front of the Mirror" to the tune of "The Bear Went Over the Mountain":
   Daddy shaves in front of the mirror;
   Daddy shaves in front of the mirror;
   Daddy shaves in front of the mirror;
   To see what he can see.

   Mother puts on her make-up;
   Mother puts on her make-up'
   Mother puts on her make-up;
   In front of the mirror.

Art

1. Let the children draw a face in a mirror by painting on aluminum foil backed by cardboard and using colored glue for paint.
2. Have children tear or cut out pictures of mirrors and paste on paper for a mirror collage.
3. Supply "mirrors" in various shapes (circle, square, rectangle) and have the children match mirrors to outline on paper and paste them on the outline.
4. Continue the mural begun in Lesson #1 Art #4. Have the use aluminum foil to add a mirror to mural. Make a frame around the mirror with bits of construction paper.

Snack

   Children watch themselves eat snack in a mirror.

Fine Motor

1. Make faces in a mirror with the children. Stand in front of a mirror with a child and have child follow your lead in sticking tongue out, moving tongue from side to side, making a kiss, winking eyes, scratching head, wiggling nose, etc. Then, switch roles and you follow child's lead.
2. Have the children make hand prints on the mirror. Put a little bit of lotion on each child's hands and then have them make hand or fingerprints on a real or aluminum foil mirror.
3. Give the children spray bottles full of water and paper towels and let them clean "mirrors."

Games

Let children pretend to be Mother and Daddy at the mirror. Supply the child with a brush and a comb. Let them style their own hair or each other's hair or do it for them. Spray a little hair spray on their hair. "Your hair is pretty!" "Don't you look nice, David!"

Storytelling

Recite this poem: "Mirror, Mirror"
Verse 1: Mirror, mirror,
On the wall,
Who's the cleanest kid of all?
Verse 2: Mirror, mirror,
On the wall,
Jack is the cleanest kid of all.
Check each child's hands and face. Let each child look at his face in the mirror. Recite second verse. Then it is Jack's turn. He recites the same verses and checks the children's faces and hands. Then it is another child's turn until everyone has a turn.

Gross Motor

Provide a full length mirror and have the children watch themselves jumping, hopping, skipping, etc., in the mirror.

Cognitive

1. Let the children look in a mirror and find their eyes, nose, mouth, ears, etc.
2. Provide mirrors (foil covered cardboard) in different sizes and have the children sequence the mirrors from smallest to largest.

Enrichment

1. Let the children look at or do mirror writing. Study letters and profiles in a mirror and on paper.
2. Discuss the uses of mirrors. What would happen if cars did not have mirrors or cameras did not have mirrors inside them.

Related Children's Records
ADVENTURES IN SOUND (MH)
"Take A Bath" from LEARNING BASIC SKILLS-HEALTHY & SAFETY (EA)
"I Looked Into the Mirror" from JAMBO (SCHOL)

Related Children's Books
Barrett, Judi. I HATE TO TAKE A BATH. Englewood Cliffs, N.J.: Four Winds Press, 1975.
Jackson, Ellen B. THE BEAR IN THE BATHTUB. Reading, Mass.: Addison-Wesley Publishing Co., 1981.
Vigna, Judith. THE LITTLE BOY WHO LOVED DIRT AND ALMOST BECAME A SUPERSLOB.
    Chicago: Albert Whitman & Co., 1975.
Yoken, Jane. NO BATH TONIGHT. New York: Thomas Y. Crowell, 1978.

Related Parenting Materials
Cansler, Dot. THE HOMESTRETCH. Winston-Salem, NC 27113-5128: Kaplan Press, 1983.

Unit 17: Mail

A developmental assessment should determine the functional levels of each child. Individual expectations are based on the assessment results.

Lesson 1: Mail Carrier

Unit Group Lesson

1. **Match Concrete Objects**
   Present two mail carriers. (If dolls or figures are not available, present pictures in items 1 and 2 and omit items 3 and 4.) Say, "This is a mail carrier." Ask each child in turn to put the mail carrier with the mail carrier. Gradually increase number of irrelevant objects from which (s)he must select mail carrier to match.

2. **Discriminate Objects**
   Present several objects. Have each child touch the mail carrier in response to verbal direction, "Touch the mail carrier."

3. **Match Pictures**
   Present several pictures of common objects. Have each child match the pictures of the mail carriers.

4. **Discriminate Pictures**
   Present a group of several unrelated pictures of objects. Have each child touch the picture of the mail carrier in response to verbal direction, "Touch the mail carrier."

5. **Figure-Ground**
   Present a "busy" picture with many visual distractions. Ask each child to find the mail carrier.

6. **Visual Closure**
   Partially cover each of several pictures with paper. Ask each child to find the picture of the mail carrier.

7. **Function**
   Ask, "What does a mail carrier do?"

8. **Association**
   Ask, "What goes with the mail carrier?" Use pictures or objects including letter, mailbox, mailbag, mail truck, etc., with several unrelated objects or pictures.

9. **Imitate Verbalization**
   Present a mail carrier and ask, "What is this? Say, 'Mail carrier'." The child will imitate "Mail carrier."

10. **Verbalize Label**
    Present a mail carrier and ask, "What is this?" The child will respond, "Mail carrier."

11. **Concept Enrichment**

Discuss what the mail carrier takes to our houses. Look at the letters, cards, and magazines that he carries. Discuss how he carries the mail. Let children try to carry a mail bag. If a mail truck comes nearby take children to look at it.

Music

Sing to the tune of "Here We Go 'Round the Mulberry Bush":
Who is knocking at our door,
At our door, at our door?
Who is knocking at our door,
Knockety knock knock knock.

Run and see who it can be,
Who it can be, who it can be,
Run and see who it can be,
Knockety knock knock knock.

The mail carrier is at our door,
At our door, at our door,
The mail carrier is at our door,
Knockety knock knock knock.

Bringing letters to our door,
To our door, to our door,
Bringing letters to our door,
Knockety knock knock knock.

(This song could be acted out. Have the children use rhythm sticks for the knocking sounds.)

Art

1. Make mail carrier hats. Use paper bags that are seven inches wide on widest side. Cut bag off about three inches from the bottom. Have the children paint the bottom portion of the bag blue. Cut out a black brim and have children staple it to the blue portion of the bag. (See fig. 17A.)
2. Make mailbags from large brown paper bags. Have each child decorate his mailbag and staple on a strap.
3. Have the children cut or tear pretty pictures from magazines to carry in their mailbags made above.

Snack

Serve the children's snack from a mailbag.

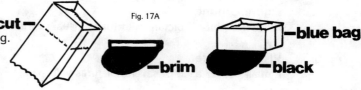

Fig. 17A
cut — — blue bag
— brim — black

Fine Motor

1. Make a worksheet with a mail carrier on it without a hat. Have children paste a blue construction paper hat on his head. Also have the children color his uniform blue.
2. Have the children decorate an envelope with Air Mail stripes and the words. . .VIA AIR MAIL. Children can trace around pre-marked guides.
3. Have each child fold paper into a seal-it note and put his name on it (following dotted letters or gluing cut out letters). The mail carrier can deliver all letters. (See fig. 17B.)

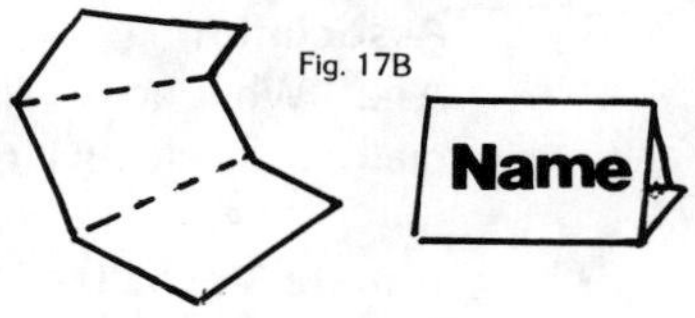

Fig. 17B

Name

Games

1. Put felt mail carrier in a blue suit without a hat on the flannel board. Put red, blue and yellow felt hats on the flannel board. Have the children put the hat which matches his suit on the mail carrier. Do this several times, then take the mail carrier down and ask the children to find the blue hat.
2. Put a mailbag and hat or uniform in the housekeeping area for dress-up.

Storytelling

1. Pantomime: "Mr. Mail Carrier":
    Good morning, Mr. Mail Carrier.
    Your bag is full I see.
    I'm looking for a letter;
    Have you anything for me?

    Yes! Here's a letter
    And here's a paper, too.
    I've others for your neighbors,
    But nothing else for you.

2. Put a mailbox and three houses, each a different color, on the flannel board. Make up a simple story about delivering the mail and emphasize the sequencing.
    For example: *"The mail carrier took mail to the red house, then the yellow house, then he went to get some mail from the mailbox."*
    Model taking the mail carrier on this sequence. Then tell another story for the child to follow on the flannel board. Vary the difficulty of the stories to suit the individual child. Some children may only be able to take the mail carrier to one house, while others may be able to follow a four step command.

Gross Motor

1. Fill envelopes with bean bags, and let the children toss them into the mail carrier's bag.
2. Let children pretend to be mail carriers and carry a partially filled mailbag (made in Art #2) through an obstacle course.

Cognitive

1. Prior to this lesson wrap two packages and address them to the class. Mail one of them. When it comes to the class, look at all the new marks on the package compared to the unmailed package.
2. From a bag of clothing, or an envelope of clothing pictures, have the children sort the mail carrier's clothing.
3. Make mailbags in several sizes and have the children sequence them.

Enrichment

1. Have the children find pictures of all things that carry mail such as mail carrier, mail bag, truck, airplane, bus, train, men and women.
2. Have the children wrap a package to be sent in the mail.

Visitor

Wait for the mail carrier to deliver the mail. Talk with him and look at his uniform.

Lesson 2: Letter and Envelope

Unit Group Lesson

NOTE: It may be necessary to teach these concepts separately.

1. **Match Concrete Objects**
    Present two letters and envelopes. Say, "This is a letter and envelope." Ask each child in turn to put the letter and envelope with the letter and envelope. Gradually increase number of irrelevant objects from which (s)he must select letter and envelope to match.

2. **Discriminate Objects**
    Present several objects. Have each child touch the letter and envelope in response to verbal direction, "Touch the letters and touch the envelopes."

3. **Match Pictures**
Present several pictures of common objects. Have each child match the pictures of the letters and envelopes.

4. **Discriminate Pictures**
Present a group of several unrelated pictures of objects. Have each child touch the picture of the letter and envelope in response to verbal direction, "Touch the letter and touch the envelope."

5. **Figure-Ground**
Present a "busy" picture with many visual distractions. Ask each child to find the letter and envelope.

6. **Visual Closure**
Partially cover each of several pictures with paper. Ask each child to find the picture of the letter and envelope.

7. **Function**
Ask, "What do we do with a letter and envelope?"

8. **Association**
Ask, "What goes with the letter and envelope?" Use pictures or objects including mail carrier, pen, mailbag, mailbox, etc., with several unrelated objects or pictures.

9. **Imitate Verbalization**
Present a letter and envelope and ask, "What is this? Say, 'Letter and envelope'." The child will imitate "Letter and envelope."

10. **Verbalize Label**
Present a letter and envelope and ask, "What is this?" The child will respond, "Letter and envelope."

11. **Concept Enrichment**
Look at many different sizes of envelopes and letter papers. Talk about big and little, big and bigger.

Music

Sing to the tune of "Where Is Thumbkin?":
    Here's a letter,
    Here's a letter,
    It's for Tony,
    It's for Tony.
    Put it in an envelope,
    Put it in an envelope,
    With a stamp,
    With a stamp.

Art

1. Have the children decorate stationery with magic markers or crayons.
2. Have the children draw a story picture and tell about their pictures. Use this picture to put in an envelope for Fine Motor #1 for today.
3. Have each child make an airmail envelope out of a plain white one by using red and blue crayon marks around the envelope. (See fig. 17C.)

Fig. 17C

Snack

Put the snack crackers in envelopes addressed to each child.

Fine Motor

1. Model folding the picture letter and help each child fold his picture letter (see Art #2). Give each child an envelope and have him put his letter in the envelope and seal it. Put a square space on the envelope for a stamp and have the child stick the stamp on it. Write the child's parents' name and address it. Mail it when you study the mailbox. (Lesson #4 Field Trip.)
2. Give the children "junk" mail to open.
3. Provide inexpensive envelopes for the children to "address." Save old advertising stamps for the children to use as stamps, to tear and paste on envelopes.

Games

1. Make a mailbox for each child of the same color as an envelope with his name on it. Write his name on the mailbox. Put the envelopes on the floor and have each child find his/her envelope and put it in his/her mailbox. Put the envelopes on the floor again and have the children choose any envelope except their own and put it in the matching mailbox.
2. Put stationery and envelopes in the housekeeping area.

Storytelling

Put five envelopes on the chalkboard ledge. Put one familiar picture in each envelope. Say, "Five pretty envelopes standing in a row. I wonder what's inside? Do you know?" Encourage children to say the rhyme. Let one child look in an envelope and tell the other children what is in it. Then have him show the picture to the other children. "Four pretty envelopes standing in a row. I wonder what's inside. Do you know?" Continue until all the envelopes have been opened.

Gross Motor

Have a relay race to the class mailbox. Have each child mail a letter, race back and tap the next child to run and mail his letter. Vary the activity by having the children, walk, skip, jump, etc.

Cognitive

1. Have the children sort letters from envelopes.
2. Send the class a letter inviting them to a special occasion such as a movie, assembly program, party, etc. Say, "Look what came in the mail for us. What should I do with it?" Open the envelope and read the letter.
3. Make a worksheet with the outline of several different sized stamps on it. Give each child "stamps" which fit and have them glue each stamp onto the correct spot.

Enrichment

Look at all kinds of mailing envelopes. Ask, "What can go inside?" Have a basket of items and let the children tell which goes with which envelope. (Include things you would not mail in an envelope - like a mirror. Discuss why not.)

Field Trip

Take a trip to buy envelopes and stamps.

Visitor

Write a letter (called an invitation) for someone to come visit. Have the visitor bring the invitation, show it to the children, read it, tell about when it arrived, etc.

Lesson 3: Mail Carrier

Unit Group Lesson

1. **Match Concrete Objects**
    Present two mail carriers. (If dolls or figures are not available, present pictures in items 1 and 2 and omit items 3 and 4.) Say, "This is a mail carrier." Ask each child in turn to put the mail carrier with the mail carrier. Gradually increase number of irrelevant objects from which (s)he must select mail carrier to match.

2. **Discriminate Objects**
    Present several objects. Have each child touch the mail carrier in response to verbal direction, "Touch the mail carrier."

3. **Match Pictures**
    Present several pictures of common objects. Have each child match the pictures of the mail carriers.

4. **Discriminate Pictures**
    Present a group of several unrelated pictures of objects. Have each child touch the picture of the mail carrier in response to verbal direction, "Touch the mail carrier."

5. **Figure-Ground**
    Present a "busy" picture with many visual distractions. Ask each child to find the mail carrier.

6. **Visual Closure**
    Partially cover each of several pictures with paper. Ask each child to find the picture of the mail carrier.

7. **Function**
    Ask, "What does a mail carrier do?"

8. **Association**
    Ask, "What goes with the mail carrier?" Use pictures or objects including letter, mailbox, mailbag, mailtruck, etc., with several unrelated objects or pictures.

9. **Imitate Verbalization**
    Present a mail carrier and ask, "What is this? Say, 'Mail carrier'." The child will imitate "Mail carrier."

10. **Verbalize Label**
    Present a mail carrier and ask, "What is this?" The child will respond, "Mail carrier."

11. **Concept Enrichment**
    Discuss fact that a mail carrier is a community helper. Discuss other community helpers and their jobs.

Music

Sing to the tune of "Mary Had A Little Lamb":
   I'm glad we have a mail carrier,
   Mail carrier, mail carrier
   I'm glad we have a mail carrier
   To bring us mail each day.

Art
1. Have each child paint a picture for the mail carrier.
2. Have each child glue the parts of a mail carrier onto an outline of a mail carrier and decorate the picture.

Snack
1. Have someone dressed as a mail carrier to serve snack.
2. Put graham crackers in clean white envelopes for snack.

Fine Motor

1. Make a path tracing activity of taking "The mail carrier to the mailbox," "The mail truck to the post office," "The mail carrier to the house," and "The mail truck to the mailbox." Vary the level of difficulty according to the skills of the children.

2. Have the children button the mail carrier's jacket. If other community helper uniforms are available, have the children fasten them.

Games

1. "The Mail Carrier's On His Way." Sing to the tune of "The Farmer in the Dell":

   The mail carrier's on his way,
   The mail carrier's on his way,
   He'll open up his letter bag
   And bring us mail today.

   One child is chosen to be the mail carrier. He walks around in the circle, as the group sings "The Mail Carrier's on His Way." At the end of the song, he stops and pulls out a letter and finds the child to whom it belongs. From: CHURCH KINDERGARTEN RESOURCE BOOKS.

2. Put a variety of community helper hats and uniforms in the dress up area.

Storytelling

For this flannel board story, five mail carriers are needed. Start with all of the mail carriers on the flannel board and have a child remove one at each verse of the poem.

   Five mail carriers standing by the store.
   One left to empty the mailbox,
   Then there were four.
   Four mail carriers looking for me.
   One took Jill a present,
   Then there were three.
   Three mail carriers dressed in blue.
   One brought mother a magazine,
   Then there were two.
   Two mail carriers walking in the sun.
   One brought daddy a letter,
   Now there is one.
   One mail carrier walking just for fun.
   He brought me a birthday card,
   Now there are none.

Gross Motor

Put "house" signs on chairs, doors, indoors or outdoors (wherever you decide) at different levels. Have one child, the mail carrier, deposit a letter at each place, reaching for some, stooping for some. The next child collects the mail; the next child delivers it again.

Cognitive

1. Make a cue sheet with a mail carrier at the top and mail carriers and other community helpers underneath. Let the children mark the mail carriers.

2. Make a large chart with a mail carrier and other community helpers on it. Have the children identify the carriers and other community helpers such as policeman, fireman, librarian, etc.

Enrichment

Talk about the Pony Express. Use a picture to stimulate discussion. Talk about how many horses and men it took to deliver a letter. Let the children dramatize the story.

Visitor

Wait for the mail carrier to come to the school. Show him the pictures that the children made for him.

Lesson 4: Mailbox

Unit Group Lesson

1. **Match Concrete Objects**
   Present two mailboxes. Say, "This is a mailbox." Ask each child in turn to put the mailbox with the mailbox. Gradually increase number of irrelevant objects from which (s)he must select mailbox to match.

2. **Discriminate Objects**
   Present several objects. Have each child touch the mailbox in response to verbal direction, "Touch the mailbox."

3. **Match Pictures**
   Present several pictures of common objects. Have each child match the pictures of the mailbox.

4. **Discriminate Pictures**
   Present a group of several unrelated pictures of objects. Have each child touch the picture of the mailbox in response to verbal direction, "Touch the mailbox."

5. **Figure-Ground**
   Present a "busy" picture with many visual distractions. Ask each child to find the mailbox.

6. **Visual Closure**
   Partially cover each of several pictures with paper. Ask each child to find the picture of the mailbox.

7. **Function**
   Ask, "What do we do with a mailbox?"

8. **Association**
   Ask, "What goes with the mailbox?" Use pictures or objects including letters, mail carriers, stamps, etc., with several unrelated objects or pictures.

9. **Imitate Verbalization**
   Present a mailbox and ask, "What is this? Say, 'Mailbox'." The child will imitate "Mailbox."

10. **Verbalize Label**
    Present a mailbox and ask, "What is this?" The child will respond, "Mailbox."

11. **Concept Enrichment**
    Discuss the sequence of taking mail to the mailbox, a mail carrier picking it up and taking it to the post office.

Music

Sing to the tune of "Here We Go 'Round the Mulberry Bush":

We will send our letter to Grandma,
Our letter to Grandma,
Our letter to Grandma,
We will send our letter to Grandma,
We'll put it in the mailbox.

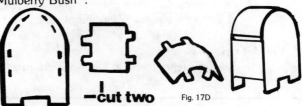

cut two   Fig. 17D

Art

1. Cut out of heavy cardboard a large mailbox that the children can assemble as a group. Have the children paint it. (See fig. 17D.)
2. Provide red, white and blue paints at the easel and let the children paint mailboxes.

Snack

Serve snack for each child in the mailboxes made in Fine Motor #3 today.

Fine Motor

1. On a worksheet have the children trace a mailbox, a letter and a stamp.
2. Give each child a full-page sized alphabet letter to color. Use the letters MAIL and have the children paste them in correct order onto the mailbox. Write the letters lightly on the mailbox so that they can paste them over the penciled letters.
3. Make mailboxes from milk cartons glued together. Have one for each child. Child makes his own name to glue on his mailbox.

Games

Give each child a different command and have the other children clap if the child follows the command correctly. For example: "Jimmy, do put the letter in the mailbox." "Tony, do not put the book in the mailbox, but do put it on the shelf."

Storytelling

Pantomime the following story. Have the children copy you in a "Follow the Leader" fashion.

"I'm writing my grandma a letter. Now I'll put it in the envelope and lick the envelope and close it. I have to find the stamp. I can't find the stamp. Let's look under Tony's chair. Let's look on the table. Let's look in the drawer. No stamps anywhere. Oh, look in Mary's hand. Mary has the stamps. Please give us each a stamp, Mary. Now let's put the stamp on the envelope. Off to the mailbox. We go out the door and down the street to the mailbox. Let's put the letter in the mailbox."

The teacher can either add to the story or simplify it depending on the children.

Gross Motor

Use the "real"-sized mailbox made in Art #1 today and have children crawl under it, and walk, run, jump and hop around it.

Cognitive

1. Ask each child to go to the mailbox, open it and mail a letter.
2. Discuss OPEN and CLOSED. Show a toy mailbox with the door open and door closed. Let each child open and close the mailbox when instructed to do so.
3. Practice putting things IN the mailbox and taking them OUT. Give each child several turns.

Enrichment

1. Make alphabet LETTER MAILBOXES. Draw two mailboxes, a large and a small one. Glue them onto boxes with lids. Make a slot in each lid. On the large mailbox write "CAPITAL LETTERS" and on the small box write "small letters." Have the children sort through the "letters" (alphabet cards) and mail them "in" proper box.

2. Make cards with 1 to 5 mailboxes on them. Cover with plastic and have children count the mailboxes on each card. Some children may be capable of matching the correct numeral to the picture and some of writing the numeral on the picture.

Field Trip
Take the letter made in Lesson 2 and mail it in the nearest mailbox.

Lesson 5: Post Office

Unit Group Lesson

1. **Match Concrete Objects**
    Present two post offices. (If only pictures are available, present pictures in items 1 and 2 and omit item 3.) Say, "This is a post office." Ask each child in turn to put the post office with the post office. Gradually increase number of irrelevant objects from which (s)he must select post office to match.

2. **Discriminate Objects**
    Present several objects. Have each child touch the post office in response to verbal direction, "Touch the post office."

3. **Match Pictures**
    Present several pictures of common objects. Have each child match the pictures of the post offices.

4. **Discriminate Pictures**
    Present a group of several unrelated pictures of objects. Have each child touch the picture of the post office in response to verbal direction, "Touch the post office."

5. **Figure-Ground**
    Present a "busy" picture with many visual distractions. Ask each child to find the post office.

6. **Visual Closure**
    Partially cover each of several pictures with paper. Ask each child to find the picture of the post office.

7. **Function**
    Ask, "What do we do at a post office?"

8. **Association**
    Ask, "What goes with the post office?" Use pictures or objects including letters, mail carriers, mailbox, etc., with several unrelated objects or pictures.

9. **Imitate Verbalization**
    Present a post office and ask, "What is this? Say, 'Post office'." The child will imitate "Post office."

10. **Verbalize Label**
    Present a post office and ask, "What is this?" The child will respond, "Post office."

11. **Concept Enrichment**
    Explain how the mail at the post office is sorted, sent to other post offices and delivered to people to whom it is addressed.

Music

Review all songs taught this week.

Art

1. Help each child make a model post office. Give each child a shoe box. Have each child paint it red or grey, cut a hole in it for a door, and paste on squares of black paper for windows. Give each child a small flag to put on top of his post office.

2. Have the class make a town mural with a post office in the town. Paint the buildings different colors, glue on signs for each building, an American flag over the post office, bricks on some buildings, mailboxes, fire hydrants, doors, windows, merchandise, etc. Let some children cut or draw their own additions and have others use pre-cut parts. (See fig. 17E.)

Snack

1. Eat something in "envelope bread" (pocket or pita bread).
2. Eat foods that are easily mailed at the post office.

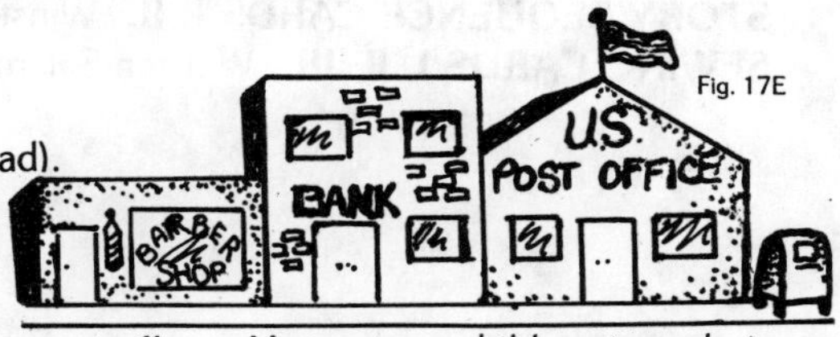

Fig. 17E

Fine Motor

1. Make a large pretend map going from the school to the post office. Have some children trace between the straight portions only and let the more advanced children do the curves and corners. They may use small cars or crayons to trace the paths.

2. Have some children draw and/or cut items for the mural in Art #2.

3. Have the children trace the dotted words POST OFFICE on a large piece of paper. (See fig. 17F.)

Fig. 17F

Games

Set up a pretend post office. Have some children sort letters (by color, number, letter or some other appropriate cue), others put them in mailbags, and others deliver them to addresses.

Storytelling

Tell a story about what happens to a letter when it's mailed. Use pictures to show the letter as it goes in to the mailbox, then into a mail truck, then to the post office, then into a bigger mail truck, then into an airplane, then into another mail truck, then to another post office, then to a mailman, and then to a house.

Gross Motor

Walk briskly to the real post office or an imaginary one. Go up the steps, open the door, mail a letter, close the door, and walk back down the steps.

Cognitive

1. Make post offices in several sizes. Have the children sequence them by size.
2. Discuss parts of a post office building. Have the children identify them on a picture.
3. Discuss materials used to build a post office. Have the children select them from materials that would never be used to build a post office.

Enrichment

1. Label places in the community on shapes. Tape along a road drawn on paper, the table or carpet. Have the children match word cards in matching shapes to the right building.

2. Arrange houses along a street. Have the children deliver mail to the right house. (See fig. 17G.)

Fig. 17G

Field Trip

Go to a post office.

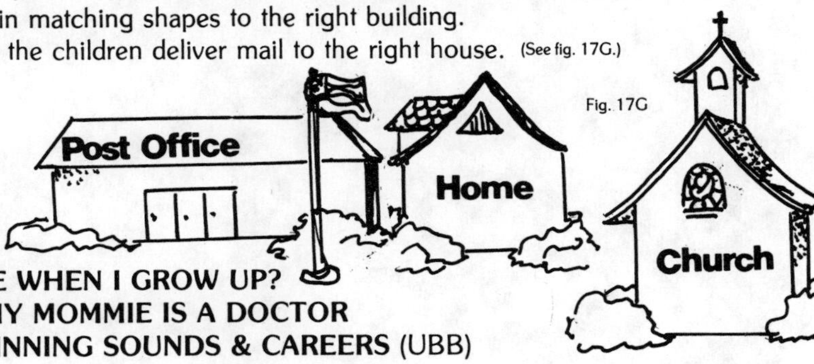

Related Children's Records

"Happy Postman" from **WHAT WILL I BE WHEN I GROW UP?**

"The Ones Who Deliver the Mail" from **MY MOMMIE IS A DOCTOR**

"Michael Mason the Mailman" from **BEGINNING SOUNDS & CAREERS** (UBB)

Related Children's Books
Keats, Ezra Jack. **A LETTER TO AMY.** Harper & row, 1968.
Scarry, Richard. **POSTMAN PIG AND HIS BUSY NEIGHBORS.** New York: Random House, 1978.
Suhl, Ur. **SIMON BOOM GETS A LETTER.** Englewood Cliffs, N.J.: Four Winds Press, 1976.

Related Parenting Materials
Cansler, Dot. **THE HOMESTRETCH.** Winston-Salem, NC 27113-5128: Kaplan Press, 1983.

Related Materials
TEACHING PICTURES. Winston-Salem, NC 27113-5128: Kaplan Press, 1983.
STORY SEQUENCE CARDS I, II. Winston-Salem, NC 27113-5128: Kaplan Press, 1983.
SEWING CARDS I, II, III. Winston-Salem, NC 27113-5128: Kaplan Press, 1983.

Unit 18: Valentines

A developmental assessment should determine the functional levels of each child. Individual expectations are based on the assessment results.

Lesson 1: Valentine

Unit Group Lesson

1. **Match Concrete Objects**
   Present two valentines. Say, "This is a valentine." Ask child to put the valentine with the valentine. Gradually increase number of irrelevant objects from which (s)he must select valentine to match.

2. **Discriminate Objects**
   Present several objects. Have each child touch the valentine in response to verbal direction, "Touch the valentine."

3. **Match Pictures**
   Present several pictures of common objects. Have each child match the pictures of the valentines.

4. **Discriminate Pictures**
   Present a group of several unrelated pictures of objects. Have each child touch the picture of the valentine, in response to verbal direction, "Touch the valentine."

5. **Figure-Ground**
   Present a "busy" picture with many visual distractions. Ask each child to find the valentine.

6. **Visual Closure**
   Partially cover each of several pictures with paper. Ask each child to find the picture of the valentine.

7. **Function**
   Ask, "What do we do with a valentine?"

8. **Association**
   Ask, "What goes with the valentine?" Use pictures or objects including kiss, cupid, etc., with several unrelated objects or pictures.

9. **Imitate Verbalization**
   Present a valentine and ask, "What is this? Say, 'Valentine'." The child will imitate "Valentine."

10. **Verbalize Label**
    Present a valentine and ask, "What is this?" The child will respond, "Valentine."

11. **Concept Enrichment**
    Discuss why we use a heart shape for valentine. (Because the heart stands for love and Valentine's Day is a day for someone you love.)

Music

Sing to the tune of "Muffin Man":
I'm looking for a Valentine, a valentine, a valentine,
I'm looking for a Valentine, to be a friend of mine.
Won't you (will you?) be my valentine, my valentine, my valentine,
Won't you (will you?) be my valentine and be a friend of mine?
One child walks (skips) around circle, stops in front of another child as group sings.

Art

1. Help each child make a valentine necklace. Give each child a large darning needle with 25 inches of yarn and a felt valentine with two holes punched in the top. Child threads yarn through holes in valentine, remove needle and tie ends of yarn together. Using Elmer's glue have the children glue a piece of paper doiley or sequins onto the valentine. (See fig. 18A.)

2. Have the children make a valentine tree. Cut a branch from a tree, place in a flower pot in plaster of paris. Decorate with child-made and commercial valentines.

3. Help everyone make valentine sachets. Have them decorate two identical hearts with bits of paper doilies, lace, sequins, glitter or other attractive things, put perfume on cotton balls and place between the two hearts and glue or staple the hearts closed. Hang from ribbon and give to Mother or a friend to say I love you.

Fig. 18A

Snack

1. Make Valentine cupcakes. Stencil a heart on top of pink or white icing by cutting a heart shape out of cardboard and gently laying on top. Sprinkle red sugar over rest of frosting.

2. Eat "hearty" sandwiches on bread cut with heart-shaped cookie cutters.

Fine Motor

1. Make felt cut-outs of hearts, circles and other shapes. Have the children match the shapes to each other and place the correct match directly on top of its mate. (See fig. 18B.)

2. Help the children make a pop-up card. Fold heart down inside when card is closed. Have them cut and decorate the card. (See fig. 18C.)

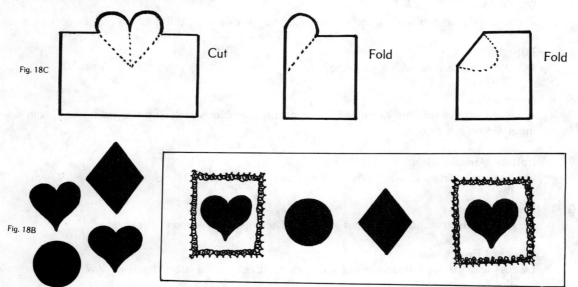

Fig. 18C   Cut   Fold   Fold

Fig. 18B

3. Have the children outline heart shapes with "Bumpy" dough, colored red, pink, or white.
   BUMPY DOUGH
   ¾ cup flour
   ¼ cup salt
   water
   tempera color of your choice
   (Cardboard shapes may be outlined or hearts can be formed and left to dry on newspaper). (See fig. 18D.)

Fig. 18D

4. Make sewing cards of a valentine and have children lace around it.

Games

Hide a plastic valentine and have the children find it. Use a simple classroom map with the location of the heart marked on it for those children who can work from a map.

Storytelling

Make a valentine man or woman by gluing felt valentines together. Use the flannel board and make up a silly story about what the valentine might do. Have the children think of things the valentine person might do. (See fig. 18E.)

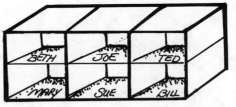
Fig. 18F

Fig. 18E

Gross Motor

Let the children toss a heart-shaped beanbag or a beanbag with a felt heart glued onto it into a decorated waste basket or box.

Cognitive

1. Provide hearts and have each child count hearts (as high as (s)he can count).
2. Let the children match hearts cut from the same designs. (Use wrapping paper, wallpaper samples, etc.).
3. Let the children make a post office of milk cartons glued together. Put child's name on each box. Provide small envelopes with children's names on them. Have the children make valentines and mail to names on post office. (See fig. 18F.)

Fig. 18G

Enrichment

Cut hearts in half and place a numeral on one half and the corresponding number of dots on the other half. Have the children match the heart pieces, the half with the numeral to the half with the correct number of dots. Make the activity self-correcting by having different numbers of notches for each heart. (See fig. 18G.)

Lesson 2: Red Valentine

Unit Group Lesson

Caution on this Lesson: Mixing the concepts red and valentine may be too high level for some children, especially after just teaching valentine.

1. **Match Concrete Objects**
   Present two red valentines. Say, "This is a red valentine." Ask each child in turn to put the red valentine with the red valentine. Gradually increase the number of irrelevant objects (or of other colors of valentines) from which (s)he must select red valentine to match.

2. **Discriminate Objects**

Present several red and non-red valentines. Have each child touch the red valentine in response to verbal direction, "Touch the red valentine."

3. **Match Pictures**

Present several pictures of common objects. Have each child match the pictures of the red valentines.

4. **Discriminate Pictures**

Present a group of pictures of several red and non-red valentines. Have each child touch the picture of the red valentine, in response to verbal direction, "Touch the red valentine."

5. **Figure-Ground**

Present a "busy" picture with many visual distractions. Ask each child to find the red valentine.

6. **Visual Closure**

Partially cover each of several pictures with paper. Ask each child to find the picture of the red valentine.

7. **Function**

Ask, "What do we do with the red valentine?"

8. **Association**

Ask, "What goes with the red valentine?" Use pictures or objects including other color valentines and several unrelated objects or pictures.

9. **Imitate Verbalization**

Present a red valentine and ask, "What is this? Say, 'Red valentine'." The child will imitate "Red valentine."

10. **Verbalize Label**

Present a red valentine and ask, "What is this?" The child will respond, "Red valentine."

11. **Concept Enrichment**

Discuss other colors for valentines, especially pink. Talk about mixing red and white to make pink.

Music

Sing to the tune of "Mary Had A Little Lamb":
    I can find a valentine,
    Valentine, valentine.
    I can find a valentine.
    My valentine is red.

Art
1. Have the children put glue on the edge of a red valentine shape and sprinkle sand on the glue.
2. Let the children use red and white paint to paint hearts and mix the paint together to make pink.
3. Let the children make red valentines using many different kinds of material such as: at the easel with red tempera paint, red construction paper, red play dough, red crayons, etc.
4. Let the children decorate the valentine tree with the red valentines made in #2 and #3 above. Have them attach strings or paper clips to the valentines for hanging.

Snack
1. Decorate heart cookies with red sugar.
2. Make red valentine punch by mixing red fruit drink with ginger ale.

Fine Motor

1. Have the children spatter-paint valentine shapes using a toothbrush and popsicle sticks. Rub stick over the toothbrush which has been dipped in red paint. Have the children do the activity inside an open box to prevent excessive spray.
2. Let the children make and wear rose-colored glasses by stapling red cellophane into 2 sections of a plastic 6-pack holder and attaching pipe cleaners for ear pieces. (See fig. 18H.)

Fig. 18H

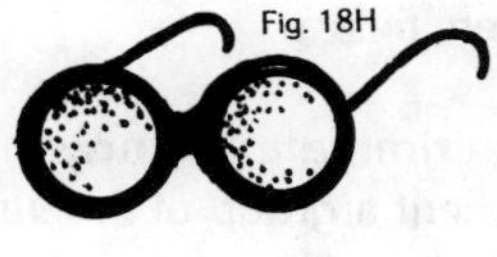

Games

Have the children pick the red valentines from the felt valentine tree on the flannel board. Have different colored valentines on the tree. (See fig. 18I.)

Fig. 18I

Storytelling

Recite "How Many Valentines?" with six heart-shaped, red felt valentines and a flannel board.

Red valentines, red valentines;
How many do you see?
Red valentines, red valentines;
Count them with me:

One for father.	(Hold up thumb.)
One for Mother.	(Hold up pointer finger.)
One for Grandma, too;	(Hold up middle finger.)
One for Sister.	(Hold up ring finger.)
One for Brother.	(Hold up little finger.)
And here is one for YOU!	(Make heart shape with thumbs and pointer fingers.)

From RHYMES FOR FINGERS AND FLANNEL BOARDS, Scott, Thompson; Webster McGraw Hill, 1960.

Gross Motor

Have a Red Heart Relay: Give a red heart valentine to first child. Have child run an obstacle course holding onto red valentine. (The obstacle course should be heart-shaped). Child returns to beginning and passes heart to next child and so on until all have had a turn.

Cognitive

1. Discuss redness of things. Look at many different red objects. Have the children select red things from non-red things.
2. Provide hearts in different colors. Have the children sort them by color or into red and non-red groups.
3. Cut out hearts for the children, two of many different colors. Give a heart to each child and have children find their partners (other child with identical heart).

Enrichment

Put some red candy hearts into small jars. Have children guess, "How many red hearts are in the jar?" Then let them count and eat the candies.

Lesson 3: Big Valentine

Unit Group Lesson

Caution: Mixing the concepts big and valentine may be too high level for some children, especially after just teaching valentine.

1. **Match Concrete Objects**
   Present two BIG valentines. Say, "This is a BIG valentine." Ask each child in turn to put the BIG valentine with the BIG valentine. Introduce small valentines from which (s)he muset select BIG valentine to match.

2. **Discriminate Objects**
Present several sizes of valentines. Have each child touch the BIG valentine in response to verbal direction, "Touch the BIG valentine."

3. **Match Pictures**
Present several pictures of different sized valentines. Have each child match the pictures of the BIG valentines.

4. **Discriminate Pictures**
Present a group of several different sized valentines. Have each child touch the picture of the BIG valentine, in response to verbal direction, "Touch the BIG valentine."

5. **Figure-Ground**
Present a "busy" picture with many visual distractions. Ask each child to find the BIG valentine.

6. **Visual Closure**
Partially cover each of several pictures with paper. Ask each child to find the picture of the BIG valentine.

7. **Function**
Ask, "What do we do with the BIG valentine?"

8. **Association**
Ask, "What goes with the BIG valentine?" Use pictures or objects including hearts, candy, etc., with several unrelated objects or pictures.

9. **Imitate Verbalization**
Present a BIG valentine and ask, "What is this? Say, 'BIG valentine'." The child will imitate "BIG valentine."

10. **Verbalize Label**
Present a BIG valentine and ask, "What is this?" The child will respond, "BIG valentine."

11. **Concept Enrichment**
Discuss "big" versus not-big things. How do the children compare to the teacher in size? Teacher is big; child is not-big. Not-big is called little.

Music

Sing to the tune of "Where Is Thumbkin?":
Here's a valentine   *(Hold up a BIG valentine.)*
Here's a valentine
It's for you
It's for you
The valentine is pretty
The valentine is pretty
It's for you
It's for you.

Art
1. Provide red felt-tip pens and have the children trace around a big cardboard valentine and paint valentine with tempera paint.
2. Have the children decorate their big valentines with lace and crushed egg shells.
3. Have the children hang big valentines on the valentine tree.

Snack
1. Make a big valentine cake using a 9" round and 9" square pan. (See fig. 18J.)

2.   Eat cookies made in Fine Motor #1, today.

Fine Motor
1.   Have everyone make big valentine cookies. Let the children help mix the dough. Then give each child some dough and a rolling pin. Help the children use a big valentine pattern to cut the cookie. Let the children ice and decorate the cookies.
2.   Make a Valentine floor puzzle. Use 22" x 28" posterboard to trace two large valentines. Cut one into pieces, then trace the outline of each piece onto the uncut puzzle to help children in placement. Let them do the puzzle.
3.   Let everyone help prepare a big valentine card. Have the children trace designs and shapes on a big piece of poster board and decorate it with bits of red ribbon and paper doilies.
      Make a big valentine today and repeat the activity tomorrow with little valentines. (See fig. 18K.)

Fig. 18K

Games
      Put several vastly different sized valentine cookie cutters in the feely box and have the children find the big valentine cookie cutter. Let the children feel and study the cutters before you put them into the feely box.

Storytelling
      Hold up a big red valentine and say, "I'm going to give this big red valentine to (child's name)." Give the child the big valentine and have him tell you what he has and to whom he's going to give it. Have him use a complete sentence as in the example given.

Gross Motor
1.   Push a cage ball or medicine ball through a big valentine. Make a very big valentine from wire and crepe paper, suspend it from the ceiling and let children push a cage ball or medicine ball through it.
2.   Make a path of big valentines and have the children hop, skip, jump, walk and run on the big valentine path. (See fig. 18L.)

Fig. 18L

Cognitive
1.   Let the children sort big valentines from not-big valentines.
2.   Have the children count big valentines on the valentine tree.
3.   Have each child find big valentines under chairs, on tables, beside the door, on the door knob etc. Have the child who finds a big valentine describe where he found it.

Fig. 18M

Enrichment
1.   Have each child cut out two big folded hearts and a cigar shape which have been outlined by teacher. Tape or glue the hearts to the "body." Draw eyes and use pipe cleaners for antennas. (See fig. 18M.)
2.   Provide big, bigger and biggest valentines and let the children sequence them by size.

Lesson 4: Little Valentine

Unit Group Lesson

1.   **Match Concrete Objects**
      Present two LITTLE valentines. Say, "This is a LITTLE valentine." Ask each child in turn to put the LITTLE valentine with the LITTLE valentine. Introduce BIG valentines from which (s)he must select LITTLE valentine to match.

2.   **Discriminate Objects**
      Present several sizes of valentines. Have each child touch the LITTLE valentine in response to verbal direction, "Touch the LITTLE valentine."

3. **Match Pictures**

Present several pictures of different sized valentines. Have each child match the pictures of the LITTLE valentines.

4. **Discriminate Pictures**

Present a group of several different sized valentines. Have each child touch the picture of the LITTLE valentine, in response to verbal direction, "Touch the LITTLE valentine."

5. **Figure-Ground**

Present a "busy" picture with many visual distractions. Ask each child to find the LITTLE valentine.

6. **Visual Closure**

Partially cover each of several pictures with paper. Ask each child to find the picture of the LITTLE valentine.

7. **Function**

Ask, "What do we do with LITTLE valentines?"

8. **Association**

Ask, "What goes with the LITTLE valentine?" Use pictures or objects including hearts, candy, etc., with several unrelated objects or pictures.

9. **Imitate Verbalization**

Present a LITTLE valentine and ask, "What is this? Say, 'LITTLE valentine'." The child will imitate "LITTLE valentine."

10. **Verbalize Label**

Present a LITTLE valentine and ask, "What is this?" The child will respond, "LITTLE valentine."

11. **Concept Enrichment**

Discuss "LITTLE" versus "BIG" things. How do the children compare to the teacher in size?

Music

Sing to the tune of "Hush Little Baby":
I love somebody, yes I do.
I love somebody, yes I do.
I love somebody, yes I do.
I love somebody, but I won't tell who.   (Shake head.)
I love somebody - and it's Y-O-U!   (Point to someone.)

Fig. 18N

Art
1. Help the children make little valentines for parents. Hold up a little photograph of each child for him to identify. Have the children make little cards using paper doilies on red and pink paper. Have each child paste his photograph on valentine.
2. Have the children hang little valentines on valentine tree.
3. Have each child prepare a valentine holder from two paper plates. Have each child cut one plate in half and staple it to the bottom half of the other plate. Decorate with gold and red hearts. (See fig. 18N.)
4. Have the children make little valentines from white cards, red cards, crayons, etc. Let the children keep what they make and "mail" in their post office later.

Snack

Fig. 18O

1. Make and cut little valentine cakes by putting a marble into muffin tins next to the cupcake paper. This forces the cake to cook in a heart-shape. Beware! Some children may try to eat the marbles. REMOVE THEM BEFORE SERVING. (See fig. 18O.)
2. Eat little valentine candies.

264

Fine Motor

1. Have the children use tweezers to pick little valentines (or candies) from a bowl.
2. Have the children cut little valentines from red paper.
3. Make the words I LOVE YOU with little heart-shaped dots and let the children connect them to spell I love you. (See fig. 18P.)

Fig. 18P

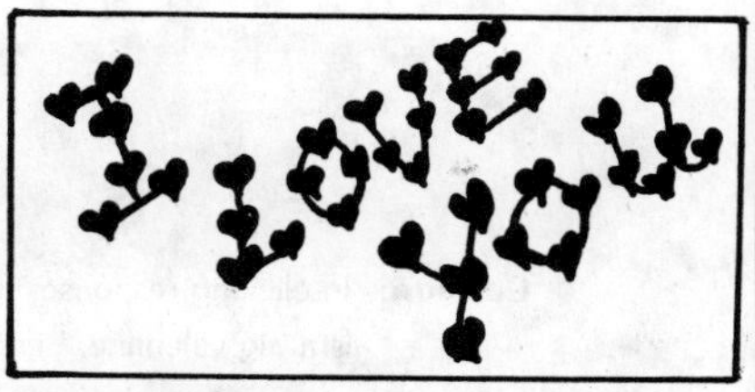

Games

Put big, little, red and blue valentines around the room. Give the children directions to find a valentine. Say, "Tony, tip-toe to the little valentine."

Storytelling

Recite "Five Little Valentines" with five heart-shaped red felt valentines:

One little valentine said, "I love you."   *(Hold up fist; extend one finger.)*
Tommy made another; then there were two.   *(Extend another finger.)*
Two little valentines, one for me;
Mary made another; then there were three.   *(Extend another finger.)*
Three little valentines said, "We need one more."
Johnny made another; then there were four.   *(Extend another finger.)*
Four little valentines, one more to arrive;
Susan made another; then there were five.   *(Extend another finger.)*
Five little valentines all ready to say,
"Be my valentine on this happy day."

From RHYMES FOR FINGERS AND FLANNELBOARDS, Scott, Thompson; Webster McGraw Hill, 1960.

Gross Motor

1. Have the children carry and deliver little valentines in the classroom vehicles.
2. Make a little valentine path and have the children walk, run, hop, skip, and/or jump on path made of little valentines.

Cognitive

1. Provide big and little valentines and have the children sort them by size.
2. Have the children count the little valentines hung on tree.
3. Make a cue sheet with a little valentine at the top and little and big valentines below. Have the children mark the little valentines.

Enrichment

1. Put instructions on WAYS TO SHOW LOVE into envelopes. Have each child choose an envelope. You read the instructions and the child acts out instruction. Some suggested instructions are:
    1. Hug (child's name) around the neck.
    2. Pat (child's name) on the back.
    3. Kiss (child's name) on the cheek.
    4. Wash the dishes for Mommy.
    5. Rake the yard.
    6. Pick up your toys.
    7. Take out the trash.
    8. Smile at your friend.
    9. Tiptoe when little brother (or sister) is asleep.
    10. Wrap a present for sister (or brother).
    11. Sing a song.
2. Provide little, littler and littlest valentines and let the children sequence them by size.

Lesson 5: Review Valentine

Unit Group Lesson

Caution: In eliciting responses from children be sure to question each concept separately. For example: "This is a red valentine." "This is a big valentine." etc.

1. **Match Concrete Objects**
   Present two valentines which are red, big or little. Say, "This is a (red,) (big,) or (little) valentine." Ask each child in turn to put the (red,) (big,) or (little) valentine with the (red,) (big,) or (little) valentine. Gradually increase the number of valentines from which (s)he must select (red,) (big,) or (little) valentine to match.

2. **Discriminate Objects**
   Present several valentines. Have each child touch the (red,) (big,) or (little) valentine in response to verbal direction, "Touch the (red,) (big,) or (little) valentine." (Be sure to do each separately.)

3. **Match Pictures**
   Present several pictures of different sized valentines. Have each child match the pictures of the valentines.

4. **Discriminate Pictures**
   Present a group of several unrelated pictures of objects and (red,) (big,) or (little) valentines. Have each child touch the picture of the (red,) (big,) or little valentine, in response to verbal direction, "Touch the (red,) (big,) or (little) valentine." (Be sure to do each separately.)

5. **Figure-Ground**
   Present a "busy" picture with many visual distractions. Ask each child to find the (red,) (big,) or (little) valentine.

6. **Visual Closure**
   Partially cover each of several pictures with paper. Ask each child to find the picture of the (red,) (big,) or (little) valentine.

7. **Function**
   Ask, "What do we do with valentines?"

8. **Association**
   Ask, "What goes with the (red,) (big,) or (little) valentine?" Use pictures or objects including red valentines, big valentines, little valentines, etc., with several related and unrelated objects or pictures.

9. **Imitate Verbalization**
   Present (red,) (big,) or (little) valentines and ask, "What is this? Say, '(Red,) (Big,) or (Little) valentine'," as the case may be. The child will imitate saying "(Red,) (Big,) or (Little) valentine."

10. **Verbalize Label**
    Present (red,) (big,) or (little) valentines and ask, "What is this?" The child will respond, "(Red,) (Big,) or (Little) valentine," appropriately.

11. **Concept Enrichment**
    Review concepts of love. We give things to people we love and do things for them.

Music

Review all songs taught this week.

Art

1. Provide the materials for cut-and-paste valentines. Let the children use hearts, stickers, doilies, glitter, etc. to make valentines for relatives or the children in the class. (Use in Cognitive #1 today.)
2. Have each child decorate a shoe box for Cognitive #1 today.
3. Use red and white paint at the easel.

Snack

1. Serve snack from a heart-shaped box.
2. Have little, big, and red heart cookies or candy.

Fine Motor

Fig. 18Q

1. Have the children put the valentines that they made for their parents into an envelope. Put a square on the envelope where the stamp belongs and help the children stick the stamp on.
2. Have the children cut zig-zags into folded heart and open and weave strips of paper in the zig-zags. (See fig. 18Q.)
3. Have the children cut big and/or little hearts depending upon their skill.

Games

Review games taught this week and have the children choose a favorite.

Storytelling

Use the flannel board and a red, a blue and a big felt valentine. Say:

 I made three valentines today
 I'll give them all away,
 The one for Mommy is red
 She'll hang it by her bed.
 The one for Daddy is little.
 It's really pretty little.
 And here's a big one just for you.

Gross Motor

Have the children deliver valentines to certain places by following directions such as: "Peter Rabbit wanted to hop to take his valentine to his mother at the window." (HOP) "Susy Duck waddled to the sand table to deliver her valentine." (WADDLE like a duck). "Price the Pony galloped to take his valentine to the door." (GALLOP like a horse.)

Cognitive

1. Help the children make a valentine train by stringing shoe boxes together (one for, and decorated by, each child with his name on it). Let the children put valentines in each child's train car.
2. Make a Valentine Lotto or Bingo game using valentines cut from a variety of wall paper patterns. (See fig. 18R.)
3. Line up red valentines, big valentines, and little valentines in a row as a model. Have each child take a turn at duplicating the pattern.

Fig. 18R

Enrichment

Make a loving tree with hearts for each child. Talk about something good each child does and write it on a heart, then put the heart on the tree. Let the children tell good things about each other and put those on tree.

Field Trip

Take parent's valentine to the nearest mailbox.

Related Children's Records
"On Valentine's Day" from **HOLIDAY SONGS** (KIM)
"Valentine's Song" from **HOLIDAY SONGS** (EA)
"Valentine Polka" from **LOOK AT THE HOLIDAYS** (GA)

Related Children's Books
Cohen, Miriam. **BE MY VALENTINE.** New York: Greenwillow Books, 1978.
Schulz, Charles. **BE MY VALENTINE, CHARLIE BROWN.** New York: Random House, 1973.
Schweinger, Ann. **THE HUNT FOR RABBIT'S GALOSH.** New York: Doubleday & Co., 1976.

Related Parenting Materials
Cansler, Dot. **THE HOMESTRETCH.** Winston-Salem, NC 27113-5128: Kaplan Press, 1983.

Related Materials
TEACHING PICTURES. Winston-Salem, NC 27113-5128: Kaplan Press, 1983.
STORY SEQUENCE CARDS I, II. Winston-Salem, NC 27113-5128: Kaplan Press, 1983.
SEWING CARDS I, II, III. Winston-Salem, NC 27113-5128: Kaplan Press, 1983.

Unit 19: Fruits

A developmental assessment should determine the functional levels of each child. Individual expectations are based on the assessment results.

Lesson 1: Apple

Unit Group Lesson

1. **Match Concrete Objects**
   Present two apples. Say, "This is an apple." Ask each child in turn to put the apple with the apple. Gradually increase number of irrelevant objects from which (s)he must select apple to match.

2. **Discriminate Objects**
   Present several objects. Have each child touch the apple in response to verbal direction, "Touch the apple."

3. **Match Pictures**
   Present several pictures of common objects. Have each child match the pictures of the apples.

4. **Discriminate Pictures**
   Present a group of several unrelated pictures of objects. Have each child touch the picture of the apple in response to verbal direction, "Touch the apple."

5. **Figure-Ground**
   Present a "busy" picture with many visual distractions. Ask each child to find the apple.

6. **Tactile Discrimination**
   Put an apple and some grossly different objects into a "feely box." Say, "Find the apple."

7. **Taste Discrimination**
   Blindfold or have the child close his eyes and put a piece of apple in his mouth. Say, "Taste the apple." While the child is blindfolded, give him two or three different things to taste and ask him to tell which is the apple.

8. **Visual Closure**
   Partially cover each of several pictures with paper. Ask each child to find the picture of the apple.

9. **Function**
   Ask, "What do we do with apples?"

10. **Association**
    Ask, "What goes with the apple?" Use pictures of a pear, banana, grapes, apple tree, etc., along with unrelated pictures.

11. **Imitate Verbalization**

Present an apple and ask, "What is this? Say, 'Apple'." The child will imitate "Apple."

12. **Verbalize Label**

Present an apple and ask, "What is this?" The child will respond, "Apple."

13. **Concept Enrichment**

Discuss different sizes and colors of apples. Discuss sweet and sour tastes. Discuss where the apples grow and how they are gathered. Discuss shape of apple and that it is a fruit.

Music

1. Sing to the tune of "Ring Around the Rosy":

   We are little apples in the apple tree,   *(Walk in a circle.)*
   When the wind blows, we all fall down.   *(Fall down.)*
   (Whe-en)

2. Sing to the tune of "Here We Go 'Round the Mulberry Bush":

   Everyone: Here we go round the apple   *(Walk in a circle holding hand around an*
             tree, apple tree, apple tree   *apple tree (pictures) with an apple on it.)*
             Here we go round the apple tree.
   Teacher: Will (child's name) go pick
             one for me?   *(Child gets apple and takes it to teacher.)*

Art

1. Make a large tree and put it on the bulletin board. Have the children make apples out of red construction paper and paste the apples on the tree. Children can cut or sprinkle red yarn on the circles.

2. Have the children make an apple "print" on a paper towel. Have them use a cut apple to make prints. Cut apples several different ways for more interesting designs. Cut this way you get an apple star. (See fig. 19A.)

3. Have the children slit a "mouth" in a peeled apple, sprinkle with lemon juice to keep from darkening. Let dry and use raisins (on a toothpick) for a nose and eyes.

Fig. 19A

Snack

1. Drink apple juice or cider.
2. Cut apples in halves, then quarters for snack. Look at the "star" the seeds form.
3. Eat apple from Art #3 above.
4. Make applesauce: 6 apples, ½ cup water, ¼ cup sugar, cinnamon, Cut, simmer 20 minutes. Mash and cool.
5. Baked Apple: Begin preparation during work time. Give each child ½ apple; core (or give cored apple). Put in a bowl. Child measures sugar into the hole. Child counts raisins and puts them in the apple. Child sprinkles cinnamon. Bake and serve at snack time. (Talk about the wonderful aroma as they cook.)

Fine Motor

1. Make a simple tree on a worksheet. Give the children several red paper apples to paste onto the tree.

2. Let the children use ½ of an apple dipped in paint to "print" apples on a large classroom tree made of poster board.

3. Make paper bag apples. Have children paint paper lunch bags red, stuff bags with crumpled newspaper, tie bag closed with green yarn, and tie in a bow to look like leaves. (Use in Gross Motor #2 today.) (See fig. 19B.)

Fig. 19B

Games

1. Have the children close their eyes or stand behind a screen, while one child hides an apple. When he had hidden it, he rings a bell, then the other children go looking for the apple.

2. Let the children go "Apple Fishing." Screw cup hooks into real apples and place in water. Let the children use strings on sticks with cup hooks or open paper clips for hooks and "fish" for apples.
3. Let the children try to bite a hanging apple.
4. Hide apples all over the room. Let children go "pick" apples and put them into a basket.

Storytelling

1. Have the children say and pantomime this poem with the teacher: "The Apple Tree"

Away up high in an apple tree;	*(Point up.)*
Two red apples smiled at me.	*(Form circles with fingers.)*
I shook that tree as hard as I could;	*(Pretend to shake tree.)*
Down came those apples,	
And mmmmm, were they good!	*(Rub tummy.)*

2. Use the flannel board and five red felt apples. Have the children say and do the following with you. They may also take turns removing the apples from the flannel board when appropriate.

"Five Red Apples"

Five red apples in a grocery store;	*(Hold up five fingers.)*
Bobby bought one, and then there were four.	*(Bend down one finger.)*
Four red apples on a apple tree;	
Susie ate one and then there were three.	*(Bend down one finger.)*
Three red apples. What did Alice do?	
Why, she ate one, and then there were two.	*(Bend down one finger)*
Two red apples ripening in the sun;	
Timmy ate one, and then there was one.	*(Bend down one finger.)*
One red apple and now we are done;	
I ate the last one, and now there are none.	*(Bend down last finger.)*

3. Read about "Johnny Appleseed."

Gross Motor

1. Have the children roll plastic apples from one tape mark on the floor to another. Adaptations: roll with elbow, roll with nose.
2. Decorate the climbing equipment on the playground or in the classroom with stuffed paper bag apples and have children climb to get them. Use apples made in Fine Motor #3.
3. After cooking apples in a crock pot, have the children put the cooked, cooled apples through a vegetable strainer or mash with a potato masher. Use for applesauce in Snack #4.

Cognitive

1. Apples are red. (For higher functioning children, talk about green and yellow apples.) Color apples red.
2. Have children identify fruit by taste alone. Let them eat with eyes closed. Ask, "What is it?"
3. Provide several varieties of apples. Have the children sort into baskets or bowls according to size or color.
4. Provide an apple puzzle the size of a poster board. Have the children fit red pieces in the outline of the apple. (See fig. 19C.)

Fig. 19C

Enrichment

1. Together Activity: Make an apple orchard. Make several large tree trunks with brown limbs. Let children add circles in varying shades of green construction paper to make the leaves. Loosely tape on apples. Several trees are called an "orchard." (See fig. 19D.)

2. Use the trees made above to have the children do activities such as: pick two green apples, count the large red apples, bring the teacher an apple, take this basket and pick all the apples, etc.

3. Dip some apples in lemon juice and some not. Have everyone observe and discuss what happens.

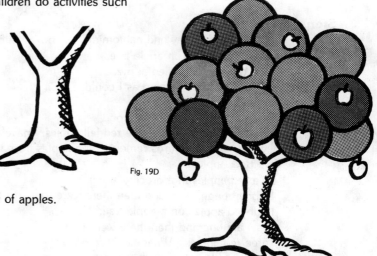

Fig. 19D

Field Trip

1. Go to the grocery store and buy a variety of apples.
2. Go to a farm and pick apples.
3. Go to a cider mill.

Lesson 2: Orange

Unit Group Lesson

1. **Match Concrete Objects**
   Present two oranges. Say, "This is an orange." Ask each child in turn to put the orange with the orange. Gradually increase number of irrelevant objects from which (s)he must select orange to match.

2. **Discriminate Objects**
   Present several objects. Have each child touch the orange in response to verbal direction, "Touch the orange."

3. **Match Pictures**
   Present several pictures of common objects. Have each child match the pictures of the oranges.

4. **Discriminate Pictures**
   Present a group of several unrelated pictures of objects. Have each child touch the picture of the orange in response to verbal direction, "Touch the orange."

5. **Figure-Ground**
   Present a "busy" picture with many visual distractions. Ask each child to find the orange.

6. **Tactile Discrimination**
   Put an orange and some grossly different objects into a "feely box." Say, "Find the orange."

7. **Taste Discrimination**
   Blindfold or have the child close his eyes and put a piece of orange in his mouth. Say, "Taste the orange." While the child is blindfolded, give him two or three different things to taste and ask him to tell which is the orange.

8. **Visual Closure**
Partially cover each of several pictures with paper. Ask each child to find the picture of the orange.

9. **Function**
Ask, "What do we do with oranges?"

10. **Association**
Ask, "What goes with the orange?" Use pictures of orange juice, other fruits, etc., along with unrelated pictures.

11. **Imitate Verbalization**
Present an orange and ask, "What is this? Say, 'Orange'." The child will imitate "Orange."

12. **Verbalize Label**
Present an orange and ask, "What is this?" The child will respond, "Orange."

13. **Concept Enrichment**
Discuss how oranges grow and are gathered, the process of making orange juice, and the purpose of the orange rind. How does the rind taste? Classify orange as a fruit. Oranges are round like a circle. Oranges are orange.

Music

Sing to the tune of "Three Blind Mice":
Verse 1: I like oranges. I like oranges.
Oranges are a fruit. Oranges are a fruit.
They are not animals, tools and such.
They are a good fruit that I like so much.
So I eat oranges. I eat oranges.

Verse 2: An orange is orange.
An orange is orange.
It is not blue.
It is not red.
It is not purple nor pink nor gray.
An orange is simply not colored that way.
An orange is orange.
An orange is orange.

Art
1. Have the children help make playdough, color it orange with food coloring and make oranges out of it.
2. Make orange finger paint and have the children make orange circles on their papers.
3. Cut sponges into circles. Dip in orange tempera paint and make "orange" sponge prints on paper.

Snack
1. Drink orange juice.
2. Eat sliced oranges.
3. Eat orange colored snacks such as: carrot "coins", pumpkin, sweet potatoes, orange gelatin, cheese, etc.
4. Buy a small orange for each child. Cut a hole in the top of each, and let the child squeeze his own orange and drink the juice. (This is a good Gross Motor activity.)

Fine Motor
1. Make 1) a worksheet with a large circle drawn on it, and 2) orange construction paper circles the same size as the circle on the worksheet. Cut the paper circles into different sections (vary the number of sections according to the child's ability). Have the child paste his sections onto the circle on his worksheet.

2. Air-dry orange peels. Let the children break them into small pieces, toss with cinnamon and put into "little pillows" for sachets. The more skilled children can make the pillows. (Or sprinkle orange extract on cotton balls and put inside.)

3. From construction paper cut a green tree top approximately 6" in diameter. Cut a brown trunk. Let children punch holes in the green tree top with puncher and glue the tree onto orange paper. Presto! Oranges on the tree!

4. Collect orange juice cans from parents. Let the children build towers and construct shapes from orange juice cans. (Play counting games with orange juice cans.) (See fig. 19E.)

5. Cut juice oranges into two pieces. Let the children use hand orange squeezer to juice the oranges. Drink juice at snack. A child may pour juice. (See fig. 19F.)

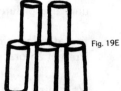

Fig. 19F

Fig. 19E

Games

1. Make a large orange paper circle and put it on the floor. Say, "Girls get on the orange," or "Boys get on the orange," or "Children with something orange on their clothes get on the orange," or "Children with belts on get on the orange," etc.

2. Chase inflated orange balloons inside classroom.

3. Use scratch 'n sniff orange stickers and orange-scented markers in activities today.

Storytelling

Put a large orange circle which has been cut into four sections on the flannel board. Pass out the pieces and say the following. (Encourage children to recite, too.)

I'm going to eat some orange.
I like it yum yum.
I'll give a piece to Mary but I still have some for me,
Because I like it, yum, yum.
I'll give a piece to Tommy but I still have some for me,
Because I like it, yum, yum.
I'll give a piece to Lisa but I still have some for me,
Because I like it, yum, yum.
I'll give a piece to John,
Oh, dear, there is none left for me and I like it yum yum.
Boo hoo hoo hoo.

Gross Motor

Use a small ladder and pantomime picking oranges from a tree.

Cognitive

1. Have children sort items that are orange-colored by placing them in an orange circle of yarn.

2. Dry orange seeds 48 hours, then soak overnight. Let children plant. Light is needed but sun not necessary.

3. Let children mix red and yellow coloring or tempera to make orange color and use the paint to paint oranges.

4. Let children sequence oranges from smallest to largest and identify the middle one of three.

Enrichment

1. Let children get seeds out of their orange half. Count and make a graph of each child's findings.

2. Use orange material with elastic at neck and bottom, stuffed with newspapers to make an "orange" costume, Make costume as a group and take turns being "Orange for the day."

3. Together Activity: Make a large tree trunk and let the children glue brown bark (bits of brown paper) to trunk. Add branches and shiny dark green paper leaves. Let the children cut the leaves if they can. Have children glue or staple leaves on trunk and put oranges (orange circles) on the tree. Make two or three trees for an orchard.

Field Trip

Go to the grocery store and buy oranges.

Unit Group Lesson

1. **Match Concrete Objects**
   Present two bananas. Say, "This is a banana." Ask each child in turn to put the banana with the banana. Gradually increase number of irrelevant objects from which (s)he must select banana to match.

2. **Discriminate Objects**.
   Present several objects. Have each child touch the banana in response to verbal direction, "Touch the banana."

3. **Match Pictures**
   Present several pictures of common objects. Have each child match the pictures of the bananas.

4. **Discriminate Pictures**
   Present a group of several unrelated pictures of objects. Have each child touch the picture of the banana in response to verbal direction, "Touch the banana."

5. **Figure-Ground**
   Present a "busy" picture with many visual distractions. Ask each child to find the banana.

6. **Tactile Discrimination**
   Put a banana and some grossly different objects into a "feely box." Say, "Find the banana."

7. **Taste Discrimination**
   Blindfold or have the child close his eyes and put a piece of banana in his mouth. Say, "Taste the banana." While the child is blindfolded, give him two or three different things to taste and ask him to tell which is the banana.

8. **Visual Closure**
   Partially cover each of several pictures with paper. Ask each child to find the picture of the banana.

9. **Function**
   Ask, "What do we do with bananas?"

10. **Association**
    Ask, "What goes with the banana?" Use pictures of other fruits, cereal, etc., along with unrelated pictures.

11. **Imitate Verbalization**
    Present a banana and ask, "What is this? Say, 'Banana'." The child will imitate "Banana."

12. **Verbalize Label**
    Present a banana and ask, "What is this?" The child will respond, "Banana."

13. **Concept Enrichment**
    Discuss different sizes of bananas, the peeling, how bananas grow upward in bunches, colors of bananas, and that bananas are fruit

Music

Sing to the tune of "Where Is Thumbkin?":

Yellow bananas, yellow bananas,
You must peel,
You must peel.
Then they taste so good,
Then they taste so good.
Yum yum yum,
Yum yum yum.

Art

1. Have the children help make yellow playdough and use it to make bananas.
2. Have the children paint large yellow bananas at the easel.
3. Have children spatter paint with toothbrush, popsicle stick and non yellow tempera paint. Place a cardboard banana on yellow construction paper in a box. Remove cardboard and yellow shape of banana is left.

Snack

1. Eat sliced bananas (add a little milk from a pitcher, sprinkle with pinch of sugar).
2. Make banana splits.
3. Spread peanut butter on bread. Arrange 5 banana slices (one in each corner and one in the middle).

Fine Motor

1. Cut out paper bananas. Let children hook them on a tree in the playground (in the class) with clothespins.
2. Have the children peel their own bananas and mash them with a fork.
3. Let children use blunt knives to cut bananas for fruit salad for snack.
4. Let children use cotton swabs to paint around a large picture of a banana.
5. Have children make bananas by sprinkling glitter over a banana stencil and cutting the bananas. These could be used in Enrichment.

Games

Play "Spin the Banana." Make a spinner out of large cardboard banana. When it points to a child, that child has to do a trick. Then he can spin the banana.

Storytelling

Use the flannel board and five yellow bananas made of flannel.

One yellow banana in the jungle grew,	(Hold up one finger.)
Out popped another, and that made two.	(Hold up two fingers.)
Two yellow bananas were all that I could see,	
But Bill found another, and that made three.	(Hold up three fingers.)
Three yellow bananas - if I could find one more,	
I'd pick the, and that would make four.	(Hold up four fingers.)
Four yellow bananas - sure as you're alive!	
Why, here is another! And now there are five!	(Hold up five fingers.)

Gross Motor

1. Pretend to be monkeys and eat bananas while on monkey bars.
2. Have a "potato race" with bananas.

Cognitive

1. Have children sort yellow from non-yellow things.
2. Have children count and measure bananas.
3. Have children pick bananas from the "HAND" of bananas. Count into a basket or grocery bag. Follow directions: Pick 4 bananas. Take 1 to (child's name) and 1 to (child's name); bring the rest to me, etc.

Enrichment

Together Activity: Make giant banana trees with "Hands" (clusters) of bananas growing on them. Have the children make the trunk with short strips of brown paper. Cut and fold leaves. On long green construction paper stalks, let children arrange bananas they have painted yellow. These are called HANDS of bananas. This is how they grow. The bananas may be stapled on the stalk at the top of the bananas. Then the children can grasp and "pick" the bananas later in a counting activity. Add the hands of bananas to the trees. Bananas grow upward. Arrange banana tree like this: (See fig. 19G.)

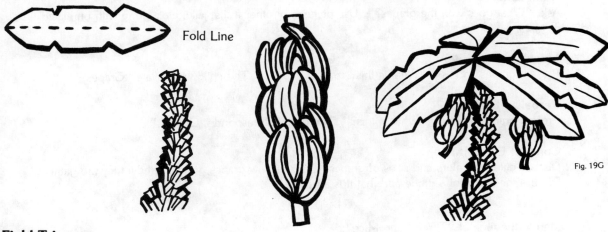

Fold Line

Fig. 19G

Field Trip

Go to the grocery store to buy bananas.

Lesson 4: Grapes

Unit Group Lesson

1. **Match Concrete Objects**
   Present two bunches of grapes. Say, "These are grapes." Ask each child in turn to put the grapes with the grapes. Gradually increase number of irrelevant objects from which (s)he must select grapes to match.

2. **Discriminate Objects**
   Present several objects. Have each child touch the grapes inresponse to verbal direction, "Touch the grapes."

3. **Match Pictures**
   Present several pictures of common objects. Have each child match the pictures of the grapes.

4. **Discriminate Pictures**
   Present a group of several unrelated pictures of objects. Have each child touch the picture of the grapes in response to verbal direction, "Touch the grapes."

5. **Figure-Ground**
   Present a "busy" picture with many visual distractions. Ask each child to find the grapes.

6. **Tactile Discrimination**
   Put grapes and some grossly different objects into a "feely box." Say, "Find the grapes."

7. **Taste Discrimination**
   Blindfold or have the child close his eyes and put a piece of grape in his mouth. Say, "Taste the grape." While the child is blindfolded, give him two or three different things to taste and ask him to tell which is the grape.

8. **Visual Closure**

   Partially cover each of several pictures with paper. Ask each child to find the picture of the grapes.

9. **Function**

   Ask, "What do we do with grapes?"

10. **Association**

    Ask, "What goes with the grapes?" Use pictures of other fruits, jelly, etc., along with unrelated pictures.

11. **Imitate Verbalization**

    Present grapes and ask, "What is this? Say, 'Grapes'." The child will imitate "Grapes."

12. **Verbalize Label**

    Present grapes and ask, "What is this?" The child will respond, "Grapes."

13. **Concept Enrichment**

    Discuss different colors and sizes of grapes. Discuss how grapes grow and how they are gathered. Discuss the shape of a grape and that it is a fruit.

Music

Sing to the tune of "Three Blind Mice":

I like grapes - I like grapes.
Grapes are a fruit - Grapes are a fruit.
They are not animals, tools or such.
They are a good fruit that I like so much.
So I eat grapes - I eat grapes.

Art

1. Together Activity: Make a grape vine on the bulletin board. Give the children the outline of a cluster of grapes and have them paste purple construction paper circles onto the outline. Then have them staple their bunch of grapes on the grape vine.

2. Together Activity: Put purple grapes on an old sheet and have the children mash them with their finger tips.

Snack

1. Serve three colors of grapes and seedless grapes, Discuss seeded and seedless varieties.
2. Serve grape juice, one or more types (red, white, purple).
3. Serve dried grapes (raisins).

Fine Motor

1. Have children trace outline of a bunch of grapes with white wax candle or crayon. Paint over with thin transparent water color (very thin lavender is pretty). The wax outline of the grapes remains white.

2. Have children make thumbprint grapes. Using green, red or purple (red and blue mixed) food coloring on a sponge, let children make thumbprints in clusters around green paper strip stems.

3. Let each child make a bumpy dough picture of grapes. Mix ¾ cup flour, ¼ cup salt, water and purple tempera. Let them glue purple balls on corrugated cardboard pieces and add leaves and a piece of vine with green magic marker. (See fig. 19H.)

Fig. 19H

Games

Have the children sit in a semi-circle and place a chair so that the child sitting in it has his back to the group. Put a bunch of plastic grapes under the chair and have the child in the chair close his eyes. Chose another child to get the grapes and get back to his place without being heard. The child in the chair then has to guess who took the grapes.

Storytelling

Do this activity as a finger play and also on the flannel board with ten felt grapes:

Ten little grapes hanging on a vine,
Sam took one, then there were nine.
Nine little grapes hanging near a gate,
Jane took one, then there were eight.
Eight little grapes looking up to heaven
Jim took one, then there were seven.
Seven little grapes hanging above the sticks,
Jill took one, then there were six.
Six little grapes hanging near a hive,
Tony took one, then there were five.
Five little grapes ready for the store,
Nanny took one, then there were four.
Four little grapes ready for me,
Pat took one, then there were three.
Three little grapes ready for you,
Annie took one, then there were two.
Two little grapes hanging in the sun,
Cathy took one, then there was one.
One little grape who was having no fun,
Betty took it, then there were none.

Gross Motor

Do a grapevine activity. Have each child put his hand on the shoulder of the child in front of him like a grapevine. Let child lead the group in hopping, skipping, jumping, walking, running, etc. around the playground.

Cognitive

1. Have each child count the grapes in two bunches of grapes and match the correct numeral to each bunch. Let him decide which bunch has more or less.
2. Have each child arrange paper grapes in sequence from smallest to largest.
3. Have the children detect verbal absurdities. Ask, "Can you ride a grape?" "Can you hammer with a grape?" "Can you taste a grape?"
4. Provide grapes in green, purple, and/or red. Have the children sort them by color.

Enrichment

1. Have the children match the stem to the bunch by matching stem with numeral on it to the correct bunch of grapes (such as #1 stem to bunch with 1 grape, #2 stem to bunch with 2 grapes, etc.).
2. Have the children mix blue and red tempera to make purple. (The color of some grapes.)
3. Together Activity: Have the children make a grape arbor. Have them cut long strips of brown paper or gather twigs from outdoors and use them to build a grape arbor on the bulletin board. Then have the children cut spirals of green paper for vines and tape them to arbor. Have them cut grape leaves from green construction paper and add to the vines. Have them cut and glue circles of purple paper in bunches on an oval of cardboard and attach to the grape vines. (See fig. 191.)

Fig. 191

Field Trip
1.   Go to the grocery store to buy some grapes.
2.   Go to a vineyard.

Lesson 5: Pear

Unit Group Lesson

1. **Match Concrete Objects**
    Present two pears. Say, "This is an pear." Ask each child in turn to put the pear with the pear.
    Gradually increase number of irrelevant objects from which (s)he must select pear to match.

2. **Discriminate Objects**
    Present several objects. Have each child touch the pear in response to verbal direction, "Touch the
    pear."

3. **Match Pictures**
    Present several pictures of common objects. Have each child match the pictures of the pears.

4. **Discriminate Pictures**
    Present a group of several unrelated pictures of objects. Have each child touch the picture of the pear
    in response to verbal direction, "Touch the pear."

5. **Figure-Ground**
    Present a "busy" picture with many visual distractions. Ask each child to find the pear.

6. **Tactile Discrimination**
    Put an pear and some grossly different objects into a "feely box." Say, "Find the pear."

7. **Taste Discrimination**
    Blindfold or have the child close his eyes and put a piece of pear in his mouth. Say, "Taste the pear."
    While the child is blindfolded, give him two or three different things to taste and ask him to tell which is
    the pear.

8. **Visual Closure**
    Partially cover each of several pictures with paper. Ask each child to find the picture of the pear.

9. **Function**
    Ask, "What do we do with pears?"

10. **Association**
    Ask, "What goes with the pear?" Use pictures of other fruits, etc., along with unrelated pictures.
    with unrelated pictures.

11. **Imitate Verbalization**
    Present pear and ask, "What is this? Say, 'Pear'." The child will imitate "Pear."

12. **Verbalize Label**
    Present pear and ask, "What is this?" The child will respond, "Pear."

13. **Concept Enrichment**
    Discuss different colors and sizes of pears. Discuss where pears grow and how they are gathered.
    Discuss shape of the pear and that it is a fruit.

Music

1.   Sing to tune of "Twinkle, Twinkle, Little Star":

How I'd like to eat a pear,
Eat it here or eat it there.
I would even climb a tree,
Then I'd have it just for me.
How I'd like to eat a pear,
Eat it here or eat it there.

2.   Sing to the tune of "Three Blind Mice":

I like pears - I like pears.
Pears are a fruit - Pears are a fruit.
They are not animals, tools or such.
They are a good fruit that I like so much.
So I eat pears - I eat pears.

Art

1.   Have the children cut pears from construction paper (if they can) and decorate with bits of tissue paper in yellow, green and red.
2.   Cut pear shapes from cardboard. Let the children use small pieces of sponge to texture print yellow and green tempera on the shapes. This gives the textured look of a pear. (Pour small amounts of tempera onto a paper plate. Cover with paper towel. When sponge is pressed on the towel it picks up just the right amount of paint.)

Snack

1.   Eat fruit salad which was made with apples and pears.
2.   Eat pear halves and gelatin or pear halves with grated cheese in the middle.
3.   Eat pear salad made in Fine Motor #1.

Fine Motor

1.   Have each child make a pear salad by using a pear for head, grape halves for eyes, banana slices for nose and mouth, appled wedges for ears and an orange slice for a tie. Lay all on a bed of lettuce. (See fig. 19J.)

Fig. 19J

2.   Let the children use table knives to cut canned pear halves into small pieces for the fruit salad.
3.   Let the children practice cutting pears from construction paper. Use these in Art #1.

Games

Use the plastic fruit and pretend to have a grocery store in the classroom. Teacher gives the children play money and asks them to buy an apple, an orange, a banana, some grapes, or a pear.

Storytelling

Use a flannelboard and cut-outs to tell this story "Are the Pears Ready to Eat?":

Once upon a time there was a lovely pear tree
It had a brown trunk   *(Place brown trunk on board.)*
With brown limbs   *(Add limbs.)*
And many, many green leaves.   *(Add leaves.)*
I asked, "Are the pears ready to eat?"
And Mother said, "Be patient. It won't be long."

Early in the spring, beautiful blossoms appeared on the tree   *(Add blossoms.)*
And I asked, "Are the pears ready to eat?"
Mother said, "Be patient. It won't be long."

And then the blossoms went away to make room for
something special   *(Take blossoms off.)*
So I asked, "Are the pears ready to eat?"
And Mother said, "Be patient. It won't be long."

Guess what began growing on the tree!
Very small green pears!   *(Put on small green circles.)*
Again, I asked, "Are the pears ready to eat?"
And Mother said, "Be patient. It won't be long."

The pears grew and grew   *(Place on green pears.)*
Surely, there were ready!
So I asked, "Are the pears ready to eat?"
Once more, Mother said, "Be patient. It won't be long."

And then - a miracle happended!
The pears became a beautiful golden color!   *(Add golden pears.)*
With big eyes, I whispered, "Are the pears ready to eat?"
And Mother said, "Yes."

Gross Motor

Wrap a pear in golden foil. Hide the "magic golden pear" out on the playground. Let the children have a "pear hunt" to look for the magic pear.

Cognitive

1. Have the children sort fruits into pears and non-pears.
2. Have each child sequence different sized pears from large to small.
3. Have each child close his eyes and taste fruits studied in this unit. Help him identify each one.

Enrichment

1. Have the children cut pears into halves and fourths depending upon the levels of the children.

2. Have the children search for "P" words.

3. Together Activity: Make pear orchard: Make several large tree trunks with brown limbs. Have the children add circles in varying shades of green construction paper to make the leaves. Loosely tape on pears. Several trees are called an "orchard." (See fig. 19K.)

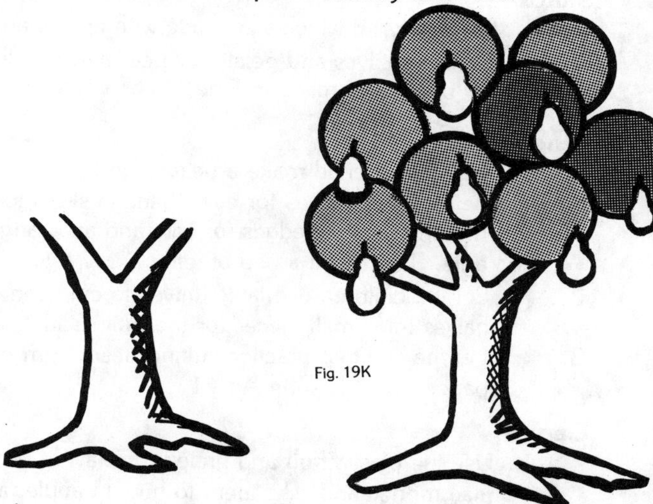

Fig. 19K

4. Use trees made above to have the children do other activities such as: pick two green pears, count the large pears, bring the teacher a pear, take this basket and pick all the pears, etc.

5. Together Activity: Cut out a giant basket. Add giant fruit paper shapes to the basket to review each fruit included in the unit. Class ends up with a lovely fruit basket. Have the children trace the basket texture. (Fruits can be made each day as that fruit is studied.) (See fig. 19L.)

Fig. 19L

Field Trip

Go to the grocery store to buy all of the fruits studied during this unit.

Unit 20: Things We Ride

A developmental assessment should determine the functional levels of each child. Individual expectations are based on the assessment results.

Lesson 1: Car

Unit Group Lesson

1. **Match Concrete Objects** (Use toys.)
   Present two cars. Say, "This is a car." Ask each child in turn to put the car with the car. Gradually increase number of irrelevant objects from which (s)he must select car to match.

2. **Discriminate Objects**
   Present several objects. Have each child touch the car in response to verbal direction, "Touch the car."

3. **Match Pictures**
   Present several pictures of common objects. Have each child match the pictures of the cars.

4. **Discriminate Pictures**
   Present a group of several unrelated pictures of objects. Have each child touch the picture of the car in response to verbal direction, "Touch the car."

5. **Figure-Ground**
   Present a "busy" picture with many visual distractions. Ask each child to find the car.

6. **Visual Closure**
   Partially cover each of several pictures with paper. Ask each child to find the picture of the car.

7. **Function**
   Ask, "What does a car do?"

8. **Association**
   Ask, "What goes with the car?" Use pictures or objects including tire, hub cap, windshield wiper, etc., with several unrelated objects or pictures.

9. **Imitate Verbalization**
   Present a car and ask, "What is this? Say, 'Car'." The child will imitate "Car."

10. **Verbalize Label**
    Present a car and ask, "What is this?" The child will respond, "Car."

11.   **Concept Enrichment**
        Introduce seat belts secured from local safety department. Discuss car safety and use of seat belts. Talk about all of the things that a car can be used to do.

Music

1.   Sing to the tune of "Row, Row Row Your Boat":
        Drive, drive, drive your car;   *(Pantomime actions.)*
        All around the town.
        Find a gas station to wait for gas,
        Then drive up hill and down.

2.   Sing to the tune of "The Wheels on the Bus Go Round and Round":
        The wheels on the car go round and round,   *(Pantomime actions.)*
        Round and round, round and round.
        The wheels on the car go round and round
        All through the town.
        Verse 2: The wipers on the car go swish, swish, swish.
        Verse 3: The horn on the car goes beep, beep, beep.

Art

1.   Give each child a small shoe box and have him count out four cardboard wheels that you have cut out and put a brad through. Help the child attach the wheels to his box. Then let him paint his car with tempera paint.
2.   Use large pieces of cardboard to make hills for the cars to coast down.
3.   Give each child a box big enough for him to sit in. Have him paint it to look like a car.

Snack

        Have a "tail-gate" picnic for snack. Eat from the back end of a station wagon.

Fine Motor

1.   Make a path tracing worksheet of taking "A car to a stop sign." and "A car to a gas station."
2.   Make a fabric-backed vinyl roadway by placing vinyl tape criss-crossed on the vinyl side of the material. Let the children drive small cars around the road, making left turns, right turns, etc. (See fig. 20A.)
3.   Teach children to fasten seat belts in a "play" car.
4.   Get an old steering wheel from a junked car. Mount it for the children to use in play.
5.   Give children starter pictures of cars and let them add the wheels and whatever each is capable of adding.

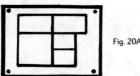

Fig. 20A

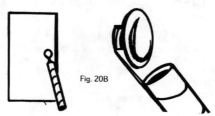

Fig. 20B

Games

1.   Play musical chairs and use the cars made out of boxes, instead of chairs.
2.   Let the children take turns hiding a toy car in the room for the other children to find.
3.   Let the children use blocks to build roads, tunnels, bridges, and a parking lot for toy cars.
4.   Help the children build a "ramp" for working on toy cars. Let children drive car up in it; use tools to work on car or wash the car. Use car wax and shine with a cloth.
5.   Let the children roll cars down inclines such as inside tubes that are taped or rubber-banded onto a door knob, then together. (See fig. 20B.)

Storytelling

1. Pretend that everyone is in the car going on a trip. Start the story and have each child tell about something he might see on the trip. For more advanced children, this could be used as a sequencing memory activity by having the children tell everything everyone else had seen when it is their turn.

2. Fingerplay:

   I'm a window wiper.   *(Bend arm.*
   this is how I go.   *Back and forth.)*
   Back and forth, back and forth
   In the rain and snow.

Gross Motor

1. Draw a "road" on the floor with chalk or masking tape. Lead the children in pretending to "drive" on road in a line. Stop at stop signs, slow for sharp corners and curves and stop for red lights.

2. Give children circles of cardboard for steering wheels in yellow, red, blue, etc. Give directions to "drive" to certain places in classroom. Use simple to complex directions according to level of child.

Cognitive

1. Make garages out of milk cartons. Put a numeral on top of each garage and each car. Have each child drive the cars to the correct garages. Color coding garages and cars simplifies the activity. This activity may be done by substituting colors or letters depending on the levels of the children (colors for lower level children, letters for higher).

2. Have each child count as many cars as he can.

Enrichment

1. Recite the poem:

   Every driver needs to know
   Red says STOP
   Green says GO

2. Cut out bottom and top of cardboard boxes and make tape streets on the floor. Let the children paint the boxes and add large wheels, headlights and a license plate. Let each child get into his car, hold it up and drive it. Have him follow stop and go signs, directions, deliver messages, drive to a specific address (the stove, church garage, etc.). (See fig. 20C.)

3. Make a bulletin board picture with trees and winding streets. Have the children cut out pictures of cars and paste them on the streets. (Let the children select car pictures from pictures of other vehicles.)

Fig. 20C

Field Trip

Have a "car hunt" or "wheel hunt" by walking in the neighborhood near the school to find cars or wheels. Count them.

Unit Group Lesson

1. **Match Concrete Objects** (Use toys.)
   Present two buses. Say, "This is a bus." Ask each child in turn to put the bus with the bus.
   Gradually increase number of irrelevant objects from which (s)he must select bus to match.

2. **Discriminate Objects**
   Present several objects. Have each child touch the bus in response to verbal direction, "Touch the bus."

3. **Match Pictures**
   Present several pictures of common objects. Have each child match the pictures of the buses.

4. **Discriminate Pictures**
   Present a group of several unrelated pictures of objects. Have each child touch the picture of the bus in response to verbal direction, "Touch the bus."

5. **Figure-Ground**
   Present a "busy" picture with many visual distractions. Ask each child to find the bus.

6. **Visual Closure**
   Partially cover each of several pictures with paper. Ask each child to find the picture of the bus.

7. **Function**
   Ask, "What do buses do?"

8. **Association**
   Ask, "What goes with the bus?" Use pictures or objects including a child, school box, tire, traffic sign, etc., with several unrelated objects or pictures.

9. **Imitate Verbalization**
   Present a bus and ask, "What is this? Say, 'Bus'." The child will imitate "Bus."

10. **Verbalize Label**
    Present a bus and ask, "What is this?" The child will respond, "Bus."

11. **Concept Enrichment**
    Discuss school bus safety. Are buses the same as cars? Count windows on the bus. Discuss the color of the school bus; why is it a bright color? Discuss the red flashing lights and the flag that comes out when it stops. What do other cars do?

Music

Sing "The Wheels on the Bus Go Round and Round":

Verse 2: The wipers on the bus go swish, swish, swish	(Make wiper movements with hands.)
Verse 3: The people on the bus go up and down,	(Bob up and down.)
Verse 4: The horn on the bus goes beep, beep, beep	(Make horn pressing.)
Verse 5: The baby on the bus goes wah-wah-wah,	(Rub hands with eyes.)
Verse 6: The mother on the bus goes sh-sh-sh,	(Place finger on lips.)
Verse 7: The driver on the bus says move on back.	(Point to rear.)

Art

1. Get a huge furniture box and cut out windows and a door. Let the children paint the bus.
2. Make a large school bus with blank windows and put it on the bulletin board. Give each child a piece of paper just the size of the bus window. Have the children draw their faces, then have each paste his picture into a window of the bus. (See fig. 20D.)

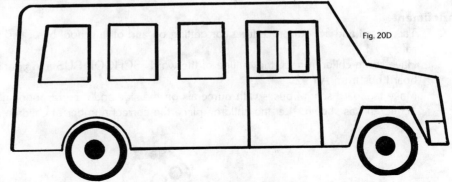

Fig. 20D

Snack

Pretend you are taking a trip on a bus. Line up chairs like the seats on a bus. Then pack snacks into small paper sacks. Get on "bus" and eat snack.

Fine Motor

1. Make a path tracing worksheet for taking "A bus to school," "A bus to a house," "A bus to church," and "A bus to the store."
2. Make a FINISH ME picture. Give children sheets with a bus shape and let them add wheels, windows, and people. (See fig. 20E.)

Fig. 20E

3. Let the children drive miniature school buses around the vinyl roadway made for Lesson #1 Fine Motor #2 of this unit.

Games

Let one child wear a bus driver's hat and have several children get into the large bus mading during Art. Then sing and pantomime "The Wheels on the Bus."

Storytelling

1. Use a flannel board with a big house, a little house, a school, a bus garage and a bus. Tell a story about the bus and have a child move the bus on the flannel board in the same sequence as the story. For example: "The bus stopped at the big house, then the little house, then it took the children to the school."
2. Have the children relate experiences that they have had on buses.

Gross Motor

Have the children in individual school buses (boxes with no bottoms). Let them drive the buses around a prescribed roadway and follow the traffic signs.

Cognitive

1. Discuss the sounds of buses and have everyone make loud and soft bus sounds.
2. Match pictures of parts of a bus to a picture of a bus. Provide two different types of buses (school and city) for some specific differences, like flashing lights and flags for a school bus.

3.　Have three children stand in the toy bus looking out of the windows. Have the children in the class close their eyes while one stoops down so he cannot be seen. Have the children guess who is missing.

4.　Ask the children if the following items can or cannot be carried on a bus: house, book, car, boy, baby, school, tree, toy, etc. Say, "Can I put a house in a bus?" etc.

Enrichment

1.　Talk about and act out procedures for getting on and off a school bus. Discuss the rules of school bus safety.

2.　Have some children trace the outline of the words SCHOOL BUS and your agency on the bulletin board bus from Art #2.

3.　Make tagboard school buses with numerals on the side and a corresponding number of slots. Make "children" as shown. Let the children place the correct number of children in each school bus. (See fig. 20F.)

Fig. 20F

Field Trip

Take the children for a trip on a public bus or board a school bus for discussion on safety rules.

Visitor

Invite the school bus driver to come talk to the children about safety rules on the bus.

Lesson 3: Train

Unit Group Lesson

1.　**Match Concrete Objects** (Use toys.)
Present two trains. Say, "This is a train." Ask each child in turn to put the train with the train. Gradually increase number of irrelevant objects from which (s)he must select train to match.

2.　**Discriminate Objects**
Present several objects. Have each child touch the train in response to verbal direction, "Touch the train."

3.　**Match Pictures**
Present several pictures of common objects. Have each child match the pictures of the trains.

4.　**Discriminate Pictures**
Present a group of several unrelated pictures of objects. Have each child touch the picture of the train in response to verbal direction, "Touch the train."

5.　**Figure-Ground**
Present a "busy" picture with many visual distractions. Ask each child to find the train.

6.　**Visual Closure**
Partially cover each of several pictures with paper. Ask each child to find the picture of the train.

7. **Function**
   Ask, "What do trains do?"

8. **Association**
   Ask, "What goes with the train?" Use pictures or objects including caboose, train track, traffic sign, luggage, etc., with several unrelated objects or pictures.

9. **Imitate Verbalization**
   Present a train and ask, "What is this? Say, 'Train'." The child will imitate "Train."

10. **Verbalize Label**
    Present a train and ask, "What is this?" The child will respond, "Train."

11. **Concept Enrichment**
    Discuss how the train moves on tracks. Discuss what can be carried by the train. Discuss how the train differs from a car and/or bus.

Music
1. Sing to the tune of "The Wheels on the Bus":
   The engine of the train goes toot, toot, toot.
   Toot, toot, toot - Toot, toot, toot.
   The engine of the train goes toot, toot, toot.
   All along the track.
2. Sing "I've Been Working on the Railroad."
3. Sing "Little Red Caboose, Chug, Chug, Chug."

Art
1. Provide several medium-sized boxes to make a train in which the children can sit. Have the children paint the boxes.
2. Make a train engine and put it on the bulletin board. Give each child a sheet of construction paper on which to write his name (provide the appropriate cues for each child). After the child has put his name on the paper, have him paste wheels onto it, decorate it and put it on the bulletin board behind the engine.

Snack
Arrange chairs in lines with an aisle between rows in the "dining car." Waiters or waitresses serve the snack on trays.

Fine Motor
1. Help the children make a milk carton "train." Open or cut off one side of carton. Punch holes in carton and "thread" them with string. The waxy coating make the "train" pull easily. The children may put objects into the "train cars."
2. Provide each child with an outline of a train. Have him put glue around the outline and sprinkle glitter on it. Then have each child tear pieces of shiny paper and glue them on the train.
3. Pretend to be trains and blow whistles.

Games
1. Let children "sell" tickets and act out going on a "train ride." Let them use "box" train made in art.
2. Use a rope (or string) to make a "train" of children.
3. Put a toy railroad set in the block area of the classroom.

Storytelling

1. Provide pictures of an engine, tank car, box car, mail car and caboose and do this fingerplay:

    Here is the engine on the track.   *(Hold up thumb.)*
    Here is the tank car, just in back.   *(Hold up pointer finger.)*
    Here is the box car to carry freight.   *(Hold up middle finger.)*
    Here is the mail car. Don't be late!   *(Hold up ring finger.)*
    Way back here at the end of the train   *(Hold up little finger.)*
    Rides the caboose through the sun and the rain.
    From *Annie's Finger Play Book.*

2. Tell "The Little Engine That Could" and encourage the children to join with you when the engine is saying, "I think I can, I think I can, I think I can, etc. - I thought I could, I thought I could," etc.

Gross Motor

Make "train stations" with "track" between them. Use chairs as the train stations and balance beams, tunnels, curved string, etc. for the "track." Let the children pretend to be trains, run on each track and sit in each station. Take turns blowing a whistle to signal the trains to move.

Cognitive

1. Make a picture of a train on the tracks with two or three cars, each with a single numeral on the side. Have each child repeat the digits in sequence - two or three depending on the child's level.
2. Make three train cars of different lengths. Let the children arrange the cars from the shortest to longest.
3. Decide which holds more, a truck or a train? Provide a truck and train which are in scale to each other and let the children fill each.

Enrichment

1. Study the uses of different types of train cars such as coal car, the car carrier, the flatbed car, the cattle car, etc.
2. Let the children sell "tickets" with play money and act out going on a train ride with a conductor, passengers, engineers, etc.
3. Help the children make a train station depot, cover roof with black or brown shingles in rows. (They may be places at random or in a specific outline.) Make red bricks for the walls and arrange chairs for a waiting area for children taking turns in the train.

Field Trip

1. Go to a railroad station.
2. Visit a hobby store to see model trains on display.

Lesson 4: Airplane

Unit Group Lesson

1. **Match Concrete Objects** (Use toys.)
    Present two airplanes. Say, "This is an airplane." Ask each child in turn to put the airplane with the airplane. Gradually increase number of irrelevant objects from which (s)he must select airplane to match.

2. **Discriminate Objects**
    Present several objects. Have each child touch the airplane in response to verbal direction, "Touch the airplane."

3.   **Match Pictures**
Present several pictures of common objects. Have each child match the pictures of the airplanes.

4.   **Discriminate Pictures**
Present a group of several unrelated pictures of objects. Have each child touch the picture of the airplane in response to verbal direction, "Touch the airplane."

5.   **Figure-Ground**
Present a "busy" picture with many visual distractions. Ask each child to find the airplane.

6.   **Visual Closure**
Partially cover each of several pictures with paper. Ask each child to find the picture of the airplane.

7.   **Function**
Ask, "What do airplanes do?"

8.   **Association**
Ask, "What goes with the airplane?" Use pictures or objects including luggage, bird, clouds, airplane pilot, etc., with several unrelated objects or pictures.

9.   **Imitate Verbalization**
Present an airplane and ask, "What is this? Say, 'Airplane'." The child will imitate "Airplane."

10.   **Verbalize Label**
Present an airplane and ask, "What is this?" The child will respond, "Airplane."

11.   **Concept Enrichment**
Review use of seat belts. Discuss different types of airplanes such as props, jets, cargo, passenger, etc.

Music

Sing to the tune of "Swing Low, Sweet Chariot":
Fly low, fly high today   *(Pantomime while singing.)*
Fly all over the sky
Fly low, fly high away
Fly low, fly high.

Art
1.   Have the children color paper and make folded paper airplanes from it.
2.   Make an airplane using a wooden clothespin and cardboard or pieces of styrofoam for a wing. (See fig. 20G.)
3.   Provide blue paper, an airplane shape and chalk. Have the children paste the airplane shape on the paper and draw in clouds above and below with white chalk dipped in water (with a little sugar to keep it from smearing).

Fig 20G

Snack

Line up chairs in rows (3 chairs on each side) with an aisle like the inside of an airplane. Have "stewards or stewardesses" serve snack on trays. (Snacks may be small a sandwich and a pickle wrapped in plastic wrap.)

Fine Motor

1. Outline the body and rudder of an airplane, as well as the wing and tail, on construction paper or styrofoam meat trays. Have the children cut them out. Cut slits in the body. Have the children assemble the airplane, attach a string to it and hang it from the ceiling. (See fig. 20H.)
2. Have children fold and staple paper to make a "ticket" folder. Have some children trace, copy or print with printing stamps the word EASTERN on the ticket folders. (See fig. 20I.)
3. Practice removing plastic wrap from "snacks."
4. Prepare for each child a plain white envelope with a border. Have the children add blue and red lines to make it an airmail envelope. Provide AIRMAIL stamps (colorful stickers) to glue on each envelope. (See fig. 20J.)

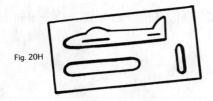

Fig. 20H

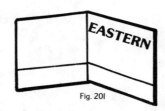

EASTERN

Fig. 20I

AIRMAIL

Fig. 20J

Games

1. Practice waiting in line to board an airplane.
2. Have an airplane race. Glue "wings" on 2 paper cups and string facing each other between 2 trees (chairs) at child's level. Mark the center with red yarn. Let the children blow the open ends of their planes along with string until they get to the center. (See fig. 20K.)

Fig. 20K

Storytelling

1. Pantomime the story of "The Airplane":

    The airplane has great big wings;   *(Arms outstretched.)*
    Its propeller spins around and sings   *(Make one arm go around.)*
    "Vvvvvvvvvvvv!"
    The airplane goes up;   *(Lift arms.)*
    The airplane goes down;   *(Lower arms.)*
    The airplane flies high;   *(Arms outstretched, turn body around.)*
    Over our town!

2. Pretend that the class is in an airplane and have each child name at least one thing that he might see when they look down.

Gross Motor

1. Have the children throw their paper airplanes into a box about five feet away.
2. Have the children throw their airplanes and run to get them. (Make airplanes from three tongue depressors and two rubber bands). (See fig. 20L.)

Fig. 20L

Cognitive

1. Make airplane hangers from oatmeal boxes and number the airplanes and hangers. Match the airplanes to their hangers. This activity can be done with colors.
2. Have the children practice announcing an airplane flight.
3. Arrange some chairs in the form of an airplane. Have each child count the chairs and count enough children to fill the chairs. The plane can range from a two-seater to one which will hold the whole class depending upon the child's level.

Enrichment

1. Discuss airplane safety and use of seat belts.
2. Have children throw their paper airplanes and measure the distance which each travels.
3. Arrange chairs like the insides of an airplane with rows of six chairs, three on each side of the aisle. Number the rows A, B, C, D etc. and the seats 1, 2, 3, 4, 5, 6. Give each child a ticket in a folder with his seat number specified such as A5, B1, C2, etc. Have the children get on the plane, find their seats with or without help from the steward(ess). When everyone is seated, fasten seat belts (old belts or strips of cloth) and prepare for take-off.

Field Trip

Visit the airport. (If you call ahead to the Public Relations Official, the group may be allowed to board an airplane.)

Lesson 5: Tricycle

Unit Group Lesson

1. **Match Concrete Objects**
Present two tricycles. Say, "This is a tricycle." Ask each child in turn to put the tricycle with the tricycle. Gradually increase number of irrelevant objects from which (s)he must select tricycle to match.

2. **Discriminate Objects**
Present several objects. Have each child touch the tricycle in response to verbal direction, "Touch the tricycle."

3. **Match Pictures**
Present several pictures of common objects. Have each child match the pictures of the tricycles.

4. **Discriminate Pictures**
Present a group of several unrelated pictures of objects. Have each child touch the picture of the tricycle in response to verbal direction, "Touch the tricycle."

5. **Figure-Ground**
Present a "busy" picture with many visual distractions. Ask each child to find the tricycle.

6. **Visual Closure**
Partially cover each of several pictures with paper. Ask each child to find the picture of the tricycle.

7. **Function**
Ask, "What do we do with a tricycle?"

8. **Association**
Ask, "What goes with the tricycle?" Use pictures or objects including wheels, handlebars, bicycle, etc., with several unrelated objects or pictures.

9. **Imitate Verbalization**

   Present a tricycle and ask, "What is this? Say, 'Tricycle'." The child will imitate "Tricycle."

10. **Verbalize Label**

    Present a tricycle and ask, "What is this?" The child will respond, "Tricycle."

11. **Concept Enrichment**

    Discuss how bicycles, tricycles, airplanes, buses, cars, and trains are different and how they are the same.

Music

Sing to the tune of "The Wheels on the Bus":
   Verse 1: The wheels on the tricycle go round and round.   *(Pantomime actions.)*
   Verse 2: The bell on the tricycle goes ding, ding, ding.

Art

1. Have the children decorate the classroom tricycles and vehicles for a parade.
2. Have the children "paint" a tricycle outside with water.

Snack

Have children deliver snack on tricycles with wagons attached.

Fine Motor

1. Give children starter pictures of tricycles. Let them add wheels. (See fig. 20M.)

Fig. 20M

2. Make a path tracing of taking "A boy to a tricycle." and "A tricycle to a playground."
3. Let the children drive miniature tricycles around streets on the vinyl roadway made in Lesson #1 Fine Motor #2 of this unit.

Games

Play "Follow the Leader" on tricycles.

Storytelling

1. Make up a story about a boy how has a bike accident because he did not look where he was going.
2. Let the children help make up an adventure that includes a child on a tricycle.

Gross Motor

Ride tricycles.

Cognitive

1. Let the children identify tricycles from unicycles and bicycles.
2. Make a road on floor with tape. Place traffic signs along the road and let the children do what the signs say to do.
3. Let the children count the wheels on unicycles, bicycles and tricycles.

Enrichment

Together Activity: During a group time, "drive" a tricycle with a wagon trailer to a child and say, "I'm carrying _____ in the wagon." What will you take in it? Each child adds something and tries to remember as many other things as he can that have already been loaded into the wagon.

Related Children's Records
"Train Is A-Coming" from **AMERICAN FOLK SONGS** (FOLKWAYS)
ADVENTURES IN SOUND (MH)
"Train Song" from **FIDDLE-EE-FEE**
"Walking On Saturday" from **FIDDLE-EE-FEE**
"I'm Not Small" from **FIDDLE-EE-FEE**
"How Are We Going" from **LEARNING BASIC SKILLS-VOC.** (EA)
"Clickety Clack" from **WITCHES' BREW**
"This Train" from **YOU'LL SING A SONG** (SCHOL)
"I've Been Working On the Railroad" from **ADVENTURES IN RHYTHM** (SCHOL)
"Barrelling On Down the Highway" from **JAMBO** (SCHOL)
"This Train" from **THIS IS RHYTHM**
"Little Red Caboose" from **THIS IS RHYTHM**
"Alex the Airplane Pilot" from **BEGINNING SOUND & CAREERS** (UBB)
"Tony the Trucker" from **BEGINNING SOUND & CAREERS** (UBB)
"A Train Ride to the Great Wall" from **I KNOW THE COLORS** by E. Jenkens (EA)

Related Children's Books
Burningham, John. **MR. GRUMPY'S MOTOR CAR.** New York: Thomas Y. Crowell, 1973.
Crews, Donald. **FREIGHT TRAINS.** New York: Greenwillow Books, 1978.
Crews, Donald. **TRUCKS.** New York: Greenwillow Books, 1978.
Kessler, Ethel and Kessler, Leonard. **BIG RED BUS.** New York: Doubleday & Co., 1957.
Piper, Watty. **THE LITTLE ENGINE THAT COULD.** New York: Platt & Munk, 1980.
Schulz, Charles. **SNOOPY'S FACTS AND FUN BOOK ABOUT PLANES.** New York: Random House, 1979.

Related Parenting Materials
Cansler, Dot. **THE HOMESTRETCH.** Winston-Salem, NC 27113-5128: Kaplan Press, 1983.

Related Materials
TEACHING PICTURES. Winston-Salem, NC 27113-5128: Kaplan Press, 1983.
STORY SEQUENCE CARDS I, II. Winston-Salem, NC 27113-5128: Kaplan Press, 1983.
SEWING CARDS I, II, III. Winston-Salem, NC 27113-5128: Kaplan Press, 1983.

Unit 21: Circus

A developmental assessment should determine the functional levels of each child. Individual expectations are based on the assessment results.

Lesson 1: Popcorn

Unit Group Lesson

1. **Match Concrete Objects**
   Present some "popped" popcorn. Say, "This is popcorn." Ask each child in turn to put the popcorn with the popcorn. Gradually increase number of irrelevant objects from which (s)he must select popcorn to match.

2. **Discriminate Objects**
   Present several objects. Have each child touch the popcorn in response to verbal direction, "Touch the popcorn."

3. **Match Pictures**
   Present several pictures of common objects. Have each child match the pictures of the popcorn.

4. **Discriminate Pictures**
   Present a group of several unrelated pictures of objects. Have each child touch the picture of the popcorn in response to verbal direction, "Touch the popcorn."

5. **Figure-Ground**
   Present a "busy" picture with many visual distractions. Ask each child to find the popcorn.

6. **Tactile Discrimination**
   Put some "popped" popcorn and some very different textured objects into a "feely box." Say, "Find the popcorn".

7. **Taste Discrimination**
   Blindfold or have the child close his eyes and put a piece of popcorn in his mouth while saying, "This is popcorn." Give child several other foods to taste and ask him to tell you when he is tasting popcorn.

8. **Visual Closure**
   Partially cover each of several pictures with paper. Ask each child to find the picture of the popcorn.

9. **Function**
   Ask, "What do we do with popcorn?"

10. **Association**
    Ask, "What goes with the popcorn?" Use pictures or objects including popcorn popper, salt, butter, etc., with several unrelated objects or pictures.

11.   **Imitate Verbalization**
      Present popcorn and ask, "What is this? Say, 'Popcorn'." The child will imitate "Popcorn."

12.   **Verbalize Label**
      Present popcorn and ask, "What is this?" The child will respond, "Popcorn."

13.   **Concept Enrichment**
      Discuss how popcorn grows and that it is a vegetable. Talk about times and places where popcorn is usually eaten.

Music
1.   Sing to the tune of "Row, Row, Row Your Boat":
            Pop-pi-ty, pop-pi-ty, pop-pi-ty pop,
            Pop, pop, pop, pop, pop.
            Pop-pi-ty, pop-pi-ty, pop-pi-ty pop,
            Pop, pop, pop, pop, pop.
2.   Sing to the tune of "Row, Row, Row Your Boat":
            Pop, pop, pop your popcorn,
            Pop it in a pan.
            Popcorn for you, popcorn for me,
            Popcorn for every man.

Art
1.   Have the children glue unpopped popcorn and popped popcorn onto construction paper to make designs.
2.   Begin a circus mural. Have the children paste popcorn dyed green with food coloring onto a mural to make trees and bushes. Leave room for a lion, clowns, elephants, and balloons and include a large circus tent in the mural.
3.   Supply a bowl of freshly-popped corn. Allow the children to create whatever they want to create.

Snack
1.   Eat popcorn from bags.
2.   Make and eat popcorn. Let the children watch corn pop. Put the popper open on a clean bed sheet and have the children sit around the sheet so they are not too close. Leave popper open. Popcorn pops out onto sheet. After popper is removed eat the popcorn off the sheet. CHILDREN MUST BE A SAFE DISTANCE AWAY FROM POPPER!

Fine Motor
1.   Have the children make popcorn balls. Let them watch as you pour melted caramel over popcorn. When cool enough let children shape into balls.
2.   Prepare "Popper Pictures." Glue popcorn at end of each of several lines. Fig. 21A
      Have the children path trace to the popped corn. (See fig. 21A.)
3.   Have the children fill bags of popcorn for snack.
4.   Have children string popcorn. Use long needles and heavy thread to string popcorn. SUPERVISE CHILDREN CLOSELY. Commerically popped popcorn has fewer hulls which makes stringing easier.

Games
1.   Have a race using a broom to sweep a piece of popcorn from one line on the floor to another.
2.   Have the children blow popcorn across the table.

Storytelling
1.   Watch popcorn popping in a popper with a plastic top. Pantomime a kernel of corn popping. Can be done as in Snack today with lid off popper or during snack.
2.   Make popcorn and put it into little bags. Have the children take turns pretending to sell it in the classroom by moving among the other children saying, "Popcorn for sale," very loudly.

Gross Motor

1. Have the children squat down and pop up and down when teacher says, "Pop, pop!"
2. Have a popcorn relay. Divide the children into two teams. Place a piece of popcorn on a napkin on the floor for each child in a long row. At given signal, one child from each team runs, kneels, eats the popcorn, and runs back to designated place. Keep going until all have had a turn.

Cognitive

1. Make popcorn counting cards for tactile stimulation. Make cards with the numerals 1-10 and glue one to ten pieces of popcorn to cards to be counted. (Make two cards for each number.) Some children can match the pairs of cards and others can match popcorn cards to the correct number cards. (See fig. 21B.)
2. Let the children use strung popcorn as an abacus (counting rod). Hang strings of popcorn. Let children slide the popcorn as they count the pieces.
3. Discuss what is needed to make popcorn. Let the children cite a popper, popcorn kernels, heat, salt, butter, etc.

Fig. 21B   Fig. 21C

Enrichment

Together Activity: Make a giant popcorn box on the wall at child level.
Let the children cut the red stripes, glue on red stripes, glue individual letters
POPCORN over outline, and glue popcorn coming out of top. (See fig. 21C.)

Field Trip

Visit a popcorn stand and buy several boxes of popcorn and share.

Lesson 2: Lion

Unit Group Lesson

1. **Match Concrete Objects**
    Present two lions (toy). Say, "This is a lion." Ask each child in turn to put the lion with the lion. Gradually increase number of irrelevant objects from which (s)he must select lion to match.

2. **Discriminate Objects**
    Present several objects. Have each child touch the lion in response to verbal direction, "Touch the lion."

3. **Match Pictures**
    Present several pictures of common objects. Have each child match the pictures of the lion.

4. **Discriminate Pictures**
    Present a group of several unrelated pictures of objects. Have each child touch the picture of the lion in response to verbal direction, "Touch the lion."

5. **Figure-Ground**
    Present a "busy" picture with many visual distractions. Ask each child to find the lion.

6. **Visual Closure**
    Partially cover each of several pictures with paper. Ask each child to find the picture of the lion.

7. **Association**
    Ask, "What goes with the lion?" Use pictures or objects including elephants, tigers, monkeys, etc., with several unrelated objects or pictures.

8. **Imitate Verbalization**
    Present a lion and ask, "What is this? Say, 'Lion'." The child will imitate "Lion."

9.   **Verbalize Label**
      Present a lion and ask, "What is this?" The child will respond, "Lion."

10.   **Concept Enrichment**
      Discuss other circus animals such as tigers, monkeys, horses, dogs, zebra, etc. Real lions are big even
      though they look small in pictures.

Music

Sing to the tune of "I've Been Working on the Railroad":
I am walking through the circus,   *(Pantomime.)*
Happy as can be.
I am walking through the circus,
Just to see what I can see.
I can see the clown laughing.
I can see the elephant, too.
I can see the lion sleeping.
Look out! He sees you.

Art

1.   Continue the circus mural begun in Lesson #1, Art #2. Give the
      children the parts of a lion cut out of gold construction paper.
      Have them paste the pieces together to make a lion, and then
      paste it onto the circus mural. Then have them glue strips of dark
      construction paper over the lion to make a cage.

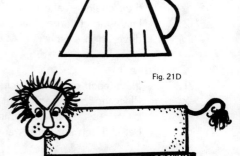

Fig. 21D

2.   Give the children yellow play dough to make lions.
3.   Use a large sheet of newsprint, four feet by four feet. Have one
      child draw a large lion on it with crayon. Then have four or five
      children paint in the lion with gold colored tempera paint. Put on bulletin board.
4.   Let each child make a "Fierce Lion" picture. Have each glue a lion's head on a triangular or
      rectangular body cut in Fine Motor #2 today. Add details and lion's mane prepared in Fine Motor #3.
      Add black strips of construction paper for a "cage" (cut in Fine Motor #4 below). (See fig. 21D.)

Snack

Eat circus foods such as popcorn, hot dogs, etc.

Fine Motor

1.   Together Activity: Lion Head
      Draw a lion face on a large sheet of newsprint or
      newspaper. Tape on wall or a table. Let the children
      take turns adding the mane with strokes of pencil,
      crayon, and water color marker. (A combination of
      these media is better than just one.) Remember the
      process is the important thing. (See fig. 21E.)

Fig. 21E

2.   Have the children cut triangles and rectangles in two
      sizes and circles for individual "Fierce Lions" for Art
      #4 above.
3.   Have the children cut yellow strips to glue around cut
      out lion's head in Art #4 above. Curl on a pencil.
4.   Have the children cut strips of black construction paper
      to glue over individual lion pictures to put them in a
      "cage" in Art #4 above.

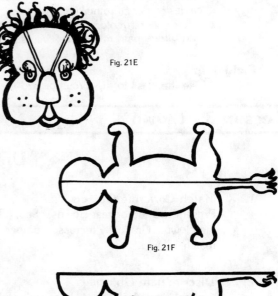

Fig. 21F

5.   Have the children cut out a lion and fringe lion head,
      draw face, fold down legs. (See fig. 21F.)

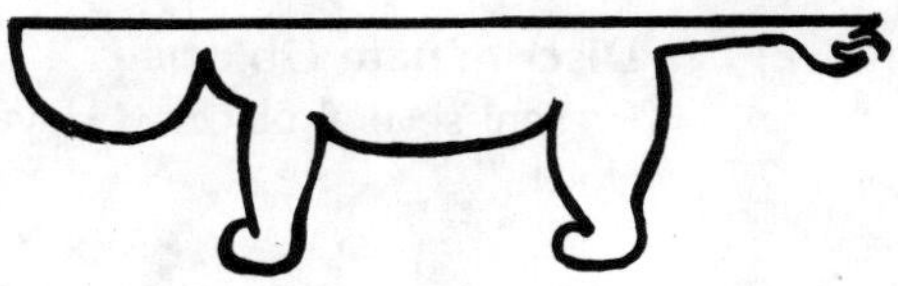

Games

1.   Choose one child to be lead lion and play follow the leader.
2.   Use a hula hoop and have the children pretend to be circus lions jumping through the hoop. Let the
      children think of other tricks that the lions might do.

Storytelling

1.   Tell the story of and pantomime "Lion Hunt."

2. Use the flannel board and five felt lions:
    Five big lions waiting at the door.   *(Hold up five fingers.)*
    One ran away, then there were four.   *(Hold up four fingers.)*
    Four big lions looking at the sea.
    One swam away, then there were three.   *(Hold up three fingers.)*
    Three big lions going to the zoo.
    One joined the circus, then there were two.   *(Hold up two fingers.)*
    Two big lions sleeping in the sun.
    One chased a monkey, then there was one.   *(Hold up one finger.)*
    One big lion chasing you for fun.
    He got lost, then there were none.   *(Hold up fist.)*

Gross Motor

1. Animal Trainer: Have children sit up on chairs. The lion trainer gives a signal for "lions" individually to pace around a designated circle. Have two or more "lions" follow each other and then return to their chairs. Take turns "taming" the lions.
2. Have the children drive the circus trucks. Have some children give directions (left, right) while others drive, then switch.

Cognitive

1. Have each child sort pictures of lions (or toy lions) from non-lions.
2. Place hoop on floor. Put small plastic (or pictures of) animals in the hoop. Let children look, then cover eyes, while one animal is removed. Ask, "What is missing?"
3. Let children sort circus animals from non-circus animals.

Enrichment

1. Help the children identify other "cats" especially wild ones such as leopards, tigers, panthers, jaguars, etc.
2. Together Activity: Make a large design of a leopard. Place on wall at child level or on table. Have the children draw "spots" on the leopard. Have some children draw circles in pencil; other children trace the pencil circles in color; other children color the spots; other children paint the leopard; and others path trace whiskers. (See fig. 21G.)

Fig. 21G

Field Trip

Take the class to the circus or zoo to see the lions.

Lesson 3: Clown

Unit Group Lesson

1. **Match Concrete Objects**
    Present two toy or real clowns. Say, "This is a clown." Ask each child in turn to put the clown with the clown. Gradually increase number of irrelevant objects from which (s)he must select clown to match.

2. **Discriminate Objects**
    Present several objects. Have each child touch the clown in response to verbal direction, "Touch the clown."

3. **Match Pictures**
    Present several pictures of common objects. Have each child match the pictures of the clown.

4. **Discriminate Pictures**

   Present a group of several unrelated pictures of objects. Have each child touch the picture of the clown in response to verbal direction, "Touch the clown."

5. **Figure-Ground**

   Present a "busy" picture with many visual distractions. Ask each child to find the clown.

6. **Visual Closure**

   Partially cover each of several pictures with paper. Ask each child to find the picture of the clown.

7. **Function**

   Ask, "What does a clown do?"

8. **Association**

   Ask, "What goes with the clown?" Use pictures or objects including balloons, lions, elephants, etc., with several unrelated objects or pictures.

9. **Imitate Verbalization**

   Present a clown and ask, "What is this? Say, 'Clown'." The child will imitate "Clown."

10. **Verbalize Label**

    Present a clown and ask, "What is this?" The child will respond, "Clown."

11. **Concept Enrichment**

    Discuss other circus performers such as jugglers, highwire walkers, trapeze artists, animal tamers, the ring master, etc., depending on the level of the children.

Music

Sing to tune of "I'm a Little Teapot":
   I'm a little clown short and fat.
   Here is my tummy, here is my hat.
   I can do a trick as you will see,
   Just turn around and look at me.
At end of song, the teacher points to a child to do a trick.

Art

1. Make simple cone-shaped hats out of posterboard. Provide crepe paper material, tissue paper, feathers, etc., for the children to paste onto their hats.
2. Use paper bags just big enough to fit over the child's head. Help the child cut the eye holes. Then have the children make clown faces on their paper bag masks.
3. Have the children use water soluble felt pens and decorate each other's faces to look like clowns, or use vaseline and real make-up.
4. Add a circus tent to the mural begun in Lesson #1 Art #2. Have the children draw and cut out clowns to paste onto the mural.

Snack

1. Eat clown sugar cookies decorated by children.
2. Make and eat clown salad. Use a peach face, cherry nose, raisin eyes and mouth banana collar and shredded carrot hair. (See fig. 21H.)

Fig. 21H

Fine Motor

1. Help children make clown hats. Roll a sheet of newspaper into a cone and staple together. Let the children cut and paste green, yellow, and red "dots" on their clown hats. (See fig. 21Q.)
2. Help the children make clown finger puppets from cardboard. Cut finger holes for clown. The children can make the finger puppet clowns jump, walk, leap, etc. (See fig. 21R.)
3. Help children make a clown picture. Give each child an outline of a head and neck drawn on paper and pre-cut clown features, hats and curls for the collar. Let each child glue parts to make a clown head. Have them glue cotton balls on the circles for the collar and hat. (Talk about "soft".) (See fig. 21I.)

Fig. 21Q Fig. 21I Fig. 21R

Games

1. Choose one child to be the lead clown and play follow the leader.
2. Five little clowns jumping on the bed. *(Jump up and down.)*
   One fell down and bumped his head. *(Hold head.)*
   Mother phoned the doctor; the doctor said,
   "No more clowns jumping on the bed."
3. Play "Pin the Nose on the Clown." Use magnetic nose or tape on the back of the nose instead of a pin and have the children put the nose on a large clown face. (Similar to "Pin the Tail on the Donkey.")

Storytelling

1. Use a flannel board and five felt clowns. Have different children remove a clown after each verse or have the children do this as a finger play:

   Five silly clowns coming through the door, *(Hold up five fingers.)*
   One ran away, then there were four. *(Fold down one finger.)*
   Four silly clowns smiling just for me, *(Hold up four fingers.)*
   One fell down, then there were three. *(Fold down one finger*
   Three silly clowns looking at you, *(Hold up three fingers.)*
   One went to the circus, then there were two. *(Fold down one finger.)*
   Two silly clowns looking for some fun, *(Hold up two fingers.)*
   One went to sleep, then there was one. *(Fold down one finger.)*
   One silly clown standing in the sun,
   She can to my house, now there are none.

2. Finger play: "The Little Clown" - (Finger and flannel board)

   This little clown is fat and gay; *(Hold up thumb.)*
   This little clown does tricks all day' *(Hold up pointer finger.)*
   This little clown is tall and strong' *(Hold up middle finger.)*
   This little clown sings a funny song; *(Hold up ring ringer and wiggle it.)*

   This little clown is wee and small; *(Hold up little finger.)*
   But he can do anything at all!!!

Gross Motor

1. Have the children wear their clown masks and have a relay race. Use one pair of large men's shoes for each team to wear.
2. Put a tumbling mat on the floor and help the children do sommersaults and other clown tricks.
3. Make a clown bean bag toss. Red yarn hair; large white circle with brightly painted eyes, cheeks, etc., open mouth cut out. Make a stand for clown face. Have children toss bean bag into clown's mouth.

Cognitive

1. Have children match real or construction paper balloons to the correct color clown. Some children will be able to identify or name the correct color.
2. Make circus tents on shoeboxes with numerals on them. Have the children put the right number of clowns in each shoebox.
3. Make several large clown feet from colored cardboard and have the children measure things using "clown feet." The desk is two clown feet long, etc.

Enrichment

1. Make a clown number match game. Match hat to clown with the correct number of dots on his collar. (See fig. 21J.)
2. Provide a dotted outline of a clown. Have the children complete and color it.
3. Together Activity: Make a giant clown and stand him at child level on the wall or bulletin board. (Give him a name after the children begin work on him.) Give children tasks according to developmental level: (See fig. 21K.)
   a. Path trace ruffles with bright colored magic marker.
   b. Cut and glue dots on his suit.
   c. Paint his shoes, hat and gloves or cover with bits of paper or wadded tissue in bright colors.
   d. Name the clown; have a child path trace the name and put it beside the clown.
   e. Cover the balloons with bits of shiny paper.

Fig. 21J

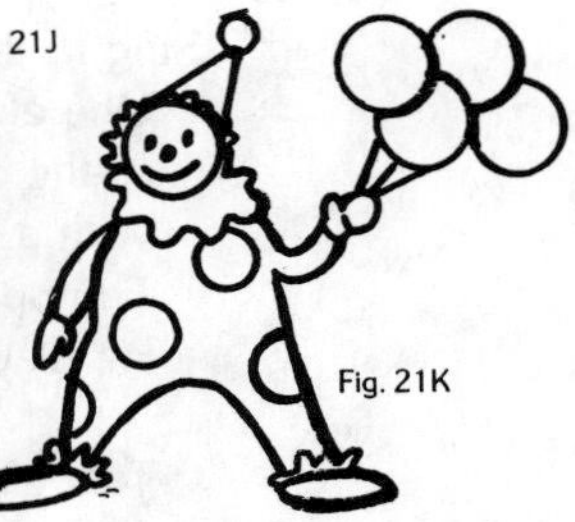

Fig. 21K

Lesson 4: Elephant

Unit Group Lesson

1. **Match Concrete Objects**
   Present two elephants (toy). Say, "This is an elephant." Ask each child in turn to put the elephant with the elephant. Gradually increase number of irrelevant objects from which (s)he must select elephant to match.

2. **Discriminate Objects**
   Present several objects. Have each child touch the elephant in response to verbal direction, "Touch the elephant."

3. **Match Pictures**
   Present several pictures of common objects. Have each child match the pictures of the elephant.

4. **Discriminate Pictures**
   Present a group of several unrelated pictures of objects. Have each child touch the picture of the elephant in response to verbal direction, "Touch the elephant."

5. **Figure-Ground**
   Present a "busy" picture with many visual distractions. Ask each child to find the elephant.

6. **Visual Closure**
   Partially cover each of several pictures with paper. Ask each child to find the picture of the elephant.

7. **Association**
   Ask, "What goes with the elephant?" Use pictures or objects including lion, clown, circus, etc., with several unrelated objects or pictures.

8. **Imitate Verbalization**
   Present an elephant and ask, "What is this? Say, 'Elephant'." The child will imitate "Elephant."

9. **Verbalize Label**
   Present an elephant and ask, "What is this?" The child will respond, "Elephant."

10. **Concept Enrichment**
    Discuss other circus animals such as lions, tigers, horses, monkeys, etc. Emphasize that elephants are very large.

Music

Sing to the tune of "This Old Man":
One elephant went out to play (el-e-phant)
At the circus for the day.
With a thump, thump, thump, thump,
Thump, thump, thump, thump, thump.
He played and played the day away.

Two elephants went out to play,
At the circus for the day,
etc.

Pantomime this song by having one child dance during the first verse and choosing another child to join in at each new verse.

Art

1. Use a large piece of newsprint four feet by six feet. Have one child draw a large elephant on it with a crayon. Then have four or five children paint in the elephant with grey tempera paint.
2. Continue the circus mural begun in Lesson #1 Art #2 of this unit. Have the children draw elephants on gray construction paper. Then have them cut the elephants out and paste them onto the mural.
3. Have the children make circus blankets for "Elsie the Elephant." Have children cut out squares of colored paper. Let them decorate them with the dots and fringes made in Fine Motor #3 today and use in Enrichment today.
4. Use shoe boxes for animal cages. Cut out bars. Glue "bars" on open side. (See fig. 21L.)

Fig. 21L

Snack

1. Eat animal crackers and drink red punch. Serve on a round tray and call it a circus ring. Have the animal crackers parade around the ring.
2. Eat peanuts and drink juice.

Fine Motor

Fig. 21M

1. Make a worksheet with the outline of an elephant on it. Give the children pieces of elephant cut out of gray construction paper to paste onto the worksheet. Divide the elephants into more pieces for children with higher-level skills.
2. Have the children cut out animal pictures and glue onto black paper. Then glue black stripes over the animal pictures for "bars" on the cage. "Bow" the "bars" out for a 3-D effect. (See fig. 21M.)
3. Have the children cut the fringes and dots (from foil paper) for the elephant blankets in Art #3 today. (See fig. 21N.)

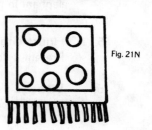
Fig. 21N

Games

1. Choose one child to be lead elephant and play follow the leader.
2. Let the children use upside down strawberry baskets as cages for plastic animals.

Storytelling

1. Fingerplay: "The Elephant"
    The elephant has a trunk for a nose,   *(Clasp hands together and extend arms.)*
    And up and down is the way it goes;   *(Raise and lower them.)*
    He wears such a saggy, baggy hide!   *(Relax body.)*
    Do you think two elephants could fit inside? *(Hold up two fingers.)*
2. Make a flannel board picture including a tree, a house, a car, and a truck. Also have a large and small elephant out of felt. Hide the small elephant behind one of the pieces on the flannel board. Give one child the large elephant and tell him a story about mother elephant looking for her baby.
    Example: "Mother Elephant lost her baby. She looked for him behind the house and behind the tree. She found him behind the car." Change the difficulty of the sequences according to the child.

Gross Motor
1. Have a Tug O' War. Have the children pretend they are elephants and wrap their trunks (arms) around the rope. Pull against the other team.
2. Have the children do an "elephant walk." Have them hold arms out to the person in front. Have them take large steps together at a slow moving pace.

Cognitive
1. Make three different sized elephants and have the children pick the largest and the smallest. (See fig. 210.)
2. Elephants are grey. Grey is a mixture of black and white. Have the children mix black and white paint to make grey paint.
3. Arrange "Elsie the Elephant" (Enrichment) shapes in a row "trunk to tail." Sequence according to numbers on the elephants. (Make elephant blankets with dots or numbers.)

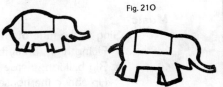
Fig. 210

Enrichment
Have each child make an "Elsie the Elephant." Have each child cut an Elsie from an outline and glue on the "blanket" made in Art #3. Have them cut elephant ears and staple on Elsie.

Lesson 5: Balloon

Unit Group Lesson

1. **Match Concrete Objects**
    Present two inflated balloons. Say, "This is a balloon." Ask each child in turn to put the balloon with the balloon. Gradually increase number of irrelevant objects from which (s)he must select balloon to match.

2. **Discriminate Objects**
    Present several objects. Have each child touch the balloon in response to verbal direction, "Touch the balloon."

3. **Match Pictures**
    Present several pictures of common objects. Have each child match the pictures of the balloon.

4. **Discriminate Pictures**
    Present a group of several unrelated pictures of objects. Have each child touch the picture of the balloon in response to verbal direction, "Touch the balloon."

5. **Figure-Ground**
    Present a "busy" picture with many visual distractions. Ask each child to find the balloon.

6. **Tactile Discrimination**
    Put an inflated balloon and some grossly different objects into a "feely box". Say, "Find the balloon".

7. **Visual Closure**
    Partially cover each of several pictures with paper. Ask each child to find the picture of the balloon.

8. **Function**
    Ask, "What do we do with balloons?"

9. **Association**
    Ask, "What goes with the balloon?" Use pictures or objects including clown, circus, birthday cake, etc., with several unrelated objects or pictures.

10. **Imitate Verbalization**

Present a balloon and ask, "What is this? Say, 'Balloon'." The child will imitate "Balloon."

11. **Verbalize Label**

Present a balloon and ask, "What is this?" The child will respond, "Balloon."

12. **Concept Enrichment**

Discuss colors, shapes and sizes of balloons. Note the difference when the balloon is inflated. Discuss the sound of a popping balloon. Discuss hot air balloons used for weather reporting.

Music

Sing to the tune of "Twinkle, Twinkle, Little Star":
Flying high, pretty big balloon,
Big balloon, please come back soon.
Up above the house and trees,
Take me with you if you please.
Flying high, pretty big balloon,
Big balloon, please come back soon.

Art

1. Have the children draw faces or designs with felt pens on balloons.
2. Continue the circus mural begun in Lesson #1 Art #2. Let each child choose a small square piece of paper (use many different colors). Model cutting off the corners to make a circle. Then let the children cut their own balloons and glue them onto the mural. Let them glue on a real string. Mark the cutting line for those children who need it.

Snack

Eat round cookies frosted in pretty colors.

Fine Motor

1. Make a path tracing worksheet of "Draw a string from a boy to a balloon," "A girl to a balloon," "A monkey to a balloon," etc.
2. Have the children trace around outlines of balloons and strings.
3. Have the children finger paint on circles of paper to make balloons.

Games

1. Put a balloon on a chair and let the children take turns trying to break it by sitting on it.
2. Toss a balloon in the air and have the children try to keep it from falling to the floor.
3. Give several balloons to one child and have him pretend to be selling them at a circus. Take turns. Have the seller shout, "Balloons for sale!"

Storytelling

1. Tell a story about a little girl holding on to a balloon and flying high in the air. Have each child tell something she saw while up in the air. Also have each child tell where she lands and how she gets home.
2. Make up a story about a little balloon that gets lost. Have the children tell how the little lost balloon finds his way home again.

Gross Motor

1. Use balloons tied with a string or piece of heavy yarn. Bounce balloons into the air and let the children catch the strings.
2. Have the children bounce balloons off each other's hands outdoors.
3. Play balloon keep away. The children keep balloon away from a designated tree or bush, etc.
4. Tie a balloon to a tree limb. Have the children throw bean bags to make it move or to break it.

Cognitive

1. Make balloons in different colors. Have the children match the balloons which are the same color.
2. Have children find a balloon on the table to match a balloon on the mural.
3. Make balloons in different sizes and have the children arrange them from smallest to largest.

Enrichment

1. Together Activity: "Balloons in the Clouds" mural.
   Provide a large sheet of mural paper or newsprint on wall at child level or on the floor. Have children finger paint or use the side of blue crayons to paint the entire paper. Add circles for balloons, strings with no balloons and dotted outlines of clouds. Have the children add strings to the balloons; cut out balloons to add to strings; trace dotted clouds with chalk, and color clouds with chalk. This mural will have lots of balloons but remember, the process is the important part. (See fig. 21P.)

2. Provide some helium filled balloons and note the differences between them and regular balloons.

Fig. 21P

Related Parenting Materials
Cansler, Dot. **THE HOMESTRETCH.** Winston-Salem, NC 27113-5128: Kaplan Press, 1983.

Related Materials
TEACHING PICTURES. Winston-Salem, NC 27113-5128: Kaplan Press, 1983.
STORY SEQUENCE CARDS I, II. Winston-Salem, NC 27113-5128: Kaplan Press, 1983.
SEWING CARDS I, II, III. Winston-Salem, NC 27113-5128: Kaplan Press, 1983.

Unit 22: St. Patrick's Day

A developmental assessment should determine the functional levels of each child. Individual expectations are based on the assessment results.

Lesson 1: Green

Unit Group Lesson

NOTE: Use identical objects of various colors, when child is first learning concept of color.

1. **Match Concrete Objects**
   Present some green things. Say, "This is green." Ask each child in turn to put the green with the green. Gradually increase number of objects of other colors from which (s)he must select green to match.

2. **Discriminate Objects**
   Present several objects. Have each child touch the green ones in response to verbal direction, "Touch the green (thing)."

3. **Match Pictures**
   Present several pictures of common objects. Have each child match the green ones.

4. **Discriminate Pictures**
   Present a group of several pictures of objects or colors. Have each child touch the green ones in response to verbal direction, "Touch the green (thing)."

5. **Figure-Ground**
   Present a "busy" picture with many visual distractions. Ask each child to find the green things.

6. **Visual Closure**
   Partially cover each of several pictures with paper. Ask each child to find the green objects.

7. **Association**
   Ask, "What things are green?" Use pictures or objects including grass, shamrock, leaves, etc. with several other colored objects or pictures.

8. **Imitate Verbalization**
   Present a green thing and ask, "What is this? Say, 'Green'." The child will imitate "Green."

9. **Verbalize Label**
   Present a green thing and ask, "What is this?" The child will respond, "Green."

10. **Concept Enrichment**
Discuss fact that green is a mix of blue and yellow. Green is associated with St. Patrick's Day. St. Patrick helped the Irish people kill snakes in Ireland.

Music
Sing "It's Not Easy Being Green" (Kermit the Frog - Sesame Street). *(Those wearing green stand up while singing.)*

Art
1. Let children paint with green paint.
2. Let children make a green collage by cutting or tearing green things out of catalogs and magazines. Also use bits of ribbon and fabric.
3. Begin a rainbow bulletin board. Outline the green strips on a large sheet of paper taped at child's level. Have children fill in between the lines with bits of green tissue paper. (See Fine Motor #4 today.)

Snack
1. Eat green jello.
2. Have a limeade or green punch.
3. Have a green salad.
4. Use green napkins.

Fine Motor
1. Have children cut green things from magazines.
2. Have children cut green lines drawn on white paper. Vary with children's skills.
3. Have children fingerpaint with yellow and blue fingerpaint.
4. Have the children cut strips of green paper and make a field beneath the rainbow on the bulletin board. (See Art #3 today.)

Games
1. Let children decorate the classroom with green streamers.
2. Play red light, green light. Use a red circle and green circle as red light and green light.

Storytelling
Make up a story about a green painter who paints everything green that is not green to get ready for St. Patrick's Day. Let each child mention something that the green painter will paint such as the sky, oranges, the sun, the ocean, clouds, etc. because it is not green.

Gross Motor
Have the children skip in time to "The Wearing of the Green."

Cognitive
1. Let children sort green from not green.
2. Let children sort green from red, yellow and blue.
3. Have the class help make a list of everything in the class which is green.

Enrichment
1. Have children bring from home objects that are green. They may bring items which are naturally green, painted green, or magazine pictures. Sort in shades of green.
2. Have children match color names to colors of the primary and secondary colors. Use color coding to simplify the activity.

Field Trip

Take a class walk. Have each child collect three green items from nature.

Visitor

Invite an artist to paint a green picture. Invite a child in the class to paint a green picture while the others watch.

Lesson 2: Shamrock

Unit Group Lesson

1. **Match Concrete Objects**
Present two shamrocks. Say, "This is a shamrock." Ask each child in turn to put the shamrock with the shamrock. Gradually increase number of objects from which (s)he must select shamrock to match.

2. **Discriminate Objects**
Present several objects. Have each child touch the shamrock in response to verbal direction, "Touch the shamrock."

3. **Match Pictures**
Present several pictures of common objects. Have each child match the shamrocks.

4. **Discriminate Pictures**
Present a group of several pictures of objects. Have each child touch the shamrock in response to verbal direction, "Touch the shamrock."

5. **Figure-Ground**
Present a "busy" picture with many visual distractions. Ask each child to find the shamrock.

6. **Visual Closure**
Partially cover each of several pictures with paper. Ask each child to find the shamrock.

7. **Function**
Ask, "What do we do with a shamrock?"

8. **Association**
Ask, "What goes with the shamrock?" Use related pictures or objects including hats, "good luck," pot of gold, etc. with several unrelated objects or pictures.

9. **Imitate Verbalization**
Present a shamrock and ask, "What is this? Say, 'Shamrock'." The child will imitate "Shamrock."

10. **Verbalize Label**
Present a shamrock and ask, "What is this?" The child will respond, "Shamrock."

11. **Concept Enrichment**
Discuss the facts that shamrocks are green and have three leaves and a stem. We associate shamrocks with Ireland and Irish people, St. Patrick's Day, "good luck."

Music

Sing to the tune of "My Bonnie Lies Over the Ocean":

My shamrock lies over the ocean.
My shamrock lies over the sea.
My shamrock lies over the ocean.
Oh bring back my shamrock to me.

Art

1. Have the children cover 3 large circles with bright green tissue or bits of paper and place them together on a green stem to make a shamrock. (Individual shamrocks can be made on sheets of construction paper.) Let those children who are able cut circles. (See fig. 22A.)
2. Give each child an outline of a shamrock. Have him cover it with glue and sprinkle with green glitter (green tempera mixed with grits or green sand).
3. Let the children paint with green paint at the easels.

Fig. 22A

Snack

1. Eat shamrock cookies which have been made in Fine Motor #5.
2. Tape shamrocks to the bottoms of the cups so the children can see them when they drink all their drink.

Fine Motor

1. Let the children trace around cardboard shamrocks on green construction paper and cut them out. Decorate the room with the children's shamrocks. Put in grass field made yesterday in Fine Motor #4.
2. Draw the outline of a large shamrock on a long piece of white paper. Let the children cut out small pieces of construction paper and glue them inside the shamrock until it is completely filled. (See fig. 22B.)
3. Let the children make shamrocks out of green pipe cleaners.

Fig. 22B

4. Have children glue green yarn around the outline of a shamrock.
5. Shamrock Necklace - Let the children trace around small cardboard patterns of shamrocks on green construction paper. Then have them cut out the shamrocks and punch holes in them with a hole puncher. Give them a long piece of green yarn and let them string their shamrocks on the yarn then tie a knot to make a necklace.
6. Let children make shamrocks using heart shapes for the leaves and strips for the stem. Cut, or let the children cut, the shapes. Give children the green hearts with the points together and have them glue the stem over the points. (See fig. 22C.)
7. Let the children make and bake shamrock cookies. Mix up the dough. Roll out the dough. Cut out the cookies and place them on the cookie sheet. Bake the cookies. When the cookies cool, let the children ice the cookies with green frosting. Eat the cookies for snack. (Write the steps for making the cookies with pictures on a large sheet of chart paper shaped like a shamrock.)

Fig. 22C

Games

Have a treasure hunt. Mark a number of items with shamrock stickers. Hide them and let the children find them.

Storytelling

Prior to storytelling partially hide large shamrock shapes around the room. Then tell this story:

Once upon a time a tiny elf called a leprechaun was looking for shamrocks.
He wanted lots of shamrocks to bring good luck to the children in his town.
He heard that there were lots of shamrocks in our room so he is coming
here to find them. (Child's name) will you go find a shamrock and we'll
put it here in this shamrock bag. Bring a shamrock and tell where you found it.

(Each child looks for a shamrock and brings it to the group saying, "I found a shamrock: beside the door, under the table, behind the books, etc.) Have a leprechaun puppet come to collect the shamrocks or leave the shamrocks in a special place to be picked up at night while everyone is asleep.

Gross Motor
Show the children how to do the Irish lilt or jig. Have the children dance to Irish music.

Cognitive
1. Have the children sort shamrocks from non-shamrocks.
2. Make a shamrock matching game. Trace and cut out different sized shamrocks from green construction paper and cover them with contact paper. Trace the outline of all the shamrocks on a large piece of poster board with a green magic marker and cover with contact paper. Give each child the shamrocks and tell him to match them to their correct places on the poster board.
3. Make shamrock put-togethers. Trace shamrocks on green construction paper and cut them out. Put two identical pictures, stickers, shapes, etc. on each side (left and right) of the shamrocks. Cover with contact paper and cut the shamrocks in half lengthwise to make puzzles. (Make sure each cut is different on each shamrock.) Then let the children put the shamrocks together by finding the identical pairs of pictures on the shamrock halves.

Enrichment
1. Ask children how many leaves does a shamrock have? How many leaves do we need to make two shamrocks? Count the multiples of three. Arrange shamrock leaves in sets of three.
2. On the backs of the shamrock put-togethers (from Cognitive #2 today) put an upper case letter on one half, and the matching lower case letter on the other half, of each shamrock. Let the children match them. They can use the identical pictures as cues if they need them.

Field Trip
Take a walk; collect three leaf clovers and press between folded wax paper.

Lesson 3: Leprechaun

Unit Group Lesson

NOTE: If only pictures are available, use pictures for number 1 and omit numbers 2 and 3.

1. **Match Concrete Objects**
    Present two leprechauns. Say, "This is a leprechaun." Ask each child in turn to put the leprechaun with the leprechaun. Gradually increase number of objects from which (s)he must select leprechaun to match.

2. **Discriminate Objects**
    Present several objects. Have each child touch the leprechaun in response to verbal direction, "Touch the leprechaun."

3. **Match Pictures**
    Present several pictures of common objects. Have each child match the leprechauns.

4. **Discriminate Pictures**
    Present a group of several pictures of objects. Have each child touch the leprechaun in response to verbal direction, "Touch the leprechaun."

5. **Figure-Ground**
    Present a "busy" picture with many visual distractions. Ask each child to find the leprechaun.

6. **Visual Closure**
    Partially cover each of several pictures with paper. Ask each child to find the leprechaun.

7. **Function**
    Ask, "What does a leprechaun do?"

8. **Association**
    Ask, "What goes with the leprechaun?" Use related pictures or objects including pot of gold, rainbow, etc. with several unrelated objects or pictures.

9. **Imitate Verbalization**
    Present a leprechaun and ask, "What is this? Say, 'Leprechaun'." The child will imitate "Leprechaun."

10. **Verbalize Label**
    Present a leprechaun and ask, "What is this?" The child will respond, "Leprechaun."

11. **Concept Enrichment**
    Discuss fact that leprechauns are believed to keep a pot of gold at the end of the rainbow and if you catch one, he has to give you his pot of gold.

Music

Sing to the tune of "Have You Ever Seen a Lassie?":

Have you ever seen a leprechaun,
A leprechaun, a leprechaun.
Have you ever seen a leprechaun,
Go this way and that.

Art
1. Have the children paint a forest for the leprechauns to live in. For some children, outline the trees.
2. Have the children cut or tear out pictures of leprechauns and make a collage.
3. Let the children color leprechauns, cut them out and add them to the rainbow bulletin board begun in Lesson #1 Art #3 of this unit. (Check card shops for a variety of leprechauns which can be used in this lesson.)
4. Have the children paint a pot outline black and put it at the end of the rainbow on the rainbow bulletin board. Leave an opening at the top.

Snack
1. Ask the children what leprechauns eat. Tell them that leprechauns like green milk and Lucky Charms cereal for breakfast. Let the children put green food coloring in their milk, mix it up and pour it over a bowl of "Lucky Charms" and eat them.
2. Eat green jello with fruit in it.

Fine Motor
1. Make leprechaun lacing cards. Glue leprechauns and pots of gold on green construction paper and cover with contact paper. Cut them out and punch holes around the edges. Let the children lace around the leprechaun with green yarn or shoe laces.
2. Make a path trace activity. Draw leprechauns on the left side of paper and pots of gold on the right side of the paper. Make paths going from the leprechauns to the pots of gold. Cover with laminating paper and give the child a green magic marker or crayon and have him trace the path the leprechaun has to take to get his gold. Wipe off with a paper towel or tissue. Vary the difficulty of the paths for different children.
3. Have the children cut coins from yellow construction paper to put in the leprechaun's pot of gold on the rainbow bulletin board from Art #4.

Games

1. Have a visit from a leprechaun. Place a pipe and a green hat in the room. Tape some small green footprints on the floor all around the room and sprinkle gold glitter around on the floor. Make small round coins out of construction paper and sprinkle them with glitter around the edges. Write each child's name on a coin, punch holes in the top of each coin and string green yarn through the coins to make a necklace. Hide the necklaces around the room. When the children come into the room, tell them there has been a visitor in the room while they were gone and have them look for clues that will tell who the visitor was. Then let them search for their gold necklaces that the leprechaun left for them.

2. Decorate a small box with green paint and shamrocks. Draw a window and a door on it. Place a small cardboard figure of a leprechaun inside the house. Show the house to the children and tell them it was found outside and that it is the home of someone very small. Then let the children take turns guessing whose house it might be. After all the children have made guesses, open up the house and show them the leprechaun. Explain what a leprechaun is and ask the children where a leprechaun might be found. Then go on a "Leprechaun Hunt" outside.

Storytelling

1. Tell the story of LEPRECHAUNS. They are believed to be little people who live in Ireland and keep a pot of gold at the end of the rainbow.

2. Make up a story about some children who tried to catch a leprechaun. Let the children help make up their adventures as they follow the leprechaun through fields, woods and over streams.

Gross Motor

1. Have the children walk, run, jump, tiptoe, etc. like a leprechaun.

2. Make a pot of gold bean bag game. Cut a large black pot from paper and tape it to the front of a box. Give each child ten bean bags on which gold sequins have been sewn and tell him they are "gold coins." Tell the child to fill the pot up by tossing the "gold coins" in. Then let the child count how many "gold coins" he gets in the pot.

Cognitive

1. Use a large leprechaun to identify body parts such as eyes, nose, mouth, ears, arms, legs, head, body, etc.

2. Discuss short versus tall. Leprechauns are short and basketball players are tall. Provide pictures of tall and short things and let the children sort short things into a box with a leprechaun and tall things into a box with a basketball player. Some tall and short pairs are flower and tree, mothers and baby, city building and ranch home, crane and bulldozer, etc.

3. Trace and cut out different sized leprechauns and laminate. Let the children hang the leprechauns on a clothesline with clothespins starting with the smallest and going to the largest. Vary the number of leprechauns given with the skills of the children.

Enrichment

1. Ask each child what they would do with a leprechaun if they caught one. Write their responses on a large piece of lined paper. At the end read the responses back to the children and see if they can identify theirs. Repeat this activity using the question, "What would you do if a leprechaun gave you his pot of gold?"

2. Make ten pots out of black construction paper and paste them on the front of empty milk cartons. Paste numerals 1-10 on the "pots." Make gold coins out of construction paper and glitter. Give the "coins" to the child and tell him to look at the numeral on each pot and count the correct number of coins into each pot.

3. What is a leprechaun's favorite color? Let the children make guesses and then tell them it is green. Discuss wearing green on St. Patrick's Day and the consequences if the person forgets! Give the children magazines and have them cut out pictures of "green things" and glue them on a large piece of paper.

Field Trip

Hide a black pot filled with small gold foil-wrapped food or toy items (one for each child). Take a trip to find the pot of gold at the end of the rainbow.

Lesson 4: Rainbow

Unit Group Lesson

NOTE: If only pictures are available, use pictures for number 1 and omit numbers 2 and 3.

1. **Match Concrete Objects**
    Present two rainbows. (Use plastic rainbows.) Say, "This is a rainbow." Ask each child in turn to put the rainbow with the rainbow. Gradually increase number of objects from which (s)he must select rainbow to match.

2. **Discriminate Objects**
    Present several objects. Have each child touch the rainbow in response to verbal direction, "Touch the rainbow."

3. **Match Pictures**
    Present several pictures of common objects. Have each child match the rainbows.

4. **Discriminate Pictures**
    Present a group of several pictures of objects. Have each child touch the rainbow in response to verbal direction, "Touch the rainbow."

5. **Figure-Ground**
    Present a "busy" picture with many visual distractions. Ask each child to find the rainbow.

6. **Visual Closure**
    Partially cover each of several pictures with paper. Ask each child to find the rainbow.

7. **Function**
    Ask, "What do we do with a rainbow?"

8. **Association**
    Ask, "What goes with the rainbow?" Use related pictures or objects including pot of gold, leprechaun, rainbow, etc. with several unrelated objects or pictures.

9. **Imitate Verbalization**
    Present a rainbow and ask, "What is this? Say, 'Rainbow'." The child will imitate "Rainbow."

10. **Verbalize Label**
    Present a rainbow and ask, "What is this?" The child will respond, "Rainbow."

11. **Concept Enrichment**
    Discuss how rainbows are formed. Talk about the leprechaun's pot of gold at the end of the rainbow.

Music

Sing "Somewhere Over the Rainbow."

Art

1. Finish the rainbow bulletin board begun in Lesson #1 Art #3 of this unit. Draw the rest of the rainbow. Have the children fill in the bands of color with crushed tissue paper in yellow, blue, violet, pink, etc.
2. Have the children make rainbow parfaits. Have them pour partially chilled gelatin in layers of different colors into clear plastic cups.
3. Let the children paint rainbows at the easels or with watercolors.

Snack

Eat the rainbow parfaits made in Art #2 today.

Fine Motor

1. Give each child an individual rainbow and let them color between the lines with different colors.
2. Make a path tracing activity to take the leprechaun over the rainbow to his pot of gold. Let the children follow the path with a leprechaun mobile (a small green car). Vary the complexity of the rainbow for the different skill levels of the children.
3. Have children practice making lines that look like a rainbow. Be sure that they work from left to right and top to bottom on a large sheet of paper.

Games

1. Provide clothes in the dress up corner in rainbow colors.
2. Make a class rainbow by having each child hold up balloons of rainbow colors. Place the different colors at different heights and put the same color in the same row. Take a picture so the children can see themselves as part of a rainbow.
3. Put on a lawn sprinkler (if it is a sunny day) and try to make a rainbow in it by positioning it between the class and the sun.

Storytelling

Let the children tell about where they saw a rainbow, where they were, what they were doing, and who was with them.

Gross Motor

Let the children run to the rainbow, skip to the rainbow, hop to the rainbow, etc.

Cognitive

1. Have the children sort the bands of rainbows by color.
2. Present rainbows of different lengths and have the children sequence them from shortest to longest.
3. Give each child one or more bands of a rainbow. Have her identify the color and find other things to match that color.

Enrichment

1. Provide several prisms for the children to use. Help them to see the rainbow colors.
2. Make a list of rainbow color words. Have matching words on cards. Let the children label things in the classroom with the appropriate color words.

Field Trip

Go to see a hill or horizon. Lie down on the grass and look up at the sky. Talk about the colors in the sky.

Visitor

Invite a singer with a guitar to sing "Somewhere Over the Rainbow."

Unit 23: Nature Hike

A developmental assessment should determine the functional levels of each child. Individual expectations are based on the assessment results.

Lesson 1: Tree

Unit Group Lesson

1. **Match Concrete Objects**
    Present two trees. Say, "This is a tree." Ask each child in turn to put the tree with the tree. Gradually increase the number of irrelevant objects from which (s)he must select the tree to match.

2. **Discriminate Objects**
    Present several objects. Have each child touch the tree in response to the verbal direction, "Touch the tree."

3. **Match Pictures**
    Present several pictures of common objects. Have each child match the pictures of the trees.

4. **Discriminate Pictures**
    Present a group of several unrelated pictures of objects. Have each child touch the picture of the tree in response to verbal direction, "Touch the tree."

5. **Figure-Ground**
    Present a "busy" picture with many visual distractions. Ask each child to find the tree.

6. **Visual Closure**
    Partially cover each of several pictures with paper. Ask each child to find the picture of the tree.

7. **Function**
    Ask, "What do trees do?" or "What do we do with trees?"

8. **Association**
    Ask, "What goes with the tree?" Use pictures or objects including leaves, bark, bird, etc. with several unrelated objects or pictures.

9. **Imitate Verbalization**
    Present a tree and ask, "What is this? Say, 'Tree'." The child will imitate "Tree."

10. **Verbalize Label**
    Present a tree and ask, "What is this?" The child will respond, "Tree."

11. **Concept Enrichment**

Discuss different sizes, types, and uses for trees. Discuss differences between some winter trees and some summer trees. Discuss types of fruit trees. Ask, "What do you like best about trees?"

Music

Sing to the tune of "Paw Paw Patch": (Make large cardboard trees for children to paint and paste apples on. Use as a "prop.")

Where, oh where is my friend (child's name)?
Where, oh where is my friend (child's name)?
Where, oh where is my friend (child's name)?

He's way down yonder behind the apple tree.   *(Named child gets behind tree.)*
She's way down yonder beside the apple tree.   *(Named child gets beside tree.)*
He's way down yonder in front of the apple tree.   *(Named child gets in front of tree.)*

Art

1. Draw trunk of tree onto a big piece of paper. Have children tear with fingers or cut construction paper leaves, then paste leaves on tree for bulletin board. (Leaves may also be made with sponge painting.) Blossoms may be made by shaking cotton balls in tempera and gluing to tree.
2. Have children paint leaf shapes cut out of brown paper. (If the paper is crumpled first it will have a veined look).
3. Have children make tree trunks from stick pretzels glued on construction paper. Add cut leaves or torn paper leaves. This is very attractive if children glue on construction paper circles of different shades of green and yellow.

Snack

1. Eat slices of apples under a tree. Discuss how apples grow on special trees.
2. Eat broccoli. Discuss how it looks like a tree.

Fine Motor

1. Draw tree trunk and branches. (Some children can make the trunks by blowing brown tempera paint with a straw.) Have children paste pre-cut leaves on tree, or thumbtack real leaves to a tree on bulletin board.
2. Place a real leaf under sheet of paper, taped to table. Have children rub with blunt side of crayon or chalk and watch the leaf design appear! Or do the same with a piece of tree bark.
3. Take branches of a tree and put into big can of sand. Have children cut out and hole-punch leaves, thread with yarn, and hang leaves on tree. (Bent paper clips make great "hangers," too!)
4. Have children pick up matching leaves and place in egg carton hole where duplicate is found. (The egg carton should be upside down with holes for the stems.) (See fig. 23A.)

Fig. 23A

Games

Play "Touch A Tree." When whistle blows, children run to a tree and touch it.

Storytelling

1. Use flannelboard and have children sing "Ten Little Trees" (model the song on "Ten Little Indians") as you put up cut-outs. Then, have a child put up cut-outs as he listens to song.
2. Use large picture cards and tell story of what happens to a leaf. Example:
   a. *Springtime leaves are green, start as little buds and then grow.*
   b. *Summer leaves are large and give us shade.*
   c. *Fall comes and leaves turn yellow, red, and brown.*

    d. *Winter and cold come. Wind blows leaves off trees to ground. Branches are bare.*

    e. *Then, when spring comes again, little green leaves start to grow again on tree.*

    Tell story and then mix up the pictures. Have children sequence pictures. Later, have children tell story, too.

3.   Use flannelboard and illustrate poem below.

        My Little Tree - by Rebecca McLeod (Adapted by Jane Findlay)

        Here is the trunk of my little tree

        And here are the branches, look and see

        When the wind blows, little tree bends and sways

        This little tree likes a windy day.

    (Read and illustrate poem once more. Next, you and children act out poem together. Then you read poem and have children act it out).

Gross Motor

1.   Play "Squirrel in a Tree." Children hold arms out in a circle. A "dog" chases squirrel until it goes into a tree. Have children take turns. Spread out the "trees" for running longer distances according to the levels of the children.

2.   Have children imitate trees in the wind, during a storm, etc.

Cognitive

1.   Have children match different types of trees. Cut basic trees from construction paper and let children match them.

2.   Have children match leaves to leaves and bark to bark after field trip.

3.   Discuss basic tree shapes: Evergreens look triangular. Oaks and fruit trees look circular. Willows look rectangular. (See fig. 23B.)

Fig. 23B

Enrichment

1.   Use tape measure to measure around a tree. Can each child find a tree to hug so that his/her hands touch?

2.   Make a display of tree products (nuts, acorns, seeds pods, cones, gum balls, bark, and leaves). Examine each with a magnifying glass.

3.   Together Activity - The Forest. Provide a large piece of mural paper with lines on it. Tape to the wall at children's level. Have children glue strips of paper over the lines in brown construction paper. Provide triangles and circles in several sizes of green paper for adding the "leaves." (As an added activity, let it "rain" in the forest with chalk or blue crayon. Remember, the process is what is important!)

Field Trip

1.   Nature Hike: Take a walk to collect different kinds of leaves and bark. Arrange in science area on return. Match leaves and bark collected by the children.

2.   a. Cut leaves of 3 different shapes, giving one to each child. (Leaf shapes may be taped on front of a paper bag).

        b. Take a "leaf hunt" walk. "Each child uses his/her bright eyes to find a leaf shaped like yours."

        c. Gather all leaves found into paper bags.

Visitor

    Invite a Forest Ranger or a tree farmer to visit the class.

Lesson 2: Rock

Unit Group Lesson

1. **Match Concrete Objects**
   Present two rocks. Say, "This is a rock." Ask each child in turn to put the rock with the rock. Gradually increase number of irrelevant objects from which (s)he must select the rocks to match.

2. **Discriminate Objects**
   Present several objects. Have each child touch the rock in response to the verbal direction, "Touch the rock."

3. **Match Pictures**
   Present several pictures of common objects. Have each child match the pictures of the rock.

4. **Discriminate Pictures**
   Present a group of several unrelated pictures of objects. Have each child touch the picture of the rock in response to verbal direction, "Touch the rock."

5. **Figure-Ground**
   Present a "busy" picture with many visual distractions. Ask each child to find the rock.

6. **Visual Closure**
   Partially cover each of several pictures with paper. Ask each child to find the picture of the rock.

7. **Function**
   Ask, "What do we do with rocks?"

8. **Association**
   Ask, "What goes with the rock?" Use pictures or objects including sand, dirt, etc., with several unrelated objects or pictures.

9. **Imitate Verbalization**
   Present a rock and ask, "What is this? Say 'Rock'." The child will imitate "Rock."

10. **Verbalize Label**
    Present a rock and ask, "What is this?" The child will respond, "Rock."

11. **Concept Enrichment**
    Discuss various sizes, weights, and colors of rocks. Discuss concepts of soft and hard.

Music
1. Sing to the tune of "Three Blind Mice":

Rocks are hard	(Pound fist on hand 3 times.)
Rocks are hard	(Pound fist on hand 3 times.)
Some are very big	(Make a big circle.)
And some are very small	(Make a small circle.)
But little or big or small or large	(Gesture appropriately.)
Rocks are hard.	

2. Sing to the tune of "Paw Paw Patch":
   We're picking up rocks and putting them in our pockets
   We're picking up rocks and putting them in our pockets
   We're picking up rocks and putting them in our pockets
   Big rocks, little rocks, hard rocks all. *(Gesture big, little, pound fist on hand 3 times.)*

Art
1. Have children paint rocks with tempera paint. Some children may wish to glue or paint faces on some of larger rocks. Use paint, Elmer's glue and felt, and/or other materials. Use as door stop, paper weight or decoration. Shellac will seal the paint.

2. Let children make a "fossil" by pushing a leaf or shell against a smooth lump of clay. Let dry.
3. Shake rock salt in a mixture of powdered paint and water. Let the children use the colored rock salt for a collage.

Snack
Let children eat rock candy.

Fine Motor
1. Have children use pincer grasp (thumb and index finger) to drop tiny rocks (gravel) into tin cans.
2. Let children cover rocks with glue with fingers, and then sprinkle glitter on rocks.
3. Let children break up rocks using a hammer.
4. Have children wash rocks and line them up on a line (masking tape on table) until they dry.

Games
1. Start a terrarium (or call it a house for plants). Let children put small rocks in the bottom layer and larger rocks as decorations in the terrarium. Have children show where the rocks are, or let children put rocks in terrarium.
2. Have the class start a rock collection: take a field trip and hunt for different kinds of rocks. Take rocks back to class and put in a big, open box, where children can re-examine rocks.
3. Hide glittered rocks and let children have a treasure hunt.

Storytelling
Tell a story with large sequence cards about rocks.
Then let children arrange cards and tell story. Example:
1. Boy rides bike.
2. Boy rides bike and runs into rock.
3. Boy falls off bike.
4. Boy picks self up and gets on bike again.

Gross Motor
1. Give ½ egg carton to each child. Let each child "Find a rock for each section" on nature walk.
2. Have children throw rocks into a creek, puddle of water, or plastic wading pool. Watch the splash and the air bubbles come out.
3. Arrange stepping "stones" on the floor or rug. Have the children cross the "creek" (maybe snack will be across the creek). The stepping stones may be changed from short steps to longer ones where jumping is necessary.

Cognitive
1. Place a can of pebbles on the table for each child in group. Have each child in turn roll dice (or turn over a card) and take out of the can the number on the dice or card. The first empty can "wins."
2. Have children arrange rocks from small to large.
3. Have children add rocks to a pan of water to see the level of water rise. (Note air bubbles as you drop in rocks).
4. Have children match rocks according to feel, color, size, etc. Note that as the characteristic on which the sorting is done changes, rocks change groups.

Enrichment
1. Together Activity: On the sand table, have the children make a stone path going from a small house to another house or a "pond." (Wet sand and draw the boundaries of the path. Paths may change with different groups. Keep sand moist so the stones can be pushed down in it.)
2. Have children weigh objects on a balance scale using rocks of fairly equal size to balance scale. Note that the doll weighs 10 rocks, etc. Relate that to the English system of stones.

Field Trip
1. Take a nature hike and have the children collect rocks.
2. Visit a museum where rocks and stones are on display.

Lesson 3: Sand

Unit Group Lesson

1. Match Concrete Objects
Present two containers of sand. Say, "This is sand." Ask each child in turn to put the sand with the sand. Present containers of irrelevant materials such as flour, sugar, etc. from which (s)he must select sand to match. Gradually increase the number of irrelevant materials presented.

2. Discriminate Objects
Present container of several materials. Have each child touch the sand in response to verbal direction, "Touch the sand."

3. Match Pictures
Present several pictures of common objects. Have each child match the pictures of the sand.

4. Discriminate Pictures
Present a group of several unrelated pictures of objects. Have each child touch the picture of the sand in response to verbal direction, "Touch the sand."

5. Figure-Ground
Present a "busy" picture with many visual distractions. Ask each child to find the sand.

6. Visual Closure
Partially cover each of several pictures with paper. Ask each child to find the picture of the sand.

7. Function
Ask, "What do we do with sand?"

8. Association
Ask, "What goes with the sand?" Use pictures or objects including dirt, plants, rocks, etc., with several unrelated objects or pictures.

9. Imitate Verbalization
Present sand and ask, "What is this? Say 'Sand'." Child will imitate "Sand."

10. Verbalize Label
Present sand and ask, "What is this?" The child will respond, "Sand."

11. Concept Enrichment
Discuss: Where do we find sand? How is sand different from rock? What are some uses of sand?

Music
1.   Sing to the tune of "Here We Go 'Round The Mulberry Bush":
  Verse 1: This is the way we pour the sand. *(Use plastic cups.)*
  Verse 2: This is the way we draw in the sand. *(Use stick for drawing.)*
  Verse 3: This is the way we make sand pies. *(Use aluminum pie pan.)*

2.   Sing to the tune of "How Dry I Am":
        Verse 1: We play in sand
                  With both our hands
                  And make some cakes
                  For us to bake.
        Verse 2: We make big hills
                  They are so big
                  I think that they
                  Will touch the sky.

Art

1.   On construction paper write names of children and/or draw geometric shapes with magic marker. Have children cover lines with glue and sprinkle sand on top of glue. Let stand. Shake sand off paper gently.
2.   Have children color sand with tempera paint powder. Each child pours sand into a jar. Add tempera paint powder and shake jar with top on. Put sand in open boxes, let children draw in sand.
3.   Let children add different colors of tempera paint powder to sand or use above sand. Pour layers of different colors into baby food jar. Fill completely to top. Makes a pretty paper weight.

Snack

Eat sugar cookies baked in Fine Motor #5 today. Sprinkle with sugar. Discuss differences and similarities between sugar and sand.

Fine Motor

1.   Have children pour sand from one container to another in sandbox. Let children use scoop-type tools.
2.   Let children make sand castles in sandbox.
3.   Make Sand Timers: Have children glue tops of 2 identical lids together. (Baby food jars are great!) Punch holes in lids with a thin nail (alternate sides in which holes are punched). Let children add sand to one jar. Screw lids on and turn jars over. (See fig. 23C.)
4.   Have children use sand paper to "sand" wooden blocks donated by lumber yard and paste pictures on block. Shellac for paperweight.
5.   Have children help make sugar cookies for snack today.

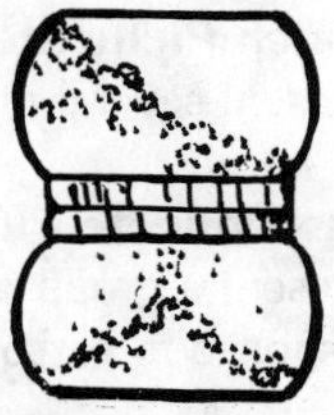

Fig. 23C

Games

"Tracks in the Sand": Fill a plastic dishpan with damp sand and have 4-5 cookie cutters. One child uses cookie cutters to make "tracks" or imprints in the sand. Another child guesses which cookie cutter was used.

Storytelling

Materials needed: 2 large pans, sand and water

Use dripping water on a sand castle to tell the story of "a boy who built a special castle for a lovely princess." The castle was built at the beach where the ocean waves sent water up to the castle. Finally, the waves washed the beautiful castle away. The little boy was very sad until he heard the lovely princess whisper, "Don't worry; now you can build another castle. Who would like to build another castle for our secret princess?"

Discuss how the water washed away the castle. Ask children if this has ever happened to them at the beach. Discuss the difference between houses of rock and sand.

Gross Motor

1.   Let children fill, carry and pour out buckets of sand into a wagon. They pull wagon, unload with scoops.
2.   Fill 2-liter plastic bottles with 2 cups of sand poured through a funnel. Children may help. Cap. Arrange outdoors and play "Bowling."

Cognitive

1.   Paint around clear plastic bottles with red nail polish. Have children fill to that line with sand, using funnel.

2.   Have children copy shapes, numbers or letters in moist sand with finger or stick.

Enrichment

Make sand letters for the children. Outline the letters of the alphabet or each child's name on paper. Have children spread with glue and sprinkle with sand. Children can use these tactile letters over and over again.

Field Trip

Take a nature hike and have children collect sand while hiking.

Lesson 4: Ant

Unit Group Lesson

1.   **Match Concrete Objects**
Present two plastic ants. Say, "This is an ant." Ask each child in turn to put the ant with the ant. Gradually increase number of irrelevant objects from which (s)he must select the ant to match.

2.   **Discriminate Objects**
Present several objects. Have each child touch the ant in response to the verbal direction, "Touch the ant."

3.   **Match Pictures**
Present several pictures of common objects. Have each child match the pictures of the ants.

4.   **Discriminate Pictures**
Present a group of several unrelated pictures of objects. Have each child touch the picture of the ant in response to verbal direction, "Touch the ant."

5.   **Figure-Ground**
Present a "busy" picture with many visual distractions. Ask each child to find the ant.

6.   **Visual Closure**
Partially cover each of several pictures with paper. Ask each child to find the picture of the ant.

7.   **Function**
Ask, "What do ants do?"

8.   **Association**
Ask, "What goes with an ant?" Use pictures or objects including ground, sand, ant hill, etc., with several unrelated objects or pictures.

9.   **Imitate Verbalization**
Present an ant and ask, "What is this? Say, 'Ant'." The child will imitate "Ant."

10.   **Verbalize Label**
Present an ant and ask, "What is this?" The child will respond, "Ant."

11.   **Concept Enrichment**
Discuss where ants live, what they eat, how they work, and move.

Music

Sing to the tune of "Frere Jacques":

Ants are working, ants are working
Very fast - Very fast
Busy, busy ants - Busy, busy ants
Don't be last!- Don't be last!

Art

1. Cut a 3-section piece of styrofoam egg carton for each child. Have children make ants by using pipe cleaners for 6 legs and two small antennaes.

2. Have children dip their thumbs on a sponge of water color and make thumbprint ants.

Snack

1. Make and eat "Ants on a Log." Have children spread peanut butter on celery and drop on raisin "ants."

2. Make and eat "Ants in the Snow." Have children spread cream cheese on crackers "poke" in raisins for ants.

Fine Motor

1. Make cardboard puzzles of an ant. Vary difficulty by varying number and size of pieces.

2. Make a path tracing activity on blackboard. Ant moves along "path" from an ant hill to crumbs or cookie.

Games

Have children play "Cootie." Simplify rules for younger or developmentally delayed children.
("Cootie" can also be used as a fine motor activity, giving children all the parts to assemble the cootie).

Storytelling

Read all or part of Ant and Bee.

Gross Motor

1. Children line up across room from teacher. Crawl as fast as possible to teacher who has treat for them.

2. Sing to the tune of "Frere Jacques" and have children act out "Ant action" as in Music:

Ants are working	(Move fast.)
Ants are working	(Move fast.)
Very fast	(Move very fast.)
Very fast	(Move very fast.)
Busy, busy ants	
Busy, busy ants	
Don't be last! Don't be last!	

Cognitive

1. Make an ant ranch. Put a paper towel tube in a jar (to keep the ants at the edge) and fill jar and tube nearly to the top with sand. Punch holes in the lid. Dab honey on a piece of cheese cloth and put on ground. When ants are on it, put them in the jar, outside the paper tube. Put another piece of cheesecloth over top of jar. Put the whole thing in a dark paperbag for 2 days. Feed ants honey, lettuce, bread and a few water drops once a week by placing on top of sand outside paper tube. The paper tube prevents the ants from building their tunnels in the center of the jar where they could not be seen. (See fig. 23D.)

2. Make ant cue sheets. Put the picture of an ant at the top of the page and ants and distractors below. Have the children mark all the ants. Vary the levels of difficulty according to the levels of the children.

Enrichment

1. Discuss organization of an ant colony.

2. Have everyone count sections of an ant's body, ant legs, etc.

Fig. 23D

Field Trip

Take a nature hike and go on an ant hunt.

Unit 24: Birds

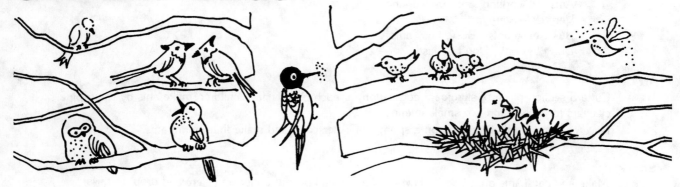

A developmental assessment should determine the functional levels of each child. Individual expectations are based on the assessment results.

Lesson 1: Bird

Unit Group Lesson

1. **Match Concrete Objects**
   Present two birds. Say, "This is a bird." Ask each child in turn to put the bird with the bird. Gradually increase number of irrelevant objects from which (s)he must select bird to match.

2. **Discriminate Objects**
   Present several objects. Have each child touch the bird in response to verbal direction, "Touch the bird."

3. **Match Pictures**
   Present several pictures of common objects. Have each child match the pictures of the birds.

4. **Discriminate Pictures**
   Present a group of several unrelated pictures of objects. Have each child touch the picture of the bird in response to verbal direction, "Touch the bird."

5. **Figure-Ground**
   Present a "busy" picture with many visual distractions. Ask each child to find the bird.

6. **Visual Closure**
   Partially cover each of several pictures with paper. Ask each child to find the picture of the bird.

7. **Function**
   Ask, "What do we do with birds?" or "What do birds do?"

8. **Association**
   Ask, "What goes with the bird?" Use pictures or objects including eggs, nest, feathers, etc. with several unrelated objects or pictures.

9. **Imitate Verbalization**
   Present a bird and ask, "What is this? Say, 'Bird'." The child will imitate "Bird."

10. **Verbalize Label**
    Present a bird and ask, "What is this?" The child will respond, "Bird."

11. **Concept Enrichment**
     Discuss homes, sounds, names, colors, sizes and foods of various birds.

Music

1. Sing to the tune of "Ten Little Indians":
    Flying, flying, flying birds
    Flying, flying, flying birds
    Flying, flying, flying birds
    Fly all away.

2. Sing to the tune of "Row, Row, Row Your Boat":
    Fly, fly, fly away,
    Happy as can be.
    Oh fly, fly, fly away,
    Then fly back to me.

Art

1. Make cardboard outline of bird and have each child spatter paint over it onto construction paper. To prevent excess over spray, place the work in a shallow box.

2. Have children cut blue, red, and brown construction paper strips. Then give each child an outline of bluebird (redbird, etc.). Model spreading of paste all over bird. Place pieces of construction paper on bird to make his feathers, wings, and tail. Real feathers may be substituted for construction paper strips.

3. Help the children make "binoculars" out of toilet tissue tubes or rolled construction paper taped or glued together. Fasten string or yarn to hang around child's neck. They can take a walk for "bird watching."

4. Have each child make a bird's nest under a pictured bird by drawing lines for the nest with brown crayons.

Snack

1. Have children prepare peanut butter balls rolled in roasted sesame or sunflower seeds. Serve from a bird feeder. Each child must "chirp-chirp" before "bird food" is offered.

2. Play tapes of bird songs softly during snack time.

Fine Motor

1. Make bird puzzles with five basic parts: head, body, two wings and tail. Divide them into two or more pieces. Depending upon the child's puzzle-skill level, give her a puzzle with two, three, four, five or more pieces.

2. Make path tracing activities of "Take a bird to his house." and "Take a bird to a nest." Make a variety of levels of difficulty depending upon the skills of the children.

3. Play record or cassette tape of bird sounds and have the children snap their fingers when they hear the bird sounds.

Games

1. Have the children form a circle and lead this activity:
    Two little bluebirds on the wall
    One is named Peter and the other's named Paul.
    Fly away Peter, fly away Paul,   *(Flap arms and fly away.)*
    Come back, Peter, come back, Paul.   *(Flap arms and return to circle.)*
    (Substitute other names for Peter and Paul.)

2. Play "Blue Bird, Blue Bird In and Out Your Window." Divide children into pairs and have them form a circle with the partners joining hands to make an arch. The "blue bird" moves in and out of the arches as the song is sung. On last line of sing, the "blue bird" is "caught" by the pair nearest him.
    Song: Blue bird, blue bird in and out our window.
           Blue bird, blue bird in and out our window.

Blue bird, blue bird in and out our window.
Oh, jolly, what a good boy (girl).

3. Make up lotto game. Have same pictures of birds and other animals on board. "Find bird and put bird on bird."

Storytelling

1. With a flannel board and cut outs recite this from *Creative Movements for the Developing Child.*

All the little birds are asleep in their nest,　　　*(Children seated in circle*
All the little birds are taking a rest,　　　*pretend to sleep.)*
They do not sing, they do not eat;
Everything is quiet on their street.

Then came the mother bird and tapped then om　　　*(Teacher taps head of*
　the head;　　　*some of the children.)*
They opened up one little eye and this is what was
　said;
"Come little birdies, it's time to learn to fly.
Come little birdies, fly way up to the sky."

Fly, fly, oh, fly away, fly, fly, fly.
Fly, fly, oh, fly away, fly away so high.　　　*(Selected children wave*
Fly, fly, oh, fly away, birds can fly best.　　　*arms as they "fly" about*
Fly, fly, oh, fly away, now fly back to your nest.　　　*room.)*

2. Fingerplay: Adapted from *Creative Movement for the Developing Child.*

This little bird is going to bed.　　　*(Place forefinger in opposite palm.)*
Down in the nest he puts his head.　　　*(Turn finger over on side.)*
He covers himself with feathers so　　　*(Put three fingers and thumb over*
　tight.　　　*forefinger.)*
This is the way he sleeps all night.
In the morning, he opens his eyes.
Back come his feathers, ready to fly.　　　*(Make fingers wiggle.)*
He hops out of the nest all dressed.　　　*(Hop finger out of palm and run up arm.)*
Then off to fly and play with the rest.　　　*(Press together thumb and other fingers*
　　　several times. Move arm up and down and
　　　around to look as if flying away.)

Gross Motor

1. Have the children hop, "fly", walk, run and move like birds.
2. Have the children jump into the "nest." Mark an area on the floor with a rug or tape. Have the children stand on the edge and jump into and out of the nest.

Cognitive

1. Have the children match, sort, and classify birds' feathers by size or color.
2. Have the children match different types of birds.
3. Make birds in several different sizes. Have the children sequence them by size.

Enrichment

1. Help the children match bird eggs to the proper birds.
2. Help the children match male to female birds of the same type.
3. Help the children cut bird shapes and wings. Let them glue on eyes and a bill to the body and string to the center of the wing. Fold the wing and staple on the bird. Let the children run to make the birds "fly." When the birds are not flying they can sit on limbs in the classroom windows or tables. (See fig. 24B.)

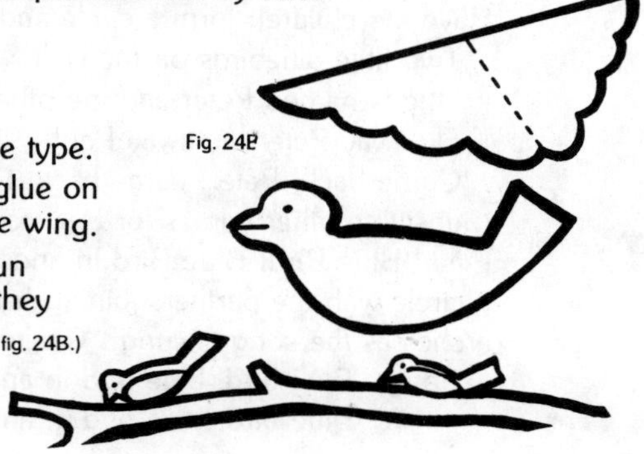

Fig. 24B

Lesson 2: Bird House

Unit Group Lesson

1. **Match Concrete Objects**
Present two bird homes. Say, "This is a bird home." Ask each child in turn to put the bird home with the bird home. Gradually increase number of irrelevant objects from which (s)he must select bird home to match.

2. **Discriminate Objects**
Present several objects. Have each child touch the bird home in response to verbal direction, "Touch the bird home."

3. **Match Pictures**
Present several pictures of common objects. Have each child match the pictures of the bird homes.

4. **Discriminate Pictures**
Present a group of several unrelated pictures of objects. Have each child touch the picture of the bird home in response to verbal direction, "Touch the bird home."

5. **Figure-Ground**
Present a "busy" picture with many visual distractions. Ask each child to find the bird home.

6. **Visual Closure**
Partially cover each of several pictures with paper. Ask each child to find the picture of the bird home.

7. **Function**
Ask, "What does a bird home do?"

8. **Association**
Ask, "what goes with the bird home?" Use pictures or objects including nest, bird home, bird, etc. with several unrelated objects or pictures.

9. **Imitate Verbalization**
Present a bird home and ask, "What is this? Say, 'Bird feeder'." The child will imitate "Bird feeder."

10. **Verbalize Label**
Present a bird home and ask, "What is this?" The child will respond, "Bird home."

11. **Concept Enrichment**
Discuss various types of bird nests and how they are built by the birds; how the bird eggs are placed in the nest; and how the baby birds are fed in the nest. Discuss the differences between the bird nest and a bird house made by a person. Emphasize that the birds make nests inside the wooden houses.

Music
1. Sing to the tune of "Did You Ever See A Lassie?":
   Did you ever see a bird home,
   A bird home, a bird home.
   Did you ever see a bird home?
   Where some birds do live?

Watch me draw a bird home,
A bird home, a bird home.
Watch me draw a bird home,
Then you can have a turn.

Draw on blackboard or big paper. Add hole in middle for bird to fly in.

2.　　Sing to the tune of "Ten Little Indians": (Use flannel birds or fingers to count.)

　　　1 little, 2 little, 3 little birdies
　　　4 little, 5 little, 6 little birdies
　　　7 little, 8 little, 9 little birdies
　　　10 little singing birdies.

Art

1.　　Have the children make a "bird cage." Let them wrap an air-filled balloon with yarn dipped in starch. When dry, pop and remove the balloon. Hang a paper bird inside.

2.　　Let the children collect small sticks, dried grass, etc., and make a pretend nest. Cut plastic gallon milk carton in half and let the children line it with grass, small sticks, etc. and add cotton balls for eggs.

3.　　Let the children make a nest of clay, let dry and paint with tempera paint.

4.　　Have each child make a bird's nest under a pictured bird by drawing lines for the nest with brown crayons. (See fig. 24A.)

Fig. 24A

Snack

Make and eat "bird nests." Melt chocolate or butterscotch chips and stir in chinese noodles. Shape into bird nests. Let cool. Eat.

Fine Motor

1.　　Have children cut out pictures of birds from books, magazines, etc.

2.　　Outline parts to a bird house and color-cued each part (example: triangle outlined in red). Have children glue pre-cut, color cued triangle, square, or circle on appropriate outline. Demonstrate assembly of bird house such as a red triangle on the red triangle outline. (See fig. 24C.)

3.　　Use several large sheets of paper (shelf paper) and have children paste a picture of a bird house in the middle and then paste on colored birds. Have each child draw a line from bird to bird house without bumping into other birds. (To individualize have some children "fly" the birds to the house; others use a dotted path made by the teacher from bird to bird house.)

4.　　Have the children participate in a bulletin board activity. Draw an outline of a bird nest and have children color the nest brown. Have children paste pre-cut paper eggs in nest. Model, emphasizing concept "in."

Fig. 24C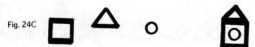

Games

1.　　Turn an old card table upside down for a bird nest. Put in some soft blankets. Let the children sit in the "nest."

2.　　Rake leaves into a "nest" outside. Let the children sit in the "nest," "fly to get some worms," etc.

Storytelling

Use flannel board and cutouts to tell this poem.

Five little blue birds sitting in the nest	*(Hold up five fingers.)*
One flew away and then there were four.	*(Fold down one finger.)*
Four little blue birds sitting in a nest	*(Hold up four fingers.)*
One flew away and then there were three.	*(Fold down one finger.)*
Three little blue birds sitting in a nest	*(Hold up three fingers.)*
One flew away and then there were two.	*(Fold down one finger.)*
Two little blue birds sitting in the sun	*(Hold up two fingers.)*
One flew away and then there was one.	*(Fold down one finger.)*
One little blue bird sitting all alone	*(Hold up one finger.)*
One flew away and then there was none.	

Gross Motor

1.   Make a bird house out of a cardboard box with a big opening. Have the children toss beanbags through the opening.
2.   Make up rhymes for baby birds to act out:
     Little birds, little birds, fly to the swings.
     Little birds, little birds, fly and flap your wings.
     Have the children act out the movements.

Cognitive

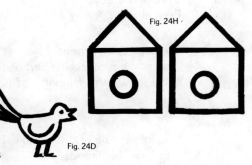

Fig. 24H

Fig. 24D

1.   Sort pictures of bird houses by color or type.
2.   Cut out bird shape. Let the children draw eyes, make feet, add marks for feathers. Have children identify the bird parts as they make them. Then have the birds sit on a string like they do outdoors. (See fig. 24D.)
3.   Make a bird house on flannel board. Have the children assemble parts. Talk about the different shapes such as circle, triangle, square. Make several bird houses and count them. Then give the children flannel board cut outs of birds and have them put one bird with each bird house and then put two birds with each bird house. Continue. (See fig. 24H.)

Enrichment

1.   Help the children make a bird nest builder. Wrap tape around the edges of a 6 inch square of wire mesh. Let children weave yarn, pine straw, pine needles, and straw in mesh. Hang outside and let birds gather materials for nest building. Birds are afraid of bright colors so use neutral colors.
2.   Bring in bird houses made from wood and "houses" the birds made (nests). Talk about the materials used for each. Emphasize that birds make nests inside the wooden houses.

Lesson 3: Bird Feeder

Unit Group Lesson

1.   **Match Concrete Objects**
     Present two bird feeders. Say, "This is a bird feeder." Ask each child in turn to put the bird feeder with the bird feeder. Gradually increase number of irrelevant objects from which (s)he must select bird feeder to match.

2.   **Discriminate Objects**
     Present several objects. Have each child touch the bird feeder in response to verbal direction, "Touch the bird feeder."

3.   **Match Pictures**
     Present several pictures of common objects. Have each child match the pictures of the bird feeders.

4.   **Discriminate Pictures**
     Present a group of several unrelated pictures of objects. Have each child touch the picture of the bird feeder in response to verbal direction, "Touch the bird feeder."

5.   **Figure-Ground**
     Present a "busy" picture with many visual distractions. Ask each child to find the bird feeder.

6.   **Visual Closure**
     Partially cover each of several pictures with paper. Ask each child to find the picture of the bird feeder.

7.   **Function**
     Ask, "What do we do with a bird feeder?"

8.   **Association**

Ask, "What goes with the bird feeder?" Use pictures or objects including seeds, peanut butter, worms, etc. with several unrelated objects or pictures.

9.   **Imitate Verbalization**

Present a bird feeder and ask, "What is this? Say, 'Bird feeder'." The child will imitate "Bird feeder."

10.   **Verbalize Label**

Present a bird feeder and ask, "What is this?" The child will respond, "Bird feeder."

11.   **Concept Enrichment**

Discuss the foods which birds eat (berries, seeds, worms, nuts, etc.). Discuss the need for bird feeders in the snowy winter months. Discuss placement of bird feeders for "bird-watching."

Music

Sing to the tune of "Row, Row, Row Your Boat":
   Eat, eat, eat the seeds
   Birds of red and blue
   Eat the seeds both big and small
   We have here for you.

Art

1.   Cut shape of bird from corrugated paper or any rough-textured materials. Place blank paper on top of bird shape. Have children rub with blunt side of crayon or chalk and a bird picture will appear.
2.   Have children trace around a cardboard bird shape on construction paper, put glue on outlined bird, place seeds on glue to make a bird picture and decorate around the bird.
3.   Help children make a bird feeder. Punch holes in bottoms of paper cups. Knot string or tie paper clip on end, hole for hanging. Have children spread peanut butter on outside of cup with fingers, roll the cup in bird seed and hang outside for birds.
4.   Let the children make necklaces of round oat cereal (like Cheerios), wear, take outside at playtime and hang on the limbs for birds.

Snack

Make "Kid Feeders." Spread apple slices with peanut butter and roll in topping. (wheat germ, raisins, ground nuts, sesame seeds, etc.). Serve from bird feeder. Encourage children to talk like birds ("Tweet, tweet") before receiving snack.

Fine Motor

Fig. 24E

1.   Let the children nail bottle caps into wood to use for bird feeders. (See fig. 24E.)
2.   Have the children mix bird seed, suet, or peanut butter with corn meal. (This keeps the peanut butter from sticking to the bird's pallet). Place mixture in a pine cone and hang from a tree.
3.   Cut plastic milk cartons (gallon-sized) to make bird feeder. Have the children attach wire or string for hanging and fill with bird seed. (See fig. 24F.)
4.   Let the children make bird pudding using ½ pound of lard, 1 cup peanut butter and enough oatmeal to make "workable." Birds love it.

Fig. 24F

Games

1.   Ask all the children to cover their eyes while you hide a toy or paper bird. Tell one child to find the bird. When she gets close, she will hear "tweet-tweet" (you and class make bird sounds). Have a helper go along if two are needed to find bird.
2.   Have the children act out and recite this action rhyme:
   Little birds, little birds fly to the wall

Little birds, little birds fly back all
Little birds, little birds hop to the door
Little birds, little birds sit on the floor.

Storytelling

Tell a story of a hungry little bird who flew and flew looking for some food. Finally, she came to your school and found the feeders that (child's name), (child's name), etc. had made for hungry birds. She ate and ate. She was so happy that she sang a lovely song for the children.

Gross Motor

1. Hide paper bird eggs around the playground so the children will have to climb, run, etc. to find them. Let the children have an egg hunt while singing to tune of "Oh-Dear! What Can The Matter Be?":
    Oh, dear, where are the birdie eggs?
    Oh, dear, where are the birdie eggs?
    Oh, dear, where are the birdie eggs?
    Hiding all over our room.
2. Have children climb to hang and fill bird feeders.

Cognitive

1. Make a bird feeder for each window in the classroom.
2. Gather materials to make a bird feeder for each child (2 jar lids, one nail, doughnut, etc.). Punch holes through the center of 2 jar lids. Have the children put a nail through the hole of one lid. Place doughnut onto nail. Then place other lid onto nail. Bend end of nail up. Tie and hang. Emphasize that each child used one doughnut, two lids and one nail for her feeder. (See fig. 24G.)

Fig 24G

3. Make a cue sheet with a bird feeder at the top and other types of "feeders" such as dishes, dog dishes, horse troughs, etc. and identical bird feeders on the bottom. Have the children mark all of the bird feeders.

Enrichment

1. Grow birdseed on a sponge and let the children cut it with scissors.
2. Make bird feeders and put a numeral on each roof. Have the children count out the correct number of birds for each feeder.

Children's Related Records
ADVENTURES IN SOUND (MH)
"Bluebird" from FOLK SONG CARNIVAL (EA)
"Birds In the Circles" from EASY DOES IT (EA)
"High & Low" from LEARNING BASIC SKILLS-VOC. (EA)
"Birds" from LEARNING BASIC SKILLS I (EA)
"Sammy" from GETTING TO KNOW MYSELF
"A Bird's Quest" from RAINDROPS (MH)
"What Flies?" from MY STREET BEGINS AT MY HOUSE
"Sing a Song of Sixpence" from NURSERY RHYMES (SCHOL)

Children's Related Books
Eastman, P.D. THE BEST NEST. New York: Random House, 1968.
Holl, Adelaide. THE REMARKABLE EGG. New York: Lothrop, Lee & Shepard Co., 1968.
Hutchins, Pat. GOOD-NIGHT OWL. New York: Macmillian Publishing Co., 1972.
Krauss, Ruth. THE HAPPY EGG. New York: J. Philip O'Hara, 1967.
Wildsmith, Brian. BIRDS BY BRIAN WILDSMITH. New York: Oxford University Press, 1980.

Unit 25: Spring

A developmental assessment should determine the functional levels of each child. Individual expectations are based on the assessment results.

Lesson 1: Flower

Unit Group Lesson

1. **Match Concrete Objects**
   Present two flowers. Say, "This is a flower." Ask each child in turn to put the flower with the flower. Gradually increase number of irrelevant objects from which (s)he must select a flower to match.

2. **Discriminate Objects**
   Present several objects. Have each child touch the flower in response to verbal direction, "Touch the flower."

3. **Match Pictures**
   Present several pictures of common objects. Have each child match the pictures of the flower.

4. **Discriminate Pictures**
   Present a group of several unrelated pictures of objects. Have each child touch the picture of the flower in response to verbal direction, "Touch the flower."

5. **Figure-Ground**
   Present a "busy" picture with many visual distractions. Ask each child to find the flower.

6. **Visual Closure**
   Partially cover each of several pictures with paper. Ask each child to find the picture of the flower.

7. **Function**
   Ask, "What do we do with a flower?"

8. **Association**
   Ask, "What goes with the flower?" Use pictures or objects including stem, leaf, petals, bee, butterfly, etc., with several unrelated objects or pictures.

9. **Imitate Verbalization**
   Present a flower and ask, "What is this? Say, 'Flower'." The child will imitate "Flower."

10. **Verbalize Label**
    Present a flower and ask, "What is this?" The child will respond, "Flower."

11. **Concept Enrichment**

Discuss the names, colors, and sizes of various flowers. Discuss the parts of a flower such as stem, leaf, and petals.

Music

1. Sing to the tune of "Here We Go Round the Mulberry Bush":

   Verse 1: This is the way we plant the seed,   *(Stoop down to "plant seed.")*
          Plant the seed, plant the seed.   *(Stoop down to "plant seed.")*
          This is the way we plant the seed.   *(Stoop down to "plant seed.")*
          For flowers so pretty and fair.   *(Cup hands like a pretty flower.)*

   Verse 2: Down comes the rain to water the   *(Move fingers from sky to ground.)*
          seed.

   Verse 3: This is the way the blossoms   *(Move slowly from squat to upright position
          grow.   with hands over head.)*

   Verse 4: This is the way we cut the   *(Use pointer and middle fingers to make
          stems.   cutting motion.)*

   Verse 5: This is the way we make a   *(Make vase with circle of fingers. Place
          bouquet.   "stems" in vase for bouquet.)*

Art

1. Give the children waxed paper and let them put flowers between two pieces. Press with a warm iron and place against glass windows.
2. Have children trace or draw flowers with crayons. Mix food coloring with water. Let children brush solution lightly over crayon picture for a lovely crayon resist! The paint colors the parts where there is no crayon.
3. Have children cut stems and leaves of green, paste on paper and add a "flower" of colored cupcake paper or balls of tissue paper.
4. Place rose petals in a bag and let the children smell them and handle them. Give each child a card with a large dot in the center. Let the children arrange and paste petals around the dot. (See fig. 25A.)

Snack

1. Roast sunflower seeds and serve.
2. Put bouquets of flowers on each table.

Fig. 25A

Fine Motor

1. Have each child assemble a puzzle of a flower. Vary the level of difficulty with the level of each child.
2. Give each child a piece of paper and have him make vertical lines with a green crayon. Give him flower seals to place at the top of each "stem" (line).
3. Have the children make flowers by punching a hole in center of one colored pre-cut egg carton section. Insert different colored pipe cleaners and put these flowers in a vase or tall glasses.
4. Let each child use an "eye dropper" to drop tempera paint onto a wet area of paper. The colors will "run" and blend into "fuzzy" pictures of flowers.

Games

1. Play a pretend game by having each child curl up on floor. One child comes around with a watering can and waters each flower (child). Each time the flower is watered, child stands up a little more.
2. Bring in potted flowers, for example: geraniums. Let each child have a turn during the week to help water the flowers.
3. Children pass large plastic flower from child to child while music plays. When the music stops, the child holding the flower must leave the circle. The last child (winner) gets to wear the "magic" flower for the rest of the day.
4. Sing and play to the tune of "Ring Around the Rosie":

   Ring around the rosie   *(Place plastic or real rose in center of
   Pocketful of posies   circle.)*
   Rainstorm, rainstorm   *(Walk in circle.)*
   We all fall down.   *(Hands move up and down.)*
                                           (All fall to floor.)

Storytelling

Make up a sequence story of a seed put in the ground. The rain rains on it; the sun shines on it. The roots go down into the earth, and a green stem breaks through the ground. The stem gets bigger and bigger. One day a bud appears and then it opens into a flower. Tell the story with pictures and modify the detail according to the level and attention span of the children. Mix the pictures and have the children put them in the correct order.

Gross Motor

Have the children make a flower for activities. Place a large circle on the floor. Give out petals to the children and let them take turns putting petals around the center. (Petals must slip under the circle.) After the flower is "complete," use with the following activities: (See fig. 25B.)

Fig. 25B

   a. Jump over the flower.
   b. Sit beside the flower.
   c. Put your hand on top of the flower.
   d. Slide your foot between the petals.
   e. Jump on the flower.
      Jump on the flower and clap your hands.
      Jump on the flower and pat your head.
      Jump on the flower and bend your knees.
      Jump on the flower, rubbing your nose, etc.

Cognitive

1. Put different flower shapes on clothes hangers. Provide a mixed "garden" of flowers on table or in a box lid. Have the children sort flowers to match cue on hanger. (Vary by colors, sizes of same flower) and hang the flower on clothes hanger with clip clothespins. (See fig. 25C.)

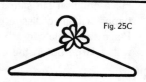

Fig. 25C

2. Make stem and flower cards for matching. Have cards with 1-5 stems and others with flowers. Children match cards with the same number of stems as flowers. (For higher level children add a 3rd set of cards with numerals to match.)

3. Plant flower seeds that grow fast. Observe and discuss their growth.

Enrichment

1. Help the children make individual pots of flowers. (See fig. 25D.)
   a. Use brown paper bags for the pots. (You may draw heavy outline of pot for cutting.)
   b. Decorate the pot.
   c. Add paper stems cut from green paper.
   d. Cut leaves, fold, and glue on stems.
   e. Add flowers of colored paper or shapes with wadded tissue in color.
   f. Line up pots in rows on the bulletin board or a wall.
   g. Add a giant sprinkling can, painted by the teacher.
   h. Children cut out water drops of blue paper to fall on the plants.

Fig. 25E

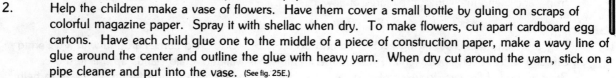

2. Help the children make a vase of flowers. Have them cover a small bottle by gluing on scraps of colorful magazine paper. Spray it with shellac when dry. To make flowers, cut apart cardboard egg cartons. Have each child glue one to the middle of a piece of construction paper, make a wavy line of glue around the center and outline the glue with heavy yarn. When dry cut around the yarn, stick on a pipe cleaner and put into the vase. (See fig. 25E.)

Field Trip

1. Visit a nursery where potted flowers are sold.
2. Visit flower garden.
3. Take a walk to find flowers beside houses.
4. Take a wild flower walk.

Fig. 25D

Visitor

Have a mother arrange or pot flowers.

Unit Group Lesson

1. **Match Concrete Objects**
   Present two bunnies. Say, "This is a bunny." Ask each child in turn to put the bunny with the bunny. Gradually increase number of irrelevant objects from which (s)he must select a bunny to match.

2. **Discriminate Objects**
   Present several objects. Have each child touch the bunny in response to verbal direction, "Touch the bunny."

3. **Match Pictures**
   Present several pictures of common objects. Have each child match the pictures of the bunnies.

4. **Discriminate Pictures**
   Present a group of several unrelated pictures of objects. Have each child touch the picture of the bunny in response to verbal direction, "Touch the bunny."

5. **Figure-Ground**
   Present a "busy" picture with many visual distractions. Ask each child to find the bunny.

6. **Visual Closure**
   Partially cover each of several pictures with paper. Ask each child to find the picture of the bunny.

7. **Function**
   Ask, "What does a bunny do?"

8. **Association**
   Ask, "What goes with the bunny?" Use pictures or objects including carrots, lettuce, Easter eggs, etc., with several unrelated objects or pictures.

9. **Imitate Verbalization**
   Present a bunny and ask, "What is this? Say, 'Bunny'." The child will imitate "Bunny."

10. **Verbalize Label**
    Present a bunny and ask, "What is this?" The child will respond, "Bunny."

11. **Concept Enrichment**
    Discuss Easter bunny. Let the children relate this understanding of the Easter bunny.

Music
1. Sing to the tune of "Frere Jacques":
   Bunny rabbit, bunny rabbit
   Hop, hop, hop,
   Hop, hop, hop.
   Bunny, bunny rabbit,
   Bunny, bunny rabbit,
   Hop, hop, hop.

   (Stand up and put hands behind head to make ears. Hop with both feet together, hands still behind head.)

2. Sing "Here Comes Peter Cottontail."

Art

1. On a large piece of construction paper, draw an outline of a rabbit. Have the children use cotton balls and glue them all over the rabbit's body and add eyes, nose, and mouth with felt-tipped pen or by gluing construction paper parts onto the cotton balls.
2. Help children use paper bags to make a bunny puppet. Have children cut out ears and glue onto bag. Mark and cut out eyes while children make whiskers by cutting pipe cleaners. Children then glue pipe cleaners on mask. Let dry. (See fig. 25F.)
3. Cut rabbit shapes out of meat trays. Paint rabbits pink, add eyes, etc. and glue on yarn ball for tail.
4. Have children make a bunny from two cotton balls, one for the head and one for the body. Have them add ears and other features, glue on an egg cut-out and draw grass or other decorations. (See fig. 25G.)

Snack

1. Eat "rabbit food" such as fresh raw vegetables which are liked by rabbits (lettuce, carrots, celery, broccoli, squash dipped in a mixture of equal parts ketchup and mayonnaise are very tasty).
2. Eat "Rabbit Salad." Grate carrots. Mix with raisins and enough honey to suit taste.
3. Eat carrots which children have helped to scrape and wash.
4. Eat sugar cookies made in Fine Motor #3.

Fine Motor

1. Glue several rabbit pictures onto cardboard and make puzzles of varying levels of difficulty.
2. Let the children use a rabbit cookie cutter and make rabbit "cookies" out of play dough.
3. Help the children make sugar cookie dough, cut out rabbits with a cookie cutter, sprinkle colored sugar on top and bake in an available oven. Eat at snack.
4. Help children cut out pink bunny ears and staple them to a band to wear around the head. (See fig. 25H.)
5. Clean and cut vegetables for snack.

Games

1. Hide a bunny in the room and let the children find it.
2. Have the children listen and do (using a stuffed rabbit):
   a. jump over rabbit
   b. walk around rabbit
   c. step over rabbit
   d. crawl around rabbit
   e. lie down behind rabbit
   f. crawl in front of rabbit
   g. put rabbit under chair
   h. put rabbit in chair

Fig. 25F

Fig 25G

Fig. 25H

Storytelling

1. Read or tell the story of Peter Rabbit using a large picture book.
2. Make up a story about a bunny who loses his fuzzy tail while running near the school. Have the children think of all the places where he could have lost it. At the end of the story, he finds his tail and is very happy.

Gross Motor

Play a musical action game. Have the children perform the stated actions while singing this song to the tune of "Twinkle, Twinkle, Little Star."

Bunny rabbit hops around
Way up high and
Close to the ground
Hops so fast and hops so slow;
Wags his fluffy tail to and fro.
Bunny rabbit hops around,
Way up high and
Close to the ground.

Cognitive

1. Make a bunny cue sheet. Put a bunny at the top of a sheet and bunnies and other things below. Have the children mark all of the bunnies (like the cue). Vary the number of items and the level of discrimination according to the abilities of the children.

2. Make paper rabbits in three different sizes. Ask the children to arrange them in order from largest to smallest and the tallest to shortest.

3. Have the children count bunnies on the flannel board.

4. Discuss concepts of front and back. For the back view of the bunny, glue a large and a small oval together; glue pipe cleaner whickers on small oval. Add ears and a cotton ball tail. For the front view, use the ovals with the whiskers on the front and features made with a felt-tip pen. No tail is visible on the front view. Have the children decide which is the front and which is the back. (See fig. 25I.)

Fig. 25I

Enrichment

1. Together Activity: Help the children make a large bunny outline and tape it to wall as though he were sitting on the ground. Have children cover bunny fur with cotton tufts and color the coat blue, paint it blue, or cover it with bits of blue paper. Cut strips of green paper and have the children make a lettuce patch from wads of green tissue paper and fringe the strips of green paper to make grass. Add large decorated eggs this Together Activity as Easter approaches. (See fig. 25J.)

Fig. 25J

2. Hide "cotton tails" (white yarn balls) near the school in places where bunnies might go - beside a tree, behind a rock, near a fence. Let children go on a cotton tail hunt to find soft, furry, bunny tails. Refer to the "Bunny Who Lost His Cotton Tail" in Storytelling.

Lesson 3: Easter Egg

Unit Group Lesson

1. **Match Concrete Objects**
    Present two Easter eggs. Say, "This is an Easter egg." Ask each child in turn to put the Easter egg with the Easter egg. Gradually increase number of irrelevant objects from which (s)he must select an Easter egg to match.

2. **Discriminate Objects**
    Present several objects. Have each child touch the Easter egg in response to verbal direction, "Touch the Easter egg."

3. **Match Pictures**
    Present several pictures of common objects. Have each child match the pictures of the Easter eggs.

4. **Discriminate Pictures**
    Present a group of several unrelated pictures of objects. Have each child touch the picture of the Easter egg in response to verbal direction, "Touch the Easter egg."

5. **Figure-Ground**
    Present a "busy" picture with many visual distractions. Ask each child to find the Easter egg.

6. **Visual Closure**
    Partially cover each of several pictures with paper. Ask each child to find the picture of the Easter egg.

7. **Function**
   Ask, "What do we do with Easter eggs?"

8. **Association**
   Ask, "What goes with the Easter egg?" Use pictures or objects including chicks, Easter bunny, basket, etc., with several unrelated objects or pictures.

9. **Imitate Verbalization**
   Present an Easter egg and ask, "What is this? Say, 'Easter egg'." The child will imitate "Easter egg."

10. **Verbalize Label**
    Present an Easter egg and ask, "What is this?" The child will respond, "Easter egg."

11. **Concept Enrichment**
    Discuss the custom of hiding Easter eggs. Discuss the fact that eggs come from chickens, ducks, and birds. Discuss how eggs hatch in the spring time.

Music

1. Sing to the tune of "Mary Had A Little Lamb":
   Hide, hide, hide the Easter egg
   Easter egg, Easter egg,
   Hide, hide, hide the Easter egg
   Can you find it, (child's name)?

   (One child gives egg to friend in the circle as group sings.)

   (Selected child looks in hands behind each friend in circle as group sings.)

   Look, look, for the Easter egg
   Easter egg, Easter egg
   Look, look, for the Easter egg
   Looking is such fun.
   (Child's name) found the egg!

   (Or if the egg is found.)

2. Give the children cut out paper eggs or let them use any of the eggs made in Art today and sing to the tune of "Ten Little Indian Boys":
   1 little, 2 little, 3 little eggs,
   4 little, 5 little, 6 little eggs,
   7 little, 8 little, 9 little eggs,
   10 pretty Easter eggs.

Art

1. Have the children color hard-boiled eggs with wax crayons, or dye eggs. Make stands for eggs by cutting toilet paper tubes.
2. Cut out egg shapes from styrofoam meat trays. Let children paint them or color them with magic markers.
3. Have the children use pieces of colored egg shell to make a mosaic by gluing on paper.
4. Cut out paper eggs. Have children decorate eggs with colored yarn, macaroni, pieces of tissue paper, scraps of ribbon, etc. Use in Music #2.
5. Make large Easter egg with a crack across it (simple or complex depending upon the child) for each child. Have each child color and cut open an egg along the crack, glue the halves on a sheet of paper, make grass with a crayon and add a chick made from cotton balls shaken with yellow tempera powder in a bag. The child adds feet and a beak to the chick. (See fig. 25K.)

Fig. 25K

Snack

Eat hard boiled eggs which were decorated in Art #1. (Save shells for mosiac in Art #3).

Fine Motor

1. Have the children make eggs out of clay or play dough and decorate them.
2. Make egg-shaped lacing cards made from heavy paper. Have the children lace them.
3. Have the children path trace designs on large eggs. Make the paths simple to complex according to levels of children. (See fig. 25M.)
4. Have the children make nest of green grass for eggs - either real or cut green paper.
5. Give child paper with egg design. Color egg, hide it in the grass. (Green stokes of crayon.) (See fig. 25L.)
6. Make "cracked egg" puzzles from simple to complex eggs according to levels of children. (See fig. 25P.)

Games

1. Have an Easter egg hunt. Hide eggs all around room and have the children hunt and find the eggs.
2. Make a "Go Fishing" game. Make eggs in different colors and put paper clips on them. Attach a string with a magnet to a dowel. Let the children fish for a red, blue, yellow or green egg.

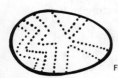
Fig. 25M

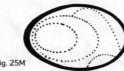

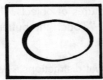

Fig. 25L

Fig. 25P

Storytelling

Make up a story of an egg in the grass cracking open and revealing a tiny yellow chicken. Use a plastic pantyhose egg with a chick made of two cotton balls sprinkled with yellow tempera powder.

Gross Motor

1. Have the children roll hard-cooked eggs with their noses with their hands behind their backs. Make an egg track on table with blocks to serve as borders to keep eggs from rolling onto floor.
2. Have the children hold a basket and hop to find 2 yellow eggs; 3 Easter eggs; all the eggs they can find, etc.
3. Have the children prepare a large basket with a bed of real grass which they have pulled up from outside. Have them take turns hopping, skipping, jumping, walking, etc. across the room to place their eggs in the basket.

Cognitive

1. Make egg cut-outs of wall paper, decorated colored paper, etc. for a matching activity. Say, "Find the egg that's exactly like this one."
2. Make different colored "eggs." Have children put all red eggs in a red yarn circle, all blue eggs in a blue yarn circle, etc.
3. Number sections of an egg carton. Have children put the correct number of paper "eggs" in each section. Include zero if children are familiar with it. (See fig. 25N.)

Fig. 25N

Enrichment

Together Activity: Outline a basket and tape it to wall at child's level. Have the children trace the basket design (vary difficulty), add grass strips cut from green construction paper in and around the basket and add decorated eggs piled in the basket and spread out in the grass. (See fig. 25O.)

Field Trip

Have an Easter egg hunt in a local park.

|||||||||||||||||||—Cut

Fig. 25O

Visitor

Have an artist come to paint designs or pictures on eggs.

Lesson 4: Butterfly

Unit Group Lesson

1. **Match Concrete Objects**
   Present two butterflies. Say, "This is a butterfly." Ask each child in turn to put the butterfly with the butterfly. Gradually increase number of irrelevant objects from which (s)he must select a butterfly to match.

2. **Discriminate Objects**
   Present several objects. Have each child touch the butterfly in response to verbal direction, "Touch the butterfly."

3. **Match Pictures**
   Present several pictures of common objects. Have each child match the pictures of the butterfly.

4. **Discriminate Pictures**
   Present a group of several unrelated pictures of objects. Have each child touch the picture of the butterfly in response to verbal direction, "Touch the butterfly."

5. **Figure-Ground**
   Present a "busy" picture with many visual distractions. Ask each child to find the butterfly.

6. **Visual Closure**
   Partially cover each of several pictures with paper. Ask each child to find the picture of the butterfly.

7. **Function**
   Ask, "What do butterflies do?"

8. **Association**
   Ask, "What goes with the butterfly?" Use pictures or objects including flowers, caterpillars, etc., with several unrelated objects or pictures.

9. **Imitate Verbalization**
   Present a butterfly and ask, "What is this? Say, 'Butterfly'." The child will imitate "Butterfly."

10. **Verbalize Label**
    Present a butterfly and ask, "What is this?" The child will respond, "Butterfly."

11. **Concept Enrichment**
    Discuss the life cycle of a butterfly from egg to caterpillar to cocoon (pupa) and then to butterfly.

Music

1. Sing to the tune of "Glow Little Glowworm":
   Eat little caterpillar
   Eat and grow.
   It will be soon you know
   That you'll become a butterfly
   Eat little caterpillar
   Eat.

Fig 25Q

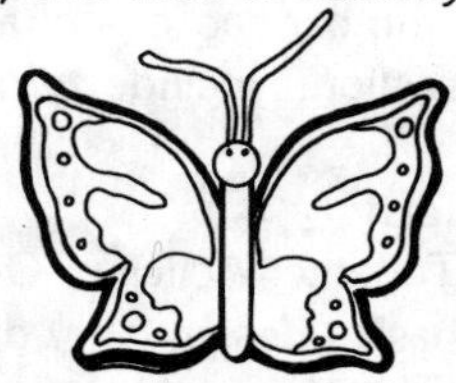

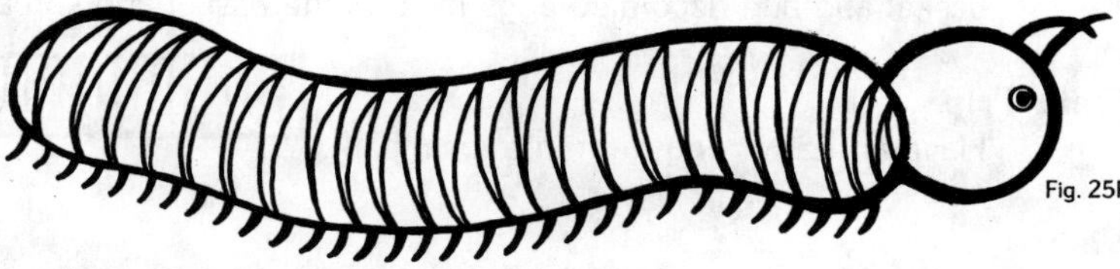

Fig. 25R

Art

1. Trace butterfly patterns on two colors of construction paper. Have the children decorate, then cut them and glue the two butterflies together in the center. Fold up 2 wings for 3-D effect.
2. Make a butterfly using brightly colored tissue paper as wings, a straight wooden clothespin as the body, and a pipe cleaner as antennae. Make eyes with a magic marker. (See fig. 25Q.)
3. Have the children make a "wiggly caterpillar." Have them draw a pair of wiggly parallel lines; draw lines inside and across the parallel lines, and add a head and legs. Label "wiggly caterpillar" and have the children add a background. (See fig. 25R.)

Snack

Make a butterfly salad. Use lettuce leaves for wings, a carrot stick for a body and raisin for decorations.

Fine Motor
1. Have the children draw irregular and triangular designs on butterfly wings.
2. Help each child make a pair of butterfly wings for Games today. Let the children staple pleated tissue paper to the top of a band of elastic big enough to go around their arms. (See Fig. 25S.)
3. Have the children decorate butterfly shapes with dots and bright colors and attach them to paper towel tubes.
4. Help each child make a caterpillar by fringing long pieces of paper on both long edges and stapling two or three together down the middle. Use larger paper for less skilled children. (See fig. 25T.)
5. Help each child make a caterpillar from four sections of an egg carton and color it with magic markers. (See fig. 25U.)

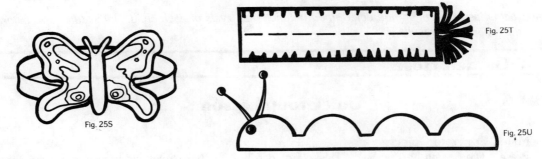

Fig. 25S   Fig. 25T   Fig. 25U

Games

Play musical flowers. Have the children move from one paper flower to another, flapping their wings (made in Fine Motor #2 today) like butterflies to slow music. Follow the same rules as musical chairs with a slow, graceful tempo.

Storytelling
1. Read *The Apple and the Moth,* by Mari, *The Very Hungry Caterpillar* or *Where Does the Butterfly Go When It Rains?* by Garelick.
2. Make up a sequence story of an egg that becomes a fuzzy, wiggly caterpillar, then a pupa and finally a beautiful butterfly. Let the children have a turn to sequence the story.

Gross Motor
1. Have the children make "Butterflies on the Floor" like "Angels in the Snow." Have children lie on their backs on the floor. The teacher rhythmically says in-out and the children move arms and legs in and out to the rhythm.
2. Let the children put on wings made in Fine Motor #2 today and fly like butterflies.
3. Use the butterflies made in Fine Motor #3 to do a rhythmic activity. Have the children fold the butterflies above their heads and make them flutter, sway and twirl.

Cognitive
1. Make butterflies cut from different colors and have children match butterflies of the same color.
2. Make a butterfly life-cycle chart showing each stage. Each child can contribute to the chart.
3. Make a series of pairs of butterflies with patterns. Let the children match the butterflies with identical patterns. Make obvious differences for lower functioning children.

Enrichment

Locate a milkweed plant with a butterfly egg on it. Put it into a cage or fish tank and watch it develop into a caterpillar. If you can find one with a Monarch cocoon on it, the class can watch a Monarch butterfly emerge. Monarch butterflies feed exclusively on milkweed.

Unit 26: Garden Tools

A developmental assessment should determine the functional levels of each child. Individual expectations are based on the assessment results.

Lesson 1: Garden Hose

Unit Group Lesson

1. **Match Concrete Objects**
    Present two garden hoses. Say, "This is a garden hose." Ask each child in turn to put the garden hose with the garden hose. Gradually increase number of irrelevant objects from which (s)he must select garden hose to match.

2. **Discriminate Objects**
    Present several objects. Have each child touch the garden hose in response to verbal direction, "Touch the garden hose."

3. **Match Pictures**
    Present several pictures of common objects. Have each child match the pictures of the garden hoses.

4. **Discriminate Pictures**
    Present a group of several unrelated pictures of objects. Have each child touch the picture of the garden hose in response to the verbal direction, "Touch the garden hose."

5. **Figure-Ground**
    Present a "busy" picture with many visual distractions. Ask each child to find the garden hose.

6. **Visual Closure**
    Partially cover each of several pictures with paper. Ask each child to find the picture of the garden hose.

7. **Function**
    Ask, "What do we do with a garden hose?"

8. **Association**
    Ask, "What goes with the garden hose?" Use pictures or objects including water, hoe, rake, shovel, lawn mower, etc. with several unrelated objects or pictures.

9. **Imitate Verbalization**
    Present a garden hose and ask, "What is this? Say, 'Garden hose'." The child will imitate "Garden hose."

10. **Verbalize Label**

Present a garden hose and ask, "What is this?" The child will respond, "Garden hose."

11. **Concept Enrichment**

Discuss color of garden hose. What other garden things are green? Identify the parts of a garden hose and explain how it works.

Music

Sing to the tune of "Campbell Soup Song":
> Water hose, water hose
> Puts lots of water on the garden.
> Puts lots of water on the grass.
> Puts lots of water on the flowers.
> Water hose, water hose
> This is how we use a water hose.   *(Pantomime.)*
> Turn on water, hold on tight   *(Pantomime.)*
> Then out comes the water, whoosh, whoosh, whoosh.   *(Make whoosh sound.)*

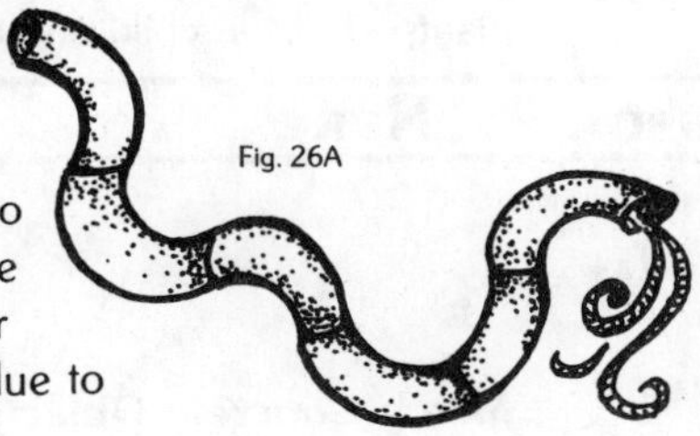

Fig. 26A

Art

1. Make a pencil outline of hose on piece of paper. Use green food coloring to make elbow macaroni green. Model for children how to cover the pencil outline with glue and then, put noodles next to one another on the glue and let dry. Draw pencil lines to indicate water coming out. Pieces of pipe cleaners or thick spaghetti on top of glue to represent water. (See fig. 26A.)

2. Let the children begin a garden mural by gluing on a long green garden hose to water the garden plants. Have them paint plants green, then glue or staple them to the mural.

3. Let children paint at the easels with green paint. Let them make wiggly, squiggly hoses.

Snack

1. Eat spaghetti noodles for snack. Have children feel before and after cooking. Eat buttered with topping.

2. Use drinking straws for pretend hoses. Drink juice through "hose."

Fine Motor

1. Let children make a hose out of clay or playdough.

2. Make a path tracing activity of "Take the water from the spigot through the hose to the flowers." This activity could be done on chalk board in varying levels of difficulty. (See fig. 26B.)

Fig. 26B

3. Let the children use a real hose to water plants, fill a school wading pool, etc.

Games

Use real hoses for play. Let children "squirt" different specific objects.

Storytelling

Tell the story about a hose using puppets on a stage. "Two friends were playing outside. One friend (Mary) saw a hose, thought it was a snake and was afraid. She then ran to her friend and told her to come and see the garden snake. Her friend told Mary that it was a hose, not a snake, but Mary did not believe her. So the friend showed Mary how the hose worked. The friend showed Mary how to use the hose to water flowers and grass. Mary wanted a turn, so she watered the flowers and grass, too. She wasn't afraid of the hose anymore."

Gross Motor

1. Wind hose into large loops two feet in diameter. Have children stand several feet away and toss a ball through the hose. Have someone on other side to catch ball. (Also use bean bags, newspaper balls, sponge balls, etc.).
2. Have children use a hose to water garden, grass and flowers.
3. Use hose which has been wound up into approximately three foot diameter loops: fasten hose securely with sturdy tape. Have children crawl through, when hose is held vertically to floor and jump into and out of the middle of hose lying horizontally on floor, one at a time.

Cognitive

1. Prepare a figure-ground activity. Hide a hose among plants. Have the children color the hose green.
2. Have the children measure different pieces of hose to each other and decide which is the longest, the shortest, and in the middle.
3. Have the children look at the color of garden hose and compare it to grass. Discuss why they are the same.

Enrichment

1. Show children several hose nozzles and let them experiment with how they work.
2. Discuss whether a hose grows and whether a garden grows.
3. Help the children to plan a garden on paper. Provide a large piece of paper and pictures of various plants. Let the children arrange the pictures.

Lesson 2: Rake

Unit Group Lesson

1. **Match Concrete Objects**
   Present two rakes. Say, "This is a rake." Ask each child in turn to put the rake with the rake. Gradually increase number of irrelevant objects from which (s)he must select rake to match.

2. **Discriminate Objects**
   Present several objects. Have each child touch the rake in response to verbal direction, "Touch the rake."

3. **Match Pictures**
   Present several pictures of common objects. Have each child match the pictures of the rakes.

4. **Discriminate Pictures**
   Present a group of several unrelated pictures of objects. Have each child touch the picture of the rake in response to the verbal direction, "Touch the rake."

5. **Figure-Ground**
   Present a "busy" picture with many visual distractions. Ask each child to find the rake.

6. **Visual Closure**
   Partially cover each of several pictures with paper. Ask each child to find the picture of the rake.

7. **Function**
   Ask, "What do we do with a rake?"

8. **Association**
   Ask, "What goes with the rake?" Use pictures or objects including dirt, hoses, hoe, shovel, lawn mower, etc. with several unrelated objects or pictures.

9. **Imitate Verbalization**
   Present a rake and ask, "What is this? Say, 'Rake'." The child will imitate "Rake."

10. **Verbalize Label**

Present a rake and ask, "What is this?" The child will respond, "Rake."

11. **Concept Enrichment**

Compare rakes to hair combs. Look at the differences and similarities in leaf rakes and garden rakes.

Music

1. Sing to the tune of "Campbell Soup Song":

    Rake the leaves, rake the leaves,   *(Pantomime.)*
    See us work, raking leaves.
    We can help, we can help,
    We can help rake the leaves.

2. Sing to tune of "Row, Row, Row Your Boat":

    Rake, rake, rake the leaves,   *(Pantomime.)*
    See us rake the leaves.
    Rake, rake, rake the leaves,
    Raking leaves is fun.

Art

1. Continue the garden mural begun in Lesson #1 Art #2. Draw trees and a boy and girl, each with a rake. Have children cut or tear different colored construction-paper leaves. Have each child come and glue or tape leaves on mural. Let some children trace lines in the garden made by a rake, or add strips of brown paper for raked dirt and some cutout rakes.
2. Have the children sand paint by raking a thin layer of sand in a shallow box with fingers or cardboard rakes.
3. Have the children finger paint with their hands bent like a rake. (See fig. 26C.)

Fig. 26C

Snack

1. Let each child spread fingers and "rake" snack to himself.
2. Use forks to rake snack from middle of the table to child's place. Use dry cereal or small crackers for snack.

Fine Motor

1. Make path tracing of "Take the rake to leaves." and "Take the rake to the garden." Make a variety of different levels.
2. Have each child trace around stencil of a rake made out of posterboard or cardboard. (See fig. 26D.)
3. Let child use fingers to "rake" through sand to find "treasures" hidden in it.
4. Help children make rakes out of pieces of drinking straws or toothpicks or sticks, glued together. Or use toothpicks stuck in styrofoam for rake head.
5. Help the children make garden rakes by cutting out the head, as shown, folding and attaching to a tube. (See fig. 26E.)

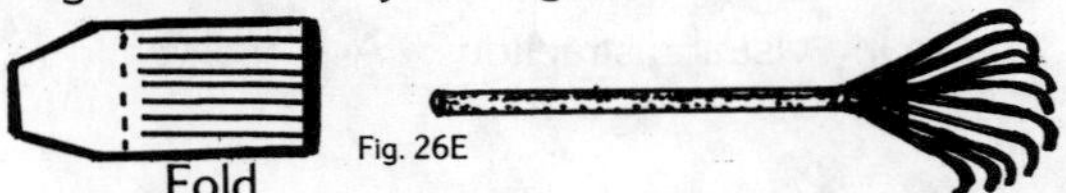

Fold   Fig. 26E 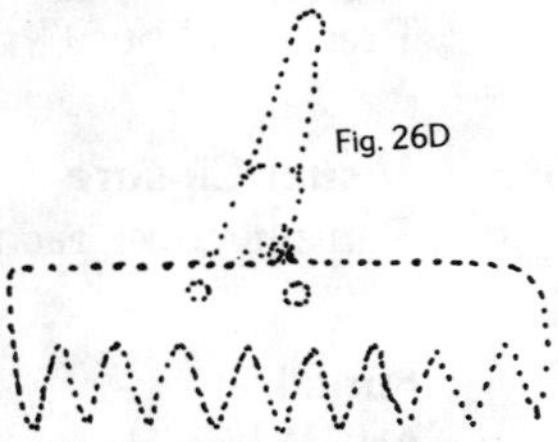   Fig. 26D

Games

1. Have a rake in housekeeping area so children can pretend to have a garden.
2. "Rake" each other's backs (scratch) with a back scratcher.

Storytelling

Use large picture cards (self drawn) to tell story about two children raking leaves. Then have children assemble pictures in the sequence you told the story. Then mix them up again and have children re-sequence. Start with a three- or four-part story to begin.

Then add more parts as children are able to sequence four-part story easily.

Example: 1. Children asking, "Mother, what can we do?" Mother suggests raking leaves.
         2. Mother and children rake leaves.
         3. Put leaves in big bags.
         4. Put bags at side of road for garbage men to take away.

Gross Motor

1. Place rake between two chairs as part of obstacle course. Have children go under, over, around rake when following directions through obstacle course. Make sure rake prongs are pointing down.
2. Use rake in relay race. Children have to touch rake and run back to line. Adult holds rake.
3. Have children rake leaves outdoors and jump into big piles of leaves.

Cognitive

1. Have children sort rakes from non-rakes.
2. Blindfold child and guide to table with objects. Let children feel each object. Then, have her find or tell which one is the rake. Say, "Tell me when you find the rake." "How can you tell its a rake?" (Tactile Discrimination)
3. Help children begin a terrarium in a fish tank. Put a layer of charcoal on the bottom. Fill ½ full of potting soil. Smooth dirt with a tiny houseplant rake or cardboard rake.

Enrichment

Rake ground that will be used for a garden.

Lesson 3: Shovel

Unit Group Lesson

1. **Match Concrete Objects**
    Present two shovels. Say, "This is a shovel." Ask each child in turn to put the shovel with the shovel. Gradually increase number of irrelevant objects from which (s)he must select shovel to match.

2. **Discriminate Objects**
    Present several objects. Have each child touch the shovel in response to verbal direction, "Touch the shovel."

3. **Match Pictures**
    Present several pictures of common objects. Have each child match the pictures of the shovel.

4. **Discriminate Pictures**
    Present a group of several unrelated pictures of objects. Have each child touch the picture of the shovel in response to verbal direction, "Touch the shovel."

5. **Figure-Ground**
    Present a "busy" picture with many visual distractions. Ask each child to find the shovel.

6. **Visual Closure**
    Partially cover each of several pictures with paper. Ask each child to find the picture of the shovel.

7. **Function**
    Ask, "What do we do with a shovel?"

8. **Association**
    Ask, "What goes with the shovel?" Use pictures or objects including rake, hoe, dirt, etc. with several unrelated objects or pictures.

9. **Imitate Verbalization**
    Present a shovel and ask, "What is this? Say, 'Shovel'." The child will imitate "Shovel."

10. **Verbalize Label**
Present a shovel and ask, "What is this?" The child will respond, "Shovel."

11. **Concept Enrichment**
Discuss different types of tools used for digging.

Music
1. Sing to the tune of "Punchinella":

What do we do with Mr. Shovel, Mr. Shovel
What do we do with Mr. Shovel, here at school?

We dig in the sand, dig and dig, dig and dig
We dig in the sand, in the sandbox outside.

We dig in the dirt, dig and dig, dig and dig
We dig in the dirt, for a garden in our yard.

2. Sing to the tune of "Merrily We Roll Along":
(Child's name) will dig a hole,   *(Pantomime)*
Dig a hole, dig a hole,
(Child's name) will dig a hole,
Now the hole is dug.

Art
1. Cut shovels out of heavy paper. Let the children sponge paint or spatter paint around cut-out of shovel. Keep shovel cut-out in place by putting small piece of masking tape on back.
2. Have children cut shovels out of catalogs and make a collage.
3. Continue the mural begun in Lesson #1 Art #2. Have children add plants to the new garden area and some shovels to represent how the holes were dug.

Snack
Have children pretend that their spoons are shovels and dig into snack.

Fine Motor
1. Make path tracing activities of "Take the shovel to the bucket." and "Take the shovel to the garden."
2. Let children use small play shovels to put sand in buckets. This is an excellent sandbox activity.
3. Have children cut out shovel shapes and attach to tubes to make shovels. (See fig. 26F.)

Games
Play "Hide and Seek" with a shovel. Hide a shovel and let the children find it.

Storytelling
1. Make up a story about planting a garden using a shovel. Use pictures to illustrate.
2. Read *The Carrot Seed* by Ruth Krauss.

Fig. 26F

Gross Motor
Have children shovel styrofoam packing material from one box to another. This can be set up as a race. Time it to see if children can beat their own time.

Cognitive
1. Blindfold a child and guide her to table with objects. Let child feel each object. Then, have her identify which one is the shovel. Say, "Tell me when you find the shovel." (Tactile Discrimination)
2. Help children continue tank garden. Use a tiny house plant shovel to dig holes for plants. Leave room for a row of seeds.

Enrichment
1. Have children continue raking and shoveling to level garden plot.
2. Have children count seeds to put in the garden.

Lesson 4: Hoe

Unit Group Lesson

1. **Match Concrete Objects**
    Present two hoes. Say, "This is a hoe." Ask each child in turn to put the hoe with the hoe. Gradually increase number of irrelevant objects from which (s)he must select hoe to match.

2. **Discriminate Objects**
    Present several objects. Have each child touch the hoe in response to verbal direction, "Touch the hoe."

3. **Match Pictures**
    Present several pictures of common objects. Have each child match the pictures of the hoe.

4. **Discriminate Pictures**
    Present a group of several unrelated pictures of objects. Have each child touch the picture of the hoe in response to verbal direction, "Touch the hoe."

5. **Figure-Ground**
    Present a "busy" picture with many visual distractions. Ask each child to find the hoe.

6. **Visual Closure**
    Partially cover each of several pictures with paper. Ask each child to find the picture of the hoe.

7. **Function**
    Ask, "What do we do with a hoe?"

8. **Association**
    Ask, "What goes with the hoe?" Use pictures or objects including rake, dirt, plants, shovel, etc. with several unrelated objects or pictures.

9. **Imitate Verbalization**
    Present a hoe and ask, "What is this? Say, 'Hoe'." The child will imitate "Hoe."

10. **Verbalize Label**
    Present a hoe and ask, "What is this?" The child will respond, "Hoe."

11. **Concept Enrichment**
    Discuss weeds and why they are not good for a garden.

Music
1.   Sing to the tune of "Row, Row, Row Your Boat":
        Hoe, hoe, hoe the garden   *(Pantomime.)*
        Hoeing all the dirt.
        Hoe, hoe, hoe away
        For our garden today.

2. Sing to the tune of "The Farmer in the Dell":
Verse 1: The farmer plants the seed.
The farmer plants the seed.
Hi ho the merry oh.
The farmer plants the seed.
Verse 2: The sun begins to shine.
Verse 3: The rain begins to fall.
Verse 4: The seed begins to grow.

Art
1. Make cutouts of hoe, using thick posterboard or cardboard. Have children trace around cutout using crayon or magic marker, fill in outline with rubber cement or white glue and use fingers to sprinkle sand over glue. Let dry and gently shake off excess.
2. Have children continue mural begun in Lesson #1 Art #2. "Plant seeds in garden." Let them use beans or seeds and glue them to dirt area to represent the planted seeds and glue on hoes.
3. Let the children make designs in the sandbox with a small hoe. (See fig. 26G.)

Snack
Use hand cupped as hoes to gather snack for each child.

Fig 26G

Fine Motor
1. Have children make hoes out of clay.
2. Make a path trace of "Take hoe to garden." and "Hoe the weeds in the garden." Vary the level of difficulty according to the skills of each child.
3. Have children cup hand and "chop" in soft sand. (See fig. 26H.)

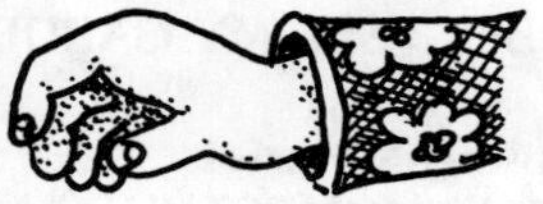

Fig. 26H

Games
1. Hoe the dirt in the garden into rows. (You will have to help children with this.) Use hose to water the rows.
2. Use hoe which is held by a child at each end. Give children directions to:
   a. jump over
   b. step over
   c. crawl under
   d. run under
   e. hop on one foot under
(Raise and lower height of hoe during game.)

Storytelling
1. Word games: What would I use if I needed to:
   a. dig a hole?
   b. gather up leaves?
   c. plant a tree?
   c. make rows for a garden?
   e. chop down weeds?
   f. water the flowers?
   g. water the grass?
Give much practice with this, even use improvisations
2. Fooler Word Game: "See If I Can Trick You"
Use above activity and make mistakes. See if children can correct you. Use props, if necessary (cutouts or pictures).

Gross Motor
Use hoes to turn over dirt in classroom garden or in sandbox.

Cognitive

1. Have children label tools as "hoes" and "not hoes" (or "rakes" and "not rakes"; etc.).
2. Blindfold child and guide to table with objects. Let child feel each object. Then, have her found the hoe. Say, "Tell me when you find the hoe."
3. Have children continue tank garden. Let them use a tiny house plant hoe to make rows for seeds. Plant seeds and then cover with soil. Water and watch grow.

Enrichment

Let the children use hoes to make holes for seeds in the garden. Cover seed when planted and water well with garden hose.

Field Trip

Take field trip to hardware store and examine garden tools studied.

Related Children's Records
ADVENTURES IN SOUND (MH)
"Mr. Yokum the Yardman" from BEGINNING SOUNDS & CAREERS (UBB)

Related Children's Books
Bond, Michael and Banbery, Fred. PADDINGTON'S GARDEN. New York: Random House, 1973.
Harwood, Pearl. MR. BUMBA PLANTS A GARDEN. Minneapolis, Minn.: Lerner Publications, 1964.
Moncure, Jane Belk. SEE MY GARDEN GROW. Elgin, Ill.: Child's World, 1976.

Related Parenting Materials
Cansler, Dot. THE HOMESTRETCH. Winston-Salem, NC 27113-5128: Kaplan Press, 1983.

Related Materials
TEACHING PICTURES. Winston-Salem, NC 27113-5128: Kaplan Press, 1983.
STORY SEQUENCE CARDS I, II. Winston-Salem, NC 27113-5128: Kaplan Press, 1983.
SEWING CARDS I, II, III. Winston-Salem, NC 27113-5128: Kaplan Press, 1983.

Unit 27: Animals

A developmental assessment should determine the functional levels of each child. Individual expectations are based on the assessment results.

Lesson 1: Dog

Unit Group Lesson

1. **Match Concrete Objects** (Use toys.)
   Present two dogs. Say, "This is a dog." Ask each child in turn to put the dog with the dog. Gradually increase number of irrelevant objects from which (s)he must select dog to match.

2. **Discriminate Objects**
   Present several objects. Have each child touch the dog in response to verbal direction, "Touch the dog."

3. **Match Pictures**
   Present several pictures of common objects. Have each child match the pictures of the dogs.

4. **Discriminate Pictures**
   Present a group of several unrelated pictures of objects. Have each child touch the picture of the dog in response to verbal direction, "Touch the dog."

5. **Figure-Ground**
   Present a "busy" picture with many visual distractions. Ask each child to find the dog.

6. **Visual Closure**
   Partially cover each of several pictures with paper. Ask each child to find the picture of the dog.

7. **Function**
   Ask, "What does a dog do?"

8. **Association**
   Ask, "What goes with the dog?" Use pictures or objects including leash, dog collar, dog food, dog bone, etc. with several unrelated objects or pictures.

9. **Imitate Verbalization**
   Present a dog and ask, "What is this? Say, 'Dog'." The child will imitate "Dog."

10. **Verbalize Label**
    Present a dog and ask, "What is this?" The child will respond, "Dog."

11. **Concept Enrichment**
    Discuss sizes of dogs, what dogs eat, colors of dogs and where dogs live. Discuss who has a dog. Discuss sounds that dogs make. Note that baby dogs are called puppies.

Music

1.   Sing to the tune of "Did You Ever See A Lassie?":
   Did you ever see a dog's tail,   *(Put hand behind you and*
   A dog's tail, a dog's tail.   *wiggle it back and forth.)*
   Did you ever see a dog's tail
   Go this way and that.
2.   Sing "Bingo."
3.   Sing "Old MacDonald."
4.   Sing "Hark, Hark, the Dogs do Bark."

Art

1.   Have each child begin an animal book. Make an outline of a dog for each child. Have each color the dog and decorate around the dog. Have each make a cover for her book by folding a large sheet of construction paper. Put child's name on her book.
2.   Help the children make dog masks from paper plates with felt and fur.
3.   Have children make dog collages by gluing pictures of dogs cut from magazines onto a piece of construction paper.

Snack

1.   Eat like a dog (with mouths, without hands) using dry cereal in a tray.
2.   Eat animal crackers.

Fine Motor

1.   Have each child pick up pieces of dried dog food using pincer grasp. (Index finger to thumb) and put it in dog's dish. When filled, let dog eat food. Some children can use tongs for this activity.
2.   Make a path tracing of "Take dog to his bone." and "Take dog to his dog house."
3.   Make puzzles of dogs with two or more pieces. Let each child work on a puzzle at her level.
4.   Have children glue small dog pictures onto tongue depressors for book marks.

Games

1.   Play "Farmer in the Dell."
2.   Play "Pin Tail on the Dog" but use a magnet or tape instead of a pin.
3.   Have two teams of "dogs" hunt hidden items. When children locate something, they must "bark" before they touch it.

Storytelling

1.   Tell this story of going on a trip. Use a flannel board to demonstrate.
   Teacher: "I'm going to Grandma's, and I will take my dog."
   Children: Repeat exactly.
   Teacher: "I'm going to Grandma's, and I will take my dog and dog food."
   Children: Repeat exactly.
   Teacher: "I'm going to Grandma's, and I will take my dog, dog food, and dog
        bowl."
   Children: Repeat exactly.
  Later, have a child act as teacher and tell what she will take.
2.   Read *My Dog Is Lost!* by Keats.
3.   Read *Harry the Dirty Dog* (series) by Gene Zion.

Gross Motor

  Make a picture of a dog's head. Cut out a big hole for the dog's mouth. Have children stand three feet away and throw a sponge ball into dog's mouth. Now move child back further and hold poster, telling child to throw ball in dog's mouth. May want to use different ball, such as tennis or rubber.

Cognitive

1.   Play "I've Got A Secret." Say, "This animal can be large or small. It barks. It eats dog food, etc." Let the children guess which animal.

2. Draw a dog's face on heavy tagboard. Make a slit in the mouth. Cut bones which are different (colors, have names on them, etc.) from tagboard. Let the children "feed" the dog certain bones according to directions such as "Feed the dog a blue bone."

3. Make dogs with numerals on them. Put them on empty milk cartons. Have the children feed each dog the correct number of dog bones (real or cardboard).

Enrichment

Help the children make a stand up dog. Cut a large piece of cardboard as shown and fold it in half. Have the children add bits of paper and fake fur to give the dog a shaggy effect. Have the children make a head and tail for the dog. (See fig. 27A.)

Fig. 27A

Field Trip

Visit an animal shelter, a pet store, or a veterinary hospital.

Lesson 2: Cat

Unit Group Lesson

1. **Match Concrete Objects** (Use toys.)
   Present two cats. Say, "This is a cat." Ask each child in turn to put the cat with the cat. Gradually increase number of irrelevant objects from which (s)he must select cat to match.

2. **Discriminate Objects**
   Present several objects. Have each child touch the cat in response to verbal direction, "Touch the cat."

3. **Match Pictures**
   Present several pictures of common objects. Have each child match the pictures of the cats.

4. **Discriminate Pictures**
   Present a group of several unrelated pictures of objects. Have each child touch the picture of the cat in response to verbal direction, "Touch the cat."

5. **Figure-Ground**
   Present a "busy" picture with many visual distractions. Ask each child to find the cat.

6. **Visual Closure**
   Partially cover each of several pictures with paper. Ask each child to find the picture of the cat.

7. **Function**
   Ask, "What does a cat do?"

8. **Association**
   Ask, "What goes with the cat?" Use pictures or objects including ball of yarn, dish of milk, cat food, cat bed, etc. with several unrelated objects or pictures.

9. **Imitate Verbalization**
   Present a cat and ask, "What is this? Say, 'Cat'." The child will imitate "Cat."

10. **Verbalize Label**
    Present a cat and ask, "What is this?" The child will respond, "Cat."

11. **Concept Enrichment**

Discuss sounds cats make and that baby cats are called kittens. Discuss sizes of cats, what cats eat, colors of cats, and where cats live. Discuss who has a cat. Discuss how cats use their whiskers.

Music

Sing "Old MacDonald Had A Farm."

Art

1. Have each child make a cat collage with different cats cut from magazines.
2. Have each child make a cat mask with fake fur and string for whiskers.
3. Give each child an outline of a cat and the pieces of a cat to glue on the outline. Give the more skilled children a cat cut into more pieces.
4. Continue the animal book begun in Lesson #1 Art #1 by having each child color and decorate a cat picture.

Snack

1. Try "lapping milk" out of a saucer like a cat.
2. Eat animal crackers.

Fine Motor

1. Make picture of cat's face. Have each part cut out. Model how to assemble. Let each child put each part of face in appropriate place (without cues, if possible): eyes, nose, mouth, ears, whiskers. Give child paste to glue them onto face.
2. Make a path tracing activity to take the cat to a dish of milk. Use more difficult paths for advanced children. Let them walk a small toy cat on the path.
3. Have children add pieces of colored tissue paper and glue on the outline of a cat.

Games

1. Play "Farmer in the Dell."
2. Play "Tape the Tail on the Cat" like "Pin the Tail on the Donkey" but substitute tape or magnets for the pins.

Storytelling

1. Tell the story of the "Three Little Kittens" using flannel board cut-outs. Then have children count kittens. "We have three kittens. Present enough mittens so that each kitten has a pair of mittens."
2. Read *The Bremen Town Musicians*.

Gross Motor

Be a cat: stretch, walk, roll like a cat.

Cognitive

1. Ask, "Who owns a cat?" Count owners and non-owners.
2. Have the children count the legs on a cat.
3. Have the children match kittens to look-alike mother cats.

Enrichment

1. Have the children make cats by cutting cardboard as illustrated. Have them fold it and make cuts for the head and tail. Have the children decorate heads and tails and add to the cat. (See fig. 27B.)
2. Make cards with numerals on one side and an appropriate number of cat stickers or pictures on the other side. Cut them in half and give each a unique cut. Let the children match the correct halves of the cards. (See fig. 27C.)

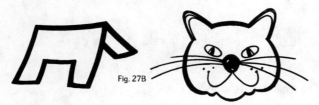

Fig. 27B

Fig. 27C

Lesson 3: Horse

Unit Group Lesson

1. **Match Concrete Objects** (Use toys.)
   Present two horses. Say, "This is a horse." Ask each child in turn to put the horse with the horse. Gradually increase number of irrelevant objects from which (s)he must select horse to match.

2. **Discriminate Objects**
   Present several objects. Have each child touch the horse in response to verbal direction, "Touch the horse."

3. **Match Pictures**
   Present several pictures of common objects. Have each child match the pictures of the horses.

4. **Discriminate Pictures**
   Present a group of several unrelated pictures of objects. Have each child touch the picture of the horse in response to verbal direction, "Touch the horse."

5. **Figure-Ground**
   Present a "busy" picture with many visual distractions. Ask each child to find the horse.

6. **Visual Closure**
   Partially cover each of several pictures with paper. Ask each child to find the picture of the horse.

7. **Function**
   Ask, "What does a horse do?"

8. **Association**
   Ask, "What goes with the horse?" Use pictures or objects including saddle, bridle, wagon, hay, etc., with several unrelated objects or pictures.

9. **Imitate Verbalization**
   Present a horse and ask, "What is this? Say, 'Horse'." The child will imitate "Horse."

10. **Verbalize Label**
    Present a horse and ask, "What is this?" The child will respond, "Horse."

11. **Concept Enrichment**
    Discuss sounds horses make and that baby horses are called colts. Discuss different types of horses. Discuss how cowboys ride horses in the west.

Music

1. Sing to the tune of "Here We Go 'Round the Mulberry Bush":
   This is a horse, his home is the barn   *(Have pictures on hand and show)*
   His home is the barn, his home is the barn.   *Have pictures on bulletin board of barn, house, school*
   This is a horse, his home is the barn,   *church, etc. Child is to find where the horse lives.)*
   Now, go show me where he lives

2. Sing to the tune of "Mary Had A Little Lamb":
   Pick a partner, then go gallop.
   Gallop, gallop, gallop, gallop.
   Pick a partner, then go gallop
   All around the room.

3. Sing "Yankee Doodle."

Art
1. Have the children draw a horse and/or decorate the outline of a horse and glue on straw for feed.
2. Help the children make a hobby horse out of an old broomstick, yardstick, large cardboard tube, etc. Stuff a paper head. Add ears, a mane, etc.
3. Continue the animal book begun in Lesson #1 Art #1. Have each child color and decorate a picture of a horse and add it to her book.

Snack
1. Eat apple and oatmeal cookies because horses like apples and oatmeal.
2. Eat shredded wheat and pretend it is hay.

Fine Motor
1. Make a barn out of a shoe box. Put small plastic animals upright in barn. Have children take only the horses out without knocking other animals over.
2. Make puzzles of a horse with two and more pieces. Let each child do a puzzle with number of pieces appropriate to her skill development.
3. Have children fringe strips of brown, black and white paper for horses manes and glue them onto a horse picture.

Games
1. Play "Tape the Tail on the Horse."
2. Bring in or make a broomstick horse and let the children ride it.

Storytelling
1. Recite with the child: "Ride, ride, ride your pony, up the hill and down. Ride him in the country, ride him in the town." Pantomime activities.
2. Read *Cowboys, What Do They Do?* by Greene.

Gross Motor
1. Have the children gallop to music. Demonstrate. (Same foot steps ahead; other foot catches up but never passes the first).
2. Use a wagon and a rope "harness" for a pony ride. Let children take turns being the pony.
3. Let the children play horse. Put rope (cloth) under arms of one child. Another holds ends and says "Giddyap." Together they gallop.
4. Play horseshoes using cardboard or wooden "shoes." Let each child toss and see who can come closest to a certain tree, pole, etc.
5. Let the children use a chair or sawhorse for a "horse" to ride or to "rope" (touch with a swinging or thrown rope).
6. Let children ride a rocking horse.

Cognitive
1. Have both horses pull the wagon. Using several cut-out horses, have two or both horses pull a wagon. Ask, "How many is both?"
2. Ask "What animal wears shoes fastened to his feet by nails? Do these nails hurt the animal's feet?"
3. Ask, "If you had a horse, where would you ride it? How would you feed it? Where would you keep it?, etc."

Enrichment
1. Provide pictures of individual horses and colts. Let the children sort the horses by type such as Clydesdales, Morgans, etc.
2. Talk about the Pony Express. Have the children pretend to be Pony Express riders and transfer mail from one to the other.

Field Trip
Visit a real stable. Hire a pony for an hour, and let the children ride.

Lesson 4: Pig

Unit Group Lesson

1. **Match Concrete Objects**
Present two pigs. Say, "This is a pig." Ask each child in turn to put the pig with the pig. Gradually increase number of irrelevant objects from which (s)he must select pig to match.

2. **Discriminate Objects**
Present several objects. Have each child touch the pig in response to verbal direction, "Touch the pig."

3. **Match Pictures**
Present several pictures of common objects. Have each child match the pictures of the pigs.

4. **Discriminate Pictures**
Present a group of several unrelated pictures of objects. Have each child touch the picture of the pig in response to verbal direction, "Touch the pig."

5. **Figure-Ground**
Present a "busy" picture with many visual distractions. Ask each child to find the pig.

6. **Visual Closure**
Partially cover each of several pictures with paper. Ask each child to find the picture of the pig.

7. **Function**
Ask, "What does a pig do?"

8. **Association**
Ask, "What goes with the pig?" Use pictures or objects including cat, dog, cow, horse, etc., with several unrelated objects or pictures.

9. **Imitate Verbalization**
Present a pig and ask, "What is this? Say, 'Pig'." The child will imitate "Pig."

10. **Verbalize Label**
Present a pig and ask, "What is this?" The child will respond, "Pig."

11. **Concept Enrichment**
Discuss sounds pigs make. Baby pigs are called piglets, boar and sow are the father and mother pig. Discuss color of pigs. Footballs are made of pigskin.

Music
Sing "Ten Little Pigs" to the tune of "Ten Little Indians."

Art
1. Outline a pig on construction paper. Let the children tear pieces of pink tissue paper, crumple it and glue pieces next to each other so the outline of the pig is filled.
2. Let children put cut-out pigs in a picture of a farm and add it to the animal book begun in Lesson #1 Art #1.
3. Let the children paint some brown mud (thick brown tempera paint) on a large paper and add cut-out pigs.

Snack

Eat "Pigs In a Blanket" (hotdog wrapped in ½ a bacon strip). Fry in an electric skillet until done.

Fine Motor

1. Make lacing cards in the shape of a pig. Two pieces of poster board glued together will make a sturdy card. Punch holes around edge. Make more holes for the more skilled children.
2. Make a path tracing of "Take a pig to the food." and "Take a pig to the pig pen." Vary the difficulty of the paths for children with different skill levels.
3. Help the children make a spool pig. Have the child cut out front and back and glue onto spool. Provide precut pieces for those who need it. (See fig. 27D.)

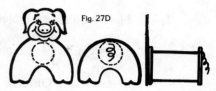

Fig. 27D

Games

1. Play "Tape the Tail on the Pig."
2. Make a "Go Fishing" game. Use a magnet on a pole for a fishing rod. Who can fish and find the pig? Prepare five to ten animals by gluing pictures on poster board and attaching paper clips to each. Place the animals face up in a box and allow children to fish for the pigs in the group.

Storytelling

1. Tell the story of "The Three Little Pigs" using flannel board and cut-outs. One-to-one correspondence: "Put up enough pigs so each pig will go with a house."
2. Recite: "Pigs are stout and pigs are pink
   and pigs are seldom clean.
   Snout in front and tail behind
   and bacon in between!"
3. Recite "To Market, To Market."
4. Recite "This Little Piggy."
5. Tell the story of *Charlotte's Web*.

Gross Motor

1. Have a relay race. Have children touch the picture of pig on the wall and run back to a line.
2. Have everyone play "Drive the pig to market" by pushing ball with a stick.
3. Talk about footballs being made of pigskin and play football.

Cognitive

1. Make animals noises and let the children guess the animal.
2. Have children sort pigs from non-pigs.
3. Have children divide animals into farm animals and house pets. Use the animals studied this week.

Enrichment

1. Discuss why pigs roll in mud.
2. Provide each child with pictures of a sow, a boar and several piglets. Let each child make up a pig family story and write the story for the child in a pig book. Let her glue her pigs on the cover and write (Child's name) PIG STORY on it. Let each child make as many accompanying pictures as she wishes.

Lesson 5: Cow

Unit Group Lesson

1. **Match Concrete Objects** (Use toys.)
   Present two cows. Say, "This is a cow." Ask each child in turn to put the cow with the cow. Gradually increase number of irrelevant objects from which (s)he must select cow to match.

2. **Discriminate Objects**
   Present several objects. Have each child touch the cow in response to verbal direction, "Touch the cow."

3. **Match Pictures**
   Present several pictures of common objects. Have each child match the pictures of the cows.

4. **Discriminate Pictures**
   Present a group of several unrelated pictures of objects. Have each child touch the picture of the cow in response to verbal direction, "Touch the cow."

5. **Figure-Ground**
   Present a "busy" picture with many visual distractions. Ask each child to find the cow.

6. **Visual Closure**
   Partially cover each of several pictures with paper. Ask each child to find the picture of the cow.

7. **Function**
   Ask, "What does a cow do?"

8. **Association**
   Ask, "What goes with the cow?" Use pictures or objects including calf, milk, cheese, butter, etc., with several unrelated objects or pictures.

9. **Imitate Verbalization**
   Present a cow and ask, "What is this? Say, 'Cow'." The child will imitate "Cow."

10. **Verbalize Label**
    Present a cow and ask, "What is this?" The child will respond, "Cow."

11. **Concept Enrichment**
    Discuss sounds cows make. Discuss fact that the name of the baby cow is calf, the mother cow is called a cow and the father is a bull. Discuss fact that cows give milk and that the milk is used to make dairy products.

Music
1. Sing "Old MacDonald Had a Farm."
2. Play Ella Jenkins' song "Did You Feed My Cow?" from the record *You'll Sing a Song.*

Art
1. Let the children paint with buttermilk and spread it all over paper. Then let them rub over it with chalk.
2. Have children make cow pictures. Cut cows out of construction paper. Let the children crumple brown and white tissue paper and glue it on the outline.
3. Finish the animal book begun in Lesson #1 Art #1. Give each child an outline of a cow and let her color the cow and decorate around it. Add it to the book and staple the book together.

Snack
1. Eat cheese, a variety of kinds.
2. Use all forms of dairy products as snack: milk, ice cream, yogurt, cottage cheese, etc.

Fine Motor
1. Make cow puzzles with two or more pieces. Have each child put together a puzzle appropriate to her level. (See fig. 27E.)
2. Have each child make a folded paper stand-up cow with a head and tail as illustrated. (See fig. 27F.)

Fig. 27E

Fig. 27F

3. Have the children trace around the outline of a cardboard cow stencil. Provide large simple stencils for children with lower-level skills.

Games
1. Sing and play like "London Bridge":
    This big bridge
    Is falling down, falling down.
    This big bridge is falling down
    On the cow.
2. Play "Mother May I" and use moos as signals.

Storytelling
1. Tell the story of Old MacDonald using flannel board characters.
2. Make up a story about a cow that gave milk. Have the children help tell about things that were done with the milk such as making yogurt, cheese, ice cream, etc.

Gross Motor
Divide children into two groups, cows and cowboys; have cowboys round up the cows by chasing and tagging and put them in a designated place called a corral.

Cognitive
1. Have children select cows from non-cows.
2. Make animal noises. Let the children guess the animal. Let children make animal noises and others guess.
3. Have the children match cows to baby cows. Have them do the same with all animals studied in this unit.

Enrichment
1. Find pictures of different kinds of cows. Talk about BEEF cows and DAIRY cows. Match milk, cheese, butter, and ice cream to DAIRY cows. Match steak, hamburger, roast beef, and meatloaf to BEEF cows.
2. Have the children sort farm animals into a group with cows and non-farm animals into another group.

Field Trip
Take a field trip to a farm.

Related Children's Records
ADVENTURES IN SOUND (MH)
"Barnyard Song" from FIDDLE-EE-FEE
"Walking on Saturday" from FIDDLE-EE-FEE
"Mouse In the House" from FIDDLE-EE-FEE
"Grandmother's Farm" from WITCHES' BREW
"Animal Sounds" from TEMPO FOR TOTS
"Did You Feed My Cow?" from YOU'LL SING A SONG

Related Children's Books
Cole, Joanna. A CALF IS BORN. New York: William Morrow & Co., 1975.
Fujikawa, Gyo. PUPPIES, PUSSY CATS AND OTHER FRIENDS. New York: Grossett & Dunlap, 1975.
Goble, Paul. THE GIRL WHO LOVED WILD HORSES. Scarsdale, N.Y.: Bradbury Press, 1978.
Holl, Adelaide. THE RAIN PUDDLE. New York: Lothrop, Lee & Shepard, Co., 1965.
Wildsmith, Brian. WILD ANIMALS. New York: Oxford University Press, 1979.

Related Parenting Materials
Cansler, Dot. THE HOMESTRETCH. Winston-Salem, NC 27113-5128: Kaplan Press, 1983.

Related Materials
TEACHING PICTURES. Winston-Salem, NC 27113-5128: Kaplan Press, 1983.
STORY SEQUENCE CARDS I, II. Winston-Salem, NC 27113-5128: Kaplan Press, 1983.
SEWING CARDS I, II, III. Winston-Salem, NC 27113-5128: Kaplan Press, 1983.

Unit 28: The Farm

A developmental assessment should determine the functional levels of each child. Individual expectations are based on the assessment results.

Lesson 1: Farmer

Unit Group Lesson

1. **Match Concrete Objects** (Use toys.)
   Present two farmers. (If only pictures are available, present pictures in items 1 and 2 and omit item 3.) Say, "This is a farmer." Ask each child in turn to put the farmer with the farmer. Gradually increase number of irrelevant objects from which (s)he must select farmer to match.

2. **Discriminate Object**
   Present several objects. Have each child touch the farmer in response to verbal direction, "Touch the farmer."

3. **Match Pictures**
   Present several pictures of common objects. Have each child match the pictures of the farmers.

4. **Discriminate Pictures**
   Present a group of several unrelated pictures of objects. Have each child touch the picture of the farmer in response to verbal direction, "Touch the farmer."

5. **Figure-Ground**
   Present a "busy" picture with many visual distractions. Ask each child to find the farmer.

6. **Visual Closure**
   Partially cover each of several pictures with paper. Ask each child to find the picture of the farmer.

7. **Function**
   Ask, "What does a farmer do?"

8. **Association**
   Ask, "What goes with the farmer?" Use pictures or objects including farm, barn, tractor, truck, chicken, etc., with several unrelated objects or pictures.

9. **Imitate Verbalization**
   Present a farmer and ask, "What is this? Say, 'Farmer'." The child will imitate "Farmer."

10. **Verbalize Label**
    Present a farmer and ask, "What is this?" The child will respond, "Farmer."

11. **Concept Enrichment**

Talk about kinds of farmers: dairy, beef, worm, tobacco, fruit, truck (raises vegetables for the market), etc. Talk about clothes farmers wear.

Music

1. Sing "Old MacDonald Had a Farm."
2. Sing to the tune of "Punchinello":

    What do you do, Mr. Farmer, Mr. Farmer,
    What do you do, Mr. Farmer, on the farm?
    I take care of Mrs. Cow, Mrs. Horse, Cat and Dog.
    I take care of Mr. Chicken and Mr. Pig.
    What else do you do, Mr. Farmer, Mr. Farmer,
    What else do you do, Mr. Farmer, on the farm?
    I grow food to eat, to eat, food to eat.
    I grow food to eat, corn and beans and hay.

Art

1. Let the children make pictures of farmer using different foods that farm animals eat (corn, oats, hay, etc.). Provide an outline of a farmer and let children glue dried corn, oats, bits of hay, etc. on the picture to fill in the farmer's clothing and background.
2. Have the children make a scarecrow.
3. Prepare a large paper for a farm mural by outlining a farmer and barn. Have the children decorate the outline of a farmer on the mural.
4. Let each child make or decorate a picture of a farmer doing one of the farmer's jobs.

Snack

1. Eat cookies made in Fine Motor #3.
2. Eat animal crackers.

Fine Motor

1. Make path tracing activities of "Take the farmer to the field" and "Take the farmer to the tractor."
2. Have each child assemble a picture of a farmer. Pre-cut the shirt, overalls, head, feet, and hands. Have child match parts to outline and then glue them on the outline. Some children may be able to do their own cutting.
3. Let children mix, roll out, cut and bake farm animal cookies to eat in Snack #1.

Games

1. Play "Farmer in the Dell." Have one child dress up as farmer and stand in middle.
2. Have "farmer dress-up clothes" (overalls, plaid shirts, straw hats, etc.) in the housekeeping corner.

Storytelling

Tell the story of "Old MacDonald" using a flannel board.

Gross Motor

1. Have the children pretend to be farmers by planting seeds in the ground. Have them bend at designated spots and "plant" a bean.
2. Have the children prepare and plant a real garden.

Cognitive

1. Tear out assorted pictures. Have each child make a booklet of things that go with the farmer. Discuss which pictures go with farmer and which do not. Then have each child cut out one thing and put in a "Farmer's Book." For example have pictures of animals, community helpers, vegetables, toys, clothing.
2. Make pictures of farmers in 3 sizes. Have rakes, hoes, shovels in graduated sizes. Let children match tools with the small-, large-, or middle-sized farmer.
3. Have the children sort farm animals from non-farm animals.

Enrichment

1.   Bring pictures from house of all things farmers help us to have. Paste in a large scrapbook.
2.   Tape long strips of paper on the floor. Have the children path trace garden rows down the paper.
       Have children follow the rows and pretend to plant seeds by leaving a dot where the seed was planted.

Field Trip

   Visit a farm.

Lesson 2: Barn

Unit Group Lesson

1.   **Match Concrete Objects** (Use toys.)
      Present two barns. Say, "This is a barn." Ask each child in turn to put the barn with the barn.
      Gradually increase number of irrelevant objects from which (s)he must select barn to match.

2.   **Discriminate Object**
      Present several objects. Have each child touch the barn in response to verbal direction, "Touch the
      barn."

3.   **Match Pictures**
      Present several pictures of common objects. Have each child match the pictures of the barns.

4.   **Discriminate Pictures**
      Present a group of several unrelated pictures of objects. Have each child touch the picture of the barn
      in response to verbal direction, "Touch the barn."

5.   **Figure-Ground**
      Present a "busy" picture with many visual distractions. Ask each child to find the barn.

6.   **Visual Closure**
      Partially cover each of several pictures with paper. Ask each child to find the picture of the barn.

7.   **Function**
      Ask, "What do we do with a barn?"

8.   **Association**
      Ask, "What goes with the barn?" Use pictures or objects including farm, farmer, tractor, truck,
      chicken, etc., with several unrelated objects or pictures.

9.   **Imitate Verbalization**
      Present a barn and ask, "What is this? Say, 'Barn'." The child will imitate "Barn."

10.   **Verbalize Label**
      Present a barn and ask, "What is this?" The child will respond, "Barn."

11.   **Concept Enrichment**
      Discuss animals which live in the barn. Ask, "Why are barns usually painted 'barn red'?" The round
      structure on the side of the barn is called a silo. It is used to hold feed for the animals.

Music

Sing to the tune of "Down by the Station":

Down by the barn,
Early in the morning,
You will see the cows
All in a row.
When the gate is opened
You will see them walking.
Moo-moo, moo-moo,
Time to eat.

Substitute other animals for cow (pigs, chicks, horse, and sheep).

Art

1. Let the children paint a large box red like a barn. Let dry, draw on doors and cut them out.
2. Have the children paint at the easel with barn red paint.
3. Have the children decorate the barn on the mural begun in Lesson #1 Art #3 with small bits of red and brown paper.

Snack

Place a bowl of french fried potatoes on the table. Talk about how the potatoes grow and where they are stored.

Fine Motor

1. Make barn puzzle in two and more pieces. Let each child work a puzzle appropriate to her skill level.
2. Make lacing cards of a barn. Make several levels of difficulty for children with different skill levels.
3. Have children make silos from brick-looking paper wrapped around cardboard cylinders
4. Let children cut around barn outlines. Vary the sizes of the barns with the skill levels of the children.

Games

1. Play "Ring Around the Barn (Rosey)."
2. Make a farm area. Put barn in farm area. Build fence (wooden bricks) around the farm. Put animals on the farm and in the barn.

Storytelling

Tell an imaginary story about the BARN family. Have each child tells the name of a friend who lives in the barn such as Polly Pony, Robert Rooster, Carrie Cow, etc.

Gross Motor

Have children dance to music or move like animals; when you clap like thunder, all the animals run to get in the barn (a designated area on the playground or building) to get in out of the rain.

Cognitive

1. Let children use shoe boxes painted "barn red" as barns for small plastic animals. Let them sort animals which go in the barn from those which do not such as lions, tigers, etc.
2. Let children identify the barn which has OPEN doors from the barn which has CLOSED doors.
3. Provide shoebox barns with numerals on them. Have each child put the correct number of animals in the barn. Some children may only be about to count one or two and some may go higher.

Enrichment

Compare barns to houses people live in and storage sheds people use.

Field Trip

Visit a barn. Have children climb into the hay loft. See different uses of barns.

Lesson 3: Truck

Unit Group Lesson

1. **Match Concrete Objects** (Use toys.)
   Present two trucks. Say, "This is a truck." Ask each child in turn to put the truck with the truck. Gradually increase number of irrelevant objects from which (s)he must select truck to match.

2. **Discriminate Objects**
   Present several objects. Have each child touch the truck in response to verbal direction, "Touch the truck."

3. **Match Pictures**
   Present several pictures of common objects. Have each child match the pictures of the trucks.

4. **Discriminate Pictures**
   Present a group of several unrelated pictures of objects. Have each child touch the picture of the truck in response to verbal direction, "Touch the truck."

5. **Figure-Ground**
   Present a "busy" picture with many visual distractions. Ask each child to find the truck.

6. **Visual Closure**
   Partially cover each of several pictures with paper. Ask each child to find the picture of the truck.

7. **Function**
   Ask, "What do trucks do?"

8. **Association**
   Ask, "What goes with the truck?" Use pictures or objects including farm, farmer, tractor, barn, chicken, etc., with several unrelated objects or pictures.

9. **Imitate Verbalization**
   Present a truck and ask, "What is this? Say, 'Truck'." The child will imitate "Truck."

10. **Verbalize Label**
    Present a truck and ask, "What is this?" The child will respond, "Truck."

11. **Concept Enrichment**
    Discuss different types and sizes of trucks. What do trucks carry?

Music

1. Sing to the tune of "Here We Go 'Round the Mulberry Bush":
   In my truck, I carry things,
   Carry things, carry things.
   In my truck, I carry things,
   All around the town.
   Have each child think of something different for the truck to carry.
2. Sing:
   Take a ride in my big red truck.
   Rattle, rattle, bang, bang.
   Don't get stuck!

Art

1. Obtain large furniture boxes to use as "trucks" that the children can get into and cut out the windows. Have the children paint the "trucks."
2. Help children make and decorate stand-up trucks. Have them fold paper and cut truck as shown. (See fig. 28A.)

 Fold   Fig. 28A    Fold

3. Have each child make a picture of a road and a sky and glue a pre-cut truck onto the road.

Snack

Place snacks in toy truck. Have each child take food from truck and drive it to friend seated beside him. Develop language concepts about the milk truck and cookie truck which delivers food.

Fine Motor

1. Make a truck using a different color of felt for each part. Have the children assemble the truck on the flannel board.
2. Put a picture of a large truck on the bulletin board. Have the children cut magazine pictures of things that can be carried in a truck and then paste them onto the truck.
3. Have children fill a toy dump truck with cubes and other small items; drive it along a path to a defined location; dump items and drive back. Let the children take turns.
4. Have the children load up toy trucks with plastic animals and drive to barn.

Games

1. Put a truck in farm area of room. Put plastic animals on truck and take them to the farm where they will stay and live.
2. Use a large toy truck and put three familiar objects in the truck. Let one child push the truck behind a screen and remove one object and push truck back to the group. Have children tell what is missing.

Storytelling

1. Use the flannel board and five felt trucks to recite. Use the names of children in the class.
   Five little trucks going into town.
   This one carried a bed for Ned.
   This one carried a table for Mable.
   This one carried a pony for Tony.
   This one carried a bone for Joan.
   This one carried a pan for Anne.
2. Say, "I'm going for a trip and I'll put a book in my truck." Then the next child says, "I'll put a book and a _____ in my truck." Keep adding an item with each turn. It may be necessary to act it out with a toy truck and actual objects in order to help the children remember the items.

Gross Motor

1. Provide circles of heavy cardboard for each child to use as a "steering wheel." Have the children "drive" truck up a hill (slowly); "drive" truck down a hill (fast); and "drive" around curves.
2. Help children set up a roadway on the floor or in the sandbox and make tunnels out of large boxes. Let them drive toy trucks through the tunnels and on the roads.
3. Let the children use inner tubes (large) from trucks to crawl through, bounce on, jump in, etc.

Cognitive

1. Provide different sized trucks and discuss which are BIG trucks and which are LITTLE trucks.
2. Create groups of three trucks each, two which match and one which is different. Have each child identify the different trucks from the group. Use pictures with some children and toy trucks with others. The more skilled children will be able to detect less obvious differences.

Enrichment

1. Discuss different types of trucks: dump trucks, gasoline trucks, milk trucks, mail trucks, flatbed trucks, refrigerated trucks, tandem trucks, etc.
2. Outline a truck shape on heavy paper. Outline wheels separately. Have children cover shape with torn bits of construction paper, paint the wheels, and glue inner circle to make tires. When completed, use in language and reasoning skill development: Ask, "What could be under the tarp?" Make several trucks to be used as a convoy. (See fig. 28B.)

Fig. 28B

Field Trip

1. Go for a walk to see different kinds of trucks.
2. Listen for truck sounds.

Lesson 4: Tractor

Unit Group Lesson

1. **Match Concrete Objects** (Use toys.)
    Present two tractors. Say, "This is a tractor." Ask each child in turn to put the tractor with the tractor. Gradually increase number of irrelevant objects from which (s)he must select tractor to match.

2. **Discriminate Object**
    Present several objects. Have each child touch the tractor in response to verbal direction, "Touch the tractor."

3. **Match Pictures**
    Present several pictures of common objects. Have each child match the pictures of the tractors.

4. **Discriminate Pictures**
    Present a group of several unrelated pictures of objects. Have each child touch the picture of the tractor in response to verbal direction, "Touch the tractor."

5. **Figure-Ground**
    Present a "busy" picture with many visual distractions. Ask each child to find the tractor.

6. **Visual Closure**
    Partially cover each of several pictures with paper. Ask each child to find the picture of the tractor.

7. **Function**
    Ask, "What do we do with a tractor?"

8. **Association**
    Ask, "What goes with the tractor?" Use pictures or objects including farm, farmer, barn, truck, chicken, etc., with several unrelated objects or pictures.

9. **Imitate Verbalization**

   Present a tractor and ask, "What is this? Say, 'Tractor'." The child will imitate "Tractor."

10. **Verbalize Label**

   Present a tractor and ask, "What is this?" The child will respond, "Tractor."

11. **Concept Enrichment**

   Discuss things that can be attached to a tractor (plow, discs, reaper, etc.). Discuss fact that a tractor has big wheels in the back and small wheels in the front. Why? Talk about how a tractor works.

Music

Sing to the tune of "Here We Go 'Round the Mulberry Bush":
   This is the way we plow our fields.

Art

1. Continue the mural begun in Lesson #1 Art #3 by having the children paint tractors and glue them on and near the mural. Provide outlines.
2. Let the children paint a classroom "tractor" made out of a box.
3. Paint tractor inner tubes with water. (This is a good outdoor warm-weather activity.)

Snack

Eat farm foods.

Fine Motor

1. Assemble pictures of a tractor. Have an outline of tractor and its parts on each child's paper. Give each child pre-cut parts which are to be matched to outline. When done correctly, have child glue parts onto outline.
2. Cut out pictures of tractors and paste on paper to put in "Farmer's Book" begun in Lesson #1 Cognitive #1.
3. Cut a large tractor tire in ½. Let the children use the two circular troughs for water play. (See fig. 28C.)

Fig. 28C

4. Make a cardboard "plow." Let children pull through sand to see "rows." (See fig. 28D.)

Fig. 28D

Games

1. Put tractor in farm area and make a cardboard area with rows. Let children drive tractor along rows.
2. Let children bring in toy farm machines to share with the class.

Storytelling

Make up a story about "Tillie the Tractor." Tillie starts the season out by plowing under all the old stalks in the field. Then she keeps working the soil until it is fairly smooth. Then she makes neat rows in the field for the seeds. Let the children contribute other ideas of what Tillie does. Be sure to include the weeding that Tillie does.

Gross Motor

Use school riding toys for dramatizing tractor riding.

Cognitive

1. Let children sort tractor pictures from other farm machinery.
2. Let children sort different kinds of tractor pictures.

Enrichment

Put Farm Journal magazines on a table. Let the children make a folder with different makes of tractors; pictures of farmers on tractors, etc.

Field Trip

Take a trip to a field just plowed by a tractor.

Visitor

Invite a tractor salesman with brochures to give the children with tractor pictures.

Lesson 5: Chicken

Unit Group Lesson

1. **Match Concrete Objects** (Use toys.)
   Present two chickens. Say, "This is a chicken." Ask each child in turn to put the chicken with the chicken. Gradually increase number of irrelevant objects from which (s)he must select chicken to match.

2. **Discriminate Object**
   Present several objects. Have each child touch the chicken in response to verbal direction, "Touch the chicken."

3. **Match Pictures**
   Present several pictures of common objects. Have each child match the pictures of the chickens.

4. **Discriminate Pictures**
   Present a group of several unrelated pictures of objects. Have each child touch the picture of the chicken in response to verbal direction, "Touch the chicken."

5. **Figure-Ground**
   Present a "busy" picture with many visual distractions. Ask each child to find the chicken.

6. **Visual Closure**
   Partially cover each of several pictures with paper. Ask each child to find the picture of the chicken.

7. **Function**
   Ask, "What do we do with a chicken?"

8. **Association**
   Ask, "What goes with the chicken?" Use pictures or objects including barn, tractor, farm, farmer, truck, etc., with several unrelated objects or pictures.

9. **Imitate Verbalization**
   Present a chicken and ask, "What is this? Say, 'Chicken'." The child will imitate "Chicken."

10. **Verbalize Label**
    Present a chicken and ask, "What is this?" The child will respond, "Chicken."

11.   **Concept Enrichment**

Eggs come from chickens and chickens come from eggs. When they are babies, they are called chicks and say, "Peep, peep." Males are called roosters and females are called hens. Note that chickens have feathers.

Music
1.   Sing "Old MacDonald Had a Farm."
2.   Sing to the tune of "Frere Jacques":
      I like chickens.
      I like chickens.
      Yes, I do.
      Yes, I do.
      The chicken's voice says "Cheep, cheep."
      The chicken's voice says "Cheep, cheep."
      Strutting on two feet.
      Strutting on two feet.
Stoop down and put hand on hips and move them like flapping wings.

Art
1.   Have children decorate shoe boxes and make them into chicken houses.
2.   Have each child make a chick in an egg shell. Have each child glue a yellow pom-pom into a foam egg carton cup. Let her glue on small pieces of black felt for eyes and orange felt for beaks. Cotton balls and construction paper may be substituted for pom-poms and felt.
3.   Have children glue real feathers on a cut-out chicken.

Snack
1.   Eat chicken-shaped cookies made in Fine Motor #2 today.
2.   Eat eggs in all forms: scrambled, poached, hard and soft baked, fried, sunny-side-up, in omelets, in quiches, etc. Talk about the yolk, the white. "What would it grow into?"

Fine Motor
1.   Have children make eggs and chicken's nests out of clay.
2.   Have children cut out chicken-shaped cookies with cookie cutters. Eat for snack.
3.   Make a path tracing activity of "Take a chicken to the chicken house" and "Take a chicken to the hen." Vary the difficulty of paths according to the skills of the children. Let each child do some at her own level.
4.   Have children put the halves of plastic eggs together. Use larger eggs for less skilled children.

Games
1.   Add chickens and chicken houses to farm area.
2.   Let children "cluck" and flap "wings" and be chickens in games.

Storytelling
1.   Read "The Little Red Hen." Help the children dramatize the story.
2.   Help the children learn "Humpty Dumpty."

Gross Motor
1.   Follow an exercise record called "Chicken Fat."
2.   Have chicken races during which children cluck, flap wings, and race around an obstacle course.

Cognitive
1.   Have the children sort chickens from other animals.
2.   Make small, medium and large chickens. Have children sequence chickens.
3.   Have children put one baby chick into each "egg." Then count how many eggs and how many chicks.

Enrichment
1. Provide large and small yellow circles. Have the children glue the shapes on large paper, draw the beaks, feet and eyes and add grass and flowers by drawing vertical lines. (See fig. 28E.)

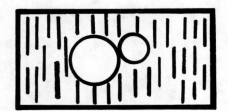

Fig. 28E

2. Have children sort pictures of feathered and non-feathered animals.

Field Trip
1. Go to farm and examine tractor, truck, barn, chicken house.
2. Go to a chicken farm. Let the children gather eggs. Let each child have her "own" egg for snack.

Visitor
Invite someone with a baby chicken to tell how to care for it, what it eats, etc.

Related Children's Records
ADVENTURES IN SOUND (MH)
"Barnyard Song" from **FIDDLE-EE-FEE**
"Farmer" from **WHAT WILL I BE WHEN I GROW UP?**
"Who Fed the Chickens?" from **I KNOW THE COLORS** by Ella Jenkins (EA)

Related Children's Books
Dunn, Phoebe and Dunn, Judy. **ANIMALS OF BUTTERCUP FARM.** New York: Random House, 1981.
Ginsburg, Mirra. **GOOD MORNING CHICK.** New York: Greenwillow Books, 1980.
Hutchins, Pat. **ROSIE'S WALK. Macmillan Publishing Co., 1968.**
Lindgren, Astrid. **THE TOMTEN.** New York: Coward, McCann & Geoghegan, 1967.
Schulz, Charles. **SNOOPY'S FACTS AND FUN BOOK ABOUT FARMS.** New York: Random House, 1980.

Related Parenting Materials
Cansler, Dot. **THE HOMESTRETCH.** Winston-Salem, NC 27113-5128: Kaplan Press, 1983.

Related Materials
TEACHING PICTURES. Winston-Salem, NC 27113-5128: Kaplan Press, 1983.
STORY SEQUENCE CARDS I, II. Winston-Salem, NC 27113-5128: Kaplan Press, 1983.
SEWING CARDS I, II, III. Winston-Salem, NC 27113-5128: Kaplan Press, 1983.

Unit 29: Vegetables

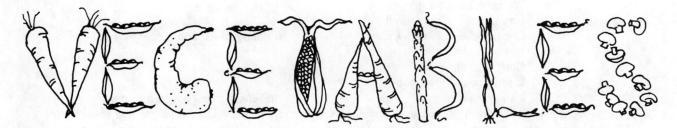

A developmental assessment should determine the functional levels of each child. Individual expectations are based on the assessment results.

Lesson 1: Corn

Unit Group Lesson

1. **Match Concrete Objects**
   Present some corn. Say, "This is corn." Ask each child in turn to put the corn with the corn. Gradually increase number of irrelevant objects from which (s)he must select corn to match.

2. **Discriminate Objects**
   Present several objects. Have each child touch the corn in response to verbal direction, "Touch the corn."

3. **Match Pictures**
   Present several pictures of common objects. Have each child match the pictures of the corn.

4. **Discriminate Pictures**
   Present a group of several unrelated pictures of objects. Have each child touch the picture of the corn in response to verbal direction, "Touch the corn."

5. **Figure-Ground**
   Present a "busy" picture with many visual distractions. Ask each child to find the corn.

6. **Visual Closure**
   Partially cover each of several pictures with paper. Ask each child to find the picture of the corn.

7. **Function**
   Ask, "What do we do with corn?"

8. **Association**
   Ask, "What goes with the corn?" Use pictures or objects including beans, carrots, etc. with several unrelated objects or pictures.

9. **Imitate Verbalization**
   Present corn and ask, "What is this? Say, 'Corn'." The child will imitate "Corn."

10. **Verbalize Label**
    Present corn and ask, "What is this?" The child will respond, "Corn."

11. **Concept Enrichment**
    Discuss how corn grows and that it is a vegetable. Talk about times and places where corn is usually eaten. Corn is yellow and white.

Music

1.   Sing to the tune of "Ring Around the Rosey":
     Verse 1: Farmer grows the corn.
               We cook corn on the stove.
               Umm-good! Umm-good!
               Oops, we've eaten it all up!   *(Pretend to eat and rub tummy.)*
     Verse 2: Corn is pretty yellow.
               Corn is pretty yellow.
               Umm-good! Umm-good!
               It's eaten all up.   *(Pretend to eat and rub tummy.)*

2.   Play musical chairs with vegetables. Play a marching music record. Lift the needle and show picture of the vegetable (corn). All children must go and find same vegetable on floor and stand on it. (To make picture stay on floor, use tape on back. Cover each picture with clear contact paper to preserve it.)

Art

1.   Work together to make a classroom scarecrow. Some children can hammer the wood, some can fasten the clothes, some can stuff the clothes with newspapers and straw, etc.

2.   Have each child make a collage of corn seen in different forms such as ears in husks, cooked ears, kernels, popcorn, creamed corn.

3.   Make a vegetable bulletin board. Have each child tape a corn picture (s)he has drawn or decorated onto the bulletin board.

Snack

1.   Eat corn in various ways: boiled or roasted on the cob, creamed, in casseroles, in cornbread, popped, etc.

2.   Make and eat cornstacks: melt two packages of butterscotch bits. Let the children stir in one can chow mein noodles and one can peanuts and drop by teaspoon onto wax paper. Cool and enjoy!

Fine Motor

1.   Have the children shuck corn and cook it.

2.   Help children open cans of corn with manual can opener; pour into pan and stir while it cooks over hot plate. Let children spoon corn onto their plates or put into a cup. CLOSE SUPERVISION NECESSARY!

3.   Help children plant corn seeds in garden dug during the unit on garden tools (Unit 26).

4.   Give children corn shapes and let them glue on dried corn to cover. (See fig. 29A.)

Fig. 29A

Games

1.   Have an over-and-under relay using real or plastic ears of corn. Form lines. One child passes corn over shoulder and next child passes corn under legs, etc.

2.   Set up grocery store in class and include vegetable stand or table.

3.   Corn Jump - Have lined up several ears of corn next to one another. Have children see if they can jump over the row of corn without touching any corn. (Use broad jump or running jump.)

4.   Add play vegetables to housekeeping corner.

Storytelling

1.   Read *What Shall I Put In The Hole That I Dig?*

2.   Read *Stone Soup* Marcia Brown.

Gross Motor

1.   Imitate corn stalks growing. They begin as little plants (curl up on floor) and stretch higher and higher.

2.   Have a corn cob relay. Each child runs an obstacle course with a corn cob. He gives it to the next child, etc. until all have had a turn.

Cognitive

1. Make cut-out corn cobs with different numbers of kernels on each and provide a shoebag or boxes with numerals on them. Have the children count the kernels and place the corn cob in the shoebag pocket or box that has the correct numeral.
2. Talk about vegetables served hot, cold, or hot and cold. How do children prefer them?
3. Have the children match other yellow things to corn and sort yellow from non-yellow things.

Enrichment

Help the children make a display of junk foods and healthful foods. Display the healthful foods in the four basic food groups and discuss the components of a good diet.

Lesson 2: Carrot

Unit Group Lesson

1. **Match Concrete Objects**
   Present two carrots. Say, "This is carrot." Ask each child in turn to put the carrot with the carrot. Gradually increase number of irrelevant objects from which (s)he must select carrot to match.

2. **Discriminate Objects**
   Present several objects. Have each child touch the carrot in response to verbal direction, "Touch the carrot."

3. **Match Pictures**
   Present several pictures of common objects. Have each child match the pictures of the carrots.

4. **Discriminate Pictures**
   Present a group of several unrelated pictures of objects. Have each child touch the picture of the carrot in response to verbal direction, "Touch the carrot."

5. **Figure-Ground**
   Present a "busy" picture with many visual distractions. Ask each child to find the carrot.

6. **Visual Closure**
   Partially cover each of several pictures with paper. Ask each child to find the picture of the carrot.

7. **Function**
   Ask, "What do we do with carrots?"

8. **Association**
   Ask, "What goes with the carrot?" Use pictures or objects including corn, peas, beans, potato, etc. with several unrelated objects or pictures.

9. **Imitate Verbalization**
   Present a carrot and ask, "What is this? Say, 'Carrot'." The child will imitate "Carrot."

10. **Verbalize Label**
    Present a carrot and ask, "What is this?" The child will respond, "Carrot."

11. **Concept Enrichment**
    Discuss how carrots grow under the soil and that they are vegetables. Talk about times and places where carrots are usually eaten. Carrots are orange. Carrots are good for the eyes.

Music

Play musical chairs with vegetable pictures as in Lesson #1 Music #2.

Art

1. Help children make carrot prints. Have them cut off part of carrot, dip in thick tempera paint or stamp pad and dab up and down. Model how to do this for children. Use shelf paper and do it on floor or long table.
2. Have children make a carrot collage with magazine pictures. Some children can cut their own.
3. Have each child cut and color a long shape into a carrot. Add it to the vegetable bulletin board begun in Lesson #1 Art #3.

Snack

1. Make and eat "Carrot Curlers." Clean and slice with a potato peeler, one carrot per child. Soak in orange juice and one teaspoon sugar. When the carrot slices curl, eat them.
2. Prepare and eat a carrot cake.
3. Make carrot salad with carrots, raisins, pineapple tidbits, sunflower (or sesame) seeds, and a mixture of yogurt, honey and lemon juice.

Fine Motor

1. Have children help make carrot salad for Snack #3. Let each child have a turn at grating carrot.
2. Have children plant carrot seeds in rows of garden begun in Unit 26.
3. Let the children cut carrots into pieces. Give each child a turn cutting and let her eat what she cuts for snack. (SUPERVISE CAREFULLY.)
4. Let the children cut and dry carrot "coins" and use for wheels in a picture.
5. Have children string carrot "coins" with dental floss (and a needle) and use as a necklace after drying 3-4 days. (SUPERVISE CAREFULLY.)

Games

1. Let children cut off top of carrot and stick toothpicks in three sides. Place carrot tops in a full glass of water and watch it grow.
2. Tasting party: blindfold child, let him taste carrot or corn. Then have him tell or show you what he ate. (Some children may not want to be blindfolded.)

Storytelling

1. Make up a story Mr. Carrot and how he grew up. Use pictures to show sequence from seed to large carrot. Tell about need for water, air, and sun.
2. Read *The Carrot Seed* by Ruth Krauss.

Gross Motor

Carrots are good for the eyes. Have children close their eyes to help them go around, under, over and through obstacles. Give verbal instructions to the children.

Cognitive

1. Provide real or paper carrots in different lengths. Have children sequence them. Some children should be given only the biggest and smallest carrots while others can sequence five or more different sizes.
2. Cut off 2 inches on large end of carrot. Core out the inside and turn upside down. Put water into hole daily (and change water every 3-4 days!). Hang up and watch the growth. (See fig. 29B.)
3. Have children sort orange things (including carrots) from non-orange things.

Enrichment

1. Together Activity: Provide long paper with line across it. Let children add carrot tops above line and carrots below the line. Have children trace or draw in roots for the carrots. (See fig. 29F.)
2. Make bunches of carrots with different numbers of carrots. (Use real or paper carrots.) Have children count the number of carrots in each bunch. Be sure that each child counts a number appropriate for his skill level.

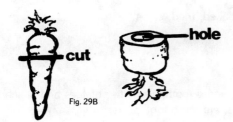

Fig. 29B

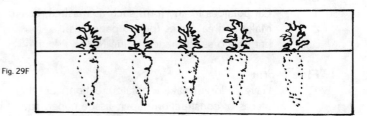

Fig. 29F

Lesson 3: Potato

Unit Group Lesson

1. **Match Concrete Objects**
   Present two potatoes. Say, "This is potato." Ask each child in turn to put the potato with the potato. Gradually increase number of irrelevant objects from which (s)he must select potato to match.

2. **Discriminate Objects**
   Present several objects. Have each child touch the potato in response to verbal direction, "Touch the potato."

3. **Match Pictures**
   Present several pictures of common objects. Have each child match the pictures of the potatoes.

4. **Discriminate Pictures**
   Present a group of several unrelated pictures of objects. Have each child touch the picture of the potato in response to verbal direction, "Touch the potato."

5. **Figure-Ground**
   Present a "busy" picture with many visual distractions. Ask each child to find the potato.

6. **Visual Closure**
   Partially cover each of several pictures with paper. Ask each child to find the picture of the potato.

7. **Function**
   Ask, "What do we do with potatoes?"

8. **Association**
   Ask, "What goes with the potato?" Use pictures or objects including beans, corn, carrots, etc., with several unrelated objects or pictures.

9. **Imitate Verbalization**
   Present a potato and ask, "What is this? Say, 'Potato'." The child will imitate "Potato."

10. **Verbalize Label**
    Present a potato and ask, "What is this?" The child will respond, "Potato."

11. **Concept Enrichment**
    Discuss how potatoes grow under the soil and that they are vegetables. Talk about times and places where potatoes are usually eaten. Potatoes are brown. Potatoes are made into french fries, chip, etc.

Music

Play musical vegetables as in Lesson #1 Music #2 and include potatoes.

Art
1. Help children make potato prints. Cut potatoes in half and have children carve out designs in potato (square, circle, triangle, etc.) with knife. Let them use the tempera paint and stamp pads and print on non-slick shelf paper. (SUPERVISE CAREFULLY.)
2. Let children make a potato collage of potatoes in different forms, cooked and uncooked.
3. Continue vegetable bulletin board begun in Lesson #1 Art #3 by adding pictures of potatoes. Give children ovals, let them paint them brown and use white dot stickers for potato eyes.

Snack

1. Eat potatoes in any form such as mashed, baked, twice baked, fried, chips.
2. Make and eat latkes (potato pancakes).
3. Eat potato salad made in Fine Motor #4.

Fine Motor

1. Have children make a potato creation. Let them insert colored toothpicks into potatoes and attach torn pieces of construction paper, tissue paper, round noodles, etc. onto toothpicks.
2. Let the children make potato faces using stick-on eyes, nose, ears, and mouth.
3. Let children scrub potatoes before cooking.
4. Let children cut up cooked potatoes for making potato salad with blunt plastic knives. Let them mix ingredients for potato salad.

Games

1. Play "Hot Potato" using varying types and sizes of balls depending on child's ability. Bean bags can also be used.
2. Help children cut off tops of potatoes and stick toothpicks into them. Fill glasses or jars with water and place potatoes so that part of them touches the water. Watch them grow.

Storytelling

1. Make up a story using flannel board about the vegetable that loved to hide. Talk about the corn, carrot, and potato cut-outs. Cover board and remove one vegetable. Ask children which one you removed. To increase difficulty, you will want to add more items. To make the story even more difficult, include both fruits and vegetables. "What is missing?" "Is it a fruit or vegetable?" "Is it brown?"
2. Help children cut off tops of potatoes and stick toothpicks into them. Fill glasses or jars with water and place potatoes so that part of them touches the water. Watch them grow. (Sweet potatoes produce pretty, fast-growing greenery.)

Gross Motor

1. Play a relay game carrying a potato on a spoon. Divide the class into teams. Have one child from each team carry the potato to a given point and back and pass it to the next team member. Continue until all children have had a turn.
2. Have the children participate in a potato race. Let them push potatoes with noses while on all fours.

Cognitive

1. Let children select from a group of potatoes the largest. Longest. Fattest. Smallest. Etc.
2. Recite with the children the "Counting Out" rhyme: "One potato, 2 potatoes, 3 potatoes, 4 . . .". Use real potatoes to count.
3. Have the children select brown and non-brown things.

Enrichment

Have children cut "eyes" from a potato. Fold back the top of a sturdy plastic garbage bag liner so it stays open and lets in sun and air. Let children put in some gravel, then soil to within 5" of the top and put in potato "eyes," cover with soil and water. Put in the sun. Poke holes in the bottom of the bag for drainage. The potatoes grow from spring until fall.

Lesson 4: Bean

Unit Group Lesson

1. **Match Concrete Objects**
   Present two beans. Say, "This is bean." Ask each child in turn to put the bean with the bean. Gradually increase number of irrelevant objects from which (s)he must select bean to match.

2. **Discriminate Objects**
    Present several objects. Have each child touch the bean in response to verbal direction, "Touch the bean."

3. **Match Pictures**
    Present several pictures of common objects. Have each child match the pictures of the beans.

4. **Discriminate Pictures**
    Present a group of several unrelated pictures of objects. Have each child touch the picture of the bean in response to verbal direction, "Touch the bean."

5. **Figure-Ground**
    Present a "busy" picture with many visual distractions. Ask each child to find the bean.

6. **Visual Closure**
    Partially cover each of several pictures with paper. Ask each child to find the picture of the bean.

7. **Function**
    Ask, "What do we do with a bean?"

8. **Association**
    Ask, "What goes with the bean?" Use pictures or objects including carrots, potatoes, corn, radishes, etc. with several unrelated objects or pictures.

9. **Imitate Verbalization**
    Present a bean and ask, "What is this? Say, 'Bean'." The child will imitate "Bean."

10. **Verbalize Label**
    Present a bean and ask, "What is this?" The child will respond, "Bean."

11. **Concept Enrichment**
    Discuss how beans grow above the soil and that they are vegetables. Talk about times and places where beans are usually eaten. Some beans are green (pole beans, string beans). Discuss other types of beans.

Music
1. Play musical vegetables as in Lesson #1 Music #2. Add beans.
2. Use tambourines made in Fine Motor #3 to keep time with music.

Art
1. Have each child write her name with magic marker or draw a geometric shape. Have her spread or squeeze glue over lines, place dried beans on top of glue and let dry. (Geometric shapes can be filled with beans.)
2. Let children make collages of different types of beans. Some children can cut their own pictures.
3. Each child makes and decorates a small picture of a bean in some form. Hang them all on the vegetable bulletin board begun in Lesson #1 Art #3.

Snack
1. Eat different forms of beans: navy, green, pinto, etc.
2. Eat snap beans prepared during Fine Motor #1 today.
3. Eat vegetables with bean dip.

Fine Motor
1. Let the children snap green beans, cook and spoon their beans onto plate.
2. Have the children plant bean seeds in rows of garden. Let them pat dirt on top of seeds and pour water on with watering can.

3. Help children make tambourines from pie tins and dried beans. Punch holes evenly spaced in edges of pie tins so the tins can be threaded together with heavy string. Have each child put beans into bottom pan, put another pie tin face down over it and thread string through holes. Knot string ends together tightly.

4. Help children make simple beanbags. Sew three sides of a cloth square or rectangle. Let children fill with beans. Sew the last side. Use for beanbag games of toss or head-carry. (See fig. 29C.)

Fig. 29C

Games

1. Throw bean bags into wooden Coke crate. Have four sections of Coke crate painted different colors. Make bean bags same color as each section. Ask child to "throw red bean bag into red square," "throw yellow bean bag into yellow square." See who can do this three feet or more away. If this is too difficult, work on tossing bean bag into trashcan, box, and into pie tin before Coke crate.

2. Play "Paw-Paw Patch." Instead of paws-paws, substitute word, "beans" and have large bean seeds on floor to pick up during game.

Storytelling

1. Play "Which One Is Missing." Show all vegetables for the week. Take one away while children are not looking. Ask, "Which one is missing?"

2. Read "Jack and the Beanstalk." Have children act out the story by climbing on chairs to go up the beanstalk and jumping off to climb down.

Gross Motor

Have children toss beanbags through circles (hula hoops, tires, etc.) hung up vertically.

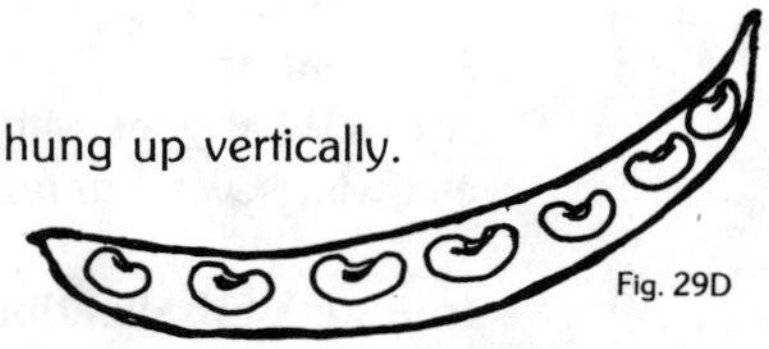

Cognitive

Fig. 29D

1. Have children sort different types of bean seeds.

2. Have children look inside a lima. Soak lima beans overnight, then open one up and see what's inside. Note the tiny lima plant waiting to sprout.

3. Give children green cardboard string beans. Let them glue beans in a row on the green cardboard bean and count the beans. Vary the bean length depending upon the children's skills. (See fig. 29D.)

Enrichment

1. Have the children plant three different types of bean seeds, observe what comes up and decide whether the plants look alike?

2. Prepare germination jars from baby food jars and blotters. Let children:
   a. soak beans overnight,
   b. put piece of blotter inside jar,
   c. put bean between the blotter and the jar,
   d. keep moist, and
   e. watch what happens.

Lesson 5: Radish

Unit Group Lesson

1. **Match Concrete Objects**
   Present two radishes. Say, "This is radish." Ask each child in turn to put the radish with the radish. Gradually increase number of irrelevant objects from which (s)he must select radish to match.

2. **Discriminate Objects**
   Present several objects. Have each child touch the radish in response to verbal direction, "Touch the radish."

3. **Match Pictures**
Present several pictures of common objects. Have each child match the pictures of the radishes.

4. **Discriminate Pictures**
Present a group of several unrelated pictures of objects. Have each child touch the picture of the radish in response to verbal direction, "Touch the radish."

5. **Figure-Ground**
Present a "busy" picture with many visual distractions. Ask each child to find the radish.

6. **Visual Closure**
Partially cover each of several pictures with paper. Ask each child to find the picture of the radish.

7. **Function**
Ask, "What do we do with a radish?"

8. **Association**
Ask, "What goes with the radish?" Use pictures or objects including beans, corn, potatoes, etc., with several unrelated objects or pictures.

9. **Imitate Verbalization**
Present a radish and ask, "What is this? Say, 'Radish'." The child will imitate "Radish."

10. **Verbalize Label**
Present a radish and ask, "What is this?" The child will respond, "Radish."

11. **Concept Enrichment**
Discuss how a radish grows and that it is a vegetable. Talk about times and places where radishes are usually eaten. Radishes are red. Discuss fact that radishes are hot. Radishes grow under the soil and the leaves grow above the soil.

Music

Play musical vegetables as in Lesson #1 Music #2 and add radishes.

Art

1. Help children make radish mobiles. Provide pre-cut red radishes out of construction paper. Let children spread glue on one radish, put yarn on glue and then put other radish on top. Pat gently. Each child should make two or three and tie to coat hanger or from ceiling. Hang up.
2. Finish vegetable bulletin board begun in Lesson #1 Art #3 by giving the children circles to cut, mark, and color as radishes. Add them to the bulletin board.
3. Paint large paper radishes red.

Snack

1. Have the salad including radishes made during Fine Motor today.
2. Have radish rosettes.

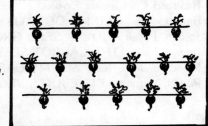
Fig. 29E

Fine Motor

1. Make lacing cards of radishes. Make some with a small number of large holes and others with a lot of small holes.
2. Let children cut and tear lettuce, carrots, radishes for salad. Small bits of cooked corn and green bean can be included. Mix together.
3. Let the children "plant the garden." Make "rows" for the garden on sheets of paper. You or skilled children can cut small slots in the drawn lines. Let the children add tiny plants just peeping out of the ground with radishes on the ends. (See fig. 29E.)

Games

1. Hide radishes around the room. Have a treasure hunt to find them.
2. Have various foods to taste. (Cover children's eyes.) Let them guess which is the radish. Be sure to use tiny pieces so the children do not burn their mouths.

Storytelling

Make up a story of a radish picked by a boy (Glen) who started to eat the whole radish. Then he heard a noise which made him jump. When he jumped, so did the radish. The radish rolled and rolled. First, it rolled across the room and into a crack on the floor. Then it rolled down the crack into a hole, but it didn't stop there. Let the children help continue and finish the story.

Gross Motor

Have a "radish run." Put radish on big spoon. Have each child walk to end of room with radish in spoon, put radish in a box, then run back and sit down.

Cognitive

1. Help children cut off top of radish and insert toothpicks in bottom of radish and put into water in glass or jar. Be sure the water touches the top of the jar. Watch radishes sprout tops.
2. Have the children sort red from non-red items. Some children may be able to sort red, green, brown, orange and yellow items.
3. Have the children identify big and small radishes from two or more radishes, depending upon their skill levels.

Enrichment

1. Radishes grow very rapidly. Have the children plant some outside or in a window box and watch them grow.
2. Help the children make large poster of "garden" vegetables. Label vegetables. Talk about dishes (recipes) made from certain vegetables. Find pictures of vegetable dishes and put on the poster.
3. Let children taste radishes and discuss other foods that are hot.

Field Trip

Go to grocery store and let each child buy one vegetable. Bring each vegetable back to school in paper bag with child's name on it. Have "show and tell." Snack could be raw vegetables with dip made from purchases.

Related Children's Records
"Carrots & Things" from COME & SEE THE PEPPERMINT TREE (EA)
"Kinds of Food" from LEARNING BASIC SKILLS-VOC. (EA)
"Alice's Restaurant" from LEARNING BASIC SKILLS-HEALTH & SAFETY (EA)

Related Children's Books
Barrett, Judi. OLD MacDONALD HAD AN APARTMENT HOUSE. New York: Atheneum, 1969.
Jordan, Helen. HOW A SEED GROWS. New York: Thomas Y. Crowell, 1960.
Krauss, Ruth. THE CARROT SEED. New York: Harper & Row, 1945.
Moncure, Jane Belk. SEE MY GARDEN GROW. Chicago: Children's Press, 1976.
Poulet, Virginia. BLUEBUG'S VEGETABLE GARDEN. Chicago: Children's Press, 1973.

Related Parenting Materials
Cansler, Dot. THE HOMESTRETCH. Winston-Salem, NC 27113-5128: Kaplan Press, 1983.

Related Materials
TEACHING PICTURES. Winston-Salem, NC 27113-5128: Kaplan Press, 1983.
STORY SEQUENCE CARDS I, II. Winston-Salem, NC 27113-5128: Kaplan Press, 1983.
SEWING CARDS I, II, III. Winston-Salem, NC 27113-5128: Kaplan Press, 1983.

Unit 30: Things for Cleaning

A developmental assessment should determine the functional levels of each child. Individual expectations are based on the assessment results.

Lesson 1: Broom

Unit Group Lesson

1. **Match Concrete Objects**
   Present two brooms. Say, "This is a broom." Ask each child in turn to put the broom with the broom. Gradually increase number of irrelevant objects from which (s)he must select broom to match.

2. **Discriminate Objects**
   Present several objects. Have each child touch the broom in response to verbal direction, "Touch the broom."

3. **Match Pictures**
   Present several pictures of common objects. Have each child match the pictures of the brooms.

4. **Discriminate Pictures**
   Present a group of several unrelated pictures of objects. Have each child touch the picture of the broom in response to verbal direction, "Touch the broom."

5. **Figure-Ground**
   Present a "busy" picture with many visual distractions. Ask each child to find the broom.

6. **Visual Closure**
   Partially cover each of several pictures with paper. Ask each child to find the picture of the broom.

7. **Function**
   Ask, "What do we do with a broom?"

8. **Association**
   Ask, "What goes with the broom?" Use pictures or objects including dust pan, dirt, floor, etc. with several unrelated objects or pictures.

9. **Imitate Verbalization**
   Present a broom and ask, "What is this? Say, 'Broom'." The child will imitate "Broom."

10. **Verbalize Label**
    Present a broom and ask, "What is this?" The child will respond, "Broom."

11. **Concept Enrichment**
    Discuss the materials that brooms are made of such as wood, straw, etc.

Music

1. Perform an action song to tune of "Row Your Boat":

   Sweep, sweep, sweep the room
   Sweep where ever you see;
   Sweep, sweep, sweep the room
   Now it's clean as can be.

   (Use both hands like holding broom and make sweeping motions.)

2. Have children use broom upside down as a horse to gallop on horseback to music.

Art

1. Let children find pictures of brooms in magazines or catalogs. Tear/cut-out and paste/glue into "Things for Cleaning" scrapbook.
2. Cut broom shapes from stiff board (tagboard, file folders, cardboard). Attach shape to large piece of newsprint, construction paper, etc. with paper clips. Have children sponge paint around shape. Remove shape and let paint dry.
3. Let the children dip brooms into water and paint designs on the playground or paved area near school.

Snack

1. Let children use broomstraws for testing doneness of snack cake. Then eat snack cake for snack.
2. Have children "sweep" crumbs off table with hands or whisk broom.

Fine Motor

1. Make path tracing activities of "Take the broom to the dust pan." and "Take the broom to the dirt." Let the children use large crayons, magic markers or large paint brushes.
2. Find large pictures of brooms and paste them onto cardboard. Cut them into two or more pieces. Have the children assemble like a puzzle. Use more pieces for more skilled children.
3. Let children use whisk brooms on tables, chairs, etc.

Games

1. Play "Pass the Broom." Have the group form a circle. Give a child-sized broom to one child. Tell child to pass the broom to the person next to him and keep it going until the music stops. The child who is holding the broom when the music stops moves out of circle and takes a turn to stop the music for the next round. Continue game until all participants have had an opportunity to stop music.
2. Put child-sized brooms in housekeeping area.

Storytelling

Before class cut out flannel shapes of broom, dust pan and mop. Have children manipulate the shapes on flannel board, and help them make up stories about them.

Gross Motor

1. Sweep (with child-sized broom) ping-pong balls, tennis balls, etc. across play area as a game.
2. Play "Broom Baseball." Have children use child-sized broom as bat and hit large ball thrown by teacher.
3. Toss paper scraps on the floor. Have children pick them up by hand and sweep them up. Let children decide which way was easier.
4. Let the children use small pine boughs as outside brooms.

Cognitive

1. Give each child several objects, including broom and one or two other articles for cleaning. Be sure each object has been introduced. Have each child put articles you clean with in one area and others in a different area. For a higher level activity, use pictures of objects and sort them into shoe boxes.
2. Provide real or cardboard brooms in two or more lengths. Have the children sequence them from shortest to tallest.
3. Measure each child against a broom. Let her decide if she is taller or shorter than the broom.

Enrichment

1. Talk about witches riding brooms. Try riding stick brooms.

2.   Make brooms with different numbers of straws. Have the children count the straws and tell how many.

Field Trip
   Visit a plant that makes brooms.

Lesson 2: Dust Pan

Unit Group Lesson

1.   **Match Concrete Objects**
   Present two dust pans. Say, "This is a dust pan." Ask each child in turn to put the dust pan with the dust pan. Gradually increase number of irrelevant objects from which (s)he must select dust pan to match.

2.   **Discriminate Objects**
   Present several objects. Have each child touch the dust pan in response to verbal direction, "Touch the dust pan."

3.   **Match Pictures**
   Present several pictures of common objects. Have each child match the pictures of the dust pans.

4.   **Discriminate Pictures**
   Present a group of several unrelated pictures of objects. Have each child touch the picture of the dust pan in response to verbal direction, "Touch the dust pan."

5.   **Figure-Ground**
   Present a "busy" picture with many visual distractions. Ask each child to find the dust pan.

6.   **Visual Closure**
   Partially cover each of several pictures with paper. Ask each child to find the picture of the dust pan.

7.   **Function**
   Ask, "What do we do with a dust pan?"

8.   **Association**
   Ask, "What goes with the dust pan?" Use pictures or objects including broom, vacuum cleaner, dirt, etc. with several unrelated objects or pictures.

9.   **Imitate Verbalization**
   Present a dust pan and ask, "What is this? Say, 'Dust pan'." The child will imitate "Dust pan."

10. **Verbalize Label**
   Present a dust pan and ask, "What is this?" The child will respond, "Dust pan."

11. **Concept Enrichment**
   A whisk broom is often used with a dust pan.

Music
   Sing an action song. Have the children use left hands as dust pan and right hands as broom, and make sweeping and picking up motions while they sing:
      Look, see I can do this!
      Look, see I can do this!
      Look, see I can do this!
      You can do it too if you watch me.

387

Art

1. Have children find pictures of dust pans in catalogs and paste them in "Things For Cleaning" scrapbook begun in Lesson #1 Art #1.
2. Let the children spatter paint around a dust pan or dust pan outline.
3. Provide dust pan shapes in several sizes. Have the children decorate them with scraps of paper and fabric and hang them on a hanger as a mobile.

Snack

Sweep up snack mess with a broom and dust pan. Use a whisk broom on the table.

Fine Motor

1. Have each child trace dotted line shape of dust pan and cut out the shape. If shape is drawn on sturdy paper, dust pan can be used to actually pick up dirt.
2. Let children use dust pan in sand box to pick up and pour sand into containers or back into sandbox.
3. Make dust pan shape sewing cards and provide shoe laces for children to sew. Make several cards to provide different levels of difficulty appropriate to children's skills.

Games

1. Place three large marbles in a circle on the floor. Have the children kneel around the circle with dust pans and push marbles back and forth to be "caught" in the dust pan. Let them use only the hand with the dust pan to catch the marble and take turns.
2. Put dust pans in the housekeeping area.

Storytelling

Use an old sheet and lamp or flashlight to tell a shadow story with broom, vacuum cleaner, mop, and dust pan. Let children manipulate the objects and contribute to the story.

Gross Motor

Have a dust pan and paper relay. Divide the class into teams of three children each. Form two lines with a team in each. Give dust pan to the child at the front of each line. Put three crumpled-up balls of newspaper in front of each line. The leaders use dust pan to pick up one ball of paper without help of other hand; take it to waste basket ten feet away, dump it in and bring dust pan back to person in front of line. First person goes to back of line while second person repeats the process. If paper ball is dropped on way to waste basket the child must pick it up again with dust pan only and get it into the waste basket. Continue until all teams have had a turn.

Cognitive

1. Have children sort dust pans from non-dust pans.
2. Have the children match whisk brooms to dust pans. Cut matching whisk brooms and dust pans from construction paper, making each set of a different color. For more advanced children use the color word on one and the color on the other. (This may be done as a shape matching activity with shapes glued onto brooms and dust pans cut of one color.)
3. Make pairs of dust pans which are identical. Show the children two alike and one which it is different and have them select the one that is different. Children with higher levels of skills can detect slighter differences.

Enrichment

Provide dust pan and small broom for the children to clean areas of the room.

Lesson 3: Mop

Unit Group Lesson

1. **Match Concrete Objects**
Present two mops. Say, "This is a mop." Ask each child in turn to put the mop with the mop. Gradually increase number of irrelevant objects from which (s)he must select mop to match.

2. **Discriminate Objects**
    Present several objects. Have each child touch the mop in response to verbal direction, "Touch the mop."

3. **Match Pictures**
    Present several pictures of common objects. Have each child match the pictures of the mops.

4. **Discriminate Pictures**
    Present a group of several unrelated pictures of objects. Have each child touch the picture of the mop in response to verbal direction, "Touch the mop."

5. **Figure-Ground**
    Present a "busy" picture with many visual distractions. Ask each child to find the mop.

6. **Visual Closure**
    Partially cover each of several pictures with paper. Ask each child to find the picture of the mop.

7. **Function**
    Ask, "What do we do with a mop?"

8. **Association**
    Ask, "What goes with the mop?" Use pictures or objects including water, soap, broom, dust pan, etc. with several unrelated objects or pictures.

9. **Imitate Verbalization**
    Present a mop and ask, "What is this? Say, 'Mop'." The child will imitate "Mop."

10. **Verbalize Label**
    Present a mop and ask, "What is this?" The child will respond, "Mop."

11. **Concept Enrichment**
    Discuss how a mop is different from a broom. Mops can be made of strings and sponge. Show both types.

Music

1. Sing an action song to the tune of "The Farmer in the Dell":
    We're mopping up the floor.   *(Make mopping motion.)*
    We're mopping up the floor.
    Stick in the mop and wring it out
    We're mopping up the floor.
2. Put on record with galloping music and let children use mop upside down as a horse and gallop to music around room or outside.

Art

1. Help each child make mop. Give each child a short piece of old broom handle, dowel, tongue depressor or popsicle stick for a handle and short pieces of colorful yarn. Have each put several pieces of yarn together and staple or tape bunch to the handle to make a miniature mop.
2. Give each child a drawn shape of a mop. Ask each one to outline shape with glue and to squeeze glue on inside of shape. Child may fill in outline with yarn or string.
3. Make small "mops" from straws and yarn stapled together. Let the children paint with them.

Snack

Serve spaghetti noodles and talk about how they look like a mop.

Fine Motor

1. Give children an opportunity to wring and squeeze water out of mop.
2. Have the children make mop pictures by gluing individual strands of yarn over outline of mop strings. Put the pictures in the "Things For Cleaning" scrapbook begun in Lesson #1 Art #1. Vary the number of strings and their curviness according to the skills of the children.

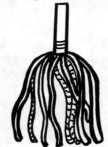

Fig. 30A

3. Make mops by stapling yarn to the end of a straw or dowel. Let the children give the mop haircuts by cutting the yarn with scissors. (See fig. 30A.)

Games

Provide real mops (rag and sponge) for children to use (slightly damp) on classroom floors.

Storytelling

Make stick puppets of Mrs. Broom, Mr. Vacuum Cleaner, and Baby Mop and begin a story for the children to finish.

Gross Motor

1. Have the children jump over the mop. Move the head of the mop back and forth on floor while each child takes a turn to jump over it as it is moved fast or slowly.
2. Let children mop the sidewalk with water from buckets.

Cognitive

1. Let the children choose pictures of mops from pictures of other cleaning items.
2. Provide mops in several sizes. Let the children identify the big one.
3. Have the children wipe up water from the floor with cloths and mops. Let them decide which is easier.

Enrichment

1. Grow grass seed in water cress seed on a sponge.
2. With equal-sized cups of water, let the children submerge different materials (such as sponge, strings, paper towels, etc.) and determine which absorbs the most water.

Lesson 4: Vacuum Cleaner

Unit Group Lesson

1. **Match Concrete Objects**

   Present two vacuum cleaners. Say, "This is a vacuum cleaner." Ask each child in turn to put the vacuum cleaner with the vacuum cleaner. Gradually increase number of irrelevant objects from which (s)he must select vacuum cleaner to match.

2. **Discriminate Objects**
    Present several objects. Have each child touch the vacuum cleaner in response to verbal direction, "Touch the vacuum cleaner."

3. **Match Pictures**
    Present several pictures of common objects. Have each child match the pictures of the vacuum cleaners.

4. **Discriminate Pictures**
    Present a group of several unrelated pictures of objects. Have each child touch the picture of the vacuum cleaner in response to verbal direction, "Touch the vacuum cleaner."

5. **Figure-Ground**
    Present a "busy" picture with many visual distractions. Ask each child to find the vacuum cleaner.

6. **Visual Closure**
    Partially cover each of several pictures with paper. Ask each child to find the picture of the vacuum cleaner.

7. **Function**
    Ask, "What do we do with a vacuum cleaner?"

8. **Association**
    Ask, "What goes with the vacuum cleaner?" Use pictures or objects including broom, vacuum cleaner bags, etc. with several unrelated objects or pictures.

9. **Imitate Verbalization**
    Present a vacuum cleaner and ask, "What is this? Say, 'Vacuum cleaner '." The child will imitate "Vacuum cleaner."

10. **Verbalize Label**
    Present a vacuum cleaner and ask, "What is this?" The child will respond, "Vacuum cleaner."

11. **Concept Enrichment**
    Discuss differences between a broom and a vacuum cleaner. There are two types of vacuum cleaners, tank and upright. Vacuum cleaners suck up the dirt like one can suck up drink with a straw. Discuss safety with electrical appliances.

Music

Sing to the tune of "Here We Go 'Round the Mulberry Bush":
The vacuum cleaner is full of air,
Full of air, full of air.
The vacuum cleaner is full of air,
It sucks up all the dirt.

Art

1. Have children assemble a vacuum cleaner. Prepare background paper by drawing shape of vacuum cleaner on it and coloring different parts different colors. Cut out parts of vacuum cleaner in different colors to fit shapes. Have children assemble vacuum cleaner by pasting shapes in proper place and add it to their "Things for Cleaning" scrapbook begun in Lesson #1 Art #1.
2. Make a path tracing for use with paint. Have each child use large paint brush and tempera to "take the vacuum cleaner to the carpet," first through a wide, straight tunnel, and then through a narrow, curved tunnel.
3. Let children decorate a vacuum cleaner bag with fabric scraps.

Snack

Use drinking straws in snack drink.

Fine Motor

1. Flannel Board - cut vacuum cleaner parts from flannel materials of different colors and have children assemble vacuum cleaner on flannel board.
2. Puzzle. Find a large picture of vacuum cleaner. Cut it out and paste it on cardboard. Cut the picture into three or four pieces. Have children put puzzle together.
3. Let the children pretend to be vacuum cleaners and blow air out. Let them use drinking straws to blow paint around on paper.

Games

1. Let the children pretend to be vacuum cleaners at work by making sucking and whirring sounds. They can move around in the room cleaning floors, chairs, blinds, etc.
2. Play an auditory discrimination game. Ask a small group to close their eyes while one child hides with vacuum cleaner and turns it on for a few seconds. Children in small group open eyes and point or tell teacher where the sound came from ("behind the piano," "out of bathroom," "under the table," "behind the book shelf," etc.).
3. Put a toy vacuum cleaner in the housekeeping area.

Storytelling

1. On cards, make a four-part sequence story of a vacuum cleaner at work. Repeat the story until the children can tell the story themselves.
2. Fingerplay:

   My vacuum cleaner has a great big tummy   *(Arms measure how big.)*
   And a very long nose   *(Hands and arms stretched forward.)*
   That sucks air up into it   *(Su, su, su, su.)*
   As the motor goes.   *(Whirr, whirr, whirr.)*

Gross Motor

Let the children use real vacuum cleaners in the classroom to clean carpet. Demonstrate both an upright and a tank if possible. Show other kinds also and explain that all of these are vacuum cleaners.

Cognitive

1. Have children learn prepositions by responding to instructions to vacuum ON, UNDER and AROUND a rug.
2. Show children other things that use sucking action such as eye dropper, baster, etc.
3. Let the children sweep up paper scraps and then vacuum them. Discuss "Which was easier?" and "Which was noisier?"

Enrichment

Make a collection of vacuum attachments. Have the children discuss their uses and later identify which one to use for various tasks.

Lesson 5: Dish Soap

Unit Group Lesson

1. **Match Concrete Objects**
   Present two containers of dish soap. Say, "This is dish soap." Ask each child in turn to put the dish soap with the dish soap. Gradually increase number of irrelevant objects from which (s)he must select dish soap to match.

2. **Discriminate Objects**
   Present several objects. Have each child touch the dish soap in response to verbal direction, "Touch the dish soap."

3. **Match Pictures**
Present several pictures of common objects. Have each child match the pictures of the dish soap.

4. **Discriminate Pictures**
Present a group of several unrelated pictures of objects. Have each child touch the picture of the dish soap in response to verbal direction, "Touch the dish soap."

5. **Figure-Ground**
Present a "busy" picture with many visual distractions. Ask each child to find the dish soap.

6. **Visual Closure**
Partially cover each of several pictures with paper. Ask each child to find the picture of the dish soap.

7. **Function**
Ask, "What do we do with dish soap?"

8. **Association**
Ask, "What goes with the dish soap?" Use pictures or objects including dishes, sink, sponge, mop, etc. with several unrelated objects or pictures.

9. **Imitate Verbalization**
Present dish soap and ask, "What is this? Say, 'Dish soap '." The child will imitate "Dish soap."

10. **Verbalize Label**
Present dish soap and ask, "What is this?" The child will respond, "Dish soap."

11. **Concept Enrichment**
Discuss reasons for using liquid dish soap rather than a powdered product. Look at clear and opaque dish soaps. Smell the different smells of dish soap especially the lemon types. Stress that dish soap should never be put in the mouth and caution children about products with lemons and such on the label that are NOT for drinking.

Music

Sing to the tune of "My Bonnie Lies Over the Ocean":
We put water into the dishpan.
We put in some dish soap, too.
We wiggle our hands in the water,
And the bubbles come tumbling through.
Soap suds, soap suds.
You feel good and clean dishes, too-oo-oo.
Soap suds, soap suds.
You feel good and clean dishes, too.

Art
1. Let the children whip up some dish soap and water to make a mixture that can be used like finger paint. The addition of food coloring, tempera, or glitter can make the activity more interesting.
2. Add sand or wood shavings to #1 for more texture.
3. Have children blow soap bubbles in a glass or on a piece of waxed paper. (See fig. 30B.)
4. Let children decorate a picture of dish soap and add it to the "Things for Cleaning" scrapbook. Let each child decorate a cover for the book.

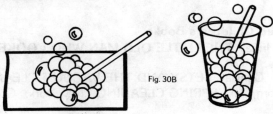
Fig. 30B

Snack

1. Eat 7-minute frosting, grits, or other food that resembles suds.
2. Use dish soap for hand washing before snack time.   Show children how one hand washes the other.

Fine Motor

1. Let the children mix dish soap with a little water and use for blowing bubbles. This helps to develop breathing skills for later pronunciation of certain words. Have children catch bubbles to help develop eye-hand coordination.
2. Let children fill empty dish soap bottles with water and squeeze the water out.
3. Let each child put title and her own name on "Things for Cleaning" scrapbook.
4. Have the children use soap suds mixture to frost a cardboard box cake or cover a milk carton house with snow.
5. Use soap suds mixture to cover small tree branches brought in from woods to make a winter scene.

Games

Place a small bottle of dish soap on table or floor. See if child can pick it up without using hands. Child may use elbows, feet, legs, etc.

Storytelling

1. Use scrapbook of "Things For Cleaning" that children have made during the week to show pictures. Have children tell about pictures by verbally labeling items and telling how they are used. Put book on book shelf for individual use next week.
2. Recite "This Little Hand":

This little hand is a good little hand	*(Raise right hand.)*
And this little hand is his brother.	*(Raise left hand.)*
They wash and they wash	*(Make washing motions.)*
And they wash and they wash.	
Each one washes the other.	

Gross Motor

Have children use dish soap to wash school's tables, dishes, doll clothes, outside equipment, etc.

Cognitive

1. Collect dish soap bottles in different sizes and have the children sequence them from smallest to largest.
2. Have children put green things with green dish soap and yellow things with yellow dish soap.
3. Use different kinds of soap (bar, liquid, etc.).

Enrichment

Blow bubbles (liquid detergent with a little sugar or glycerin to hold bubble shapes) using spools, drinking straws splayed at the end, plastic 6-pack holders, etc. Compare different results.

Field Trip

1. Take a trip to a department store, hardware store, or appliance store to see items studied this week.
2. Visit a cosmetic factory or a store selling soap.

Related Children's Records
ADVENTURES IN SOUND (MH)
"Shake the Papaya Down" from FOLK SONG CARNIVAL (EA)

Related Children's Books
Black, Irma. **THE LITTLE OLD MAN WHO COOKED AND CLEANED.** Chicago: Albert Whitman & Co., 1970.
Wolde, Gunilla. **BETSY AND THE VACUUM CLEANER.** New York: Random House, 1978.
Tornborg, Pat. **SPRING CLEANING.** New York: Golden Press, 1980.

Unit 31: Fire Fighter

A developmental assessment should determine the functional levels of each child. Individual expectations are based on the assessment results.

Lesson 1: Fire Fighter

Unit Group Lesson

1. **Match Concrete Objects** (Use dolls.)
Present two fire fighters. Say, "This is a fire fighter." Ask each child in turn to put the picture of the fire fighter with the picture of the fire fighter. Gradually increase number of pictures of irrelevant objects from which (s)he must select fire fighter to match.

2. **Discriminate Objects**
Present several objects. Have each child touch the fire fighter in response to verbal direction. "Touch the fire fighter."

3. **Match Pictures**
Present several pictures of common objects. Have each child match the pictures of the fire fighters.

4. **Discriminate Pictures**
Present a group of several unrelated pictures of objects. Have each child touch the picture of the fire fighter in response to verbal direction, "Touch the fire fighter."

5. **Figure-Ground**
Present a "busy" picture with many visual distractions. Ask each child to find the fire fighter.

6. **Visual Closure**
Partially cover each of several pictures with paper. Ask each child to find the picture of the fire fighter.

7. **Function**
Ask, "What does a fire fighter do?"

8. **Association**
Ask, "What goes with the fire fighter?" Use pictures or objects including boots, hat, coat, fire truck, etc., with several unrelated objects or pictures.

9. **Imitate Verbalization**
Present a fire fighter and ask, "What is this? Say, 'Fire fighter'." The child will imitate "Fire fighter."

10. **Verbalize Label**
Present a fire fighter and ask, "What is this?" The child will respond, "Fire fighter."

11.   **Concept Enrichment**

Fire fighters are also called firemen and public safety officers. Discuss differences between the job a fire fighter does and the jobs done by other community helpers such as police persons, mail carriers, etc.

Music

Sing to the tune of "Here We Go 'Round the Mulberry Bush":
The fire fighter puts the fire out,
Fire out, fire out.
The fire fighter puts the fire out,
To keep us safe from harm.

Art

1.   Have children color picture of a fire fighter.
2.   Cut out construction paper uniform, boots and helmet for fire fighter. Give each child a picture of undressed fire fighter. Let her paste pieces in appropriate place to dress fire fighter. Color-code pieces for children with lower skill levels.
3.   Help the children make a giant firetruck from a large box. Have them cover it with red scraps of paper and add black wheels.

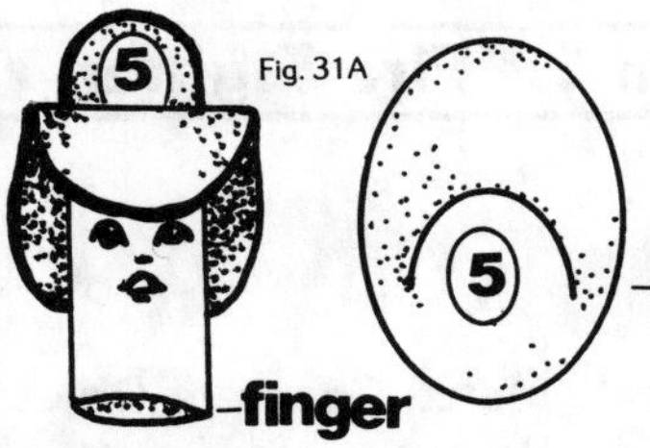

Fig. 31A

Snack

Eat bag lunches that a fire fighter might take to the station.

Fine Motor

1.   Let children tear small pieces of red construction paper and paste them on a large sheet for fire. Have each child glue a square of red cellophane paper over collage for additional fire effect.
2.   Help children cut out fire fighter's boots, helmets, etc.
3.   Have each child make a fire fighter finger puppet. Let each make a cylinder out of white paper and cut out fire hat on red paper that fits finger, add features on cylinder and glue on hat. (See fig. 31A.)

Games

Provide fire hat, boots, and coats for children to use in dramatic play.

Storytelling

1.   Read a story about fire fighters that tells what they wear, what they do, and where they live.
2.   Recite poem:
          The fire fighter is waiting ready
          Near his engine good and stout
          And should there be a fire tonight
          He'll rush to put it out
3.   Perform finger play:
          Five little fire fighters sleeping in a row.   *(Close fingers of one hand.)*
          Ding Dong goes the bell,   *(Use other hand to pull down two times.)*
          And off to the fire they go.   *(Put one hand on top of other and do*
                                                            pole slide motion with hands.)

Gross Motor

1.   Let children use old hose on playground and climb ladders to put out fires.
2.   Have a fire fighter's helmet relay: use two discarded fire fighter's helmets. Divide children into two lines and let each one have a turn to run, get helmet, and bring to next person in line. Continue until all children have had a turn.
3.   Boot race: use fire fighter's boots or men's large shoes and let children race to fence, sandbox, etc. and back.

Cognitive

1.   Have children select fire fighters from pictures of community helpers.
2.   Make a cue sheet with the fire fighter pictured at the top and repeated below several times. Make a variety of levels of difficulty suitable to the children's skills.

3. Have children sort fire fighter's clothing from non-fire fighters clothing.
4. Use bell to events certain signal. Have the children count times the bell rings to determine what the signal means. For example, one bell means change centers, two bells means eating time, etc.

Enrichment

Look at fire hydrants, fire alarm boxes, fire detectors, etc., in and near the school.

Field Trip

Talk about taking a trip to a fire station. (Trip is in Lesson #4 of this unit.) The children will be most interested in a fire fighter's hat, coat, boots, ladder, hose, bell, siren and truck. Do not try to go into too much detail when visiting a fire station.

Visitor

Invite a fire fighter to come dressed in uniform to your class. Talk about the fact that women can be (and are) fire fighters, too!

Lesson 2: Fire Truck

Unit Group Lesson

1. **Match Concrete Objects**
   Present two fire trucks. Say, "This is a fire truck." Ask each child in turn to put the fire truck with the fire truck. Gradually increase number of irrelevant objects from which (s)he must select fire truck to match.

2. **Discriminate Objects**
   Present several objects. Have each child touch the fire truck in response to verbal direction, "Touch the fire truck."

3. **Match Pictures**
   Present several pictures of common objects. Have each child match the pictures of the fire trucks.

4. **Discriminate Pictures**
   Present a group of several unrelated pictures of objects. Have each child touch the picture of the fire truck in response to verbal direction, "Touch the fire truck."

5. **Figure-Ground**
   Present a "busy" picture with many visual distractions. Ask each child to find the fire truck.

6. **Visual Closure**
   Partially cover each of several pictures with paper. Ask each child to find the picture of the fire truck.

7. **Function**
   Ask, "What do we do with a fire truck?"

8. **Association**
   Ask, "What goes with the fire truck?" Use pictures or objects including ladder, fire fighter, fire hose, etc., with several unrelated objects or pictures.

9. **Imitate Verbalization**
   Present a fire truck and ask, "What is this? Say, 'Fire truck'." The child will imitate "Fire truck."

10. **Verbalize Label**
    Present a fire truck and ask, "What is this?" The child will respond, "Fire truck."

11. **Concept Enrichment**
What kind of noises do fire trucks make?

Music

Sing to the tune of "Wheels on the Bus":
Verse 1: The wheels on the fire truck
Go round, round, round
round, round, round
round, round, round
The wheels on the fire truck go
round, round, round
All around the town.
Verse 2: The horn. . .beep, beep, beep.
Verse 3: The bell. . .ding, ding, ding.
Verse 4: The hose. . .squirt, squirt, squirt.
Verse 5: The siren. . .(siren noises).

Art

1. Have children paint fire truck at the easel.
2. Help the children make a giant fire truck from a large box. Have them cover it with red paper pieces and add black wheels.
3. Make a fire station from a big box. Cut doors for trucks to go in and out. Paint red. Write name of station on front such as NURSERY SCHOOL STATION 1.

Snack

Bring snack to the table on the classroom fire truck.

Fine Motor

1. Have children paint with red tempera or finger paint.
2. Have children paste fire fighter picture on fire truck to associate fire fighter with fire truck.
3. Have children use fire truck cookie cutters to cut play dough fire trucks.
4. Have children find outlines of hose, axes, ladder, fire fighter, etc., that have been drawn on a large fire truck and glue on matching cut out shapes.

Games

1. Put toy fire trucks, fire fighters, helmets, boots, pieces of hose, etc., into block center or outside to encourage dramatic play.
2. Add ladders, hoses, etc., to the fire truck made in Art #2.
3. Put toy fire trucks in block play area.

Storytelling

Make large flannel fire truck cut-out and small cut-outs of tools and fire fighters. Use them to tell a flannel board story. Leave this material out for several days so that children may tell their own stories to each other or use it individually.

Gross Motor

1. Cut out large cardboard or wooden shape of fire truck. Cut out back of truck so that children can use it for bean bag toss. (See fig. 31B.)
2. Make roads on floor with masking tape for children to drive toy fire trucks.
3. At the sound of a fire bell have the children run to a designated spot to get in the truck to go "fight" a fire.

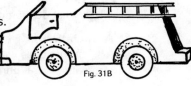
Fig. 31B

Cognitive

1. Make toy fire stations out of milk cartons. Have Station #1, #2, etc. Have children drive toy fire trucks with same numbers into proper fire station.
2. Have children put fire trucks IN fire stations.
3. Teach prepositions by having children put toy fire truck, IN, UNDER, ON, and BEHIND a barrel, box, shelf, etc.

Enrichment

1.   Discuss why a fire truck has a siren.
2.   Discuss the tools kept on a fire truck and their uses.

Visitor

Have a fire truck visit the school.

Lesson 3: Fire Hose

Unit Group Lesson

NOTE: If only pictures are available then use them in item 1 and omit items 2 and 3.

1.   **Match Concrete Objects**
     Present two fire hoses. Say, "This is a fire hose." Ask each child in turn to put the fire hose with the fire hose. Gradually increase number of irrelevant objects from which (s)he must select fire hose to match.

2.   **Discriminate Objects**
     Present several objects. Have each child touch the fire hose in response to verbal direction, "Touch the fire hose."

3.   **Match Pictures**
     Present several pictures of common objects. Have each child match the pictures of the fire hoses.

4.   **Discriminate Pictures**
     Present a group of several unrelated pictures of objects. Have each child touch the picture of the fire hose in response to verbal direction, "Touch the fire hose."

5.   **Figure-Ground**
     Present a "busy" picture with many visual distractions. Ask each child to find the fire hose.

6.   **Visual Closure**
     Partially cover each of several pictures with paper. Ask each child to find the picture of the fire hose.

7.   **Function**
     Ask, "What do we do with a fire hose?"

8.   **Association**
     Ask, "What goes with the fire hose?" Use pictures or objects including fire, fire fighter, ladder, fire truck, etc., with several unrelated objects or pictures.

9.   **Imitate Verbalization**
     Present a fire hose and ask, "What is this? Say, 'Fire hose'." The child will imitate "Fire hose."

10. **Verbalize Label**
     Present a fire hose and ask, "What is this?" The child will respond, "Fire hose."

11. **Concept Enrichment**
     Show and discuss different types of fire hoses, fire hydrants, fire extinguishers.

Music

1.   Sing to the tune of "Here We Go 'Round the Mulberry Bush":
     This is the way we squirt the hose.   *(Pantomime squirting hose while singing.)*

2. Give the children pieces of water hose to sing through. This changes the sound of their voices and is fun.

Art
1. Let children do a blow painting with short pieces of hose. Put small spoon of tempera paint on large piece of construction paper. Have child put one end of hose near paint and blow through the other and watch the paint scatter across the paper to make designs. Use several colors.
2. Let children use play dough or clay to make long hose. Let dry. Paint.
3. Let children make a collage of a hose using pieces of elbow macaroni glued next to each other.

Snack
1. Serve noodles for snack. Let the children feel them before and after cooking. Eat buttered or with topping.
2. Let the children use drinking straws for pretend hoses. Drink juice through "hose."

Fine Motor
1. Have children glue string over a picture of fire hose attached to a hydrant. Vary the level of difficulty according to the children's skills. (See fig. 31C.)
2. Make a figure-ground activity as above but cover the hose with distractors. Let the children outline the hose with magic markers. Vary the complexity of the hose and distractors according to the skill levels of the children.
3. Have children use tongs and tweezers to pick up pretend fire hose (rope, string, etc.).

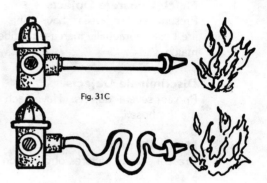

Fig. 31C

Games
Use real hoses for play. Let children "squirt" out pretend fires in the play yard, using either imagination or real water.

Storytelling
Make up a story about a fire hose which saves a family's house by putting out a fire in the house.

Gross Motor
1. Have the children roll up long garden hose.
2. Put two long pieces of hose on ground side by side. Have the children jump over them. Spread two hose pieces five or six inches apart and see who can still jump over without getting feet inside. Continue spreading hose pieces further apart until nobody can jump over the span.
3. Use a rope for a hose. Let children walk "hose" forward and backward (straight and in a circle), hop over "hose," and move along a curvy (rope) "hose."

Cognitive
1. Use a real hose to water plants, fill a school wading pool, wash teacher's car, etc.
2. Provide different lengths of hose and let the children decide which is the longest and shortest.
3. Have each child shape a length of hose into her initial.

Enrichment
1. Show children a nozzle and let them experiment with how it works.
2. Decide whether a hose can grow. The fire hose sometimes looks like it is growing as it is being pulled out of the truck.

Field Trip
1. Show children fire hydrants and talk about their purpose. See one being used if possible.
2. Visit the fire station, look for the hose.

Visitor
A fireman.

Unit Group Lesson

1. **Match Concrete Objects**
Present two ladders. Say, "This is a ladder." Ask each child in turn to put the ladder with the ladder. Gradually increase number of irrelevant objects from which (s)he must select ladder to match.

2. **Discriminate Objects**
Present several objects. Have each child touch the ladder in response to verbal direction, "Touch the ladder."

3. **Match Pictures**
Present several pictures of common objects. Have each child match the pictures of the ladders.

4. **Discriminate Pictures**
Present a group of several unrelated pictures of objects. Have each child touch the picture of the ladder in response to verbal direction, "Touch the ladder."

5. **Figure-Ground**
Present a "busy" picture with many visual distractions. Ask each child to find the ladder.

6. **Visual Closure**
Partially cover each of several pictures with paper. Ask each child to find the picture of the ladder.

7. **Function**
Ask, "What do we do with a ladder?"

8. **Association**
Ask, "What goes with the ladder?" Use pictures or objects including hose, fire fighter, fire truck, etc., with several unrelated objects or pictures.

9. **Imitate Verbalization**
Present a ladder and ask, "What is this? Say, 'Ladder'." The child will imitate "Ladder."

10. **Verbalize Label**
Present a ladder and ask, "What is this?" The child will respond, "Ladder."

11. **Concept Enrichment**
Look at and discuss different types of ladders, such as: stepladders, aerial ladders, extension ladders, etc.

Music

Sing to the tune of "Did You Ever See a Lassie":
Did you ever see a ladder   *(Motion with arms up and down.)*
A ladder, a ladder
Did you ever see a ladder
Go up and down.

Art

1. Let children make a crayon drawing of a ladder. Then have them paint over it with red food coloring and water.

2. Draw picture of ladder. Have children outline shape with glue then sprinkle on sand or glitter. Let them decorate around the ladder.

3. Let children make a ladder by gluing cotton swabs in ladder - shape and use pipe cleaner "fire fighters" for "climbing."

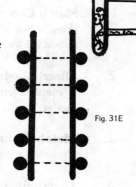

Fig. 31D

Snack

Make and eat "ladders" made from carrots, celery sticks, pretzels, bananas, etc. Cut food in strips and place on plates in ladder design. The children can prepare the "ladder treats." (See fig. 31D.)

Fine Motor

1. Paste picture of ladder on stiff cardboard. Cut into two or more pieces. Have children assemble ladder puzzles which are appropriate to their ability.

2. Have children glue strips on construction paper onto ladder for rungs.

3. Let children make ladders from Tinkertoys.

Fig. 31E

4. Let children make ladders from peas and toothpicks. Soak green peas overnight. Let children build a ladder and let dry completely. The peas will harden like glue.

5. Give each child a page with two vertical lines. Let them make a ladder from these lines. (For some children include dots of the ladder's rungs.) (See fig. 31E.)

Games

1. Lay ladders down on top of wagons to make fire trucks. Attach pieces of hose, rubber, axe, etc. Pretend these are fire trucks and play fire fighter.

2. Put several ladders of different heights on the playground. Use them for climbing games.

Storytelling

Make up a story about "Larry the Ladder." Larry works for the fire department and he helps them in many ways. Help the children name things which Larry does such as help rescue cats from trees, help firemen put out fires, etc.

Gross Motor

1. Use ladders as part of obstacle course. Children have to climb OVER, UNDER and THROUGH ladders.

2. Place a ladder on the floor (or make one with masking tape). Have children walk between rungs, put two feet in each square, have one foot in a square and one outside, etc.

3. Let children climb small, stable ladders.

Cognitive

1. Have children sort fire fighter's tools from doctor's tools or baker's tools.

2. Have the children count rungs on ladders and the spaces between the rungs. Vary the number of rungs according to each child's skill.

3. Auditory Closure: Have children find missing part of word when you say fire _____ or _____ fighter. Grammatic: Have children repeat a model sentence (example) "This is a fire fighter." Visual: Show picture of fire fighter with a body part missing (arm, leg, foot, nose, and eye). Ask child to find part that is missing.

Enrichment

Count the rungs on the ladder. Have ladders with different numbers of rungs. Have the children lay loose rungs on those pictured and tell how many rungs on each ladder. use stick pegs or strips of paper for matching rungs. (See fig. 31F.)

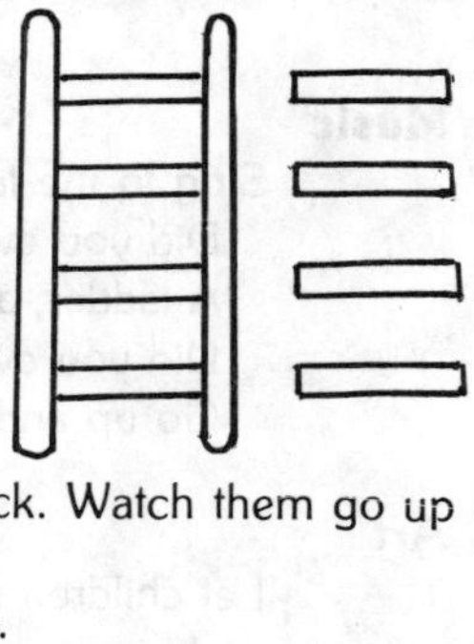

Fig. 31F

Field Trip

1. Visit fire station. Have fire fighter show the ladders on the hook and ladder truck. Watch them go up and down.

2. Look for ladders around the neighborhood. Go to construction sites if possible.

3. Look at bunk beds (home, store) which use ladders. Let children climb up to the top bed.

Lesson 5: Fire

Unit Group Lesson

1. **Match Pictures**

   Present two pictures of fire. Say, "This is a fire." Ask each child in turn to put the picture of the fire with the picture of the fire. Gradually increase number of pictures of irrelevant objects from which (s)he must select fire to match.

2. **Discriminate Pictures**

   Present a group of several unrelated pictures of objects. Have each child touch the picture of the fire in response to verbal direction, "Touch the fire."

3. **Figure-Ground**

   Present a "busy" picture with many visual distractions. Ask each child to find the fire.

4. **Visual Closure**

   Partially cover each of several pictures with paper. Ask each child to find the picture of the fire.

5. **Function**

   Ask, "What do we do with a fire?"

6. **Association**

   Ask, "What goes with the fire?" Use pictures or objects including fire fighter, fire hose, fire truck, etc., with several unrelated objects or pictures.

7. **Imitate Verbalization**

   Present a picture of fire and ask, "What is this? Say, 'Fire'." The child will imitate "Fire."

8. **Verbalize Label**

   Present a picture of fire and ask, "What is this?" The child will respond, "Fire."

9. **Concept Enrichment**

   Fire is hot. Talk about safety around fire.

Music
1. Review unit's music.
2. Sing to the tune of "Three Blind Mice":
   Fire is hot.
   Fire is hot.
   Touch it not.
   Touch it not.

Art
1. Have children make candle holders from play dough or clay and stick candles in them.
2. Help children make candles in paper cups or milk cartons. Melt paraffin (hot!) and old crayons of one color. Pour into containers over a wick. When cool, peel container off. SUPERVISE CAREFULLY.
3. Let children paint with red and yellow paint at the easel.

Snack
1. Eat "red hots" for snack.
2. Use candles on the table, talk about the need to be careful of the fire on the candle.

Fine Motor

1. Let children use cut up drinking straws and pre-cut red construction paper shapes to string onto yarn for a necklace.
2. Have children pour cold and warm water from one container to another.
3. Light birthday or other candles. Let children blow them out.
4. Let children blow out candles that re-light.

Games

1. Play "Hot Potato" with ball outside or small potato inside.
2. Divide the group into two groups. One group is flaming fire and the others are fire fighters. Have children pantomime fire fighters squirting water on the flaming fire. The flaming fire gets smaller and smaller.

Storytelling

1. Prepare a story about the trip to the fire station. Use photographs or other available pictures to prepare for or recall the experience of going to the fire station.
2. Make up a story about "Felix Fire." Felix does very good things for people. He keeps them warm, cooks their food and lights the night. However, Felix will burn things if he gets too near to them. He has no control over where he goes so people must help him to stay under control. He gets very sad if he gets out of control. Have children think up some ideas to help keep Felix under control.

Gross Motor

Make a pretend fire using sticks and red cellophane paper. Dance around it. Run around it, etc.

Cognitive

1. Give children pictures of things used to fight fires (hose, ladders, etc.) and things not used to fight fires (spoon, toothbrush, etc.). Let children sort pictures.
2. Let children find pictures of all the places you can build a fire safely.
3. Help children make a list of things fire can do. (warm, etc.).

Enrichment

1. Show children that fire needs air to burn. Light two identical candles and put a glass jar over one. Why did one stay lighted and the other go out?
2. Discuss safety around fire.

Field Trip

Visit a home with an open fireplace. Build a fire. Talk about precautions as you watch fire.

Visitor

Invite an Eagle Scout to produce fire with flint stones, sticks or a mirror.

Related Parenting Materials

Cansler, Dot. **THE HOMESTRETCH.** Winston-Salem, NC 27113-5128: Kaplan Press, 1983.

Related Materials

TEACHING PICTURES. Winston-Salem, NC 27113-5128: Kaplan Press, 1983.
STORY SEQUENCE CARDS I, II. Winston-Salem, NC 27113-5128: Kaplan Press, 1983.
SEWING CARDS I, II, III. Winston-Salem, NC 27113-5128: Kaplan Press, 1983.

Unit 32: Things for Mealtime

A developmental assessment should determine the functional levels of each child. Individual expectations are based on the assessment results.

Lesson 1: Spoon

Unit Group Lesson

1. **Match Concrete Objects**
   Present two spoons. Say, "This is a spoon." Ask each child in turn to put the spoon with the spoon. Gradually increase number of irrelevant objects from which (s)he must select spoon to match.

2. **Discriminate Objects**
   Present several objects. Have each child touch the spoon in response to verbal direction, "Touch the spoon."

3. **Match Pictures**
   Present several pictures of common objects. Have each child match the pictures of the spoons.

4. **Discriminate Pictures**
   Present a group of several unrelated pictures of objects. Have each child touch the picture of the spoon in response to verbal direction, "Touch the spoon."

5. **Figure-Ground**
   Present a "busy" picture with many visual distractions. Ask each child to find the spoon.

6. **Visual Closure**
   Partially cover each of several pictures with paper. Ask each child to find the picture of the spoon.

7. **Function**
   Ask, "What do we do with a spoon?"

8. **Association**
   Ask, "What goes with the spoon?" Use pictures or objects including fork, knife, bowl, etc. with several unrelated objects or pictures.

9. **Imitate Verbalization**
   Present a spoon and ask, "What is this? Say, 'Spoon'." The child will imitate "Spoon."

10. **Verbalize Label**
    Present a spoon and ask, "What is this?" The child will respond, "Spoon."

11.   **Concept Enrichment**
Discuss the best kinds of foods to eat with a spoon. Discuss other uses of spoons, such as serving, and look at slotted spoons, etc.

Music
1.   Sing "Hey, Diddle Diddle, the Cat and the Fiddle" and use flannel cut-outs along with song.
2.   Model "playing spoons." Let children play spoons with you. (Put two spoons back to back or use one spoon as a drumstick.)

Art
1.   Have children cut out pictures of spoons from catalogs and start a "Thing for Mealtime," book.
2.   Let children use spoons with play dough.
3.   Have children make spoon puppets. Let them draw face on bowl of a wooden spoon then make a dress, add hair, etc.   (See fig. 32A.)

Fig. 32A

Snack
1.   Eat soup, apple sauce, jello, pudding, yogurt, etc. with a spoon.
2.   Eat spoon bread made in Fine Motor #4 today.
3.   Set aside a special table at lunchtime for people who know mealtime manners. Use real place mats, cloth napkins, napkin ring, real silver and a lighted candle. Two at a time earn the privilege of eating at the special table. Continue this throughout the week.

Fine Motor
1.   Make table setting puzzle with two or more pieces. Have each child put together a puzzle appropriate to her skill level.
2.   Let children spoon up sand, finger paint, mashed potatoes, etc. Have child say, "We use a spoon to pick up mashed potatoes."
3.   Model how to hold spoon and dip food and take it to mouth. Say, "This is the way we eat with a spoon." Have each child imitate with spoon. Pretend to feed doll with spoon.
4.   Have children help make spoonbread. Eat for snack.

Games
1.   Use spoons in games. Carry potatoes, hard boiled eggs, etc. on spoons.
2.   Let children feed each other using spoons.
3.   Have silverware in housekeeping area and in sand play area.

Storytelling
Recite "Hey Diddle Diddle the Cat and the Fiddle." Let children recite the nursery rhyme as they put flannel pieces on flannel board. Let the children dramatize the story by acting out the motions.

Gross Motor
Have each child carry large bean in spoon from table to door and back without spilling it.

Cognitive
1.   Classification Activity: Use two shoe boxes to separate things for eating from things not for eating. Put all objects for eating in one box and all objects not for eating in the other box. "Name the things for eating?" Teacher models by picking up spoon and saying, "This is a spoon?"
2.   Model where to put spoon on place mat. Have child imitate teacher. Give child place mat with plate and spoon shape drawn in proper place. Have child put real spoon on outline. Give child place mat with drawn plate and have child put spoon in proper place with no cues. Have child say, "This is where the spoon goes."
3.   Let children stir things with a spoon (water, cake mix, lemonade, etc.) and count the number of "stirs."

Enrichment
1.   Have the children associate different spoons with their uses.
2.   Have children begin place mats with designs drawn on each. Let them fringe the sides of the place mat and put on a spoon outline. (See fig. 32B.)

3.   Have them "set" the table, sit at the table, and pretend to eat and use appropriate table behavior. (See fig. 32C.)

Fig. 32B

Fig. 32C

Field Trip

Visit a restaurant and take notice of place mats, table setting, seats, etc.

Lesson 2: Fork

Unit Group Lesson

1. **Match Concrete Objects**
Present two forks. Say, "This is a fork." Ask each child in turn to put the fork with the fork.
Gradually increase number of irrelevant objects from which (s)he must select fork to match.

2. **Discriminate Objects**
Present several objects. Have each child touch the fork in response to verbal direction, "Touch the fork."

3. **Match Pictures**
Present several pictures of common objects. Have each child match the pictures of the forks.

4. **Discriminate Pictures**
Present a group of several unrelated pictures of objects. Have each child touch the picture of the fork in response to verbal direction, "Touch the fork."

5. **Figure-Ground**
Present a "busy" picture with many visual distractions. Ask each child to find the fork.

6. **Visual Closure**
Partially cover each of several pictures with paper. Ask each child to find the picture of the fork.

7. **Function**
Ask, "What do we do with a fork?"

8. **Association**
Ask, "What goes with the fork?" Use pictures or objects including spoon, knife, meat, plate, etc., with several unrelated objects or pictures.

9. **Imitate Verbalization**
Present a fork and ask, "What is this? Say, 'Fork'." The child will imitate "Fork."

10. **Verbalize Label**
Present a fork and ask, "What is this?" The child will respond, "Fork."

11. **Concept Enrichment**
Forks come in big sizes for farm work called pitchforks.

Music

Sing to the tune of "Here We Go 'Round the Mulberry Bush":
  This is the way we eat
  with a fork, (spoon, etc.).

Art

1.   Give each child a construction paper place mat with a pre-drawn place setting. Have child color fork, spoon, knife, plate and napkin.

2.   Make path tracing activities of "Take the fork to the meat." and "Take the fork to the mouth." Vary the level of difficulty according to the skills of the children.

3.   Have children make soft play dough balls, clay balls, etc. and use a fork to "spear" them.

Snack

1.   Use forks for "spearing" foods (diced ham, peas, pieces of cake, cut up hot dogs, pieces of bananas, etc.).

2.   "Spear" snack foods with toothpicks.

Fine Motor

1.   Cut out shapes of forks in cardboard. Punch holes around edges and let the children use as a sewing card. Let them use shoe string to sew. Vary the number and size of the holes for different levels of skills.

2.   Prepare a shoe box of grits, lentils, rice, beans, spaghetti and let children use fork to see which items can be picked up with forks and which can not.

3.   Show children how forks hold food for knives to cut. Let child hold fork while teacher uses knife to cut food.

Games

Play "Knife, Knife, Fork" like "Duck, Duck, Goose" game. Have children form a circle; one child is "it" and march around circle saying, "knife, knife, fork." He says this several times, then on the word "fork" he touches someone in circle who must run after him. If "it" gets back to empty space before being caught, the chaser becomes "it" and repeats games. If chaser catches "it" then "it" has to get inside circle until another "it" is caught and put inside.

Storytelling

1.   Make flannel cut-out of table setting. Let children assemble items on flannel board and make up a story about them.

2.   Finger play:
  Here are mother's knives and forks.   *(Interlock fingers, palms up.)*
  This is father's table.   *(Interlock fingers, palm down.)*
  This is sister's drinking glass.   *(Touch all fingers on one hand to thumb leaving open at top of hand.)*
  This is the gravy ladle.   *(Extend one arm down and cup hand up.)*

3.   Pretend to be a fork named "Florrie Fork" and describe all the things which "Florrie Fork" does.

Gross Motor

1.   Use a real or play pitchfork to pick up hay, dirt or styrofoam pellets.

2.   Make a "Find-the-fork obstacle course." Have children go over an obstacle course until they get to the fork at the end.

Cognitive

1.   Teach each child to set the table and place the fork properly.

2.   Have the children sort things for eating from other things.

3.   Make large forks with three and four tines. Have the children match three-tined forks to those with three tines and four-tined forks to those with four tines.

Enrichment

Add the outline of a fork to the place mat begun in Lesson #1 Enrichment #2.

Field Trip

Take a walk and find forked sticks to take back to school.

Lesson 3: Knife

Unit Group Lesson

1. **Match Concrete Objects**
   Present two knives. Say, "This is a knife." Ask each child in turn to put the knife with the knife. Gradually increase number of irrelevant objects from which (s)he must select knife to match.

2. **Discriminate Objects**
   Present several objects. Have each child touch the knife in response to verbal direction, "Touch the knife."

3. **Match Pictures**
   Present several pictures of common objects. Have each child match the pictures of the knives.

4. **Discriminate Pictures**
   Present a group of several unrelated pictures of objects. Have each child touch the picture of the knife in response to verbal direction, "Touch the knife."

5. **Figure-Ground**
   Present a "busy" picture with many visual distractions. Ask each child to find the knife.

6. **Visual Closure**
   Partially cover each of several pictures with paper. Ask each child to find the picture of the knife.

7. **Function**
   Ask, "What do we do with a knife?"

8. **Association**
   Ask, "What goes with the knife?" Use pictures or objects including spoon, fork, meat, plate, etc., with several unrelated objects or pictures.

9. **Imitate Verbalization**
   Present a knife and ask, "What is this? Say, 'Knife'." The child will imitate "Knife."

10. **Verbalize Label**
    Present a knife and ask, "What is this?" The child will respond, "Knife."

11. **Concept Enrichment**
    Discuss knife safety.

Music

Sing "Three Blind Mice."

Art

1. Have children glue pre-cut shapes of knife, fork, spoon, and plate onto construction paper model for table setting and decorate the edges.
2. Have children cut out shapes of knives and use pinking shears to make a blade with teeth.
3. Have children practice spreading by spreading finger paint on paper using popsicle sticks as spreaders.

Snack

1. Have children use plastic knives to spread foods for snack such as peanut butter, cream cheese, pimento cheese, honey butter, etc.
2. Have children use plastic knives for cutting bananas, cheese, cooked apples, etc.

Fine Motor

1. Have children use table knives without teeth with play dough.
2. Show children how forks hold food for knives to cut, but do not expect children to do both actions. Hold the food with a fork while the child cuts.
3. Have children trace around the dotted outline of a large knife.

Games

Have a knife hunt. Hide a knife while children close their eyes. Give clues as to where knife is while children hunt for knife. Finder gets to hide knife next time.

Storytelling

Hold up a knife (or picture). Have the children each tell a one-line story about what the knife did: at a picnic, at a watermelon party, at a birthday party, at the bakery, when Johnny was eating pancakes, etc.

Gross Motor

Play tag or ride tricycles outdoors.

Cognitive

1. Help children learn to place a knife in the proper location in a table setting.
2. Have the children sort out utensils in trays used for silverware.
3. Have the children match knives with different and same silverware patterns.
4. Help children learn to hold knives by the handle.

Enrichment

1. Add an outline of a knife to the place mat begun in Lesson #1 Enrichment #2.
2. Show a Swiss army knife and identify all of the gadgets.

Field Trip

Take group to the cafeteria. Let each child select three items for table setting (spoon, fork, knife) and set a place on the table for lunch.

Lesson 4: Plate

Unit Group Lesson

1. **Match Concrete Objects**
Present two plates. Say, "This is a plate." Ask each child in turn to put the plate with the plate. Gradually increase number of irrelevant objects from which (s)he must select plate to match.

2. **Discriminate Objects**
Present several objects. Have each child touch the plate in response to verbal direction, "Touch the plate."

3. **Match Pictures**
Present several pictures of common objects. Have each child match the pictures of the plates.

4. **Discriminate Pictures**

Present a group of several unrelated pictures of objects. Have each child touch the picture of the plate in response to verbal direction, "Touch the plate."

5. **Figure-Ground**

Present a "busy" picture with many visual distractions. Ask each child to find the plate.

6. **Visual Closure**

Partially cover each of several pictures with paper. Ask each child to find the picture of the plate.

7. **Function**

Ask, "What do we do with a plate?"

8. **Association**

Ask, "What goes with the plate?" Use pictures or objects including spoon, fork, knife, etc., with several unrelated objects or pictures.

9. **Imitate Verbalization**

Present a plate and ask, "What is this? Say, 'Plate'." The child will imitate "Plate."

10. **Verbalize Label**

Present a plate and ask, "What is this?" The child will respond, "Plate."

11. **Concept Enrichment**

Discuss materials from which plates are made. Discuss different sizes of plates and other types of china (bowl, cups, etc.). Discuss different types of foods such as junk foods and nutritional foods.

Music

Have children balance a paper plate on their heads while marching to music.

Art

1. Have children make paper plate face mobiles to hang in room.
2. Help children make wax paper place mats by placing cut-outs of knife, spoon, fork and plate between two rectangles of wax paper and press with a warm iron. This mat may be used for follow-up teaching of proper place setting as child puts real object on appropriate shape each day.
3. Have children use paper plates to create masks, puppets, animal faces, wreaths, musical instruments (tambourine, bells), etc.
4. Have children make stick puppets by gluing a tongue depressor onto paper plate and adding yarn, construction paper pieces, sequins, fabric, etc. to make people or animal faces.

Snack

1. Use plates for holding snacks.
2. Pass cookies on a plate.
3. Have a cake the class made served on a plate.

Fine Motor

1. Make a path tracing activity of "Take a plate to a table." and "Take the food to a plate." Vary the difficulty of the paths according to the skills of the children.
2. Have children lace a teacher-made plate-shape sewing card or sew around a sturdy paper plate with holes punched in it.
3. Let the children use magic markers and paper plates to practice making circles.
4. Have each child decorate a paper plate according to a design so the class creates a "set" of paper plates. Have them glue on design according to a pattern.

Games

1. Have children stand a certain distance from a waste basket (3 to 4 ft.) and throw in paper plate.

2.   Play "Hot Plate" like "Hot Potato."
3.   Put plates in dramatic play center as well as sand play area.

Storytelling

Make up a story about a plate which ran away from the other plates. "She started out on the table and slid down the table cloth." Let the children describe her adventures until she happily returns to the other plates.

Fig. 32D

Gross Motor

Let the children use small sturdy paper plates as throwing discs.

Cognitive

1.   Help children learn where plates belong in a table setting.
2.   Have the children use plates in the study of circles.
3.   Have the children sort plates by size, small, medium, and large.
4.   Have the children match designs on cardboard cups and plates. (See fig. 32D.)
5.   Have the children match real cups to plates.

Enrichment

1.   Help each child make a plate "turtle" by adding head, tail and four legs to a small paper plate.
2.   Have children glue cut-out foods on paper plates to make a junk food plate and a healthful plate.
3.   Have children add a plate and glass outline to the place mat begun in Lesson #1 Enrichment #2.

Field Trip

Visit a department store to see sets of dishes. Talk about appropriate behavior at department store.

Lesson 5: Napkin

Unit Group Lesson

1.   **Match Concrete Objects**
Present two napkins. Say, "This is a napkin." Ask each child in turn to put the napkin with the napkin. Gradually increase number of irrelevant objects from which (s)he must select napkin to match.

2.   **Discriminate Objects**
Present several objects. Have each child touch the napkin in response to verbal direction, "Touch the napkin."

3.   **Match Pictures**
Present several pictures of common objects. Have each child match the pictures of the napkins.

4.   **Discriminate Pictures**
Present a group of several unrelated pictures of objects. Have each child touch the picture of the napkin in response to verbal direction, "Touch the napkin."

5.   **Figure-Ground**
Present a "busy" picture with many visual distractions. Ask each child to find the napkin.

6.   **Visual Closure**
Partially cover each of several pictures with paper. Ask each child to find the picture of the napkin.

7. **Function**

   Ask, "What do we do with a napkin?"

8. **Association**

   Ask, "What goes with the napkin?" Use pictures or objects including plate, hand, mouth, etc., with several unrelated objects or pictures.

9. **Imitate Verbalization**

   Present a napkin and ask, "What is this? Say, 'Napkin'." The child will imitate "Napkin."

10. **Verbalize Label**

    Present a napkin and ask, "What is this?" The child will respond, "Napkin."

11. **Concept Enrichment**

    Look at different sizes and types of napkins and discuss their uses.

Music

Have children wave napkins (fast, slow, high, etc.) in time to music.

Art

1. Let the children use crayons or magic markers to decorate napkins.
2. Make potato prints or rubberstamp prints on napkins. Napkins are very absorbent and so make an excellent painting paper.
3. Let children make cloth napkins for themselves or others using fabric crayons.

Snack

Put napkins on children's laps during snack time (it may necessary to attach napkin to child so it will not slip off onto the floor).

Fine Motor

1. Have children fold paper and/or cloth napkins with different numbers and types of folds depending upon the skill levels.
2. Have children use napkins for parachutes. Let them attach string to the four corners and then to a plastic figure. Use in Gross Motor #1.
3. Let children use napkins to wipe up spills during the day.
4. Let children make paper napkins by fringing paper towels with scissors.

Games

1. Play "Drop the Napkin" like "Drop the Handkerchief."
2. Put napkins in the housekeeping area.
3. Play musical napkins like musical chairs. Put large dinner napkins in a circle on floor. Ask children to sit on a napkin. When music starts children stand up and march around napkin circle. Remove one napkin. When music stops whoever does not have napkin to sit on must move out of circle. Game continues until only one person is left, the winner.

Storytelling

Make up a story about "Natalie Napkin" going on a picnic (or someplace else). Let the children make up things that Natalie does.

Gross Motor

Have children climb to top of jungle gym, stairs, or slide and drop parachutes made in Fine Motor #2 today.

Cognitive

1. Have children sort sets of napkins by matching textures, design, etc.

2.   Let children count napkins and pass out napkins for snack or lunch, and set table, etc.
3.   Let the children sequence napkins by size.

Enrichment

Add napkin outline to place mat begun in Lesson #1 Enrichment #2. Before or after laminating, write child's name in upper left hand corner. Have each child learn to place her place setting on the design.
(See fig. 32E.)

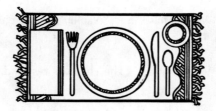

Fig. 32E

Related Children's Records
"All on the Table Before You" from **LEARNING BASIC SKILLS-VOC.** (EA)

Related Children's Books
Petersham, Maude and Petersham, Mishka. **THE CIRCUS BABY.** New York: Macmillan   Publishing Co., 1950.
Hoban, Lillian. **BREAD AND JAM FOR FRANCIS.** New York: Scholastic Book Services, 1964.
Krasilovsky, Phyllis. **THE MAN WHO DIDN'T WASH HIS DISHES.** New York: Doubleday & Co., 1950.
Watanabe, Shigeo. **WHAT A GOOD LUNCH.** Cleveland, Oh.: William Collins Publishers, 1978.
Weissman, Cynthia. **BREAKFAST FOR SAMMY.** Englewood Cliffs, N.J.: Four Winds Press,   1978.

Related Parenting Materials
Cansler, Dot. **THE HOMESTRETCH.** Winston-Salem, NC 27113-5128: Kaplan Press, 1983.

Related Materials
TEACHING PICTURES. Winston-Salem, NC 27113-5128: Kaplan Press, 1983.
STORY SEQUENCE CARDS I, II. Winston-Salem, NC 27113-5128: Kaplan Press, 1983.
SEWING CARDS I, II, III. Winston-Salem, NC 27113-5128: Kaplan Press, 1983.

Unit 33: Camping

A developmental assessment should determine the functional levels of each child. Individual expectations are based on the assessment results.

Lesson 1: Tent

Unit Group Lesson

1. **Match Concrete Objects**

   Present two tents. Say, "This is a tent." Ask each child in turn to put the tent with the tent. Gradually increase number of irrelevant objects from which (s)he must select tent to match.

2. **Discriminate Objects**

   Present several objects. Have each child touch the tent in response to verbal direction, "Touch the tent."

3. **Match Pictures**

   Present several pictures of common objects. Have each child match the pictures of the tents.

4. **Discriminate Pictures**

   Present a group of several unrelated pictures of objects. Have each child touch the picture of the tent in response to verbal direction, "Touch the tent."

5. **Figure-Ground**

   Present a "busy" picture with many visual distractions. Ask each child to find the tent.

6. **Visual Closure**

   Partially cover each of several pictures with paper. Ask each child to find the picture of the tent.

7. **Function**

   Ask, "What do we do with a tent?"

8. **Association**

   Ask, "What goes with the tent?" Use pictures or objects including stakes, tent poles, sleeping bags, etc., with several unrelated objects or pictures.

9. **Imitate Verbalization**

   Present a tent and ask, "What is this? Say, 'Tent'." The child will imitate "Tent."

10. **Verbalize Label**

    Present a tent and ask, "What is this?" The child will respond, "Tent."

11. **Concept Enrichment**

    Discuss fact that tents are for sleeping in to keep insects away, rain off, have privacy, etc.

Music

Sing to the tune of "The Bear Went Over the Mountain":
We're sleeping inside our tent.
We're sleeping inside our tent.
We're sleeping inside our tent.
We are on a camping trip.

Art

1. Let the children use shoe boxes to make miniature tents. Have each child cut out window and door and paint her tent shoebox.
2. Have each child begin a "Camping Book" by finding pictures of tents in catalogs and pasting onto paper.
3. Have each child make stick puppets of her family members to use for camping stories.

Snack

1. Eat "trail mix" prepared in Cognitive #2, today.
2. Eat snack inside or next to a tent.

Fine Motor

1. Make a path tracing activity of "Take the sleeping bag to the tent" and "Take the child to the tent." Vary the levels of difficulty according to each child's skill levels.
2. Allow children to zip and unzip windows and doors of a real tent.
3. Let children put together tent poles.

Games

1. Set up the housekeeping area as a campsite for this unit. Set up a pup tent. Bring in one or two sleeping bags, a first aid kit, wood, red cellophane paper and flashlight to make pretend campfire, and a toy camper truck.
2. Put a real tent in playground for the unit so that children may do dramatic play around camping.
3. Let the children go fishing while camping out. Let them use a stick, string, and hook made from a paper clip, "Fish" in a pretend pond or bucket of water, with a magnet for paper fish (with paper clips attached). Pretend to catch fish, cook and eat for supper.

Storytelling

1. Encourage children who have been camping to talk about it and bring picture to school to share with group.
2. Let children use stick puppets made in art to tell camping stories.

Gross Motor

1. Let children pretend to paddle a canoe (large box).
2. Make a cardboard box into an open-topped tent and let the children toss bean bags into the "tent."

Cognitive

1. Have children sort tents from other camping gear.
2. Help children prepare a "trail mix." Have each child count out raisins, nuts and round oat cereal into a plastic bag to take tenting with them.
3: Pack a backpack with camping items such as an axe, bed rolls, clothing, pajamas, toothbrush, canteen, etc. Have children reach in, take out an item, tell what it is and what it is used for.

Enrichment

Help children make a tent bag:
   a. Putting a sheet over a card table. Pin up a corner for the door of the tent.
   b. Drape a sheet, bedspread, etc. over a line strung between 2 trees (chairs). Use for a tent.
   c. Put 4 chairs back to back, a short distance apart (form a square). Drape blanket or sheet or bedspread over tent.

Field Trip

1.   Go to a park "trail." Follow the trail, have a picnic.
2.   Visit a store and look at camping supplies.

Lesson 2: Sleeping Bag

Unit Group Lesson

1. **Match Concrete Objects**

Present two sleeping bags. Say, "This is a sleeping bag." Ask each child in turn to put the sleeping bag with the sleeping bag. Gradually increase number of irrelevant objects from which (s)he must select sleeping bag to match.

2. **Discriminate Objects**

Present several objects. Have each child touch the sleeping bag in response to verbal direction, "Touch the sleeping bag."

3. **Match Pictures**

Present several pictures of common objects. Have each child match the pictures of the sleeping bags.

4. **Discriminate Pictures**

Present a group of several unrelated pictures of objects. Have each child touch the picture of the sleeping bag in response to verbal direction, "Touch the sleeping bag."

5. **Figure-Ground**

Present a "busy" picture with many visual distractions. Ask each child to find the sleeping bag.

6. **Visual Closure**

Partially cover each of several pictures with paper. Ask each child to find the picture of the sleeping bag.

7. **Function**

Ask, "What do we do with a sleeping bag?"

8. **Association**

Ask, "What goes with the sleeping bag?" Use pictures or objects including tent, campfire, pillow, cot, etc., with several unrelated objects or pictures.

9. **Imitate Verbalization**

Present a sleeping bag and ask, "What is this? Say, 'Sleeping bag'." The child will imitate "Sleeping bag."

10. **Verbalize Label**

Present a sleeping bag and ask, "What is this?" The child will respond, "Sleeping bag."

11. **Concept Enrichment**

Discuss fact that sleeping bags are for sleeping in instead of a bed. Sleeping bags are warm inside. The inside of the sleeping bag is soft.

Music

Sing to tune of "Muffin Man":
Oh, do you have a sleeping bag?
A sleeping bag, a sleeping bag?
Oh, do you have a sleeping bag?
To sleep in all night long.

Art

1. Have children make a sleeping bag collage and add it to the "Camping Scrapbook" begun in Lesson #1, Art #1.
2. With tempera paint, let children path trace boy to sleeping bag, first with straight paths, then with curved paths. Vary the difficulty of the paths according to the children's skills.
3. Let children paint sleeping bags at the easel. Provide outlines.
4. Have children tie dye "sleeping bag fabric."

Snack

1. Make "sleeping bags" for snack by eating hot dogs or other snack in a bun, cheese rolled around bacon bits or bacon rolled around piece of cheese.
2. During snack, go to edge of playground or into nearby wood on a "camping" trip. Take blankets if sleeping bags not available. Have snack there or a bag lunch.

Fine Motor

1. Paste a picture of a sleeping bag on a piece of cardboard. Punch holes around edges and let child use as a lacing card. Vary the number of holes according to the skills of each child.
2. Let children zip and unzip the sleeping bags.
3. Let the children put paper dolls or small dolls into sock sleeping bags.
4. Let the children roll up sock sleeping bags.

Games

Provide real sleeping bags in housekeeping center, block center, or outside.

Storytelling

Cut out pictures of boy, girl, mother, father, tent, camper, sleeping bags, and first aid kit. Glue pictures to cardboard and attach to tongue depressors to make stick puppets. Let children use them to tell their own stories about going camping.

Gross Motor

1. Roll up in towels for sleeping bags or sew 2 towels together and let children practice getting in and out.
(See fig. 33A.)

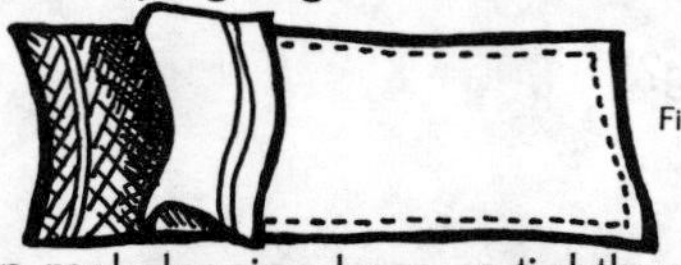

Fig. 33A

2. Let children roll up real sleeping bags as tightly as they are able.
3. Have a sack race using small sleeping bags instead of sacks.

Cognitive

1. Cut off sock tops. Let children use lower halves as sleeping bags for paper dolls mounted on cardboard. Provide people dressed for various occasions and have children slip the appropriately dressed dolls into sleeping bags.
2. Let children put one doll in one sleeping bag. Provide small dolls and doll-sized sleeping bags or use socks and paper dolls as above.
3. Let children organize a sequence story about getting ready for bed in a sleeping bag.

Enrichment

1. Let children take naps in "sleeping bags."

2.	Together Activity: Have children prepare a "camp site" with many pine trees and make fold-over sleeping bags. Then have them put paper dolls into the sleeping bags and staple them closed and place among the pine trees. (See fig. 33B.)

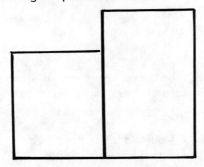 

Fig. 33B

Field Trip

Visit a camping store. Look at the equipment.

Visitor

Invite a hiker with a back pack to demonstrate how he carries and rolls his sleeping bag.

Lesson 3: Campfire

Unit Group Lesson

1.	**Match Concrete Objects**
Present two campfires. Say, "This is a campfire." Ask each child in turn to put the campfire with the campfire. Gradually increase number of irrelevant objects from which (s)he must select campfire to match.

2.	**Discriminate Objects**
Present several objects. Have each child touch the campfire in response to verbal direction, "Touch the campfire."

3.	**Match Pictures**
Present several pictures of common objects. Have each child match the pictures of the campfires.

4.	**Discriminate Pictures**
Present a group of several unrelated pictures of objects. Have each child touch the picture of the campfire in response to verbal direction, "Touch the campfire."

5.	**Figure-Ground**
Present a "busy" picture with many visual distractions. Ask each child to find the campfire.

6.	**Visual Closure**
Partially cover each of several pictures with paper. Ask each child to find the picture of the campfire .

7.	**Function**
Ask, "What do we do with a campfire?"

8.	**Association**
Ask, "What goes with the campfire?" Use pictures or objects including pots, tent, sleeping bag, camper, etc., with several unrelated objects or pictures.

9. **Imitate Verbalization**

Present a campfire and ask, "What is this? Say, 'Campfire'." The child will imitate "Campfire ."

10. **Verbalize Label**

Present a campfire and ask, "What is this?" The child will respond, "Campfire."

11. **Concept Enrichment**

Discuss safety with fires; they are hot so one has to be careful near them. It is important to be sure that the fire is completely put out by drowning it with water and covering with dirt.

Music

Sing to the tune of "She'll Be Coming Around the Mountain":
Verse 1: We'll be putting up our tent when she comes, when she comes
We'll be putting up our camp tent when she comes, when she comes
We'll be putting up our camp tent,
We'll be putting up our camp tent,
We'll be putting up our camp tent when she comes.
Verse 2: We'll be dancing around the campfire when she comes. . .
Verse 3: We'll be roasting marshmallows when she comes. . .
Verse 4: We'll get into sleeping bags when she comes. . .

Art

1. Have children complete pictures of a campfire to add to the "Camping Scrapbook" begun in Lesson #1 Art #1.
2. Have children stack and glue popsicle sticks to make a miniature pretend campfire and stick in red cellophane paper or tissue paper for flames.
3. Help children make campfire logs from rolled newspaper and paint them brown, red and yellow.

Snack

1. Make a real campfire in a small portable grill. Let children roast marshmallows or wieners over fire. This will require close supervision with only two or three children roasting food at a time.
2. Eat "red hots."

Fine Motor

1. Let children use clay to make pretend sticks for campfire.
2. Provide a picture of logs. Have children add red fire and path trace "heat" radiating from fire. (See fig. 33C.)

Fig. 33C

3. Have children roll paper into miniature logs with their fingers.

Games

1. Make a small campfire on the ground. Let children sing and dance around campfire. Let children help put out fire. Stress the importance of making sure fire is out before leaving it.
2. Let children build a pretend campfire with a few small logs, tinfoil, and red, yellow and orange tissue paper.

Storytelling

1. Read a story about "Smokey the Bear" or other story about camping.
2. Sit around a real or pretend campfire and tell stories. Have each child tell a little story about herself. Provide as much assistance as the child needs.

Gross Motor

1. Let children have a relay race to gather logs for a fire.
2. Let children dance around the campfire.
3. On the playground have children gather small twigs of wood to use to start a fire.

Cognitive

1. Have each child count twigs into bundles of 3, 5, 10 or whatever number is appropriate for her counting level.
2. Provide pictures of many settings such as city, hillside, flower garden, kitchen, ocean etc. Let children pick out the places appropriate for making a campfire and tell why.
3. Have children make a mural of equipment to cook food on a campfire.
4. Make cue sheets with pictures of campfires and other camping equipment. Have the children mark the campfires with red. Vary the levels of difficulty of the cue sheets according to the skills of the children.

Enrichment

Help children make campfire logs. Let children cut log shapes from brown construction paper. Let them tear red and yellow tissue paper and glue them on for "flames," arrange logs in fire shape and sit around the campfire and sing.

Visitor

Invite an Eagle Scout to come build a real campfire and prepare sticks for roasting marshmallows. Roast marshmallows together.

Lesson 4: First Aid Kit

Unit Group Lesson

1. **Match Concrete Objects**
   Present two first aid kits. Say, "This is a first aid kit." Ask each child in turn to put the first aid kit with the first aid kit. Gradually increase number of irrelevant objects from which (s)he must select first aid kit to match.

2. **Discriminate Objects**
   Present several objects. Have each child touch the first aid kit in response to verbal direction, "Touch the first aid kit."

3. **Match Pictures**
   Present several pictures of common objects. Have each child match the pictures of the first aid kits.

4. **Discriminate Pictures**
   Present a group of several unrelated pictures of objects. Have each child touch the picture of the first aid kit in response to verbal direction, "Touch the first aid kit."

5. **Figure-Ground**
   Present a "busy" picture with many visual distractions. Ask each child to find the first aid kit.

6. **Visual Closure**
   Partially cover each of several pictures with paper. Ask each child to find the picture of the first aid kit.

7. **Function**
   Ask, "What do we do with a first aid kit?"

8. **Association**

   Ask, "What goes with the first aid kit?" Use pictures or objects including tent, gauze, scissors, bandaids, etc., with several unrelated objects or pictures.

9. **Imitate Verbalization**

   Present a first aid kit and ask, "What is this? Say, 'First aid kit'." The child will imitate "First aid kit."

10. **Verbalize Label**

    Present a first aid kit and ask, "What is this?" The child will respond, "First aid kit."

11. **Concept Enrichment**

    Discuss when to use a first aid kit. Discuss treatment for different types of hurts such as cuts, bruises, sprains, etc.

Music

Sing to the tune of "Campbell Soup Song":
First aid kit,
First aid kit,
What do you need when camping?
A first aid kit.

Art

1. Provide jewelry boxes or small shoe boxes. Let each child make, paint and label a first aid kit from one of the boxes.
2. Put out large roll of cotton so that children can pinch off small amounts to roll and make cotton balls. Let them use the cotton balls to paint around stencils.
3. Have the children use cotton swabs, cotton balls, bandaids and other items from a first aid kit to make a collage.

Snack

Drink orange juice for snack and eat nutritious foods.

Fine Motor

1. Put out a large roll of cotton and have the children pinch off small amounts to make cotton balls for the first aid kits. Have children put bandaids, cotton balls, etc. in the boxes prepared in Art #1.
2. Give each child two bandaids. Have her peel off paper end and put band-aid on herself, a friend, or a doll.
3. Tear up pieces of sheet into strips (start and let children finish). Let children roll strips into bandage rolls and use it to bandage doll legs, arms, heads, etc. (See fig. 33D.)

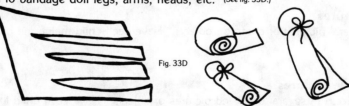

Fig. 33D

Games

Make large cardboard box first aid kit with big opening in top. Have children stand several feet away and throw in cotton balls.

Storytelling

Make up a story about a child falling from her tricycle. Let the children help finish it. Ask, "Where did she get hurt? Who did she call? What did she say? How did she sound?"

Gross Motor

1. Have a relay to get the first aid kit in a "hurry." Walk instead of "run" so you will not get hurt.
2. Put the first aid kit in special places. Give directions to go get it such as climb up the slide, etc.

Cognitive

1. Let each child count the number of bandages in the bandaid box. Have a number appropriate to each child's skill level.

2. Let child discriminate alcohol from other liquids by smell. Which are same color as alcohol such as vinegar or water or blindfold child and use other liquids (orange juice).

3. Dump out all items from a first aid kit and mix with other small items. Ask each child to pick up all first aid items and put back in kit.

Enrichment

Place numerals one through ten on bandaid boxes (metal ones are sturdy). Have the children put the correct number of bandaids in each box.

Visitor

Have an emergency vehicle visit the school (Rescue Squad) and show children a first aid kit.

Lesson 5: Camper

Unit Group Lesson

1. **Match Concrete Objects** (Use toys.)
Present two campers. Say, "This is a camper." Ask each child in turn to put the camper with the camper. Gradually increase number of irrelevant objects from which (s)he must select camper to match.

2. **Discriminate Objects**
Present several objects. Have each child touch the camper in response to verbal direction, "Touch the camper."

3. **Match Pictures**
Present several pictures of common objects. Have each child match the pictures of the campers.

4. **Discriminate Pictures**
Present a group of several unrelated pictures of objects. Have each child touch the picture of the camper in response to verbal direction, "Touch the camper."

5. **Figure-Ground**
Present a "busy" picture with many visual distractions. Ask each child to find the camper.

6. **Visual Closure**
Partially cover each of several pictures with paper. Ask each child to find the picture of the camper.

7. **Function**
Ask, "What do we do with a camper?"

8. **Association**
Ask, "What goes with the camper?" Use pictures or objects including sleeping bag, campfire, tent, first aid kit, etc., with several unrelated objects or pictures.

9. **Imitate Verbalization**
Present a camper and ask, "What is this? Say, 'Camper'." The child will imitate "Camper."

10. **Verbalize Label**
Present a camper and ask, "What is this?" The child will respond, "Camper."

11. **Concept Enrichment**

Look at and discuss different types of campers such as pop-up tent campers, travel trailers, motor homes, etc.

Music

1. Sing to the tune of "Jack and Jill":

   Jack and Jill went up the hill
   Riding in a camper.
   Jack jumped out,
   Then Jill jumped out,
   As fast as she could scamper.

2. Sing to the tune of "The Wheels on the Bus Go Round and Round":

   Verse 1: The wheels on the camper go round and round. . .
   Verse 2: The horn on the camper goes beep, beep, beep. . .
   Verse 3: The children in the camper bounce up and down. . .
   Verse 4: The baby in the camper goes wa-wa-wa, wa-wa-wa. . .

Art

1. Help the children make a trailer park mural. Designate a large area in the center for a lake. Color blue. Make a sign for the trailer park. Have children cut out green triangles and glue in series to make pine trees. Have children cut out camper pictures and add to mural around the lake. (See fig. 33E.)

Fig. 33E

2. Have each child make background on individual camper pictures by gluing strips of brown construction paper around camper and adding green pine needles.

Snack

Let children take snacks of small sandwiches or bags of trail mix for camping from a picnic hamper. Drink juice from paper cups. Place wrappers and cups in trash container.

Fine Motor

1. Prepare figure-ground activities for each child. Give each child a worksheet that has several sizes of camper shapes drawn among shapes of several other vehicles (motorcycle, car, etc.). Ask child to find all the camper shapes and outline them.

2. Paste pictures of camper onto cardboard. Cut into two or more pieces (for puzzles) depending upon skill levels of children.

3. Have children paste wheels on camper pictures.

Games

1. Make masking tape roads in block center or housekeeping area for toy camper trucks to use in dramatic play. Also make roads outside and use toy campers there.

2. Let the children use wagon as camper and load up sleeping bags, first aid kits, etc. Haul to "pretend campsite" (jungle gym with blanket or canvas over top).

Storytelling

Make up a story about "the little camper that could" and include facts about all of the equipment inside of a camper truck (names of objects, their uses, how they work, etc.).

Gross Motor

Have the children make several "campers" out of medium-sized cardboard boxes with top and bottom folded in. Paint and glue on wheels. Children step in box, pull it up and hold it with hands and travel down the "highway" (highway may be on the playground or tape on the floor). Children make "rest" stops along the way to buy gas, go to the restroom, change drivers. On the highway they can go around another camper by blowing their horn.

Cognitive

1. Help children discriminate toy campers from other toy vehicles.
2. Have children match letters TRASH or LITTER to letter printed on a strip of paper. Glue letters on the tape. Tape strips to trashcan. Be sure children use the trashcan.
3. Make a list of towns or places where she can drive to camp. Write each child's name beside the place he choses.
4. Think of an appropriate name for the trailer park mural and place the name on the mural.

Enrichment

1. Provide a large posterboard with roads and places to see drawn in and several small cardboard "campers." Have children turn over numbered cards to see where to put their campers along the road. (See fig. 33F.)

Fig. 33F

2. Find pictures of national forests and parks in National Geographics. Place on discovery table.

Field Trip

Ask a parent or friend to bring their camper to school so children may go inside and see what it is like.

Related Children's Records
FOLK SONG CARNIVAL (EA)
AMERICAN FOLK SONGS FOR CHILDREN (FLKW)
ABIYOYO (FLKW)
JAMBO AND OTHER CALL-AND-RESPONSE (SCHOL)

Related Children's Books
Brinkloe, Julie. **GORDON GOES CAMPING.** New York: Doubleday & Co., 1975.
Mayer, Mercer. **JUST ME AND MY DAD.** New York: Golden Press, 1977.
Shulevitz, Uri. **DAWN.** New York: Farrar, Straus & Grioux, 1974.

Related Parenting Materials
Cansler, Dot. **THE HOMESTRETCH.** Winston-Salem, NC 27113-5128: Kaplan Press, 1983.

Related Materials
TEACHING PICTURES. Winston-Salem, NC 27113-5128: Kaplan Press, 1983.
STORY SEQUENCE CARDS I, II. Winston-Salem, NC 27113-5128: Kaplan Press, 1983.
SEWING CARDS I, II, III. Winston-Salem, NC 27113-5128: Kaplan Press, 1983.

Unit 34: Parade

A developmental assessment should determine the functional levels of each child. Individual expectations are based on the assessment results.

Lesson 1: American Flag

Unit Group Lesson

1. **Match Concrete Objects**
    Present two American flags. Say, "This is an American flag." Ask each child in turn to put the American flag with the American flag. Gradually increase number of irrelevant objects from which (s)he must select the American flag to match.

2. **Discriminate Objects**
    Present several objects. Have each child touch the American flag in response to verbal command, "Touch the American flag."

3. **Match Pictures**
    Present several pictures of common objects. Have each child match the pictures of the American flag.

4. **Discriminate Pictures**
    Present a group of several unrelated pictures of objects. Have each child touch the picture of the American flag in response to verbal direction, "Touch the American flag."

5. **Figure-Ground**
    Present a "busy" picture with many visual distractions. Ask each child to find the American flag.

6. **Visual Closure**
    Partially cover each of several pictures with paper. Ask each child to find the picture of the American flag.

7. **Function**
    Ask, "What do we do with an American flag?"

8. **Association**
    Ask, "What goes with the American flag?" Use pictures or objects including flag pole, majorette, etc., with several unrelated objects or pictures.

9. **Imitate Verbalization**
    Present an American flag and ask, "What is this? Say, 'American flag'." The child will imitate "American flag."

10.   **Verbalize Label**
       Present an American flag and ask, "What is this?" The child will respond, "American flag."

11.   **Concept Enrichment**
       Compare the American flag to other flags.

Music
1.   Sing "My Country 'Tis of Thee" and wave small flags.
2.   Sing "The Star Spangled Banner."
3.   Play marching music and let children march and carry flags.

Art
1.   Give children pre-cut parts of American flag. Let them assemble flag by pasting parts on flag shape. (Cover with clear contact paper to use for placemats.) Vary the number of pieces and difficulty of the cuts with the children's skills.
2.   Have children paint with red, white, and blue paint at the easel to encourage painting flags.
3.   Give each child an outline of an American flag and crayons (red, white and blue) and let them color the flag.

Snack
1.   Eat star-shaped sandwiches or cookies.
2.   Use placemats made in Art #1 today.

Fine Motor
1.   Have children put flag puzzles together. Make flag puzzles by gluing flags onto cardboard and cutting into two or more pieces. Make several different levels of difficulty.
2.   Glue medium-sized gold stars on a blue sheet of construction paper.
3.   Have children wave small flags.
4.   Have children cut out red and white stripes and arrange in sequence for a flag.

Games
1.   Have a flag relay race. Let the children race and pass a flag to the next child.
2.   Let children raise the flag at school this week.

Storytelling
1.   Read a story about a parade.
2.   Tell the story of Betsy Ross sewing the first flag.
3.   Teach the children "The Pledge of Allegiance to the Flag."

Gross Motor
1.   Have everyone march in a circle to marching music.
2.   Have a parade.

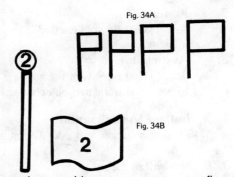

Fig. 34A

Fig. 34B

Cognitive
1.   Have children sequence flags according to size. This activity can be varied by using two, or more flags depending upon the level of the children. (See fig. 34A.)
2.   Have children match flags to flag poles. Put numerals on the poles and matching numerals on the flags. (See fig. 34B.)
3.   Have children learn flag colors. Have them collect white items in one basket, blue in another, red in another and identify red, white and blue on American flag.
4.   Have children sequence red and white color strips to create an alternating pattern.

Enrichment
1.   Show children flags from other countries and note differences.
2.   Talk about National Flag Day on June 14.

Field Trip

Visit a state or city government building. Find flag pole. Watch the flag flying in the breeze.

Visitor

Invite a Boy Scout to bring the American flag and demonstrate the proper method of folding a flag.

Lesson 2: Soldier

Unit Group Lesson

1. **Match Concrete Objects**

    Present two soldiers. Say, "This is an soldier." Ask each child in turn to put the soldier with the soldier. Gradually increase number of irrelevant objects from which (s)he must select the soldier to match.

2. **Discriminate Objects**

    Present several objects. Have each child touch the soldier in response to verbal command, "Touch the soldier."

3. **Match Pictures**

    Present several pictures of common objects. Have each child match the pictures of the soldier.

4. **Discriminate Pictures**

    Present a group of several unrelated pictures of objects. Have each child touch the picture of the soldier in response to verbal direction, "Touch the soldier."

5. **Figure-Ground**

    Present a "busy" picture with many visual distractions. Ask each child to find the soldier.

6. **Visual Closure**

    Partially cover each of several pictures with paper. Ask each child to find the picture of the soldier.

7. **Function**

    Ask, "What do soldiers do?"

8. **Association**

    Ask, "What goes with the soldier?" Use pictures or objects including medals, tanks, uniforms, etc., with several unrelated objects or pictures.

9. **Imitate Verbalization**

    Present a soldier and ask, "What is this? Say, 'Soldier'." The child will imitate "Soldier."

10. **Verbalize Label**

    Present a soldier and ask, "What is this?" The child will respond, "Soldier."

11. **Concept Enrichment**

    Look at uniforms of different soldiers. Look at American soldiers uniforms as they have changed through history.

Music

1.   Divide class into two groups. Let one group be band members and other group be soldiers. Band members choose an instrument and make music for soldiers to march. Then soldiers become band

members and band members become soldiers for another round of marching.

2. Sing to the tune of "Mary Had A Little Lamb":
   We are soldiers marching along,
   Marching along, marching along.
   We are soldiers marching along
   In the big parade.

Fig. 34C

Fig. 34D

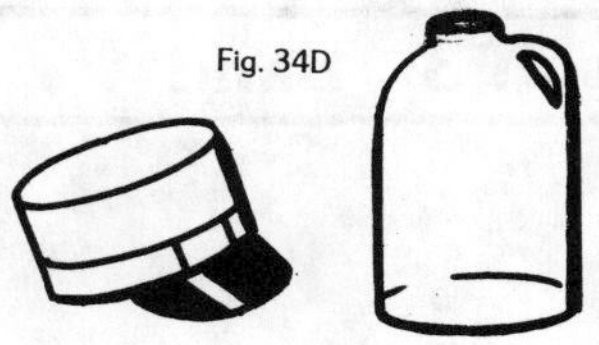

Art

1. Cut hole in top of a large brown grocery bag for head and one hole in each side for arms for each child. Let children decorate bag uniforms with crayon, tempera paint, magic markers or paste on collage materials to make a soldier uniform to wear in parade on Friday. (See fig. 34C.)

2. Help children make soldier caps. Cut a cap from a bleach bottle. Have children glue on a band of colored paper and make a buckle of cardboard covered with aluminum foil. (See fig. 34D.)

Snack

Eat graham crackers and peanut butter. Place peanut butter at one end and stand crackers in row like soldiers in a parade. Have children line up to pick up a soldier to eat.

Fine Motor

1. Paste pictures of soldiers on cardboard, punch holes around edges of pictures. Let children use for sewing cards. Vary the levels of difficulty according to the skills of the children.

2. Paste pictures of soldiers on cardboard. Cut into two or more pieces. Let children assemble puzzles appropriate to their skill levels.

3. Prepare a path tracing activity of "Take a soldier to his drum." and "Take a drum to the soldier." Vary the levels of difficulty of the paths appropriate to the childrens skills.

Games

Play an action game:

Five little soldiers standing in a row;	*(Five children stand in a row.)*
First they bow to the Captain so.	*(Children bow.)*
They march to the left,	
They march to the right,	
And then they all stand ready to fight.	*(Stand straight and tall.)*
Along came a man with a big long gun.	*(Another child comes with a toy gun.)*
Do you think those little soldiers would run?	
No, not one!	*(Stand straight with hands on hips.)*

Storytelling

Read the story of "The Toy Soldier." Play the story on record or show filmstrip of story.

Gross Motor

Play a marching record. Talk about marching IN PLACE, IN LINE, and IN PARADE. Have children practice each of these.

Cognitive

1. Have children line up toy soldiers in sets of 2, 4, 6, and 8.
2. Make soldiers in several sizes and have the children sequence them by size.
3. Give each child cue sheet with pictures of soldiers and pictures of other men. Ask child to color all of the soldiers. Vary the level of difficulty according to the skill level of the children.
4. Make soldiers with different colors or patterns of uniform. Have children sort soldiers according to uniform. Select task according to child's skill level.

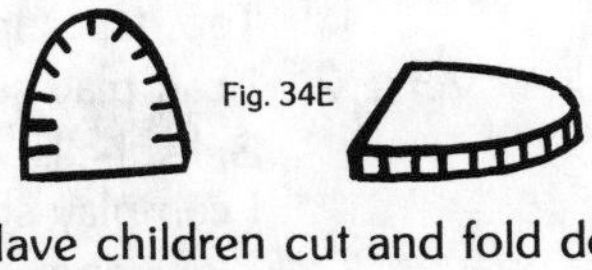

Fig. 34E

Enrichment

Talk about epaulets. Make yellow shapes with magic marker lines. Have children cut and fold down sides. Put on shoulders with masking tape. March to marching music. (See fig. 34E.)

Lesson 3: Band

Unit Group Lesson

1. **Match Concrete Objects**
   Present two pictures of a band. Say, "This is a band." Ask each child in turn to put the band with the band. Gradually increase number of irrelevant pictures from which (s)he must select the band to match.

2. **Match Pictures**
   Present several pictures of common objects. Have each child match the pictures of the bands.

3. **Discriminate Pictures**
   Present a group of several unrelated pictures of objects. Have each child touch the picture of the band in response to verbal direction, "Touch the band."

4. **Figure-Ground**
   Present a "busy" picture with many visual distractions. Ask each child to find the band.

5. **Visual Closure**
   Partially cover each of several pictures with paper. Ask each child to find the picture of the band.

6. **Function**
   Ask, "What do bands do?"

7. **Association**
   Ask, "What goes with bands?" Use pictures or objects including instruments, music, music stands, etc., with several unrelated objects or pictures.

8. **Imitate Verbalization**
   Present a picture of a band and ask, "What is this? Say, 'Band'." The child will imitate "Band."

9. **Verbalize Label**
   Present a picture of a band and ask, "What is this?" The child will respond, "Band."

10. **Concept Enrichment**
    Discuss the various band instruments and the categories to which they belong such as percussion, wind, brass, etc.

Music
1. Let children play band instruments to accompany "Old MacDonald Had a Band."
2. Let children play marching music with instruments and march.
3. Perform this action song "I Can Play" to the tune of "London Bridge is Falling Down":
   Verse 1: I can play some rhythm sticks,
   Rhythm sticks, rhythm sticks.
   I can play some rhythm sticks,
   Tap, tap, tap, tap.
   Verse 2: I can play some bells,
   Bells, bells.
   I can play some bells,
   Ring, ring, ring-a-ling.

Verse 3: I can play a drum,
Drum, drum.
I can play a drum,
Boom, boom, boom, boom, boom.

Verse 4: I can play some cymbals,
Cymbals, cymbals.
I can play some cymbals,
Bing-bang, bing-bang, bing-bang.

Art
1. Have children find pictures of musical instruments and paste them in "Band Scrapbook."
2. Have children decorate the cover of band scrapbook. (See fig. 34F.)
3. Have children make band instruments from play dough.

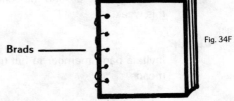

Fig. 34F

Brads ————

Snack
Listen to marching music played by band while eating snack.

Fine Motor
1. Let children blow a real horn (trumpet) and push down buttons.
2. Provide each child with a dotted outline of a band instrument and have him trace around it. Use more complex instruments for children with higher skill levels. For example a cymbal is simple and a trumbone is very difficult.
3. Have children design and build a route for a band to march along. Place a large piece of paper on the floor and let the children draw roads, sidewalks, etc. for a parade.

Games
Play musical chairs to band music.

Storytelling
Make up a story about a band. When you get to the name of an instrument, use that instrument to make the sound and have children say the name. For example:

Once upon a time there was a man who wanted to have a band. He went out to look for instruments. Soon he heard a boom, boom. (Reach in a mystery box on her lap and strike drum.) Children say, "Drum." The man said, "Mr. Drum will you be in my band?" Mr. Drum said, "Yes," so the man went on. Pretty soon he heard a ding-a-ling, children say, "Bell." The man said, "Mrs. Bell, will you be in my band?" Mrs. Bell said, "Yes," so the man went on. Pretty soon he heard a tap, tap, tap. Children say, "Rhythm sticks." "Mr. Rhythm Sticks will you be in my band?" Mr. Rhythm Sticks said, "Yes," so the man went on. Pretty soon he heard a root-toot-toot-toot. Children say, "Horn." The man said, "Miss Horn, will you be in my band?" Miss Horn said, "Yes," so the man went on. . . .etc. The next day all the instruments got together at the man's house and their music was so beautiful that they were asked to be in the big parade downtown.

Gross Motor
1. Have everyone gloriously act out playing a trombone, beating a large drum, conducting the band, and playing cymbals.
2. Have children march in double-time to marching music.
3. Have children take turns leading the band.

Cognitive
1. Have children sort band instruments from other things. Some children will need objects to sort and some will be skilled enough to sort pictures.
2. Provide pictures of pairs of instruments. Have the children match instruments which are alike.
3. Have children listen to instrument sounds and identify the instruments. Play one instrument at a time and have each child point to a picture or name the instrument depending upon her skill level.

4. Play a sequence of two to five sounds on a xylophone depending upon the individual's skill. Have each each child match the sequence.

5. Beat the drum a given number of times depending upon the child's counting skill. Have the child tell how many times the teacher beat the drum.

Enrichment

1. Discuss orchestra and band instruments. Have children identify band instruments from orchestra and band instruments.

2. Have children listen to orchestra and band music and identify band music.

3. Discuss conducting an orchestra and leading a band.

Field Trip

Have a parade around the school building. Let children use and wear all the things they have made this week.

Visitor

Invite a band member in full uniform with instruments. Ask her to talk about band practice and what it means.

Lesson 4: Majorette

Unit Group Lesson

NOTE: Use dolls if possible. If only pictures are available, substitute pictures in 1 and omit 2 and 3.

1. **Match Concrete Objects**
Present two majorettes. Say, "This is a majorette." Ask each child in turn to put the majorette with the majorette. Gradually increase number of irrelevant pictures from which (s)he must select the majorette to match.

2. **Discriminate Objects**
Present several objects. Have each child touch the majorette in response to verbal command, "Touch the majorette."

3. **Match Pictures**
Present several pictures of common objects. Have each child match the pictures of the majorette.

4. **Discriminate Pictures**
Present a group of several unrelated pictures of objects. Have each child touch the picture of the majorette in response to verbal direction, "Touch the majorette."

5. **Figure-Ground**
Present a "busy" picture with many visual distractions. Ask each child to find the majorette.

6. **Visual Closure**
Partially cover each of several pictures with paper. Ask each child to find the picture of the majorette.

7. **Function**
Ask, "What do majorettes do?"

8. **Association**
Ask, "What goes with the majorette?" Use pictures or objects including baton, band, etc., with several unrelated objects or pictures.

9. **Imitate Verbalization**

Present a majorette and ask, "What is this? Say, 'Majorette'." The child will imitate "Majorette."

10. **Verbalize Label**

Present a majorette and ask, "What is this?" The child will respond, "Majorette."

11. **Concept Enrichment**

Look at majorettes' uniform, hat, boots, baton. Discuss the fact that the majorette often leads the marching band.

Music

Sing to the tune of "Twinkle, Twinkle, Little Star":
    Marching, marching with the band
    Turning my baton with only one hand
    Twirling, twirling all around
    Then I split right to the ground
    Marching, marching with the band
    Turning my baton with only one hand.

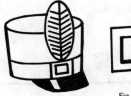

Fig. 34G

Art

1. Have children make paper bag majorette puppets. Use yarn for hair, sequins, and buttons for eyes, rick-rack, ribbon, etc. for other decoration.
2. Have children make majorette costumes for parade tomorrow from paper bags. Use the same procedures as for the soldier costumes made in Lesson #2 Art #1.
3. Have children make batons from paper towel tubes. Paint tube and sprinkle with glitter on the ends.
4. Have children make majorette hats from bleach bottles. Cut a visor and add a colored band. Let the children make silver buckles from cardboard shapes covered with aluminum foil. Let children add plumes cut from colored paper folded in middle. (See fig. 34G.)

Snack

Eat good nutritious foods like a majorette must in order to have energy and bounce.

Fine Motor

1. Have children cut up drinking straws and small geometric shapes from construction paper and lace necklaces for majorettes.
2. Let children twirl a baton like a majorette.
3. Make path tracing activities of "Take the baton to the majorette." and "Take the majorette to the band." Vary the level of difficulty according to the skills of the children.
4. Have the children make paper epaulets and gold buttons to wear. Put on with masking tape. (See fig. 34H.)

Games

Have children take turns leading the band in a parade.

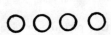

Fig. 34H

Storytelling

Let the children help make up a story about a majorette looking for a band to lead. Once upon a time a band majorette came to town. She needed a band to lead. She went to the grocery store. She saw (have children name items that are appropriate) but there wasn't a band to lead. The groceryman told her to go to the bakery. She went to the bakery. She saw (have children name items that are appropriate), but there wasn't a band to lead. The baker said go to the doctor, etc. At last she finds a band at the football game.

Gross Motor

1. Have children practice twirling batons again.
2. Have children practice high-stepping, prancing and twirling a baton.

Cognitive

1. Have children count out four gold buttons for each majorette's uniform. Put four buttons on each child with masking tape or pins.
2. Let children count pairs of epaulets.
3. On a series of majorettes (paper doll figures) "give" each one a baton. (Cut-outs.)
4. Make majorette hats with different colored plumes. Have children sort the majorette hats by plume color. (See fig. 34l.)

Enrichment

Help children learn left and right movements and to march forward, backward, etc.

Field Trip

Watch a band practice.

Visitor

Invite a band majorette.

Fig. 34l

Lesson 5: Parade

Unit Group Lesson

1. **Match Pictures**
   Present two pictures of a parade. Say, "This is a picture of a parade." Ask each child in turn to put the picture of a parade with the picture of a parade. Gradually increase number of irrelevant pictures from which (s)he must select the picture of a parade to match.

2. **Discriminate Pictures**
   Present a group of several unrelated pictures or objects. Have each child touch the picture of a parade in response to verbal direction, "Touch the parade."

3. **Figure-Ground**
   Present a "busy" picture with many visual distractions. Ask each child to find the parade.

4. **Visual Closure**
   Partially cover each of several pictures with paper. Ask each child to find the picture of the parade.

5. **Function**
   Ask, "Why do we have a parade?"

6. **Association**
   Ask, "What goes with a parade?" Use pictures or objects including flags, majorettes, bands, etc., with several unrelated objects or pictures.

7. **Imitate Verbalization**
   Present a picture of a parade and ask, "What is this? Say, 'Parade'." The child will imitate "Parade."

8. **Verbalize Label**
   Present a picture of a parade and ask, "What is this?" The child will respond, "Parade."

9. **Concept Enrichment**
   Discuss all the reasons for having a parade such as July 4th, Memorial Day, Thanksgiving Day, etc. Concentrate on days important in your community.

Music

Listen to and play all kinds of marching band music.

Art

1. Have children prepare a float on a wagon, cut a fringe and tape it around the outside, and put dolls dressed in costume to ride on the float. (See fig. 34J.)
2. Have children put fringe, plumes, and "decorations" on trucks and cars in play area to be part of the parade. (Talk about "decorate" and let the children have a free range in decorating the vehicles.)
3. Have children continue to work on costumes for parade, soldier hats, epaulets, and plumes.

Snack

Serve popcorn or anything that might be eaten at a parade.

Fine Motor

1. Have children cut fringe for the floats and costumes.
2. Have children cut buttons, epaulets, plumes and so on for costumes for majorettes, soldiers and clowns to be used in the parade.
3. Have the children trace numerals for float number cards to be used in Cognitive #1.
4. Have children string pieces of straws, sequins and beads to make decorations for costumes.

Games

Have a parade.

Fig. 34J

Storytelling

Describe a cold windy, blustery day. The Jones family with daddy, mom, Sue, Johnny and baby Tommy are going to the parade. Make up a story about the family related to the following words:

CLOTHING   (What to wear, why? Kind of shoes, etc.)
CAR   (Where to park, streets roped off, parade route.)
FOOD   (What to take, where to buy food at parade.)
SEE   (What will you see?)

Have the children add information related to each of these.

Gross Motor

Have The Parade. Line up participants and "floats," etc., in sequence. March to music around a parade route.

Cognitive

1. Have the children give each float a number card and arrange them in sequence. Use cards made in Fine Motor #3.
2. Have children identify the FIRST and LAST in lines of objects.
3. Have the children select the FIRST and LAST thing for the parade.
4. Have children count all people in the parade, floats in the parade, etc.
5. Have children plan the parade route and make a map of it.

Enrichment

1. Have children help plan floats that advertise items of interest to the children.
2. Talk about advertisement. Have children look for things advertised in magazines and papers.
3. Have children make floats to advertise items and decorate with ads from magazines.

Field Trip

Go to a parade!

Related Children's Records
"Bean Bag Parade" from **BEAN BAG ACTIVITIES & CO-ORD. SKILLS** (KIM)
"Circus Parade" from **DO IT YOURSELF KIDS CIRCUS** (KIM)
"Clowns" from **DO IT YOURSELF KIDS CIRCUS** (KIM)
"Marching Band" from **DO IT YOURSELF KIDS CIRCUS** (KIM)
"Mod Marches" by **HAP PALMER** (EA)
"Let's Make a Flag" from **FLAG DAY FROM HOLIDAY SONGS** (KIM)
"Star Spangled Banner" from **HOLIDAY SONGS** (EA)
"Shape Up Parade" from **SHAPES IN ACTION**

Related Parenting Materials
Cansler, Dot. **THE HOMESTRETCH.** Winston-Salem, NC 27113-5128: Kaplan Press, 1983.

Related Materials
TEACHING PICTURES. Winston-Salem, NC 27113-5128: Kaplan Press, 1983.
STORY SEQUENCE CARDS I, II. Winston-Salem, NC 27113-5128: Kaplan Press, 1983.
SEWING CARDS I, II, III. Winston-Salem, NC 27113-5128: Kaplan Press, 1983.

Unit 35: Hairdresser

A developmental assessment should determine the functional levels of each child. Individual expectations are based on the assessment results.

Lesson 1: Hairdresser

Unit Group Lesson

Unit Group Lesson

1. **Match Concrete Objects**
   Present two hairdressers. Say, "This is a hairdresser." Ask each child in turn to put the hairdresser with the hairdresser. Gradually increase number of irrelevant objects from which (s)he must select hairdresser to match.

2. **Discriminate Objects**
   Present several objects. Have each child touch the hairdresser in response to verbal direction, "Touch the hairdresser."

3. **Match Pictures**
   Present several pictures of common objects. Have each child match the pictures of the hairdressers.

4. **Discriminate Pictures**
   Present a group of several unrelated pictures of objects. Have each child touch the picture of the hairdresser in response to verbal direction, "Touch the hairdresser."

5. **Figure-Ground**
   Present a "busy" picture with many visual distractions. Ask each child to find the hairdresser.

6. **Visual Closure**
   Partially cover each of several pictures with paper. Ask each child to find the picture of the hairdresser.

7. **Function**
   Ask, "What does a hairdresser do?"

8. **Association**
   Ask, "What goes with the hairdresser?" Use pictures or objects including brush, scissors, hair dryer, etc. with several unrelated objects or pictures.

9. **Imitate Verbalization**
   Present a hairdresser and ask, "What is this? Say, 'Hairdresser'." The child will imitate "Hairdresser."

10. **Verbalize Label**
    Present a hairdresser and ask, "What is this?" The child will respond, "Hairdresser."

11.   **Concept Enrichment**

Discuss things which a hairdresser can do in addition to cutting hair. Discuss other names for hairdressers, such as barber, beautician, hair stylist.

Music

1.   Sing to the tune of "Here We Go 'Round the Mulberry Bush":

This is the way the barber works	*(Snip with scissors.)*
Barber works, barber works.	*(Snip with scissors.)*
This is the way the barber works	*(Snip with scissors.)*
So early in the morning.	*(Snip with scissors.)*

2.   Play "Harry the Hairstylist" from *Beginning Sounds & Careers (MH)*.

Art

1.   Help children make potato animals. Scoop out the top of a large white potato. Let the children stick four inverted golf tees into bottom of potato for feet; fill scooped out section with dirt; plant grass seed; and finish up potato animal by punching thumb tacks in one end for eyes and pipe cleaner in other end for tail. When grass grows tall enough give animals hair cuts. (See fig. 35A.)

Fig. 35A

2.   Let children make a hair collage. Have them dye pasta (rice, spaghetti, etc.) different colors and glue onto picture of a head.
3.   Have the children tie-dye old shirts to use as hairdresser smocks.
4.   Begin a "Hairdresser" scrapbook. Have the children cut or tear pictures of hairdressers from magazines and glue onto a hairdresser page.

Snack

1.   Cook spaghetti noodles. Talk about the shape of the noodles (like hair). Eat for snack. Be sure to examine before and after cooking.
2.   Use grated carrots, cheese, or coconut for "hair" on bread, fruit or cracker faces.

Fine Motor

1.   Have the children trim hair on wigs with scissors.
2.   Have the children comb and brush doll's hair.
3.   Let the children braid rope, large yarn or each others hair.

Games

1.   Set up the housekeeping area as hairdressing shop. Bring in old clippers, magazines, powders, brush, cloth, comb, etc. Put up barber poles. Let children role play with make-up, cotton balls, shampoo, bottles, wigs, clip-on rollers, and colored water in nail polish bottles.
2.   Play "The Hairdresser in the Dell."
3.   Have children role play being hairdressers. Let them put towels around "customer's" necks and pretend to wash, cut and set hair.

Storytelling

1.   Read a story about a barber.

2.   Fingerplay:
        Five little barbers standing in a row.   *(Hold up all fingers on one hand.)*
        This little barber stubbed his toe.   *(Pointer finger.)*
        This little barber cried, "Oh! Oh!"   *(Middle finger.)*
        This little barber laughed and was   *(Ring finger.)*
            glad.
        This little barber cried and was sad.   *(Pinky finger.)*
        But this little barber who was kind and   *(Use thumb.)*
            good.
        He ran for the doctor as fast as he could.

Gross Motor

Make a hairdresser obstacle course by placing hairdresser equipment (or pictures) at different levels. Have the children reach up to touch or reach down to touch depending upon where the item is placed.

Cognitive

1.   Have the children sort hairdressers from non-hairdressers.
2.   Have the children select hairdresser tools from non-hairdresser tools.
3.   Provide pictures of a variety of community helpers and have the children sort them into groups.
4.   Provide pictures of barber, postman, fireman, nurse and other community helpers and pictures of dog, ball, apple, banana, etc. Ask each child to put all community helper pictures in one pile and all other pictures in another pile.

Enrichment

1.   Make pictures of hairdressers and customers. Place a numeral on each hairdresser and have the children match the correct number of customers to each hairdresser.
2.   Provide a series of before-and-after pictures of people who have been to a hairdresser. Have the children match the correct before-and-after pictures.

Field Trip

Take a walk to a barber shop or beauty shop.

Visitor

Ask a hairdresser to come to your class to talk with children and show the tools (s)he uses.

Lesson 2: Scissors

Unit Group Lesson

Unit Group Lesson

1.   **Match Concrete Objects**
Present two pairs of scissors. Say, "This is a scissors." Ask each child in turn to put the scissors with the scissors. Gradually increase number of irrelevant objects from which (s)he must select scissors to match.

2.   **Discriminate Objects**
Present several objects. Have each child touch the scissors in response to verbal direction, "Touch the scissors."

3.   **Match Pictures**
Present several pictures of common objects. Have each child match the pictures of the scissors.

4.   **Discriminate Pictures**
Present a group of several unrelated pictures of objects. Have each child touch the picture of the scissors in response to verbal direction, "Touch the scissors."

5. **Figure-Ground**
   Present a "busy" picture with many visual distractions. Ask each child to find the scissors.

6. **Visual Closure**
   Partially cover each of several pictures with paper. Ask each child to find the picture of the scissors.

7. **Function**
   Ask, "What do we do with scissors?"

8. **Association**
   Ask, "What goes with the scissors?" Use pictures or objects including hair, hair dryer, comb, brush, hairdresser, etc. with several unrelated objects or pictures.

9. **Imitate Verbalization**
   Present scissors and ask, "What is this? Say, 'Scissors'." The child will imitate "Scissors."

10. **Verbalize Label**
    Present scissors and ask, "What is this?" The child will respond, "Scissors."

11. **Concept Enrichment**
    Look at different types of scissors such as hair-cutting scissors, thinning shears, pinking shears, etc.

Music

Sing to the tune of "Baa, Baa Black Sheep":
Snip, snip, snip, snip
Take the scissors up.
The barber used the scissors
To give me a haircut.

Art

1. Let children find pictures of scissors in catalogs and paste onto a page for the "Hairdresser" scrapbook begun in Lesson #1 Art #4.
2. Let the children use scissors to cut different kinds of paper (newspaper, tissue paper, construction paper, wax paper, foil, cellophane paper) and decorate a picture.
3. Draw large faces on paper. Attach to wall at child level. Let children cut straight or curly hair and put it around one of the faces. (See fig. 35B.)

Fig. 35B

Snack

1. Use clean scissors for cutting up foods for snack.
2. Cut up long foods for snack (long french fries, pieces of bread, etc.).

Fine Motor

1. Let children use tongs to develop back and forth movement useful for scissors skills.
2. Let children press play dough through a garlic press and snip with scissors. (Use the commerical play dough barber shop press and people if available and let the children cut the hair with scissors.)
3. Make doll (cardboard) with yarn hair. Let children cut "hair."
4. Let each child cut out a paper doll and use scissors to fringe doll's hair. (See fig. 35C.)

Fig. 35C

Games

Continue the hairdresser shop in the housekeeping area and let the children continue to role play being hairdressers. (Be careful that the children do not actually cut real hair. Confine their activities to wigs, etc.)

Storytelling

Make up story about "The Little Scissors That Would Not Cut." The mother didn't know why scissors wouldn't cut; the father didn't know; sister didn't know; brother didn't know. They took the scissors to Mr. Brown, the hairdresser who said; "Uh-huh, these scissors are too dull to cut. Let's sharpen them."

Gross Motor

1. Have a scissor hunt. Hide several pairs of blunt scissors around room. Have children find them. Hide scissors so that children must crawl, walk and climb while looking.

2. Have the children pretend their legs and arms are scissors and do scissor moves with them. "Open." "Shut."

Cognitive

1. Put several tools including blunt scissors into feely box. Ask each child to stick hand into hole and get out scissors. Start with only blunt scissors at first, then add other objects.

2. Provide scissors in several sizes. Have the children sequence them according to size.

3. Cut small amount of your hair. Look at hair under a magnifying glass.

Enrichment

Let the children try out a variety of scissors such as thinning shears, pinking shears, etc. on paper to see the differences in how they cut.

Lesson 3: Hair Dryer

Unit Group Lesson

Unit Group Lesson

1. **Match Concrete Objects**

   Present two hair dryers. Say, "This is a hair dryer." Ask each child in turn to put the hair dryer with the hair dryer. Gradually increase number of irrelevant objects from which (s)he must select hair dryer to match.

2. **Discriminate Objects**

   Present several objects. Have each child touch the hair dryer in response to verbal direction, "Touch the hair dryer."

3. **Match Pictures**

   Present several pictures of common objects. Have each child match the pictures of the hair dryers.

4. **Discriminate Pictures**

   Present a group of several unrelated pictures of objects. Have each child touch the picture of the hair dryer in response to verbal direction, "Touch the hair dryer."

5. **Figure-Ground**

   Present a "busy" picture with many visual distractions. Ask each child to find the hair dryer.

6. **Visual Closure**

   Partially cover each of several pictures with paper. Ask each child to find the picture of the hair dryer.

7. **Function**

   Ask, "What do we do with a hair dryer?"

8. **Association**

   Ask, "What goes with the hair dryer?" Use pictures or objects including brush, scissors, hairdresser, etc. with several unrelated objects or pictures.

9. **Imitate Verbalization**

   Present hair dryer and ask, "What is this? Say, 'Hair dryer'." The child will imitate "Hair dryer."

10. **Verbalize Label**

    Present hair dryer and ask, "What is this?" The child will respond, "Hair dryer."

11. **Concept Enrichment**

    Look at different types of hair dryers. Discuss what portable means. Decide which are portable. Discuss fact that a hair dryer heats the water until it evaporates off the hair into the air.

Music

Sing to the tune of "Here We Go 'Round the Mulberry Bush":
This is the way we dry our hair,   *(Pantoimime using a blow dryer.)*
Dry our hair, dry our hair.
This is the way we dry our hair,
With a hair dryer in the morning.

Art

1. Provide outlines of hair dryers and let the children paint them and decorate them.
2. Continue the "Hairdresser" scrapbook by having the children make hair dryer collages and add them to the book.

Snack

Have the children wash their hands for snack and dry them with a hair dryer.

Fine Motor

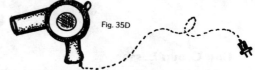

Fig. 35D

1. Prepare a path tracing of "Take the cord to a wall plug." Vary the difficulty for children with different skill levels. (See fig. 35D.)
2. Provide an old hair dryer for the children to turn on and off. (Do not plug it in while they use the switch.)
3. Have the children blow ping pong balls like a hair dryer would.

Games

Use hair dryer to blow ping pong balls for children to "catch."

Storytelling

Use flannel board and flannel board pictures to tell a story about a hairdresser whose hair dryer would not work. Let the children help figure out that she needs to plug it into the wall socket.

Gross Motor

Let the children chase ping pong balls blown around by a hair dryer.

Cognitive

1. Give each child a hair dryer and several lighter weight objects. Have her identify the heavy object. Begin with a hair dryer and a very, very lightweight object and gradually add objects that are closer in weight to the hair dryer.
2. Provide pictures of hair dryers of different types and other non-related objects. Have the children sort the hair dryers from non-hair dryers.
3. Make hair dryers in different colors and let the children sort them by color.

Enrichment

Let the children dry wet spots on a black board with a hair dryer. Discuss evaporation.

Field Trip
    Visit a beauty parlor. Let the children take turns sitting under dryer.

Lesson 4: Shampoo

Unit Group Lesson

Unit Group Lesson

1. **Match Concrete Objects**
    Present two bottles of shampoo. Say, "This is shampoo." Ask each child in turn to put the shampoo with the shampoo. Gradually increase number of irrelevant objects from which (s)he must select shampoo to match.

2. **Discriminate Objects**
    Present several objects. Have each child touch the shampoo in response to verbal direction, "Touch the shampoo."

3. **Match Pictures**
    Present several pictures of common objects. Have each child match the pictures of the shampoos.

4. **Discriminate Pictures**
    Present a group of several unrelated pictures of objects. Have each child touch the picture of the shampoo in response to verbal direction, "Touch the shampoo."

5. **Figure-Ground**
    Present a "busy" picture with many visual distractions. Ask each child to find the shampoo.

6. **Visual Closure**
    Partially cover each of several pictures with paper. Ask each child to find the picture of the shampoo.

7. **Function**
    Ask, "What do we do with shampoo?"

8. **Association**
    Ask, "What goes with the shampoo?" Use pictures or objects including comb, hair, scissors, brush, etc. with several unrelated objects or pictures.

9. **Imitate Verbalization**
    Present shampoo and ask, "What is this? Say, 'Shampoo'." The child will imitate "Shampoo."

10. **Verbalize Label**
    Present shampoo and ask, "What is this?" The child will respond, "Shampoo."

11. **Concept Enrichment**
    Discuss similarities and differences between shampoo and soap.

Music

    Sing to the tune of "Mary Had A Little Lamb":
        The hairdresser has some shampoo,
        Some shampoo, some shampoo,
        The hairdresser has some shampoo,
        To make hair clean and shiny.

Art
1.   Let the children make suds with shampoo and add food coloring. Then they can finger paint with it.

2. Continue the "Hairdresser" scrapbook by letting the children make shampoo collages and add them to the book.
3. Mix tempera powder into shampoo and let the children paint with it.

Snack
Wash hands with shampoo before snack.

Fine Motor
1. Let the children blow bubbles with shampoo.
2. Prepare a figure-ground activity with bottles of shampoo. Make simple to complex versions for children with different skill levels. Have the children glue pre-cut shampoo bottles onto the outline of the shampoo bottle. (See fig. 35E.)

Fig. 35E

3. Let the children screw and unscrew caps from shampoo bottles.

Games
Fill several empty shampoo bottles with water. (Be sure the bottles have squeeze tops.) Make a target on pavement or on an outside wall and let the children squirt the water at the target.

Storytelling
Make up a story about how the hairdresser uses shampoo to wash people's hair. Use flannel board and cut-outs to illustrate. Have children participate.

Gross Motor
1. Have a shampoo relay. Let the children run with a bottle of shampoo and pass it to the next person.
2. Place several containers of shampoo on floor or ground about three to four feet apart and have children jump or hop over containers. Spread them further apart as children become more proficient with game.

Cognitive
1. Provice a variety of empty shampoo containers with labels. Let the children match shampoo labels.
2. Provide or make shampoo bottles in several different sizes. Have the children sequence them from small to large.
3. Collect empty shampoo bottles with caps. Let the children match the correct cap to the correct bottle and put it on the bottle.

Enrichment
1. Compare shampoo and laundry powder, dish liquid, bar soap, etc. Note similarities (they all make suds) and differences (some are easier to dissolve).
2. Together Activity: Let the children make a giant shampoo bottle. Some can cut it out; some can paint it; some can label it. (See fig. 35F.)

Fig. 35F

Field Trip

    Visit a drug or grocery store to find shampoo.

Visitor

    Invite a parent to shampoo a child or dog.

Lesson 5: Brush

Unit Group Lesson

Unit Group Lesson

1. **Match Concrete Objects**
   Present two brushes. Say, "This is a brush." Ask each child in turn to put the brush with the brush. Gradually increase number of irrelevant objects from which (s)he must select brush to match.

2. **Discriminate Objects**
   Present several objects. Have each child touch the brush in response to verbal direction, "Touch the brush."

3. **Match Pictures**
   Present several pictures of common objects. Have each child match the pictures of the brushes.

4. **Discriminate Pictures**
   Present a group of several unrelated pictures of objects. Have each child touch the picture of the brush in response to verbal direction, "Touch the brush."

5. **Figure-Ground**
   Present a "busy" picture with many visual distractions. Ask each child to find the brush.

6. **Visual Closure**
   Partially cover each of several pictures with paper. Ask each child to find the picture of the brush.

7. **Function**
   Ask, "What do we do with brush?"

8. **Association**
   Ask, "What goes with the brush?" Use pictures or objects including comb, shampoo, hairdresser, scissors, etc. with several unrelated objects or pictures.

9. **Imitate Verbalization**
   Present a brush and ask, "What is this? Say, 'Brush'." The child will imitate "Brush."

10. **Verbalize Label**
    Present a brush and ask, "What is this?" The child will respond, "Brush."

11. **Concept Enrichment**
    Discuss and show pictures of different kinds of brushes. Discriminate hair brushes from other types of brushes such as clothes brushes, floor brushes, etc. Identify the parts of a brush, such as handle, bristles, etc.

Music

Sing to tune of "Row, Row, Row Your Boat":
Brush, brush, brush my hair.
Brush my hair so neat.
Brush, brush, brush my hair.
Brush my hair so neat.

Art

1. Have the children make a brush from clay or play dough.
2. Let the children use hair brushes for painting on large paper.
3. Complete the "Hairdresser" scrapbook by having the children make hair brush collages and adding them. Have each child paint a picture of a hairdresser shop and use it as the book cover for the scrapbook.

Snack

1. Eat a snack which has been washed with a vegetable brush.
2. Have toast on which the children have brushed melted butter with a pastry brush.

Fine Motor

1. Make brush puzzles by gluing pictures of brushes onto cardboard and cutting them into pieces. Vary the number of pieces according to the skill levels of the children. Have each child work a puzzle at her own skill level.
2. Make brush sewing cards by cutting out brush shapes and punching holes around edges. Let children lace. Use more holes for children with higher skills in lacing and less for beginners.
3. Have children brush each other's hair, animal's hair and doll's hair.

Games

Use a wire brush to make designs in sand or on a piece of velour.

Storytelling

Fingerplay:

Five little brushes standing in a row.	*(Put up five fingers.)*
They all work for Barber Joe.	*(Wiggle fingers.)*
They go swish, swish here,	*(Brush right side of head and neck.)*
And swish, swish there.	*(Brush left side of head and neck.)*
They brush on the powder, and	*(Rub hand on face.)*
They brush off the hair.	*(Wave hand away from face and neck.)*

Gross Motor

Have a hair brush relay. Divide the class into teams. One child from each team carries a hair brush to a given point and back and gives the brush to a teammate. Continue until all children have had a turn.

Cognitive

1. Make cue sheets. Make a brush shape at the top of the paper and brushes and other hairdresser's tools (clippers, powder) beneath. Ask child to mark all the brushes which look the same as the brush at top of page. Vary the level of difficulty of the cue sheets according to the skills of the children. (See fig. 35G.)

Fig 35G

2.   Make brush numeral peg boards. Cut brush shapes in wood. Put a numeral on each handle and make holes for the appropriate number of golf tees. Let the children count golf tees and place them in brushes. (See fig. 35H.)

Fig. 35H

Enrichment
Collect a variety of brushes and discuss how they are used.

Field Trip
1.   Visit a beauty shop.
2.   Visit a variety store, find all kinds of brushes.
3.   Visit a car wash and look for a big brush.

Visitor
Invite a parent to demonstrate how to wash your hair brush. Take turns washing brushes.

Related Children's Records
"Harry the Hairstylist" from **BEGINNING SOUNDS & CAREERS** (UBB)

Related Children's Books
Freeman, Don. **DANDELION.** New York: Viking Press, 1964.
Freeman, Don. **MOP TOP.** New York: Viking Press, 1955.
Rockwell, Anne and Rockwell, Harlow. **MY BARBER.** Macmillan Publishing Co., 1981.

Related Parenting Materials
Cansler, Dot. **THE HOMESTRETCH.** Winston-Salem, NC 27113-5128: Kaplan Press, 1983.

Related Materials
TEACHING PICTURES. Winston-Salem, NC 27113-5128: Kaplan Press, 1983.
STORY SEQUENCE CARDS I, II. Winston-Salem, NC 27113-5128: Kaplan Press, 1983.
SEWING CARDS I, II, III. Winston-Salem, NC 27113-5128: Kaplan Press, 1983.

Unit 36: Ball Games

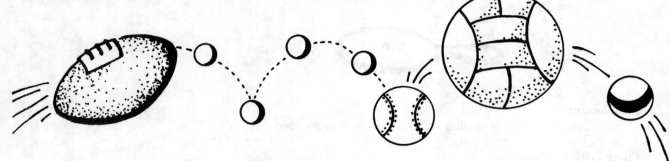

A developmental assessment should determine the functional levels of each child. Individual expectations are based on the assessment results.

Lesson 1: Soccer

Unit Group Lesson

1. **Match Concrete Objects**
   Present two soccer balls. Say, "This is a soccer ball." Ask each child in turn to put the soccer ball with the soccer ball. Gradually increase number of irrelevant objects from which (s)he must select soccer ball to match.

2. **Discriminate Objects**
   Present several objects. Have each child touch the soccer ball in response to verbal direction, "Touch the soccer ball."

3. **Match Pictures**
   Present several pictures of common objects. Have each child match the pictures of the soccer ball.

4. **Discriminate Pictures**
   Present a group of several unrelated pictures of objects. Have each child touch the picture of the soccer ball in response to verbal direction, "Touch the soccer ball."

5. **Figure-Ground**
   Present a "busy" picture with many visual distractions. Ask each child to find the soccer ball.

6. **Visual Closure**
   Partially cover each of several pictures with paper. Ask each child to find the picture of the soccer ball.

7. **Function**
   Ask, "What do we do with a soccer ball?"

8. **Association**
   Ask, "What goes with the soccer ball?" Use pictures or objects including goal, soccer field, soccer shoes, etc. with several unrelated objects or pictures.

9. **Imitate Verbalization**
   Present a soccer ball and ask, "What is this? Say, 'Soccer ball'." The child will imitate "Soccer ball."

10. **Verbalize Label**
    Present a soccer ball and ask, "What is this?" The child will respond, "Soccer ball."

11.   **Concept Enrichment**

Discuss the goal (the cage into which the ball is kicked). Discuss scoring a goal in soccer and the field on which soccer is played.

Music

Play a musical game of pass the soccer ball. Form a circle with small group. Give one child a soccer ball. Start musical record. Have children move ball around circle by gently kicking it from one child to the next. Child with back turned to group stops the music. The child who has the ball must "trap" it between her feet and she becomes the record stopper.

Art

1.   Give each child ball shapes (from various sports). Have her put "same on same" and paste shapes in place. Vary difficulty by adding more shapes and different shapes dependent upon child's ability. Let child decorate paper.
2.   Have children find pictures of soccer balls, cut out and paste into "Our Game Book."
3.   Have children make soccer balls from clay or play dough.

Snack

Serve a snack you might be able to purchase at a soccer game such as bags of popcorn and lemonade.

Fine Motor

1.   Make sewing cards in the shape of a soccer ball and let children lace string around the ball. Vary the levels of difficulty according to the skills of the children.
2.   Give child puzzle of a soccer player and let him put whole pieces such as arms, legs, etc. back in place.
3.   Draw shape of soccer ball on peg board. Have child put pegs along lines to outline soccer ball shape.
4.   Give child a picture with several pre-drawn shapes of soccer balls and some lines drawn over them to partially cover shapes. Ask child to find all the ball shapes and outline them with magic marker or give child soccer ball shapes and ask him to find all the soccer ball shapes and paste soccer ball on soccer ball. (Figure-Ground)

Games

1.   Put soccer uniforms and shoes in dress-up corner.
2.   Pantomime soccer: Show group how to dribble and kick and run with soccer ball. Let each child imitate actions. "How is this different from basketball?"

Storytelling

Read a story about a soccer game. Make flannel pieces to go with story to get children involved.

Gross Motor

1.   Let children play a soccer game and include kicking, running, trapping, passing. The sponge rubber balls are good for this.
2.   Let child stand several feet away from wastebasket or large box turned on its side and kick soccer ball into it. Move goal farther away as child's ability increases.
3.   Have a soccer relay. Let the children kick the ball from one child to the next.
4.   Soccer is the one game where the ball can be hit with the head. Use a sponge soccer ball and let the children practice using their head to move the ball.
5.   Tape a goal area on wall. Have children take turns getting a sponge soccer ball into goal while "goalie" works to keep it out. Give one point for each goal. Keep score to see how many goals the class can make.

Cognitive

1.   Have children match numerals on soccer shirts to soccer balls with the same numeral. (See fig. 36A.)
2.   Have children match colors of soccer shirts.

Fig. 36A

3. Put soccer shirts on cut-outs with same number. (See fig. 36B.)
4. Have children match soccer shirt designs. For more advanced children make the differences very subtle. (See fig. 36N.)

Fig. 36B

Enrichment
1. Have children collect newspaper pictures of soccer and make a soccer book or a giant soccer poster.
2. Have children compare soccer players and basketball players. How do basketball players, soccer shoes and tennis shoes, compare. Inflate a soccer ball with an air pump.
3. Mark down goals made in soccer game. Have children count the marks to get the score.
4. Help the children think of names for soccer teams. Make a list of the names such as Blazers, Runners, Whirlwind. Provide upper case letters to match the first letter of each name. Take turns matching correctly.
5. Inflate a soccer ball with an air pump.

Fig. 36N

Field Trip
1. Take class to a soccer game.
2. Watch soccer game on television.

Visitor
Invite a soccer player to come in his playing clothes with soccer ball and goalie equipment.

Lesson 2: Basketball

Unit Group Lesson

1. **Match Concrete Objects**
Present two basketballs. Say, "This is a basketball." Ask each child in turn to put the basketball with the basketball. Gradually increase number of irrelevant objects from which (s)he must select basketball to match.

2. **Discriminate Objects**
Present several objects. Have each child touch the basketball in response to verbal direction, "Touch the basketball."

3. **Match Pictures**
Present several pictures of common objects. Have each child match the pictures of the basketball.

4. **Discriminate Pictures**
Present a group of several unrelated picture of objects. Have each child touch the picture of the basketball in response to verbal direction, "Touch the basketball."

5. **Figure-Ground**
Present a "busy" picture with many visual distractions. Ask each child to find the basketball.

6. **Visual Closure**
Partially cover each of several pictures with paper. Ask each child to find the picture of the basketball.

7. **Function**
Ask, "What do we do with a basketball?"

8. **Association**
    Ask, "What goes with the basketball?" Use pictures or objects including basketball net, basketball sneakers, etc. with several unrelated objects or pictures.

9. **Imitate Verbalization**
    Present a basketball and ask, "What is this? Say, 'Basketball'." The child will imitate "Basketball."

10. **Verbalize Label**
    Present a basketball and ask, "What is this?" The child will respond, "Basketball."

11. **Concept Enrichment**
    Discuss the basket. If necessary, repeat the above format substituting basket for basketball. Discuss how to make and score a basket. Talk about the basketball team.

Music
1. Play marching music and let children bounce basketballs to music.
2. Sing to the tune of "The Farmer in the Dell":
    We bounce (throw, shoot) the basketball!
    We bounce the basketball!
    We move across the floor
    And bounce the basketball.

Fig. 36C

Art
1. Provide sheet of paper with shape of basketball already drawn. Ask child to draw shapes that will look just like the one on the paper.
2. Let children blow up a large balloon, tie it, and cover it with papier-mache to make a basketball.
3. Help children make and stuff paper basketballs. (See fig. 36C.)
4. Let children make basketball collages to add to "Our Game Book."

Snack
1. Eat basketball-shaped cookies made in Fine Motor #3.
2. Eat basketballs made from peanut butter play dough made in Fine Motor #4.
3. Throw trash (papers at snacktime) into trash cans. "Can you make a slam dunk?"

Fine Motor
1. Give child pre-drawn shapes of basketball, football and tennis ball to cut out then sort according to kind of ball.
2. Make a Geoboard with nails put in a circle. Have child put rubber bands on nails to form circle. Add an inner circle of nails to make smaller circle.
3. Have children make basketball cookies for snack and decorate with chocolate frosting.
4. Have children make basketballs from peanut butter play dough. (Peanut butter play dough is made from peanut butter, confectioners sugar and honey to taste.)
5. Have children make clay basketballs.

Games
1. Put basketball uniforms and shoes in the dress-up area.
2. Pantomime to show the group how to dribble and throw basketball. Let each child imitate actions. Ask, "How is this different from soccer?"

Storytelling
Make up a story about a basketball that could not bounce because he needed more air.

Gross Motor
1. Hot Ball - children must keep ball moving on floor or ground with feet. Children cannot touch "hot ball" with hands.
2. Let children stand several feet from a large wastebasket and throw basketball into it. Move child further

away as his ability improves.

3.   Attach a round laundry basket (with the bottom cut out) to a tree close to the ground. Let children play basketball using the basket as a hoop.

4.   Let children throw soft sponge basketballs into bucket "baskets" or laundry baskets.

5.   Let children practice passing and dribbling with real basketballs as well as rubber balls.

Cognitive

1.   Make a set of goal cards with numbers, letters, colors or items to match on goal card. Provide a set of basketballs to match the goal cards. Have each child match ball to goal card. (The children can make the card sets and balls in art.)

2.   Make card sets of a variety of balls. Have children pick out two that match. Pick out basketballs. Play concentration.

3.   Make several basketball teams with different uniforms. Have the children sort the teams.

4.   Make basketball socks in different colors and patterns. Mix them up and let the children match the pairs.

Enrichment

Make a basket. Have letters or numerals on basketballs cut from construction paper. The child scores a basket and makes a point for each basketball he can correctly identify. (See fig. 36D.)

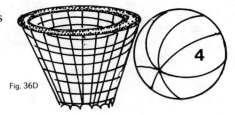

Fig. 36D

Field Trip

Take class to a basketball game.

Visitor

Invite a basketball player to come in uniform, help children learn to dribble, to hold ball, etc. Ask him to talk about the color of his uniform and what it means.

Lesson 3: Baseball

Unit Group Lesson

1.   **Match Concrete Objects**
Present two baseballs. Say, "This is a baseball." Ask each child in turn to put the baseball with the baseball. Gradually increase number of irrelevant objects from which (s)he must select baseball to match.

2.   **Discriminate Objects**
Present several objects. Have each child touch the baseball in response to verbal direction, "Touch the baseball."

3.   **Match Pictures**
Present several pictures of common objects. Have each child match the pictures of the baseballs.

4.   **Discriminate Pictures**
Present a group of several unrelated picture of objects. Have each child touch the picture of the baseball in response to verbal direction, "Touch the baseball."

5.   **Figure-Ground**
Present a "busy" picture with many visual distractions. Ask each child to find the baseball.

6.   **Visual Closure**
Partially cover each of several pictures with paper. Ask each child to find the picture of the baseball.

7. **Function**

Ask, "What do we do with a baseball?"

8. **Association**

Ask, "What goes with the baseball?" Use pictures or objects including baseball bat, baseball glove, catcher's mask, etc. with several unrelated objects or pictures.

9. **Imitate Verbalization**

Present a baseball and ask, "What is this? Say, 'Baseball'." The child will imitate "Baseball."

10. **Verbalize Label**

Present a baseball and ask, "What is this?" The child will respond, "Baseball."

11. **Concept Enrichment**

Discuss baseball bat and a baseball glove. If necessary, repeat the above format substituting baseball bat or baseball glove for baseball. Talk about a baseball diamond, how to score a point in baseball, how many players are on the team, etc.

Fig. 36F

Music

Sing "Take Me Out To the Ball Game."

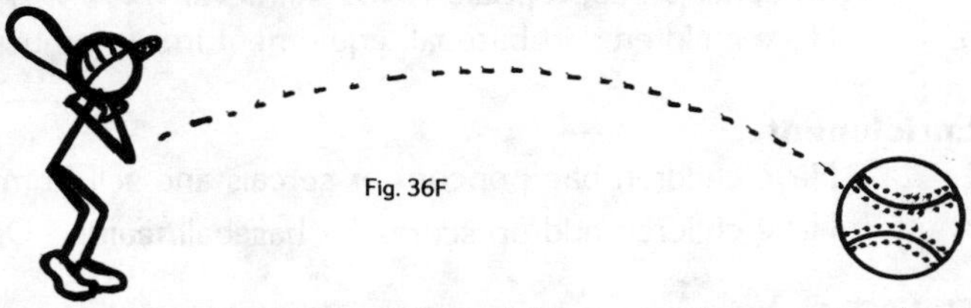

Art

1. Draw shapes of baseballs on different colors of construction paper. Have children cut them out and use them for Cognitive #1 of this lesson.
2. Have children find pictures of baseballs and basketballs and paste them in "Our Game Book."
3. Have children make baseballs and basketballs from play dough and compare sizes.

Snack

Eat popcorn, hotdogs, etc. like one would at a baseball game.

Fig. 36E   METS

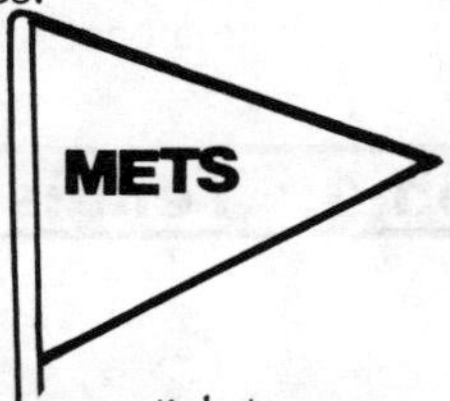

Fine Motor

1. Let each child make a baseball cap for herself with her name on it.
2. Have children cut triangles to make pennants with team names. Put on walls or on a stick to wave. Let children write over team name or write team name. (See fig. 36E.)
3. On blackboard draw stick figure player hitting ball. Have children take turns path tracing and erasing for next child. For some draw dots. Allow others to draw the line from bat to ball. (See fig. 36F.)

Games

1. Put a baseball uniform, masks and gloves in the dress-up area.
2. Use large plastic bat to begin with and let children hit ball. Later on you may let children run to base, etc.
3. Pantomime to show the group how to hold and run in baseball as well as how to hit and pitch the ball. Let each child imitate how to pitch, run, and bat. "How is this different from what we do with a tennis ball or basketball?"

Storytelling

1. Cut out flannel figures of enough baseball players to make a team. Cut strips and squares to make a baseball diamond on flannel board. Make baseball bat and ball. Use this to tell the story of "Casey At the Bat," your own story, or help the children make up a story.
2. Fingerplay (use flannel board cut-outs).

Five little baseballs sitting near a bat
The first one said, now would you look at that.   *(Point to bat.)*
The second one said, I'll punch him in the nose.   *(Take second ball and punch handle of bat.)*
The third one said, I'll pull his little toes.   *(Take third ball and make pulling motion at end of bat.)*

The fourth one hid behind a big oak tree while
The fifth one counted 1, 2, 3.

Gross Motor
1. Get a T-ball tee for children to use to practice batting.
2. Hang a ball (of newspaper) in a tree or in a doorway. Let children use cardboard tubes as bats and "bat" the ball.
3. Play "Home Run." Let the children run to a certain "base." (Tree, bench, etc.)

Cognitive
1. Use shapes that were cut in Art #1 of this lesson. Put colored baseballs on table or ground if outside. Have children stand ten to twelve feet away. Keep a shape in each color, hold up one color, and say to each child, one at a time, "Use your eyes, use your eyes. Quickly look and see. Run get a ball the color of mine and bring it back to me."
2. Make balls and bats with matching colors, numbers or alphabet letters. Have children match balls and bats that go together. This activity can be done for all the mentioned concepts and each child can work on concepts appropriate to his skill level. (See fig. 36G.)
3. Have children sort baseball equipment from non-baseball equipment.

Fig. 36G

Enrichment
1. Have children bag popcorn or cereals and sell from a vendor's stand or sale box. (See fig. 36H.)
2. Have children add up scores for baseball teams. Decide which team has more and is the winner.

Field Trip
Go to a real game or visit the dug-out at a ball park.

Visitor
Invite a baseball player to visit.

Fig. 36H

Lesson 4: Tennis

Unit Group Lesson

1. **Match Concrete Objects**
   Present two tennis balls. Say, "This is a tennis ball." Ask each child in turn to put the tennis ball with the tennis ball. Gradually increase number of irrelevant objects from which (s)he must select tennis ball to match.

2. **Discriminate Objects**
   Present several objects. Have each child touch the tennis ball in response to verbal direction, "Touch the tennis ball."

3. **Match Pictures**
   Present several pictures of common objects. Have each child match the pictures of the tennis balls.

4. **Discriminate Pictures**
   Present a group of several unrelated pictures of objects. Have each child touch the picture of the tennis ball in response to verbal direction, "Touch the tennis ball."

5. **Figure-Ground**
   Present a "busy" picture with many visual distractions. Ask each child to find the tennis ball.

6. **Visual Closure**
Partially cover each of several pictures with paper. Ask each child to find the picture of the tennis ball.

7. **Function**
Ask, "What do we do with a tennis ball?"

8. **Association**
Ask, "What goes with the tennis ball?" Use pictures or objects including tennis racket, tennis net, tennis shoes, tennis clothes, etc., with several unrelated objects or pictures.

9. **Imitate Verbalization**
Present a tennis ball and ask, "What is this? Say, 'Tennis ball'." The child will imitate "Tennis ball."

10. **Verbalize Label**
Present a tennis ball and ask, "What is this?" The child will respond, "Tennis ball."

11. **Concept Enrichment**
Discuss tennis rackets, tennis net, tennis shoes, etc. If necessary, repeat the above format substituting tennis rackets for tennis balls. Talk about how to score in tennis, what a tennis court looks like, etc.

Music
Use record, xylophone, autoharp, or piano to make fast and slow music while children pretend to be tennis balls and bounce (hop up and down) around the room.

Art
1. Let each child decorate a tennis cap. (See fig. 36I.)
2. Have children cut out pictures of tennis equipment and players and make a collage to add to "Our Game Book."
3. Let children dip tennis balls into paint and print with them.

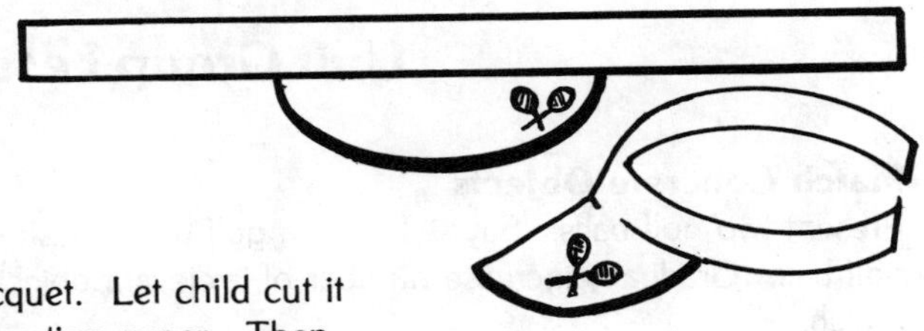

Snack
Serve crackers on a tennis racket.

Fine Motor
1. Let children draw picture of tennis racquet. Let child cut it out and paste on large piece of construction paper. Then use round sponge and white paint to sponge-paint shapes of tennis balls around and on the tennis racquet. (See fig. 36J.)
2. Have children make faces on tennis balls.
3. Have children pack tennis balls into tennis ball cans.
4. Have children zip racket into tennis racket cover.
5. Provide screw-on wooden tennis racket covers, and let children tighten screws to hold the racket.
6. On tennis racket outline, path trace string lines. (See fig. 36N.)

Fig. 36I

Fig. 36J

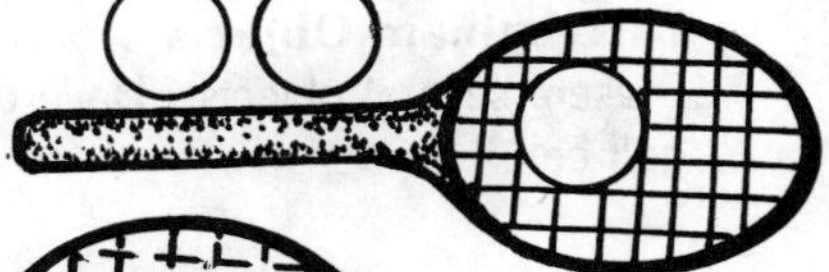

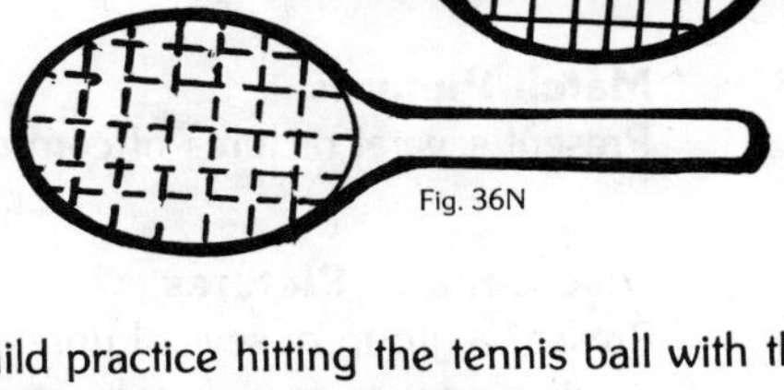

Fig. 36N

Games
1. Model how to use tennis racquet with ball. Then let each child practice hitting the tennis ball with the racquet. You many need to start with a large paper or yarn ball before using a tennis ball.
2. Let children throw tennis balls into wastebasket or holes in cardboard that are graduated in size.
3. Cover a coathanger with a stocking to make a racket. Let children hit sponge rubber balls to each other. (A net may be made from "net" material hung between two chairs.) (See fig. 36K.)

Storytelling
Show filmstrip or short movie about tennis game.

Fig. 36K

Gross Motor
1.   Give the children badminton rackets, tennis rackets or racquetball rackets to practice tennis swings.
2.   Put up net in playground. Let children throw or hit balls over it.
3.   Suspend a whiffle ball from a ceiling or doorway. Let children use small rackets or cardboard tubes to hit the ball.
4.   Hang a bell in a tree. Have children throw tennis balls and ring the bell.

Cognitive
1.   Let children sort tennis balls by color.
2.   Let children count tennis balls or how many times the tennis ball bounces.
3.   Let children count three balls into tennis ball cans and work on the concept of three.

Enrichment
1.   Provide sports clothes in a suitcase. Have child pick out tennis outfit from other items of clothing.
2.   Provide tennis bag with attached cover for tennis racket. Have children learn to pack the racket and clothing for tennis.
3.   Let children look in newspaper and sports magazines for ads about tennis equipment and use them to make a tennis "catalog."

Field Trip
Take children to tennis court or tennis match. This may be a good time to ask two tennis-playing parents to put on a demonstration game.

Visitor
Have a tennis player come in tennis clothing with his equipment in his bag. Let him explain why he wears wristband, headband, how he stores the racket and balls.

Lesson 5: Golf

Unit Group Lesson

1.   **Match Concrete Objects**
Present two golf balls. Say, "This is a golf ball." Ask each child in turn to put the golf ball with the golf ball. Gradually increase number of irrelevant objects from which (s)he must select golf ball to match.

2.   **Discriminate Objects**
Present several objects. Have each child touch the golf ball in response to verbal direction, "Touch the golf ball."

3.   **Match Pictures**
Present several pictures of common objects. Have each child match the pictures of the golf balls.

4.   **Discriminate Pictures**
Present a group of several unrelated picture of objects. Have each child touch the picture of the golf ball in response to verbal direction, "Touch the golf ball."

5.   **Figure-Ground**
Present a "busy" picture with many visual distractions. Ask each child to find the golf ball.

6.   **Visual Closure**
Partially cover each of several pictures with paper. Ask each child to find the picture of the golf ball.

7. **Function**
   Ask, "What do we do with a golf ball?"

8. **Association**
   Ask, "What goes with the golf ball?" Use pictures or objects including golf balls, golf shoes, golf bag, etc., with several unrelated objects or pictures.

9. **Imitate Verbalization**
   Present a golf ball and ask, "What is this? Say, 'Golf ball'." The child will imitate "Golf ball."

10. **Verbalize Label**
    Present a golf ball and ask, "What is this?" The child will respond, "Golf ball."

11. **Concept Enrichment**
    Discuss golf clubs and golf shoes. If necessary, repeat the above format substituting golf club for golf ball. Discuss how golf is scored, what a golf course looks like, golf carts, etc.

Music

Sing to the tune of "Row, Row, Row Your Boat":
Hit, hit, hit the ball
Knock it in the hole.
Hit, hit, hit the ball
Knock it in the hole.

Art

1. Draw pictures of golf course. Draw partially hidden golf balls in serveral places on the course. Ask child to find and mark every golf ball he sees and decorate the picture.
2. Have children find pictures of golf balls or other golf items and paste in the "Our Games" scrapbook.
3. Provide circle of styrofoam. Have children make dents in the styrofoam all over (with a ballpoint pen) to make golf balls.

Snack

Eat golf balls made from peanut butter play dough.

Fine Motor

1. Find and glue onto one large piece of cardboard one picture each of a soccer ball, baseball, basketball, tennis ball and golf ball. Cut the pictures into five or six pieces and use as puzzle.
2. Use the same picture as in #1. Do not cut apart. Punch holes around edges of each ball and use as pegboard or lacing board.
3. Let children use colored golf tees to make and copy patterns in pegboard.
4. Let children poke golf tees into styrofoam.

Games

Make a wide (2 ft.) path on the floor with two pieces of masking tape or draw two lines on the ground. Let child use a child-size broom to move the golf ball from one end of path to other end. You may want to use real golf clubs later to see if child is able to manipulate the smaller object.

Storytelling

Make a set of sequence cards of the steps in getting ball across the course to the hole. Tell the story to the group. Mix up the cards and let children put them back in order. (See fig. 36L.)

Gross Motor

1. Sink a cup into a hole in the ground. Let children use a broom, croquet mallet, or golf club to hit a ball into the hole.

Fig. 36L

2.	Tape circles on the sidewalk. Let children use small brooms or hockey sticks to push balls or jar lids into the circles.
3.	Have children play croquet.
4.	Make a golf hole by laying a can on its side, then have children roll golf balls into it.

Cogntive
1.	Have the children count the number of times it takes to hit the ball into the cup. (If the number gets too high, have the children repeat after you.)
2.	Make cardboard golf clubs with numbers, 1, 2, 3, 4, and 5 (reinforce handle with plastic drinking straws) and golf balls with the same numbers. Have children match balls to clubs. (See fig. 36M.)
3.	Place golf clubs in a golf "bag." Have children take them out according to directions of teacher such as "Give me number two, number five, etc." Place back in the golf bag according to directions.

Enrichment
Help children learn golf words such as irons, tee, range, course, clubs, putt, drive, etc.

Field Trip

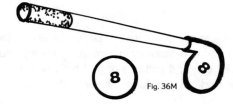
Fig. 36M

1.	Play Putt-Putt golf.
2.	Take a ride on golf carts.
3.	Take a walk on a golf course.
4.	Visit a driving range to watch golfers practice.

Visitor
Invite a parent who plays golf to bring golf clubs, golf shoes, gloves, etc. and demonstrate "putting."

Related Children's Records
ADVENTURES IN SOUND (MH)
"Take Me Out to the Ballgame" from SONGS IN MOTION-HOLIDAY (EA)
"In the Basket" from SHAPES IN ACTION (EA)
"Quentin Quick the Quarterback" from BEGINNING SOUNDS & CAREERS (UBB)
"Mr. Underwood the Umpire" from BEGINNING SOUNDS & CAREERS (UBB)

Related Children's Books
Baker, Eugene. I WANT TO BE A TENNIS PLAYER. Chicago: Children's Press, 1973.
Gemme, Leila Boyle. T-BALL IS OUR GAME. Chicago: Children's Press, 1978.
Isadora, Rachel. MAX. New York: Macmillan Publishing Co., 1976.
Kessler, Leonard. KICK, PASS AND RUN. New York: Harper & Row, 1966.
Parnish, Peggy. PLAY BALL AMELIA BEDELIA. New York: Harper & Row, 1972.

Related Parenting Materials
Cansler, Dot. THE HOMESTRETCH. Winston-Salem, NC 27113-5128: Kaplan Press, 1983.

Related Materials
TEACHING PICTURES. Winston-Salem, NC 27113-5128: Kaplan Press, 1983.
STORY SEQUENCE CARDS I, II. Winston-Salem, NC 27113-5128: Kaplan Press, 1983.
SEWING CARDS I, II, III. Winston-Salem, NC 27113-5128: Kaplan Press, 1983.

Unit 37: Doctor and Nurse

A developmental assessment should determine the functional levels of each child. Individual expectations are based on the assessment results.

Lesson 1: Doctor

Unit Group Lesson

1. **Match Concrete Objects** (Use dolls.)
   Present two doctors. Say, "This is a doctor." Ask each child in turn to put the doctor with the doctor. Gradually increase number of irrelevant objects from which (s)he must select doctor to match.

2. **Discriminate Objects**
   Present several objects. Have each child touch the doctor in response to verbal direction, "Touch the doctor."

3. **Match Pictures**
   Present several pictures of common objects. Have each child match the pictures of the doctors.

4. **Discriminate Pictures**
   Present a group of several unrelated pictures of objects. Have each child touch the picture of the doctor in response to verbal direction, "Touch the doctor."

5. **Figure-Ground**
   Present a "busy" picture with many visual distractions. Ask each child to find the doctor.

6. **Visual Closure**
   Partially cover each of several pictures with paper. Ask each child to find the picture of the doctor.

7. **Function**
   Ask, "What does a doctor do?"

8. **Association**
   Ask, "What goes with the doctor?" Use pictures or objects including white coat, nurse, stethoscope, etc. with several unrelated objects or pictures.

9. **Imitate Verbalization**
   Present a doctor and ask, "What is this? Say, 'Doctor'." The child will imitate "Doctor."

10. **Verbalize Label**
    Present a doctor and ask, "What is this?" The child will respond, "Doctor."

11.   **Concept Enrichment**

Emphasize that doctors work to keep us healthy. Children are often fearful of doctors. This is a good time to help them discuss some of their concerns. For example, doctors wear white coats because they can be made germ-free and cover the doctor's street clothes which are not so germ-free.

Music

1.   Sing to the tune of "Frere Jacques":

Busy doctor, busy doctor.

Makes us better.

Makes us better.

Busy, busy doctor.

Busy, busy doctor.

Helps us when we're sick.

Helps us when we're sick.

2.   Sing "Three Little Monkeys" (jumping on the bed).
3.   Sing "Miss Polly Had A Dolly" (who was sick, sick, sick).
4.   Listen to "My Mommie Is a Doctor" from *My Mommie Is A Doctor*.

Art

1.   Give children pictures of doctors which are missing white coats, stethoscopes, etc. Let them add pre-cut missing parts and decorate the doctor's office.
2.   Let children use white paint at the easel today.
3.   Let children draw and paint pictures of doctors.

Snack

1.   Eat popsicles made with tongue depressor sticks.
2.   Eat snack from lunch boxes ("doctor's bags"). Talk about differences between medicine and food.

Fine Motor

1.   Make doctor puzzles by gluing pictures of doctors onto cardboard. Cut into two or more pieces. Let each child do a puzzle that is appropriate to her skill level.
2.   Make path tracing activities of "Take a sick girl to the doctor." and "Take a sick boy to the doctor." Make a variety of difficulties in the paths according to the skills of the children. Let each child do appropriate path tracings.
3.   Let children fill and empty neede-less syringes with water.

Games

Put nurse's caps, medical kits, glasses without lenses, tape, gauze, cotton, bandages, tongue depressors, stethoscopes, white coats, and bags with handles in the dress-up area of the room.

Storytelling

1.   Choose two children, one to be the doctor and one to be the child. Narrate a story about what happens at a check-up and have children perform actions. For example, the doctor looks in your ears, then he looks in your mouth, etc.
2.   Read *My Doctor* by Rockwell.

Gross Motor

Have children "Take the baby to the doctor." Have each child decide on a way to get to the doctor such as hop, slide, jump, back-up, etc. Have the child carry a doll in arms while getting to the doctor.

Cognitive

1.   Have children sort doctors from non-doctors.

2. Make several lotto games. Use pictures of male doctor, female doctor, male nurse, female nurse, scales, stethoscope, medicine, otoscope, etc. Make a game board with from three to twelve pictures and make matching pieces. The children may use them for matching or as a regular lotto game. (Vinyl photo album pages are available in two to nine pockets and can be used to make lotto games.) (See fig. 37A.)

3. Fill doctor's bags with different amounts of material. Let children decide which is the heaviest of each of a pair of bags.

Fig. 37A

doctor (female)	scales	nurse (male)
nurse (female)	steth.	doctor (male)

Enrichment

Help children make a chart of things that they can do to keep healthy such as eat good foods; have regular checkups; exercise; wear proper clothing, etc. Discuss the various things in detail.

Field Trip

Visit a pediatrician's office, a hospital, or rescue squad center.

Visitor

Invite a woman doctor to visit.

Lesson 2: Nurse

Unit Group Lesson

1. **Match Concrete Objects** (Use dolls.)
Present two nurses. Say, "This is a nurse." Ask each child in turn to put the nurse with the nurse. Gradually increase number of irrelevant objects from which (s)he must select nurse to match.

2. **Discriminate Objects**
Present several objects. Have each child touch the nurse in response to verbal direction, "Touch the nurse."

3. **Match Pictures**
Present several pictures of common objects. Have each child match the pictures of the nurses.

4. **Discriminate Pictures**
Present a group of several unrelated pictures of objects. Have each child touch the picture of the nurse in response to verbal direction, "Touch the nurse."

5. **Figure-Ground**
Present a "busy" picture with many visual distractions. Ask each child to find the nurse.

6. **Visual Closure**
Partially cover each of several pictures with paper. Ask each child to find the picture of the nurse.

7. **Function**
Ask, "What does a nurse do?"

8. **Association**
Ask, "What goes with the nurse?" Use pictures or objects including doctor, stethoscope, etc. with several unrelated objects or pictures.

9. **Imitate Verbalization**
Present a nurse and ask, "What is this? Say, 'Nurse'." The child will imitate "Nurse."

10.   **Verbalize Label**
        Present a nurse and ask, "What is this?" The child will respond, "Nurse."

11.   **Concept Enrichment**
        Discuss basic procedures when one is sick: rest, keep away from other people, use a tissue to cover your nose when you sneeze or cough, etc. Talk about male nurses.

Music
1.   Sing to the tune of "Who Is That Knocking at Our Door?":
        Nurse shows us how to brush our teeth
        Brush and brush and brush those teeth
        Nurse shows us how to take our medicine
        Open, open, mouth and swallow
        She is a helper to the doctor
        She is a helper to the doctor
        The nurse is our friend, indeed
        The nurse is our friend, indeed.
2.   Listen to "Mrs. Nicholson the Nurse" from *Beginning Sounds & Careers.*

Art
1.   Let children use a syringe without a needle as a paint squirter to paint a giant piece of paper. Hang paper on the wall and use in Lesson #3 Art #2.
2.   Have children crumple tissues in different colors and glue on paper for a design.
3.   Have children make a nurse collage by cutting or tearing pictures of nurses from catalogs and gluing then onto paper.

Snack
        Eat foods which are nutritious such as fruits, vegetables, etc.

Fine Motor
1.   Have children open bandages and put them on dolls.
2.   Have children use adhesive tape to hold sterile pads on dolls.
3.   Have children make faces from paper plates, glue a tissue over nose, and then glue paper hand on top. Talk about covering mouth and nose for coughs/sneezes.

Games
1.   Emphasize nurse's cap in dress-up corner. Make out of paper and put on with bobby pins.
2.   "Nurse" pet animals or dolls in housekeeping area.

Storytelling
        Make up a story about someone who gets a cold and feels terrible. He sneezes all over and gives his cold to other people. Finally, he goes to see the nurse and she takes his temperature and gives him some medicine to make him feel better. She also shows him how to cover his nose with tissues.

Gross Motor
        Create an obstacle course. Have first child run the course to take a drinking straw "thermometer" and place it under arm of doll in chair. The next person takes it out and back to the next nurse. Continue until all children have had a turn.

Cognitive
1.   Let the children use the lotto game made in Lesson #1 Cognitive #2.
2.   Ask, "What are jobs a nurse does?" Talk about some such as gives shots, brings bedpans, gives baths, takes temperature, etc.

3.	Have children associate appropriate items with a nurse. Let them glue a nurse in the middle of a page and glue items which are suitable around the nurse.

Enrichment
Talk about nursing homes. Make gifts to take to people who live there who need nursing.

Field Trip
Visit a nursing station or doctor's office with nurses.

Visitor
Have a nurse visit, preferably a male nurse.

Lesson 3: Stethoscope

Unit Group Lesson

1.	**Match Concrete Objects**
Present two stethoscopes. Say, "This is a stethoscope." Ask each child in turn to put the stethoscope with the stethoscope. Gradually increase number of irrelevant objects from which (s)he must select stethoscope to match.

2.	**Discriminate Objects**
Present several objects. Have each child touch the stethoscope in response to verbal direction, "Touch the stethoscope."

3.	**Match Pictures**
Present several pictures of common objects. Have each child match the pictures of the stethoscopes.

4.	**Discriminate Pictures**
Present a group of several unrelated pictures of objects. Have each child touch the picture of the stethoscope in response to verbal direction, "Touch the stethoscope."

5.	**Figure-Ground**
Present a "busy" picture with many visual distractions. Ask each child to find the stethoscope.

6.	**Visual Closure**
Partially cover each of several pictures with paper. Ask each child to find the picture of the stethoscope.

7.	**Function**
Ask, "What do we do with a stethoscope?"

8.	**Association**
Ask, "What goes with the stethoscope?" Use pictures or objects including doctor, nurse, etc. with several unrelated objects or pictures.

9.	**Imitate Verbalization**
Present a stethoscope and ask, "What is this? Say, 'Stethoscope'." The child will imitate "Stethoscope."

10.	**Verbalize Label**
Present a stethoscope and ask, "What is this?" The child will respond, "Stethoscope."

11.   **Concept Enrichment**
      Talk about putting things in one's ears, what things are appropriate and what things are not appropriate.

Music

1.   To the tune of "She'll Be Comin' Round the Mountain", sing "All the Doctors Use Stethoscopes":
     Verse 1: All the doctors use stethoscopes.
     Verse 2: Listen and you'll hear that boom, boom, boom.
     Verse 3: That's your heart that's going boom, boom, boom.

2.   Have someone make "heart sound" music (on drums) "Dum-dum, dum-dum." The others move or walk to music.

Art

1.   Have each child make a yarn and toilet tissue tube "stethoscope." Let them decorate the toilet tissue tube with magic markers.   (See fig. 37B.)
2.   Make a doctor collage on the paper painted in Lesson #2 Art #1. Put a doctor in the middle of the picture and have the children decorate around him with pictures of things associated with doctors.
3.   Let children make stethoscope prints by laying a stethoscope on paper and spatter painting around it with a toothbrush. Put the whole thing in a shallow box to prevent excessive spattering.

Snack

Serve fizzy drinks and let children listen to them with stethoscopes.

Fig. 37B

Fine Motor

1.   Have each child learn to put a stethoscope in his ears.
2.   Have each child make a stethoscope out of yarn or string and one section of an egg carton. "Listen" to everyone's heart beat.
3.   Help children find pulses on necks, wrists.

Games

Put stethoscopes in the dress up area. Encourage the children to listen to their own hearts.

Storytelling

Make up story about a doctor and include a stethoscope in action.

Gross Motor

Have children do "jumping jacks" and listen to or feel their stronger heart beats.

Cognitive

1.   Have children use a real stethoscope and describe how a heart sounds.
2.   Have children count beats of a metronome or drum. Count as a group.
3.   Present pictures of doctor's equipment including stethoscopes. Have the children identify the equipment as doctor's equipment.

Enrichment

Count each child's heart rate in the class and let the children make a bar graph of the heart rates. Compare them.

Field Trip

Visit a store or place where blood pressure is checked. Watch it being done.

Visitor

Invite public health nurse to bring stethoscope to listen to heart beats. Take turns hearing heart beats.

Unit Group Lesson

1. **Match Concrete Objects**
   Present some medicine. Say, "This is medicine." Ask each child in turn to put the medicine with the medicine. Gradually increase number of irrelevant objects from which (s)he must select medicine to match.

2. **Discriminate Objects**
   Present several objects. Have each child touch the medicine in response to verbal direction, "Touch the medicine."

3. **Match Pictures**
   Present several pictures of common objects. Have each child match the pictures of the medicines.

4. **Discriminate Pictures**
   Present a group of several unrelated pictures of objects. Have each child touch the picture of the medicine in response to verbal direction, "Touch the medicine."

5. **Figure-Ground**
   Present a "busy" picture with many visual distractions. Ask each child to find the medicine.

6. **Visual Closure**
   Partially cover each of several pictures with paper. Ask each child to find the picture of the medicine.

7. **Function**
   Ask, "What do we do with medicine?"

8. **Association**
   Ask, "What goes with medicine?" Use pictures or objects including doctor's bag, bandaids, rubber gloves, tongue depressor, etc. with several unrelated objects or pictures.

9. **Imitate Verbalization**
   Present some medicine and ask, "What is this? Say, 'Medicine'." The child will imitate "Medicine."

10. **Verbalize Label**
    Present some medicine and ask, "What is this?" The child will respond, "Medicine."

11. **Concept Enrichment**
    Discuss other things that doctors use: bandaids, rubber gloves, tongue depressors, otoscope, etc. Children can be fearful about the things used in a doctor's examination. This is a good time to help them become familiar with these things. Talk about medicine and pills. Stress: Do not take ANY unless the doctor gives them to your parents.

Music

Sing "Doctors and Medicine" to the tune of "She'll Be Coming' Round the Mountain":
   Verse 1: Doctor will use medicine to make us well.
      Doctor will use medicine to make us well.
      Doctor will use medicine, doctor will use medicine, doctor will use medicine
      To make us well.
   Verse 2: He'll keep the medicine in a cabinet in an office. . .
   Verse 3: We must be careful when taking medicine. . .

Art

1. Have children make giant collage of different forms of medicine. Paste/glue pictures and real objects. Display in room.
2. Let children make tongue depressor puppets. (See fig. 37C.)
3. Let children use a syringe without a needle as a paint squirter.

Fig. 37C

Snack

Talk about medicines and pills. They should only be taken when the doctor tells your parent to give them to you because medicines are bad for you if you do not need them. Eat non-medicines and non-pills because, "We NEVER take medicine or pills unless an appropriate adult gives them to us."

Fine Motor

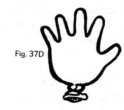

Fig. 37D

1. Give out bandaids and let children open them and put them on.
2. Blow rubber gloves up as balloons. (See fig. 37D.)
3. Have children pick up small candies with tweezers.

Games

1. Encourage children to play with first aid kit in dress-up area. Let "pretend" doctor give first aid to children. Be sure children understand they never take real medicine without adult supervision.
2. Have someone put on a doctor's mask. See if children can guess "who's behind the mask."
3. Let children wear hospital gloves while trying to do a task.

Storytelling

Use puppet to tell children a story about medicine. Include concepts such as why we take it, types of medicines (shots, pills, liquid). Stress safety precautions with and about medicine.

Gross Motor

Have children push a medicine ball around the play area. (Medicine balls are large, heavy balls which elementary, junior high schools and high schools use in their physical education programs.)

Cognitive

1. Let each child have a "first aid box" with bandaids, cotton swabs, tongue depressors, etc. Have children sort items. Provide cued trays for those children who need them.
2. Have children sort medicine from non-medicine. Use bottles etc. that have had real medicine in them.
3. Give children bandaids in different sizes and let them sequence them from BIG to LITTLE.
4. Label empty cotton swab boxes with numbers and have children put the appropriate number of cotton swabs in each box.

Enrichment

1. Prepare Cognitive #4 for higher numerals.
2. Have children learn to dial the emergency phone number in your community. Emphasize that they would only call those numbers in an emergency.

Lesson 5: Scale

Unit Group Lesson

1. **Match Concrete Objects**

    Present two scales. Say, "This is a scale." Ask each child in turn to put the scale with the scale. Gradually increase number of irrelevant objects from which (s)he must select scale to match.

2. **Discriminate Objects**

    Present several objects. Have each child touch the scale in response to verbal direction, "Touch the scale."

3. **Match Pictures**

    Present several pictures of common objects. Have each child match the pictures of the scale.

4. **Discriminate Pictures**

    Present a group of several unrelated pictures of objects. Have each child touch the picture of the scale in response to verbal direction, "Touch the scale."

5. **Figure-Ground**

    Present a "busy" picture with many visual distractions. Ask each child to find the scale.

6. **Visual Closure**

    Partially cover each of several pictures with paper. Ask each child to find the picture of the scale.

7. **Function**

    Ask, "What do we do with a scale?"

8. **Association**

    Ask, "What goes with a scale?" Use pictures or objects including doctor, nurse, stethoscope, etc. with several unrelated objects or pictures.

9. **Imitate Verbalization**

    Present a scale and ask, "What is this? Say, 'Scale'." The child will imitate "Scale."

10. **Verbalize Label**

    Present a scale and ask, "What is this?" The child will respond, "Scale."

11. **Concept Enrichment**

    Discuss fact that the unit of weight is pounds. Discuss scales for weighing fruits and vegetables, weighing trucks, weighing babies, etc.

Music

Sing to the tune of "Baa, Baa Black Sheep":
   Nurse, oh nurse, have you any scales?
   Yes sir, yes sir, stand right here.
   Let's look and see now, how much do you weigh?
   Oh, you're so big now, you weigh 43.

Art

1. Help children make scales using a homemade spinner on a brad for each. Let them paint the scales and indicate where the feet go "Weigh yourself." (See fig. 37E.)

2. Have children finger paint and use a balance scale to compare the weight of a completed finger painting with clean finger paint paper of the same size.

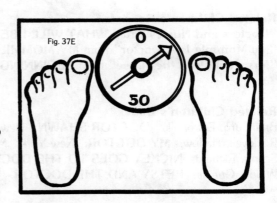
Fig. 37E

Snack

Weigh food to be eaten for snack on a food scale.

Fine Motor

1. Make path tracing activities of "Take a child to the scale to weigh her." and "Take the scale to the doctor." Vary the level of difficulty and have each child do an activity at the appropriate level.
2. Make several lacing cards, each shaped like a doctor's office scale. Vary the level of difficulty of the cards and have each child do a card appropriate to her level.
3. Have child trace over or make numerals for a scale.

Games

1. Emphasize scales in dress-up area. Weigh children.
2. Use different kinds of scales in the classroom such as baby, postage, etc.

Storytelling

Make large picture cards to illustrate visit to doctor's office. Tell story and have children sequence cards in correct order. Show:
a. Child sick in bed with sore throat. Mother says, "We'll have to see the doctor."
b. Nurse says, "Hello" and weighs child.
c. Doctor examines child and gives child medicine.
d. Nurse waves good-bye.

Gross Motor

Have children balance equal or unequal objects in outstretched hands and walk with objects. (See fig. 37F.)

Fig. 37F

Cognitive

1. Have children compare weights of pairs of children and decide who is the heaviest.
2. Have children make classroom scales using a coat hanger and weigh blocks, rocks, classroom items. "Which weighs more? Less?" Weigh "funny things" too such as shoes, dolls, mittens, etc. (See fig. 37G.)
3. Measure and weigh all the children in the class. Help children make a graph.

Enrichment

Help children collect and study a variety of scales. Have children make a chart of possible uses of the different scales.

Field Trip

Go to doctor's clinic. Talk to nurse and doctor. See scale, stethoscope, etc.

Fig. 37G

Visitor

Invite parent, baby and baby scale. Have her weigh the baby.

Related Children's Records

"Doctors and Nurses" from **WHAT WILL I BE WHEN I GROW UP?**
"My Mommie Is A Doctor" from **MY MOMMIE IS A DOCTOR**
"Mrs. Nicholson the Nurse" from **BEGINNING SOUNDS & CAREERS**

Related Children's Books

Breinburg, Petronella. **DOCTOR SHAWN.** New York: Thomas Y. Crowell, 1975.
Rockwell, Harlow. **MY DOCTOR.** New York: Macmillan Publishing Co., 1973.
Scarry, Richard. **NICKEY GOES TO THE DOCTOR.** Western Publishing Co., 1972.
Wolde, Gunilla. **BETSY AND THE DOCTOR.** New York: Random House, 1978.

Unit 38: Use of the Telephone

A developmental assessment should determine the functional levels of each child. Individual expectations are based on the assessment results.

Lesson 1: Use of the Telephone

Note: Some local phone companies have special phone sets for use in classrooms. These provide two or more phones which are connected to a board and ring when dialed. They demonstrate rings and busy signals.

Unit Group Lesson

1. **Match Concrete Objects**
   Present two telephones. Say, "This is a telephone." Ask each child in turn to put the telephone with the telephone. Gradually increase number of irrelevant objects from which (s)he must select telephone to match.

2. **Discriminate Objects**
   Present several objects. Have each child touch the telephone in response to verbal direction, "Touch the telephone."

3. **Match Pictures**
   Present several pictures of common objects. Have each child match the pictures of the telephones.

4. **Discriminate Pictures**
   Present a group of several unrelated pictures of objects. Have each child touch the picture of the telephone in response to verbal direction, "Touch the telephone."

5. **Figure-Ground**
   Present a "busy" picture with many visual distractions. Ask each child to find the telephone.

6. **Visual Closure**
   Partially cover each of several pictures with paper. Ask each child to find the picture of the telephone.

7. **Function**
   Ask, "What do we do with a telephone?"

8. **Association**
   Ask, "What goes with the telephone?" Use pictures or objects including ear, mouth, etc. with several unrelated objects or pictures.

9. **Imitate Verbalization**
   Present a telephone and ask, "What is this? Say, 'Telephone'." The child will imitate "Telephone."

10. **Verbalize Label**

Present a telephone and ask, "What is this?" The child will respond, "Telephone."

11. **Concept Enrichment**

Talk about telephone manners. Listen to the phone ringing. Ask, "What else rings?" Listen to a busy signal. Ask, "What does that mean?"

Music

1. Sing "This Is the Way We Use the Phone" to the tune of "This Is the Way We Wash Our Clothes":
   Verse 1: This is the way we dial a phone,
   Dial a phone, dial a phone.
   This is the way we dial a phone,
   To make a telephone call.
   Verse 2: This is the way we hold the receiver. . .
2. Sing "Phone Number" to the tune of "Mary Had A Little Lamb":
   (Child's name) has a phone number,
   Phone number, phone number.
   (Child's name) number is (child's number).
3. Sing "Goodbye":
   Goodbye, (child), yes indeed, yes indeed, yes indeed;
   Goodbye, (child), yes indeed
   Goodbye, (child)
4. Sing "Hello" first thing in the morning and "Good-bye" before going home each day.
5. Listen to *Adventures in Sound* (MH).

Art

1. Have each child paste a dial on a telephone ditto and decorate the telephone.
2. Make a group collage. Have children paste pictures of people using the telephone on a posterboard.
3. Make cut-out houses with each child's name, address and telephone number on it. Let the children decorate it. (See fig. 38A.)
4. Make cut-out telephone with each child's name and telephone number. Have each child decorate his own. (See fig. 38B.)
5. Make a classroom phone book. Don't forget teachers, too! Have each child decorate his own page of the phone book.
6. Make and decorate a classroom phone booth from a large box. Everyone can help paint it.

Fig. 38A   Fig. 38B

Snack

1. Pretend a celery stalk is a telephone (wide part is mouthpiece). Make and eat celery boats. Fill celery stalk with cream cheese. Eat from "mouthpiece" to the "earpiece."
2. Eat snack in and near the classroom phone booth made in art.
3. Telephone for a pizza for snack.

Fine Motor

1. Have each child dial his telephone number on a play or real telephone.
2. Have children draw "cords" (straight or coiled) on telephones. Provide exercises with and without dots to follow. (See fig. 38C.)
3. Have each child connect dots that make her telephone number. (See fig. 38D.)
4. Make path tracing activities of "Take a child to a telephone," and "Take a receiver to the telephone." Vary the level of difficulty according to the skills of the children.

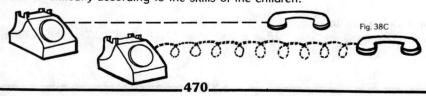

Fig. 38C

5. After child has learned his telephone number or during the process, let the child dial his home telephone number. Child can dial from memory, dial the numbers the teacher tells him, or dial the numbers he sees written on a piece of paper.

6. Let the children make "telephones" from tubes and sections from egg cartons for the mouthpiece and berry baskets and cardboard dials for the bases. (See fig. 38E.)

7. Have children send a message by touch. Have one child sit before a large piece of paper. Another child or teacher sits behind first child and draws "message" on her back (X or O or !). Child then draws the message she felt onto the paper.

8. Help children make tin can telephones using tin cans and wire or string. Take all paper off the cans; punch a hole in each can's bottom; cut a length of string; thread each end in a can; and knot the string on the inside of the can. Let the children talk from one room to another.

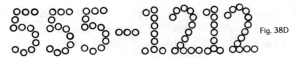 Fig. 38D

 Fig. 38E

Games
1. Let the children whisper from person to person around circle. (Play "Telephone.")
2. Let the children use tubes from toilet tissue or paper towels to whisper through around the circle.
3. In the housekeeping corner, you and children can pretend to use the telephone. Say, "Ring, ring" and answer phone, "Hello." Then pretend the call is for a child and call that child to the telephone. After you have modeled the pretend play, give each child a turn at answering the phone.
4. Place three objects, including a telephone, on a table. Blindfold a child or ask child to close his eyes. Instruct child to find the telephone by feeling the objects. (Tactile Discrimination.)
5. Use two phones to pantomime use of the telephone by calling a child in the group. Pick up the receiver, dial a number, wait for the phone to ring, and say, "Hello, (child)." Child picks up her "receiver" and talks to you. If a child needs help in the pantomiming, pick up child's hand and put it to her ear. Then have a child make a call, either to you or another child.

Storytelling
1. Make up a story of a little boy who saw a fire and reported it. He dialed "0" for operator for help. The firemen came and put the fire out. Use pictures or flannel cut-outs to illustrate. Let the children add details.
2. Make up a story of the little girl whose mother became ill. The little girl dials "0" for operator for help. Use pictures to illustrate and let the children add details.
3. Make up a story of a little girl and a little boy who call their grandmother by long distance. Let the children add details.

Gross Motor
1. Let children be telephone repair persons and drive vehicles to repair telephones.
2. Have the children move (jump, skip, walk, run, etc.) when the phone is ringing and stand still when they hear a busy signal. Tape record the sounds for use in this activity.

Cognitive
1. Present the ringing of the telephone, using a real telephone and the taped sound. Present two sounds (telephone ringing and a drum). Ask children to raise their hands when they hear the telephone ringing. Present three sounds, then four sounds. Each time ask children to raise their hands when they hear the telephone ringing. Make the task even harder by presenting sounds that are similar, (for example: dinner bell, school bell, church bells, jingle bells, etc.).
2. Have children listen to taped sounds, including the sound of a telephone ringing. Upon request, have children match the sound of the actual object (telephone) from other objects and to the picture of the telephone. (Matching.)
3. Make flash cards with the children's phone numbers on them. Show a child the flash cards for identification of his telephone number. (The telephone numbers should be quite different from each other.) Have child read numbers aloud. Then ask, "Is that your telephone number?" Child responds, "Yes" or "No."

4.   Have children look up children's names (and numbers) in a phone book.
5.   Have each child learn to get the operator.
6.   Telephone Skills Practice:

a. Answer "Hello."	Model use of telephone using a real telephone and play telephone. Call child on telephone. Child answers, "Hello." If child does not answer, initiate conversation, "Hello (child.)." Reinforce child's response by continuing conversation.
b. Say "Good Bye."	After conversation is finished in #a above, end telephone call with "Good-bye, (child)." Child responds, "Good-bye."
c. Answer and bring person to telephone.	Children and teacher will practice answering telephone during play in the housekeeping corner. Children practice skill at home. Bring proper person in to telephone.
d. Dial number.	Instruct children how to dial a telephone. For practice, have the child dial his telephone number, weather service number, or time service number.
e. Ask for person called.	Child will ask, "May I speak to (person), please," after the initial greeting.
f. Verbalize own telephone number.	When asked, "What is your telephone number," child will respond with his correct telephone number.

Enrichment
1.   Talk about the job of an operator.
2.   Use old tubing (garden hose). Put a funnel in each end held on by rubber bands. Let children talk/hear with funnels.
3.   Pretend a good fairy is on the line and the child can make any kind of wish, but only one!
4.   Do a village on bulletin board with houses, etc. and streets. Add telephone poles. Connect string telephone wires on push pins. (See fig. 38F.)

Fig. 38F

Field Trip
1.   Visit a telephone exchange.
2.   Walk to a phone booth and call parents or school.

Visitor
Invite a telephone man from the telephone company to show his tools and different kinds of telephones.

Related Children's Records
ADVENTURES IN SOUND (MH)

Related Children's Books
Harrison, David. **MY FUNNY BUNNY.** New York: Golden Press, 1980.
Kunhardt, Dorothy. **THE TELEPHONE BOOK.** New York: Golden Press, 1970.
Sharr, Christine, Illus. **TELEPHONES.** New York: Wonder-Treasure Books, 1971.
Sipherd, Ray. **ERNIE'S TELEPHONE CALLS.** Racine, Wis.: Western Publishing Co., 1978.

Related Parenting Materials
Cansler, Dot. **THE HOMESTRETCH.** Winston-Salem, NC 27113-5128: Kaplan Press, 1983.

Unit 39: Things We Read

A developmental assessment should determine the functional levels of each child. Individual expectations are based on the assessment results.

Lesson 1: Book

Unit Group Lesson

1. **Match Concrete Objects**
    Present two books. Say, "This is a book." Ask each child in turn to put the book with the book. Gradually increase number of irrelevant objects from which (s)he must select book to match.

2. **Discriminate Objects**
    Present several objects. Have each child touch the book in response to verbal direction, "Touch the book."

3. **Match Pictures**
    Present several pictures of common objects. Have each child match the pictures of the books.

4. **Discriminate Pictures**
    Present a group of several unrelated pictures of objects. Have each child touch the picture of the book in response to verbal direction, "Touch the book."

5. **Figure-Ground**
    Present a "busy" picture with many visual distractions. Ask each child to find the book.

6. **Visual Closure**
    Partially cover each of several pictures with paper. Ask each child to find the picture of the book.

7. **Function**
    Ask, "What do we do with a book?"

8. **Association**
    Ask, "What goes with the book?" Use pictures or objects including magazine, newspaper, pencil, letter, etc. with several unrelated objects or pictures.

9. **Imitate Verbalization**
    Present a book and ask, "What is this? Say, 'Book'." The child will imitate "Book."

10. **Verbalize Label**
    Present a book and ask, "What is this?" The child will respond, "Book."

11.   **Concept Enrichment**

Discuss different types of books such as picture books, word books, books that have pretend stories, etc. Look at different types of books. Find the words in the books. Talk about the care of books: turning pages, clean hands, book marks, etc.

Music

1.   Sing "Read Your Book" to the tune of "Row, Row, Row Your Boat":
Read, read, read your book;   *(Pantomime reading a book.)*
Read your book.
Read, read, read your book;
Read your book.

2.   Sing "Read, Read, Read Your Book" to the tune of "Skip To My Lou":
Read, read, read your book;   *(Pantomime reading a book.)*
Read, read, read your book;
Read, read, read your book;
And look at the pictures too!

3.   Sing "A Book" to the tune of "A-Tisket, A-Tasket":
A book, a book;
I have a book.
It's fun to read,
And fun to look at;
I have a book.

Art

1.   Help children cut a corner from an envelope, decorate and use for a bookmark. (Slip it over the corner of a book page.) (See fig. 39A.)

2.   Take pictures of the children. Put in a classroom book. Put each child's name under his/her picture. Let each child decorate her own page. Let children "read" the book at storytelling time.

3.   Help children make books. Have children cut or tear pictures from magazines and catalogs or draw their own. Let children paste the pictures on paper. Help them bind pages with yarn. On each page record what child says about that page and use for storytelling. (See fig. 39F.)

4.   Have children match a picture of a book to its partially hidden outline. Increase difficulty by adding more pictures and more outlines. (Figure-ground)

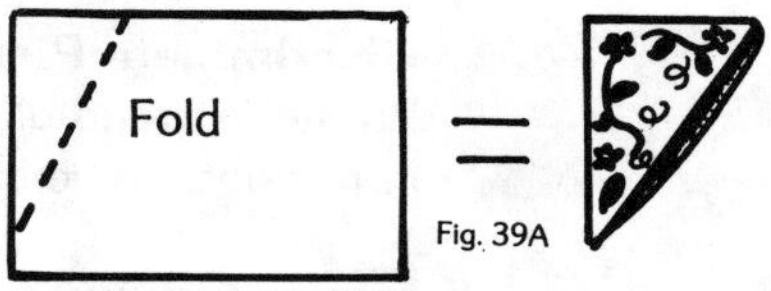

Snack

1.   Use bread to make a peanut butter "book" (sandwich) for snack.
2.   Listen to a book during snack.

Fold   =   Fig. 39A

Fine Motor

1.   Help children learn to turn the pages of a book individually.
2.   Have children lace "book" sewing cards. Paste the fronts of book jackets on cardboard and punch holes around the edges. Vary the number of holes for children with different skill levels.
3.   Have children cut circles and make "B. A. Bookworm" out of circles. (See fig. 39B.)

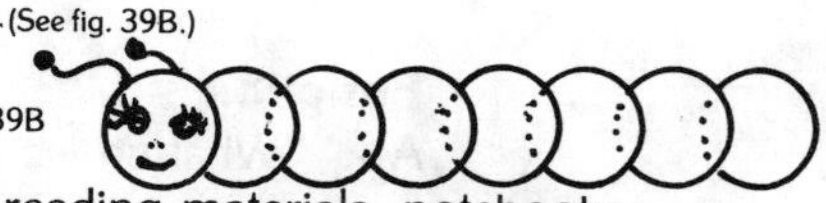

Games

Fig. 39B

1.   Play "Find a Book." Place various items on a table, include different reading materials, notebooks, paper, etc. Ask child to find a book. Help child find book and bring it back to the teacher. Give each child a turn.

2.   Play "Find the Book." Display books on a table, include books about animals, holidays, and children. Ask child to find a book about cats. Assist child in locating book if necessary. Each child gets a turn to go to the table.

Storytelling

1.   Have children pick a book to be read. Ask, "What book do you want to read?"
2.   Read the children's books made in art.

3. Always read and identify Title, Author, and Illustrator of each book read. ("Today our story is by a man named Ezra Jack Keats. Do you remember other books he wrote? Well, today our story is _____.)

Gross Motor
1. Have children carry a large book over an obstacle course.
2. Have children place books on book shelves.

Cognitive
1. Arrange four picture grouping on a bulletin board. Group pictures according to things we eat, things for play, things we read, and things we ride. Give each child a chance to place a picture of a book with the proper group. Ask the child, "Where does the book belong? Does it belong with the things we eat, with the toys, with the things we read, or with the things we ride?"
2. Have children sort books of different sizes.
3. Have children make color books. Let them assemble pictures of things which have one color, mount them on paper and make a book.
4. Have children make number books and/or letter books. Put in pictures to represent each number or letter.

Enrichment
1. Cut pictures from old cards (holiday, greeting, etc.). Let children glue pictures into a book made from folded paper. Let children tell a story about the picture and record it in child's book.
2. Talk about the library book's date due card. Make "library cards" for books at school. Play library with a child as librarian with a date-due stamp to use. Make a classroom library.
3. Sequence favorite activities of the children, let them illustrate the sequence steps, place in binder, and give books titles.

Field Trip
1. Take the children to a library or bookmobile. Let them select books to borrow for home or for the classroom.
2. Attend a story hour at a library.

Lesson 2: Magazine

Unit Group Lesson

1. **Match Concrete Objects**
Present two magazines. Say, "This is a magazine." Ask each child in turn to put the magazine with the magazine. Gradually increase number of irrelevant objects from which (s)he must select magazine to match.

2. **Discriminate Objects**
Present several objects. Have each child touch the magazine in response to verbal direction, "Touch the magazine."

3. **Match Pictures**
Present several pictures of common objects. Have each child match the pictures of the magazines.

4. **Discriminate Pictures**
Present a group of several unrelated pictures of objects. Have each child touch the picture of the magazine in response to verbal direction, "Touch the magazine."

5. **Figure-Ground**

Present a "busy" picture with many visual distractions. Ask each child to find the magazine.

6. **Visual Closure**

Partially cover each of several pictures with paper. Ask each child to find the picture of the magazine.

7. **Function**

Ask, "What do we do with a magazine?"

8. **Association**

Ask, "What goes with the magazine?" Use pictures or objects including book, letter, newspaper, pencil, etc. with several unrelated objects or pictures.

9. **Imitate Verbalization**

Present a magazine and ask, "What is this? Say, 'Magazine'." The child will imitate "Magazine."

10. **Verbalize Label**

Present a magazine and ask, "What is this?" The child will respond, "Magazine."

11. **Concept Enrichment**

Discuss a class magazine. How often would one publish it? What kind of paper would it be printed on? How is this different from a newspaper?

Music

Sing "We Read Magazines" to the tune of "Here We Go 'Round the Mulberry Bush":
We read magazines, magazines, magazines;
We read magazines,
At school and at home.

Art

1. Have children cut different pictures from magazines and glue on paper to make a scene (dog from one magazine, cat from another, boy from another). (See fig. 39C.)
2. Have children cut simple pictures out of magazines and add to them or finish them.
3. Have children match a picture of a magazine to its partially hidden outline. Increase difficulty of task by adding more pictures and more outlines. (Figure-Ground)
4. Help children make a table decoration out of a small magazine (T.V. Guide, Reader's Digest). Have children fold diagonally each page twice, paint glue on edge and sprinkle colored grits on edge. Stand on end, using clay to help balance it. (See fig. 39D.)

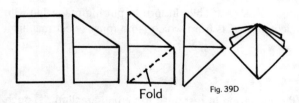

Fold   Fig. 39D

Fig. 39C

Snack

Eat snack foods which match some found in magazine pictures.

Fine Motor

1. Have children tear or cut out pictures they like from a magazine. Have them paste the pictures on paper. Let them tell the class why they liked the pictures.
2. Have children look at magazines and turn magazine pages.
3. Cut pictures from a magazine of half of a human body. Let children draw the other half. Cut the body vertically if children are older. (See fig. 39E.)

Fig. 39E

Games

Give each child a magazine. Have children race to find a picture in their magazine. "Find a girl." "Find a dog." Make sure every magazine has the picture.

Storytelling

1. Show children a copy of a child's magazine. Read appropriate articles to them and show pictures.
2. Cut out bright-colored pictures. Have children make up stories about the pictures.
3. Have copies of National Geographic available. Find an interesting action picture. Have children tell a story about that picture. Model storytelling if necessary.

Gross Motor

1. Cut out magazine pictures of people doing activities. Have children imitate what the person in the picture is doing.
2. Have children walk from one designated area to another with a magazine on their head. Let everyone be a winner.

Cognitive

1. Have children name objects in magazine pictures.
2. Arrange four groups of objects according to things we eat, things for play, things we read, and things we ride. Give each child a chance to place a picture of a magazine with the proper group. Ask the child, "Where does the magazine belong. Does it belong with the things we eat, with the toys, with the things we read, or with the things we ride?"
3. Have children select children's magazines from other magazines.
4. Have children sort or classify magazines (McCALLS, TIME, FAMILY CIRCLE, etc.). Notice characteristics.

Enrichment

Make school magazine about the people and what they are studying. Let children dictate stories to go into the magazine, draw illustrations, and cut out magazine pictures for the stories.

Fig. 39F

Field Trip

Visit a magazine stand. Have children look for TIME magazine, GOOD HOUSEKEEPING, photography magazines, sailing magazines, etc.

Visitor

A parent with a bag of magazines they read at their home. Tell why. (For example SPORTS ILLUSTRATED, TIME, WOMEN'S MAGAZINE, SCIENCE MAGAZINE, etc.).

Unit Group Lesson

1. **Match Concrete Objects**
    Present two newspapers. Say, "This is a newspaper." Ask each child in turn to put the newspaper with the newspaper. Gradually increase number of irrelevant objects from which (s)he must select newspaper to match.

2. **Discriminate Objects**
    Present several objects. Have each child touch the newspaper in response to verbal direction, "Touch the newspaper."

3. **Match Pictures**
    Present several pictures of common objects. Have each child match the pictures of the newspapers.

4. **Discriminate Pictures**
    Present a group of several unrelated pictures of objects. Have each child touch the picture of the newspaper in response to verbal direction, "Touch the newspaper."

5. **Figure-Ground**
    Present a "busy" picture with many visual distractions. Ask each child to find the newspaper.

6. **Visual Closure**
    Partially cover each of several pictures with paper. Ask each child to find the picture of the newspaper.

7. **Function**
    Ask, "What do we do with a newspaper?"

8. **Association**
    Ask, "What goes with the newspaper?" Use pictures or objects including magazine, book, letter, pencil, etc. with several unrelated objects or pictures.

9. **Imitate Verbalization**
    Present a newspaper and ask, "What is this? Say, 'Newspaper'." The child will imitate "Newspaper."

10. **Verbalize Label**
    Present a newspaper and ask, "What is this?" The child will respond, "Newspaper."

11. **Concept Enrichment**
    Discuss ideas for a class newspaper. What stories might be involved? How is a newspaper different than a magazine?

Music

1. Sing "Newspapers, Books and Magazines" to the tune of "There's a Tavern in the Town":
    Newspapers, books and magazines - mag-a-zines,
    Newspapers, books and magazines - mag-a-zines,
    We read all of these
    Newspapers, books and magazines.

2. Sing "A Newspaper" to the tune of "A-Tisket, A-Tasket":
   A newspaper, a newspaper;
   I have a newspaper.
   It's fun to read,
   And look at the comics,
   I have a newspaper.

Art
1. Have children print on newspaper with stamps, sponge or potato prints.
2. Have children help make papier-mache stripes, using strips of newspaper, and decorate them.
3. Have children crumple newspaper and glue pieces together to make a sculpture.

Snack
Serve a snack from a food section of a newspaper.

Fine Motor
1. Cover table with newspaper. Let children scribble with bright colors (crayons, markers).
2. Have children roll newspapers and put on rubber bands. Use in Gross Motor.
3. Help children fold a newspaper into a hat. Take several sheets of newspaper for each hat and fold as illustrated. (See fig. 39G.)
4. Have children path trace the natural borders of white on newspapers.
5. Have children write over large headline letters in the newspaper. Select letters for less skilled children.

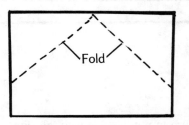 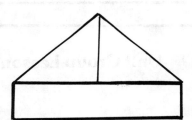 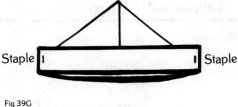

Fig 39G

Games
1. Have newspapers in the housekeeping corner. Try to find smaller ones for children to handle.
2. Designate places in room to be "houses." Have children toss newspaper from bag to the houses from a marked area on floor. (Collect and do this again with each child taking turns tossing and collecting newspapers).

Storytelling
1. Read the Sunday comics to the children. Ask them if their Mother or Daddy reads the comics from the newspaper to them.
2. Subscribe to a weekly preschool newspaper equivalent to "Weekly Reader."
3. Make up a story about a child who delivers newspapers in his neighborhood. Ask children if they have a big brother or sister who delivers newspapers. Use pictures to illustrate story. Ask children to "Find the newspaper" or "Touch newspaper."

Gross Motor
Play "Paperboy (girl)." A child takes all of the rolled newspapers (see Fine Motor #2) and puts them in a sack. Child then delivers the newspapers. (Aim for target.) Children take turns being paperboy (girl). The target may be a house drawn on the blackboard or a cardboard box.

Cognitive
1. Make sequence stories out of simple comic strips. Mount on cardboard, and let the children put them in the correct sequence.
2. Use newspaper pictures (sports, comics, cars, etc.) for children to discuss.

3. Cover a bulletin board with newspaper. Some children can underline words, others circle letters of the alphabet. Have a magnifying glass for looking for letters in the small print. Have children outline squares and rectangles on the ad pages.

4. Get two newspapers exactly alike. Cut out one into ads or large words to be matched on the other paper.

Enrichment

1. Let children find the letters of their names in a newspaper, cut them out and paste onto paper. Provide a model for those children who need it. (Simplify the activity by letting children locate their initials.)

2. Use comics: a. Cut out segments and let children put in order.
    b. Use white paint to cover the comics' words. Let children make up their own words.
    c. Let children draw an addition to the comic strip.

3. Help the children make a classroom newspaper.

Field Trip

1. Visit a newspaper to see it being put together.
2. Locate a newspaper vending machine and put in a quarter to buy one.

Visitor

Invite a paperboy with his bicycle with special bag or racks for newspapers. Let him demonstrate how he works.

Lesson 4: Signs

Unit Group Lesson

1. **Match Concrete Objects**
   Present two signs. Say, "This is a sign." Ask each child in turn to put the sign with the sign. Gradually increase number of irrelevant objects from which (s)he must select sign to match.

2. **Discriminate Objects**
   Present several objects. Have each child touch the sign in response to verbal direction, "Touch the sign."

3. **Match Pictures**
   Present several pictures of common objects. Have each child match the pictures of the signs.

4. **Discriminate Pictures**
   Present a group of several unrelated pictures of objects. Have each child touch the picture of the sign in response to verbal direction, "Touch the sign."

5. **Figure-Ground**
   Present a "busy" picture with many visual distractions. Ask each child to find the sign.

6. **Visual Closure**
   Partially cover each of several pictures with paper. Ask each child to find the picture of the sign.

7. **Function**
   Ask, "What does a sign do?"

8. **Association**

    Ask, "What goes with the sign?" Use pictures or objects including magazines, books, words, etc., with several unrelated objects or pictures.

9. **Imitate Verbalization**

    Present a sign and ask, "What is this? Say, 'Sign'." The child will imitate "Sign."

10. **Verbalize Label**

    Present a sign and ask, "What is this?" The child will respond, "Sign."

11. **Concept Enrichment**

    Talk about different types of signs: traffic signs, store signs, building signs.

Music

1. Sing "Big, Red Sign" to the tune of "This Is the Way We Wash Our Clothes":
    The big, red sign says stop, says stop,   *(Hold hand out gesturing stop.)*
    And that's what we'll do. STOP!   *(Stand still in place when teacher*
                                                                          or child shows stop sign.)

2. Sing "Sign, Sign" to the tune of "Row, Row, Row Your Boat":
    Sign, sign, read the sign.   *(Hold up stop sign.)*
    What does it say?
    Sign, sign, read the sign.
    What does it say?
    Ask child what sign says; have children "read" other signs such as Hardee's sign, etc.

Art

1. Have children match stop signs (cut from red construction paper) to their partially hidden outlines. Increase difficulty of task by adding more pictures and more outlines. (Figure-ground.)
2. Have children color a picture of a "stop" sign and a "go" sign.
3. Have children make a sign collage from signs they find in magazines, drawing, books, etc.

Snack

Follow signs for snack: sit down, drink, eat, clean up, etc.

Fine Motor

1. Have children connect dots in the shape of stop sign and color it red.
2. Help children make a stop sign from a square of red construction paper by cutting the corners from the square. (See fig. 39H.)
3. Let children match various signs to their outlines.

Fig. 39H

Games

1. Play "Follow the Leader." When the leader shows a stop sign the children "read" the sign and stop; when the leader shows a "go" sign, they go. Let children take turns being leader.
2. Give each child a different sign. Place identical signs on chairs. Have children sit in the chair that has the sign that matches theirs. Then have children exchange signs and find their new chairs.

Storytelling

With a collection of pictures of various signs, (Hardee's, McDonalds, stop, railroad, etc.). Tell a story of a little girl who visits her grandmother. The little girl talks about all the signs she sees. As a sign is mentioned, hold up its picture.

Gross Motor

Make classroom signs. Have children ride trikes and cars and "do what the signs say."

Cognitive

1. .Help children learn to identify common signs by their shape: yield, (8 sides) stop, etc.
2. Use classroom signs which have words and ones which have pictures.
3. Have children find pictures of signs (traffic, advertisements), identify the signs, and put each one on a popsicle stick. Let them hold up signs and let other children tell what the sign says. (See fig. 391.)

Enrichment

1. Put a large piece of paper up and make a large sign out of it. Select a simple word and have children fill in block letters with bits of paper and color the background.
2. Make a large "billboard." Talk about the kind to make, where it would be located, etc. (If there is a billboard company in your area, they may have discards of left over billboards which they would give to your center or school. Lay one out in the parking lot and let the children walk on it.)

Field Trip

1. Look for signs in the neighborhood. "Read" them.
2. Look for billboards.

Visitor

Invite a sign painter.

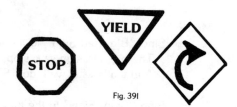

Fig. 391

Lesson 5: Letters

Unit Group Lesson

1. **Match Concrete Objects**
    Present two letters. Say, "This is a letter." Ask each child in turn to put the letter with the letter. Gradually increase number of irrelevant objects from which (s)he must select letter to match.

2. **Discriminate Objects**
    Present several objects. Have each child touch the letter in response to verbal direction, "Touch the letter."

3. **Match Pictures**
    Present several pictures of common objects. Have each child match the pictures of the letters.

4. **Discriminate Pictures**
    Present a group of several unrelated pictures of objects. Have each child touch the picture of the letter in response to verbal direction, "Touch the letter."

5. **Figure-Ground**
    Present a "busy" picture with many visual distractions. Ask each child to find the letter.

6. **Visual Closure**
    Partially cover each of several pictures with paper. Ask each child to find the picture of the letter.

7. **Function**
    Ask, "What do we do with a letter?"

8. **Association**
    Ask, "What goes with the letter?" Use pictures or objects including book, pen, pencil, ink, eraser, etc., with several unrelated objects or pictures.

9. **Imitate Verbalization**

   Present a letter and ask, "What is this? Say, 'Letter'." The child will imitate "Letter."

10. **Verbalize Label**

    Present a letter and ask, "What is this?" The child will respond, "Letter."

11. **Concept Enrichment**

    Read some letters to the class. Have the class compose a letter to someone they all know.

Music

1. Sing "Letter" to the tune of "Campbell's Soup Song":
   Read your letter,
   Read your letter.
   Open up the envelope,
   And read your letter.

2. Sing "Mailman Brought Me A Letter" to the tune of "This Is the Way We Wash Our Clothes":
   The mailman brought me a letter,
   A letter, a letter,
   The mailman brought me a letter;
   I'll open it up and read it.

Art

1. Have children decorate stationary and envelopes to match with small drawings or stickers.
2. Have each child make and decorate a mailbox out of a shoe box.
3. Have children paint a class mailbox from a large box or carton in blue and red to look like a real one.

Snack

"Mail" each child a graham cracker "letter" in an envelope.

Fine Motor

1. Have each child "write" a letter, fold it, put it in an envelope, seal the envelope and put on a stamp.
2. Learn to make XX's and OO's (kisses and hugs) on letters to mail to relatives.
3. Have each child make an airmail envelope by making red and blue marks around a white envelope.
4. Have children fold a piece of paper to make their own envelopes. (See fig. 39J.)

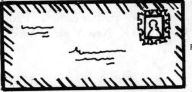

Fig. 39J

Games

1. Have child dictate a letter and write it down. Have the child fold the letter, put it in an envelope, and seal the envelope. Have the child deliver it to her classmate or put in classmate's mailbox.
2. Play "Mailman." It is similar to "Drop the Handkerchief." Children form a circle, holding their hands cupped behind them. Mailman goes around circle touching their hands saying, "Letter, letter." The mailman finally drops a letter in a hand. He is chased around circle and back to empty space. Children take turns being mailman.

Storytelling

1. Read letters from Games #1 to children.
2. Have various people send letters to the class. (For example: a neighbor writes a letter about her dog and sends a picture; a friend sends a postcard from a vacation; etc.). Read the letters to the class.
3. Look at "A Child's World of Strangers," De Press, and look at stamps.

Gross Motor

1. Get a mailbag and deliver letters around the building. Use classroom vehicles for mail trucks.

2.   Write the class a letter with exercise instructions in it. Read it to the class and have them follow the instructions.

Cognitive
1.   Have children match letters to envelopes. Put together a collection of stationery with one envelope and letter sheet which match. Mix the pairs up and let the children match the sets.
2.   Write a group story-letter to a child who is sick or has moved or to someone else.
3.   Provide a shoebag with numerals on the pockets and letters with numerals on them. Have the children put each letter in the correct pocket.

Enrichment
1.   Write letters and mail to children. Talk about having the correct information (address and return address) and stamp on the envelope.
2.   Make a large cardboard post office. Cut a door and windows. Fold back a corner. Cut openings for mail slots. Tape shoeboxes behind to catch the letters.
3.   Make cards, letters, or thank-you notes for friends and relatives.
4.   Provide a shoebag with numerals on each pocket. Have the children mail the correct number of letters in each pocket.

Field Trip
Go to a real mailbox and mail a letter.

Visitor
1.   Invite a letter carrier with a bag full of letters.
2.   Invite a parent to bring letters they have received; show kinds: personal, bills, advertisement, etc.

Related Children's Records
"Did You Ever Think" from **MY MOMMIE IS A DOCTOR**
"Lori the Librarian" from **BEGINNING SOUNDS & CAREERS** (UBB)

Related Children's Books
Dugan, William. **THE SIGN BOOK.** New York: Golden Press, 1968.
Funks, Tom. **I READ SIGNS.** New York: Holiday House, 1962.
Keats, Ezra Jack. **A LETTER TO AMY.** New York: Harper & Row, 1968.
Numeroff, Laura. **BEATRICE DOESN'T WANT TO.** New York: Franklin Watts, 1981.

Related Parenting Materials
Cansler, Dot. **THE HOMESTRETCH.** Winston-Salem, NC 27113-5128: Kaplan Press, 1983.

Related Materials
TEACHING PICTURES. Winston-Salem, NC 27113-5128: Kaplan Press, 1983.
STORY SEQUENCE CARDS I, II. Winston-Salem, NC 27113-5128: Kaplan Press, 1983.
SEWING CARDS I, II, III. Winston-Salem, NC 27113-5128: Kaplan Press, 1983.

Unit 40: Tools

A developmental assessment should determine the functional levels of each child. Individual expectations are based on the assessment results.

Lesson 1: Hammer

Unit Group Lesson

1. **Match Concrete Objects**
   Present two hammers. Say, "This is a hammer." Ask each child in turn to put the hammer with the hammer. Gradually increase number of irrelevant objects from which (s)he must select hammer to match.

2. **Discriminate Objects**
   Present several objects. Have each child touch the hammer in response to verbal direction, "Touch the hammer."

3. **Match Pictures**
   Present several pictures of common objects. Have each child match the pictures of the hammers.

4. **Discriminate Pictures**
   Present a group of several unrelated pictures of objects. Have each child touch the picture of the hammer in response to verbal direction, "Touch the hammer."

5. **Figure-Ground**
   Present a "busy" picture with many visual distractions. Ask each child to find the hammer.

6. **Visual Closure**
   Partially cover each of several pictures with paper. Ask each child to find the picture of the hammer.

7. **Function**
   Ask, "What do we do with a hammer?"

8. **Association**
   Ask, "What goes with the hammer?" Use pictures or objects including wood, saw, nail, pliers, screwdriver, etc., with several unrelated objects or pictures.

9. **Imitate Verbalization**
   Present a hammer and ask, "What is this? Say, 'Hammer'." The child will imitate "Hammer."

10. **Verbalize Label**
    Present a hammer and ask, "What is this?" The child will respond, "Hammer."

11. **Concept Enrichment**

Discuss different types of hammers. Hammers vary from small tack hammers to large sledge hammers. Discuss hammer safety.

Music

1. Sing "Hammer, Hammer, Hammer" to the tune of "Campbell Soup Song":

   Hammer, hammer, hammer,   *(Pantomime holding a nail and hammering*
   Hammer, hammer, hammer,   *it.)*
   Hammer, hammer, hammer,
   I will hammer a nail.

2. Sing "Hammer A Nail" to the tune of "Twinkle, Twinkle, Little Star":

   Hammer, hammer, hammer, hammer,   *(Pretend to hammer nail into wood.)*
   Hammer a nail into the wood.   *(Pretend to hammer nail into wood.)*
   Hammer, hammer, hammer, hammer,   *(Pretend to hammer nail into wood.)*
   Be careful not to hit your finger!   *(Pretend to hit finger. Grimace.)*
   Hammer, hammer, hammer, hammer,   *(Pretend to hammer nail into wood.)*
   Hammer a nail into the wood.   *(Pretend to hammer nail into wood.)*

3. Sing "Hammer the Nail" to the tune of "Row, Row, Row Your Boat":

   Hammer the nail into the wood,
   Hammer, hammer, hammer.
   Hammer the nail into the wood,
   Hammer, hammer, hammer.
   Sing song while hammering nails into wood.

4. Play drums.

Art

1. Have children put bits and pieces of crayon in a paper sack and pound the sack with a hammer. Then have them put the small pieces of crayon on a piece of paper, fold it, and iron over the paper. Help with ironing. Open the paper while still warm. Display the children's designs. SUPERVISE CAREFULLY.

2. Have children tear or cut out pictures of hammers and paste on paper. Use department store and hardware store tool catalogs.

3. Have children create sculpture by pounding pieces of styrofoam with hammers.

Snack

1. Put cookies (graham crackers, Saltines) in brown lunch bags. Let children hammer to crush and make crumbs for use in snack. Roll bananas in crumbs or put on top of casserole or cake. Eat.

2. Have children use a hammer to pound ice in a bag for snack drink.

Fine Motor

1. With a real child-sized hammer, have the children hammer real nails into a piece of soft wood, an old tree stump, piece of exterior sheating, or styrofoam. SUPERVISE CAREFULLY.

2. Let children hammer pegs using a commerical toy workbench.

3. Have children connect dots in the shape of a hammer.

4. Let children pull nails from wood with a claw hammer.

5. Have children hammer golf tees into scraps of soft wall board to make things or to follow a pattern.

6. On strip of cardboard trace around a hammer. Cut into three pieces. Let children put together puzzle. (See fig. 40A.)

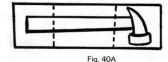

Fig. 40A

Games

Provide carpenters hats, tool aprons, and tool boxes for the children.

Storytelling

1. Tell the story of "The Three Little Pigs" using pictures to illustrate. Emphasize the pigs, "building" their houses using their tools. Have children pretend to build a house. Have children find the tools in the picture. Say, "Find the pig's hammer."
2. Read *Katy No Pockets*.

Gross Motor

1. Let children hammer rocks or ice in a bag to break them up. Use a small sledge hammer for the stronger children.
2. Let children hammer golf tees and stakes into the ground.

Cognitive

1. Let children sort different sized hammers and nails into boxes.
2. Arrange four groups of objects on a table. The four groups will be tools, dolls, food and clothes. Give a child a hammer and say, "Where does the hammer go?" or "Put the hammer on the table where it belongs." Child should put the hammer with the other tools. Ask, "Is a hammer a tool?" or "What is a hammer?" The child should answer, "Tool," "A tool," or "It's a tool."
3. Have assorted sizes and weights of hammers. Have the children sort them according to weight.
4. Ask what other things might be used as hammer? (Stick, shoe, rock, etc.).

Enrichment

1. Have children identify tools in catalogs that are used for building houses and paste on the shape of a house.
2. Collect all kinds of hammers. Let children find out how they are used.
3. Let children take pictures of certain tools to a hardware store. Find the tools.

Field Trip

1. Visit site of house being built. Watch workman with tools.
2. Visit a hardware store.

Visitor

Invite a maintenance person to visit your class. Have him/her bring his/her carpenter's tools and repair an item in the classroom.

Lesson 2: Saw

Unit Group Lesson

1. **Match Concrete Objects**
   Present two saws. Say, "This is a saw." Ask each child in turn to put the saw with the saw. Gradually increase number of irrelevant objects from which (s)he must select saw to match.

2. **Discriminate Objects**
   Present several objects. Have each child touch the saw in response to verbal direction, "Touch the saw."

3. **Match Pictures**
   Present several pictures of common objects. Have each child match the pictures of the saws.

4. **Discriminate Pictures**
   Present a group of several unrelated pictures of objects. Have each child touch the picture of the saw in response to verbal direction, "Touch the saw."

5. **Figure-Ground**
   Present a "busy" picture with many visual distractions. Ask each child to find the saw.

6. **Visual Closure**
   Partially cover each of several pictures with paper. Ask each child to find the picture of the saw.

7. **Function**
   Ask, "What do we do with a saw?"

8. **Association**
   Ask, "What goes with the saw?" Use pictures or objects including lumber yard, wood, etc., with several unrelated objects or pictures.

9. **Imitate Verbalization**
   Present a saw and ask, "What is this? Say, 'Saw'." The child will imitate "Saw."

10. **Verbalize Label**
    Present a saw and ask, "What is this?" The child will respond, "Saw."

11. **Concept Enrichment**
    Discuss different types of saws, cross cut, hacksaw, tree saw, etc.

Music
1. Sing "I Am Cutting With My Saw" to the tune of "Twinkle, Twinkle Little Star":
   Saw, saw, saw, saw,
   I am cutting with my saw.
   See the sawdust on the ground,
   Hear the saw make a cutting sound.
   Saw, saw, saw, saw,
   I am cutting with my saw.
2. Sing "Saw, Saw, Saw" to the tune of "Campbell Soup Song":
   Saw, saw, saw,
   Saw, saw, saw,
   I am cutting with my saw.

Art
1. Let the children tear or cut out pictures of saws and paste on paper as a collage. Provide department store and hardware store tool catalogs.
2. Help the children make sawdust pictures. Let the children make designs on colored construction paper with glue and a paintbrush; shake sawdust on glue and shake off excess; and let pictures dry. Display the pictures.
3. Mix sawdust in paint to make texture. Let the children feel it and pour it, paint with it, etc.

Snack
Let the children "saw" food for snack using plastic knives. Such things as cheese, cream cheese, bananas, or jello square could be sawed.

Fine Motor
1. Have each child saw a piece of soft wood, wallboard, or styrofoam with a child-sized saw. SUPERVISE CLOSELY.

2.   Have children "saw" cake with a knife. SUPERVISE CAREFULLY.

3.   Make path tracing activities of "Take a saw to a board" and "Take a child to a saw." Vary the difficulty of the paths according to the skills of the children.

4.   Give children a picture of a table with a leg sawed off. Let them complete the leg. (See fig. 40B.)

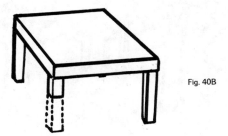

Fig. 40B

Games

Play "Find a Tool." Hide tools or pictures of tools in the room. Have children find the tool named.

Storytelling

Emphasize sawing wood for house construction. Make up a story about the saw who had no teeth. He could not help his owner build a treehouse, etc. Finally he gets some teeth and can help his owner. Let children suggest ways for the saw to get his teeth. Use pictures or felt cut-outs. (See fig. 40C.)

Fig. 40C

Gross Motor

1.   Let the children use cardboard saws to pretend to saw down playground trees.

2.   Let two children hold both hands facing each other and be a "saw" going back and forth. (See fig. 40D.)

Fig. 40D

Cognitive

1.   Cut out and number several saws. Let children decide how many limbs each saw can cut. (The number on the saw tells how many.) Let the children match the correct number of limbs to each saw. (See fig. 40E.)

Fig. 40E
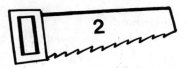

2.   Provide saws in several sizes. Let the children sequence saws from smallest to largest.

3.   Let the children saw down the largest tree in the forest. To "saw" they must draw a line through the trunk of the largest tree. (See fig. 40F.)

Fig. 40F

Enrichment
1. Help the children make a saw collection.
2. Help the children use a "C" clamp to control wood and saw a set of blocks for the classroom.

Field Trip
Go to a lumber yard. Watch circular, jig and other saws at work.

Visitor
Invite a carpenter to demonstrate several types of saws.

Lesson 3: Pliers

Unit Group Lesson

1. **Match Concrete Objects**
   Present two pairs of pliers. Say, "This is a pair of pliers." Ask each child in turn to put the pliers with the pliers. Gradually increase number of irrelevant objects from which (s)he must select pliers to match.

2. **Discriminate Objects**
   Present several objects. Have each child touch the pliers in response to verbal direction, "Touch the pliers."

3. **Match Pictures**
   Present several pictures of common objects. Have each child match the pictures of the pliers.

4. **Discriminate Pictures**
   Present a group of several unrelated pictures of objects. Have each child touch the picture of the pliers in response to verbal direction, "Touch the pliers."

5. **Figure-Ground**
   Present a "busy" picture with many visual distractions. Ask each child to find the pliers.

6. **Visual Closure**
   Partially cover each of several pictures with paper. Ask each child to find the picture of the pliers.

7. **Function**
   Ask, "What do we do with a pair of pliers?"

8. **Association**
   Ask, "What goes with the pliers?" Use pictures or objects including hammer, saw, screwdriver, etc., with several unrelated objects or pictures.

9. **Imitate Verbalization**

Present a pair of pliers and ask, "What is this? Say, 'Pliers'." The child will imitate "Pliers."

10. **Verbalize Label**

Present a pair of pliers and ask, "What is this?" The child will respond, "Pliers."

11. **Concept Enrichment**

Look at different sizes and types of pliers.

Music

1. Sing "With Your Pliers" to the tune of "There's A Tavern in the Town":

Pull out the nail with your pliers, with your pliers.

Tighten the bolt with your pliers, with your pliers.

Show me what you can do.

Can do with your pliers, with your pliers.

Either pantomime the suggested activity, show a picture of somone doing the activity, or actually perform the suggested activity while singing the song.

2. Sing "Hold the Pliers" to the tune of "Campbell Soup Song":

Hold (grip) the pliers.

Hold (grip) the pliers.

Show me how you hold the pliers.

Art

1. Let each child make a pair of pliers using a ditto picture of pliers and cardboard. Put in toolbox.
2. Make a toolbox out of a shoe box. Let children paint toolbox and tear or cut out pictures of different tools and put in box. Have each child write her name on top.
3. Let children tear or cut out pictures of pliers and paste on paper.

Snack

1. Have children use kitchen tongs to pick up snack items (grapes, cookies, etc.).
2. Have children use real pliers for opening lids.
3. Have children squeeze oranges (lemons, limes, etc.) with hands before using for snack.

Fine Motor

1. Let children pull large nails out of styrofoam with child-sized pliers.
2. Let children pull toothpicks out of styrofoam with tweezers.
3. Have children use tongs from the kitchen to pick up things such as cotton balls, large nails, etc.
4. Let children use tweezers to pick up small things such as pieces of yarn, toothpicks, etc.
5. Let children pull golf tees out of pegboards with pliers.
6. Let children pick up objects with pliers.

Games

1. Make tool dominoes. Each domino should picture two tools. Let one or more children play. Each child draws a card and matches it to another card, (for example: hammer to hammer, pliers to pliers, saw to saw, etc.). Continue as in dominoes. (See fig. 40G.)

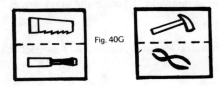

Fig. 40G

2. Toolbox Game:

a. Put one tool in a toolbox and sit in front of children. Hold toolbox up to one child, quickly open box, let child see tool, and close box. Have child tell which tool he saw.

b. Put two tools in toolbox. Let child see the tools and close box. Open and remove one tool. Let child look in the box and tell which tool is missing.

3.   Get some pipes and elbows from a plumber. Let children put them together.

Storytelling
    Make up a story about a man going to the hardware store to buy a pair of pliers.

Gross Motor
1.   Let children squeeze soft balls. Get an exerciser for squeezing. Let the children try it.
2.   Let children cut soft wire with pliers bending it back and forth.

Cognitive
1.   Let children sort pliers from other tools.
2.   Let children sequence small to large pliers. (Either pictures or actual tools.)
3.   Let children count how many turns it takes to remove a screw from a board using pliers.

Enrichment
1.   Let the children sort different types of pliers.
2.   Discuss which workers need pliers. (For example, the electrician, the florist) and why?

Field Trip
    Go to a hardware store and look at all kinds of pliers.

Visitor
    Invite an electrician to show how (s)he uses pliers.

Lesson 4: Screwdriver

Unit Group Lesson

1. **Match Concrete Objects**
    Present two screwdrivers. Say, "This is a screwdriver." Ask each child in turn to put the screwdriver with the screwdriver. Gradually increase number of irrelevant objects from which (s)he must select screwdriver to match.

2. **Discriminate Objects**
    Present several objects. Have each child touch the screwdriver in response to verbal direction, "Touch the screwdriver."

3. **Match Pictures**
    Present several pictures of common objects. Have each child match the pictures of the screwdrivers.

4. **Discriminate Pictures**
    Present a group of several unrelated pictures of objects. Have each child touch the picture of the screwdriver in response to verbal direction, "Touch the screwdriver."

5. **Figure-Ground**
    Present a "busy" picture with many visual distractions. Ask each child to find the screwdriver.

6. **Visual Closure**
    Partially cover each of several pictures with paper. Ask each child to find the picture of the screwdriver.

7. **Function**
    Ask, "What do we do with a screwdriver?"

8. **Association**

Ask, "What goes with the screwdriver?" Use pictures or objects including hammer, pliers, saw, paintbrush, etc., with several unrelated objects or pictures.

9. **Imitate Verbalization**

Present a screwdriver and ask, "What is this? Say, 'Screwdriver'." The child will imitate "Screwdriver."

10. **Verbalize Label**

Present a screwdriver and ask, "What is this?" The child will respond, "Screwdriver."

11. **Concept Enrichment**

Make a paper or cloth screw to show children that a screw is a nail with an inclined plane around it. Talk about advantages of a screw over a nail and a nail over a screw. (See fig. 40K.)

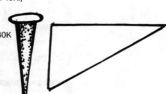
Fig. 40K

Music

1. Sing "Turn the Screw" to the tune of "London Bridge":
   Verse 1: Turn the screw with the screwdriver, screwdriver, screwdriver,
   Turn the screw with the screwdriver,
   We work with our tools.
   Verse 2: Hammer the nail with the hammer..........
   Verse 3: Saw the wood with the saw................
   Verse 4: Tighten the bolt with the pliers.........

2. Sing to the tune of "Old MacDonald Had a Farm":
   Verse 1: Susie Jones had some tools.
   This I know.
   With a turn, turn here
   And a turn, turn there
   Here a turn, there a turn,
   Everywhere a turn, turn,
   Susie Jones had some tools,
   This I know.
   Verse 2: And in her toolbox she had a hammer
   This I know.
   With a hammer, hammer, here, and a hammer, hammer, there.......
   Repeat verse 1.
   Verse 3: And in her toolbox she had a saw
   This I know.
   With a saw, saw, here, and a saw, saw, there.......
   Repeat verse 2, then verse 1.
   Verse 4: And in her toolbox she had some pliers
   This I know.
   With a pull, pull, here, and a tighten, tighten, there.......
   Repeat verses 3, 2 and then 1.
   Substitute the children's names in song and look in children's "toolboxes" as the song is sung.

Art

1. Have each child make a screwdriver and screw collage by pasting different sizes of screwdrivers and screws on paper.
2. Have each child create a sculpture by using screwdriver to put screws into styrofoam blocks.
3. Let children use screwdrivers to spread finger paint.

Snack

Allow children to practice coring apples.

Fine Motor

1. Have children turn a screw into styrofoam, or a soft piece of wood. Start the screw, if necessary.
2. Have children put large nuts and bolts together.
3. Let children use Fisher Price wind-up drive which comes with screwdrivers and plastic screws.

Games

1. Provide old clocks and radios with twist turn-on knobs for the children to use.
2. Provide wind-up toys and games.

Storytelling

Make up a story about the screwdriver that was left out in the rain. Make a sequence story using simple pictures to illustrate it. (See fig. 40H.)

a. Girl fixes wheel on wagon with screwdriver.
b. She leaves screwdriver outside.
c. If rains on screwdriver.
d. Screwdriver gets all wet in rain puddle.
e. Girl remembers screwdriver. She brings a towel outside to dry it off.
f. Girl puts screwdriver away.

Fig. 40H

Gross Motor

Let children demonstrate the action of using a screwdriver. Let your body show the way a screwdriver turns. Turn left to remove screws. Turn right to put them tightly in place.

Cognitive

1. Provide different width jars with screw-on lids. Let children match lids to jars and screw lids on.
2. Provide large buttons or washers. Let children sort them by color or size and put them into bottles and screw on the lids.
3. Let children sort screws.
   a. Give a child a sack of very large and very small screws. Let child sort the screws into two boxes or two bowls.
   b. Give a child a sack of very long and very short screws. Have child sort the screws into two boxes or two bowls.
   c. Give a child a sack of two, three, and four different kinds of screws. Let the child sort them.
4. Put tool in a cloth bag (laundry bag). Let each child feel tool and identify it. Some children may only be able to point to the picture of the tool they feel.

Enrichment

Help children make a screwdriver and screw collection. Discover the screwdriver best for each screw. Divide which screwdrivers will work for which screws. Be sure to include Phillips head screws and screwdrivers.

Field Trip

Look for screws to tighten around the school. Take a tool kit and tighten them.

Visitor

Invite a carpenter to put together wood rising screws.

Lesson 5: Paintbrush

Unit Group Lesson

1. **Match Concrete Objects**
   Present two paintbrushes. Say, "This is a paintbrush." Ask each child in turn to put the paintbrush with the paintbrush. Gradually increase number of irrelevant objects from which (s)he must select paintbrush to match.

2. **Discriminate Objects**
   Present several objects. Have each child touch the paintbrush in response to verbal direction, "Touch the paintbrush."

3. **Match Pictures**
   Present several pictures of common objects. Have each child match the pictures of the paintbrushes.

4. **Discriminate Pictures**
   Present a group of several unrelated pictures of objects. Have each child touch the picture of the paintbrush in response to verbal direction, "Touch the paintbrush."

5. **Figure-Ground**
   Present a "busy" picture with many visual distractions. Ask each child to find the paintbrush.

6. **Visual Closure**
   Partially cover each of several pictures with paper. Ask each child to find the picture of the paintbrush.

7. **Function**
   Ask, "What do we do with a paintbrush?"

8. **Association**
   Ask, "What goes with the paintbrush?" Use pictures or objects including paint, ladder, drop cloth, etc., with several unrelated objects or pictures.

9. **Imitate Verbalization**
   Present a paintbrush and ask, "What is this? Say, 'Paintbrush'." The child will imitate "Paintbrush."

10. **Verbalize Label**
    Present a paintbrush and ask, "What is this?" The child will respond, "Paintbrush."

11. **Concept Enrichment**
    Talk about different types of brushes. Brush hair, clothes, shoes, etc.

Music
1. Sing "Turn the Screw" to the tune of "London Bridge" from Lesson #4 and add:
   Verse 5: Paint the wall with the paintbrush.......
2. Sing to the tune of "Old MacDonald Had A Farm" as in Lesson #4 and add:
   Verse 5: And in her toolbox she had a brush,
   This I know. This I know.
   With a brush, brush here, and a brush, brush there.......
   This I know. This I know.
   Repeat Verses 1-4.

3.　Sing "Tool Box Song" to the tune of "Hokey Pokey":
　　　First you take your hammer out of the toolbox.　*(Pantomime use of tool as it is*
　　　Then you take the pliers and screwdriver out.　　　*mentioned.)*
　　　Don't forget the saw and the paintbrush, too!
　　　Then you hammer, pull, saw, paint and screw.
　　　Then you put your hammer back in the box.
　　　Remember the plier and screwdriver.
　　　Don't forget the saw and paintbrush too!
　　　And now you know what, you're all through.
　　Sings song as children remove and put back their "tools" in their toolboxes.　Stop singing after each
　　tool is mentioned to give the children time to follow the activity.

Art
1.　Let children paint with different sized paintbrushes, either on an easel or on a large sheet of mural
　　paper.　Use large house brush, 1-inch easel brush, eyeliner brush, small glue brush, medium house
　　paintbrush, etc.
2.　Have children paint a "house."　Cut a large cardboard shipping box so that it looks like a house with
　　doors and windows.　Let children paint the house white.　Have them paint the entire house.　Use
　　medium-sized paintbrushes.
3.　Have children use toothbrushes for spatter painting.　(Rub popsicle sticks across bristles which have
　　been dipped in paint.)　Put painting in a shallow box so that spatters do not spread far.

Snack
1.　Eat left-over chocolate pudding from Fine Motor #4.
2.　Eat sugar cookies made in Fine Motor #5 today.

Fine Motor
1.　Have children paint a circle and a straight line on a piece of cardboard.
2.　Have children drop paintbrushes into an empty paint can.
3.　Let the children use pastry brushes to baste foods being cooked.
4.　Let children finger paint with chocolate pudding, lick fingers clean and eat the remaining pudding for
　　snack.
5.　Let children make sugar cookies, paint on frosting such as egg yolk paint (egg yolk, beaten with food
　　color), or evaporated milk paint (evaporated milk with food color).　Let them use pastry or other small
　　clean brushes.

Games
1.　Find the paintbrush.　Hide paintbrushes of different sizes around the room.　"Find the large
　　paintbrush."　"Find all the paintbrushes."
2.　Hang child-sized tools on a pegboard when not in use.　Have the outline of the tool painted on the
　　pegboard.　Children take turns putting up the tools.　Child must match tool to its outline.　(See fig. 40I.)
3.　Wear painters' caps (free from paint stores).

 Fig. 40I

Storytelling
　　Make up a story about a paintbrush that painted a big house and a little house.　Use pictures or felt cut-
　　outs on a flannel board to illustrate.　(See fig. 40J.)

Fig. 40J
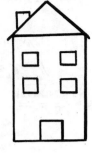

Gross Motor
1. Use large paintbrushes or wall paper brushes to paint the sidewalks and school building with water.
2. Paint a car with tempera, then use brushes to wash it.

Cognitive
1. Put out tools of different sizes and shapes. Let children sort according to use: all hammers together, all screwdrivers together, all paintbrushes together, etc., or size: all big, medium, etc.
2. Put five tools (hammer, saw, pliers, screwdriver, paintbrush) in a box or paper sack. Have child reach in and pull out a tool. Ask, "What tool is that?" "How do you use that tool?" Have child pantomime the use of the tool, using the tool.
3. Make tool cards, a deck of cards with a tool on each card. Let one or more children play. Mix cards and place face down. Let children take turns drawing cards. The child must pantomime the use of the tool pictured.

Enrichment
1. Provide a canvas for painting. Let children paint with acrylics.
2. Collect different sized paint cans. Let the children match brush sizes to paint cans.

Field Trip
1. Visit a hardware store or the hardware department of a department store.
2. Watch workmen build and paint a house.

Visitor
Invite someone to paint a wall in the school.

Related Children's Records
"Carpenter" from **FINGER GAMES** (EA)
"Hammer, Hammer, Hammer" from **LITTLE JOHNNY BROWN** (SCHOL)

Related Children's Books
Barton, Byron. **BUILDING A HOUSE.** New York: Greenwillow Books, 1981.
Rockwell, Anne and Rockwell, Harlow. **THE TOOLBOX.** New York: Macmillan Publishing Co., 1971.
Spier, Peter. **OH! WERE THEY EVER HAPPY!** New York: Doubleday & Co., 1978.
Wolde, Gunilla. **TOMMY BUILDS A HOUSE.** Boston: Houghton-Mifflin Co., 1971.

Related Parenting Materials
Cansler, Dot. **THE HOMESTRETCH.** Winston-Salem, NC 27113-5128: Kaplan Press, 1983.

Related Materials
TEACHING PICTURES. Winston-Salem, NC 27113-5128: Kaplan Press, 1983.
STORY SEQUENCE CARDS I, II. Winston-Salem, NC 27113-5128: Kaplan Press, 1983.
SEWING CARDS I, II, III. Winston-Salem, NC 27113-5128: Kaplan Press, 1983.

Unit 41: Traffic Safety

A developmental assessment should determine the functional levels of each child. Individual expectations are based on the assessment results.

Lesson 1: Stop Sign

Unit Group Lesson

1. **Match Concrete Objects**
   Present two stop signs. Say, "This is a stop sign." Ask each child in turn to put the stop sign with the stop sign. Gradually increase number of irrelevant objects from which (s)he must select stop sign to match.

2. **Discriminate Objects**
   Present several objects. Have each child touch the stop sign in response to verbal direction, "Touch the stop sign."

3. **Match Pictures**
   Present several pictures of common objects. Have each child match the pictures of the stop signs.

4. **Discriminate Pictures**
   Present a group of several unrelated pictures of objects. Have each child touch the picture of the stop sign in response to verbal direction, "Touch the stop sign."

5. **Figure-Ground**
   Present a "busy" picture with many visual distractions. Ask each child to find the stop sign.

6. **Visual Closure**
   Partially cover each of several pictures with paper. Ask each child to find the picture of the stop sign.

7. **Function**
   Ask, "What does a stop sign mean?"

8. **Association**
   Ask, "What goes with the stop sign?" Use pictures or objects including car, traffic light, yield sign, etc., with several unrelated objects or pictures.

9. **Imitate Verbalization**
   Present a stop sign and ask, "What is this? Say, 'Stop sign'." The child will imitate "Stop sign."

10. **Verbalize Label**
    Present a stop sign and ask, "What is this?" The child will respond, "Stop sign."

11.   **Concept Enrichment**
       Stop signs are red and white. Look at other traffic signs and discuss what they mean.

Music
1.   Sing to the tune of "Baa, Baa Black Sheep":
          Stop, stop, boys and girls,
          Don't you see the signs?
          Yes sir, yes sir,
          Just in time.
          One sign for master,
          One for the dame,
          One for the little boy who lives in the lane.
          Stop, stop, boys and girls,
          Don't you see the signs?
          Yes sir, yes sir,
          Just in time.

2.   Sing to the tune of "One Little, Two Little, Three Little Indians":
          1 little, 2 little, 3 little stop signs
          4 little, 5 little, 6 little stop signs
          7 little, 8 little, 9 little stop signs
          Stand by the road
       To get children involved, make and use construction-paper or cardboard stop signs and a road.

Art
1.   Let children make stop signs to use in Music #2.
2.   Have children paint stop signs at easel.
3.   Have children paint stop signs with finger paint.
4.   Draw a lay-out of several streets on large paper. Have children find pictures of stop signs and other traffic signs and paste them at the appropriate places.

Snack
       Eat stop sign cookies or a stop sign cake.   (See fig. 41A.)

 Fig. 41A

Fine Motor
1.   Let children do a crayon rubbing over a sandpaper stop sign.
2.   Let children make classroom "stop" signs. Glue them on popsicle sticks or tongue depressors and stand in a clay base. Use them in Games #2.
3.   Make finger caps with stop signs and other traffic signs. Have each child touch her thumb to the finger which has the same cap as the teacher is showing.

Games
1.   Show stop sign to group. Point out that it is red. Say, "Red says stop." Have children imitate the sentence. Let children run, hop, crawl and march. Hold up stop sign anytime during the action. This means children must stop. When stop sign is taken down children may move again. Teacher talks to a child who has stopped at the stop sign and ask, "Why did you stop here?" or "What does that sign say?"
2.   Put small stop signs in the block area to use with cars and trucks.

Storytelling
       Read or make up a story about traffic safety.

Gross Motor
1.   Set up a roadway with Stop signs. Let children ride school vehicles and follow signs.

2. Set up several stop signs along the path chosen for a group march. Put on marching music and let children march and stop when ever they get to a stop sign. Change positions of signs.

Cognitive
1. Make stop-sign cue sheets. Put a stop sign at the top and stop signs and distractors on the bottom. Have each child mark the stop signs that are like the one at the top. Be sure to vary the difficulty of the cue sheets.
2. Make stop signs in several different sizes and have the children sequence them according to size.

Enrichment
1. Talk about traffic signs. Say, "We use our eyes to keep us safe." Learn to "read" traffic signs. What do traffic signs say? Glue sign on paper and write the word under it that tells what it "says." Let children who are able do the writing.
2. Find a stop sign low enough for the children to reach it (or hold the children up). Let them feel the letters S-T-O-P as the teacher says them. Make a sandpaper Stop sign for the classroom.

Field Trip
Talk a walk in your school neighborhood to see stop signs and to see how traffic obeys the signs.

Lesson 2: Traffic Light

Unit Group Lesson

1. **Match Concrete Objects**
Present two traffic lights. Say, "This is a traffic light." Ask each child in turn to put the traffic light with the traffic light. Gradually increase number of irrelevant objects from which (s)he must select traffic light to match.

2. **Discriminate Objects**
Present several objects. Have each child touch the traffic light in response to verbal direction, "Touch the traffic light."

3. **Match Pictures**
Present several pictures of common objects. Have each child match the pictures of the traffic lights.

4. **Discriminate Pictures**
Present a group of several unrelated pictures of objects. Have each child touch the picture of the traffic light in response to verbal direction, "Touch the traffic light."

5. **Figure-Ground**
Present a "busy" picture with many visual distractions. Ask each child to find the traffic light.

6. **Visual Closure**
Partially cover each of several pictures with paper. Ask each child to find the picture of the traffic light.

7. **Function**
Ask, "What does a traffic light mean?"

8. **Association**

   Ask, "What goes with the traffic light?" Use pictures or objects including car, stop sign, yield sign, etc., with several unrelated objects or pictures.

9. **Imitate Verbalization**

   Present a traffic light and ask, "What is this? Say, 'Traffic light'." The child will imitate "Traffic light."

10. **Verbalize Label**

    Present a traffic light and ask, "What is this?" The child will respond, "Traffic light."

11. **Concept Enrichment**

    Traffic lights are red, green and yellow. Red is on top. Yellow is in the middle and green is on the bottom.

Music

1. Sing to the tune of "Where is Thumbkin?"

   Teacher: Where is my red light?
   Where is my red light?
   Children: Here I am.   *(Hold up red circle.)*
   Here I am.   *(Hold up red circle.)*
   Teacher: Tell me what you say, sir.
   Tell me what you say, sir.
   Children: I say stop.
   I say stop.

   Repeat with green and yellow light. Cut out green, red, and yellow circles so each child may have a color. Have the child hold up circle at appropriate time in the song.

2. Sing Ella Jenkins song, "Stop and Go."

Art

1. Give children pre-cut red, yellow and green circles and a large piece of cardboard or construction paper. Ask them to paste circles on paper to make traffic light. Encourage children to use them in block center and outside. Let them decorate around light.
2. Have children use red, green and yellow play dough to make traffic light.
3. Get a tall cardboard box and cut out three holes from one side. Have children paint boxes and cover holes with red, yellow and green cellophane paper. Use flashlight inside of box to make the green, yellow or red light light up.

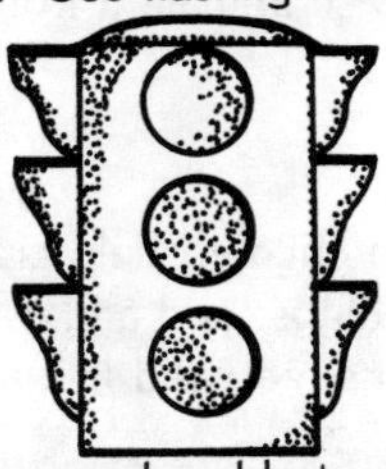

Snack

1. Eat traffic light cake made in Fine Motor #4.
2. Eat traffic light cookies made in Fine Motor #3.

Fig. 41B

Fine Motor

1. Make the traffic light for Game #1. Some children may be able to cut the circles while others can glue them together on the sticks. (See fig. 41B.)
2. Have children trace around a dotted picture of a traffic light and color it the correct colors.
3. Let children make traffic light cookies. Have them drop red, yellow and green Life Savor candies into cookies shaped like traffic lights. Bake. The candies will melt and look transparent.
4. Let children make a cake and ice it to look like a traffic light.

Games

1. Cut out large circles of red, green and yellow (8" or so). Put on sticks "lollipop" fashion. Use for "stop" and "go" and "be careful" games such as those below.
2. Play "Traffic Director." Child (teacher) holds up one of the colors. Children walk, stop or pause.
3. Play game of having children pat heads, stamp feet, etc. on green light and stop when red light is presented.

4. Play game of "1, 2, 3, 4 Red Light." Children line up. The leader stands 25 or 30 feet away, turns back to group and says "1, 2, 3, 4 Red Light" while children run towards leader. Leader turns around quickly at end of verse. Anyone caught still running has to go back to starting point. First person to reach leader wins and becomes leader.

Storytelling

1. Make up a story about a red light and make sequence cards to use with story.
    Once there was a red light who was lost and trying to find out where he belonged. He went into a Toy Store but couldn't find where a red light might fit. He went into a Furniture Store but didn't see any red lights. As he was walking down the street he saw cars whizzing through a traffic light. Looking up at the traffic light he saw something missing. He knew where he belonged then. He must be the red light that makes it safe for cars on the street.

2. Recite poem "Stop and Go":
    The traffic lights we see ahead
    Are sometimes green and sometimes red.
    Red on top, green below.
    The red means stop.
    The green means go.
    Green below, go, go, go.
    Red on top, stop, stop, stop.
    By Marie Louise Allen, *Church Kindergarten Resource Book,* 1964.

Gross Motor

1. "What is a crosswalk?" "How can we use them?" Put two pieces of tape on the floor and let the children use them for a cross walk.
2. Give children red, yellow and green beanbags or yarn balls to toss into a "traffic light." Try to get the red where the red light goes, etc. Make the "traffic light" out of a cardboard carton. Cut large "lights" and paint cue colors around holes.

Cognitive

1. Have children match red circles to red circles, yellow circles to yellow circles, and green circles to green circles.
2. Talk about top, bottom, and middle. Have children identify top, bottom, and middle on a variety of pictures.
3. Teach color green. Discriminate it from red. Teach function of green and red light. "Green says go," "Red says stop."

Enrichment

Together Activity: Let children help create a town on a large piece of paper. Let them draw streets, cut out and color buildings, and add a traffic light. Let children add sidewalk lines or path trace (in the lines) pull toy cards in street, and talk about safety at the corner. (See fig. 41C.)

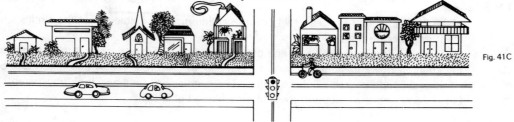

Fig. 41C

Field Trip

Go watch a traffic light "at work." Talk about the colors, about having the cars "take turns," etc.

Visitor

Invite a highway patrolman to come in his patrol car.

Unit Group Lesson

1. **Match Concrete Objects**
   Present two red lights. Say, "This is a red light." Ask each child in turn to put the red light with the red light. Gradually increase number of irrelevant objects from which (s)he must select red light to match.

2. **Discriminate Objects**
   Present several objects. Have each child touch the red light in response to verbal direction, "Touch the red light."

3. **Match Pictures**
   Present several pictures of common objects. Have each child match the pictures of the red lights.

4. **Discriminate Pictures**
   Present a group of several unrelated pictures of objects. Have each child touch the picture of the red light in response to verbal direction, "Touch the red light."

5. **Figure-Ground**
   Present a "busy" picture with many visual distractions. Ask each child to find the red light.

6. **Visual Closure**
   Partially cover each of several pictures with paper. Ask each child to find the picture of the red light.

7. **Function**
   Ask, "What does a red light mean?"

8. **Association**
   Ask, "What goes with the red light?" Use pictures or objects including car, street, etc., with several unrelated objects or pictures.

9. **Imitate Verbalization**
   Present a red light and ask, "What is this? Say, 'Red light'." The child will imitate "Red light."

10. **Verbalize Label**
    Present a red light and ask, "What is this?" The child will respond, "Red light."

11. **Concept Enrichment**
    Discuss crossing the street with the traffic light. If red is facing you - STOP!

Music
1. Sing to the tune of "Three Blind Mice":
   Three red lights
   Three red lights
   See how they work
   See how they work
   They stop all the cars and the buses, too
   They're busy working for me and you
   Three red lights
2. Sing Hap Palmer's "Colors."

Art

1. Help children cut squares of construction paper and circles out of the middle of the squares. Have them cover circles with red cellophane paper; tape against classroom window so sun can shine through the cellophane paper and prints the word "stop" on strip of paper and places under the light.
2. Have children make an all-red collage.
3. Let children punch holes in a piece of dark construction paper and shine a red light through them.

Snack

Eat cherry gelatin, red apples, tomatoes, and/or red berries.

Fine Motor

1. Make path tracing activities of "Take the car to the red light" and "Take the child to the red light." Vary the difficulty according to the needs of the children. Make them large enough for small cars to travel the paths.
2. Make several traffic light pegboards out of cardboard. Ask each child to put green pegs around green light, yellow pegs around yellow light and red pegs around red light. Vary the level of difficulty of each pegboard and size of pegs required appropriate to the skills of the children.
3. Let children build bridges, gates and other structures with small blocks. Let them start when shown a green light and stop when shown a red light.

Games

1. Play "Freeze" game using red light as a freeze signal.
2. Play "Red Rover."

Storytelling

1. Make up story about a red light and make sequence cards to use with story.
2. Recite poem:
   Hippity hop,
   Hippity hop,
   Green says go;
   Red says stop;

   And that is why
   We always know
   When to stop
   And when to go.
3. Read *Clifford, the Big Red Dog* (series).
4. Read *The Red Balloon.* Play with red balloons.

Gross Motor

1. Show red light to group. Point out that it is red. Say, "Red says stop." Have children imitate the sentence. Let children run, hop, crawl, and march. Hold up red light anytime during the action. This means children must stop. When red light is taken down children may move again.
2. Play "Red Light; Green Light."

Cognitive

1. Have "Red Day" when everyone (teacher, too) wears red or brings something red.
2. Let children use red all day long such as red paint, red chalk, red markers, etc.
3. Let the children sort red from non-red things.

Enrichment

Have children learn the rhyme:

Every driver needs to know
Red says STOP.
Green says GO.

Pass out red and green circles. When the word RED is said, the children hold high the red circle. When GREEN is said, they hold high the green circle. Let them take turns saying the rhyme. Rhyming words.

Lesson 4: Yellow Light

Unit Group Lesson

1. **Match Concrete Objects**
   Present two yellow lights. Say, "This is a yellow light." Ask each child in turn to put the yellow light with the yellow light. Gradually increase number of irrelevant objects from which (s)he must select yellow light to match.

2. **Discriminate Objects**
   Present several objects. Have each child touch the yellow light in response to verbal direction, "Touch the yellow light."

3. **Match Pictures**
   Present several pictures of common objects. Have each child match the pictures of the yellow lights.

4. **Discriminate Pictures**
   Present a group of several unrelated pictures of objects. Have each child touch the picture of the yellow light in response to verbal direction, "Touch the yellow light."

5. **Figure-Ground**
   Present a "busy" picture with many visual distractions. Ask each child to find the yellow light.

6. **Visual Closure**
   Partially cover each of several pictures with paper. Ask each child to find the picture of the yellow light.

7. **Function**
   Ask, "What does a yellow light mean?"

8. **Association**
   Ask, "What goes with the yellow light?" Use pictures or objects including stop light, stop sign, etc., with several unrelated objects or pictures.

9. **Imitate Verbalization**
   Present a yellow light and ask, "What is this? Say, 'Yellow light'." The child will imitate "Yellow light."

10. **Verbalize Label**
    Present a yellow light and ask, "What is this?" The child will respond, "Yellow light."

11. **Concept Enrichment**

Discuss traffic safety. Talk about being careful, especially near streets and parking lots.

Music

1. Sing to the tune of "Campbell's Soup Song":
   Watch out.
   Watch out.
   The yellow light says
   Watch out.

2. Sing to the tune of "Where is Thumbkin?"
   Teacher: Where is yellow light
          Where is yellow light
   Children: Here I am   *(Hold up yellow circles.)*
           Here I am   *(Hold up yellow circles.)*

3. Sing "The Yellow Rose of Texas."
   Tell me what you do, sir
   Tell me what you do, sir
   I say watch out.
   I say watch out.

Art

1. Let children use yellow finger paint.
2. Have children use tempera to paint traffic lights.
3. Have children cut yellow construction paper circles to use with game in Games #1.
4. Have children find, cut out and glue pictures of yellow things onto yellow paper.

Snack

Drink and eat lemonade, bananas, eggs, custard, lemon gelatin, pineapple juice, squash, grapefruit, etc.

Fine Motor

1. Make several cardboard traffic light sewing cards for the children to lace. Vary the difficulty according to the skills of the children.
2. Find large pictures of traffic lights. Glue large pictures of traffic lights onto cardboard, cut into two or more pieces. Have each child assemble a puzzle suitable to his skill level.
3. Have each child crumple yellow tissue paper and glue it on an outline of a yellow light.

Games

1. Collect several items and place them in a mystery box along with several yellow circles. Have a child reach in, pull out an item, and hold it up. The group calls out the name of the item. Example: show ball; children say "ball." When the yellow circle is pulled out all children say "Careful." Continue game for several rounds.
2. Let children play traffic game using a traffic light. Talk to a child who has stopped his tricycle at the yellow light. Ask, "Why did you stop here?" or "What does that light say?"

Storytelling

Tell this story:

Once upon a time I went to look for my friend Be-Careful Yellow. Be-Careful was easy to see because he was always yellow. I went to friend "Go-Green" and said, "Go-Green have you seen Be-Careful Yellow?" He said, "Yes, I saw him over at the curb beside the fire hydrant." I went to see and sure enough, there he was all along the sidewalk to help people be careful not to park there. I said, "Hello." Then I went on my way and I saw him again, right in the middle of the street flashing on-off, on-off to tell people to be careful not to cross without looking both ways. "Hello, Be-Careful Yellow," I said, "Thank you for helping us cross at this intersection." Then I went on my way to the school house. Children were leaving school. They wanted to cross the street. I looked up and there was Be-Careful Yellow on a sign to tell cars to slow down because the children were crossing the street.

Storytelling

"Thank you," I said and waved as I crossed the street, "for helping school children get home." "I'll see you again," he answered. My dad came to pick me up, and we started driving home. We were going around the curve on the hill by our house and suddenly I saw Be-Careful Yellow again. He was running along the road in front of the car to tell my Daddy not to pass any cars. Soon we saw him disappear, and I turned and yelled, "Thank you for helping my Dad, Be-Careful!" I think that it is nice that Be-Careful goes everywhere to help us. Where have you seen Be-Careful?"

Gross Motor

Show traffic light to group. Point out that it is yellow. Say, "Yellow says careful." Have children imitate the sentence. Let children run, hop, crawl, march. Hold up a yellow light anytime during the action. This means children must slow down and be careful. When light turns green children may move again in a regular manner.

Cognitive

1. Have the children match yellow to yellow. "Put yellow on yellow."
2. Have children discriminate yellow from other colors by marking the yellow things.
3. Associate yellow with watch out. "This is yellow." Yellow says be careful. Touch yellow. Touch "Be careful." Use the traffic light made earlier and flashlight to light up yellow. Ask, "What color is this?" and "What does it say?" (See fig. 41D.)
4. Have "Yellow Day." Have everyone wear and bring yellow things to school.
5. Have child select the MIDDLE item from groups of three items.

Fig. 41D

Enrichment

Talk about safety colors; during this unit use red, yellow, green, in all the signs around the room, school building, etc.

Lesson 5: Green Light

Unit Group Lesson

1. **Match Concrete Objects**
   Present two green lights. Say, "This is a green light." Ask each child in turn to put the green light with the green light. Gradually increase number of irrelevant objects from which (s)he must select green light to match.

2. **Discriminate Objects**
   Present several objects. Have each child touch the green light in response to verbal direction, "Touch the green light."

3. **Match Pictures**
   Present several pictures of common objects. Have each child match the pictures of the green lights.

4. **Discriminate Pictures**
   Present a group of several unrelated pictures of objects. Have each child touch the picture of the green light in response to verbal direction, "Touch the green light."

5. **Figure-Ground**
   Present a "busy" picture with many visual distractions. Ask each child to find the green light.

6. **Visual Closure**
   Partially cover each of several pictures with paper. Ask each child to find the picture of the green light.

7. **Function**
   Ask, "What does a green light mean?"

8. **Association**
   Ask, "What goes with the green light?" Use pictures or objects including car, street, red light, yellow light, etc., with several unrelated objects or pictures.

9. **Imitate Verbalization**
   Present a green light and ask, "What is this? Say, 'Green light'." The child will imitate "Green light."

10. **Verbalize Label**
    Present a green light and ask, "What is this?" The child will respond, "Green light."

11. **Concept Enrichment**
    Discuss traffic safety. Green means go. The green light is on the bottom.

Music
1. Sing to the tune of "Where Is Thumbkin?" as in Lesson #2 Music #1.
2. Sing to the tune of "Old MacDonald Had A Farm":
   Old MacDonald had a light
   E-I-E-I-O
   And on that light he had some green
   E-I-E-I-O
   With a go, go here   *(Hold up green circle.)*
   And a go, go there   *(Hold up green circle.)*
   Here a go   *(Hold up green circle.)*
   There a go   *(All children hold up circles.)*
   Everywhere a go, go
   Old MacDonald had a light
   E-I-E-I-O
3. *Sing "It's Not That Easy Being Green" from Sesame Street.*

Art
1. Let children finger paint with green paint.
2. Hold up a green "light," as a signal for the children to paint on their papers. Hold up a red "light," as a signal to stop painting.
3. Help children cut squares of construction paper and circles out of the middle. Let them cover the circles with green cellophane paper and tape in the classroom window below the red circles made in Lesson #3 Art #1.

Snack
Eat green grapes, lime gelatin, peppers, pickles, lettuce, celery, cucumbers, avocado, spinach, zucchini, etc.

Fine Motor
1. Make up a sheet with several traffic lights and several stop signs. Ask children to find and outline all of the traffic lights. Let children use green markers, crayons, etc.
2. Let children fill clear plastic bottles with green beads or pegs.
3. Let children use clay to make green "lights."

Games
Play a traffic light game. Let the children pat heads, stomp feet, and clap hands when the green circle is held up and stop when the red circle is held up.

Storytelling
1. Make up or read a story about traffic safety.
2. Read *Go Dog Go,* Eastman.

Gross Motor
1. Show green light to group. Point out that it is green. Say "Green says go." Have children imitate the sentence. Let children run, hop, crawl and march. Hold up green light during the action. When the green light goes down children must stop. When green light goes up the children move again.
2. Play "Red Light; Green Light."
3. Have children get inside cardboard boxes to play car. Provide "roads" with traffic lights and stop signs for them to move along. (See fig. 41E.)

Fig. 41E

Cognitive
1. Make cue sheets with green lights at the top and green lights and distractions on the bottom. Have children find and mark all of the go or green lights on the page. Vary the levels of difficulty in accordance with the skill levels of the children.
2. Have children sort items, placing green items within a green yarn circle.
3. Repeat the above activity, with three yarn circles: red, yellow and green.
4. Have "Green Day." Have everyone wear and bring in green items.

Enrichment
1. Traffic light. Cut out red, yellow, and green circles and put on a shoebox top. Tape to a paper tube. (Play traffic game using cars on taped road on floor.)
2. Practice traffic safety rules with the children.

Field Trip
Go for a walk to a traffic light and a stop sign.

Related Children's Records
"Stop, Look & Listen" from **FINGERPLAY FUN** (EA)
"Stop, Look & Listen" from **LEARNING BASIC SKILLS-HEALTH & SAFETY** (EA)
"Colors" from **LEARNING BASIC SKILLS-VOL. 1** (EA)
"Green Light, Red Light" from **TEMPO FOR TOTS**
"Stop and Go" from **PLAY YOUR INSTRUMENTS** (SCHOL)

Related Children's Books
MacDonald, Golden. **RED LIGHT, GREEN LIGHT.** New York: Doubleday & Co., 1944.
McClosky, Robert. **MAKE WAY FOR DUCKLINGS.** New York: .Viking Press, 1969.
Poulet, Virginia. **BLUEBUG'S SAFETY BOOK.** Chicago: Childrens' Press, 1973.
Tester, Sylvia. **MAGIC MONSTER LEARNS ABOUT SAFETY.** Elgin. Ill.: Child's World, 1979.

Unit 42: Money

A developmental assessment should determine the functional levels of each child. Individual expectations are based on the assessment results.

Lesson 1: Dollar

Unit Group Lesson

1. **Match Concrete Objects.**
   Present two dollars. Say, "This is a dollar." Ask each child in turn to put the dollar with the dollar. Gradually increase number of irrelevant objects from which (s)he must select dollar to match.

2. **Discriminate Objects**
   Present several objects. Have each child touch the dollar in response to verbal direction, "Touch the dollar."

3. **Match Pictures**
   Present several pictures of common objects. Have each child match the pictures of the dollars.

4. **Discriminate Pictures**
   Present a group of several unrelated pictures of objects. Have each child touch the picture of the dollar in response to verbal direction, "Touch the dollar."

5. **Figure-Ground**
   Present a "busy" picture with many visual distractions. Ask each child to find the dollar.

6. **Visual Closure**
   Partially cover each of several pictures with paper. Ask each child to find the picture of the dollar.

7. **Function**
   Ask, "What do we do with a dollar?"

8. **Association**
   Ask, "What goes with the dollar?" Use pictures or objects including penny, nickle, dime, quarter, etc., with several unrelated objects or pictures.

9. **Imitate Verbalization**
   Present a dollar and ask, "What is this? Say, 'Dollar'." The child will imitate "Dollar."

10. **Verbalize Label**
    Present a dollar and ask, "What is this?" The child will respond, "Dollar."

11. **Concept Enrichment**
    Talk about George Washington. Talk about his picture on a dollar bill.

Music

1. Sing "I Gave My Friend" to the tune of "This Is The Way We Wash Our Clothes":

   I gave my friend one dollar,
   One dollar,
   One dollar.
   I gave my friend one dollar,
   One dollar.

2. Sing "I Have Some Money" to the tune of "Hurry on Down to Hardee's":

I have some money,	*(Point to self.)*
And it's a dollar.	*(Children and teacher wave a dollar bill.)*
I have some money,	*(Point to self.)*
And its a dollar.	*(Wave dollar bill.)*
I can buy a book,	*(Pretend to read a book.)*
Or some food to cook.	*(Rub stomach as if you were hungry.)*
I can buy a ball,	*(Make circle with hands.)*
Or a picture for my wall.	*(Point to wall.)*
I have some money,	*(Point to self.)*
And it's a dollar.	*(Wave dollar bill.)*

3. Sing "A Dillar A Dollar" from *Nursery Rhymes* (SCHOL).

Art

1. Make play dollar bills. Have children cut out green rectangles. With a black crayon or felt tip pen, they write "1" on their "dollar bills." The children use this "money" to play store. See Games #1.

2. Have children make paper wallets. Let them fold and staple paper, put child's names on them and decorate. (See fig. 42A.)

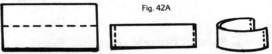

Fig. 42A

Snack

Let children purchase their snack with play dollars.

Fine Motor

1. Have children connect dots in the shape of a dollar bill, then paste a play dollar in the outline. Put more than one dollar on the page and arrange them in different directions.

2. Give children play dollar bills to put in their wallets.

3. Let the children make dollar bills from green construction paper and use them in dramatic play.

Games

1. Set up a store and let children buy the items with their "dollars." Label every item in two ways: with the actual amount $2.00 and with a picture of the amount. Help child count the dollars in the picture and then count out the money needed to buy the item. For example, a book costs $2.00. Say, "John, your money. One, two dollars (laying it on the table)." John takes the two dollars to the child with the cash register and pays for his book. Child at cash register takes money and puts book in a paper bag. "John, you bought a book with your two dollars!" If using inexpensive items, the teacher may want the children to keep the items.

2. Put different amounts of play dollars in each child's wallet (see Art 2). Let children count their money.

3. Play "Dollar, Dollar." Play like "Drop the Handkerchief." Have children chant, "Dollar, dollar, who has the dollar?" Use play money.

4. Put old pocketbooks in the housekeeping area for the children's "money."

Storytelling

Make up a story about a little girl (or boy) who gets a dollar for her birthday. She goes to a toy store and cannot decide what to buy. Let the children offer suggestions as to what she might like to buy.

Gross Motor

Divide the class into teams. Have a child from each team race to a wallet, take out a dollar and bring it back to the next child on the team. Have that child race back to the wallet and place the dollar in it. Continue until all children have had a turn.

Cognitive

1. Arrange four groups such as (a) blocks, (b) money, (c) jewelry and (d) small toys. Give each child a dollar and ask, "In which group does the dollar belong: the group of blocks, the group of money, the group of jewelry or the group of toys?" Point to each group as it is mentioned. Child should respond, "Money." When the child responds correctly, let him "buy" a piece of candy from the teacher.

2. Make "dollar" cue sheets by placing a dollar at the top of a page and dollars and other items on the bottom. Have children mark an "X" on every dollar on the page. Vary the difficulty according to the skills of the children. (See fig. 42B.)

3. Have children count dollar bills into wallets labeled with numerals 1 through 5.

4. Have child identify which item costs more between two items labeled with prices.

Fig. 42B

Enrichment

Help the children learn how many $1 are in $5, $10, and $20 bills.

Field Trip

1. Go to a store and find things that cost $1.
2. Go to a bank and exchange a $5, $10, and $20 bill for dollar bills.

Lesson 2: Penny

Unit Group Lesson

1. **Match Concrete Objects.**
   Present two pennies. Say, "This is a penny." Ask each child in turn to put the penny with the penny. Gradually increase number of irrelevant objects from which (s)he must select penny to match.

2. **Discriminate Objects**
   Present several objects. Have each child touch the penny in response to verbal direction, "Touch the penny."

3. **Match Pictures**
   Present several pictures of common objects. Have each child match the pictures of the pennies.

4. **Discriminate Pictures**
   Present a group of several unrelated pictures of objects. Have each child touch the picture of the penny in response to verbal direction, "Touch the penny."

5. **Figure-Ground**
   Present a "busy" picture with many visual distractions. Ask each child to find the penny.

6. **Visual Closure**
   Partially cover each of several pictures with paper. Ask each child to find the picture of the penny.

7. **Function**
   Ask, "What do we do with a penny?"

8. **Association**
   Ask, "What goes with the penny?" Use pictures or objects including dollar, nickel, dime, quarter, etc., with several unrelated objects or pictures.

9. **Imitate Verbalization**
   Present a penny and ask, "What is this? Say, 'Penny'." The child will imitate "Penny."

10. **Verbalize Label**
    Present a penny and ask, "What is this?" The child will respond, "Penny."

Gross Motor

Have the children pitch pennies into oatmeal box decorated to look like Lincoln's hat. For less skilled children, use large pennies made of corrugated cardboard or small bean bags with a penny picture. (See fig. 42C.)

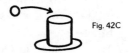

Fig. 42C

Cognitive

1. Put pennies (a penny) in each child's hand appropriate to the child's counting skills. Have each child count her pennies with help, if it is needed.
2. Label egg carton sections with numerals and have children count pennies into the egg carton sections.
3. Make several charts with pennies and other money. Have the children match the pennies to the pennies. Vary the levels of difficulty for children with different levels of skills as with a cue sheet.

Enrichment

1. Let children drop pennies into water and watch what happens.
2. Discuss "heads" and "tails" of coins. Have children dump pennies from a cup. Ask, "How many heads? Tails?"
3. Let each child glue a penny to the top of a popsicle stick, add a tall black hat and use as a Lincoln puppet. Tell the story of Abraham Lincoln.

Lesson 3: Nickel

Unit Group Lesson

1. **Match Concrete Objects.**
   Present two nickels. Say, "This is a nickel." Ask each child in turn to put the nickel with the nickel. Gradually increase number of irrelevant objects from which (s)he must select nickel to match.

2. **Discriminate Objects**
   Present several objects. Have each child touch the nickel in response to verbal direction, "Touch the nickel."

3. **Match Pictures**
   Present several pictures of common objects. Have each child match the pictures of the nickels.

4. **Discriminate Pictures**
   Present a group of several unrelated pictures of objects. Have each child touch the picture of the nickel in response to verbal direction, "Touch the nickel."

5. **Figure-Ground**
   Present a "busy" picture with many visual distractions. Ask each child to find the nickel.

6. **Visual Closure**
   Partially cover each of several pictures with paper. Ask each child to find the picture of the nickel.

7. **Function**
   Ask, "What do we do with a nickel?"

8. **Association**
   Ask, "What goes with the nickel?" Use pictures or objects including dollar, penny, dime, quarter, etc., with several unrelated objects or pictures.

9. **Imitate Verbalization**
   Present a nickel and ask, "What is this? Say, 'Nickel'." The child will imitate "Nickel."

10. **Verbalize Label**
    Present a nickel and ask, "What is this?" The child will respond, "Nickel."

11.   **Concept Enrichment**

Talk about a penny's copper color, smooth edges, and Lincoln's picture.

Music

1.   Sing "In Our Bank" to the tune of "Mary Had A Little Lamb":

Verse 1: (Child's name) had a penny,
        A penny, a penny.
        (Child's name) had a penny,
        And she put it in her bank.

Everyone sings as a child (named in song) puts a penny in a bank. Every child puts one penny in bank.

Verse 2: We have our pennies in our bank,
        In our bank, in our bank.
        We have pennies in our bank,
        Pennies in our bank.

2.   Sing "A Penny Is One Cent" to the tune of "The Farmer in the Dell":

A penny is one cent,
A penny is one cent.
Oh yes, I know that it is so.
A penny is one cent.

3.   Sing "I Gave My Friend" to the tune of "This Is The Way We Wash Our Clothes":

I gave my friend a penny
A penny,
A penny.
I gave my friend a penny,
A penny.

4.   Sing "A Shiny Penny" from *Come & See the Peppermint Tree* (EA.)

Art

1.   Have children tear or cut out circles representing pennies. Make them out of brown paper. Give each child a sheet of brown paper with circle and 1¢ signs already marked. Say, "Pennies are round." It may be necessary to make the pennies larger than actual size. Let children make a penny collage from pennies.

2.   Help each child make a bank. Cut a hole in top of a box. Have children decorate outside of the box and glue play money on the outside, collage-like. Oatmeal boxes, tea cans, and bandage boxes make good banks.

3.   Give children pennies and outlines of stick figures. Let them make penny people by gluing pennies on the outline and decorating them as they wish. (See fig. 42D.)

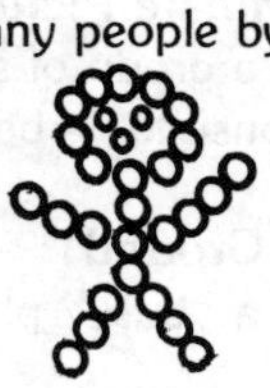

Fig. 42D

Snack

Eat "pennies" made in Fine Motor #3.

Fine Motor

1.   Have children connect dots in the shape of a penny and then paste a penny on the outline. Put more then one penny on a page.

2.   Put a bubble gum bank or machine in the room. Give each child a penny to get some gum. Child must put penny in the slot and pull lever.

3.   Make "pennies" for snack from peanut butter play dough (peanut butter, dry milk and honey to taste) or chocolate cookie dough.

Games

1.   Continue play store begun in Lesson #1 Games #1. Label items in pennies such as 2¢ or 1¢. Follow the same procedure and use real money.

2.   Have children sort old and new pennies. Get new pennies at the bank and put twenty new pennies and twenty old pennies in a bowl. Let the children sort old and new pennies into two other bowls. Initiate activity by putting a penny in each bowl if necessary.

Storytelling

Tell a simple story of Abe Lincoln, whose picture is on the penny.

11.   **Concept Enrichment**

Discuss a nickel's silver color, Jefferson's picture and Monticello. Discuss the concept of five, relate that a nickel and five pennies are equal to the same amount of money.

Music

Sing "In Our Bank" to the tune of "Mary Had A Little Lamb":
Verse 1: (Child's name) had a nickel,
            A nickel, a nickel.
            (Child's name) had a nickel,
            And she put it in her bank.
Everyone sings as named child puts a nickel in the bank. Sing the song for all the children.
    Verse 2: We have nickels in our bank,
                in our bank, in our bank.
                We have nickels in our bank,
                Nickels in our bank.

Art

1.   Have children tear or cut nickels from gray or silver paper and use them to make a nickel collage.
2.   Let children make crayon rubbings of nickels. Obtain the large plastic nickels if possible. Otherwise, cut nickel sized holes in shirt cardboard, put nickels in the holes and tape paper securely over the nickels. Let the children rub the side of a crayon over the paper and the nickels will appear.

Snack

Use nickels to buy snack foods.

Fine Motor

1.   Give each child a bank and a handful of nickels. Have the child put the nickels in the bank. Change the activity by putting the nickels on the table and have the child pick up nickels with thumb and forefinger.
2.   Have children toss, drop, and roll nickels. Some children may learn to spin nickels, too.
3.   Have children make stacks of nickels, etc. "How high can you stack nickels?" (See fig. 42E.)
4.   Have children balance nickels on finger and walk with them. (See fig. 42F.)

Fig. 42E

Games

1.   Continue the play store begun in Lesson #1 Games #1. Price items in nickels. Such as 5¢ or 5¢ + 5¢. Some children may be able to determine that two nickels are 10¢. Make some items 6¢. (5¢ + 1¢), 7¢ (5¢ + 1¢ + 1¢), 5¢ (1¢ + 1¢ + 1¢ + 1¢ + 1¢).
2.   Let children sort pennies and nickels into two bowls. Initiate sorting by putting a nickel in one bowl and a penny in the other.

Storytelling

1.   Make up a story about a little girl who finds a nickel at the playground. At first she decides to keep the nickel, then she decides to find the person who lost it. At the end she finds the person, another little girl, who decides to buy ice cream cones for each of them. Let the children make up some of her adventures.
2.   Read *A Pickle for A Nickel* and eat pickles.

Gross Motor

Have children push nickels from one side of a room to other with a stick. Continue until each child has had several turns.

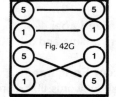
Fig. 42G

Fig. 42F

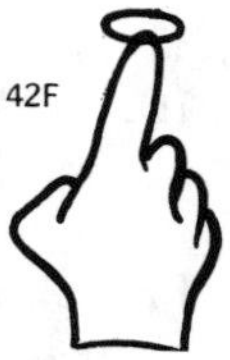

Cognitive

1.   Arrange four groups such as (a) blocks, (b) money, (c) jewelry, (d) small toys. Give each child a nickel and ask, "In which group does the nickel belong: the group of blocks, the group of money, the group of jewelry, or the group of toys?" Point to each group as it is mentioned. Child should respond, "Money." When the child responds correctly have him "buy" a piece of candy from the teacher. (See fig. 42G.)
2.   Let children pick out nickels from a bowl of coins.
3.   Have child match nickels to nickels and pennies to pennies. Give each child a sheet of paper with the same number of pennies and nickels. Mix up the coins and paste them in two columns. Have child draw a line from penny to penny and from nickel to nickel.

Enrichment

1. Bring in something nickel-plated. Talk about how a nickel got its name.
2. Display five pennies and one nickel. Have the children count the pennies. Stress that the nickel equals five pennies. Let the children practice buying 5¢ items at the play store with nickels or five pennies.

Lesson 4: Dime

Unit Group Lesson

1. **Match Concrete Objects.**
   Present two dimes. Say, "This is a dime." Ask each child in turn to put the dime with the dime. Gradually increase number of irrelevant objects from which (s)he must select dime to match.

2. **Discriminate Objects**
   Present several objects. Have each child touch the dime in response to verbal direction, "Touch the dime."

3. **Match Pictures**
   Present several pictures of common objects. Have each child match the pictures of the dimes.

4. **Discriminate Pictures**
   Present a group of several unrelated pictures of objects. Have each child touch the picture of the dime in response to verbal direction, "Touch the dime."

5. **Figure-Ground**
   Present a "busy" picture with many visual distractions. Ask each child to find the dime.

6. **Visual Closure**
   Partially cover each of several pictures with paper. Ask each child to find the picture of the dime.

7. **Function**
   Ask, "What do we do with a dime?"

8. **Association**
   Ask, "What goes with the dime?" Use pictures or objects including dollar, penny, nickel, quarter, etc., with several unrelated objects or pictures.

9. **Imitate Verbalization**
   Present a dime and ask, "What is this? Say, 'Dime'." The child will imitate "Dime."

10. **Verbalize Label**
    Present a dime and ask, "What is this?" The child will respond, "Dime."

11. **Concept Enrichment**
    Talk about words that rhyme with dime: chime, time, etc. Discuss Franklin Roosevelt's picture on the dime.

Music

1. Sing "What Can You Buy" to the tune of "Here We Go 'Round the Mulberry Bush":
   What can you buy with a dime, a dime?   *(Hold up a dime.)*
   What can you buy with a dime, a dime?
   What can you buy with a dime, a dime?
   You can buy a _____.   *(Point to a child who will name an item.)*
2. Repeat songs "In Our Bank" and "A Penny Is One Cent" from Lesson #2 Music #1 and #2.

516

Art
1. Give each child a dime and some clay. After she makes a "pancake" with her clay, have her press the dime into it. Have her make dime prints all over the clay.
2. Have children make dime collages by cutting or tearing dimes from silver or grey paper.
3. Let the children paint with silver-colored paint.

Snack
Pay for snack with dimes.

Fine Motor
1. Have children connect dots in the shape of a circle in different sizes.
2. Have each child pick dimes up from the table and put into a bank.
3. Let children play tiddley winks by flipping dimes into containers.

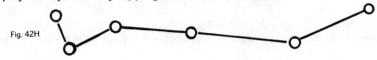

Fig. 42H

Games
1. Continue the play store begun in Lesson #1 Games #1. Label items in dimes (10¢ or 5¢ + 5¢, 20¢ or 10¢ + 10¢, and 30¢ or 10¢ + 10¢ +10¢). Label some items in nickels and some in pennies. Label some items with all three currency amounts (10¢ + 10¢ or 5¢ + 5¢ or 1¢ + 1¢ + 1¢ + 1¢ + 1¢ + 1¢ + 1¢ + 1¢ + 1¢ + 1¢). In each case help the child count his money.
2. Play bank and let the "Teller" give 10 pennies in exchange for a dime or vice versa, 2 nickels for a dime or vice versa, etc.

Storytelling
Make up a story about a child who goes to an amusement park. He has five dimes. With the dimes he buys five tickets. Let the children describe the rides he rides at the park.

Gross Motor
Tape large dimes to the floor at intervals. Have the children step or jump from dime to dime. (See fig. 42H)

Cognitive
1. Cut out pictures of items "For Sale." Let children "purchase" the items in dimes. The more advanced children can use pennies and nickels, too.
2. Put a dime in every child's hand. Say, "Here is a dime. How many dimes do you have?" Child answers "One." Later, say, "You have ten cents." Then put ten pennies in every child's hand and let him count pennies. Some children may associate ten pennies with a dime.
3. Children sort pennies, nickels and dimes into three bowls. Put a penny, nickel and dime into bowls as a model of which coin goes into which bowl.

Enrichment
1. Help each child make a "coin" purse. Let her staple or glue sides, fold down top and decorate. The children can make theirs look like leather by using the side of a crayon. (See fig. 42I.)
2. Make parking meters from boxes and wrapping paper rolls. Tape to the walls and have the children drive cars, park them by the meters and put dimes in the meters. (See fig. 42J.)

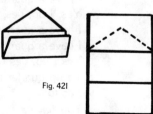

Fig. 42I

Fig. 42J

Field Trip
Take a walk to look at parking meters. Use dimes to show how they work.

Lesson 5: Quarter

Unit Group Lesson

1. **Match Concrete Objects.**
Present two quarters. Say, "This is a quarter." Ask each child in turn to put the quarter with the quarter. Gradually increase number of irrelevant objects from which (s)he must select quarter to match.

2. **Discriminate Objects**

   Present several objects. Have each child touch the quarter in response to verbal direction, "Touch the quarter."

3. **Match Pictures**

   Present several pictures of common objects. Have each child match the pictures of the quarters.

4. **Discriminate Pictures**

   Present a group of several unrelated pictures of objects. Have each child touch the picture of the quarter in response to verbal direction, "Touch the quarter."

5. **Figure-Ground**

   Present a "busy" picture with many visual distractions. Ask each child to find the quarter.

6. **Visual Closure**

   Partially cover each of several pictures with paper. Ask each child to find the picture of the quarter.

7. **Function**

   Ask, "What do we do with a quarter?"

8. **Association**

   Ask, "What goes with the quarter?" Use pictures or objects including dollar, penny, nickel, dime, etc., with several unrelated objects or pictures.

9. **Imitate Verbalization**

   Present a quarter and ask, "What is this? Say, 'Quarter'." The child will imitate "Quarter."

10. **Verbalize Label**

    Present a quarter and ask, "What is this?" The child will respond, "Quarter."

11. **Concept Enrichment**

    A quarter is worth twenty-five pennies, five nickels, or two dimes plus one nickel. George Washington's picture is on the quarter. Talk about eagles and why an eagle is on the back of a quarter.

Music

1. Sing "I Have A Quarter" to the tune of "Are You Sleeping":
   I have a quarter.
   I have a quarter.
   Yes, I do, yes, I do.
   I have a quarter.
   I have a quarter.
   Yes I do, yes I do.

   Hold up quarter and sing song. Give every child a coin studied this week. Sing song again changing words to:

   You have a _____ (Point to child and have her fill in blank by naming the coin she is holding.)
   Yes you do,
   Yes you do.

2. Repeat the songs taught in this unit and sing them for all coins taught.

Art

1. Let the children spatter paint around quarters and other coins. Have children ask for specific coins.
2. Give each child a paper with coin outlines and play money. Have children match and paste the coins to their outlines.
3. Help children make giant coins from aluminum pie tins. Let them create the design on the back by pushing with a popsicle stick. They will need to reverse any lettering.

Snack

1. Show a movie and let the children buy popcorn for a quarter a bag and eat while watching the movie.

2. Press foil around a quarter. Use as mold and fill with chocolate, melted cheese, etc. Let children eat "coin." If a large plastic souvenir coin is available use it as a mold instead.
3. Have children purchase something at a real store worth 25¢ for snack.

Fine Motor
1. Teach children to flip quarters. Model activity and then, place coin on the child's thumb. Tell him to "flip" his thumb.
2. Help the children glue a quarter on the end of a popsicle stick, add cotton for hair and beard, and add a tricornered hat for head. Use as a Washington puppet.
3. Have each child cover a quarter with foil and rub until the design shows.

Games
1. Continue the play store begun in Lesson #1 Games #1. Label items in quarters (25¢ + 25¢ or 2 quarters). Have each child count out quarters and pay for the items.
2. Have children toss quarters through holes of a cardboard target. Have five holes. Above each hole have an item the child might be inclined to buy. Children "buy" the items by tossing the quarters through the holes. Children will need to stand close to the target.

Storytelling
Make up a story about a little boy who goes to the grocery store for his mother to buy some bread. He puts two quarters in his pocket but when he gets to the store, he finds his pocket has a hole in it and he has lost his money.

Gross Motor
Place vehicles around the classroom or playground and have children buy rides with real money. Label prices with actual amounts and pictures.

Cognitive
1. Have children sort quarters from non-quarters.
2. Have children match real coins to their corresponding shape on a "game board."
3. Have children count quarters. Let each count a number appropriate to her counting skills.

Enrichment
1. Make price tags and tie on objects on a table. Have children pick up objects and tell how much they cost (range from 1¢ to 25¢). Have them choose something that costs more than (a penny), less than (a dime), or the same as (a quarter). (See fig. 42K.)
2. Have children stack pennies or nickels in paper coin wrap folders.
3. Have children exchange pennies, nickels, dimes and combinations of these for quarters.

Field Trip
1. Go to a grocery store or a store and buy the snack for today with a quarter.
2. Go to an arcade and let children each play a 25¢ game.
3. Buy a newspaper from a wire vendor machine with a quarter.

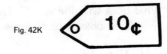
Fig. 42K

Related Children's Records
"A Shiny Penny" from **COME & SEE THE PEPPERMINT TREE** (EA)
"Money Money Money" from **OOOO WE'RE HAVING FUN** (RP)
"See Saw Margery Daw" from **NURSERY RHYMES** (SCHOL)
"A Dillar A Dollar" from **NURSERY RHYMES** (SCHOL)

Related Children's Books
Aldridge, Josephine. **PENNY AND A PERIWINKLE.** Oakland, Cal.: Parnassus Press, 1961.
Brenner, Barbara. **THE FIVE PENNIES.** New York: Alfred A. Knopf, 1964.
Rose, Anne. **AS RIGHT AS RIGHT CAN BE.** New York: Dial Press, 1976.
Viorst, Judith. **ALEXANDER, WHO USED TO BE RICH LAST SUNDAY.** New York: Atheneum, 1978.
Hintz, Sandy and Hintz, Martin. **WE CAN'T AFFORD IT.** Milwaukee, Wis.: Raintree Publisher, 1977.

Unit 43: Things in the Sky

A developmental assessment should determine the functional levels of each child. Individual expectations are based on the assessment results.

Lesson 1: Sun

Unit Group Lesson

1. **Match Pictures**
   Present two pictures of the sun. Say, "This is the sun." Ask each child in turn to put the sun with the sun. Gradually increase number of irrelevant objects from which (s)he must select sun to match.

2. **Discriminate Pictures**
   Present a group of several unrelated pictures of objects. Have each child touch the picture of the sun in response to verbal direction, "Touch the sun."

3. **Figure-Ground**
   Present a "busy" picture with many visual distractions. Ask each child to find the sun.

4. **Visual Closure**
   Partially cover each of several pictures with paper. Ask each child to find the picture of the sun.

5. **Function**
   Ask, "What does the sun do?"

6. **Association**
   Ask, "What goes with the sun?" Use pictures or objects including moon, stars, clouds, etc., with several unrelated objects or pictures.

7. **Imitate Verbalization**
   Present a picture of the sun and ask, "What is this? Say, 'Sun'." The child will imitate "Sun."

8. **Verbalize Label**
   Present a picture of the sun and ask, "What is this?" The child will respond, "Sun."

9. **Concept Enrichment**
   The sun is in the sky. The sun gives us light, keeps us warm and grows our food. The sun is yellow.

Music
1. Sing the "Itsy Bitsy Spider" song.
2. Sing "You Are My Sunshine."

Art

1. Help the children make a giant circle "Together picture" with yellow, red, and orange paint. Let them paint colors on or dab with pieces of sponge held with clothespins and sprinkle with glitter.
2. Have each child decorate a cut-out of a sun with glue and glitter, glue it onto paper and add strips cut in Fine Motor #3 as sun rays. (See fig. 43A.)

Fig. 43A

Snack

1. Serve cheese circles with shredded cheese for children to arrange like the sun and sun rays on toast, on a napkin or paper plate.
2. Make sun tea, let tea sit in sun. Drink.

Fine Motor

1. Have children draw a clothesline with clothes attached to dry in the sun. (May cut clothing out of the catalog or magazines.) (See fig. 43B.)

Fig. 43B

2. Have children cut suns from yellow paper.
3. Have children cut strips of yellow paper for use in Art #2.

Games

Set up "housekeeping" corner with beach clothing and straw hats for pretend activities on the beach.

Storytelling

Make up a story about a trip to the beach.

Gross Motor

1. Have children take a walk wearing sunglasses.
2. Creative Movement: Form a "ball" (children) on floor; let the "sun" rise and shine to the sound of music.

Cognitive

1. Let children study and pick out circles the color of the sun.
2. Let children pick out things the color of the sun.
3. Have children identify things which are warm and cold.

Enrichment

1. Help children learn "warm" colors.
2. Put a saucer of water in window and see what happens to the water.
3. Let children make a collection of sunglasses.
4. Let children study shadows.

Field Trip

Go out in the sun.

Visitor

Invite a mother or volunteer to visit and show things to protect us from sun (lotion, sunscreen, hats, beach umbrella).

Lesson 2: Clouds

Unit Group Lesson

1. **Match Pictures**
   Present two pictures of clouds. Say, "This is a cloud." Ask each child in turn to put the cloud with the cloud. Gradually increase number of irrelevant objects from which (s)he must select cloud to match.

2. **Discriminate Pictures**
   Present a group of several unrelated pictures of objects. Have each child touch the picture of the cloud in response to verbal direction, "Touch the cloud."

3. **Figure-Ground**
   Present a "busy" picture with many visual distractions. Ask each child to find the cloud.

4. **Visual Closure**
   Partially cover each of several pictures with paper. Ask each child to find the picture of the cloud.

5. **Function**
   Ask, "What do clouds do?"

6. **Association**
   Ask, "What goes with the cloud?" Use pictures or objects including moon, sun, sky, etc., with several unrelated objects or pictures.

7. **Imitate Verbalization**
   Present a picture of a cloud and ask, "What is this? Say, 'Cloud'." The child will imitate "Cloud."

8. **Verbalize Label**
   Present a picture of a cloud and ask, "What is this?" The child will respond, "Cloud."

9. **Concept Enrichment**
   Clouds move because the wind blows them and the earth is moving. Clouds are white, gray and black.

Music

Have children "float" to soft music with arms making floating movements.

Art
1. Let children do a detergent painting. Let them make a paste of laundry detergent and use on dark blue paper.
2. Let children make clouds with white chalk on blue paper.
3. Let children make clouds with white crayon and paint over them with thin blue water color for a crayon-resist cloud painting.

Snack
1. Eat popcorn and look at cloud shapes.
2. Have a whipped cream "cloud" on a chocolate cookie or piece of fruit.

Fine Motor
1. Have children blow bubbles with spools and saucers of soapy water. Let children blow bubbles up gently and ask, "What fills the bubble?" Blow bubbles outside on the first pretty day. Let them watch bubbles "fly."

2. Let children pull apart whisps of cotton to glue on a large cloud shape.
3. Let children staple a cover of waxed paper on a picture to make a "cloudy day."

Games

Set up water table or dish pans outdoors. Make bubble bath or detergent suds in water. Let children blow them away with a straw and watch them float away.

Storytelling

Let the children tell what they could see while riding on a cloud looking down at the room, the playground, the street, etc.

Gross Motor
1. Movement: Let children move like happy clouds, floating gently or angry clouds, moving faster.
2. Let children lie down on grass or on sheets outdoors to watch clouds go over.

Cognitive
1. Let children sort soft things from hard things.
2. Talk about a cloudy day.
3. Let children select things that are white like clouds.

Enrichment

Help children make a "cloud" chart calendar. Look at the sky everyday. Paste on a cloud (cotton wad) everyday you can see a cloud in the sky.

Lesson 3: Star

Unit Group Lesson

1. **Match Concrete Objects**
   Present two stars. Say, "This is a star." Ask each child in turn to put the star with the star. Gradually increase number of irrelevant objects from which (s)he must select star to match.

2. **Discriminate Objects**
   Present several objects. Have each child touch the star in response to verbal direction, "Touch the star."

3. **Match Pictures**
   Present several pictures of common objects. Have each child match the pictures of the stars.

4. **Discriminate Pictures**
   Present a group of several unrelated pictures of objects. Have each child touch the picture of the star in response to verbal direction, "Touch the star."

5. **Figure-Ground**
   Present a "busy" picture with many visual distractions. Ask each child to find the star.

6. **Visual Closure**
   Partially cover each of several pictures with paper. Ask each child to find the picture of the star.

7. **Function**
   Ask, "What do stars do?"

8. **Association**
Ask, "What goes with the star?" Use pictures or objects including moon, sun, clouds, etc., with several unrelated objects or pictures.

9. **Imitate Verbalization**
Present a star and ask, "What is this? Say, 'Star'." The child will imitate "Star."

10. **Verbalize Label**
Present a star and ask, "What is this?" The child will respond, "Star."

11. **Concept Enrichment**
Stars are distant suns that are so far away that we can only see them at night.

Music

Sing "Twinkle, Twinkle Little Star." Have children move their fingers above head to "twinkle."

Art

1. Have children paste yellow triangles on a yellow circle to form a star. (See fig. 43C.)

Fig. 43C

2. Let the children make enough stars to cover the ceiling by putting glue and sprinkling glitter on stars, and hanging by string from ceiling.
3. Let children make a giant star and "dab" paint on it with sponges.

Snack

Serve star cut sandwiches with egg salad on them.

Fine Motor

1. Let the children path trace star shapes. Provide dots as needed.
2. Let children cut out triangles and circles to make stars in Art #1.
3. Let children match star shapes to star-shape outlines on a large board.

Games

Play "Reach for the Stars." Place star shapes in hiding places and on walls high enough to "reach for them." Play music as children "reach for" as many stars as they can find.

Storytelling

Make up a story about all the things that happen after the stars are out. Let children help tell the story.

Gross Motor

Arrange stars on floor. Give the children directions to jump over, sit beside, hop around, skip around, take giant steps to, etc., the various stars.

Cognitive

1. Let children match star shapes.
2. Make stars in several sizes and let the children sequence the stars from smallest to largest.
3. Have the children count the points on the stars.

Enrichment

1. Talk about what "shining" means.
2. Make up a tale about what can make a star "shine."
3. Have everyone look for stars around school and on clothing.

Field Trip

Visit planetarium.

Visitor

Invite an astronomer or someone with a telescope.

Lesson 4: Moon

Unit Group Lesson

1. **Match Concrete Objects**

   Present two moons. Say, "This is a moon." Ask each child in turn to put the moon with the moon. Gradually increase number of irrelevant objects from which (s)he must select moon to match.

2. **Discriminate Objects**

   Present several objects. Have each child touch the moon in response to verbal direction, "Touch the moon."

3. **Match Pictures**

   Present several pictures of common objects. Have each child match the pictures of the moons.

4. **Discriminate Pictures**

   Present a group of several unrelated pictures of objects. Have each child touch the picture of the moon in response to verbal direction, "Touch the moon."

5. **Figure-Ground**

   Present a "busy" picture with many visual distractions. Ask each child to find the moon.

6. **Visual Closure**

   Partially cover each of several pictures with paper. Ask each child to find the picture of the moon.

7. **Function**

   Ask, "What does the moon do?"

8. **Association**

   Ask, "What goes with the moon?" Use pictures or objects including stars, sun, clouds, etc., with several unrelated objects or pictures.

9. **Imitate Verbalization**

   Present a moon and ask, "What is this? Say, 'Moon'." The child will imitate "Moon."

10. **Verbalize Label**

    Present a moon and ask, "What is this?" The child will respond, "Moon."

11. **Concept Enrichment**

    The moon is in the sky at night. It reflects sunlight. Men have flown to the moon in rockets.

Music

Play soft slow music and let the children pretend to be walking like the men who have walked on the moon.

Art

1. Cut out "full" moon and "crescent" moon from cardboard. Make as large as a poster sheet allows. Let children use clothespins to pick up cotton balls, dip in yellow paint, and "dab" paint on the moon shapes (taking turns).
2. When the above has dried, let children glue bits of yellow paper tissue made in Fine Motor #1 on moon shapes and hang the crescent up in the room.

Snack

Eat moon sandwiches made in Fine Motor #3.

Fine Motor

1. Have children tear up bits of yellow paper and crumple yellow tissue paper to use on moon shapes in Art #2.
2. Have children path trace full moon and crescent shapes. Vary the size and width of the paths according to the skills of the children.
3. Let children use a cookie cutter to cut out round bread shapes for snack. Cover with yellow margarine mixed with honey.

Games

Pretend to be on the moon and have children follow the leader in making motions one might make on the moon such as moon walking, etc.

Storytelling

Tell "Hey Diddle Diddle, the Cat and the Fiddle."

Gross Motor

1. Act out "Hey Diddle Diddle" using the giant moon crescent or circle made in Art.
2. Have children follow special directions such as jump over the moon, walk around the moon, sit on the moon, move the moon to, etc.

Cognitive

1. Make dice with sun, cloud, star, moon. Have children roll the dice, choose the matching shape from a basket of matching shapes. (See fig. 43D.)
2. Have children match moon shapes from stages of moon.
3. Use the same dice from Cognitive #1 today. Make a sentence using the symbol such as "The sun shines;" "The clouds are soft and white;" etc.

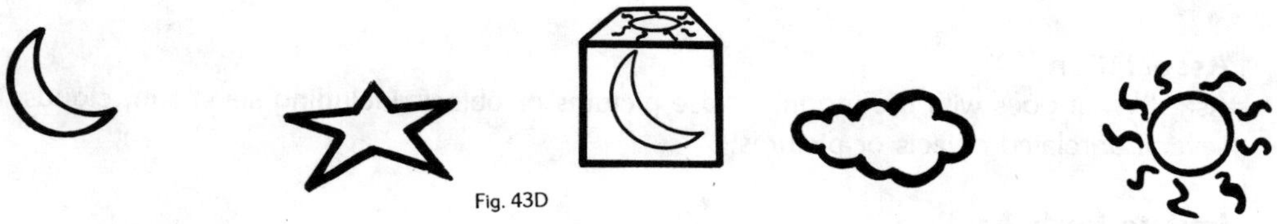

Fig. 43D

Enrichment

1. Help children make a moonscape. Draw a large circle on playground in a sandy area. Build a "moonscape" by collecting rock, sand and placing in circle.
2. Discuss "full" moon, compare shapes of moon.

Lesson 5: Rocket

Unit Group Lesson

1. **Match Concrete Objects**
    Present two toy rockets. Say, "This is a rocket." Ask each child in turn to put the rocket with the rocket. Gradually increase number of irrelevant objects from which (s)he must select rocket to match.

2. **Discriminate Objects**
    Present several objects. Have each child touch the rocket in response to verbal direction, "Touch the rocket."

3. **Match Pictures**
    Present several pictures of common objects. Have each child match the pictures of the rockets.

4. **Discriminate Pictures**
    Present a group of several unrelated pictures of objects. Have each child touch the picture of the rocket in response to verbal direction, "Touch the rocket."

5. **Figure-Ground**
    Present a "busy" picture with many visual distractions. Ask each child to find the rocket.

6. **Tactile Discrimination**
    Put toy rocket and some grossly different objects into a "feely box." Say, "Find the rocket."

7. **Visual Closure**
    Partially cover each of several pictures with paper. Ask each child to find the picture of the rocket.

8. **Function**
    Ask, "What does a rocket do?"

9. **Association**
    Ask, "What goes with the rocket?" Use pictures or objects including sky, moon, stars, etc., with several unrelated objects or pictures.

10. **Imitate Verbalization**
    Present a rocket and ask, "What is this? Say, 'Rocket'." The child will imitate "Rocket."

11. **Verbalize Label**
    Present a rocket and ask, "What is this?" The child will respond, "Rocket."

12. **Concept Enrichment**
    Rockets come in many sizes. Big ones take men into space and have taken men to the moon.

Music

Play "Star Wars" music and allow the children free expression of movement to the music.

Art

1. Let children paint shoe boxes to be used for "oxygen" tanks on a space trip. Attach cloth bands to be worn like a backpack. (See fig. 43F.)

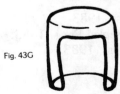
Fig. 43G

Fig. 43F

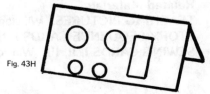
Fig. 43H

2. Let children decorate helmets made from large plastic milk bottles. (They fit a child's head perfectly.) Have different sizes and colors of stars to be glued on helmets. (See fig. 43G.)

3. Have children paint 2 large cardboard boxes to use for mission control panels. (See fig. 43H.)

Snack

Eat dehydrated fruits such as peaches, apricots, pears, prunes like the astronauts eat. Soak some in water to see the difference.

Fine Motor

1. Give children a "rocket control board" with buttons to push, dials to turn, etc. (See fig. 43I.)
2. Let children glue dials and knobs to an outlined control board.
3. Let children trace around letters "SPACE SHIP" for the rocket in Games.

Games

For dramatic play, provide a round card table with cone shape taped to it. Cover table leaving a place to enter. Put one control board inside, other on another part of room near table. Children pretend to be in rocket wearing helmets and oxygen tanks on their backs. (See fig. 43J.)

Fig. 43J

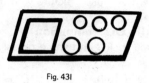

Fig. 43I

Storytelling

Make up a story about how fast you can go in a rocket. Let each child tell where he wants to go "fast!"

Gross Motor

Let children pretend to be rockets. Let them squat down and as you count down, "10, 9, 8, 7, 6, 5, 4, 3, 2, 1," stretch up and jump.

Cognitive

1. Have the children match buttons for control board.
2. Have the children count parts of the control board.

Enrichment

Make a collection of pictures taken from space or of the astronauts. Have children glue on a large mural.

Field Trip

Visit a museum or planetarium if possible.

Related Parenting Materials

Cansler, Dot. **THE HOMESTRETCH.** Winston-Salem, NC 27113-5128: Kaplan Press, 1983.

Related Materials

TEACHING PICTURES. Winston-Salem, NC 27113-5128: Kaplan Press, 1983.
STORY SEQUENCE CARDS I, II. Winston-Salem, NC 27113-5128: Kaplan Press, 1983.
SEWING CARDS I, II, III. Winston-Salem, NC 27113-5128: Kaplan Press, 1983.

Unit 44: Seashore

A developmental assessment should determine the functional levels of each child. Individual expectations are based on the assessment results.

Lesson 1: Beach Sand

Unit Group Lesson

1. **Match Concrete Objects**
   Present two containers of beach sand. Say, "This is beach sand." Ask each child in turn to put the beach sand with the beach sand. Present containers of irrelevant materials such as dirt, flour, etc. from which (s)he must select beach sand to match. Gradually increase the number of irrelevant materials presented.

2. **Discriminate Objects**
   Present containers of several materials. Have each child touch the beach sand in response to verbal direction, "Touch the beach sand."

3. **Match Pictures**
   Present several pictures of common objects. Have each child match the picture of the beach sand.

4. **Discriminate Pictures**
   Present a group of several unrelated pictures of objects. Have each child touch the picture of the beach sand in response to verbal direction, "Touch the beach sand."

5. **Figure-Ground**
   Present a "busy" picture with visual distractions. Ask each child to find the beach sand.

6. **Visual Closure**
   Partially cover each of several pictures with paper. Ask each child to find the picture of the beach sand.

7. **Function**
   Ask, "What do we do with beach sand?"

8. **Association**
   Ask, "What goes with the beach sand?" Use pictures or objects including pail, shovel, etc. with several unrelated objects or pictures.

9. **Imitate Verbalization**
   Present beach sand and ask, "What is this? Say, 'Beach sand.'." The child will imitate "Beach sand."

10. **Verbalize Label**
    Present beach sand and ask, "What is this?" The child will respond, "Beach sand."

11.   **Concept Enrichment**

Discuss the beach, water, shells, etc. Discuss what sand feels like. Are there other materials that feel similar? Talk about how sand is different from dirt. Can you plant potatoes in sand? Can you dig a hole better in sand or dirt? Why? Which can the wind blow more easily?

Music

1.   Sing to the tune of "By the Sea, By the Sea, By the Beautiful Sea":
>   On the beach, on the beach
>   On the sandy beach
>   You and me, you and me
>   Oh how happy we'll be.

2.   Dress in beach hats, sunglasses etc. Dance to "Beach" rock music. (Songs of the Beach Boys made about swimming and surfing, etc.)

Art

Fig. 44A

1.   Have children make sand sculptures. Let them pack wet sand into containers and turn over for sculpture. Use wet "dribbled" sand to enhance the design.
2.   Wet sand surface. Make smooth by pulling a ruler over it. Let children use different tools to make designs - forks, sticks, shells, potato mashers or special sand "combs" cut from wood or cardboard. (See fig. 44A.)
3.   Have each child make a hand or foot impression in sand and fill with plaster of paris. In about an hour the impression can be removed.
4.   Begin a seashore mural with a sandy beach. Have the children paint on large paper and sprinkle with sand. When dry hang on wall at child level.

Fig. 44B

Snack

Eat "sand" cookies (sugar cookies with wheat germ topping).

Fine Motor

1.   Have the children make a sand painting. Have them spread glue and sprinkle with sand mixed with different colors of powdered tempera.
2.   Make sandpaper letters, numbers and shapes for children to feel.
3.   Spread colorful terrarium sand on the bottom of a shoe box lid. Let children make letters or designs in the sand.
4.   Have the children pour sand from one container to another.
5.   Prepare large circles with dots in the center. Have the children make colorful beach balls from the circles by drawing lines and coloring between the lines. (See fig. 44B.)
6.   Paint eyes and mouth on child's fist to make it look like it is a sand crab. Let the sand crab travel across the sand to find objects in the sand such as shells, boats, pebbles, etc. You can say, "The sand crab crawls to get the shell." "The sand crab crawls to pick up the boat." (See fig. 44C.)

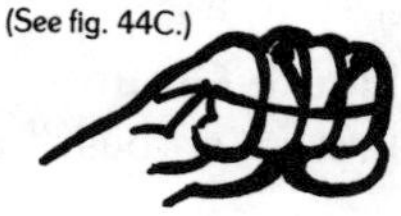

Fig. 44C

Games

1.   Plant "treasures" in the sand and have children dig or sift for them. Partially hide the "treasures" and let children guess what they are. Gradually reveal item until the children can identify it.
2.   Designate a place on the playground to be the "beach"; another part to be the ocean. Play beach games and pretend to "see" things in the ocean, such as ships, dolphins, whales, etc.

Storytelling

1.   Listen to a record that has beach sounds on it. Try to identify the sounds.
2.   Tell this story of a beach ball who did not like sand. Let the children figure out a solution for the ball.
>   *"Benny Beach Ball did not like the gritty feeling of sand. When he got wet in the ocean, the sand would stick to him and make him very heavy. It also poked into his skin. It was hard for him to bounce when he was heavy with sand and the sand dug into his skin."*

Ask the children for suggestions to help Benny Beach Ball.

Gross Motor

Use sand bags to make an obstacle course. Have the children help make the sand bags by filling plastic locking bags with sand and putting them inside cloth bags to make them less slippery. Then have everyone make the obstacle course.

Cognitive
1. Have children identify FULL and EMPTY by observing containers which are empty or filled with sand.
2. Have each child use his sandpaper letters to spell his name.
3. Place seashells and pebbles from the beach in a sand table. Talk about how they wash up on the sand. Sort out the seashells according to type (Use 3, 6, 8, or 10 types of shells according to the developmental level of the child).

Enrichment
1. Spread sand and small nails on table top (in box or lid) and move magnet slowly through mixture. Note that sand is not attracted to the magnet, but the nails are.
2. Have children sort small containers of materials by feel. Use materials such as sand, salt, flour, powder, sugar, confectioners sugar, pebbles, small shells, etc. Notice that sand, sugar and salt feel similar as do powder, flour, and confectioners sugar.

Field Trip
1. Take a walk to find "sandy" places.
2. Go to a park to play in a sandpile.

Lesson 2:   Shell

Unit Group Lesson

1. **Match Concrete Objects**
   Present two shells. Say, "This is a shell." Ask each child in turn to put the shell with the shell. Gradually increase number of irrelevant objects from which (s)he must select shell to match.

2. **Discriminate Objects**
   Present several objects. Have each child touch the shell in response to verbal direction, "Touch the shell."

3. **Match Pictures**
   Present several pictures of common objects. Have each child match the picture of the shells.

4. **Discriminate Pictures**
   Present a group of several unrelated pictures of objects. Have each child touch the picture of the shell in response to verbal direction, "Touch the shell."

5. **Figure-Ground**
   Present a "busy" picture with visual distractions. Ask each child to find the shell.

6. **Visual Closure**
   Partially cover each of several pictures with paper. Ask each child to find the picture of the shell.

7. **Function**
   Ask, "What do we do with a shell?"

8. **Association**

Ask, "What goes with the shell?" Use pictures or objects including beach sand, fish, bathing suit, etc. with several unrelated objects or pictures.

9. **Imitate Verbalization**

Present a shell and ask, "What is this? Say, 'Shell'." The child will imitate "Shell."

10. **Verbalize Label**

Present a shell and ask, "What is this?" The child will respond, "Shell."

11. **Concept Enrichment**

Look at different types of seashells. Talk about creatures who live in the shells especially hermit crabs who borrow unused shells.

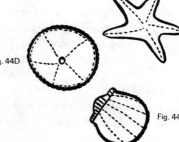

Fig. 44E

Fig. 44D

Music

Sing to the tune of "By the Sea, By the Sea, By the Beautiful Sea":

On the beach, on the beach
On the sandy beach
Shells you'll see, shells you'll see
Oh how happy you'll be.

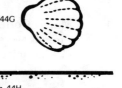

Fig. 44F

Art
1. Have each child make a shell collage using real shells or pictures of shells.
2. Draw a sand dollar. Have children trace lines, cut out and add to seashore mural begun in Lesson #1 Art #4. (See fig. 44D.)
3. Draw a starfish. Have children trace dots, and color. Cut around and add to seashore mural. (See fig. 44E.)
4. Make shell designs and have the children complete them and add them to the seashore mural. (See fig. 44F.)
5. Provide starfish shapes and have the children glue beans on them.

Fig 44G

Snack

Eat snack out of a half shell.

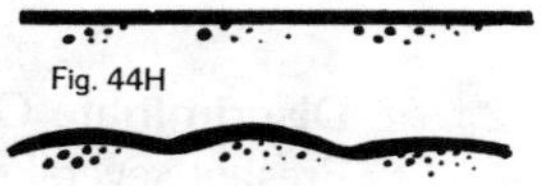

Fine Motor
1. Have the children complete shells. See Art #4 today.
2. Have the children open and close a shell. (See fig. 44G.)
3. Have the children line up tiny shells on a seashore which is provided for them. (See fig. 44H.)
4. Place shells in a tub. Let the children play with shells in water.

Fig. 44H

Games
1. Play the shell game. Have the children guess which shell has the object under it. Start with two shells and then use three. Move them slowly so children can follow the movements.
2. Put a hermit crab in the science area of the class.

Storytelling

Make up a story about a hermit crab looking for a new shell and the adventures which he has.

Gross Motor

Simulate the motion of the ocean water in and out of a shellfish's mouth by playing "In and Out My Window." Have the children form a circle, hold hands and keep them high to form other shells. The "leader" child goes in and out the "shellfish's mouth" in sequence around the circle.

Cognitive
1. Have the children sort shells by type, with or without a guide, on the different trays. The activity is higher level without the guide. Remember to work from greater to lesser differences depending upon child's level.

2. Have the children sort shells by size as above.
3. Shell Sequences: Have the children match a sequence of shells glued on a piece of heavy paper. (Pictures may also be used). For example: a clam shell, scallop shell, mollusk shell are placed in that order and child places the same beneath each one in the model.
4. Study the concepts OPEN and CLOSED by looking at shells which are opened and shells which are closed.
5. Place a shell on a table and others in a cloth bag. Have each child feel the shells in the bag to find all which are shaped like the cue. This activity can be done with one shell in the bag and other objects.

Enrichment
1. Provide a book of shell pictures and a box of shells. Have children match the shells to the pictures and tell why they are alike.
2. Have children bring shells to make a class "collection."
3. Together Activity: Hang a fish net from ceiling or drape on bulletin board. Have the children make stuffed fish, star fish, octopus, etc. from balled up paper, paper, yarn or string to put in the fish net.

Field Trip
1. Visit a local seafood restaurant decorated with shells.
2. Visit a museum exhibiting a shell collection.

Visitor
Invite a collector to bring a shell collection.

Lesson 3: Fishing Pole

Unit Group Lesson

1. **Match Concrete Objects**
   Present two fishing poles. Say, "This is a fishing pole." Ask each child in turn to put the fishing pole with the fishing pole. Gradually increase number of irrelevant objects from which (s)he must select fishing pole to match.

2. **Discriminate Objects**
   Present several objects. Have each child touch the fishing pole in response to verbal direction, "Touch the fishing pole."

3. **Match Pictures**
   Present several pictures of common objects. Have each child match the picture of the fishing pole.

4. **Discriminate Pictures**
   Present a group of several unrelated pictures of objects. Have each child touch the picture of the fishing pole in response to verbal direction, "Touch the fishing pole."

5. **Figure-Ground**
   Present a "busy" picture with visual distractions. Ask each child to find the fishing pole.

6. **Visual Closure**
   Partially cover each of several pictures with paper. Ask each child to find the picture of the fishing pole.

7. **Function**
   Ask, "What do we do with a fishing pole?"

8. **Association**

Ask, "What goes with the fishing pole?" Use pictures or objects including fish, hook, fishing line, etc. with several unrelated objects or pictures.

9. **Imitate Verbalization**

Present a fishing pole and ask, "What is this? Say, 'Fishing pole'." The child will imitate "Fishing pole."

10. **Verbalize Label**

Present a fishing pole and ask, "What is this?" The child will respond, "Fishing pole."

11. **Concept Enrichment**

Discuss other ways and places to catch fish besides with a fishing pole at the seashore.

Music

Sing "Three Little Fishes":
Way down yonder in an iddy biddy pool
Swam three fishes and a momma fishy, too.
Swim, said the momma fishy, swim if you can
And they swam, and they swam, all over the dam.
Boop-boop-didden doturn what-un shoo
Boop-boop-didden doturn what-un shoo
Boop-boop-didden doturn what-un shoo
And they swam and they swam all over the dam.

Art
1. Make a class mural. Lay a large piece of paper on the floor. Tie brushes to fishing pole lines. Let children dip them in paint and then paint on mural.
2. Cut out fish shapes and let children sponge paint the fish shapes.
3. Continue the mural begun in Lesson #1 Art #4 by having the children cut out pictures of people fishing and placing them on the mural.

Fig. 44l

Snack
1. Eat fish.
2. Eat goldfish crackers.

Fine Motor
1. Have the children catch floating sponge fish with clothespins.
2. Let the children wind a reel.
3. Make a fishing pole out of a dowel and string. Use a paper clip for a hook. Let the children help tie string. One child fishes and another child clips a fish onto the line.
4. Draw an octopus face on each child's fist and have his fingers move across the sand table like an octopus.
5. Give each child a picture with boy or girl holding a pole. Have him draw lines to water and draw fish on line. (See fig. 44l.)

Games
1. Play "Go Fishing." Put a magnet on a string attached to a pole. Have the children catch poster board fish with paper clips on them.
2. Hide fish which are tied to the end of a long string. Have children hold string in hands and follow it to the fish.

Storytelling

Have the children make up a story about a little boy who went fishing and put all the wrong things on his hook. Have each child name things fish do not eat. The last child says "worm" and the fish gets caught.

Gross Motor
1. Let the children fish for exercises. Write activities (jump 10 ft., hop on left foot, jump two feet, etc.) on fish and let children use fishing pole and magnet to select their activity.
2. Teach the children to cast a line (with a weight but NO HOOK).

Cognitive
1. Spread a variety of fish made from different colors and textures in a "lake." Give a child a fishing pole with a magnet and have him catch the blue fish, green fish, rough fish, shiny fish, etc. (See fig. 44J.)

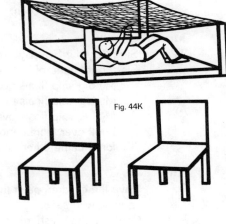

Fig. 44J

2. Continue the above activity but change the concepts to "Catch the fish beside the blue fish. below the yellow fish, etc."
3. Match different shapes and colors of fish.

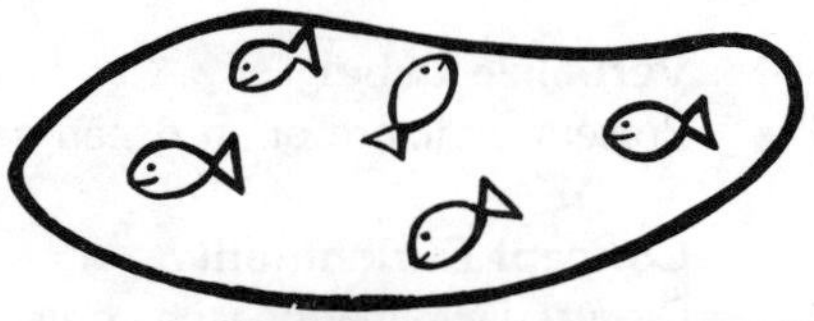

Enrichment
1. Have the children do fish net weaving. Tack fish net to the legs of a table turned upside down and have children weave strips of cloth through the net as they lie on pillow underneath it. Have other children sit in chairs to wait their turn. (See fig. 44K.)

Fig. 44K

2. Make a giant fish shape and put it on a table. Have the children cover the fish with scales they have made by tearing small pieces of paper. (The fish may be divided into a part for each child to do with his name on it, and he must find his own name). (See fig. 44L.)

Field Trip
1. Go to the fish market. Talk about fish caught on poles, fish caught in nets.
2. Visit an aquarium in a fish store.

Fig. 44L

Visitor
Have a fisherman bring his tackle box and fishing pole to show to the children.

Lesson 4: Ocean

Unit Group Lesson

1. **Match Pictures**
    Present two pictures of the ocean. Say, "This is an ocean." Ask each child in turn to put the ocean with the ocean. Gradually increase number of irrelevant objects from which (s)he must select ocean to match.

2. **Discriminate Pictures**
    Present a group of several unrelated pictures of objects. Have each child touch the picture of the ocean in response to verbal direction, "Touch the ocean."

3. **Figure-Ground**
    Present a "busy" picture with visual distractions. Ask each child to find the ocean.

4. **Visual Closure**
    Partially cover each of several pictures with paper. Ask each child to find the picture of the ocean.

5. **Function**
    Ask, "What do we do at the ocean?"

6. **Association**

   Ask, "What goes with the ocean?" Use pictures or objects including sand, bathing suit, shells, etc. with several unrelated objects or pictures.

7. **Imitate Verbalization**

   Present a picture of an ocean and ask, "What is this? Say, 'Ocean'." The child will imitate "Ocean."

8. **Verbalize Label**

   Present a picture of an ocean and ask, "What is this?" The child will respond, "Ocean."

9. **Concept Enrichment**

   Discuss facts that oceans contain salt water and cover most of the earth. Explain that fish, whales, plants live in the ocean.

Music
1. Sing "By the Sea, By the Sea, By the Beautiful Sea."
2. Sing to the tune of "My Bonnie Lies Over the Ocean":
   My big ship floats over the ocean.
   My big ship floats over the sea.
   My big ship floats over the ocean.
   Look over there...and you'll see...
   (Children name other things that can be seen on the ocean such as whale, fish, submarine, etc.)

Art
1. Have the children paint the inside of shoe box tops sea blue, glue on shells, paint with glue, and sprinkle with sand.
2. Continue the seashore mural with ocean waves. Have the children paint ocean waves with blue paint. Some children may make boats to add to the ocean.
3. Provide blue and white paint at the easels today and have the children paint pictures of oceans. (See fig. 44M.)

Fig 44M

Snack
Drink juice poured from thermos bottles; eat "picnic" from paper bags.

Fine Motor
1. Have the children make beach balls by cutting construction paper wedges that fit together on the back of a paper plate. Let children combine colors and glue in place for three dimensional beach balls. Use on the beach mural.
2. Have the children pattern trace scales or put scales all over fish. (See fig. 44P.)
3. Bulletin Board: Have children cut blue strips of ocean (drawn by teacher). Arrange overlapping on bulletin board. Children can add boats, swimmers, or a fish. (See fig. 44N.)

Fig. 44N

Fig. 44P

Games
1. Pin fish shapes on children in different colors and sizes. Spread a sheet on the floor and have some children "get in the ocean." Have other children "catch" fish by following specific directions given by you or a child such as "catch the yellow fish." From the edge of the sheet without getting in the water, the child tries to "catch" the "fish" by throwing a nerf ball.
2. Outdoor Fishing. . .Some children are fish, some are fishermen. The fishermen chase and tag fish and take them to a designated place until all the fish are caught.

Storytelling
Make up a story about a little boat lost in a big ocean. The boat sailed and sailed and sailed and sailed, but never saw land. One day a big storm blew the boat to some land.

Gross Motor

1.　　Twist like ocean waves. Play a record of ocean waves during the activity.
2.　　Get on the floor and imitate swimming. Do a frog stroke to teacher's rhythmic in-out commands.

Cognitive

1.　　Sort ocean things (shells, seaweed, boats, etc.) from non-ocean things.
2.　　Taste salty ocean water.

Enrichment

1.　　Which can water move more easily - sand or dirt? Try an "experiment" with sand and dirt. Pour water over them side by side and see what happens.
2.　　Oceans are made up of salt water. Let the children taste the salt water and try other things which are salty. Have them name all the things which are salty and make a salty collage.
3.　　Things float more easily in salt water. Let the children float objects in regular water and salt water to determine which things will float in one but not the other. (Make a strong salt solution). Children with cuts on their hands should not put their hands in the salt water.

Lesson 5: Bathing Suit

Unit Group Lesson

1.　　**Match Concrete Objects**
Present two bathing suits. Say, "This is a bathing suit." Ask each child in turn to put the bathing suit with the bathing suit. Gradually increase number of irrelevant objects from which (s)he must select bathing suit to match.

2.　　**Discriminate Objects**
Present several objects. Have each child touch the bathing suit in response to verbal direction, "Touch the bathing suit."

3.　　**Match Pictures**
Present several pictures of common objects. Have each child match the picture of the bathing suits.

4.　　**Discriminate Pictures**
Present a group of several unrelated pictures of objects. Have each child touch the picture of the bathing suit in response to verbal direction, "Touch the bathing suit."

5.　　**Figure-Ground**
Present a "busy" picture with visual distractions. Ask each child to find the bathing suit.

6.　　**Visual Closure**
Partially cover each of several pictures with paper. Ask each child to find the picture of the bathing suit.

7.　　**Function**
Ask, "What do we do in a bathing suit?"

8.　　**Association**
Ask, "What goes with the bathing suit?" Use pictures or objects including beach sand, ocean, shells, etc. with several unrelated objects or pictures.

9. **Imitate Verbalization**

Present a bathing suit and ask, "What is this? Say, 'Bathing suit'." The child will imitate "Bathing suit."

10. **Verbalize Label**

Present a bathing suit and ask, "What is this?" The child will respond, "Bathing suit."

11. **Concept Enrichment**

Discuss boy and girl bathing suits. Talk about one- and two- piece bathing suits. Look at old time pictures when everyone wore bathing suits that covered most of the body. They were very heavy when wet.

Music

1. Sing "I am Going Swimming" to the tune of "Mary Had A Little Lamb":

   I am going swimming,
   Swimming, swimming, swimming.
   I am going swimming,
   And this is what I'll wear.   *(Hold up a bathing suit.)*

2. Sing to the tune of "This Is the Way We Wash Our Clothes":

   Verse 1: "Put on my swim suit...on a hot summer day."
   This is the way I put on my swim suit,   *(Pantomime motions.)*
   Put on my swim suit, put on my swim suit.
   Repeat
   On a hot summer day.

   Verse 2: Going to swim...on a hot summer day.
   This is the way I am going to swim,   *(Pantomime motions.)*
   Going to swim, going to swim.
   Repeat
   On a hot summer day.

Art

1. Have each child make a collage of beach clothes cut from magazines.
2. Have each child decorate construction paper with sponge prints or shell prints to make pretend beach towels and use in Fine Motor #2.
3. Color swim suits done in Fine Motor #1.

Snack

1. Eat round cookies and call them beach ball cookies.
2. Wear bathing suits to snack.

Fine Motor

Fig. 440

1. On a ditto sheet, have each child connect the dots of a bathing suit. Then use in Art #3.
2. Have the children make pretend beach towels by fringing construction paper decorated in Art #1 today.
3. Let the children glue bathing suits cut out of fabric onto paper and let each child draw the rest of the person.
4. Make paper dolls with swim suits and let the children make stripes, dots, and designs on suits. (See fig. 440.)

Games

1. Place a variety of bathing suits in the dress up area of the classroom.
2. Play a squirt game: Outside the teacher squirts the child wearing the "green swim suit," the "striped swim suit," etc. The teacher announces who will be squirted or may just want their feet wet.

Storytelling

Flannel board. Display a variety of swim suits (big, little, red, blue, bikini, etc.) Pretend to own a swim suit store. Have the children come to the store to buy swim suits and describe the suit they want. Give it to them after description.

Gross Motor

1. Go swimming at a local neighborhood, private or YMCA pool. (Some motels will let groups swim in their pools).
2. Set up a plastic wading pool on the playground. Let children swim in it.
3. Have the children change into their swimsuits and squirt them with a hose while they run and race around.
4. Have the children wear bathing suits and stand in a circle outside. Let them toss a wet sponge to each other.
5. Have children run in a circle, through a plastic wading pool. When lifeguard blows whistle, the person caught in pool is out.

Cognitive

1. Make two-piece swim suits of different colors. Have the children match top to bottom.
2. Sort seashore from non-seashore things.
3. Have the children match color names to correct swim suit. Have each child work on colors at his readiness level. Use color coding (the color name is written in its color) for some children.

Enrichment

1. Talk about places you wear a swim suit. Show weather pictures of spring, fall, winter, summer. Talk about when you wear a swim suit. Why?
2. Have a pile of fabrics. Let children pick out good fabric for swim suits and tell why.

Field Trip

Go swimming in local pool or a motel pool.

Visitor

Invite a lifeguard to talk about safe games to play in the water and water safety.

Related Parenting Materials

Cansler, Dot. **THE HOMESTRETCH.** Winston-Salem, NC 27113-5128: Kaplan Press, 1983.

Related Materials

TEACHING PICTURES. Winston-Salem, NC 27113-5128: Kaplan Press, 1983.
STORY SEQUENCE CARDS I, II. Winston-Salem, NC 27113-5128: Kaplan Press, 1983.
SEWING CARDS I, II, III. Winston-Salem, NC 27113-5128: Kaplan Press, 1983.

Appendix I - Methods and Principles

INTRODUCTION TO METHODS AND PRINCIPLES

This section of the curriculum guide contains descriptions of some of the principles on which teaching is based. These basic principles on which good teaching are based include the following:

1. Preparing Instructional Objectives
2. Task Analysis of skills being taught.
3. Error-free Learning Techniques including Positive Reinforcement for assured success for each child.

PREPARING INSTRUCTIONAL OBJECTIVES (Adapted from Robert F. Mager)

In writing education objectives three questions must be answered:
  (1) What is it that we must teach? (BEHAVIOR)
  (2) What materials and procedures will work best to teach what we wish to teach? (CONDITIONS)
  (3) How will we know when we have taught it? (CRITERIA)

Before writing these objectives, it's important to understand the terminology. Some terms used include:

Behavior - refers to any observable activity displayed by a learner (student).

Terminal behavior - refers to the behavior you would like your learner to be able to demonstrate at the time your influence over him ends or when you have finished teaching him.

Criterion - is an acceptable level of performance (a test) by which behavior is evaluated.

Objective - an intent communicated by a statement describing a proposed change in learner behavior; a statement of what the learner will be able to do when he has successfully completed a learning experience; a description of a pattern of behavior we want the learner to be able to demonstrate.

Steps in writing instructional objectives:

1. Identify the behavior specifically by name and specify the behavior which will be accepted as evidence that the learner has achieved the objective. What will the learner be DOING and what will the teacher be OBSERVING when the student has achieved the objective? (Be sure to use a verb in describing the behavior; the student will be able to "choose," "identify," "point to," etc.

2. Try to further define the desired behavior by describing the important conditions under which the behavior will be expected to occur. State the conditions you will impose upon the learner when he is demonstrating his mastery of the objectives. Ask these questions:
   (a) What will be provided to the learner? Example: Given the A.A.M.D., definition. . .
   (b) What will the learner be denied? Example: Without looking at the book. . .
   (c) Are there any skills which you are specifically not trying to develop? Does the objective exclude such skills? Example: Given the following job application, print, (do not write). . .

3. Specify the criteria of acceptable performance by describing how well (or how much, or in what amount of time) the learner must perform to be considered acceptable. Example: Given the following list of 25 words the student must be able to correctly read 20 of the words.

TASK ANALYSIS IN THE PRESCHOOL AND FOR THE HANDICAPPED

Assuming that learning represents a process of change in the learner's behavior, an examination of teacher procedures for effecting change seems appropriate. No longer can the teacher be a combination of educational philosopher and social worker. The role of instructor calls for a highly trained technician who is responsible for a unique contribution to the child's welfare - that of teaching him essential concepts and skills (Engelmann, 1969).

Task analysis represents a logical educational technique for effecting change in conceptual and skill development. The process of Task Analysis involves several basic steps:

1. Identification of appropriate behavioral objectives.
2. The break-down of objectives into constituent concepts.
3. Sequential development of tasks.
4. Manipulation of variables.
5. Evaluation.

Identification of Appropriate Learning Objectives.

Mager (1962) defines an objective as "an intent communicated by a statement describing a proposed change in a learner - a statement of what the learner is to be like when he has successfully completed a learning experience."

Since the teacher becomes the formulator of appropriate objectives, the first pre requisite involves sophistication in knowledge of subject matter. In the preschool for handicapped children, the normative data supplied by experts of child development (Gesell, 1940) provide a hierarchy of tasks which may become possible objectives for the individual student. The appropriateness of these tasks is determined by the child's developmental level, the task's meaningful relationship to the learner's environment, and the likelihood of reinforcement in daily life. For instance, the communication "hi" may be expressed in several developmental levels (gesture, utterance and gesture, or verbalization). This task is relevant to all environmental situations, and certainly will be reinforced by those about him.

A necessary component of the formulation of objectives involves the pre-test. The pre-evaluation may necessitate adjustment on instructional objectives - deleting some, adding some, or modifying criteria. Without pre-assessment, a teacher may run several risks. He may attempt to teach competencies already possessed by his learner or assume pre-requisite skills or entry behaviors not in his student's pre-instruction repertoire (Popham, 1970).

The identification of the specific learner behaviors that will indicate the attainment of certain skills aids the teacher in: (1) efficient evaluation of her strategies; (2) a sound basis for selecting appropriate materials; (3) effective instructional methodology; (4) the reduction of incorrect or ambiguous interpretation of objectives; and (5) evaluation of pupil progress. The statement of precise behavioral objectives is essential to an effective teaching program. Illusive, broad, vague objectives hamper specific instructional planning. As Mager points out, "the machinist does not select a tool until he knows what operation he intends to perform."

Breakdown of Objectives Into Constituent Concepts.

A behavioral analysis of the task to be taught demands the breakdown of objectives into specific sub-components. A rigorous analysis of each task includes the identification of the pre requisites to performance. What behaviors will demonstrate the attainment of this concept? These behaviors usually will depend upon the successful mastery of one or more sub-objectives. Task analysis prompts examination of the child's existing skills which can be utilized. The teacher must consider how isolation of the task can be achieved to insure the prevention of assumptions and conceptual leaps; what sub-components of this task are appropriate for this individual child?

Sequential Development of Tasks.

Once the specific behaviors comprising the sub-objectives of the task have been identified, the curriculum designer must decide on the order of presentation. The teacher must determine the "planned sequence of experiences leading to proficiency in terms of stimulus-response relationships." The term "planned sequence" implies that the teacher determines "not only what experiences the student should have - but also in what order they should occur." (Espech and Williams, 1967.)

Gagne (1967) suggests that comple cognitive behaviors are invariably composed of simpler tasks, and that attainment of these tasks is necessary before the complex behavior can be demonstrated. Gagne has analyzed behavior into a hierarchy proceeding from the simplest kind of learning through the most complex. He hypothesizes that for learning any given task a structure exists. This structure includes the critical subtasks that a learner masters on his way to criterion performance. It is instructionally wise to attempt to identify subtasks for any instructional objective in order to avoid failures in mastery. (Popham, 1970.) Determination of the hierarchy of these subtasks is the critical issue of sequencing, and it is in this area where teachers frequently err. The development of a logical, orderly, analytical and systematic sequence of instruction requires a methodical approach to design.

Manipulation of Variables.

A variable is a behavior or feature of the environment that is subject to change. The teacher's challenge is the scientific manipulation of variables affecting learning to increase the probability of evoking the correct response. In teaching the retarded preschooler, the variables of size, texture, position, color, novelty, shape, brightness, material, function, symmetry or number may be used in cueing. Obviously the use of the order and number of variables is crucial in determining sequential development or ability to focus on the relevant task.

A stimulus is anything that elicits, or results in, a reaction from an organism. A response is, quite simply, the reaction to the stimulus. (Epech, 1967.) The teacher's responsibility is to manipulate the variables of the stimuli to evoke the desired response. This requires an analysis of the strength and type of responses elicited by various stimuli.

The preschool handicapped child may have to be taught to attend to the relevant stimulus dimensions. To accomplish this, it is essential to keep the relevant dimension constant from task to task. The manipulation of variables can be used to aid in this focus. For instance, in teaching a color to the handicapped preschooler, the isolation of the task is achieved by teaching only one color at a time. Red may be presented in various forms of size, number, texture, shape, etc., but the variable which remains constant and to which the child ultimately attends is color.

Since the handicapped preschooler utilizes the visual discrimination modality in many of his learning experiences, the studies of Zeaman (1960) on visual discrimination learning of the retarded provides significant insight for consideration in the manipulation of variable. Here is a summary of his conclusions:

1. The retardate's discrimination learning is mediated, not by verbal behavior, but by attention to relevant stimulus dimensions.
2. Retardates prefer to attend to position.
3. Their attention focuses (when it does) on broad classes of stimuli, on whole dimensions, not specific cues. They attend to color, not red and green, to form, not square and triangle.
4. Approach tendencies to positive cues are formed more rapidly early in learning than avoidance of negative cues.
5. The nature of stimuli provides a powerful determinant of retardate visual discrimination learning:
   a. Stimulus novelty is a discriminable aspect of stimuli that can facilitate discrimination.
   b. The absolute size of stimuli and figure-to-ground relationship controls discrimination learning of colors and forms. The bigger the better.
   c. Form is a stronger dimension than color.
   d. Some aspects of form, such as symmetry, make for good discrimination.
   e. Three-dimensional figures are more easily discriminated than otherwise equivalent two-dimensional figures.
   f. Relational cues (such as oddity and similarity) are exceedingly difficult.
   g. Redundancy facilitates. The greater the number of relevant dimensions, the greater the likelihood of learning.
   h. The greater the number of variables, irrelevant dimensions, the poorer the performance.
6. Transfer operations, such as reversal and intra- and extra- dimensional shifts, are sensitive determinants of retardate visual discrimination learning.
7. Pairing the discriminative stimulus with a junk stimulus (multidimensionally different) strengthens the attention to the relevant cue.

This summary of Zeaman's findings can provide a basis for structuring the manipulative variables of the learning task in a hierarchy of steps. With this knowledge the teacher analyzes the relative strength of each stimulus in evoking the desired response and sequences her lesson accordingly.

Evaluation.

A complete analysis of each learning task includes evaluative procedures which measure the effectiveness of the instructional design. Evaluation considers the following questions:

Was the behavioral objective appropriate for this child?
Did the child exhibit an observable change in behavior?
Did he meet the criteria for acceptable performance?
Did the learning materials facilitate focus on the task, or were they too stimulating?

An example of the task-analysis process in the preschool for the handicapped may be seen in the hypothetical objective of teaching the concept square. The behavioral objective states: "When presented with five pairs of stimuli, the learner can visually discriminate and touch the square in response to verbal direction, 'touch square'. Criteria of performance are four correct responses in five trials."

The teacher's first objective is to elicit attending behavior in the learner. No verbal direction is given until the child maintains eye contact with the teacher.

The learning task is then isolated, as the teacher states, "This is square." Superfluous verbalizations are avoided. Any further comment, such as "big, red square," becomes "verbal garbage" (Lawler, 1970), which inhibits focus on the task.

The teacher then models the response as she directs, "Touch square." Already an assumption is made that the child possesses the touching response. If touching behavior is not present in his repertoire of skills, then it becomes a sub-objective.

Attention to the relevant dimension of "square" must now be developed. Initially, multidimensional cues are utilized in developing a hierarchy of responses which insure positive, successful experiences for the child.

A design for the process of discrimination must now be developed by the teacher. Use of three-dimensional, large, colored, novel, carefully-positioned, redundant cues tends to elicit a positive response. Analytical manipulation of the cues will maintain attention to "square." The initial pairing of "square" with a position-cued multi-dimensional junk stimulus represents a low-level task. As the similarity of relevant dimensions increases, the difficulty of the discriminative task increases.

For instance, the discrimination hierarchy may begin with the pairing of a large, red, wooden, textured square, placed near the child, with a small uncolored picture of a line, away from the learner. A higher level of discrimination would present a pair of identically placed pictures - a pencil-drawn square with a pencil-drawn pentagon. Removed are the cues of color, form, texture, size and position. The child must focus on the shape square.

Summary.

With this concept of the teacher as an engineer of instructional design, the responsibility for student learning rests with her ability to set appropriate behavioral objectives, break down these objectives into prerequisite subcomponents, sequence the sub-objectives in a hierarchy of tasks, effectively manipulate the variable to insure a positive response, and objectively evaluate the effectiveness of her lesson.

It is in the task analysis process that the true logic, skill, knowledge, ingenuity, creativity and excitement of teaching the handicapped and preschooler express itself.

Bibliography.

Ellis, Norman R. **INTERNATIONAL REVIEW OF RESEARCH IN MENTAL RETARDATION.** Academic Press, NY: 1966.

Engelmann, Siegfried. **PREVENTING FAILURE IN THE PRIMARY GRADES.** S.R.A., Chicago, IL, 1969.

Espech, James E. and Williams, Bill. **DEVELOPING PROGRAMMED INSTRUCTIONAL MATERIALS.** Fearon Publishers, Palo Alto, California, 1967.

Gesell, Arnold. **THE FIRST FIVE YEARS OF LIFE.** New York: Harper & Row, 1940.

Gibson, Janice T. **EDUCATIONAL PSYCHOLOGY.** Appleton-Century-Crofts, NY, 1968.

Lawler, Julia. "Application of Operant Principles to Education." Paper presented at M.R.T.I. Workshops, Chapel Hill, NC, Nov., 1970.

Mager, Robert F. **PREPARING INSTRUCTIONAL OBJECTIVES.** Fearon Publishers, Inc., Palo Alto, CA, 1962.

Markle, Susan Meyer. **GOOD FRAMES AND BAD.** John Wiley & Sons, Inc., NY, 1969.

Popham, W. James and Baker, Eva L. **SYSTEMATIC INSTRUCTION.** Prentice-Hall, Inc., Englewood Cliffs, NJ, 1970.

Skinner, B.J. Verbal Behavior. Appleton-Century-Crofts, NY, 1957.

Zeaman, D. and House, B.J. "An attention theory of retardate discrimination" In N.R. Ellis (Ed.), **HANDBOOK OF MENTAL DEFICIENCY,** McGraw Hill, NY, 1963.

TOILET TRAINING: TASK ANALYSIS

Assumption: That the child is phsycially able to control the muscles involved.

   In shaping the toileting behavior we break the task down in order to insure success for the child and opportunity for reward. This task breakdown moves from the last step in the sequence to the next-to-last, and so on. The following is a step by step routine for training. It should be noted that the untrained child should be taken to the bathroom frequently; especially after certain activities such as eating times, long walks, play time, nap time, and any other times when success is likely.

Step 1.   Some children may need a reward for going into the bathroom or approaching the toilet without resistance.

Step 2.   Once in the bathroom, assist the child in sitting on the toilet and reward him for sitting a few minutes, whether or not he performs. If, indeed, he does perform, reward him with praise or food or a combination as soon as evacuation occurs so that he becomes aware of the desired behavior. This, of course, means that you do not leave the child sitting on the toilet, because close observation and immediate reinforcement are vital in the training. While sitting opposite the child you may need to offer the child a reward such as a book or toy to establish sitting response.

Step 3.   Now you want the child to seat himself. Accompany him to the toilet and say, "Sit on the toilet, Mary." This will also be programmed so that the child understands your request and seats himself. In the early training sessions you will remain near, ready to reward performance of sitting quietly, and evacuation.

Step 4.   The child is now aware of the desired behavior, is able to sit and performs successfully at least part of the time. You walk the child to the bathroom and begin programming for pulling down pants by decreasing your assistance as the child acquires skills of pulling down part way to completely. Unsnapping, unzipping, or unbuckling are all skills which may need a great deal of training. Don't assume that because the child knows how to sit and what is required after sitting, that he can manipulate his clothing. He could wet his pants while trying frantically to unbuckle his belt!

Step 5.   The child is able to pull down his pants, seat himself, perform; and now you program for manipulating the clothing after toileting everyday. The closures of buttoning, zipping and buckling should be taught at other times during the day until the child acquires these skills. Reward all newly acquired skills as well as those just previously acquired. Note: To achieve the target toileting behavior more quickly, you may want a particular child to wear pants with elasticized waistbands only. This should only be necessary for the child with severe fine motor deficits.

Step 6.   Go to the bathroom door with the child and wait. Reward his behavior; make a big deal out of his independent efforts. The child may still need imediate reinforcement as you approvingly observe these new skills. Flushing the toilet may become a reward.

Step 7.   Program now for taking the child to the bathroom and leaving him with or without the door closed. Be observant and careful to praise the child on leaving the bathroom. You have gradually increased the distance between you and the child.

Step 8.   The child should now be ready to indicate his need to you and to go unassisted to the bathroom. Reward him for initiating the toileting behavior.

Eventually the child will express his need to go to the bathroom when you are outside the school environment, and he should be rewarded for this behavior. Should the child have an accident, change him as soon as you become aware of it so that he becomes accustomed to dry pants and uncomfortable with wet ones. The family should be working with you in this training and should be informed in writing of the precise skill being programmed and the precise techniques and language being used to keep consistency between home and school.

Keep accurate records on the daily routine, the number of successes and the accidents; and if possible, chart the success/accident behaviors. This will give you an accurate and graphic evaluation of your toileting program. Individual charts on the children being trained may be kept on a wall in the bathroom or some other location convenient for immediate recording.

CUTTING WITH SCISSORS: TASK ANALYSIS

Fig. 1A

Prerequisite Skills: Use of tongs and pinching clothespins together.

Use double scissors to help the child get the idea of "how to cut." (See fig. 1A.)

Step 1.   Take long strip of construction paper and partially cut through it. Take double scissors, teacher's fingers in outer holes, child's fingers in inner holes. Make one cut (1 closure of double scissors) and piece falls off strip. Tell child he cut paper and praise him! Do this many times, so child gets lots of practice in cutting motion. (See fig. 1B.)

Step 2.   When child can do this consistently, have him make 2 cuts (2 closures of double scissors) and then pieces fall off strip. Again, reinforce his learning how to cut. Teacher should begin to give less assistance in cutting motion so child learns to do it independently. (See fig. 1C.)

Step 3.   After much practice on Step 2, increase to three cuts or closures of scissors to make piece fall off strip. Move to primary scissors when you think child has mastered the cutting stroke and can make cuts consistently.

Step 4.   Go through Steps 1 - 3 again, using primary scissors. Child does the cutting independently. Teacher may help by holding the strip of paper for child while he makes the cuts.

Step 5.   Then, have child learn to hold paper in one hand and cut with other.

Step 6.   Increase length of cuts till child can cut through whole piece of paper on his own.

Step 7.   This step begins learning to cut on a line. Draw a straight wide line with a magic marker to indicate where to cut. Show the child how to cut on the line. Then child has a turn to cut "on the line." (See fig. 1D.)

Step 8.   Decrease width of line slowly until child can cut approximately on a thick primary pencil line. (See fig. 1E.)

Step 9.   Now have child cut on a very thick curved line drawn with a magic marker. Show him how to turn the paper around with the free hand. (See fig. 1F.)

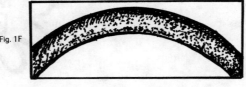

Step 10.   Decrease widths of curved lines gradually. Give lots of practice cutting out magazine pictures. Child can put his "cuttings" in a plastic bag and take them home to show. (See fig. 1G.)

Fig. 1G

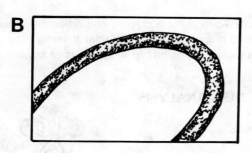

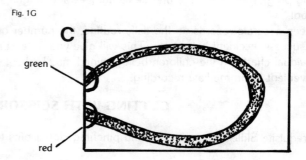

green

red

TASK ANALYSIS OF "NAME READING"

Objective: To be able to visually discriminate and touch child's printed name when shown 5 names including his own.

The breakdown of the objective into sub-objectives for this task would include the following:
1. Read name with no cues.
2. Match name with name with cues.
3. Touch and label name.
4. Visually discriminate name from other names with cues.
5. Match name to name with child's picture attached.
6. Discriminate name from other names with no cues.

The sequencing of the sub-objectives for this task include the following:
1. Touch and label name.
2. Match name to name with child's picture attached (see example).
3. Match name to name with cues.
4. Visually discriminate name from other names with cues.
5. Discriminate printed name with no cues.
6. Discriminate printed name from other names without cues.

Manipulating variables such as size, color, form, and novelty is quite important in teaching this task and evaluation of the results is vital to determine whether the child has achieved the desired goal.

Procedure:
  Choose a symbol for the child. Select something he likes - truck, wagon, doll, flower, etc. Have a different symbol for each child. Write the child's name in the middle of the flower (symbol). Use construction paper to make symbols.

1. Attach a picture of child to the flower under her name. Teacher says, "This says Mary." "Touch Mary." "What did you read?" "What does this say . . . Mary?" (See fig. 1H.)

     Cues:
       Form
       Color - Red
       Size - Big
       Novelty
       Picture
       Symbol

Fig. 1H

2. Both teacher and child have similar flower picture. Give child the flower and label the child's flower and say, "Put Mary on Mary." Model how to do it if child does not understand. (See fig. 1J.)

Cues:
Form
Color
Size
Novelty
Picture
Symbol

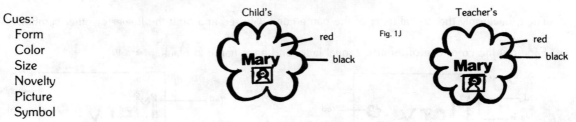

Child's

red

black

Fig. 1J

Teacher's

red

black

Teacher - "Yes, you did it! This says Mary and you read Mary." Give lots of practice here.

3. In this step, have child match his name and symbol to the appopriate name and symbol in a two object discrimination task. The teacher would have a red flower with Mary written on it and a blue truck with Fred written on it.

Cues:
Form
Color
Size
Novelty
Symbol
Cues Faded:
Picture of Child

Repeat above but use 2, then 3 other name and symbols.

4. Use another shape such as circle, triangle, or jigsaw shape. Keep the color of the flower the same. In this case it was red. (See fig. 1K.)

Cues:
Symbol
Size of Symbol
Color of Symbol
Cues Faded:
Form
Picture
Novelty
Color

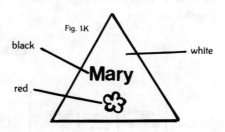

Fig. 1K

black

white

red

Mary

This enables the child to pick out his name because of his symbol. We have paired the name and the symbol. This step may be broken down further by (1) Teacher labeling and modeling: "This says Mary." "Put Mary on Mary." (2) Matching the symbol.

5. Use another shape such as 4" x 7" index card. Color cue the child's name by outlining the black letters with red. The flower remains red. (See fig. 1L.)

Cues:
Symbol
Color of Symbol
Size of Symbol
Cues Faded:
Form
Picture
Novelty
Color

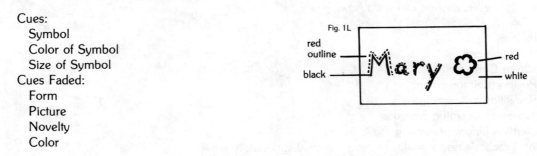

Fig. 1L

red outline

black

Mary

red

white

a. Begin to fade out the red outline cues, starting with the last letter of the name. Continue to use the flower symbol but decrease its size gradually. (See fig. 1M. – fig. 1O.)

b. Then, have only the capital letter of the name cued with red and omit the flower or other symbol. (See fig. 1P.)

6. Fade out the color cue of the first capital letter and have name in black. (See fig. 1Q.)

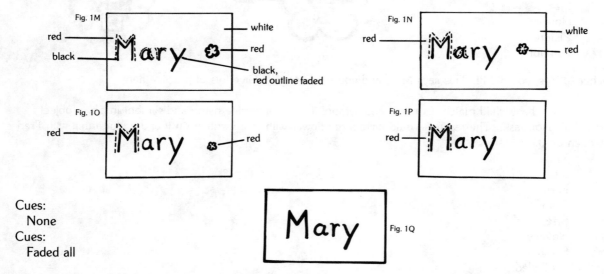

Cues:
  None
Cues:
  Faded all

7. Have child discriminate his own printed name from printed names of other children without cues.

Use this method and apply the index cards on the following, which child sees and uses each day:
  a. Place where child hangs coat.
  b. Chair and/or desk.
  c. Glasses used for snack and lunch (plastic).
  d. Can which holds child's toothbrush and toothpaste.
  e. Crayon box.

ERROR-FREE LEARNING

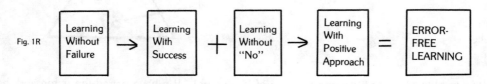

"Error-free Learning" is a unique method for learning and teaching. It is appropriate for all children, but most appropriate for children who are behind in acquiring appropriate age-level skills. The child in a day care center for handicapped children, or the child identified as having developmental lags, can profit most from "error-free free learning." (See fig. 1R.)

Acquisition of skills for teaching in the "Error-free Learning" method requires planning, practice and evaluation. However, anyone can learn how!

Basic Principles
1. Isolate the concept.
2. Move from Concrete to Abstract.
3. Use Positive Reinforcement.
4. Use Repetition in teaching.
5. Develop Short Learning Sessions.
6. Get attention before presenting the task.
7. It is the Teacher's responsibility to have the child succeed.

Four Specific Techniques: **MODELING**
 PROMPTING
 CUEING
 POSITIVE REINFORCEMENT

Unit: Body Parts

Task #3: "Touch nose"

1. **MODELING**
 Teacher demonstrates what she wants child to do.

> Task ► "touch nose"

Example of modeling: Teacher would touch her own nose.

The teacher is a model and demonstrates exactly what the child is expected to do.

2. **PROMPTING**
 Teacher gives physical assistance in discriminating the appopriate response.

> Task ► "touch nose"

Child doesn't know what to do. He sits there or starts to touch his eyes.

Example of prompting: Teacher takes child's hand/fingers and puts finger on child's nose.

The teacher supplies the child with the answer by physically moving his hand and fingers to touch his nose.

3. **CUEING**
 Teacher gives cue or hint to child as to the correct response. Some cues are: size, shape, position, number, proximity, junk stimuli, pointing with finger.

> Task ► "touch nose"

Example of cueing: Teacher makes a mask of construction paper and puts it over her face. The only cut out part of the mask is the hole for the nose.

Cues given by the teacher in this instance would be: position (of nose through mask over face); shape (of nose); size (of nose); color (of nose) and no other distracting drawing or holes in the mask.

4. **POSITIVE REINFORCEMENT**
 That reward which follows a behavior and makes that behavior more likely to happen again.

Two types of positive reinforcement that all teachers can use:

Verbal	Non-Verbal
"Wow - great work!"	smile
"That's the way."	hug
"Good working."	handshake
"Just right!"	clapping
"I like the way you did that."	nodding of head
"What a smart girl!"	pat on back, shoulder, hand
"You're really getting big now."	wink
"I like the way you're sitting."	
(name appropriate behavior	
"Good writing."	

POSITIVE REINFORCEMENT
CATCH THE CHILD BEING GOOD!

By David G. Tinsley, student and John P. Ora, Assistant Professor, Department of Psychology, George Peabody College for Teachers, Nashville, Tenn.

Every day the classroom teacher faces a wide variety of behavior from disruptive horseplay to outstanding work. In recent years, psychologists have studied the effects of teacher responses on pupil behavior. The results indicate that each teacher has a potent means of obtaining the behavior he desires. Most encouraging, the results have confirmed that to succeed in obtaining desirable behaviors from their students, most teachers need not learn any new responses, gimmicks, or tricks of the trade. They need learn only to alter systematically the timing of their usual basic response, attention, or "social reinforcement."

In various classroom settings, the social reinforcement technique has effectively modified the behavior of students ranging in age from three to eleven. Specifically, the technique has been used to increase such things as cooperative play, attention span, and studying and to reduce regressive crawling, crybaby outbursts, sulking, pestering other children, inappropriate talking, blurting out, making noises, and so on.

The initial step of the social reinforcement technique is to define the behavior to be modified. The term behavior indicates the focus of the technique; the procedure is designed to modify directly what people do that can be observed and measured. As behavior changes, attitudes and feelings will probably change also, but we cannot directly measure such internalized responses. The behavior must be defined in terms of observable overt responses and must be stated unambiguously.

To illustrate, if a teacher is concerned with general inappropriate behavior, he should list the different responses he considers inappropriate, such as "out of seat," defined perhaps as "ceases to touch chair." Then he is no longer concerned with a "bad child," but with reducing "number of times out of seat." Finally, he should adhere to the original definition at all times so that any change in recorded behavior will not be due to a change in definition.

Defined by what is observable, a behavior is easily measured. The most frequently used measure is a count of the number of times the behavior occurs in a specified length of time. For some behavior, the most appropriate measure is its duration in seconds within a specified time period. Graphs give the most meaningful representations of the measures.

Such objective measurement procedures are necessary and worth every bit of the time and energy they consume. Without them, the teacher is too easily influenced by his own feelings and moods or by an outstanding response or series of responses by a student. In short, objective measurements greatly reduce the subjective error in evaluating a child's behavior.

Daily measurements also afford the teacher frequent feedback on his application of the technique. If an observation session yields results substantially disparate from previous observations of that experimental stage, the teacher is alerted to the possiblity of his misapplication of the technique or of the interference of some other factor with the results.

Once the teacher has defined the behavior and selected the method of measurement, he can obtain the current rate of the behavior. This rate is called the baseline. During the baseline stage, the teacher makes no change in his own behavior other than to record student behavior. He measures the target behavior by the predetermined method and compares its rate to that of all subsequent measurements. A baseline should contain enough observations to help the teacher decide whether or not changes of behavior during reinforcement are due to random fluctuations.

Giving attention to desired behaviors and ignoring undesired behaviors are the main elements of the social reinforcment technique. The teacher should select the attention to make the child feel praised, competent, or appreciated. A positive physical contact, like a pat on the back; friendly verbal interaction; and praise, such as "Very good," and "You're doing fine," are effective forms of attention. If these responses are awkward or disruptive in a situation, friendly facial expressions and hand gestures are the best alternatives. Smiling and giving the OK sign are examples of such responses.

Whatever its form, the positive attention should be given the child while he is still engaged in the desired behavior or immediately after he completes it. The teacher should place emphasis on "catching the child being good" (as researchers Madsen, Becker, and Thomas have expressed it). Even if the child has just previously misbehaved, any present appropriate behavior should be reinforced. The teacher who uses a variety of attentive behaviors in a spontaneous and warm manner will increase the effectiveness of the technique.

All schools of education support positive approaches to teaching, and most teachers practice them somewhat, but far from enough. Thus, in applying the social reinforcement technique, the first change in timing involves a large increase in the frequency and immediacy of positive teacher attention. The second involves the teacher's ignoring (directing his attention away from) "bad" behavior.

The idea of ignoring inappropriate behavior may seen inconsistent with common sense. However, recent studies indicate that reprimands maintain or even increase the rates of the very behaviors they are intended to eliminate. Further, a substantial body of evidence shows that physical punishment as applied in the school is an ineffective technique for controlling behavior. Hence the teacher's only practical alternative response to inappropriate behavior is to ignore it - not punitively and as if by deliberation - but by acting as if he is involved with other matters. The idea is to appear unaware of the presence of the misbehaving child. This is easy for the teacher who is occupied with praising other children's good behavior.

Initially, ignoring may lead to an increase in the "bad" behavior as the child tests the teacher. But, especially when others are bing praised for doing at the teacher wishes, most children soon join in the race for teacher attention on the teacher's terms.

In summary, attending to and ignoring are used together. The teacher gives attention to the desired behaviors and ignores the undesired. The golden moment for reinforcement occurs whenever one child is indulging in a particular misbehavior at the same instant that his neighbor is indulging in its opposite.

Sometimes a student never or almost never give the desired response. In such a case, the teacher must shape the behavior by successive approximations. This procedure calls for his initially giving attention to any first sign of the appropriate behavior. He then reinforces only those behaviors that are closer and closer approximations of the desired behavior. By this method the teacher moves the student from a weak starting point to the desired behavior. For example, to reinforce in - seat behavior in a child who is always up, first praise his being near his seat.

For a variety of reasons, when shaping a response to a broad class of stimuli, it may be best to reinforce responses to just one stimulus. After the response to this stimulus increases to the desired level, the teacher can generalize the response to other stimuli by introducing them as he continues to reinforce.

To illustrate, suppose that the desired behavior were an increase in cooperative play for a boy of a minority group. If the boy felt less shy toward members of his own sex group, the teacher initially would increase his responses to these members by praising his approaches until he acquired the cooperative play response. Once this response was well-established, the teacher would generalize it to the other groups in the class by gradually introducing members from those groups into the group the boy approached.

In shaping behavior, it is usually desirable to begin by reinforcing as many of the child's appropriate behaviors as possible. Because the teacher has so many other demands on his attention, he probably will not be able to reinforce every appropriate response. Nonetheless, during behavior shaping, the child is likely to receive an undue share of attention temporarily.

To maintain the behavior, the teacher can decrease the frequency of reinforcement or, in technical terms, make it more intermittent. There is nothing fancy about this procedure; the crucial point is simply to decrease the frequency very gradually., If you have been praising a child every time he has done an arithmetic problem, as soon as he works steadily, you should drop first to praising four out of five instances, then to three out of five, and so on, watching your graph to be sure that the number of correct problems does not decline markedly. Continue to decrease the frequency of reinforcement until the child works throughout the period. Perhaps your sole reinforcement would be to stand with your hand on the child's shoulder once or twice while you survey the class and check his work. Intermittent reinforcement not only results in a response that is more easily controlled, but also in one that is much more durable.

In several studies, the social reinforcement technique has been successfully applied to an entire class. This implies that the technique could be used as a general way of handling classes - praise and attention for desired behavior and none for the undesired. Indications are that, generally, the more praise the better, as long as it follows appropriate behavior.

For a general, everyday group approach, the teacher would not have to collect data. With an individual or a group that continued to misbehave or failed to perform well in some respect, the teacher could apply the technique more systematically.

The above experimentally verified principles go against much of the lore of the teacher's lounge. Their application requires some faith and some patience. Reprimanding a child stops his misbehavior promptly, even if only for a little while. That is obious, and reinforcing to the teacher. Ignoring the child's bad behavior and, above all, praising behavior that our culture says he "should" produce without thanks have effects that are not so obvious and that with some children might appear impossible.

As procedures, praise and ignoring take longer. This can cause impatience. But in the long run, the positive social reinforcement technique can turn the teacher's original dream of motivation into reality.

Appendix II - Specific Skills

PART 1
FIGURE GROUND

Figure-Ground is a visual discrimination task which requires the child to pick out the important visual symbol (figure) from a busy background (ground). Why use figure-ground activities?

1. It is a component of reading and other higher level visual tasks.
2. To develop attending skills.
3. To develop fine motor skills when pasting is involved.
4. To provide a structured art activity for those children whose developmental levels require more structure.
5. To provide for enjoyment and success, especially for children functioning on a lower developmental level.

Like all tasks it is necessary to task analyze Figure-Ground activities so that each child is given activities appropriate to his own level of skill. This is an example of sequencing figure-ground activities in order of difficulty and the variable affecting the levels of difficulty:

Day's Concept: Banana

Variables

1. size: large
   number: one
   cues: color outline yellow
   hiding lines: simple, few
   position: right side up (See fig. 2A.)

2. size: smaller
   number: increased
   cues: color outline yellow
   hiding lines: more
   position: turned in two different directions (See fig. 2B.)

3. size: smaller
   number: increased
   cues: color cue faded, no outline
   hiding lines: more complex
   position: turned in several different directions (See fig. 2C.)

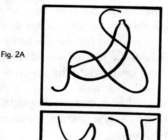

Fig. 2A

Fig. 2B

Fig. 2C

yellow cutout to paste on

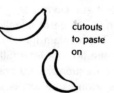
cutouts to paste on

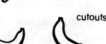
cutouts

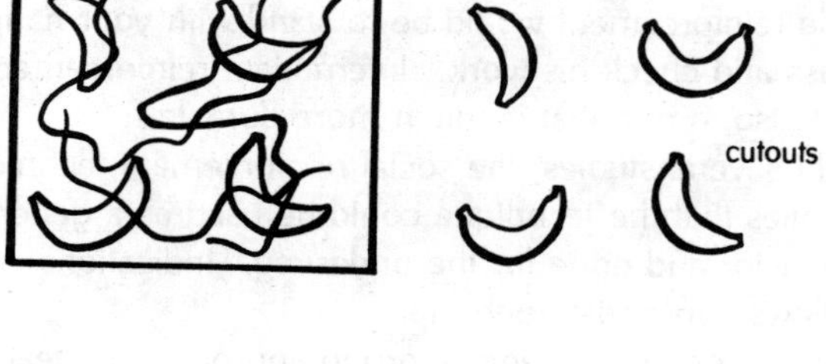

PART 2
PATH TRACING

Path Tracing requires the child to follow a guide from one point to another. It is an important pre-writing skill because it involves the drawing of lines required in writing the alphabet. These lines are the following: (See fig. 2D.)

Fig. 2D

1. _____ (horizontal)
2.  ~‿ (curved)
3. | (vertical)
4. ∟ ꓜ (angular)

Other Reasons for Using Path Tracing Activities:

1. To develop eye-hand coordination.
2. To develop the left to right and top to bottom progression.
3. To develop attending skills.

Sequencing Path Tracing Activites in Order of Difficulty:

1. Horizontal and Vertical Paths - Make a large newsprint 'map' with a straight road about 18" long and 3" wide. Put a picture of a house (or green spot) at one end and a picture of a school (or a red spot) at the other. Have the children drive a toy car from the house to the school without going off the road. Always start at the left side of the paper with horizontal roads. Teach the commands "Go" and "Stop", "Top" and "Bottom." As child masters 3" paths decrease the width to 2 inches, 1 inch, ½ inch, then ¼ inch. Use felt pens or crayons, finally pencils on ½ and ¼ inch paths. (See fig. 2E.)

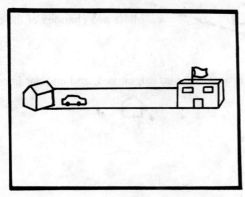

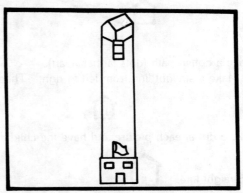

Fig. 2E

2. Curved Paths - After children have mastered horizontal and vertical paths, use another large 'map' and have the car go on a curved road to the school. This lesson introduces the curved line. As a child's skill increases, decrease the width of the curved paths to 2", 1", ½", and ¼". Again, begin with car, then use felt pens, crayons, and finally pencils on ¼ inch paths. A dotted, colored line may be used as a cue. (See fig. 2F.)

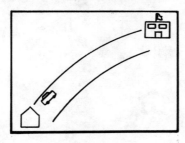
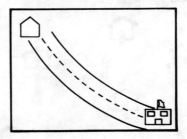

Fig. 2F

3. Angular and/or Change of Direction Paths - Use the same process as with horizontal, vertical and curved paths, moving from 3 inch paths to ¼ inch paths. Always remind the child to "stay on the road." (See fig. 2G.)

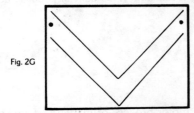
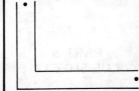
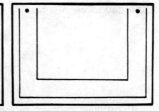

Fig. 2G

4. Dotted Path (with the dots close together) and Primary Pencil -
   a. Make a straight line from left to right. Use color cues by having child always start at a green dot and stop at a red dot.

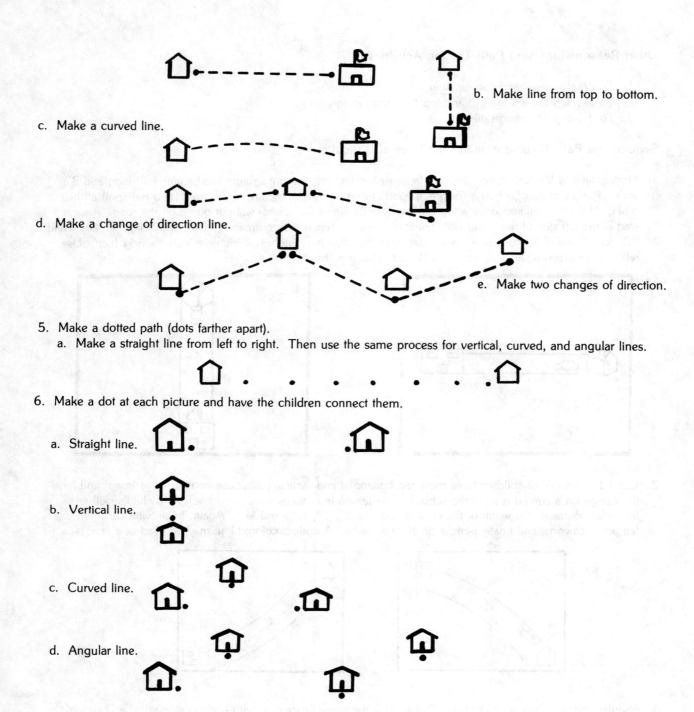

b. Make line from top to bottom.

c. Make a curved line.

d. Make a change of direction line.

e. Make two changes of direction.

5. Make a dotted path (dots farther apart).
   a. Make a straight line from left to right. Then use the same process for vertical, curved, and angular lines.

6. Make a dot at each picture and have the children connect them.

   a. Straight line.

   b. Vertical line.

   c. Curved line.

   d. Angular line.

Use color cues by having child always start on a green dot and stop on a red dot. This activity is easily adapted to the concept of the day in each lesson.

PART 3
CUE SHEETS

Cue sheets require a cognitive process of matching to a cue and a fine motor process of marking. Cue sheets train the child to identify identical shapes, figures and symbols. The symbol at the top of the page is the "cue." The task is to find all those symbols on the page which are identical to the "cue" symbol. Design cue sheets to fit the levels of the children. Your cue may be the same for all the children but the levels of difficulty may be different. Therefore, the worksheets will look somewhat different.

I. Beginning Level -

A.   Teach the child the meaning of "mark" by demonstration on the chalkboard. Teacher makes a mark (/ or X). Have the children come to the board and make the "mark."

B.   Give children a picture and ask them to mark the picture as they did on the board.

C.   Give children a piece of paper with two or three pictures (dog, house, girl). "Mark the girl." "Mark the house." "Mark the dog."

II. Level Two -

Give children a cue sheet such as this. Point to the circle. "Find the shape that is the same as this one and mark it." (See fig. 2H.)

III. Level Three -

Add a few more distractors which are significantly different. (See fig. 2I.)

IV. Level Four -

Now add to the number of distractors on the paper. (See fig. 2J.)

Fig. 2K

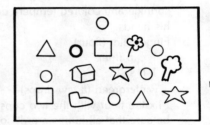

V. Level Five -

More difficult because the distractors are more similar to the cue. (See fig. 2K.)

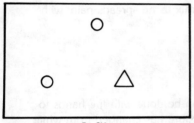

Fig. 2H

Fig. 2I

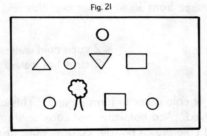

Fig. 2J

Note that cue sheets can be designed with pictures of different sizes on them. For children with lower level skills use bigger pictures and fewer distractors than for more highly skilled children. This activity is adaptable to the concepts of the day in each lesson.

PART 4
ART ACTIVITIES FOR THE YOUNG CHILDREN

The following eight categories of art activities are listed in sequence beginning with gross motor activities, which involve many parts of the body, and ending with the fine motor tasks such as using primary pencils.

1. Sand play
2. Fingerpainting
3. Water play
4. Chalk
5. Clay or playdough
6. Tempera painting
7. Crayons and Magic Markers
8. Tearing, cutting, pasting, and fastening

I. Sand

1.   Provide a sand box inside and outside the room for daily use. If a commerical sandbox is not available, you may use a child's small inflatable swimming pool, aluminum or plastic dishpan or sturdy cardboard box. Later on you may add sand toys and especially containers for pouring sand from one into the other.

2. Sand painting - Add dry tempera to sifted dry sand. Place the colored sand in a salt shaker with holes made large by driving a nail through them. The children may draw a picture or use a plain piece of paper. Let them cover the picture with paste and sift sand over it. They may cover various areas with different colors of sand. Salt, grits or sand-dust may be substituted for the sand.

3. Sand numbers and alphabets - Have large squares of cardboard pre-cut with large blocked numbers or alphabets printed on. (You may use a cardboard from laundered shirts.) Allow each child to choose a number or alphabet and fill in with glue or rubber cement then cover with colored sand. This makes good tactile materials for teaching numbers and alphabets. (See fig. 2L.)

4. Individual sandboxes - Shoe boxes, sturdy gift boxes or Kodak Carousel slide tray boxes make excellent individual sand boxes for a child to draw or write in using his fingers.

Fig. 2L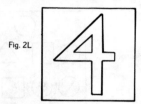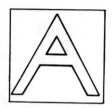

II. Fingerpainting

1. Recipes

    a. An excellent fingerpaint may be made using about 2 teaspoons of polycell (or any cellulose wallpaper adhesive) to a pint of water. Put a spoonful of this on slick shelf paper and let child sprinkle any colored tempera desired from a salt shaker over this and mix as he spreads paint with his hands.

    b. Fingerpaint (flour)

1 cup flour	2 cups cold water
1 t. salt	2 cups hot water
wintergreen (a few drops)	

    Mix the flour with the two cups of cold water to form a paste. This can be done with the hands to be sure that all lumps are dissolved. Add hot water and cook until mixture has changed from white color to darker color. Add food coloring or powder color. A few drops of wintergreen takes away the flour smell.

2. Activities

    a. Mono-Print - Let the children fingerpaint on a tray or table. Then lay a clean sheet of paper on the fingerpaint and press. When you remove the paper there will be a reverse design on it.

    b. Texture Painting - Add some materials such as sand, sand-dust, or corn meal to the fingerpaint before using it.

    c. Mixing Colors - Allow children to paint with two primary colors using free, rhythmic movements and noticing the creation of a new color when the two primaries are mixed.

    d. Soapsuds Painting -

    1 cup of hot water in a pan

    soap flakes

    Gradually add soap flakes while beating the mixture with an eggbeater until it is the consistency of whipped cream. Place mixture on the table. The children use their hands to make designs with it. Food coloring or tempera may be added for color.

    e. Automatic Fingerpainting - Make an arrangement of strings, dried leaves, etc. on a table top. Lay them out flat. Cover the fingerpaint paper with fingerpaint and lay it on top of the arrangement of string, dried leaves, etc. Hold the paper by an edge to keep it from slipping and pull a squeegee (piece of cardboard) over the painted surface. The paint will be picked up where the underlying shapes press against the squeegie but will remain undisturbed in other places. (See fig. 2M.)

squeegee

Finger
Paint
Paper

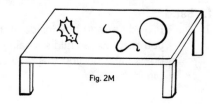

Fig. 2M

III. Water

1. Provide a water area inside and outside the room for daily use. If a commerical water table is not available you may use a child's small inflatable swimming pool or aluminum or plastic dishpan. Put out water accessories for pouring, weighing, measuring, soaking, coloring, brushes for painting with water, etc.

2. Chalk and water - Give the child large pieces of chalk, a small container of water, and a large piece of construction paper. Child should dip one end of chalk in water then make a design or picture on the paper.

3. Provide many sizes of brushes and a pail of water for the children to use to paint pieces of wood, rocks, trees, and walls outside and even their tricycles or wagons. Remember this will be clear water that will dry quickly. For some handicapped children you may need a styrofoam cylinder or top of a Clorox bottle to make the handle more convenient for the child. (See fig. 2N.)

4. Mixing Colors - Water is an excellent medium for showing how two colors can produce a third color. Just add food coloring or easter egg dye. (See fig. 2O.)

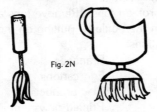
Fig. 2N

Fig. 2O

IV. Chalk

1. Draw with white or colored chalk on blackboard.
2. Dip chalk in milk (plain or buttermilk) and draw designs or pictures.
3. Use several colors of chalk to draw on wet paper. Chalk will smear if not "fixed." A fixative made of equal parts of liquid starch and water may be sprayed on with an atomizer or pump type sprayer or brushed on. A thin mixture of powdered milk sprayed on will act as a fixative. There are also commercial fixatives.

V. Clay and Playdough

1. Amaco clay is a commercial potter's clay that is mixed with water and kept indefinitely in a covered container or plastic bag.
2. Commercial playdough can be bought in small cans or large cans.
3. Uncooked playdough - Mix ½ cup salt, 1 cup flour (sifted), 1½ T. salad oil, ⅓ cup plus 2 T. water, 2 t. food coloring. Add food coloring to water, if tempera paint is used it can be added to the water. Add oil last.
4. Encourage children to manipulate clay or playdough by pressing, squeezing, pounding, rolling and other exploratory actions.
5. Make stabiles by squeezing a small lump of clay or old playdough into a shape and choosing some things to stick into it. (Either things child brings from home or he finds, or other things the teacher may provide like, popsicle sticks, pipe cleaners, straws, bottle caps, shells, buttons, beads, etc.) (See fig. 2P.)

Fig. 2P

6. For an interesting substance for the children to handle mix cornstarch and water. Experiment with different consistencies.

VI. Tempera Paint

1. Blob Painting - Prefold paper, drop thick paint onto paper from tongue depressors, spoons, or brushes. Refold paper, press and open. Several colors may be used.

2. String Painting Magic - Dip short lengths of string in bowl of paint. (String may be tied to large stick for easier holding.) Let dipped string fall on one side of pre-folded paper. Cover string with other side of paper. Hold one hand on paper and pull string out from between the open ends. Very interesting designs will appear.

3. Object Printing - Collect such items as thread spools, sponges, potato mashers, hair curlers, tooth brushes and such vegetables as white potatoes, apples, bell peppers, celery, carrots. Cut interesting designs on vegetables. Dip any of these objects or vegetables into various colors of tempera paints set up in muffin tins or small containers. Blot on paper towel or newspaper. Press on paper. This idea is especially good for making wrapping paper for celebrations and for just plain fun of watching the shapes appear.

4. Roller Painting (Gross Motor) - Purchase small sash rollers at the paint store, roll in tempera and let children paint large boxes, newspaper, large murals, etc.

5. Roll On Painting - Use deodorant bottles with roll-on tops. Remove tops and fill bottles with paint. Several colors may be used and paint stored in the bottle by putting on the top.

6. Try painting on many surfaces. Some suggestions:

Paper towels	Branches
Sea shells	Egg cartons
Wallpaper	Clay products
Woodwork products	Printed newsprint
Fingerpaint paper	Scrap lumber
Colored construction paper	Pine cones
Stones	Magazine pages
Paper bags	Playdough products
Cardboard boxes	

VII. Crayons and Magic Markers

1. Allow children to use crayons at the easel. It provides more space, creativity, and excitement.

2. Crayon Textures - Place objects under paper and with the side of crayon go back and forth on top of paper to get the impression. Be sure to remove paper from around crayons. Suitable objects would be cut-outs made from plastic lids, screen wire, corrugated cardboard, linoleum, burlap, keys, string, plastic doilies and cut up stove top protectors.

3. Draw with Magic Markers on various textures of paper.

4. Crayon Resist - Draw heavy design on paper with crayons. Paint over this with a very thin water color paint. Paint should not adhere to crayon markings.

VIII. Tearing, Cutting, Pasting, and Fastening, Etc.

1. Allow children to freely tear paper of many textures.

2. How to cut is discussed under Task Analysis in Appendix I.

3. Cereal Mosaic - Beautiful pictures may be made using different types of dry cereal. Draw picture and glue on different types of dry cereal to form mosaic or just glue cereal in any design desired.

4. Sock Horse - 1. Stuff sock full of cotton batting or old nylon stockings. 2. Push a yard length of broomstick well up through the stuffing. Tie opening at cuff of sock and tack to broomstick. 3. From an old glove, cut off two fingers. Stuff and sew into place for the ears. 4. Sew on buttons for eyes and fasten strips of leather, shoestrings, or ½'' ribbon in place for bridle and reins. Paint on nostrils and teeth. (McCall's) (See fig. 2Q.)

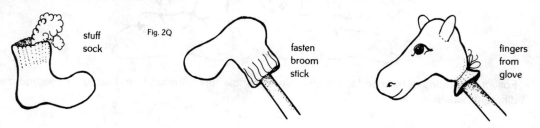

stuff sock   Fig. 2Q   fasten broom stick   fingers from glove

5.   Handkerchief Parachute - Cut four lengths of string about 12" long. Tie one piece of string to each corner of handkerchief. For man who jumps, paint design of wooden clothespin, using poster paints. Then tie the loose ends of all four strings to the top of the clothespin. Roll up parachute and throw as high as you can. (McCall's) (See fig. 2R.)

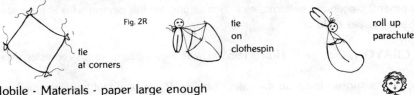

Fig. 2R   tie at corners   tie on clothespin   roll up parachute

6.   Body Part's Mobile - Materials - paper large enough to trace a child's body; construction paper for face parts; string; a piece of coathanger. Trace a child's body. Have the children help assemble parts to make a person. Have them find their own and find parts of a friend (e.g., "Mary, show me Joe's hair.") Talk about the relation of body parts to one another. (See fig. 2S.)

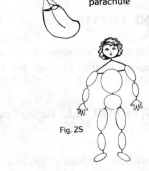

Fig. 2S

7.   Papier-Mache Eggs - Divide a newspaper page into fourths; then cut strips of newspaper about 1" wide. Three or four strips are needed for each egg. The child is given a piece of the divided newspaper, and he crumples it into an egg shape. Then the strips of newspaper are wrapped around the egg. Continue this process until the egg is as large as the child wants it.

8.   Christmas Bell - Cut egg cartons into 12 cups. The children trim them in holdiay colors and, if they wish, add glitter. A hole is punched in the top and yarn drawn through to form a hanger. (Wylie)

9.   Hand Puzzles - Materials - heavy cardboard; exacto-blade; enamel paint; glue. Glue 2 cardboards together to create backing. Cut out hands and fingers. Paint hands with enamel and contrast the background. Use for counting, one to one correspondence, right-left identification.

Listed here are some books which would be excellent if you want to build a library for children's art. Your local book store would probably order most of these for you or you can write the company which publishes the book and they will invoice you or send the book C.O.D.

1.   **ART ACTIVITIES FOR THE VERY YOUNG,** F. Louis Hoover, David Publications, Inc. Worcester, Mass.

     This is an excellent book on art for the 3 to 6 year old. Hoover lists helpful hints to the parent and teacher, describes about 15 art activities, and points out several activities for the special occasions.

2.   **THE PSYCHOLOGY OF CHILDREN'S ART,** by Rhoda Kellogg with Scott O'Dell Random House Publishers, 1967.

     Rhoda Kellogg is a leading nursery-school educator and internationally know authority on children's art. She has collected more than a million samples of art, the largest known collection of child art in the world. She has selected 250 of these for this book. It is beautiful. . .

3.   **CREATIVE ART FOR HOME AND SCHOOL,** Pauline McDonald and Doris V. Brown. Du-Mor Publishers, 3614 Motor Ave., Los Angles, Calif.

     This well illustrated (pictures of many of the activities) book has chapters on painting, drawing, collage, construction, modeling, and mounting and displaying pictures. It also has 25 pages of holiday projects.

4.   **EXPERIENCING ART IN KINDERGARTEN,** George F. Horn, 1971. Davis Publications, Inc., Worcester, Mass.

     A beautifully illustrated pamphlet book which all teachers of kindergarten age children should have to refer to. Horn describes the 5 year old kindergarten child then suggests an art program with purpose.

5. **ANALYSING CHILDREN'S ART,** Rhoda Kellogg, National Press, 850 Hansen Way, Palo Alto, Calif., 94340.

This is a thorough study of Kellogg's analysis of children's art with detailed descriptions of stages of art development, placement patterns, etc. Something for the person who is interested to know more about how Kellogg sees child art.

6. **THE CRAYON,** George F. Horn, 1969, Davis Publications, Inc. Worcester, Mass.

This is one of those "icing on the cake" books. It is a beautiful book devoted to use of the crayon by young children through the intermediate grades. Many new ideas which could be adapted for other children.

7. **ARTS FOR ALL,** Randy Friedman-Granovetter, Educaide, Route 7, Box 121, Chapel Hill, NC 27514.

This book includes "kitchen" activities, visual art activities, creative movement, music and drama activities oriented to enjoyment of the art experience.

Activities in this section have been compiled from materials supplied by Anne Sanford, Randall Crump, Annie Pegram, and Mrs. Sarah Hoffman. Additional sources are Engel; Mary E. Platts (Create - A Handbook for Teachers of Elementary Art); Evelyn G. Hershoff (It's Fun to Make Things from Scrap Material); Jeanne Wylie (A Creative Guide for Preschool Teachers); F.L. Hoover (Art Activities for the Very Young); The New Nursery School; Grade Teacher Magazine; McCall's Make-It Book (by John Peter)' Barbara Bucher Linse (Arts and Crafts for all Seasons); The Day Care Unit, Child Welfare, State Department of Public Instruction, Raleigh, NC, Department of Family Relations and Child Development OSU and Marilyn and Joseph Spanlings, Art and Young Children 1968.

PART 5
HOME FOLLOW-UP ACTIVITIES

PROGRAM FOR HOME FOLLOW-UP

This week Emily has been working on the concepts (1) path tracing; (2) writing; (3) numbers 1, 2; (4) jumping, kicking.

Your child can exhibit the following behaviors:

(1) If she is paying attention to task, Emily can follow V-shape paths without crossing line.
(2) Emily can trace letters Emi.
(3) She can recognize number 1 and associate number with object. She is beginning number 2.

Suggested activities which may be carried out at home to reinforce these concepts are:

(1) Make 90° V-shape paths - 1 inch in width. Ask Emily to go from "green" to "red". "Stay on path, don't cross the line." (See fig. 2T.)

Fig. 2T

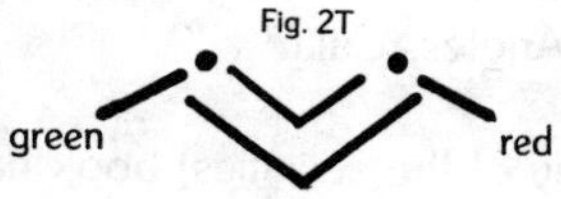

green   red

(2) Make letters Emi 1½" high ⌐mi for her to trace.

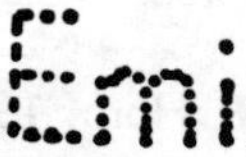

(3) Ask Emily to point out 1 object or give you 1 object. (ex: 1 book, 1 cup).
(4) Have her step up on stool or other object close to floor (10 to 12") and jump down unassisted. Roll a large ball toward her and ask her to kick it.

PROGRAM FOR HOME FOLLOW-UP

This week Emily has been working on the concepts (1) self-help skills; (2) saying her name with three syllables.

Your child can exhibit the following behaviors:

(1) Emily is learning to sew and thread a large needle. She is able to sew on lines when shown where to put the needle using your finger.
(2) Emily is practicing her cutting skills using a knife and fork.
(3) Emily can mop, sweep, and vacuum.
(4) Emily can say her name with three syllables when modeled for her.

Suggested activities which may be carried out at home to reinforce these concepts are:

(1) Emily is just beginning to sew with yarn on burlap. She likes it a lot. You may want to use this activity at home on weekends! She can really stay with this task a long time.
(2) Using playdough, which you and Emily could make together, Emily could use a knife and fork and practice her skills in cutting at home. She loves this and is doing well independently! (Playdough recipe: 2 cups flour; 1 cup salt; 1 T oil; and ½ cup water.) Roll playdough around into shape of a hot dog and put it on a plate to cut.
(3) Let Emily help you mop, sweep and vacuum. She's so good at these, I know she's had some good training here at home.
(4) Work with Emily on saying her name. Let her watch your mouth as you say "Emily". Do not accept a two-syllable response.

PROGRAM FOR HOME FOLLOW-UP

This week Emily has been working on the concepts (1) clothing; (2) big-little.

Your child can exhibit the following behaviors:

(1) Emily has been working on pants, shirt, dress and skirt. She can consistently touch a named item of clothing and can imitate its name. She has just begun to work on parts of clothing - sleeve and collar.
(2) Emily can consistently touch "big" objects and pictures and say "big" when so requested.

Suggested activities which may be carried out at home to reinforce these concepts are:

(1) As she dresses or undresses, show her the sleeve and collar. Tell her its label. Then ask her to "find the sleeve" or "find the collar" on her clothes, your clothes, or brothers' and sisters' clothes.
(2) A game to reinforce the concept of big can be played by you and other members of the family - brothers and sisters. It goes like this: Say, "Look, look and see, find the big one and give it to me!" Use blocks of the same color, or pictures from Sears catalogs on cards of the same thing. For example: a big red dress and a little red dress; a big black suitcase and a little black suitcase.

For additional home activities that correlate with this Curriculum Guide see Home Stretch by Dorothy Cansler, published by Kaplan Press.

Appendix III

CHARTING THE UNIT GROUP LESSONS

The form on the opposite page is presented to help the care givier in charting the accomplishments of the children performing the Unit Group Lesson.

The space at the top is to be filled in with the unit name, number and lesson. Select the columns which are appropriate to the lesson of the day. For each child check those levels (s)he has mastered. If you are concerned with "a gesture" vs "a verbal" response indicate same by using a capital "G" and "V" where appropriate.

You will notice the spaces are small however there is room for comments should you desire to use them. This form may be duplicated.

UNIT _____

CONCEPT _____

Child's Name	Match Concrete Objects	Discriminate Objects	Locate Own	Match Pictures	Discriminate Pictures	Figure-Ground	Tactile Discrimination	Taste Discrimination	Visual Closure	Function	Association	Imitate Verbalization	Verbalize Label

NOTES

NOTES

NOTES

NOTES

NOTES

NOTES

NOTES

NOTES

NOTES

NOTES